Lecture Notes in Computer Science 15883

Founding Editors

Gerhard Goos
Juris Hartmanis

AF167704

The series Lecture Notes in Computer Science (LNCS), including its subseries Lecture Notes in Artificial Intelligence (LNAI) and Lecture Notes in Bioinformatics (LNBI), has established itself as a medium for the publication of new developments in computer science and information technology research, teaching, and education.

LNCS enjoys close cooperation with the computer science R & D community, the series counts many renowned academics among its volume editors and paper authors, and collaborates with prestigious societies. Its mission is to serve this international community by providing an invaluable service, mainly focused on the publication of conference and workshop proceedings and postproceedings. LNCS commenced publication in 1973.

Michał Baczyński · Bernard De Baets ·
Michal Holčapek · Vladik Kreinovich ·
Jesús Medina
Editors

Advances in Fuzzy Logic and Technology

14th Conference of the European Society for Fuzzy Logic and
Technology, EUSFLAT 2025, Riga, Latvia, July 21–25, 2025
Proceedings, Part I

 Springer

Editors
Michał Baczyński 🆔
University of Silesia in Katowice
Katowice, Poland

Bernard De Baets 🆔
Ghent University
Ghent, Belgium

Michal Holčapek 🆔
University of Ostrava
Ostrava, Czech Republic

Vladik Kreinovich 🆔
The University of Texas at El Paso
El Paso, TX, USA

Jesús Medina 🆔
University of Cádiz
Cádiz, Spain

ISSN 0302-9743   ISSN 1611-3349 (electronic)
Lecture Notes in Computer Science
ISBN 978-3-031-97224-9   ISBN 978-3-031-97225-6 (eBook)
https://doi.org/10.1007/978-3-031-97225-6

This Springer imprint is published by the registered company Springer Nature Switzerland AG
The registered company address is: Gewerbestrasse 11, 6330 Cham, Switzerland

If disposing of this product, please recycle the paper.

Preface

It is with great pleasure that we present the proceedings of the 14th Conference of the European Society for Fuzzy Logic and Technology (EUSFLAT 2025), held in Riga, Latvia, from July 21 to 25, 2025. This biennial conference continued the tradition of bringing together researchers, practitioners, and students from around the world who work in the broad area of fuzzy logic and related fields, including soft computing, computational intelligence, uncertainty modeling, and approximate reasoning. The event served as a platform for the exchange of ideas, dissemination of new results, and the strengthening of collaborations across academic, scientific, and industrial domains.

Nearly 26 years ago, the inaugural EUSFLAT-ESTYLF Joint Conference was convened in Palma de Mallorca from September 22 to 25, 1999. That event marked the first official conference of the European Society for Fuzzy Logic and Technology (EUSFLAT), following its establishment earlier that same year. Since then, the Society has organized successful conferences in Leicester (2001), Zittau (2003), Barcelona (2005), Ostrava (2007), Lisbon (2009), Aix-les-Bains (2011), Milan (2013), Gijón (2015), Warsaw (2017), Prague (2019), Bratislava (2021), and again Palma de Mallorca (2023). The fourteenth edition was hosted in Riga, organized by the University of Latvia, in cooperation with EUSFLAT.

The papers included in these proceedings underwent a rigorous peer-review process. Each submission was reviewed by at least two qualified experts, using a single-blind review protocol and adhering to strict conflict-of-interest policies. In addition, all submissions were carefully evaluated by the program chairs. As a result of this review process, 53 submissions were accepted and are presented across the two volumes of the proceedings. Topics covered include, but are not limited to, fuzzy sets and systems, knowledge representation, fuzzy control, decision-making, machine learning, data analysis, and applications in engineering, economics, and the social sciences.

The EUSFLAT conference series has served as a central forum for the community since its inception, promoting interdisciplinary collaboration and addressing new challenges in science and technology through fuzzy logic and soft computing. The 2025 edition stood out not only for the quality of its scientific contributions but also for its location – Riga, a city known for its rich cultural heritage, architectural beauty, and its growing role as a hub for science and innovation in the Baltic region. The Local Organizing Committee worked tirelessly to ensure a warm, efficient, and memorable experience for all participants.

In addition to regular paper sessions, EUSFLAT 2025 featured invited talks by distinguished researchers, special sessions on emerging topics, tutorials, and panel discussions. These components were designed to offer attendees a well-rounded and intellectually stimulating experience that combined depth with breadth. The program included keynote lectures by:

- Bernard De Baets (Ghent University, Belgium),
- Irina Perfilieva (University of Ostrava, Czech Republic),

- Humberto Bustince (Public University of Navarre, Spain),
- Óscar Cordón (University of Granada, Spain),
- Katarzyna Kaczmarek-Majer (Systems Research Institute, Polish Academy of Sciences, Warsaw, Poland),
- Ulrich Bodenhofer (University of Applied Sciences Upper Austria, Hagenberg, Austria),
- Andris Ambainis (University of Latvia, Latvia).

We are deeply grateful to all authors for submitting their research and sharing their insights with the community. We sincerely thank the reviewers and Program Committee members for their time, expertise, and thoughtful feedback, and we acknowledge the special session organizers for their initiative and commitment. Our appreciation also goes to the invited speakers for their inspiring presentations and to the session chairs for their essential role in ensuring the smooth flow of the technical program. Special thanks go to the Local Organizing Committee members for their dedication in preparing and hosting the conference. Their professionalism, attention to detail, and hospitality were instrumental in creating a successful and enjoyable event.

Last but not least, we would like to dedicate these proceedings to the late Alexander Šostak, who was an exemplary member of our society and a great researcher, and who was very happy and delighted that this fourteenth edition was going to be held in his city. Unfortunately, he is no longer with us, but his magnificent research group, and Olga Grigorenko in particular, have made great efforts for the organization of a splendid conference that would have made Alexander very proud. We hope that these proceedings will not only serve as a record of the work presented at EUSFLAT 2025, but will also stimulate future research, foster continued dialogue, and encourage new developments in the field of fuzzy logic and soft computing.

May 2025

Michał Baczynski
Bernard De Baets
Michal Holčapek
Vladik Kreinovich
Jesús Medina

Organization

General Chairs

Martin Štěpnička	University of Ostrava, Czech Republic
Susana Montes	University of Oviedo, Spain
Svetlana Asmuss	University of Latvia, Latvia

Organizing Chairs

Olga Grigorenko	University of Latvia, Latvia
Slawomir Zadrozny	Polish Academy of Sciences, Poland

Publication Chairs

Jesús Medina	University of Cádiz, Spain
Michal Baczynski	University of Silesia in Katowice, Poland

EUSFLAT Programme Chairs

Bernard De Baets	Ghent University, Netherlands
Vladik Kreinovich	University of Texas at El Paso, USA
Michal Holčapek	University of Ostrava, Czech Republic

Publicity Chairs

Vladik Kreinovich	University of Texas at El Paso, USA
Katarzyna Kaczmarek-Majer	Polish Academy of Sciences, Poland

Advisory Board

Radko Mesiar	Slovak University of Technology in Bratislava, Slovakia
Janusz Kacprzyk	Polish Academy of Sciences, Poland

Vilém Novák	University of Ostrava, Czech Republic
Marek Reformat	University of Alberta, Canada
Gabriella Pasi	University of Milano-Bicocca, Italy
Przemyslaw Grzegorzewski	Warsaw University of Technology, Poland
Susana Vieira	Universidade de Lisboa, Portugal
María Ángeles Gil	University of Oviedo, Spain
Peter Sussner	University of Campinas, Brazil

Organizing Committee

Elīna Buliņa	University of Latvia, Latvia
Reinis Isaks	University of Latvia, Latvia
Māris Krastiņš	University of Latvia, Latvia
Ingrīda Uļjane	University of Latvia, Latvia
Mārtiņš Zemlītis	University of Latvia, Latvia

SS1: Interval Uncertainty. Organizers

Martine Ceberio	University of Texas at El Paso, USA
Christoph Lauter	University of Texas at El Paso, USA
Vladik Kreinovich	University of Texas at El Paso, USA

SS2: Representing and Managing Uncertainty: Different Scenarios, Different Tools. Organizers

Davide Ciucci	University of Milano-Bicocca, Italy
Chris Cornelis	Ghent University, Belgium
Jesús Medina	University of Cádiz, Spain
Dominik Slezak	University of Warsaw, Poland

SS3: Mathematical Fuzzy Logic. Organizers

Matteo Bianchi	Università degli Studi di Milano, Italy
Tommaso Flaminio	IIIA-CSIC, Barcelona, Spain
Amanda Vidal	IIIA-CSIC, Barcelona, Spain

SS4: Soft Methods in Statistical Inference and Data Analysis. Organizers

Przemyslaw Grzegorzewski	Warsaw University of Technology, Poland
Katarzyna Kaczmarek-Majer	Polish Academy of Sciences, Poland
Antonio Calcagni	University of Padova, Italy

SS5: Fuzzy Implication Functions. Organizers

Michal Baczyński	University of Silesia in Katowice, Poland
Balasubramaniam Jayaram	Indian Institute of Technology Hyderabad, India
Raquel Fernández-Peralta	Universitat de les Illes Balears, Spain

SS6: Information Fusion Techniques Based on Aggregation Functions, Preaggregation Functions and their Generalizations. Organizers

Humberto Bustince	Universidad Publica de Navarra, Spain
Graçaliz Pereira Dimuro	Universidade Federal do Rio Grande, Brazil
Javier Fernández	Universidad Publica de Navarra, Spain
Tiago da Cruz Asmus	Universidade Federal do Rio Grande, Brazil
Giancarlo Lucca	Universidade Católica de Pelotas, Brazil
Benjamin Bedregal	Universidade Federal do Rio Grande do Norte, Brazil

SS7: Fuzzy Metric Spaces and their Generalizations: Theory and Applications. Organizers

Juan José Miñana	Universitat Politècnica de València, Spain
Jesús Rodríguez López	Universitat Politècnica de València, Spain
Almanzor Sapena	Universitat Politècnica de València, Spain

SS8: New Contexts in Aggregation Theory. Organizers

Bernard De Baets	Ghent University, Belgium
Raúl Pérez-Fernández	University of Oviedo, Spain

SS9: Modeling Complex Dynamics: Adapting Analytical Tools for Diverse Scenarios. Organizers

Martina Daňková	University of Ostrava, Czech Republic
Babak Shiri	Neijiang Normal University, China
Zahra Alijani	University of Ostrava, Czech Republic
Petra Števuliáková	University of Ostrava, Czech Republic

SS10: Soft Computing, Uncertainty and Imprecision in Image Processing. Organizers

Irina Perfilieva	University of Ostrava, Czech Republic
Javier Montero	Universidad Complutense de Madrid, Spain
Humberto Bustince	Universidad Publica de Navarra, Spain
Isabelle Bloch	Sorbonne Université, France
Olivier Strauss	Université de Montpellier, France
Carlos Lopez Molina	Public University of Navarra, Spain

SS11: Fuzzy Relations and Applications. Organizers

Halis Aygün	Kocaeli University, Turkey
Elif Güner	Kocaeli University, Turkey
Ingrīda Uļjane	University of Latvia, Latvia
Oscar Valero	University of the Balearic Islands, Spain

SS12: The Role and Value of Information in Decision Making

Dmitry Gromov	University of Latvia, Latvia

SS13: Generalized Quantifiers, Logical Syllogisms and Applications. Organizers

Vilém Novák	University of Ostrava, Czech Republic
Petra Murinová	University of Ostrava, Czech Republic
Karel Fiala	University of Ostrava, Czech Republic

SS4: Advancements and Applications of Fuzzy Theory and Fuzzy Control. Organizers

Chin-Wang Tao	National Ilan University, Taiwan
Chen-Chia Chuang	National Ilan University, Taiwan

Program Committee

Akbarzadeh-T., M.-R.	Ferdowsi University of Mashhad, Iran
Acampora, Giovanni	Università degli Studi di Napoli Federico II, Italy
Aliev, Rafik Aziz	Azerbaijan State Oil and Industry University, Azerbaijan
Allahviranloo, Tofigh	Istinye University, Turkey
Alijani, Zahra	University of Ostrava, Czech Republic
Alonso, Jose Maria	Universidad de Santiago de Compostela, Spain
Angelov, Plamen	Lancaster University, UK
Asmus, Tiago da Cruz	Universidade Federal do Rio Grande, Brazil
Asmuss, Svetlana	University of Latvia, Latvia
Atanassov, Krassimir	Bulgarian Academy of Sciences, Bulgaria
Balas, Valentina	Academy of Romanian Scientists, Romania
Baczyński, Michal	University of Silesia in Katowice, Poland
Bargiela Andrzej	University of Nottingham, UK
Bedregal, Bejamin	Universidade Federal do Rio Grande do Norte, Brazil
Beliakov, Gleb	Deakin University, Australia
Běhounek, Libor	University of Ostrava, Czech Republic
Bělolávek, Radim	Palacký University Olomouc, Czech Republic
Bianchi, Matteo	Università degli Studi di Milano, Italy
Bloch, Isabelle	Sorbonne Université, CNRS, France
Bobillo, Fernando	Universidad de Zaragoza, Spain
Bordogna, Gloria	Consiglio Nazionale delle Ricerche, Italy
Boffa, Stefania	University of Milano-Bicocca, Italy
Bouchon-Meunier, Bernadette	Sorbonne Université, France
Bronselaer, Antoon	Ghent University, Belgium
Bustince, Humberto	Universidad Pública de Navarra, Spain
Calvo, Tomasa	Universidad de Alcalá, Spain
Calganì, Antonio	University of Padova, Italy
Carlsson, Christer	Institute for Advanced Management Systems Research, Finland
Carvalho, Joao Paulo	Universidade de Lisboa, Portugal
Castellano, Giovanna	Università degli studi di Bari Aldo Moro, Italy

Castillo, Oscar   Tijuana Institute of Technology, Mexico
Ceberio, Martine   University of Texas at El Paso, USA
Chen, Guoqiang   Tsinghua University, China
Ciucci, Davide   University of Milano-Bicocca, Italy
Cordero, Pablo   Universidad de Málaga, Spain
Cordón, Oscar   Universidad de Granada, Spain
Cornelis, Chris   Ghent University, Belgium
Dankova, Martina   University of Ostrava, Czech Republic
De Baets, Bernard   Ghent University, Belgium
De Tré, Guy   Ghent University, Belgium
De Cock, Martine   University of Washington, Tacoma, USA
Diaz, Irene   Universidad de Oviedo, Spain
Dick, Scott   University of Alberta, Canada
Dimuro, Graçaliz   Universidade Federal do Rio Grande, Brazil
Dubois, Didier   Centre National de la Recherche Scientifique,
                                          France
Durante, Fabrizio   Università del Salento, Italy
Escano, Juan Manuel   Universidad de Sevilla, Spain
Ekel, Petr   Pontifícia Universidade Católica de Minas Gerais,
                                          Brazil
Fernandez, Javier   Universidad Pública de Navarra, Spain
Fiala, Karel   University of Ostrava, Czechia
Figueroa-García, Juan C.   Universidad Distrital Francisco José de Caldas,
                                          Colombia
Flaminio, Tommaso   IIIA - CSIC, Spain
Gaeta, Matteo   Università degli Studi di Salerno, Italy
Gagolewski, Marek   Deakin University, Poland
Garibaldi, Jonathan M.   University of Nottingham, UK
Gerla, Brunella   Università degli Studi dell'Insubria, Italy
Godo, Lluis   Artificial Intelligence Research Institute, IIIA -
                                          CSIC, Spain
Gomide, Fernando   Universidade Estadual de Campinas, Brazil
Greco, Salvatore   University of Catania, Italy
Grigorenko, Olga   University of Latvia, Latvia
Gromov, Dmitry   University of Latvia, Latvia
Grzegorzewski, Przemyslaw   Warsaw University of Technology, Poland
Güner, Elif   Kocaeli University, Turkey
Halaš, Radomír   Palacký University Olomouc, Czech Republic
Halčinová, Lenka   University of Pavol Jozef Šafárik, Slovakia
Halis, Aygün   Kocaeli University, Turkey
Hall, Larry   University of South Florida, USA
Herrera, Francisco   Universidad de Granada, Spain

Herrera-Viedma, Enrique	Universidad de Granada, Spain
Hirota, Kaoru	Beijing Institute of Technology, Japan
Holčapek, Michal	University of Ostrava, Czech Republic
Holeňa, Martin	Czech Academy of Sciences, Czech Republic
Huellermeier, Eyke	Ludwig Maximilian University of Munich, Germany
Hutník, Ondrej	Pavol Jozef Šafárik University, Slovakia
Inuiguchi, Masahiro	Osaka University, Japan
Ishibuchi, Hisao	Southern University of Science and Technology, China
Jayaram, Balasubramaniam	Indian Institute of Technology Hyderabad, India
Jin, Lesheng	Nanjing Normal University, China
Kaczmarek-Majer, Katarzyna	Polish Academy of Sciences, Poland
Kacprzyk, Janusz	Polish Academy of Sciences, Poland
Kahraman, Cengiz	Istanbul Technical University, Turkey
Kalina, Martin	Slovak University of Technology, Slovakia
Kaymak, Uzay	Eindhoven University of Technology, Netherlands
Keller, Jim	University of Missouri, USA
Kerre, Etienne	Ghent University, Belgium
Khastan, Alireza	Institute for Advanced Studies in Basic Sciences, Iran
Kim, Sungshin	Pusan National University, South Korea
Klawonn, Frank	Ostfalia University of Applied Sciences, Germany
Klement, Erich Peter	Johannes Kepler University Linz, Austria
Koczy, Laszlo T.	Budapest University of Technology and Economics, Hungary
Kolesárová, Anna	Slovak University of Technology, Slovakia
Kreinovich, Vladik	University of Texas at El Paso, USA
Krídlo, Ondrej	Pavol Jozef Šafárik University, Slovakia
Kruse, Rudolf	Otto von Guericke University Magdeburg, Germany
Lauter, Christophe	University of Alaska Anchorage, USA
Lesot, Marie-Jeanne	Sorbonne Université, France
Li, Jun	University of China, China
Liu, Xinwang	Southeast University, China
Loia, Vincenzo	University of Salerno, Italy
López-Molina, Carlos	Universidad Pública de Navarra, Spain
Lu, Jie	Australian Artificial Intelligence Institute, Australia
Lucca, Giancarlo	Catholic University of Pelotas, Brazil
Luo, M.	China Jiliang University, China
Madrid, Nicolas	University of Cádiz, Spain

Magdalena Layos, Luis	Universidad Politécnica de Madrid, Spain
Marcelloni, Francesco	University of Pisa, Italy
Marsala, Christophe	Sorbonne University, France
Martínez, Luis	Universidad de Jaén, Spain
Masulli, Francesco	University of Genoa, Italy
Massanet, Sebastia	Universitat de les Illes Balears, Spain
Medina, Jesús	Universidad de Cádiz, Spain
Mendel, Jerry	University of Southern California, USA
Merigo, Jose	University of Chile, Chile
Mesiar, Radko	Slovak University of Technology, Slovakia
Michalíková, Alzbeta	Matej Bel University, Slovakia
Miñana, Juan José	Universitat Politècnica de València, Spain
Možkoš, Jiří	University of Ostrava, Czech Republic
Montero, Javier	Universidad Complutense de Madrid, Spain
Montes, Susana	Universidad de Oviedo, Spain
Moreno-García, Juan	University of Castilla-La Mancha, Spain
Murinová, Petra	University of Ostrava, Czech Republic
Navara, Mirko	Czech Technical University, Czech Republic
Nguyen, Hung T.	University of Connecticut, USA
Niskanen, Vesa	University of Helsinki, Finland
Noguera, Carles	University of Siena, Italy
Novák, Vilém	University of Ostrava, Czech Republic
Nurmi, Hannu	University of Turku, Finland
Oh, Sung-Kwun	Suwon University, South Korea
Ojeda-Aciego, Manuel	Universidad de Málaga, Spain
Olivas, José Angel	Universidad de Castilla-La Mancha, Spain
Pal, Nikhil K.	Indian Statistical Institute, Kolkata, India
Pal, Sankar R.	Indian Statistical Institute, Kolkata, India
Pasi, Gabriella	University of Milano-Bicocca, Italy
Pedrycz, Witold	University of Alberta, Canada
Pókala, Barbara	University of Silesia in Katowice, Poland
Pérez-Fernández, Raúl	Universidad de Oviedo, Spain
Perfilieva, Irina	University of Ostrava, Czech Republic
Petrosino, Alfredo	University of Naples Parthenope, Italy
Platoš, Jan	Technical University of Ostrava, Czechia
Pocs, Jozef	Pavol Jozef Šafárik University, Slovakia
Portmann, Edy	University of Fribourg, Switzerland
Prade, Henri	Centre national de la recherche scientifique, France
Ralescu, Dan	University of Cincinnati, USA
Ralescu, Anca	University of Cincinnati, USA
Reformat, Marek	University of Alberta, Canada

Riera-Clapés, Juan Vicente	Universitat de les Illes Balears, Spain
Rodriguez, Rosa María	University of La Laguna, Spain
López, Jesús Rodríguez	University Pablo de Olavide, Spain
Romero, Francisco P.	Universidad de Castilla-La Mancha, Spain
Rovetta, Stefano	University of Genova, Italy
Ruiz-Aguilera, Daniel	Universitat de les Illes Balears, Spain
Sadeghian, Alireza	Toronto Metropolitan University, Canada
Sanchez, Daniel	Universidade Estadual de Campinas, Brazil
Sapena, Almanzor	Polytechnic University of Valencia, Spain
Seising, Rudolf	Deutsches Museum, Germany
Serrano-Guerrero, Jesús	Universidad de Castilla-La Mancha, Spain
Skowron, Andrzej	University of Warsaw, Poland
Slezak, Dominik	University of Warsaw, Poland
Słowiński, Roman	Poznań University of Technology, Poland
Snášel, Václav	Technical University of Ostrava, Czechia
Šostak, Alexander	University of Latvia, Latvia
Sotirov, Sotir	Paisii Hilendarski University of Plovdiv, Bulgaria
Sozzo, Sandro	University of Udine, Italy
Šešelja, Branimir	University of Novi Sad, Serbia
Štěpnička, Martin	University of Ostrava, Czech Republic
Števuliáková, Petra	University of Ostrava, Czech Republic
Straccia, Umberto	Istituto di Scienza e di Tecnologie dell'Informazione, Italy
Strauss, Olivier	University of Montpellier, France
Stupňanová, Andrea	Slovak University of Technology, Slovakia
Su, Shun-Feng	National Taiwan University of Science and Technology, Taiwan
Sussner, Peter	Universidade Estadual de Campinas, Brazil
Szmidt, Eulalia	Polish Academy of Sciences Poland
Takáč, Zdenko	Slovak University of Technology, Slovakia
Torra, Vicenç	Umeå University, Sweden
Tsai, Ching-Chih	National Chung Hsing University, Taiwan
Uļjane, Ingrīda	University of Latvia, Latvia
Valero, Oscar	University of the Balearic Islands, Spain
Verdegay, José Luis	Universidad de Granada, Spain
Vetterlein, Thomas	Johannes Kepler University Linz, Austria
Verma, Amanda	UNITY College of Teacher Education, India
Vidal, Amanda	Artificial Intelligence Research Institute, Spain
Watada, Junzo	Waseda University, Japan
Wilbik, Anna	Maastricht University, Netherlands
Yager, Ronald R.	Iona University, USA
Ying, Hao	Wayne State University, USA

Yoon, Jin Hee	Sejong University, South Korea
Zadrozny, Sławomir	Systems Research Institute, Poland
Zemankova, Andrea	Slovak Academy of Sciences, Slovakia
Zhang, Guangquan	University of Technology Sydney, Australia

Additional Reviewers

Sérgio Marcelino
Paolo Baldi
Kavit Nanavati

Sponsoring Institutions

EUSFLAT (European Society for Fuzzy Logic and Technology)
Investment and Tourism Agency of Riga, Latvia
University of Latvia, Faculty of Exact Sciences and Technology, Department of Mathematics, Latvia
MDPI AG, Basel, Switzerland
Latvian Council of Science, project "A fuzzy logic based approach to the value of information estimation in optimal control problems under uncertainty with applications to ecological management", project No. lzp-2024/1-0188.

Contents – Part I

Fuzzy Transforms

Generalized Quantifiers, Logical Syllogisms and Applications

Fuzzy Entropy

Fuzzy Metric Spaces and Their Generalizations

Information Fusion Techniques

Mathematical Fuzzy Logic

Contents – Part II

Soft Methods in Statistical Inference and Data Analysis

Type 2 Fuzzy Sets

Advancements and Applications of Fuzzy Theory

Fuzzy Relations and Applications

Functors from Fuzzy Structures Categories into Categories of Fuzzy Topological Spaces with Continuous Fuzzy Relations

Jiří Močkoř[(✉)] [iD]

Institute for Research and Applications of Fuzzy Modeling, University of Ostrava,
30. dubna 22, 701 03 Ostrava 1, Czech Republic
jiri.mockor@osu.cz
http://irafm.osu.cz/

Abstract. This paper deals with categories of L-fuzzy structures, such as L-fuzzy closure and interior operators, L-fuzzy pretopologies and co-pretopologies, L-fuzzy relations, or spaces with L-fuzzy partitions and transformations of these categories into the categories of L-fuzzy topological spaces. Unlike traditional approaches that use mappings in the category of L fuzzy topological spaces as morphisms, continuous L-fuzzy relations are used, aligning with the actual trends in fuzzy set theory. Functors transforming the categories of the above-mentioned structures into the category of L-fuzzy topological spaces with a continuous L-fuzzy relation are presented, and some properties of these functors are investigated.

Keywords: Fuzzy topology · Continuous fuzzy relation ·
Transformation functors

1 Introduction

In L-fuzzy set theory, where L is the unital commutative quantale, there are many examples of structures that are related to L-fuzzy topological structures or are based on the use of various operators related to these structures. Typical examples of these structures are various L-fuzzy approximation spaces, L-fuzzy closure and interior operators, L-fuzzy pretopological operators, and L-fuzzy rough sets, and their various modifications and combinations (for example, see [1,9–12]. Although these structures are generally based on the common basis of different topological spaces and their modifications, the tools and languages they use are often very different, and it is difficult to identify deeper relationships between different types of structures and their topological backgrounds. It is obvious that the use of new tools and theories from the field of various types of topological spaces would allow for expanding the spectrum of standard methods used within individual structures, and thus expand the applicability of these structures to other areas. As an example of a possible application of

M. Baczyński et al. (Eds.): EUSFLAT 2025, LNCS 15883, pp. 3–14, 2025.
https://doi.org/10.1007/978-3-031-97225-6_1

topological tools, we can consider the category of spaces with L-fuzzy partitions ([6], for example), which represent one type of structure based on principles similar to those of general topological structures. This category forms the ground category for the so-called F-transforms, which are used in both the theory and applications of fuzzy sets. If we can transform this category into a subcategory of L-fuzzy topological spaces, we can also use this transformation for applications of F-transforms to various types of topological structures, including the definition of a continuity theory for these F-transforms.

Although fuzzy topological spaces were introduced more than 50 years ago, the issue of continuity between these structures has changed little. As in the original definition [2], continuity is generally understood as the continuity of maps between fuzzy topological spaces. However, recently, a number of results have emerged in the theory of fuzzy sets, which are based on the application of *fuzzy relations* instead of mappings. Unfortunately, very few publications address the issue of continuous fuzzy relations, and most of these publications are written in the language of category theory.

In this study, we focused on the possible transformation of categories that have a certain relationship with topological structures. Namely, we deal with categories **K** of L-fuzzy closure and interior operators, L-fuzzy pretopologies and co-pretopologies, L-fuzzy relations, and spaces with L-fuzzy partitions. We demonstrate how these categories can be transformed into the category **Top** of L-fuzzy topological spaces. These transformations are defined as functors, $F :$ **K** $\to$ **Top**. However, in contrast to the standard transformation results, instead of continuous mappings as morphisms in **Top**, we use new definitions of *continuous L-fuzzy relations* between L-fuzzy topological spaces as morphisms. This result represents the main contribution of this study. We also show (Proposition 1) that all of these transformations F have a universal form, that is, the L fuzzy topology in the topological space $F(X)$ is the set of fixed points of some mapping $L^X \to L^X$.

2   Preliminaries

In this section, we repeat the basic properties of the quantale as the main value-set structure and recall the definitions of principal structures representing various concepts of proximity, which are frequently used in L-valued fuzzy set theory, including interior and closure operators, pretopologies, co-pretopologies, and fuzzy partitions. We also discuss the categories of these structures. Unlike classical categories of this type, where morphisms are mappings with various properties, in [7] we presented a generalization of these categories, where morphisms are L-fuzzy relations with various properties.

A principal value-set lattice structure L used in the paper is the *unital commutative quantale*, (see [13], for example), that is the structure $(L, \otimes, \vee, 1_L)$, where $(L, \vee)$ is a complete lattice and $(L, \otimes, 1_L)$ is a commutative semigroup, satisfying the distributivity $a \otimes \vee_{i \in I} b_i = \vee_{i \in I} a \otimes b_i$, for arbitrary set $\{a_i : i \in I\} \subseteq L$. L-fuzzy set s in a crisp set X is a mapping $s : X \to L$. The set of all L-fuzzy sets in X is denoted as L^X. For $s \in L^X$, we set $core(s) = \{x \in X : s(x) = 1_L\}$:

The binary operation $\otimes$ defines the adjoint relation $\varphi \dashv \varphi^*$, here $\varphi, \varphi^* : L \to L$ are such that for arbitrarily $a, b, c \in L$

$$\varphi(a) = a \otimes b, \quad \varphi^*(c) = \bigvee\{x : x \otimes b \le c\} =: b \nearrow c,$$
$$\varphi(a) \le c \Leftrightarrow a \le \varphi^*(c).$$

Recall that by the L-fuzzy relation Q from a set X to the set Y is the mapping $Q : X \to L^Y$, denoted by $Q : X \rightsquigarrow Y$. For L-fuzzy relations $P : X \rightsquigarrow Y$ and $Q : Y \rightsquigarrow Z$ their composition $Q \otimes P : X \rightsquigarrow Z$ is defined by

$$x \in X, z \in Z, \quad (Q \otimes P)(x)(z) = \bigvee_{y \in Y} P(x)(y) \otimes Q(y)(z),$$

and the identity L-fuzzy relation $\eta_X : X \rightsquigarrow X$ is defined by

$$\eta_X(x)(y) = \begin{cases} 1_L, & x = y, \\ 0_L, & x \ne y, \end{cases}.$$

The adjoint $\varphi \dashv \varphi^*$ can be used to extend any L-fuzzy relation $Q : X \rightsquigarrow Y$ and its inverse $Q^{-1} : Y \rightsquigarrow X$ onto adjoint pairs of mappings

$$^\uparrow Q \dashv Q^\Uparrow, \quad ^\Downarrow Q \dashv Q^\downarrow,$$

where $^\uparrow Q, Q^\downarrow : L^X \to L^Y$ and $^\Downarrow Q, Q^\Uparrow : L^Y \to L^X$. These adjoint pairs are frequently used in L-fuzzy set theory; for example, see [4–6,12] and many others. We now recall the definitions of these mappings. For the L-fuzzy relation $Q : X \rightsquigarrow Y$ by Q^{-1} we denote the L-fuzzy relation $Y \rightsquigarrow X$ such that $Q^{-1}(y)(x) = Q(x)(y)$.

Definition 1. *Let $Q : X \rightsquigarrow Y$ be an L-fuzzy relationship.*

1. Extensions of Q defined by the adjoint $\varphi \dashv \varphi^*$:
   (a) Left extension $^\uparrow Q : L^X \to L^Y$:

$$s \in L^X, y \in Y, \quad {}^\uparrow Q(s)(y) = \bigvee_{x \in X} s(x) \otimes Q(x)(y).$$

   (b) Right extension $Q^\Uparrow : L^Y \to L^X$:

$$t \in L^Y, x \in X, \quad Q^\Uparrow(t)(x) = \bigwedge_{y \in Y} Q^{-1}(y)(x) \nearrow t(y).$$

2. Extensions of Q^{-1} defined by the adjoint $\varphi \dashv \varphi^*$:
   (a) Left extension $^\Downarrow Q : L^Y \to L^X$:

$$t \in L^Y, x \in X, \quad {}^\Downarrow Q(t)(x) = \bigvee_{y \in Y} t(y) \otimes Q^{-1}(y)(x).$$

   (b) Right extension $Q^\downarrow : L^X \to L^Y$:

$$s \in L^X, y \in Y, \quad Q^\downarrow(s)(y) = \bigwedge_{x \in X} Q(x)(y) \nearrow s(x).$$

In the following proposition, we recall some properties of these extensions that are useful for various applications.

Proposition 1. *Let* $Q : X \rightsquigarrow Y$ *and* $P : Y \rightsquigarrow Z$ *be L-fuzzy relations and let* $T : X \rightsquigarrow X$ *be a reflexive L-fuzzy relation. Let* $s, s_i \in L^X, t, t_i \in L^Y$, $i \in I$

1. *All extended mappings from Definitions 1 are order-preserving.*
2. $^\uparrow Q(Q^\Uparrow(t)) \leq t$,
3. $Q^{\Uparrow\uparrow}(Q(s)) \geq s$,
4. $Q^\downarrow(\bigcup_i s_i) \geq \bigcup_i Q^\downarrow(s_i), \quad Q^\downarrow(\bigcap_i s_i) = \bigcap_i Q^\downarrow(s_i)$,
5. $Q^\Uparrow(\bigcup_i s_i) \geq \bigcup_i(Q^\uparrow(s_i), \quad Q^\uparrow(\bigcap_i s_i) = \bigcap_i Q^\uparrow(s_i)$,
6. $^\Downarrow Q(\bigcup_i t_i) = \bigcup_i {}^\Downarrow Q(t_i), \quad {}^\Downarrow Q(\bigcap_i t_i) \leq \bigcap_i {}^\Downarrow Q(t_i)$,
7. $Q^\Uparrow(\bigcup_i t_i) \geq \bigcup_i Q^\Uparrow(t_i), \quad Q^\Uparrow(\bigcap_i t_i) = \bigcap_i Q^\Uparrow(t_i)$,
8. $^\uparrow P(^\uparrow Q(s)) = {}^\uparrow(P \otimes Q)(s)$,
9. $^\Downarrow Q(^\Downarrow P(t)) = {}^\Downarrow(P \otimes Q)(t)$,
10. $T^\downarrow(s) \leq s \leq {}^\uparrow T(s) \quad T^\uparrow(s) \leq s \leq {}^\downarrow T(s)$,
11. $T^\Uparrow(t) \leq t \leq {}^\Downarrow T(t), \quad T^\Downarrow(t) \leq t \leq {}^\Uparrow T(t)$.

To facilitate the orientation of the potential reader in the following section of this paper, we recall the definitions of basic structures that present various concepts of proximity, which are frequently used in L-fuzzy set theory. These structures are presented in a number of publications, for example, [1,6,11] and many others. For $\alpha \in L$, $\underline{\alpha} \in L^X$ is defined as $\underline{\alpha}(x) = \alpha$ for an arbitrary $x \in X$.

Definition 2. *1. The map* $i : L^X \to L^X$ *is called a Čech (L-fuzzy) interior operator, if for every* $\underline{\alpha}, u, v \in L^X$, *it fulfils:*
   (a) $i(\underline{\alpha}) = \underline{\alpha}$,
   (b) $i(u) \leq u$,
   (c) $i(u \wedge v) = i(u) \wedge i(v)$.
A Čech interior operator $i : L^X \to L^X$ *is said to be a strong Čech–Alexandroff interior operator if:*

$$i(\underline{\alpha} \nearrow u) = \alpha \nearrow i(u) \quad and \quad i(\bigwedge_{j \in J} u_j) = \bigwedge_{j \in J} i(u_j).$$

2. *The map* $c : L^X \to L^X$ *is called a Čech (L-fuzzy) closure operator, if for every* $\underline{\alpha}, u, v \in L^X$, *it fulfils:*
   (a) $c(\underline{\alpha}) = \underline{\alpha}$,
   (b) $c(u) \geq u$,
   (c) $c(u \vee v) = c(u) \vee c(v)$.
A Čech closure operator $c : L^X \to L^X$ *is said to be a strong Čech–Alexandroff closure operator, if*

$$c(\underline{\alpha} \otimes u) = \alpha \otimes c(u) \quad and \quad c(\bigvee_{j \in J} u_j) = \bigvee_{j \in J} c(u_j).$$

3. *An L-fuzzy pretopology on X is a set of functions $\tau = \{p_x \in L^{L^X} : x \in X\}$, such that for all $u, v \in L^X, \alpha \in L$ and $x \in X$,*
   (a) $p_x(\underline{\alpha}) = \alpha$,
   (b) $p_x(u) \leq u(x)$,
   (c) $p_x(u \wedge v) = p_x(u) \wedge p_x(v)$.
   An L-fuzzy pretopological space (X, τ) is said to be a strong Čech–Alexandroff L-fuzzy pretopological space if:

$$p_x(\underline{\alpha} \nearrow u) = \alpha \nearrow p_x(u) \quad and \quad p_x(\bigwedge_{j \in J} u_j) = \bigwedge_{j \in J} p_x(u_j).$$

4. *A set $\mathcal{A}$ of normal fuzzy sets $\{A_\alpha : \alpha \in \Lambda\}$ in X is an L-fuzzy partition of X, if:*
   (a) The corresponding set of ordinary subsets $\{core(A_\alpha) : \alpha \in \Lambda\}$ is a partition of X, and
   (b) $Core(A_\alpha) = core(A_\beta)$ implies $A_\alpha = A_\beta$.
   Instead of using the index set Λ from $\mathcal{A}$ we use $|\mathcal{A}|$. By $w_{\mathcal{A}}$ we denote the mapping $w_{\mathcal{A}} : X \rightarrow |\mathcal{A}|$ such that $A_{w_{\mathcal{A}}(x)}(x) = 1_L$.

5. *An L-fuzzy co-pretopology on X is a set of functions $\eta = \{p^x \in L^{L^X} : x \in X\}$, such that for all $u, v \in L^X, \alpha \in L$ and $x \in X$,*
   (a) $p^x(\underline{\alpha}) = \alpha$,
   (b) $p^x(u) \geq u(x)$,
   (c) $p^x(u \vee v) = p^x(u) \vee p^x(v)$.
   An L-fuzzy co-pretopological space (X, τ) is said to be a strong Čech–Alexandroff L-fuzzy co-pretopological space if:

$$p^x(\underline{\alpha} \otimes u) = \alpha \otimes p^x(u) \quad and \quad p^x(\bigvee_{j \in J} u_j) = \bigvee_{j \in J} p^x(u_j).$$

3 *L*-Fuzzy Topological Spaces with Continuous *L*-Fuzzy Relation

As mentioned in the Introduction, our goal is to show how the category of *L*-fuzzy topological spaces can be constructed from individual categories of spaces with proximity properties, such as spaces with closure and internal operators or pretopological properties and various spaces with fuzzy partitions. For many examples of these proximity properties, this problem has already been solved [3]. However, in all these examples, the categories of spaces with proximities and *L*-fuzzy topological spaces have morphisms in the form of mappings or continuous mappings. Therefore, the question of whether similar transformations can also be performed for categories with *relations or continuous relations* as morphisms. The issue of categories with *L*-fuzzy relations as morphisms is currently topical because it expands the possibilities of applying these structures without the user being limited by the very strict properties of mappings, in contrast to the more free definition of a fuzzy relation.

In our previous publication [7], we showed how categories of proximistic structures with relations as morphisms can be defined and the relationships between these categories. In this section, we show *how these categories with L-fuzzy relations as morphisms can be embedded into L-fuzzy topological spaces with continuous L-fuzzy relations as morphisms.*

Unlike the standard concept of continuous mapping between L-fuzzy topological spaces, the concept of continuous L-fuzzy relations is not completely common. To date, this concept has been introduced only for the so-called Q *distributors in quantaloid-enriched categories* [14] and was developed for the issue of L fuzzy relations in the submitted publication [8]. In the following section, we first demonstrate how to define the notion of a continuous L-fuzzy relation in the L-fuzzy topological space. Owing to space constraints, we consider only one type of L-fuzzy topological space, namely, Chang L-fuzzy topological spaces, introduced in Chang's paper [2].

Definition 3. *[2] A Chang L-fuzzy topology in a set X is a subset $T \subseteq L^X$ such that*

1. $\{s_i : i \in I\} \subseteq T \Rightarrow \bigcup_{i \in I} s_i \in T$,
2. $u, v \in T \Rightarrow u \cap v \in T$,
3. $\underline{0_L}, \underline{1_L} \in T$.

The elements of T are open L-fuzzy sets and the elements of $T^c = \{\neg s : s \in T\}$ are closed L-fuzzy sets. Pair (X, T) is called the Chang L-fuzzy topological space or L-fuzzy topological space.

In the following definition, we introduce the notion of a continuous L-fuzzy relation. This definition is based on two basic variants of adjoints, $^\uparrow Q \dashv Q^\Uparrow$ and $^\Downarrow Q \dashv Q^\downarrow$, and we obtain two variants of continuous L-fuzzy relations.

Definition 4. *Let (X, T) and (Y, F) be L-fuzzy topological spaces and let $Q : X \rightsquigarrow Y$ be an L-fuzzy relation.*

1. *Q is called $\Uparrow$-continuous L-fuzzy relation, if the following implication holds:*

$$t \in F^c \quad \Rightarrow \quad Q^\Uparrow(t) \in T^c.$$

2. *Q is called $\Downarrow$-continuous L-fuzzy relation, if the following implication holds:*

$$t \in F \quad \Rightarrow \quad ^\Downarrow Q(t) \in T.$$

To show how the categories with fuzzy relations presented in [7] can be transformed into categories of L-fuzzy topological spaces with continuous L-fuzzy relations, we first recall how these categories are defined. In the following, we denote these sets by X, Y, and . is the composition of the morphisms from the standard category **Set**.

Definition 5. *[7]*

1. *The category* **Int** *is defined by:*
   (a) *Objects are pairs* (X, i), *where* $i : L^X \to L^X$ *is a strong Čech-Alexandroff L-fuzzy interior operator,*
   (b) $Q : (X, i) \to (Y, j)$ *is a morphism, if* $Q : X \rightsquigarrow Y$ *is an L-fuzzy relation and*
   $$Q^{\downarrow}.i \geq j.Q^{\downarrow}.$$

2. *The category* **Clo** *is defined by:*
   (a) *Objects are pairs* (X, c), *where* $c : L^X \to L^X$ *is a strong Čech-Alexandroff L-fuzzy closure operator,*
   (b) $Q : (X, c) \to (Y, d)$ *is a morphism, if* $Q : X \rightsquigarrow Y$ *is an L-fuzzy relation, and*
   $$^{\uparrow}Q.c \leq d.^{\uparrow}Q.$$

3. *The category* **PreTop** *is defined by:*
   (a) *Objects are strong Čech–Alexandroff L-fuzzy pretopological spaces* (X, ρ),
   (b) $Q : (X, \rho) \to (Y, \sigma)$ *is a morphism, where* $\rho = \{p_x \in L^{L^X} : x \in X\}$, $\sigma = \{q_y \in L^{L^Y} : y \in Y\}$ *and* $Q : X \rightsquigarrow Y$ *is an L-fuzzy relation such that for all* $s \in L^X, y \in Y$,
   $$q_y(Q^{\downarrow}(s)) \leq \bigwedge_{x \in X} Q(x)(y) \nearrow p_x(s).$$

4. *The category* **coPreTop** *is defined by:*
   (a) *Objects are L-fuzzy strong Čech–Alexandroff co-pretopological spaces* (X, ρ),
   (b) $Q : (X, \rho) \to (Y, \sigma)$ *is a morphism, where* $\rho = \{p^x \in L^{L^X} : x \in X\}$, $\sigma = \{q^y \in L^{L^Y} : y \in Y\}$ *and* $Q : X \rightsquigarrow Y$ *is an L-fuzzy relation such that for all* $x \in X, y \in Y$,
   $$q^y(^{\uparrow}Q(s)) \geq p^x(s) \otimes Q(x, y).$$

5. *The category* **Rel** *is defined by:*
   (a) *Objects are pairs* (X, S), *where* S *is a reflexive L-fuzzy relation on* X,
   (b) $Q : (X, S) \to (Y, T)$ *is a morphism, where* $Q : X \rightsquigarrow Y$ *is an L-fuzzy relation such that*
   $$Q \otimes S \geq T \otimes Q.$$

6. *The category* **SFP**$^{\uparrow}$ *is defined by:*
   (a) *Objects are sets with an L-fuzzy partition* $(X, \mathcal{A})$,
   (b) $(Q, \Psi) : (X, \mathcal{A}) \to (Y, \mathcal{B})$ *is a morphism if* $Q : X \rightsquigarrow Y$ *and* $\Psi : |\mathcal{A}| \rightsquigarrow |\mathcal{B}|$ *are L-fuzzy relations such that*
   (a) *For all* $x \in X, y \in Y$,
   $$\Psi(w_{\mathcal{A}}(x))(w_{\mathcal{B}}(y)) = Q(x)(y),$$

(b) For each $\alpha \in |\mathcal{A}|, \beta \in |\mathcal{B}|, x \in X, y \in Y$

$$A_\alpha(x) \otimes Q(x)(y) \le B_\beta(y) \otimes \Psi(\alpha)(\beta). \tag{1}$$

7. *The category* $\mathbf{SFP}^\downarrow$ *is defined by:*
   (a) Objects are sets with an L-fuzzy partition $(X, \mathcal{A})$,
   (b) $(Q, \Psi) : (X, \mathcal{A}) \to (Y, \mathcal{B})$ is a morphism if $Q : X \rightsquigarrow Y$ and $\Psi : |\mathcal{A}| \rightsquigarrow |\mathcal{B}|$ are L-fuzzy relations such that
      i. For all $x \in X, y \in Y$,

$$\Psi(w_\mathcal{A}(x))(w_\mathcal{B}(y)) = Q(x)(y),$$

   ii. For each $\alpha \in |\mathcal{A}|, \beta \in |\mathcal{B}|, x \in X, y \in Y$

$$A_\alpha(x) \otimes \Psi(\alpha)(\beta) \le B_\beta(y) \otimes Q(x)(y). \tag{2}$$

In the following theorem, we formulate the main results of the study. As follows from Definition 5, the categories defined in this definition are diverse; some have implicit relationships to fuzzy topologies, and for some (e.g., spaces with fuzzy partitions), it is not entirely obvious. However, the vast majority of publications dealing with the issue of these structures and their relationships to categories of fuzzy topological spaces deal only with categories in which morphisms are continuous mappings. In the following theorem, we show that these categories can be embedded into the categories of fuzzy topological spaces with ⇑- or ⇓-continuous relations as morphisms.

Theorem 1. *There exist the following transformation functors from categories of L-fuzzy structures with L-fuzzy relations as morphisms into categories of L-fuzzy topological spaces* $\mathbf{Top}^\Downarrow$ *or* $\mathbf{Top}^\Uparrow$ *with* ⇓*– or* ⇑*-continuous L-fuzzy relations as morphisms, respectively.*

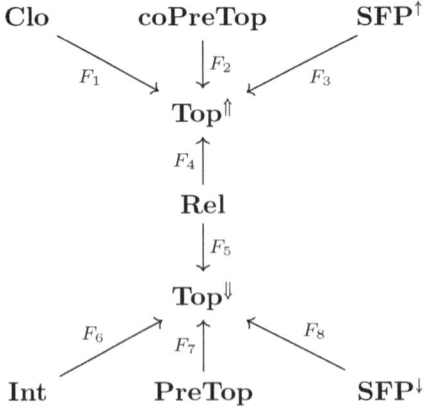

Proof. Instead of the proof, we show only how these functors are defined and what type of continuity of the L-fuzzy relations they represent.

(1) Functor F_1: Let $Q : (X, c) \rightsquigarrow (Y, d)$ be a morphism in category **Clo**. The functor F_1 is defined by

$$F_1(X, c) = (X, \mathcal{T}_c), \quad \mathcal{T}_c = \{\neg s \in L^X : c(s) = s\},$$
$$F_1(Q) = Q.$$

Then, $Q : (X, \mathcal{T}_c) \rightsquigarrow (Y, \mathcal{T}_d)$ is ⇑-continuous in category **Top**$^{\Uparrow}$.

(2) Functor F_2: Let $Q : (X, \rho) \rightsquigarrow (Y, \sigma)$ be a morphism in category **coPreTop**, where $\rho = \{p^x \in L^{L^X} : x \in X\}$ and $\sigma = \{q^y \in L^{L^Y} : y \in Y\}$. The functor F_2 is defined by

$$F_2(X, \rho) = (X, \mathcal{T}_\rho), \quad \mathcal{T}_\rho = \{\neg s \in L^X : \forall x \in X, p^x(s) = s(x)\},$$
$$F_2(Q) = Q.$$

Then, $Q : (X, \mathcal{T}_\rho) \rightsquigarrow (Y, \mathcal{T}_\sigma)$ is ⇑continuous morphism in **Top**$^{\Uparrow}$.

(3) Functor F_3: Let $(Q, \Psi) : (X, \mathcal{A}) \rightsquigarrow (Y, \mathcal{B})$ be a morphism in category **SFP**$^{\uparrow}$. The functor F_3 is defined by

$$F_3(X, \mathcal{A}) = (X, \mathcal{T}_{\mathcal{A}}), \quad F_3(Q, \Psi) = Q,$$
$$\mathcal{T}_{\mathcal{A}} = \{\neg s \in L^X : \forall x \in X, \overline{s}(x) := \bigvee_{x' \in X} s(x') \otimes A_{w_{\mathcal{A}}(x')}(x) = s(x)\}.$$

Then, $Q : (X, \mathcal{T}_{\mathcal{A}}) \rightsquigarrow (Y, \mathcal{T}_{\mathcal{B}})$ is the ⇑-continuous morphism in category **Top**$^{\Uparrow}$.

(4) Functor F_4: Let $Q : (X, S) \rightsquigarrow (Y, T)$ be a morphism in category **Rel**. This implies that $Q \otimes S \leq T \otimes Q$. We define the functor F_4 by

$$F_4(X, S) = (X, \mathcal{T}_S), \quad \mathcal{T}_S = \{\neg s \in |L^X : {}^{\uparrow}S(s) = s\},$$
$$F_4(Q) = Q.$$

Then, $Q : (X, \mathcal{T}_S) \rightsquigarrow (Y, \mathcal{T}_T)$ is ⇓-continuous in category **Top**$^{\Uparrow}$.

(5) Functor F_5: Let $(X, S) \rightsquigarrow (Y, T)$ be a morphism in **Rel**; The functor F_5 is defined by

$$F_5(X, S) = (X, \mathcal{F}_S), \quad \mathcal{F}_S = \{s \in L^X : {}^{\Downarrow}S(s) = s\}, \tag{3}$$
$$F_5(Q) = Q. \tag{4}$$

Then, $Q : (X, \mathcal{F}_S) \rightsquigarrow (Y, \mathcal{F}_t)$ is contnuous in the category **Top**$^{\Downarrow}$.

(6) Functor F_6: Let $Q : (X, i) \rightsquigarrow (Y, j)$ be a morphism in **Int**. The functor F_6 is defined by

$$F_6(X, i) = (X, \mathcal{F}_i), \quad \mathcal{F}_i = \{s \in L^X : i(s) = s\}, \quad F_6(Q) = Q.$$

Then, $Q : (X, \mathcal{F}_i) \rightsquigarrow (Y, \mathcal{F}_j)$ is ⇓-continuous in category **Top**$^{\Downarrow}$.

(7) Functor F_7: Let $Q : (X, \rho) \rightsquigarrow (Y, \sigma)$ be a morphism in the category **PreTop**, where $\rho = \{p_x \in L^{L^X} : x \in X\}$ and $\sigma = \{q_y \in L^{L^Y} : y \in Y\}$. The functor F_7 is defined by

$$F_7(X, \rho) = (X, \mathcal{F}_\rho), \quad \mathcal{F}_\rho = \{s \in L^X : \forall x \in X, p_x(s) = s(x)\}, \quad F_7(Q) = Q.$$

Subsequently, $Q : (X, \mathcal{F}_\rho) \rightsquigarrow (Y, \mathcal{F}_\sigma)$ is $\Downarrow$-continuous in **Top**$^{\Downarrow}$.

(8) Functor F_8: Let $Q : (X, \mathcal{A}) \rightsquigarrow (Y, \mathcal{B})$ be the morphism of **SFP**$^{\downarrow}$. The functor F_8 is defined by

$$F_8(X, \mathcal{A}) = (X, \mathcal{F}_\mathcal{A}),$$
$$\mathcal{F}_\mathcal{A} = \{s \in L^X : \forall x \in X, \underline{s}(x) := \bigwedge_{x' \in X} A_{w_A(x)}(x') \nearrow s(x') = s(x)\},$$
$$F_8(Q, \Psi) = Q.$$

Then, $Q : (X, \mathcal{F}_\mathcal{A}) \rightsquigarrow (Y, \mathcal{F}_\mathcal{B})$ is $\Downarrow$-continuous in **Top**$^{\Downarrow}$.

$\square$

The fuzzy topologies defined in the previous theorem have, in addition to the common property expressed in the form of $\Downarrow$- or $\Uparrow$-continuous relations, one more common property. This property is that each of these fuzzy topologies $\mathcal{T} \subseteq L^X$ is defined as the set of fixed points of some mappings $L^X \to L^X$ defined by L-fuzzy relations. In the following proposition, we show how these mappings are defined for individual L-fuzzy topological spaces $F_i(\mathcal{K}) \hookrightarrow \mathbf{Top}^{\Uparrow}$, $i=1-3$, or $F_j(\mathcal{K}) \hookrightarrow \mathbf{Top}^{\Downarrow}$, $j = 6 - 8$, where $\mathcal{K}$ are categories from Theorem 1.

Proposition 2. *1. Let $\mathcal{K}_i$ be one of the categories **Clo**, **SFP**$^{\uparrow}$ and **coPreTop** of Theorem 1 that defines the functor F_i, $i=1,2,3$. Then, there exists a functor $G_i : \mathcal{K}_i \to \mathbf{Rel}$ such that the diagram commutes*

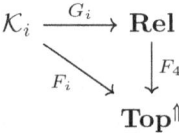

*2. Let L be the complete MV-algebra. Let $\mathcal{L}_i$ be one of the categories **Int**, **SFP**$^{\downarrow}$ and **PreTop** of Theorem 1, which defines functor F_i, $i = 6, 7, 8$. Then, there exists a functor $H_i : \mathcal{K}_i \to \mathbf{Rel}$ such that the diagram commutes*

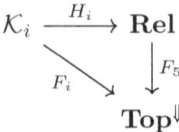

Proof. Instead of the proof, we show only how the object functions of functors G_i and H_i are defined, and how the corresponding topology is defined by the fixed points.

(1) Functor $G_1 : \mathbf{Clo} \to \mathbf{Rel}$. For $(X, c) \in \mathbf{Clo}$ we set

$$G_1(X, c) = (X, R_c), \quad R_c : X \rightsquigarrow X, \quad R_c(x)(x') = c(\eta_X(x))(x')$$
$$\text{Then } \mathcal{T}_c = \{\neg s \in L^X : {}^{\uparrow}R_c(s) = s\}.$$

(2) Functor $G_2 : \mathbf{coPreTop} \to \mathbf{Rel}$. For $(X, \rho) \in \mathbf{coPreTop}$, $\rho = \{p^x \in L^{L^X} : x \in X\}$, we set

$$G_2(X, \rho) = (X, R_\rho), \quad R_\rho : X \rightsquigarrow X, \quad R_\rho(x)(x') = p^x(\eta_X(x')),$$
$$\text{Then } \mathcal{T}_\rho = \{\neg s \in L^X : {}^{\Uparrow}R_\rho(s) = s\}.$$

(3) Functor $G_3 : \mathbf{SFP}^{\uparrow} \to \mathbf{Rel}$. For $(X, \mathcal{A}) \in \mathbf{SFP}$, $\mathcal{A} = \{A_\alpha : \alpha \in |\mathcal{A}|\}$, we set

$$G_3(X, \mathcal{A}) = (X, R_\mathcal{A}), \quad R_\mathcal{A} : X \rightsquigarrow X, \quad R_\mathcal{A}(x)(x') = A_{w_\mathcal{A}(x)}(x'),$$
$$\text{Then } \mathcal{T}_\mathcal{A} = \{\neg s \in L^X : {}^{\uparrow}R_\mathcal{A}(s) = s\}.$$

(4) Functor $H_6 : \mathbf{Int} \to \mathbf{Rel}$. For $(X, i) \in \mathbf{RFInt}$ we set

$$H_6(X, i) = (X, S_i), \quad S_i : X \rightsquigarrow X, \quad S_i(x)(x') = \neg i(\neg \eta_X(x))(x'),$$
$$\text{Then } \mathcal{F}_i = \{s \in L^X : S_i^{\downarrow}(s)(x) = s(x)\}.$$

(5) Functor $H_7 : \mathbf{PreTop} \to \mathbf{Rel}$. For $(X, \rho) \in \mathbf{PreTop}$, $\rho = \{p_x \in L^X : x \in X\}$ we set

$$H_7(X, \rho) = (X, S_\rho), \quad S_\rho : X \rightsquigarrow X, \quad S_\rho(x)(x') = \neg p_x(\neg \eta_X(x')),$$
$$\text{Then } \mathcal{F}_\rho = \{s \in L^X : S_\rho^{\downarrow}(s) = s\}.$$

(6) Functor $H_8 : \mathbf{SFP}^{\downarrow} \to \mathbf{Rel}$. For $(X, \mathcal{A}) \in \mathbf{SFP}^{\downarrow}$, $\mathcal{A} = \{A_\alpha : \alpha \in |\mathcal{A}|\}$, we set

$$H_8(X, \mathcal{A}) = (X, S_\mathcal{A}), \quad S_\mathcal{A} : X \rightsquigarrow X, \quad S_\mathcal{A}(x)(x') = A_{w_\mathcal{A}(x')}(x),$$
$$\text{Then } \mathcal{F}_\mathcal{A} = \{s \in L^X : S_\mathcal{A}^{\downarrow}(s) = s\}.$$

$\square$

Disclosure of Interests. The author declares that he has no known competing financial interests or personal relationships that could have appeared to influences the work reported in this study.

References

1. Bělohávek, R.: Fuzzy closure operators. J. Math. Anal. Appl. **262**, 473–491 (2001)
2. Chang, C.: Fuzzy topological spaces. J. Math. Anal. Appl. **24**, 182–190 (1968)
3. De Cock, M., K.E.: Fuzzy topologies induced by fuzzy relation based modifiers. In: Reusch, B. (eds.) Theory and Applications. Fuzzy Days 2001. Lecture Notes in Computer Science, vol. 2206. Springer (2001)

4. Huang, B., Guo, C.X., Li, H.X., Feng, G.F., Zhou, X.Z.: Hierarchical structures and uncertainty measures for intuitionistic fuzzy approximation space. Inf. Sci. **336**, 92–114 (2016)
5. Mahato, S., Tiwari, S.P.: On bijective correspondence between fuzzy reflexive approximation spaces and fuzzy transformation systems. New Math. Nat. Comput. **16**(2), 291–304 (2020)
6. Močkoř, J.: Spaces with fuzzy partitions and fuzzy transform. Soft. Comput. **21**(13), 3479–3492 (2017). https://doi.org/10.1007/s00500-017-2541-7
7. Močkoř, J.: Functors among relational variants of categories related to l-fuzzy partitions, l-fuzzy pretopological spaces and l-fuzzy closure spaces. Axiom **9**(2), 63 (2020)
8. Močkoř, J.: Kan extensions in the context of new types of fuzzy sets (2024, submitted)
9. Perfilieva, I., Ramadan, A., Elkorda, E.: Categories of l-fuzzy Čech closure spaces and l-fuzzy co-topological spaces. Mathematics **8**(8), 1274 (2020)
10. Perfilieva, I., Singh, A., Tiwari, S.: On the relationship among f-transform, fuzzy rough set and fuzzy topology. Soft. Comput. **21**, 3513–3523 (2017)
11. Perfiljeva, I., Ramadan, A., Elkordy, E.: Categories of l-fuzzy Čech closure spaces and l-fuzzy co-topological spaces. Soft Comput. **8**(1274) (2020)
12. Ramadan, A.A., Elkordy, E.H., El-Dardery, M.: L-fuzzy approximation spaces and l-fuzzy topological spaces. Iran. J. Fuzzy Syst. **13**(1), 115–129 (2016)
13. Rosenthal, K.: Quantales and Their Applications. Longman Scientific & Technical, Pitman Research Notes in Mathematics Series, 234 edn. (1990)
14. Shen, L.: Q-closure spaces. Fuzzy Sets Syst. **300**, 102–133 (2016)

On the Existence of Non-trivial Monometrics on Betweenness Relations: Some Sufficient Conditions

Kavit Nanavati[1] (ID), Megha Gupta[2]([✉]) (ID), and Balasubramaniam Jayaram[1] (ID)

[1] Department of Mathematics, Indian Institute of Technology Hyderabad,
Kandi 502284, India
`ma20resch01004@iith.ac.in, jbala@maths.iith.ac.in`
[2] Insight Research Ireland Centre for Data Analytics, School of Computer Science,
University College Dublin, Dublin D04 V1W8, Ireland
`megha.gupta@ucd.ie`

Abstract. In the recent past, a special type of distance function, namely monometrics, has garnered a lot of attention because of its value and interest in both theory and applications. The key challenge lies in finding a monometric w.r.t. an arbitrary betweenness relation. To address this, the constructions of non-trivial monometrics on various types of betweenness relations have been explored. While it was shown that a non-trivial monometric may not always exist on arbitrary betweenness relations, the study of such betweenness relations has not been undertaken. In this paper, we take a step towards filling this gap by partially characterizing betweenness relations that will not give rise to non-trivial monometrics. By addressing this fundamental question, we hope to provide a clearer framework for understanding when monometrics can be defined.

Keywords: Distance Function · Monometric · Betweenness Relation

1 Introduction

The concept of betweenness relations dates back to works done more than a century ago to that of Pasch [18], and Huntington and Kline [12]. The idea was further developed by Huntington [11], Pitcher and Smiley [22], and Transue [25] in which various types of transitivities of betweenness were proposed. These relations were introduced to capture the notion of betweenness amongst a triplet of elements that were either related geometrically or through an order.

Betweenness relations on a set not only help us in relating triplets of elements but also provide a framework for evaluating the compatibility of other mathematical objects w.r.t. it, particularly distance functions. A special class of such distance functions - that are compatible over a set equipped with a betweenness relation - known as monometrics, has been of significant interest in both theory [17,21] and applications, see [9,13,19,20].

© The Author(s), under exclusive license to Springer Nature Switzerland AG 2025
M. Baczyński et al. (Eds.): EUSFLAT 2025, LNCS 15883, pp. 15–25, 2025.
https://doi.org/10.1007/978-3-031-97225-6_2

Recently, efforts have been made to address the problem of obtaining such distance functions. For instance, [8] demonstrated the existence of pseudo-monometric on an arbitrary strict betweenness relation using fuzzy binary relations, in particular, non-T-transitive Fuzzy Compatible Relations.

Another key approach to obtaining distance functions is through associative, commutative, and monotonically increasing fuzzy logic connectives (FLCs), an idea that dates back to 1984 [3,4]. Taking cue from this, in [15], the authors explored the construction of distance functions obtained from fuzzy implications on $[0, 1]$, that turn out to be monometrics w.r.t. the betweenness relation induced from a partially ordered set (poset).

Towards this end, a comprehensive survey by Nanavati et al. [16] examines the conditions under which such distance functions [1–4] yield monometrics w.r.t. the betweenness relation induced from a poset. Additionally, they offered newer constructions of monometrics using pairs of FLCs such as fuzzy implications and t-conorms, and monotonic FLCs and fuzzy negations. The study of monometrics have also been extended w.r.t. lattice betweenness relations [10].

1.1 Motivation for and Contributions of this Work

The above discussed approaches for constructing non-trivial monometrics have largely relied on additional assumptions about betweenness relations—either by restricting them to specific structural settings such as posets or lattices or by imposing extra properties such as transitivity. This reliance on special conditions highlights a gap in the broader understanding of the existence of monometrics.

Towards this end, it has recently been shown that certain betweenness relations preclude the existence of non-trivial monometrics [14]. However, these betweenness relations themselves have not been thoroughly studied. Motivated by this, our work aims to characterise such relations, with the goal of bridging the gap in the study of existence and construction of non-trivial monometrics on arbitrary betweenness relations. By addressing this fundamental question, we hope to provide a clearer framework for understanding when and how monometrics can be defined.

1.2 Outline of this Work

In Sect. 2, we present a brief introduction to partially ordered relations, betweenness relations, and monometrics on such relations. We also present some rather simple examples of besets and monometrics w.r.t. them. Following these, in Sect. 3, we propose the concepts of loops, P-diagrams, and P-structures which, as can be seen in the sequel, help us in partially characterising betweenness relations that preclude the existence of non-trivial monometrics. Finally, in Sect. 4, we present some conclusions and plans for future work.

2 Preliminaries

In this section, we will initially review relevant concepts within order theory. Following this, definitions of betweenness relation and monometric will be presented, along with corresponding examples.

2.1 Partially Ordered Relations

Definition 1 (cf. [23]). *Let $\mathcal{X} \neq \emptyset$. A **pseudo-partial order** on $\mathcal{X}$ is a binary relation $\unrhd$ on $\mathcal{X}$ such that, for all $x, y \in \mathcal{X}$, the following properties hold:*

- *Reflexivity: $x \unrhd x$,*
- *Antisymmetry: If $x \unrhd y$ and $y \unrhd x$, then $x = y$.*

We shall denote the pseudo-partially ordered set (psoset, for short) by $(\mathcal{X}, \unrhd)$.

Definition 2. *Let $\mathcal{X} \neq \emptyset$. A **partial order** on $\mathcal{X}$ is a pseudo-partial order relation $\preceq$ on $\mathcal{X}$ such that, for all $x, y, z \in \mathcal{X}$, the following property holds:*

- *Transitivity: If $x \preceq y$ and $y \preceq z$, then $x \preceq z$.*

We shall denote the partially ordered set (poset, for short) by $(\mathcal{X}, \preceq)$.

It is well known that posets can be represented through Hasse Diagrams [7]. In [26], the authors showed that not only posets but psosets can also be represented by appropriate manipulation of Hasse diagrams.

Although mentioned in [26], we shall clarify a couple of points concerning the Hasse Diagram representation of psosets.

- Consider the psoset $(\mathcal{X}, \unrhd)$, and let $x, y \in \mathcal{X}$ such that $x \unrhd y$ and $y \unrhd z$. If $\unrhd$ is a partial order relation, then $x \unrhd z$, due to transitivity. If $\unrhd$ is just a pseudo-partial order relation, transitivity might not hold and $x \ntrianglerighteq z$. A dotted line is then drawn between x and z in the diagram to represent the absence of relation between the elements.
- Furthermore, there is a possibility in the case above that $z \unrhd x$. In such a scenario, an arrowed line is drawn from z to x.

Example 1. Let $\mathcal{X} = \{a, b, c, d\}$. Following are a couple of pseudo-partially ordered relations defined on $\mathcal{X}$.

(i) $R_1 := \{(a,a), (b,b), (c,c), (d,d), (a,b), (a,c), (b,d), (c,d)\}$. Note that the relation is not transitive since $a \unrhd b$, and $b \unrhd d$, but $a \ntrianglerighteq d$. The dotted line between a and d in Fig. 1(i) signify that a and d are not related.

(ii) $R_2 := \{(a,a), (b,b), (c,c), (d,d), (a,b), (b,c), (c,d), (d,b)\}$. Note that the relation is not transitive since $a \unrhd b$, and $b \unrhd c$, but $a \ntrianglerighteq c$. The dotted line between a and c in Fig. 1(ii) signify that a and c are not related (similarly for a and d). Note here that $d \unrhd b$ and hence the arrowed line from d to b.

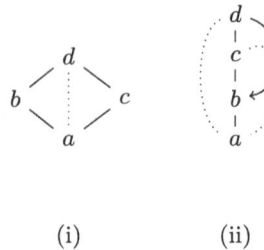

(i)   (ii)

Fig. 1. Hasse diagrams of $(\mathcal{X}, \unrhd)$, given in Example 1.

2.2   Betweenness Relations

Betweenness relations were introduced to capture the notion of a point being in between two other points on a line.

In this section, we introduce the concept of betweenness relations on a set $\mathcal{X}$ with some simple examples. Then we shall look at a way of obtaining psoset, defined in the above section, from a betweenness relation.

Definition 3 (cf. [22]). *Let* B *be a ternary relation on an* $\mathcal{X} \neq \emptyset$. *Then* B *is said to be a **betweenness** relation if it satisfies the following for any* $x, y, z \in \mathcal{X}$:

$$(x, y, z) \in \mathrm{B} \iff (z, y, x) \in \mathrm{B} \ , \tag{BS}$$
$$(x, y, z) \in \mathrm{B} \wedge (x, z, y) \in \mathrm{B} \iff y = z \ . \tag{BU}$$

Remark 1. (i) $(\mathcal{X}, \mathrm{B})$ is known as a beset. We shall use the terms **beset** and **betweenness set** interchangeably. Also, $(x, y, z) \in \mathrm{B}$ is read as 'y is in between x and z'.

(ii) The minimal betweenness relation B_0 on $\mathcal{X}$ is defined as follows:

$$\mathrm{B}_0 = \{(x, y, z) \in \mathcal{X}^3 \mid x = y \ \vee \ y = z\} \ .$$

(iii) For every betweenness relation B on $\mathcal{X}$, $\mathrm{B}_0 \subseteq \mathrm{B}$.

Example 2. In this example, we discuss betweenness relations obtained from diverse mathematical objects.

(i) Consider the real vector space $\mathbb{R}$. Let

$$\mathrm{B}_{\mathbb{R}} = \{(x, y, z) \mid y = \lambda x + (1 - \lambda)z, \ 0 \le \lambda \le 1\} \ . \tag{1}$$

Then $\mathrm{B}_{\mathbb{R}}$ is a betweenness relation, called the algebraic betweenness relation [cf. page 27, [5,24]]. Note that $(x, y, z) \in \mathrm{B}_{\mathbb{R}}$ implies y is a convex combination of x and z.

(ii) Consider a semimetric space $(\mathcal{X}, d)$. Let

$$\mathrm{B}_d = \{(x, y, z) \mid d(x, y) + d(y, z) = d(x, z)\} \ . \tag{2}$$

Then B_d is a betweenness relation called the metric betweenness relation [cf. page 36, [6]].

(iii) A betweenness relation B can be defined from a pseudo-partial order $\unrhd$ on $\mathcal{X}$ as follows:

$$B_{\unrhd} = B_0 \cup \{(x, y, z) \in \mathcal{X}^3 \mid x \unrhd y \unrhd z \text{ or } z \unrhd y \unrhd x\} . \tag{3}$$

(iv) Consider the lattice $(L, \vee, \wedge)$. Let

$$B_L = \{(x, y, z) \mid (x \vee y) \wedge (y \vee z) = y = (x \wedge y) \vee (y \wedge z)\} . \tag{4}$$

Then B_L is a betweenness relation, called the lattice betweenness relation [cf. part II, [22]].

In Example 2(iii), we saw how we can obtain besets from psosets. In the following remark, we see the converse, i.e., how to obtain psosets from besets.

Remark 2. Let $(\mathcal{X}, B)$ be a beset. For an arbitrary but fixed $x \in \mathcal{X}$, $\unrhd_x$ defined as follows is a pseudo-partial order on $\mathcal{X}$:

$$y \unrhd_x z \iff (x, y, z) \in B . \tag{5}$$

Note here that for any $x \in \mathcal{X}$, $x \unrhd_x y$ for all $y \in \mathcal{X}$. In other words $(\mathcal{X}, \unrhd_x)$ is bounded below by x.

In [14], it was shown that a betweenness relation can be represented as a family of pseudo-partial order relations.

Theorem 1 ([14]). *A ternary relation B is a betweenness relation on a set $\mathcal{X}$ if and only if it is induced by a family of pseudo-partially ordered relations $\{\unrhd_x\}_{x \in \mathcal{X}}$ on $\mathcal{X}$ satisfying $y \unrhd_x z \iff y \unrhd_z x$ for any $x, y, z \in \mathcal{X}$.*

Example 3. Let $\mathcal{X} = \{a, b, c, d\}$. Consider the betweenness relation

$$B = B_0 \bigcup \{(a, c, d), (d, a, b), (d, c, a), (b, d, c), (c, d, b), (b, c, a), (b, a, d), (a, c, b)\}$$

on $\mathcal{X}$. The family of psosets obtained from B are represented in the Hasse Diagrams given in Fig. 2.

2.3 Monometrics

In this section, we begin by introducing the concept of a distance m on $\mathcal{X}$ that is compatible over a beset $(\mathcal{X}, B)$, along with some examples.

Definition 4 (cf. [15, 19]). *Consider a beset $(\mathcal{X}, B)$. A function $m : \mathcal{X} \times \mathcal{X} \to [0, \infty)$ is called a **monometric** (w.r.t. B) if it satisfies the following properties for any $x, y, z \in \mathcal{X}$:*

$$x = y \iff m(x, y) = 0 , \tag{P2}$$

and for every $(x, y, z) \in B$,

$$\max(m(x, y), m(y, z)) \leq m(x, z) . \tag{MC}$$

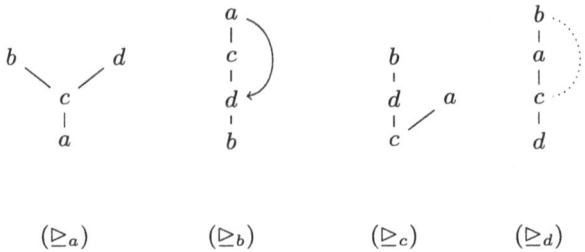

$$(\trianglerighteq_a) \qquad\qquad (\trianglerighteq_b) \qquad\qquad (\trianglerighteq_c) \qquad\qquad (\trianglerighteq_d)$$

Fig. 2. Hasse diagrams of $(\mathcal{X}, \trianglerighteq_x)$ obtained from B given in Example 3.

Remark 3. Note that the trivial metric d_k, defined on a non-empty set $\mathcal{X}$, given as follows:

$$d_k(x,y) = \begin{cases} 0, & \text{if } x = y, \\ k, & \text{otherwise.} \end{cases}$$

where $k > 0$, is a monometric on any beset $(\mathcal{X}, \text{B})$. If $k = 1$, we shall call it a discrete metric. We shall refer to distances which are not trivial as non-trivial distances.

Example 4. In this example, we shall take a look at monometrics defined on some of the besets given in Example 2.

(i) For the algebraic beset $(\mathbb{R}, \text{B}_{\mathbb{R}})$, $m : \mathbb{R}^2 \to \mathbb{R}^{\geq 0}$ defined as $m(x,y) = ||x - y||$, where $||.||$ is any norm on the vector space, acts a monometric.
(ii) For metric betweenness relation B_d, d itself acts as a monometric.
(iii) Let $(L, \preceq)$ be a lattice. Define $m : L \times L \to \mathbb{R}^{\geq 0}$ as

$$m(x,y) = f(x \vee y) - f(x \wedge y) \, ,$$

where $f : (L, \preceq) \to (\mathbb{R}, \leq)$ is an order-preserving function. Then m is a monometric on the beset (L, B_L) [10].

Remark 4. Note that the construction of monometrics on betweenness relations induced from psosets is not readily available. In the next section, we answer it partially by characterizing the betweenness relations that only allow trivial monometrics.

3   Existence of Non-trivial Monometrics on Betweenness Relations

In this section, we begin by introducing the concept of P-structure defined on a beset $(\mathcal{X}, \text{B})$. Next, we discuss the impossibility of having a non-trivial monometric on a beset.

3.1   P-Structure

Note that in Example 1 (ii), $b \trianglerighteq c \trianglerighteq d \trianglerighteq b$. In such situations, we say that the set $\{b, c, d\}$ forms a *loop*. We formalise the notion of *loop* in Definition 5.

In [26], the authors defined the relation $x \precsim y$ if there exists a finite sequence $(x_1, ..., x_n)$ such that $x \trianglerighteq x_1 \trianglerighteq ... \trianglerighteq x_n \trianglerighteq y$. In this work, we shall allow arbitrary sets instead of finite sequences.

Definition 5. *Let $\mathcal{X} \neq \emptyset$, and $x, y \in \mathcal{X}$. We say that $x \precsim y$ if there exists a totally ordered set $\{x_i \mid i \in I\} \subseteq X$, where I is an arbitrary non-empty index set, such that $x \trianglerighteq ... \trianglerighteq x_i \trianglerighteq ... \trianglerighteq y$. If $x \precsim x$, we say that $\{x, x_i \mid i \in I\}$ forms a* **loop.**

Definition 6. *Consider the psoset $(\mathcal{X}, \trianglerighteq)$. Let $a \in \mathcal{X}$ such that $a \trianglerighteq z$ for some $z \in \mathcal{X}$. We say that it is a P-**diagram** if $\mathcal{X} \setminus \{a\}$ forms a loop, and for all $y \in \mathcal{X}$, $y \not\trianglerighteq a$.*

Example 5. (i) Example 1(ii) is a P-diagram since $\{b, c, d\}$ forms a loop. Notice that $b \trianglerighteq c \trianglerighteq d \trianglerighteq b$. The corresponding Hasse diagram can be seen in Fig. 1(ii).

(ii) In Example 3, $\trianglerighteq_b$ is a P-diagram. Notice that $\{d, c, a\}$ forms a loop since $d \trianglerighteq_b c \trianglerighteq_b a \trianglerighteq_b d$. The corresponding Hasse diagram can be seen in Fig. 2($\trianglerighteq_b$).

Definition 7. *Let $(\mathcal{X}, \mathrm{B})$ be a beset. $(\mathcal{X}, \mathrm{B})$ is said to have a P-**structure** if every psoset $(\mathcal{X}, \trianglerighteq_a)$, $a \in \mathcal{X}$ is a P-diagram.*

Example 6. In [14], the following example was provided. Let $\mathcal{X} = \{a, b, c, d, e\}$. Define

$$\mathrm{B} = \mathrm{B}_0 \bigcup \{(a, b, c), (a, c, d), (a, d, e), (a, e, b),$$
$$(b, e, a), (b, a, d), (b, d, c), (b, c, e),$$
$$(c, b, a), (c, d, b), (c, a, e), (c, e, d),$$
$$(d, c, a), (d, e, c), (d, a, b), (d, b, e),$$
$$(e, d, a), (e, c, b), (e, a, c), (e, b, d)\}$$

The family of psosets obtained from B are represented in the Hasse Diagrams given in Fig. 3. Since every psoset is a P-diagram, $(\mathcal{X}, \mathrm{B})$ has a P-structure.

3.2   Existence of Monometrics

In this section, we begin by characterising the properties of a betweenness relation whose preclusion ensures the existence of non-trivial monometrics. Next, we partially characterise the betweenness relations on which non-trivial monometrics cannot be defined.

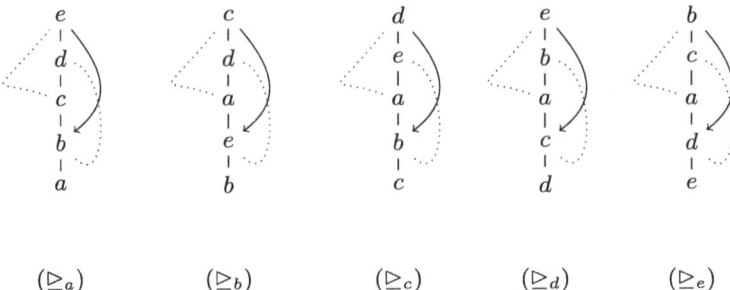

$(\unrhd_a)$ $\qquad$ $(\unrhd_b)$ $\qquad$ $(\unrhd_c)$ $\qquad$ $(\unrhd_d)$ $\qquad$ $(\unrhd_e)$

Fig. 3. Hasse diagrams of $(\mathcal{X}, \unrhd_x)$, $x \in \mathcal{X}$, given in Example 6.

Theorem 2. *Let* $(\mathcal{X}, B)$ *be a beset. Then there exists a non-trivial monometric on* $(\mathcal{X}, B)$ *if* $(\mathcal{X}, B)$ *does not satisfy any of the following properties:*

(α) *if for every* $a, b \in \mathcal{X}$, *there exists a* $p \in \mathcal{X} \setminus \{a, b\}$ *s.t.* $(a, p, b) \in B$.
(η) *if for every* $a, b \in \mathcal{X}$, *there exists a* $q \in \mathcal{X} \setminus \{a, b\}$ *s.t.* (a, b, q)
$\quad \in B$ *or* $(q, a, b) \in B$.

Proof. 1. Suppose (α) is not satisfied. Then there exists a pair $a, b \in \mathcal{X}$ such that for no $p \in \mathcal{X} \setminus \{a, b\}$, $(a, p, b) \in B$.

$$\text{Let } d(x, y) := \begin{cases} 0, & \text{if } x = y, \\ 1, & \text{if } (x, y) = (a, b), \\ 2, & \text{otherwise.} \end{cases} \text{ Then } d \text{ is a monometric on } (\mathcal{X}, B).$$

2. Suppose (β) is not satisfied. Then there exists a pair $a, b \in \mathcal{X}$ such that for no $q \in \mathcal{X} \setminus \{a, b\}$, $(a, b, q) \in B$ or $(q, a, b) \in B$.

$$\text{Let } d(x, y) := \begin{cases} 0, & \text{if } x = y, \\ 2, & \text{if } (x, y) = (a, b), \\ 1, & \text{otherwise.} \end{cases} \text{ Then } d \text{ is a monometric on } (\mathcal{X}, B).$$

The above result shows that if one cannot define a non-trivial monometric on a given beset, then clearly both the conditions (α) and (β) of Theorem 2 are satisfied. The following results show that the presence of a P-structure is one such situation which leads to the satisfaction of these properties and hence gives us a quick way of identifying besets over which non-trivial monometrics cannot be defined.

Theorem 3. $(\mathcal{X}, B)$ *has a P-structure* $\implies$ $(\mathcal{X}, B)$ *has properties (α) and (β).*

Theorem 4. $(\mathcal{X}, B)$ *has a P-structure* $\implies$ $(\mathcal{X}, B)$ *has NO non-trivial monometric.*

Note that the converse of the above theorem is not true, as illustrated in the following example.

Example 7. Let $\mathcal{X} = \{a, b, c, d, e\}$. Define

$$\begin{aligned}
\mathrm{B} = \mathrm{B}_0 \bigcup \{&(a, f, b), (a, d, b), (a, b, c), (a, c, d), (a, b, e), (a, e, f), \\
&(b, f, a), (b, d, a), (b, e, c), (b, c, d), (b, f, e), (b, d, f), \\
&(c, b, a), (c, e, b), (c, e, d), (c, a, e), (c, d, f), \\
&(d, c, a), (d, e, b), (d, e, c), (d, a, e), (d, e, f), \\
&(e, b, a), (e, f, b), (e, a, c), (e, a, d), (e, c, f), \\
&(f, c, e), (f, e, d), (f, d, c), (f, d, b), (f, e, a).\}
\end{aligned}$$

The Hasse diagrams corresponding to B are given in Fig. 4. It can be easily verified that $(\mathcal{X}, \mathrm{B})$ does not form a P-structure since $(\mathcal{X}, \trianglerighteq_f)$ does not form a P-diagram. However, with some effort, it can be proven that there does not exist a non-trivial monometric on it. Notice that B satisfies both the properties (α) and (β).

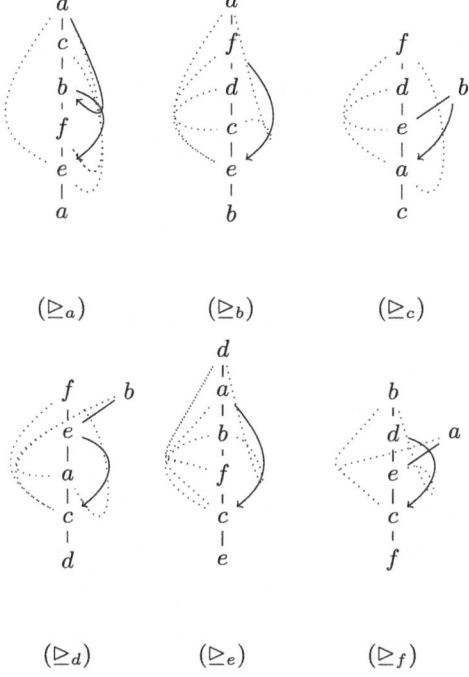

Fig. 4. Hasse diagrams of $(\mathcal{X}, \trianglerighteq_x)$, $x \in \mathcal{X}$, given in Example 7.

4   Concluding Remarks

In this work, we have identified the properties of a betweenness relation whose preclusion ensures the existence of non-trivial monometrics. In the literature, it has been shown by an example that the existence of a non-trivial monometric on an arbitrary betweenness relation is not always guaranteed. In this work, we bridge this gap and partially characterise such betweenness relations.

We believe that the aforementioned properties (α) and (β) would play a significant role in providing a complete characterization of such betweenness relations. Additionally, we intend to construct non-trivial monometrics on betweenness relations induced by psosets and characterise such betweenness relations.

Acknowledgements. The second author would like to acknowledge that this publication has emanated from research supported under the European Union's Horizon 2020 research and innovation programme under the Marie Skłodowska-Curie grant agreement No 101034252.

References

1. Aguiló, I., Calvo, T., Martín, J., Mayor, G., Suñer, J.: On distances derived from symmetric difference functions. In: 2015 Conference of the International Fuzzy Systems Association and the European Society for Fuzzy Logic and Technology (IFSA-EUSFLAT-15), pp. 632–637. Atlantis Press (2015)
2. Aguiló, I., Martín, J., Mayor, G., Suñer, J.: On distances derived from t-norms. Fuzzy Sets Syst. **278**, 40–47 (2015)
3. Alsina, C.: On quasi-copulas and metrics. In: Distributions With Given Marginals and Statistical Modelling, pp. 1–8. Springer, Heidelberg (2002)
4. Alsina, C.: On some metrics induced by copulas. In: General Inequalities, vol. 4, pp. 397–397. Springer, Heidelberg (1984)
5. Banach, S.: Théorie des opérations linéaires. Gauthier-Villars (1932)
6. Blumenthal, L.M.: Distance geometries. Univ. Missouri Stud. **13**(2) (1938)
7. Davey, B., Priestley, H.: Introduction to Lattices and Order. Cambridge University Press, Cambridge (1990)
8. Gupta, M., Jayaram, B.: Fuzzy compatibility relations and pseudo-monometrics: some correspondences. Fuzzy Sets Syst. **451**, 342–360 (2022)
9. Gupta, M., Jayaram, B.: Appropriateness of distances in nearest neighbour classification: a monometric perspective. Pattern Anal. Appl. **28**(1), 7 (2025)
10. Gupta, M., Nanavati, K., Jayaram, B.: Monometrics on lattice betweenness using fuzzy implications. In: Fuzzy Logic and Technology, and Aggregation Operators: 13th Conference of the European Society for Fuzzy Logic and Technology, EUSFLAT 2023, and 12th International Summer School on Aggregation Operators, AGOP 2023, Palma de Mallorca, Spain, 4–8 September 2023, Proceedings, pp. 667–678. Springer, Heidelberg (2023)
11. Huntington, E.V.: A new set of postulates for betweenness, with proof of complete independence. Trans. Am. Math. Soc. **26**(2), 257–282 (1924)
12. Huntington, E.V., Kline, J.R.: Sets of independent postulates for betweenness. Trans. Am. Math. Soc. **18**(3), 301–325 (1917)
13. Jayaram, B., Klawonn, F.: Can unbounded distance measures mitigate the curse of dimensionality? Int. J. Data Mining Model. Manag. **4**(4), 361–383 (2012)
14. Nanavati, K.: Monometrics on betweenness sets: a general construction. Fuzzy Sets Syst. **482**, 108911 (2024)

15. Nanavati, K., Gupta, M., Jayaram, B.: Pseudo-monometrics from fuzzy implications. Fuzzy Sets Syst. **466**, 108429 (2023)
16. Nanavati, K., Gupta, M., Jayaram, B.: Distance functions from fuzzy logic connectives: a state-of-the-art survey. Fuzzy Sets Syst. **490** (2024)
17. Nekvinda, A., Zindulka, O.: Monotone metric spaces. Order **29**(3), 545–558 (2012)
18. Pasch, M.: Vorlesungen über neuere Geometrie, vol. 23. Teubner, Leipzig (1882)
19. Pérez-Fernández, R., De Baets, B.: The role of betweenness relations, monometrics and penalty functions in data aggregation. In: 2017 Joint 17th World Congress of International Fuzzy Systems Association and 9th International Conference on Soft Computing and Intelligent Systems (IFSA-SCIS), pp. 1–6. IEEE (2017)
20. Pérez-Fernández, R., De Baets, B.: On the role of monometrics in penalty-based data aggregation. IEEE Trans. Fuzzy Syst. **27**(7), 1456–1468 (2019)
21. Pérez-Fernández, R., De Baets, B., Gagolewski, M.: A taxonomy of monotonicity properties for the aggregation of multidimensional data. Inf. Fusion **52**, 322–334 (2019)
22. Pitcher, E., Smiley, M.: Transitivities of betweenness. Trans. Am. Math. Soc. **52**(1), 95–114 (1942)
23. Skala, H.: Trellis theory. Algebra Universalis **1**, 218–233 (1971)
24. Smiley, M.F.: A comparison of algebraic, metric and lattice betweenness. Bull. Am. Math. Soc. **49**, 246–252 (1943)
25. Transue, W.: Remarks on transitivities of betweenness. Bull. Am. Math. Soc. **50**(2), 108–109 (1944)
26. Zedam, L., De Baets, B.: Weaker forms of increasingness of binary operations and their role in the characterization of meet and join operations. Fuzzy Sets Syst. **497**, 109116 (2024)

A Few Notes to the Fuzzy Best-Worst Method

Jana Špirková$^{(\boxtimes)}$ and Igor Kollár

Faculty of Economics, Matej Bel University in Banská Bystrica,
Tajovského 10, 975 90 Banská Bystrica, Slovakia
{jana.spirkova,igor.kollar}@umb.sk

Abstract. Multi-criteria decision-making is essential in both research and practical applications, with a key challenge being the precise determination of criterion weights. Various approaches exist, including both exact and approximative methods, such as the Saaty method, the Best-Worst Method, and its fuzzy adaptation known as the Fuzzy Best-Worst Method. The fuzzy variant enhances the ability to manage uncertainty by assigning interval values to the importance of criteria.

This study explores fundamental issues related to the assignment of fuzzy numbers to linguistic terms, the consistency of these numbers in computational processes, and the suitability of criteria for weight determination. The discussion is framed within the context of transportation mode selection, a problem that has been previously examined in both classical and fuzzy environments. Refinements in the Fuzzy Best-Worst Method, particularly through the use of triangular fuzzy numbers, have been introduced to enhance decision-making accuracy. The objective of this research is to contribute to the advancement of this method and encourage discussions on its precision and practical applicability.

Keywords: Fuzzy number · Fuzzy Best-Worst Method · Indicators · Weights

1 Introduction

Within the framework of multi-criteria decision-making, a relatively large number of methods for determining the weights of individual indicators, or criteria, are known. We can mention the exact Saaty method [12,13], but also the so-called approximate Saaty method, which is very easy to apply if we do not have the Solver function available in MS Office Excel. An essential part of these methods is also the Thurstone method of pairwise comparison, [14].

Currently, the so-called Best-Worst method, introduced by Jafar Rezaei, [9], is very popular. He is constantly improving his initial procedures and his ideas can be found in the articles [9–11] and [15].

All of the above methods are based on assigning importance values to individual indicators or criteria using Likert scales. Very popular scale is from 1 to

© The Author(s), under exclusive license to Springer Nature Switzerland AG 2025
M. Baczyński et al. (Eds.): EUSFLAT 2025, LNCS 15883, pp. 26–38, 2025.
https://doi.org/10.1007/978-3-031-97225-6_3

9 or just odd numbers from this scale. Of course, the choice of scale depends on the data with which the researcher is working. This numerical scale can also be expressed in terms of the verbal meaning or importance of a criterion or indicator. Saaty in [12] points out that the human mind is able to meaningfully compare approximately 7 ± 2 indicators.

Currently, considerable attention is also paid to the so-called fuzzy best-worst method, which assigns not a single number to individual indicator importances but intervals of importance values using fuzzy numbers. The first paper on fuzzy sets was published in 1965, although ideas about this type of indeterminacy from a philosophical point of view had been discussed and published earlier, [16]. The word 'fuzzy' is well known in the mathematical community and conveys vagueness, including ambiguity, lack of sharpness, blurriness, and fogginess. The same applies to multi-criteria decision-making. We assign a value of, e.g., 3 to some indicator, or we can consider that it is approximately 3 and then we can think about assigning a suitable interval of the number 3, i.e., the construction of a fuzzy number.

This contribution is also based on the idea that was 'imposed' on us by the authors Guo and Zhao, in the article [5] and later by the authors Dong, Wan, and Chen, v [3], who extended and refined the original theory. Reading these inspiring articles, we came up with a few ideas that we want to share with the mathematical fuzzy community.

This concerns primarily: 1. Are the linguistic terms corresponding to fuzzy numbers really correctly chosen, especially with regard to the term - weakly important? 2. Are disjoint fuzzy numbers taken into account in programming, or are the same upper and lower extremes used that are superimposed on each other? Is this correct with regard to the properties of fuzzy numbers and the operations with them? 3. Is it really enough to consider it appropriate to determine the weights of criteria, or indicators, if the value of the so-called graded mean integration representation of the Fuzzy Consistency Ratio $R(FCR) < 0.1$ and the individual weights are determined using fuzzy numbers that have large differences between the lower and upper values?

We are convinced that our contribution will also find its readers who will help us improve this theory regarding the fuzzy best-worst method. The entire discussion in this article is based on the solution of the problem - the Transportation Mode Selection, which was first solved by Jafar Rezaei in [9] and subsequently [3,5] in a fuzzy environment.

The paper is organized as follows. Section 2 - Preliminaries offers basic definitions, information about the Fuzzy Best-Worst Method based on triangular fuzzy numbers, and moreover mathematical programming model w.r.t. [3]. Section 3 - Our contribution to this topic gives our contribution to the fuzzy Best-Worst Method in the form of a discussion on the assignment of triangular fuzzy numbers to the corresponding linguistic terms. In this section, we offer our short analysis based on linguistic terms and the choice of the corresponding fuzzy numbers. Section 4 - Conclusion gives gives our further possible improvement and practical use of this topic.

2 Preliminaries

To begin, we recall the basic definitions of mathematical concepts that are an integral part of our topic - a triangular fuzzy number, triangular mean integration representation, and also a normalized fuzzy weight vector.

2.1 Basic Definitions

Definition 1 [4]. *A triangular fuzzy number* $\tilde{a} = (a^l, a^m, a^u)$ *is a fuzzy set defined on the set R of real numbers, whose membership function is defined as follows*

$$\mu_{\tilde{a}}(x) = \begin{cases} (a^u - x)/(a^u - a^m) & \text{if } a^m \leq x \leq a^u, \\ (x - a^l)/(a^m - a^l) & \text{if } a^l \leq x \leq a^m, \\ 0 & \text{if } x > a^u \text{ or } x < a^l. \end{cases} \tag{1}$$

where a^l, a^m, *and* a^u *are called the lower bound, the mode, and the upper bound of the triangular fuzzy number* $\tilde{a} = (a^l, a^m, a^u)$, *respectively, and* $a^l \leq a^m \leq a^u$. *If* $a^l \geq 0$, *then the triangular fuzzy number* $\tilde{a} = (a^l, a^m, a^u)$ *is called a positive triangular fuzzy number. If* $a^u \leq 0$, *then the triangular fuzzy number* $\tilde{a} = (a^l, a^m, a^u)$ *is called a negative triangular fuzzy number.*

The following graded mean integration representation is beneficial as it simplifies the complex and tedious process of the original membership function, making fuzzy multi-criteria decision-making more practical and widely accepted.

Definition 2 [5,7]. *The graded mean integration representation (GMIR)* $R(\tilde{a})$ *of a triangular fuzzy number* $\tilde{a} = (a^l, a^m, a^u)$ *is defined as follows*

$$R(\tilde{a}) = \frac{1}{6} \cdot (a^l + 4 \cdot a^m + a^u) \tag{2}$$

The concept of a normalized fuzzy weight vector plays a crucial role in fuzzy decision-making processes. The following definition formalizes this notion by establishing the necessary conditions for a triangular fuzzy weight vector to be considered normalized.

Definition 3 [1]. *Let* $\tilde{w}_j = (w_j^l, w_j^m, w_j^u)$ *be a triangular fuzzy number* $(j = 1, 2, \ldots, n)$. *A triangular fuzzy weight vector* $\tilde{w} = (\tilde{w}_1, \tilde{w}_2, \ldots, \tilde{w}_n)$ *is called a normalized fuzzy weight vector if for every* $(j \in 1, 2, \ldots, n)$, *the following holds:*

$$\sum_{j=1}^{n} w_j^m = 1, w_j^u + \sum_{i=1, i\neq j}^{n} w_i^l \leq 1, w_j^l + \sum_{i=1, i\neq j}^{n} w_i^u \geq 1. \tag{3}$$

2.2 Fuzzy Best-Worst Method Based on Triangular Fuzzy Numbers

In this section, we recall the Fuzzy Best-Worst method based on triangular fuzzy numbers, which was introduced by [5] and proofreading was offered by [3] with the title A new fuzzy BWM based on triangular fuzzy numbers for multicriteria decision making.

Steps of a New Fuzzy Best-Worst Method. We recall the basic steps of this method, although we understand that for a detailed understanding of the whole issue it is necessary to know all the details from [3].

The following steps are also taken from [3].

Step 1. Decide a set $C = (C_1, C_2, \ldots, C_n)$ of decision criteria.

Step 2. Decide the best (the most important) criterion and the worst (the least important) criterion.

Step 3. Perform fuzzy reference comparisons for the best criterion, where the fuzzy Best-to-Others vector A_B is obtained as follows:

$$\tilde{A}_B = (\tilde{a}_{B1}, \tilde{a}_{B2}, \ldots, \tilde{a}_{Bn}),\tag{4}$$

where $\tilde{a}_{Bj}$ is a triangular fuzzy number denoting the fuzzy preference of the best criterion C_B over criterion C_j, $\tilde{a}_{Bj} = (a_{Bj}^l, a_{Bj}^m, a_{Bj}^u)$, $j = 1, 2, \ldots, n$ and $\tilde{a}_{BB} = (1, 1, 1)$.

Step 4. Perform fuzzy reference comparisons for the worst criterion, where the fuzzy Others-to-Worst vector A_W is obtained as follows:

$$\tilde{A}_W = (\tilde{a}_{1W}, \tilde{a}_{2W}, \ldots, \tilde{a}_{nW}),\tag{5}$$

where $\tilde{a}_{jW}$ is a triangular fuzzy number denoting the fuzzy preference of criterion C_j over the worst criterion C_W, $\tilde{a}_{jW} = (a_{jW}^l, a_{jW}^m, a_{jW}^u)$, $j = 1, 2, \ldots, n$ and $\tilde{a}_{WW} = (1, 1, 1)$.

Step 5. Get the optimal fuzzy weight vector $\tilde{\mathbf{w}}_1^* = (\tilde{w}_1^*, \tilde{w}_2^*, \ldots, \tilde{w}_n^*)$ is a triangular fuzzy number denoting the optimal fuzzy weight of criterion C_j, $j = 1, 2, \ldots, n$.

$$s.t. \begin{cases} \min k^* \\ \left| \dfrac{\tilde{v}_B}{\tilde{w}_j} - \tilde{a}_{Bj} \right| \leq k^* \\ \left| \dfrac{\tilde{v}_j}{\tilde{w}_W} - \tilde{a}_{jW} \right| \leq k^* \\ \displaystyle\sum_{j=1}^{n} R(\tilde{w}_j) = 1 \\ w_j^l \leq w_j^m \leq w_j^u, w_j^l \geq 0; j = 1, 2, \ldots, n. \end{cases}\tag{6}$$

After solving (6), the optimal fuzzy weight vector $\tilde{\mathbf{w}}_1^* = (\tilde{w}_1^*, \tilde{w}_2^*, \ldots, \tilde{w}_n^*)$ is obtained.

The authors in [3] point out certain drawbacks of the Fuzzy Best-Worst method presented in [5], and therefore offer a new Fuzzy Best-Worst method based on triangular fuzzy numbers.

2.3   Construct the Mathematical Programming Model w.r.t [3]

The optimal weight for each criterion is one, where for each pair $\dfrac{\tilde{w}_B}{\tilde{w}_j}$ and $\dfrac{\tilde{w}_j}{\tilde{w}_W}$, it should have $\dfrac{\tilde{w}_B}{\tilde{w}_j} = \tilde{a}_{Bj}$ and $\dfrac{\tilde{w}_j}{\tilde{w}_W} = \tilde{a}_{jW}$. Of course, these equalities are very difficult to achieve. If we rewrite these equations in product form, it is possible to determine the weights as accurately as possible, and therefore we will use fuzzy equations

$$(w_B^l, w_B^m, w_B^u) \cong (w_j^l, w_j^m, w_j^u) \cdot (a_{Bj}^l, a_{Bj}^m, a_{Bj}^u) \tag{7}$$

$$(w_j^l, w_j^m, w_j^u) \cong (a_{jW}^l, a_{jW}^m, a_{jW}^u) \cdot (w_W^l, w_W^m, w_W^u) \tag{8}$$

where the symbol $\cong$ has the linguistic interpretation "fuzzy equal to". Then previous equations are equivalent to the following fuzzy equations

$$w_B^l - w_j^l \cdot a_{Bj}^l \cong 0, w_B^m - w_j^m \cdot a_{Bj}^m \cong 0, w_B^u - w_j^u \cdot a_{Bj}^u \cong 0 \tag{9}$$

and

$$w_j^l - a_{jW}^l \cdot w_W^l \cong 0, w_j^m - a_{jW}^m \cdot w_W^m \cong 0, w_j^u - a_{jW}^u \cdot w_W^u \cong 0 \tag{10}$$

With respect to [3] let

$$
\begin{aligned}
R(w_j^l) &= w_B^l - w_j^l \cdot a_{Bj}^l \cong 0, & Q(w_j^l) &= w_j^l - a_{jW}^l \cdot w_W^l \cong 0, \\
R(w_j^m) &= w_B^m - w_j^m \cdot a_{Bj}^m \cong 0, & Q(w_j^m) &= w_j^m - a_{jW}^m \cdot w_W^m \cong 0, \\
R(w_j^u) &= w_B^u - w_j^u \cdot a_{Bj}^u \cong 0, & Q(w_j^u) &= w_j^u - a_{jW}^u \cdot w_W^u \cong 0.
\end{aligned}
\tag{11}
$$

To simplify the notation, the variables w_j^l, w_j^m, w_j^u are unified into w_j^t; $t = l, m, u$ and the parameters d_j^l, d_j^m, d_j^u are unified into d_j^t; $t = l, m, u$.

Then the membership functions for the fuzzy Eqs. (11) can be rewritten as follows

$$
\mu(R(w_j^t)) = \begin{cases} 1, & \text{if } R(w_j^t) = 0, \\ 1 - \dfrac{R(w_j^t)}{d_j^t}, & \text{if } 0 \le R(w_j^t) \le d_j^t, \\ 1 + \dfrac{R(w_j^t)}{d_j^t}, & \text{if } -d_j^t \le R(w_j^t) < 0, \\ 0 & \text{otherwise,} \end{cases}
\tag{12}
$$

where the tolerance parameter $d_j^t > 0$ for $j = 1, 2, \ldots, n, t = l, m, u$, and

$$
\mu(Q(w_j^t)) = \begin{cases} 1, & \text{if } Q(w_j^t) = 0, \\ 1 - \dfrac{Q(w_j^t)}{q_j^t}, & \text{if } 0 \le Q(w_j^t) \le q_j^t, \\ 1 + \dfrac{Q(w_j^t)}{q_j^t}, & \text{if } -q_j^t \le Q(w_j^t) < 0, \\ 0 & \text{otherwise,} \end{cases}
\tag{13}
$$

where the tolerance parameter $q_j^t > 0$ for $j = 1, 2, \ldots, n, t = l, m, u$.

According to Bellman and Zadeh's extension principle of fuzzy sets [2], a fuzzy decision S can be regarded as a fuzzy set $S = \{\tilde{\mathbf{w}}, \mu_S(\tilde{\mathbf{w}})\}$, where

$$\mu_S(\tilde{\mathbf{w}}) = \min\{\mu(R(w_j^t)), \mu(Qw_j^t))\}; j = 1, 2, \ldots, n, t = l, m, u. \tag{14}$$

Let
$$\beta = \min\{\mu(R(w_j^t)), \mu(Qw_j^t))\}; j = 1, 2, \ldots, n, t = l, m, u. \qquad (15)$$

Then (14) can be transformed into

$$\max \beta$$

$$\begin{cases} \mu(R(w_j^t)) \geq \beta, j = 1, 2, \ldots, n, t = l, m, u \\ \mu(Q(w_j^t)) \geq \beta, j = 1, 2, \ldots, n, t = l, m, u \\ 0 \leq \beta < 1. \end{cases} \qquad (16)$$

where β denotes the minimal satisfaction degree of the fuzzy constraints. In order to obtain the optimal fuzzy weight vector $\tilde{\mathbf{w}}^* = (\tilde{w}_1^*, \tilde{w}_2^*, \ldots, \tilde{w}_n^*)$, the authors proposed a mathematical programming model by maximizing the minimal satisfaction degree β.

2.4   How to Solve the Constructed Mathematical Programming Model?

Because equations $\mu(R(w_j^t))$ and $\mu(Q(w_j^t))$ are piecewise functions, solving (16) depends on the risk attitude of the decision maker. In the article by the authors [3] all options for selecting parts of functions for $\mu(R(w_j^t))$ and $\mu(Q(w_j^t))$ are described, but to illustrate our observations we choose only one option, which is given in the original article as the Pessimistic approach Case 1.

For a pessimistic decision maker, by plugging $\mu(R(w_j^t)) = 1 + \frac{R(w_j^t)}{d_j^t}$ of (12) and $\mu(Q(w_j^t)) = 1 + \frac{Q(w_j^t)}{q_j^t}$ of (13) into (16), which is converted into the following linear programming model:

$$\max \beta$$

$$\begin{cases} 1 + \dfrac{w_B^t - w_j^t \cdot a_{Bj}^t}{d_j^t} \geq \beta, -d_j^t \leq w_B^t - w_j^t \cdot a_{Bj}^t < 0, j = 1, 2, \ldots, n, t = l, m, u \\ 1 + \dfrac{w_j^t - a_{jW}^t \cdot w_W^t}{q_j^t} \geq \beta, -q_j^t \leq w_j^t - a_{jW}^t \cdot w_W^t < 0, j = 1, 2, \ldots, n, t = l, m, u \\ 0 \leq \beta \leq 1 \\ \displaystyle\sum_{i=1}^{n} w_i^m = 1, w_j^u + \sum_{i=1, i \neq j}^{n} w_i^l \leq 1, w_j^l + \sum_{i=1, i \neq j}^{n} w_i^u \geq 1, j = 1, 2, \ldots, n, t = l, m, u \end{cases}$$

$$(17)$$

The authors in [3] used Lingo Version 11 software. We use Lingo Version 21 in our application solution. The resulting weights are denoted in the following text as (w_1^*, w_2^*, w_3^*), see Table 2.

2.5 Fuzzy Consistency Index

Since we are working with fuzzy numbers, we determine the fuzzy consistency index FCI for each fuzzy number that we use as linguistic terms, see Table 1, based on the system of equations [3] as follows

$$\begin{cases} (a^l_{BW} - \xi^u)^2 = a^l_{BW} + \xi^l \\ (a^m_{BW} - \xi^m)^2 = a^m_{BW} + \xi^m \\ (a^u_{BW} - \xi^l)^2 = a^u_{BW} + \xi^u \end{cases} \tag{18}$$

2.6 Fuzzy Consistency Ratio

Given (6) we need to determine the fuzzy deviation. We will do this according to the proposal of [3] as follows

$$\xi'^l = \frac{1}{2n} \sum_{j=1}^{n} (|w^{*l}_B - w^{*l}_j \cdot a^l_{Bj}| + |w^{*l}_j - a^l_{jW} \cdot w^{*l}_W|) \tag{19}$$

$$\xi'^m = \frac{1}{2n} \sum_{j=1}^{n} (|w^{*m}_B - w^{*m}_j \cdot a^m_{Bj}| + |w^{*m}_j - a^m_{jW} \cdot w^{*m}_W|) \tag{20}$$

$$\xi'^u = \frac{1}{2n} \sum_{j=1}^{n} (|w^{*u}_B - w^{*u}_j \cdot a^u_{Bj}| + |w^{*u}_j - a^u_{jW} \cdot w^{*u}_W|), \tag{21}$$

where ξ'^l, ξ'^m, ξ'^u represent the possible lower bound, possible mode and possible upper bound of the fuzzy deviation. Arrange them by size, and we get fuzzy deviation. We take the following

$$\xi^{*l} = \min\{\xi'^l, \xi'^m, \xi'^u\}, \xi^{*m} = \text{median}\{\xi'^l, \xi'^m, \xi'^u\}, \xi^{*u} = \max\{\xi'^l, \xi'^m, \xi'^u\}. \tag{22}$$

$$\tilde{\xi}^* = (\xi^{*l}, \xi^{*m}, \xi^{*u}) \tag{23}$$

Definition 4. *The fuzzy consistency ratio FCR is defined as*

$$FCR = \frac{\tilde{\xi}^*}{\tilde{\xi}} = \left(\frac{\xi^{*l}}{\xi^u}, \frac{\xi^{*m}}{\xi^m}, \frac{\xi^{*u}}{\xi^l} \right) \tag{24}$$

The graded mean integration representation of the FCR is then given by

$$R(FCR) = \frac{1}{6} \left(\frac{\xi^{*l}}{\xi^u} + 4\frac{\xi^{*m}}{\xi^m} + \frac{\xi^{*u}}{\xi^l} \right). \tag{25}$$

If $R(FCR) \leq 0.1$, then the comparisons are acceptable consistent.

3   Our Contribution to This Topic

In this section, we recall an example that was already presented by J. Rezaei in [9] and was also used by the authors in [3,5]. Within this task, we offer from our point of view and from the mathematical point of view, more correct solution. Of course, our solution can certainly provoke further discussion. The main issue is which fuzzy numbers are suitable for solving such a task and their lower and upper boundaries. Undoubtedly, the modal value also plays a very important role. But also that these fuzzy numbers should be disjoint, because the product of fuzzy numbers is in this mathematical model the product of disjoint fuzzy numbers. We recall that the original authors did not observe this condition. And what is more, from our point of view, seems practically unusable, is that the weights of the criteria are determined by the original authors as fuzzy weights with a huge difference between the lower and upper bounds. And this is precisely what makes no sense for us in determining the range of weights.

In our discussion, we offer our initial view of this issue. The main reason why we started investigating fuzzy weights is that in the aforementioned articles the weights were determined as e.g. $\tilde{w}_1^* = (0.0941, 0.2000, 0.2589)$, $\tilde{w}_2^* = (0.1411, 0.4000, 0.6471)$ and $\tilde{w}_3^* = (0.0941, 0.4000, 0.7647)$, respectively. After adjusting to $R(FCR) < 0.1$ these weights are $\tilde{w}_1^* = (0.08, 0.20, 0.30)$, $\tilde{w}_2^* = (0.00, 0.40, 0.70)$ and $\tilde{w}_3^* = (0.00, 0.40, 0.85)$, ([3], page 1095, the second round). We see that the fuzzy weights overlap each other. We think this is because the original fuzzy numbers of the linguistic terms also overlapped. Although these fuzzy numbers also have their membership functions, we doubt whether they are suitable for the appropriate selection of criterion weights from a practical point of view.

In our considerations, we pay mainly attention to Table 1.

1. For the linguistic term Equally importance, it is obvious that it is completely okay to consider the fuzzy number $(1, 1, 1)$, because it expresses the importance, or rather. significance of the criterion to itself. And we also know that these linguistic terms have an increasing tendency within the cardinality. Therefore, within our perception of the problem for the linguistic term - Weakly important, we still have doubts whether it is relevant to use the modal value 1 and consider the lower bound to be a number less than 1 and then the upper bound to be greater than 1. We perceive it emotionally as if the criterion to which we assign weakly importance could be a little more important, or just a little more significant, but on the other hand also less important, than the criterion that has the linguistic term Equally importance. We remind you that we are talking about the Fuzzy Best-Worst method, where we really arrange the individual criteria Best to Others and Others to the Worst.

2. Furthermore, the lower and upper values are the same and overlap in the calculations, so the corresponding fuzzy numbers are not disjoint, which violates the mathematical multiplication of fuzzy numbers as used in the original article [3].

Table 1. Linguistic terms and their corresponding triangular fuzzy numbers w.r.t. original authors in [3,5]

linguistic terms	Equally importance (EI)	Weakly important (WI)	Fairly important (FI)	Very important (VI)	Absolutely important (AI)
triangular fuzzy numbers	$(1,1,1)$	$(2/3,1,3/2)$	$(3/2,2,5/2)$	$(5/2,3,7/2)$	$(7/2,4,9/2)$

3.1   Application Example – Transportation Mode Selection

In this section, we recall one part of the original solution to the problem - *Transportation mode selection* - which is solved in their articles by all the aforementioned authors [3,5,9].

Transportation Mode Selection: A company desires to select an optimal transportation mode to deliver the products to a market. This company uses three criteria, including *load flexibility* - C_1 *accessibility* - C_2 and *cost* - C_3 to evaluate the transportation mode. In our case, we have 3 criteria - C_1, C_2 and C_3, where C_1 is considered the worst criterion and C_3 the best.

Specifically, we focus on the so-called pessimistic approach, and finally, we offer our solution and point out the differences, or rather our motives, why we solved the problem with other fuzzy numbers for linguistic terms.

3.2   Pessimistic Approach in Our Understanding

Tables 2 and 3 present optimal weights under a pessimistic approach for two different scenarios. The fuzzy numbers $\tilde{a}$ represent pairwise comparison values, and the final fuzzy weights w^* determine relative importance of the criteria C_1, C_2, C_3. The optimal weights (w_1^*, w_2^*, w_3^*) for the individual criteria were determined using the linear programming model (17) using Lingo Version 21. We investigated the determination of weights using the pessimistic approach - scenario 1 and the pessimistic approach - scenario 2.

In the pessimistic approach - scenario 1, the weights (w_1^*, w_2^*, w_3^*) decrease gradually for C_1 and C_2 across different cases. Criterion C_3 sees an increase in weight allocation, showing that it becomes more significant under pessimistic conditions. The highest weight for this criterion is in the most pessimistic case, showing a shift in importance.

In the pessimistic approach - scenario 2, the weights show a similar pattern but with more pronounced differences. Criterion C_3 holds an even higher dominance in all pessimistic cases than in the pessimistic approach - scenario 1. The highest weight for C_3, $w_3^* = 0.6430364$, reinforcing that C_3 gains increasing importance under more extreme pessimistic conditions.

Table 2. Optimal weights w.r.t. Pessimistic approach - scenario 1

Pessimistic 1	$\tilde{a}_{BW} = (2.6, 3.0, 3.4)$	$\tilde{a}_{B2} = (1.6, 2.0, 2.4)$	$\tilde{a}_{BB} = (1, 1, 1)$	
	$\tilde{a}_{WW} = (1, 1, 1)$	$\tilde{a}_{2W} = (1.6, 2.0, 2.4)$	$\tilde{a}_{BW} = (2.6, 3.0, 3.4)$	
(17)	C_1	C_2	C_3	w.r.t.
w_1^*	0.1890569	0.3024911	0.4839858	formula (25)
w_2^*	0.1890569	0.3024911	0.508452	$R(FCR)$
w_3^*	0.2135231	0.3024911	0.508452	0.071550
Pessimistic 2	$\tilde{a}_{BW} = (2.7, 3.0, 3.3)$	$\tilde{a}_{B2} = (1.7, 2.0, 2.3)$	$\tilde{a}_{BB} = (1, 1, 1)$	
	$\tilde{a}_{WW} = (1, 1, 1)$	$\tilde{a}_{2W} = (1.7, 2.0, 2.3)$	$\tilde{a}_{BW} = (2.7, 3.0, 3.3)$	
	C_1	C_2	C_3	
w_1^*	0.1865213	0.2962397	0.5036074	
w_2^*	0.1865213	0.2962397	0.5172391	$R(FCR)$
w_3^*	0.2001529	0.2962397	0.5172391	0.059911
Pessimistic 3	$\tilde{a}_{BW} = (2.8, 3.0, 3.2)$	$\tilde{a}_{B2} = (1.8, 2.0, 2.2)$	$\tilde{a}_{BB} = (1, 1, 1)$	
	$\tilde{a}_{WW} = (1, 1, 1)$	$\tilde{a}_{2W} = (1.8, 2.0, 2.2)$	$\tilde{a}_{BW} = (2.8, 3.0, 3.2)$	
	C_1	C_2	C_3	
w_1^*	0.1863705	0.2899096	0.5218373	
w_2^*	0.1863705	0.2899096	0.5237199	$R(FCR)$
w_3^*	0.1863705	0.2917922	0.5237199	0.049443
Pessimistic 4	$\tilde{a}_{BW} = (2.9, 3.0, 3.1)$	$\tilde{a}_{B2} = (1.9, 2.0, 2.1)$	$\tilde{a}_{BB} = (1, 1, 1)$	
	$\tilde{a}_{WW} = (1, 1, 1)$	$\tilde{a}_{2W} = (1.9, 2.0, 2.1)$	$\tilde{a}_{BW} = (2.9, 3.0, 3.1)$	
	C_1	C_2	C_3	
w_1^*	0.180046	0.2748071	0.5221335	
w_2^*	0.180046	0.2798159	0.5401381	$R(FCR)$
w_3^*	0.180046	0.2978205	0.5451469	0.028199

The triangular fuzzy numbers represent the range of uncertainty in the comparisons. A higher spread in the pessimistic approach - scenario 2 suggests a wider range of expert opinions compared to the pessimistic approach - scenario 1. In all these scenarios, the value $R(FCR) < 0.1$, meaning the data is consistent, ensuring that the weights can be confidently used in multicriteria decision making.

Table 3. Optimal weights w.r.t. Pessimistic approach - scenario 2

Pessimistic 1	$\tilde{a}_{BW} = (4.0, 5.0, 6.0)$	$\tilde{a}_{B2} = (2.1, 3, 3.9)$	$\tilde{a}_{BB} = (1, 1, 1)$	
	$\tilde{a}_{WW} = (1, 1, 1)$	$\tilde{a}_{2W} = (2.1, 3, 3.9)$	$\tilde{a}_{WB} = (4.0, 5.0, 6.0)$	
(17)	C_1	C_2	C_3	w.r.t.
w_1^*	0.140000	0.266667	0.560000	formula (25)
w_2^*	0.140000	0.266667	0.593333	$R(FCR)$
w_3^*	0.17333	0.266667	0.593333	0.071550
Pessimistic 2	$\tilde{a}_{BW} = (4.2, 5, 5.8)$	$\tilde{a}_{B2} = (2.3, 3, 3.7)$	$\tilde{a}_{BB} = (1, 1, 1)$	
	$\tilde{a}_{WW} = (1, 1, 1)$	$\tilde{a}_{2W} = (2.3, 3, 3.7)$	$\tilde{a}_{WB} = (4.2, 5, 5.8)$	
	C_1	C_2	C_3	
w_1^*	0.1394443	0.2546374	0.585666	
w_2^*	0.1394443	0.2546374	0.6059183	$R(FCR)$
w_3^*	0.1596966	0.2546374	0.6059183	0.039947
Pessimistic 3	$\tilde{a}_{BW} = (4.5, 5, 5.6)$	$\tilde{a}_{B2} = (2.5, 3.0, 3.5)$	$\tilde{a}_{BB} = (1, 1, 1)$	
	$\tilde{a}_{WW} = (1, 1, 1)$	$\tilde{a}_{2W} = (2.5, 3, 3.5)$	$\tilde{a}_{WB} = (4.5, 5, 5.6)$	
	C_1	C_2	C_3	
w_1^*	0.1395782	0.2456576	0.6141439	
w_2^*	0.1395782	0.2456576	0.6147643	$R(FCR)$
w_3^*	0.1401985	0.2456576	0.6147643	0.032239
Pessimistic 4	$\tilde{a}_{BW} = (4.8, 5, 5.2)$	$\tilde{a}_{B2} = (2.9, 3, 3.1)$	$\tilde{a}_{BB} = (1, 1, 1)$	
	$\tilde{a}_{WW} = (1, 1, 1)$	$\tilde{a}_{2W} = (2.9, 3, 3.1)$	$\tilde{a}_{WB} = (4.8, 5, 5.2)$	
	C_1	C_2	C_3	
w_1^*	0.1286073	0.2283563	0.6173149	
w_2^*	0.1286073	0.2412171	0.6301757	$R(FCR)$
w_3^*	0.6173149	0.6301757	0.6430364	0.017345

4   Conclusion

Although we have offered a kind of introductory discussion on the topic of Fuzzy Best-Worst method in the article, we believe that this method will also have its practical use if we can gradually establish certain rules that will provide us with optimal weights in multi-criteria decision-making. The basic conclusions that follow from our research are that the weights of a given criterion decrease as the interval of fuzzy numbers gradually decreases. This is especially true for criteria that are less important, in our case C_1 and C_2. Conversely, narrowing the intervals increases the weight of the best criterion, in our case C_3. That is, the criterion with a larger variance of the interval has a higher weight. According to theoretical assumptions, d and q should be sufficiently small. The original authors used the number 1 for both tolerance parameters. Our goal is also to verify to what extent these tolerance parameter values affect the resulting weights. As for the tolerance parameters d and q, when choosing a value below

0.4, the Lingo Version 21 programme did not always offer a solution, but we got the same results for other choices of these parameters. Increasing the tolerance parameters no longer affects our results. Our ambition is to continue a much deeper study of this issue and apply it in determining the weights of various criteria and indicators in economics.

The ongoing development of the fuzzy Best-Worst Method highlights the need for more precise and consistent decision-making frameworks, particularly in handling uncertainty. By incorporating intuitionistic fuzzy sets [6], and α-cut interval-based approaches, [8], recent studies have enhanced weight optimization techniques, improving reliability in multi-criteria decision-making. Future research should explore hybrid models that integrate machine learning and advanced fuzzy logic to further refine decision consistency and expand practical applications across diverse industries.

Acknowledgments. The work of Jana Špirková has been supported by the Slovak Scientific Grant Agency VEGA no. 1/0124/24.

References

1. Bas, E., Egrioglu, E., Yolcu, U., Grosan, C.: Type 1 fuzzy function approach based on ridge regression for forecasting. Granular Comput. **4**, 629–637 (2019). https://doi.org/10.1007/s41066-018-0115-4
2. Bellman, R.E., Zadeh, L.A.: Decision-making in a fuzzy environment. Manag. Sci. **17**(4), 141–164 (1970)
3. Dong, J., Wan, S., Chen, S.M.: Fuzzy best-worst method based on triangular fuzzy numbers for multi-criteria decision-making. Inf. Sci. **547**, 1080–1104 (2021). https://doi.org/10.1016/j.ins.2020.09.014
4. Dubois, D., Prade, H.: Fuzzy Sets and Systems: Theory and Applications. Academic Press, Boston (1980)
5. Guo, S., Zhao, H.: Fuzzy best-worst multi-criteria decision-making method and its applications. Knowl-Based Syst. **121**, 23–31 (2017). https://doi.org/10.1016/j.knosys.2017.01.010
6. Cheng, X., Chen, Ch.: Decision making with intuitionistic fuzzy best-worst method. Expert Syst. Appl. **237**(Part A), 121215 (2024). https://doi.org/10.1016/j.eswa.2023.121215
7. Liao, M.S., Liang, G.S., Chen, C.Y.: Fuzzy gray relation method for multiple criteria decision-making problems. Qual. Quant. **47**, 3065–3077 (2013). https://doi.org/10.1007/s11135-012-9704-5
8. Ratandhara, H.M., Kumar, M.: An α-cut intervals based fuzzy best-worst method for multi-criteria decision-making. Appl. Soft Comput. **159**, 111625 (2024). https://doi.org/10.1016/j.asoc.2024.111625. ISSN 1568-4946
9. Rezaei, J.: Best-worst multi-criteria decision-making. Omega **53**, 49–57 (2014). https://doi.org/10.1016/j.omega.2014.11.009
10. Rezaei, J.: Best-worst multi-criteria decision-making method: some properties and a linear model. Omega **64**, 126–130 (2016). https://doi.org/10.1016/j.omega.2015.12.001

11. Rezaei, J.: Best Worst Method. BWM Solvers (2016b). https://bestworstmethod. com/software/
12. Saaty, T.L.: A scaling method for priorities in hierarchical structures. J. Math. Psychol. **15**(3), 234–281 (1977). https://doi.org/10.1016/0022-2496(77)90033-5
13. Saaty, T.L.: Theory and Applications of the Analytic Network Process: Decision Making with Benefits, Opportunities, Costs, and Risks. RWS publications (2009)
14. Thurstone, L.L.: A law of comparative judgment. Psychol. Rev. **34**, 273–286 (1927)
15. Wu, Q., Liu, X., Zhou, L., Quin, J., Rezaei, J.: An analytical framework for the best-worst method. Omega **123**, 102974 (2024). https://doi.org/10.1016/j.omega. 2023.102974
16. Zadeh, L.A.: Fuzzy sets. Inf. Control **8**(3), 338–353 (1965). https://doi.org/10. 1016/S0019-9958(65)90241-X

Chatbots with Character - An Implementation of Fuzzy Conversational Character Computing

Sophie Hundertmark[1]([envelope])[iD], Ramón Christen[1][iD], and Edy Portmann[2][iD]

[1] Lucerne University of Applied Sciences and Arts, 6002 Lucerne, Switzerland
sophie.hundertmark@hslu.ch
[2] University of Fribourg, 1700 Fribourg, Switzerland

Abstract. Despite the advancements in conversational AI, most chatbots fail to adapt dynamically to users' emotions and personalities. This paper presents the Fuzzy Conversational Character Computing (FCCC) framework, which integrates Fuzzy Logic, Computing with Words and Perceptions, and Character Computing to enable chatbots to deliver adaptive, sentiment-sensitive responses. By leveraging Large Language Models (LLMs) and real-time sentiment analysis, FCCC fosters more empathetic and personalized interactions.

Through an experimental evaluation in the healthcare domain, we demonstrate that FCCC-enhanced chatbots positively influence user sentiment and satisfaction, outperforming traditional bots in perceived empathy and adaptability. These findings establish FCCC as a breakthrough in conversational AI, with broad potential for applications in healthcare, customer service, and beyond. Future research will focus on scaling the framework and exploring its integration with advanced AI technologies.

Keywords: Chatbot · Character Computing · Large Language Model

1 Introduction and Research Question

Chatbots, as an archetype of conversational AI systems, have been a topic of scientific interest since 1966 when Joseph Weizenbaum developed the first chatbot, ELIZA, as part of a psychology experiment [11]. ELIZA's operational framework was fundamentally different from the capabilities of today's chatbots. It did not leverage Artificial Intelligence (AI) or Large Language Model (LLM)s. However, its underlying goal remains a cornerstone of chatbot research: developing systems capable of natural language communication [4].

Building on this foundation, more advanced theoretical approaches have been developed to address the inherent limitations of earlier conversational systems. One such framework is Fuzzy Conversational Character Computing (FCCC), which integrates interdisciplinary concepts such as Fuzzy Logic (FL) and Computing with Words and Perceptions (CWP) [5].

M. Baczyński et al. (Eds.): EUSFLAT 2025, LNCS 15883, pp. 39–53, 2025.
https://doi.org/10.1007/978-3-031-97225-6_4

FL distinguishes itself by moving beyond the rigid binary nature of traditional logic systems, enabling chatbots to process degrees of truth and ambiguity. This makes them particularly suited to handling nuanced and imprecise user inputs, which are common in natural language communication. FL allows for modelling human-like reasoning, such as interpreting "somewhat satisfied" or "mostly true" in conversational contexts [14].

CWP, as a subset of FL, further enhances this capability by focusing on the interpretation of linguistic variables rather than strict numerical data. This enables chatbots to engage in conversations that incorporate subjective, vague, or context-dependent information, such as emotional states or perceptions. CWP allows for more dynamic and context-sensitive interactions by interpreting the "fuzzy" meaning behind user inputs [15].

By incorporating FL and CWP, the FCCC framework enables the creation of chatbots that go beyond simple command execution or rigid response structures. Instead, these systems adapt dynamically to users' personality traits, emotions, and situational contexts [5]. Inspired by systems theory, it operates as a self-regulating system, minimizing the need for external interventions and focusing on personalized, efficient interactions [1]. This approach shifts the paradigm of chatbot design, making them not only more empathetic but also more adaptable than traditional rule-based or intent-driven systems.

This research transitions from theory to practice by technically implementing and testing a chatbot using FCCC. Additionally the study evaluates how such adaptive systems foster positive changes in users' sentiment. Since previous research already mentioned advancements of LLMs, such as ChatGPT, to further enhance the system's capabilities [5], the technically implementation also makes use of these advancements and uses LLMs. The presented study applies FCCC to meet unique emotional and informational needs of users.

In particular, this research is driven by the overarching questions:

1. How can the principles of Fuzzy Logic, as applied in Fuzzy Conversational Character Computing, be operationalized to process ambiguous user inputs, dynamically adapting to personality traits and emotional states within a chatbot?
2. Does the capability of dynamically adapting the personality, character, and situation in combination with chatbot reply reformulation have a measurable influence on chat characteristics and even foster positive sentiment changes among users?

The research questions are addressed by first modelling the conceptual framework and subsequently implementing it within a chatbot. Afterwards, a laboratory experiment using the newly developed chat interface evaluates both the technical implementation and the impact of character adaptations.

In chapter two an overview of the key theories underpinning the FCCC framework and exploring the integration of LLMs is given. Chapter three extends the FCCC framework by formalizing it into a mathematical model, which serves as the foundation for the technical evaluation and experimental study conducted in chapter four. The paper concludes with a summary of the findings and a discussion of open research questions, highlighting areas for future investigation.

2   Related Work

The concept of FCCC is rooted in the integration of several disciplines—FL, CWP, and Character Computing (CC)—to create a more nuanced and adaptable conversational AI. FCCC builds on the foundational work of Zadeh's Fuzzy Logic [12], which extends classical logic by allowing variables to take on a range of values rather than being limited to binary states (true or false). This flexibility is essential for addressing the inherent uncertainties and ambiguities of human conversation [12]. Unlike rigid traditional AI approaches, FCCC leverages fuzzy sets to handle the vagueness in human communication effectively by integrating existing technologies as follows:

Computing with Words and Perceptions (CWP) are other integral components of FCCC, focuses on processing and reasoning using imprecise, natural language terms and fuzzy concepts, as described by Zadeh [13]. Instead of requiring rigid numeric inputs, CWP allows systems to work with linguistic information such as "mostly satisfied" making interactions more natural and aligned with human communication [8]. Additionally, the integration of Zumstein's multidimensional fuzzy classifications into FCCC is another key to achieve adaptability. By representing a user's context across modalities such as emotional state, personality traits, and situational factors through linguistic variables, FCCC minimizes the reliance on rigid classifications and enables smoother transitions between states [15]. Zumstein's work on fuzzy classification demonstrates its utility in real-world applications such as customer relationship management. For example, linguistic variables like "customer satisfaction" can be modelled as fuzzy sets, enabling businesses to segment users into categories with overlapping boundaries. This approach is adapted to FCCC to handle user classifications based on personality traits and situational context, leading to more personalized and effective interactions [15].

Similarly, Pangaro's Conversational Theory provides the theoretical foundation for understanding how conversational systems can adaptively build trust and rapport with users [8]. Although the theory does not technically belong to the fields of computing it is a fundamental theory describing the conversation mechanism between humans to obtain collaboration between them. Thus, it is a good inspiration for the FCCC helping developers to design chatbots that not only respond to user inputs but also guide interactions toward mutually beneficial outcomes [2].

Character Computing (CC), as a cornerstone of FCCC, transcends merely processing user inputs by modelling and predicting user behaviour. It considers stable personality traits, emotional states, and situational factors [3]. Unlike Affective Computing [9], which primarily focuses on recognizing and responding to emotional cues, CC provides a holistic view by integrating situational and motivational factors that influence behaviour [3]. For instance, the Character-Behaviour-Situation (CBS) triad proposed by El Bolock et al. demonstrates how user behaviour can be predicted based on personality and situational context. This dynamic adaptation contrasts with traditional AI systems, which rely on static user profiles and extensive datasets.

Integration of Large Language Models (LLMs) allows to extend the functionality of chatbots. The FCCC framework integrates LLMs to enhance conversational adaptability. While LLMs excel at generating contextually relevant responses, FCCC refines these outputs by aligning them with user-specific traits and emotional states. FCCC employs FL to estimate user expressions, as shown in Fig. 1 for a set of three character traits (T1, T2, T3), enabling LLMs to adjust tone and content dynamically. By combining probabilistic LLMs outputs with FCCC's fuzzy classifications, chatbots can deliver empathetic and nuanced interactions resulting in more human-like dialogues.

3   The FCCC Framework

In the FCCC framework, character estimation implies consideration of three particular aspects: the behaviour (B), instant message character (C) and situation (S). Thereby, the situation equals the chat history, including all queries and rephrased replies. The behaviour indicates the present sentiment of a chat user and may change depending on chat replies. In contrast, the character presents the character estimation of the most recent query only. Together, the three aspects build the triad defining the requirements (i.e. the parameters) for a sentiment adapted reply.

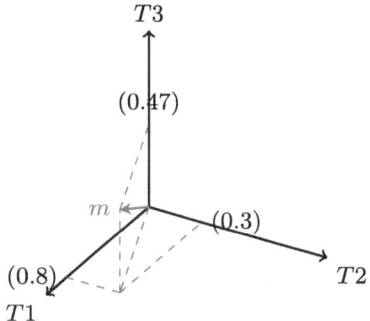

Fig. 1. Character estimation by mapping a particular message character vector (m) to a set of 3 character traits $(T1, T2, T3)$. The exemplary estimation results a membership character vector (C) for the three traits of $[0.8, 0.3, 0.47]$.

The situation is the collection of the whole passed conversation. Consequently, it is the sum of all messages m composing all queries and answers. Mathematically, the situation (S) can be formulated as the sum of all messages (m) by the formula:

$$S = \sum_i m_i \tag{1}$$

Applying a fuzzy membership function on considered character traits allows for dynamic character estimation of particular messages. As schematically presented in Fig. 1, the character estimation results a vector of membership values in the range of $[0, 1]$ for all considered character traits, such as for T1, T2, T3 in the figure. That means, the character vector of a message (m) is mapped on each character trait by applying a fuzzy membership function. In theory, since all of the considered traits can overlay independent of each other, all can be treated separately with different type of membership functions. Yet, as default implementation of the FCCC framework in the proof of concept, we assumed a left trapeziodal function (L-function) resulting 0 at the intersection and 1 for a full distinctive trait. Mathematically, the definition of the membership character vector (C) considering a given set of traits $T = t_1, t_2, t_3, ..., t_n$ is defined by the membership function applied to each trait in Formula 2 and the character vector composition given in Formula 3:

$$\mu_x(m) = max(min(\frac{m - 0}{1 - 0}, 1), 0) \tag{2}$$

$$C_{(m)} = \{\mu_1(m), \mu_2(m), \mu_3(m), \mu_4(m), \mu_5(m)\} \tag{3}$$

According the FCCC framework, the behaviour (B) represents the current sentiment of the chat user based on the character of n recent queries. To this extent, the behaviour presents the trend of the character (C). For a first implementation of the FCCC framework, we go for the arithmetic mean of n previous and the current queries. Mathematically, the behaviour can be formulated as:

$$B = \frac{1}{n + 1} \sum_{i=-n}^{-1} C_i + \frac{C}{n + 1} \tag{4}$$

The chat history is recorded to the situation (S) whereas the FCCC framework estimates the character vector of the most recent query (C) for every new input. In a second step, the framework calculates the behaviour character vector (B) based on n previous query character vectors $C_{-1}, C_{-2}, ..., C_{-n}$ and the most recent vector C.

Finally, all three compartments, the behaviour, character and situation, are factors that influence the phrasing style of a reply. In fact, the reply (R) generated by a chatbot applying the FCCC framework relies on a function f considering all three aspects such as:

$$R = f_{(B,C,S)} \tag{5}$$

Thus, the function f requires that all factors used for rephrasing the reply are calculated in advance in the following order: 1. situation update, 2. character and 3. behaviour estimation before matching replies to a particular sentiment situation. The technical implementation of the mathematical FCCC framework description is proved by an experimental setup, where the function f in Formula 5 represents the rephrasing returned from a chatbot. The following Sect. 4 discusses the experiment setup in detail.

4   Evaluation of the Technical Framework

The concept of the FCCC framework describes a new behaviour of chatbots that reacts on the sentiment of chatbot users. In fact, the concept allows for adapting chatbot appearance to the situational sentiment by rephrasing replies based on character estimations. In doing so, the context of chatbot replies remains unchanged while being able to influence the conversation positive.

In a laboratory experiment with a modified chatbot, we prove the technical implementation of the concept and evaluate qualitatively the effect of the FCCC framework. By recording the character estimations used by the FCCC framework during conversations, we assess the capabilities of influencing conversations with appropriate phrasing.

4.1   Experiment Setup

Controlling the chat process and user experience requires effective sentiment estimation throughout the interaction. This experiment focuses on adapting responses to various character traits and manipulating the chat progress to maintain a relaxed conversational tone.

Effective sentiment control relies on continuous feedback that reflects the current sentiment state, providing a distance to the desired level. This iterative process estimates sentiment after each user input (i.e., the query) to guide the conversation effectively.

The FCCC framework introduces three components to adjust replies adequately: character (C), reflecting the traits of a query; behaviour (B), capturing recent trends in input; and situation (S), representing the chat history. For reliable evaluation, the experiment integrates all these factors, with an emphasis on character estimation (C), described through five major properties.

John et al. [6] propose a character measure based on the Big Five traits: neuroticism, extraversion, openness, agreeableness, and conscientiousness. These traits are normalized into a vector format for comparative analysis across interactions, as outlined in Sect. 3. This quantitative representation enables the measurement of differences, changes, and trends in character properties.

Despite advances in character representation, the literature lacks technical methods for estimating character from short-text sequences like chat messages. To address this, we employed a generative AI service to estimate character (C) and behaviour (B). A ChatGPT bot was initialized to analyse text inputs and transform results into predefined character vectors.

To test sentiment development through phrasing alternatives, we developed a web application[1] overlaying a generative AI chatbot. The application randomly enables character analysis and reply rephrasing, conducted by a third chatbot that matches the phrased response to the desired character vector. This setup transforms replies into a format that aligns with the sentiment control goals, as depicted in Fig. 2.

---

[1] Source code: https://github.com/amishorn/char.bot.demo.git.

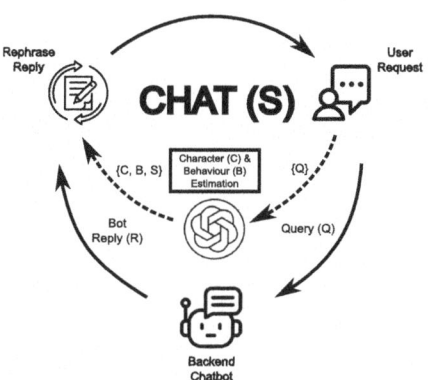

Fig. 2. Concept of the experiment framework implemented in the web application for evaluating the FCCC framework.

The experimental environment involves a proprietary chat interface and a background framework that organizes three ChatGPT bots: a plain backend chatbot (BCB), a character estimation bot (CEB), and a reply rephrasing bot (RRB). The workflow consists of three sequential steps shown in Fig. 2: 1. The user's query (Q) is forwarded to the BCB for a raw reply and the CEB for character estimation. The CEB generates character (C) and behaviour (B) vectors based on the most recent and last three inputs, respectively. 2. The results from the BCB and CEB are passed to the RRB, which rephrases the BCB's reply to match the sentiment of the current chat progress, relying on the C, B, and S vectors. 3. The rephrased reply is returned to the proprietary chat interface, ensuring the user perceives only the refined response.

Using this proprietary interface hides the backend process and ensures unbiased user interaction. Randomly disabling the rephrasing process allows for control experiments to evaluate the FCCC framework's impact [5].

This experimental design demonstrates the potential for integrating sentiment control into conversational AI systems, leveraging character computing and iterative sentiment estimation to enhance user experience.

4.2 Results

The experimental study involved a sample of 14 participants, selected randomly through an open online call. The participants, characterized by a predominantly digital professional background, had a mean age of 36 years. Gender distribution was balanced, ensuring equal consideration of male and female individuals. Grounded in the theoretical framework of Norman Nielsen, the selection of these participants aims to establish a robust foundation for addressing the research question while identifying avenues for further investigation. According to Nielsen [7], even fewer than five individuals may need to be surveyed to obtain meaningful results. Nielsen argues that due to the unique behaviour of

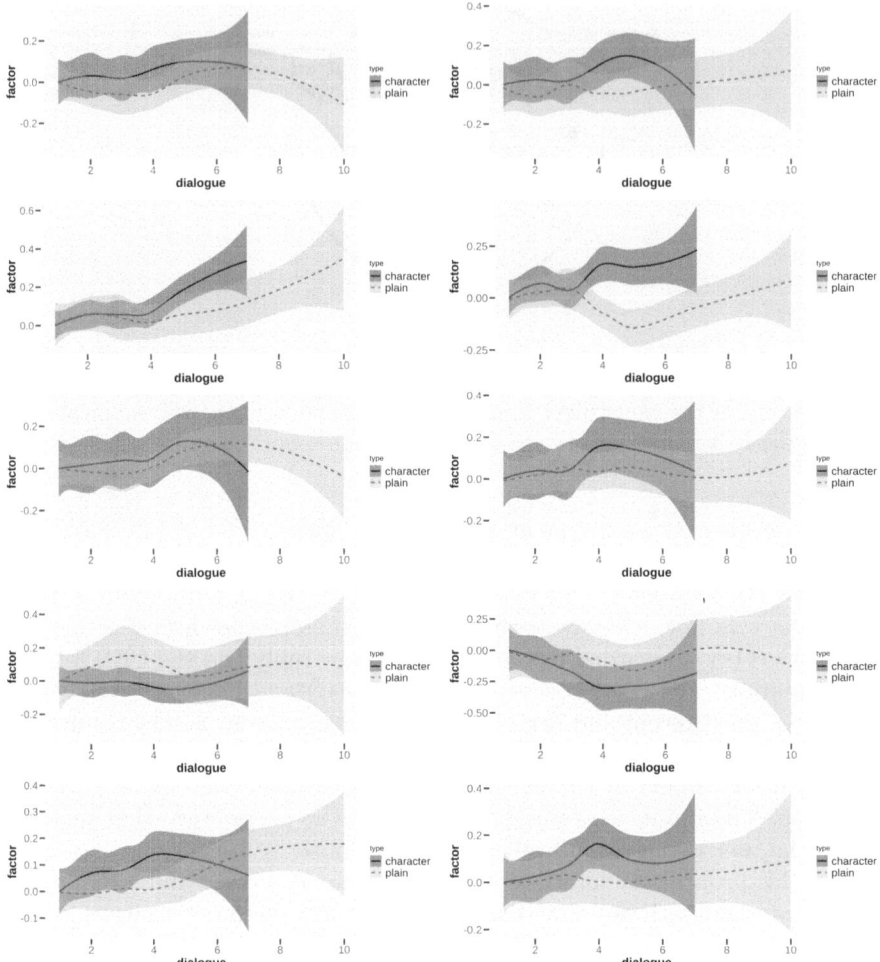

Fig. 3. Comparison of averaged progress of **agreeableness, conscientiousness, extraversion, neuroticism** and **openness** (rows 1 to 5) for B-Vectors (left) and C-Vectors (right) between all recorded conversations with (character) and without (plain) applied FCCC framework.

each test user and the diminishing insights gained from each additional participant, researchers can achieve sufficient understanding with a very small test group [7]. In this study, each participant chatted with a Backend Chat Chatbot (BCB) that received an identical instruction set. Yet, the participants were randomly selected to be served with rephrased chatbot replies from Reply Rephrase Chatbot (RRB) instead of the straight BCB reply.

Each participant engaged in four distinct dialogues with the chatbot. For evaluating the user perception and therewith the FCCC framework capabilities, the chat history as well as all estimated character vectors are recorded. The qualitative analysis of the character changes through all engaged dialogues considers all five factors of character vectors separately. As a result, there are five different graphs comparing the progress of a particular factor between all participants. From all the line graphs available, we calculated the median and the 95% confidence interval band, as shown in Fig. 3 for the B- and C-Vectors across all different character properties. Since this study represents the first evaluation of the framework, we followed an approach common in UX research by combining various qualitative methods for analysis and placing less emphasis on statistical metrics [10]. For full transparency, we calculated the trends of the character progress across all experiments individually for character and plain modes. Consequently, variations in dialogue lengths result in differing lengths of trends and larger confidence band widths towards the ends. This latter effect primarily results from reduced sample sizes for longer dialogues.

A detailed examination of the graphs led to in-depth insights into patterns of interaction and emotional trends, providing valuable qualitative context beyond mere numerical data. Additionally, discussions with experts in psychology helped us to interpret findings in light of the goal that the chatbot should foster positive emotional changes. These expert consultations provided crucial perspectives on potential psychological implications of character changes induced by the chatbot. Moreover, each participant was provided with an open-ended questionnaire. This questionnaire was pre-tested to ensure clarity and validity. Responses were qualitatively analysed and incorporated into the overall findings, enriching the dataset with direct user feedback. By triangulating these methods—graph analysis, expert discussions, and qualitative questionnaire evaluation—we were able to deepen our understanding of the user interactions with the chatbot, following best practices from UX research as outlined by Nielsen Norman Group, where qualitative depth often compensates for smaller sample sizes.

4.3   Key Findings

The FCCC framework uses FL to map user's character and situation to a membership vector of fuzzyfied character traits. These insights are combined with CC methods to adapt the chatbot's character and behaviour to each user's unique traits and context. The use of FCCC framework demonstrated a successful integration of character adaption into a chatbot. All experiment participants were able to interact with the chatbot, obtaining medically relevant responses that were aligned with their tonal preferences. Furthermore, participants reported the chatbot's empathetic responses and adaptability. The majority noticing perceptible changes in the chatbot's behaviour over the course of the conversation. By this, the first research question is answered and the successful integration of the FCCC framework combining FL, CWP and CC and using as an assistance LLM for character estimation is demonstrated. Apart from technical implementation, we reported following findings throughout the conversations about chatbot adaptability and behavioural impact:

Dynamic Character and Behaviour Parameters: The analysis of character (C) and behaviour (B) parameters during each conversation revealed dynamic adaptations. Each user interaction encompassed at least five fuzzy parameter sets (initial state + four dialogues). Results (Fig. 3) showed that character values adapted quickly to inputs, whereas behaviour parameters evolved gradually, reflecting cumulative dialogue influences. This supports the FCCC framework's design, where FL and CWP enables nuanced adaptations in character values to individual dialogues and behaviour values to cumulative trends, contrasting with the rigidity of sharp values.

Adaptation: In Fig. 3 different behaviour among the two chatbots (BCB and RRB) during the conversation progress is clearly shown. This indicates that text-based chatbots applying FCCC, have the capacity to adapt their dialogues with those of the user, as envisioned in the theoretical model proposed by [5]. This approach represents an advancement. Historically, chatbots have exhibited limited capability to adapt to the tonal preferences of their users, achieving at best minor tonal alignment. The application of CC, to date, has largely depended on supplementary sensors (e.g. body temperature, shaking level) for accurate implementation [3].

Behavioural Impact: To prove that FCCC-based chatbots can positively influence user emotions, we conducted three expert interviews with psychologists. Two of the experts are practitioners actively working with patients, while the third expert conducts research in the field of behavioural science. In the interviews we compared normal FCCC chatbots with an enhanced version that included additional parameters for specific character adaptation that brings the user in a more positive sentiment. Table 1summarizes the findings emerged for the five character traits used in FCCC framework.

Thanks to these answers the second research question is answered. The laboratory study shows, that chatbots combining FL, CWP and CC using additional specific instructions - in the case the task to foster a positive mood - are able to fulfil that task and to evoke positive emotions. Additionally the study proves that the technical implementation of FCCC is a useful method to make this character shit within chatbots possible.

5   Conclusion

Findings of this study highlight the successful technical implementation of the FCCC framework, demonstrating its feasibility in real-world applications. The experiment provide evidence that chatbots using the FCCC framework and combining FL, CWP and CC influence user behaviour and sentiment positively. Specifically, participants noted that the chatbot's empathy and adaptability contributed to a more engaging and supportive interaction experience.

While the technical implementation was fully realized, it is important to note that the observations regarding the chatbot's empathy and behavioural adaptation were based on a small-scale laboratory experiment with a limited number of participants. Although the results are promising, future studies should aim to quantify these findings through larger-scale experiments.

These findings suggest that FCCC-based chatbots not only adapt to user personalities but can also be tailored to achieve specific behavioural outcomes. Future work should explore the integration of domain-specific parameters and validate the effectiveness of such adaptations in diverse application areas.

To simplify the evaluation in this study, personality traits were assessed using ChatGPT. This choice was motivated by ChatGPT's high ratings and ease of integration at the time of the technical implementation. Future research should investigate not only the integration of additional LLMs but also how these LLMs affect the performance of the character and behaviour components.

Additionally, the overall FCCC framework as proposed in [5] integrates external influences such as knowledge databases. For practical applications in enterprise environments, it is crucial to enable the attachment of custom content or knowledge bases. While this study exclusively utilized ChatGPT's inherent knowledge, future research must evaluate technical methods that ensure that the chatbot, relies solely on fixed, predefined knowledge sources when generating responses. This approach would enhance control and precision in content delivery, aligning with specific organizational requirements.

Finally, the FCCC framework includes higher-level considerations such as ethical and cultural influences, legal and regulatory requirements, economic factors, and internal organizational conditions. For a complete technical implementation, these components must also be represented within the system. Future

Table 1. Observed effects of recorded character traits among all conversations with plain chatbot and character computing: Agreeableness (A), Conscientiousness (C), Extraversion (E), Neuroticism (N) and Openness (O).

	plain chatbot	character computing
A	Generally lower: limited ability for effective influence	Reducing over course of conversation: balance between harmony and assertiveness being necessary for encouraging behavioural change
C	Higher volatility: lacks in trust and reliability	Constant on neural level: supports trust and reliability; avoids overly controlling behaviour
E	No dominating behaviour identified	No dominating behaviour identified
N	Higher level: more stressful conversation	Constant low level: indicates stress-free (calm) and supportive interaction
O	Significantly lower: lacks of creativity	Significantly higher (being creative): chatbot is able to foster positive emotional changes

research should address how to technically integrate these overarching factors into the FCCC framework, ensuring that it aligns with the multifaceted requirements of real-world deployments.

By combining theoretical rigour with practical implementation, this study advances the understanding of adaptive conversational AI and demonstrates the transformative potential of the FCCC framework in real-world settings.

A   Integrating Fuzzy Logic Theory with the Healthcare Scenario

In the healthcare context, adaptive communication is essential for addressing patient concerns effectively. This integration leverages the Fuzzy Conversational Character Computing (FCCC) framework, underpinned by fuzzy logic, to enhance the capabilities of healthcare chatbots. By interpreting emotional cues and behavioral trends dynamically, the chatbot personalizes interactions, ensuring more empathetic and effective responses.

Scenario: Adaptive Healthcare Chatbot

Consider a healthcare chatbot designed to assist patients by tailoring its responses to their emotional state and communication style. For example:

1. A patient expresses anxiety about persistent symptoms.
2. The chatbot employs fuzzy logic to evaluate the emotional intensity, translating subjective language into measurable degrees of anxiety. This enables the chatbot to adjust its tone and content dynamically.

Step-by-Step Application

1. Situation (S): Aggregating Chat History:

Formula:

$$S = \sum_i m_i \tag{6}$$

Example messages:

m1 [User]: "I am really anxious about these new symptoms I have been feeling lately."

m2 [ChatBot]: ...

m3 [User]: "I have been feeling shortness of breath and chest tightness."

m4 [ChatBot]: "Thank you for sharing your symptoms. I understand that shortness of breath and chest tightness can be alarming. I recommend you consult a healthcare provider immediately if these symptoms worsen. Can I help you locate a nearby clinic or provide more advice?"

The chatbot aggregates these messages $m_1, m_2, ..., m_n$. The focus remains on identifying patterns like anxiety and severity in the user's input.

Thus:

$$S = m_1 + m2 + ... + m_n \tag{7}$$

Interpretation:
The chatbot uses S to create a cumulative picture of the dialogue's emotional state and severity of symptoms.

2. Character (C): Estimating Membership Values for Recent Input:

Formula:

$$C_{(m)} = \sum_{t \in T} max(min(\frac{m - 0}{1 - 0}, 1), 0) \tag{8}$$

Where $T = \{t_1, t_2, t_3, t_4, t_5\}$ represents character traits comprising agreeableness, conscientiousness, extraversion, neuroticism and openness.

Example:
For the most recent user input, "I have been feeling shortness or breath and chest tightness.":

Agreeableness: 0.4 (low) - The user is concerned and seeks help but without much positivity.
Conscientiousness: 0.6 (moderate) - User performs actions with moderate integrity.
Extraversion: 0.1 (very low) - Being introvert and feeling uncomfortable when being the centre of attention.
Neuroticism: 0.9 (high) - Indicates significant anxiety.
Openness: 0.7 (moderate-high) - Willingness to share detailed symptoms.

3. Behaviour (B): Aggregating Recent Trends:

Formula:

$$B = \frac{\sum C_{[-1,...,-n]}}{n} + \frac{C}{n} \tag{9}$$

Where $C[-1, ..., n-1]$ is the previous behaviour state, C is the current character vector, and n is the number of recent user inputs.

Example:
Previous Behaviour: $C_{[-1]} = [0.6, 0.9, 0.45, 0.75, 0.95]$
$C_{[-2]} = [0.7, 0.9, 0.35, 0.9, 0.9]$
agreeableness, conscientiousness, extraversion, neuroticism, openness.

Current Character (C): $[0.4, 0.6, 0.1, 0.9, 0.7]$
Updated Behaviour (B): $with\ n = 3, B = [0.55, 0.8, 0.3, 0.85, 0.85]$

$$B = [0.43, 0.6, 0.26, 0.55, 0.61] + \frac{[0.4, 0.6, 0.1, 0.9, 0.7]}{3} = [0.55, 0.8, 0.3, 0.85, 0.85] \quad (10)$$

This behaviour vector (B) reflects a *trend* of increasing neuroticism, decreasing extraversion and openness while indicating moderate agreeableness and rather constant conscientiousness.

4. Generating Response (R):

Formula:

$$R = f(B, C, S) \quad (11)$$

Here, function $f(...)$ adapts the response tone and content based on the computed behaviour (B), character (C), and aggregated situation (S).

Example Response for a Rule-Based Bot:

"I see that you are worried about your symptoms. Please consider consulting a healthcare provider for further assistance. Would you like me to provide you with contact details for nearby clinics?"

Example Response for a FCCC-Enhanced Bot:

"I understand that you're feeling increasingly concerned about your symptoms, and it's completely valid to feel this way. Let me help you by suggesting a nearby clinic or connecting you with a healthcare professional to address this quickly and effectively."

References

1. Bleicher, K. (ed.): Organisation als System. Gabler Verlag, Wiesbaden (1972). https://doi.org/10.1007/978-3-322-86022-4
2. Colombo, M.: Phenotropic interaction. In: Phenotropic Interaction. Fuzzy Management Methods, pp. 21–32. Springer, Cham (2024). https://doi.org/10.1007/978-3-031-42819-7_2
3. El Bolock, A.: Defining character computing from the perspective of computer science and psychology. In: Proceedings of the 17th International Conference on Mobile and Ubiquitous Multimedia, Cairo, Egypt, pp. 567–572. ACM (2018). https://doi.org/10.1145/3282894.3289721
4. Hundertmark, S., Hafner, N.: Gestaltung automatisierter Kundendialoge im Spannungsfeld von Kosten und Customer Experience. In: Bruhn, M., Hadwich, K. (eds.) Gestaltung des Wandels im Dienstleistungsmanagement. Forum Dienstleistungsmanagement, pp. 219–238. Springer Fachmedien Wiesbaden, Wiesbaden (2023). https://doi.org/10.1007/978-3-658-41815-1_9
5. Hundertmark, S., Portmann, E., Hafner, N.: Fuzzy conversational character computing: Für Chat- und voicebots. Informatik Spektrum **46**(3), 163–175 (2023). https://doi.org/10.1007/s00287-023-01538-8

6. John, O.P., Naumann, L.P., Soto, C.J.: Paradigm shift to the integrative big five trait taxonomy: history, measurement, and conceptual issues. In: Handbook of Personality: Theory and Research, 3rd edn, pp. 114–158. The Guilford Press, New York (2008)
7. Nielsen, J.: Estimating the number of subjects needed for a thinking aloud test. Int. J. Hum. Comput. Stud. **41**(3), 385–397 (1994). https://doi.org/10.1006/ijhc.1994.1065
8. Pangaro, P.: Rethinking design thinking. PICNIC Festival, Amsterdam (2010)
9. Picard, R.W.: Affective Computing. MIT Press (2000)
10. Rohrer, C.: When to use which user-experience research methods. Nielsen Norman Group **12**, 21 (2014)
11. Weizenbaum, J.: ELIZA—a computer program for the study of natural language communication between man and machine. Commun. ACM **9**(1), 36–45 (1966). https://doi.org/10.1145/365153.365168
12. Zadeh, L.: Fuzzy sets. Inf. Control **8**(3), 338–353 (1965). https://doi.org/10.1016/S0019-9958(65)90241-X
13. Zadeh, L.: Fuzzy logic = computing with words. IEEE Trans. Fuzzy Syst. **4**(2), 103–111 (1996). https://doi.org/10.1109/91.493904
14. Zimmermann, H.J.: Fuzzy Set Theory—and Its Applications. Springer, Dordrecht (2001). https://doi.org/10.1007/978-94-010-0646-0
15. Zumstein, D.: Customer Performance Measurement - Analysis of the Benefit of a Fuzzy Classification Approach in Customer Relationship Management (2007). https://doi.org/10.13140/RG.2.2.15682.58560

Generating Modular Relaxed Pseudo-metrics by Aggregation

M. D. M. Bibiloni-Femenias[1,2]([✉]) [ID], G. Jaume-Martin[1,2] [ID],
and O. Valero[1,2] [ID]

[1] Mathematics and Computer Science Department, Universitat de les Illes Balears,
Ctra. Valldemossa km. 7.5, 07122 Palma, Spain
{m.bibiloni,o.valero}@uib.es, gabriel.jaume@uib.cat
[2] Institut d'Investigació Sanitària Illes Balears (IdISBa), Hospital Universitari Son
Espases, 07120 Palma, Illes Balears, Spain

Abstract. The aggregation of different pieces of information is a well-
known practice in the field of applied sciences. Frequently, such information is obtained from metrics and, consequently, the goal is to merge
a collection of metrics into a global one. In recent studies, the addition
of a parameter to the distance measurement has been essential. Modular metrics completely meet this requirement. Therefore, in this paper
we introduce and solve the aggregation problem for a new type of modular metric: the modular relaxed pseudo-metric. This new concept has
been introduced to provide a less restrictive distance measurement that
does not need to fulfill the axiom of reflexivity, with the aim of covering a wider range of applications. Thus, we characterize the functions
that aggregate modular relaxed pseudo-metrics, which we call modular relaxed pseudo-metric aggregation functions. We also compare the
results with the modular (pseudo-)metric case. We find that properties
such as subadditivity and preservation of triangular triplets are necessary
conditions for modular relaxed pseudo-metric aggregation functions, but
not sufficient conditions. This shows a difference with modular (pseudo-)
metric aggregation functions.

Keywords: modular pseudo-metric · modular relaxed pseudo-metric ·
aggregation · monotony · subadditivity · triangular triplet

1 Introduction

The aggregation of different pieces of information is a well-known practice in
applied sciences. In multiple scenarios, the aforesaid pieces of information at
our disposal is expressed by means of metrics. In such scenarios, a frequent
goal is to merge different metrics into a global one. Particularly, this is the
case in many techniques regarding the optimal decision making. The practical
advantages granted by the use of the aforementioned type of distances have

---

Dedicated to the memory of Professor Alexander Sostak.

M. Baczyński et al. (Eds.): EUSFLAT 2025, LNCS 15883, pp. 54–65, 2025.
https://doi.org/10.1007/978-3-031-97225-6_5

inspired several researchers to study how can they be aggregated. Examples can be found in [17,18], where a characterization of pseudo-metric aggregation functions is provided, and in [13], where several characterizations of quasi-metric aggregation functions are obtained.

While working in specific physical applications, the notion of metric may fall short. This is why, the concept of modular metric, detailed in Definition 1, was introduced in the literature (see [6,7]). The use of this new kind of distances enables the possibility of measuring with respect to a positive parameter, which can become critical to getting a complete picture of the situation in some applications. For further information regarding studies about modular metrics, please refer to [2,3,6–8,12,16,19]. Furthermore, readers may consult the works in [1,6,7,9,11,14,15,20] for insights into some applications.

Next we introduce the key notion in our subsequent study.

Definition 1. *A modular pseudo-metric on a non-empty set X, is a function $d :]0, +\infty[\times X \times X \to [0, +\infty]$ which satisfies, for all $x, y, z \in X$, the conditions below:*

(MPM1) $d(t, x, x) = 0$ *for all $t > 0$,*
(MPM2) $d(t, x, y) = d(t, y, x)$ *for all $t > 0$,*
(MPM3) $d(t + s, x, z) \leq d(t, x, y) + d(s, y, z)$ *for all $t, s > 0$.*

When the axiom (MPM1) is replaced by the following one,

(MM1) $d(t, x, y) = 0$ *for all $t > 0 \Leftrightarrow x = y$,*

then d is called a modular metric on X.

It is worth noticing that the value $d(t, x, y)$ can be interpreted as the distance between x and y with respect to the value $t \in]0, +\infty[$ of the parameter.

The introduction of this new generalization of metric to the literature, led to the study of the characterization of those functions that aggregate modular (pseudo-)metrics in [2] (see also [3]). Accordingly, the researchers adapted the concept of (pseudo-)metric aggregation function given in [17,18] as described below.

Definition 2. *Let $n \in \mathbb{N}$ ($\mathbb{N}$ denotes the set of all positive integer numbers). A function $F : [0, +\infty]^n \to [0, +\infty]$ is a modular (pseudo-)metric aggregation function provided that, for each collection of modular (pseudo-)metrics $\{d_i\}_{i=1}^n$ defined on the same set X, the function $F \circ \widetilde{d}$ is a modular (pseudo-)metric on X, where $\widetilde{d} :]0, +\infty[\times X \times X \to [0, +\infty]^n$ is given, for all $x, y \in X$ and for all $t > 0$, by $\widetilde{d}(t, x, y) = (d_1(t, x, y), \ldots, d_n(t, x, y))$.*

The notions that are typically studied while facing the aggregation problem for metrics are: triangular triplets and their transformation, the subadditivity and the monotony. With the goal to facilitate the comprehension of the rest of paper, we recall below the aforesaid notions.

As described in [4], given $a, b, c \in [0, +\infty]^n$, then (a, b, c) forms an n-triangular triplet whenever $a \preceq b + c$, $b \preceq a + c$ and $c \preceq a + b$. Observe that we denote that $a \preceq b$ if, and only if, $a_i \leq b_i$ for all $i \in \{1, \ldots, n\}$, where $\leq$ is the usual partial order on the extended set of positive real numbers $[0, +\infty]$. In addition, we will say that a function $F : [0, +\infty]^n \rightarrow [0, +\infty]$ transforms n-triangular triplets into a 1-triangular triplet as long as $(F(a), F(b), F(c))$ is a 1-triangular triplet whenever (a, b, c) is an n-triangular triplet. Furthermore, a function $F : [0, +\infty]^n \rightarrow [0, +\infty]$ will be referred to as monotonic if it fulfills that $F(a) \leq F(b)$ whenever $a \preceq b$ with $a, b \in [0, +\infty]^n$. What is more, we will call a function $F : [0, +\infty]^n \rightarrow [0, +\infty]$ subadditive if it satisfies that $F(a + b) \leq F(a) + F(b)$ for all $a, b \in [0, +\infty]^n$, where $+$ denotes the usual addition in $[0, +\infty]^n$. Finally, we will use 0_n to represent the element $(0, \ldots, 0) \in [0, +\infty]^n$.

The exposed concepts exhibit certain equivalences between them. A collection of such relations was presented in [2], as shown in the lemma below.

Lemma 1. *Let $n \in \mathbb{N}$ and let $F : [0, +\infty]^n \rightarrow [0, +\infty]$ be a monotone function such that $F(0_n) = 0$. Then the following assertions are equivalent:*

(1) *F is subadditive.*
(2) *$F(c) \leq F(a) + F(b)$ for all $a, b, c \in [0, +\infty]^n$ with $c \preceq a + b$.*
(3) *F transforms n-triangular triplets into 1-triangular triplet.*

Taking advantage of the previous equivalences a characterization of pseudo-metric aggregation functions was provided in [2], as shown in the following theorem.

Theorem 1. *Let $n \in \mathbb{N}$ and let $F : [0, +\infty]^n \rightarrow [0, +\infty]$ be a function. Then the following assertions are equivalent:*

(1) *F is a modular pseudo-metric aggregation function.*
(2) *$F(0_n) = 0$, F is monotone and subadditive.*
(3) *$F(0_n) = 0$ and $F(c) \leq F(a) + F(b)$ for all $a, b, c \in [0, +\infty]^n$ with $c \preceq a+b$.*
(4) *$F(0_n) = 0$, F is monotone and transforms n-triangular triplets into 1-triangular triplet.*

In addition, also in [2], a characterization of modular metric aggregation functions was provided as detailed below.

Theorem 2. *Let $n \in \mathbb{N}$ and let $F : [0, +\infty]^n \rightarrow [0, +\infty]$ be a function. The following assertions are equivalent:*

(1) *F is a modular metric aggregation function.*
(2) *$F(0_n) = 0$, F is monotone and subadditive. Moreover, if $a \in [0, +\infty]^n$ and $F(a) = 0$, then $a_i = 0$ for some $i \in \{1, \ldots, n\}$.*
(3) *$F(0_n) = 0$ and, in addition, $F(c) \leq F(a) + F(b)$ for all $a, b, c \in [0, +\infty]^n$ with $c \preceq a + b$. Moreover, if $a \in [0, +\infty]^n$ and $F(a) = 0$, then $a_i = 0$ for some $i \in \{1, \ldots, n\}$.*
(4) *$F(0_n) = 0$, F is monotone and transforms n-triangular triplets into a 1-triangular triplet. Moreover, if $a \in [0, +\infty]^n$ and $F(a) = 0$, then $a_i = 0$ for some $i \in \{1, \ldots, n\}$.*

It is interesting to note that functions that merge modular metrics will also merge modular pseudo-metrics. However, the converse is not generally true (see Example 1 in [2]).

Inspired by the work done in [2], and the practical advantages that could come from removing condition **(MPM1)** in Definition 1, the goal of this paper will be to introduce a generalization for modular pseudo-metrics and solve its related aggregation problem. In particular, the paper is organized in three sections, subsequent to the Introduction. Section 2 presents a new concept of modular metric, which we will designate as modular relaxed pseudo-metric. In addition, the functions that aggregate these kind of distances are characterized and several examples of them are provided. Section 3 establishes the relationship between the functions that aggregate the modular relaxed pseudo-metrics and the modular (pseudo-)metrics mentioned above. This relationship is also supported by several examples of functions that aggregate or fail to aggregate modular relaxed pseudo-metrics. As for the last section (Sect. 4), the conclusions that we derive from the work carried out and the study that is being developed to extend it are presented.

2   The Aggregation of Modular Relaxed Pseudo-metrics

In the literature, the scope of the modular pseudo-metric aggregation problem has been extended to new type of metrics which do not need to comply with some of the axioms from Definition 1. In particular, in [3] the symmetry of modular pseudo-metrics was removed and the associated problem of aggregation was solved, providing a complete description of the functions that merge the modular pseudo-metrics obtained in this new framework. Notice that this asymmetry can result necessary in order to measure speed in some physical processes ([19]). In [5], the notion of relaxed pseudo-metric was introduced (see also [10]). Such distances extend the notion of pseudo-metric by means of deleting the typical reflexivity. Let us recall that a relaxed pseudo-metric on a non-empty set X is a function $d : X \times X \rightarrow [0, +\infty]$ that fulfills for all $x, y, z \in X$ the following conditions:

(i) $d(x, y) = d(y, x)$,
(ii) $d(x, y) \leq d(x, z) + d(z, y)$.

In this section, our target is twofold. On the one hand, we introduce a new type of distance which extends the notion of relaxed pseudo-metric to the modular framework. On the other hand, we address the aggregation problem for such distances and establish a few relationships with the modular pseudo-metric aggregation problem. Accordingly, we define the concept of modular relaxed pseudo-metric as follows.

Definition 3. *A modular relaxed pseudo-metric on a non-empty set X, is a function $d :]0, +\infty[\times X \times X \rightarrow [0, +\infty]$ which satisfies, for all $x, y, z \in X$, the conditions **(MPM2)** and **(MPM3)**.*

It should be noted that the preceding definition extends the notion of relaxed pseudo-metric to the modular framework. Moreover, every modular (pseudo-) metric is also a modular relaxed pseudo-metric that satisfies the reflexivity axiom (condition (MPM1)).

In light of the notion of modular relaxed pseudo-metric, it is necessary to introduce the concept of modular relaxed pseudo-metric aggregation function in order to address the problem of how to merge this type of distances. Consequently, the next definition is derived.

Definition 4. *Given $n \in \mathbb{N}$, a function $F : [0, +\infty]^n \to [0, +\infty]$ is a modular relaxed pseudo-metric aggregation function provided that, for each collection of modular relaxed pseudo-metrics $\{d_i\}_{i=1}^n$ defined on the same set X, the function $F \circ \tilde{d}$ is a modular relaxed pseudo-metric on X, where $\tilde{d} :\ ]0, +\infty[\times X \times X \to [0, +\infty]^n$ is given, for all $x, y \in X$ and for all $t > 0$, by $\tilde{d}(t, x, y) = (d_1(t, x, y), \ldots, d_n(t, x, y))$.*

Making use of the previous definition, we are able to provide a characterization of the functions that aggregate modular relaxed pseudo-metrics.

Theorem 3. *Let $n \in \mathbb{N}$. If $F : [0, +\infty]^n \to [0, +\infty]$ is a function, then the following assertions are equivalent:*

(1) *F is a modular relaxed pseudo-metric aggregation function.*
(2) *$F(a) + F(b) \geq F(c)$ for all $a, b, c \in [0, +\infty]^n$ with $c \preceq a + b$.*

Proof. (1) $\Rightarrow$ (2). Let $a, b, c \in [0, +\infty]^n$ with $c \preceq a + b$. We will prove that $F(a) + F(b) \geq F(c)$.

Set $X = \{x, y, z\}$ with x, y, z all different from each other, and let $\{d_i\}_{i=1}^n$ be a family of modular relaxed pseudo-metrics on X defined, for all $i \in \{1, \ldots, n\}$, by

$$d_i(t, x, y) = d_i(t, y, x) = \begin{cases} a_i + b_i, & \text{if } 0 < t \leq 1 \\ c_i, & \text{if } t > 1 \end{cases},$$

$$d_i(t, y, z) = d_i(t, z, y) = \begin{cases} a_i, & \text{if } 0 < t \leq 1 \\ \min(a_i, c_i), & \text{if } t > 1 \end{cases},$$

$$d_i(t, x, z) = d_i(t, z, x) = \begin{cases} b_i, & \text{if } 0 < t \leq 1 \\ \min(c_i, b_i), & \text{if } t > 1 \end{cases},$$

$$d_i(t, x, x) = d_i(t, y, y) = d_i(t, z, z) = 0, \text{ for all } t > 0.$$

Let us see that each d_i is a modular relaxed pseudo-metric on X. It is clear that (MPM2) is fulfilled. Next we see that (MPM3) is also satisfied. Fix $i \in \{1, \ldots, n\}$ and let $t, s > 0$. Obviously, for all $u, v \in X$ we get:

$$d_i(t + s, u, v) \leq d_i(t + s, u, v) + 0 \leq d_i(t, u, v) + d_i(s, v, v).$$

The other case is analogous by the symmetry of each d_i.

Hence, we only need to consider the cases where $u, v, w \in X$ are all different from each other.

- If $0 < t + s \leq 1$, then $0 < t, s \leq 1$ and we get:

$$d_i(t, u, w) + d_i(s, w, v) \geq a_i + b_i \geq d_i(t + s, u, v),$$

for all $u, v, w \in X$, being all different from each other.
- If $t + s > 1$ and the parameters satisfy that either $0 < t \leq 1$ or $0 < s \leq 1$:

$$d_i(t, u, w) + d_i(s, w, v) \geq c_i \geq d_i(t + s, u, v),$$

for all $u, v, w \in X$, being all different from each other.
- If $t + s > 1$ and $t, s > 1$:

$$d_i(t, u, w) + d_i(s, w, v) \geq \min(c_i, a_i) + \min(c_i, b_i) \geq c_i \geq d_i(t + s, u, v),$$

for all $u, v, w \in X$, being all different from each other.

Since F is a modular relaxed pseudo-metric aggregation function, then $F \circ \widetilde{d}$ is a modular relaxed pseudo-metric on X and, hence, it satisfies condition (**MPM3**) from Definition 1. Thus,

$$F(a) + F(b) = F(d_1(1, y, z), \ldots, d_n(1, y, z)) + F(d_1(1, z, x), \ldots, d_n(1, z, x))$$
$$\geq F(d_1(2, x, y), \ldots, d_n(2, x, y)) = F(c).$$

(2) $\Rightarrow$ **(1)**. Let $F(a) + F(b) \geq F(c)$ for all $a, b, c \in [0, +\infty]^n$ with $c \preceq a + b$. Let $\{d_i\}_{i=1}^n$ be a family of modular relaxed pseudo-metrics on X. We will prove that $F \circ \widetilde{d}$ is a modular relaxed pseudo-metric on X. With this aim, let $x, y, z \in X$ and let $s, t > 0$. Then we have the following:

It is clear that $F(d_1(t, x, y), \ldots, d_n(t, x, y)) = F(d_1(t, y, x), \ldots, d_n(t, y, x))$, since each d_i satisfies that $d_i(t, x, y) = d_i(t, y, x)$. Whence we deduce that $F \circ \widetilde{d}$ fulfills condition (**MPM2**).

Since each d_i satisfies that $d_i(t, x, y) + d_i(s, y, z) \geq d_i(t + s, y, x)$ we obtain, from condition **(2)**, that

$$F(d_1(t, x, y), \ldots, d_n(t, x, y)) + F(d_1(s, y, z), \ldots, d_n(s, y, z)) \geq$$
$$F(d_1(t + s, y, x), \ldots, d_n(t + s, y, x)).$$

So condition (**MPM3**) is hold by $F \circ \widetilde{d}$.

In order to further extend the reader's understanding about modular relaxed pseudo-metric aggregation functions, we present some samples of such functions in Example 1 (see also Examples 2 and 3).

Example 1. Let $n \in \mathbb{N}$. The functions $F : [0, +\infty]^n \to [0, +\infty]$ bellow are instances of modular relaxed pseudo-metric aggregation functions.

(1) $F(a) = \sum_{i=1}^n \lambda_i \cdot a_i$, with all $\lambda_i \geq 0$ for all $i \in \{1, ..., n\}$.
(2) $F(a) = \max(\lambda_1 \cdot a_1, ..., \lambda_n \cdot a_n)$, with all $\lambda_i \geq 0$ for all $i \in \{1, ..., n\}$.
(3) $F(a) = \begin{cases} 0, & \text{if } a = 0_n \\ +\infty, & \text{if } a \neq 0_n \end{cases}.$

3   Modular Relaxed Pseudo-Metric and Modular (Pseudo-)metric Aggregation Functions: The Relationship

In this section, we aim to discern what is the relationship between modular relaxed pseudo-metric aggregation functions, studied in Sect. 2, and the modular (pseudo-)metric aggregation functions characterized in [2]. The necessary results to this matter, characterizations provided by Theorems 1 and 2, are recalled in Sect. 1. In addition, based on both characterizations, we provide several examples along with certain conditions that can be used to either ensure or discard that a function is a modular relaxed pseudo-metric aggregation function.

Let us start with the study of the relationship between the aforementioned aggregation functions.

Proposition 1. *Let $n \in \mathbb{N}$. If $F : [0, +\infty]^n \to [0, +\infty]$ is a function, then the following assertions satisfy (1) $\Rightarrow$ (2):*

  (1) *F is a modular (pseudo-)metric aggregation function.*
  (2) *F is a modular relaxed pseudo-metric aggregation function.*

Proof. **(1)** $\Rightarrow$ **(2).** Any modular (pseudo)metric aggregation function F needs to satisfy that $F(a) + F(b) \geq F(c)$ for all $a, b, c \in [0, +\infty]^n$ with $c \preceq a + b$, as stated in Theorems 1 and 2. Then, by Theorem 3, F is also a modular relaxed pseudo-metric aggregation function.

The converse of Proposition 1 is not true in general, as shown in the following example.

Example 2. Let $F : [0, +\infty]^2 \to [0, +\infty]$ be the function defined by

$$F(a) = \begin{cases} 1, \text{ if } a = (0,0) \\ \frac{1}{2}, \text{ otherwise} \end{cases}.$$

Clearly $F(a) + F(b) \geq F(c)$ for all $a, b, c \in [0, +\infty]^2$. It follows from Theorem 3 that F is a modular relaxed pseudo-metric aggregation function. However, F is not monotone and $F(0,0) = 1 \neq 0$. Hence, by Theorems 1 and 2, it is clear that F is not a modular (pseudo-)metric aggregation function.

In order to generalize Example 2, we provide a family of non monotone modular relaxed pseudo-metric aggregation functions below.

Example 3. Let $n \in \mathbb{N}$. Consider $\alpha, \gamma \in]0, +\infty[$ such that $\beta \in [\frac{1}{2}, 1[$ and $\beta \cdot \alpha \leq \gamma \leq 2 \cdot \beta \cdot \alpha$. Define the function $F_{\alpha,\beta,\gamma} : [0, +\infty]^n \to [0, +\infty]$ as follows:

$$F_{\alpha,\beta,\gamma}(a) = \begin{cases} \alpha, & \text{if } a = 0_n, \\ \beta \cdot \alpha, & \text{if } a \neq 0_n \text{ and } a_i = 0 \text{ for some } i \in \{1, \ldots, n\}, \\ \gamma, & \text{if } a_i \neq 0 \text{ for all } i \in \{1, \ldots, n\}. \end{cases}$$

It is easy to prove that F satisfies assertion (2) in Theorem 3 and, hence, it is a modular relaxed pseudo-metric aggregation function. Nevertheless, F is not monotone. Indeed, $F(0_n) = \alpha > \alpha\beta = F(1, 0, \ldots, 0)$.

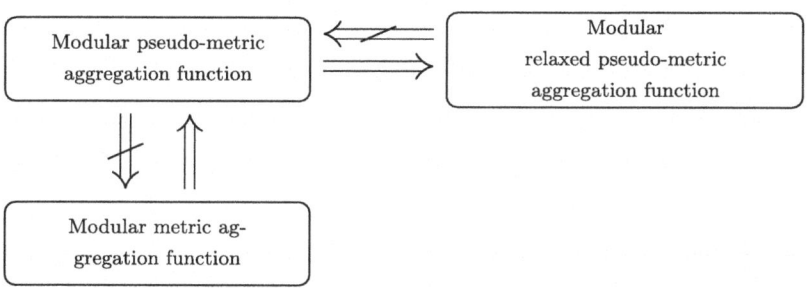

Fig. 1. Conceptual map about the relationship between modular relaxed pseudo-metric aggregation functions and modular (pseudo-)metric aggregation functions.

Please refer to Fig. 1, which summarizes the relationships previously highlighted.

Next result shows that a function F is required to be subadditive in order to be a modular relaxed pseudo-metric aggregation function.

Proposition 2. *Let* $n \in \mathbb{N}$. *If* $F : [0, +\infty]^n \to [0, +\infty]$ *is a function, then the following assertions satisfy* **(1)** $\Rightarrow$ **(2)**:

(1) $F(a) + F(b) \geq F(c)$ *for all* $a, b, c \in [0, +\infty]^n$ *with* $c \preceq a + b$.
(2) F *is subadditive.*

Proof. Assume that $a, b \in [0, +\infty]^n$, then if we choose $c_i = a_i + b_i$ for all $i \in \{1, \ldots, n\}$, it becomes obvious that $c \preceq a + b$. Hence, $F(a + b) = F(c) \leq F(a) + F(b)$, concluding that F is subadditive.

Another reason why there are functions that are modular relaxed pseudo-metric aggregation functions but they are not modular pseudo-metric aggregation function is given by the fact that the converse of Proposition 2 is not true. This is shown in Example 4, where subadditivity does not imply condition (1) in the previously mentioned lemma.

Example 4. Consider the function $F : [0, +\infty]^2 \to [0, +\infty]$, defined below:

$$F(a) = \begin{cases} 5, & \text{if } a = (0,0) \\ 1, & \text{if } a \neq (0,0) \end{cases}.$$

It is direct to prove that F is subadditive. Let us consider all possible cases:

- If $a = (0,0)$ and $b = (0,0)$, then $F(a + b) = 5 \leq 5 + 5 = F(a) + F(b)$.
- If either $a \neq (0,0)$ or $b \neq (0,0)$, the $F(a + b) = 1 \leq 1 + 1 \leq F(a) + F(b)$.

Nevertheless, $c = (0,0)$, $a = (1,1)$ and $b = (1,1)$ fulfill the condition that $c \preceq a + b$, but $F(c) \geq F(a) + F(b)$. Proving that the reciprocal of Proposition 2 is not true, in general.

Similarly to subadditivity, the following lemma shows that modular relaxed pseudo-metric aggregation functions transform n-triangular triplets into 1-triangular triplets.

Proposition 3. *Let $n \in \mathbb{N}$. If $F : [0, +\infty]^n \to [0, +\infty]$ is a function, then the following assertions satisfy* **(1)** $\Rightarrow$ **(2)**:

(1) $F(a) + F(b) \geq F(c)$ for all $a, b, c \in [0, +\infty]^n$ with $c \preceq a + b$.
(2) F transforms n-triangular triplets into 1-triangular triplet.

Proof. Assume that $a, b, c \in [0, +\infty]^n$ satisfy $a \preceq b + c$, $b \preceq a + c$ and $c \preceq a + b$. Then, condition **(1)** ensures that $(F(a), F(b), F(c))$ is a 1-triangular triplet.

As can be seen in the example below, the reciprocal of the Proposition 3 is not true, in general. This is proven by presenting a function that transforms n-triangular triplets into 1-triangular triplet, but it is not a modular relaxed pseudo-metrics aggregation function.

Example 5. Consider the function $F : [0, +\infty]^2 \to [0, +\infty]$ defined below:

$$F(a) = \begin{cases} 0, & \text{if } a = (0,0) \\ 2, & \text{if } a = (2,2) \\ 1, & \text{otherwise} \end{cases}.$$

Let us see by cases that, indeed, F transforms n-triangular triplets into 1-triangular triplets.

- Let $a \neq (0,0)$ and $b \neq (0,0)$ and $c \neq (0,0)$. Then, if we consider $u, v, w \in \{a, b, c\}$, it is satisfied that, $F(u) \leq 2 \leq F(v) + F(w)$.
- Let $a = (0,0)$ or $b = (0,0)$ or $c = (0,0)$. Without lost of generality suppose that $a = (0,0)$. Notice that if $a, b, c \in [0, +\infty]^2$ is a triangular triplet and $a = (0,0)$, then $c \preceq b$ and $b \preceq c$. Consequently, $b = c$. In such a case, we obtain the following results:

$$F(c) \leq F(a) + F(c) = F(a) + F(b) \qquad F(b) \leq F(a) + F(b) = F(a) + F(c),$$

$$0 = F(a) \leq F(c) + F(b).$$

Thus, F transforms n-triangular triplets into 1-triangular triplets. Nevertheless, if $a = (0,0)$, $b = (3,3)$ and $c = (2,2)$, we have that $c \preceq a + b$, but, $2 = F(c) \geq F(a) + F(b) = 1$. Therefore, F does not satisfy that $F(a) + F(b) \geq F(c)$ whenever $a, b, c \in [0, +\infty]^n$ such that $c \preceq a + b$ and, consequently, F is not a modular relaxed pseudo-metric aggregation function.

When the function F is monotone and satisfies that $F(0_n) = 0$, the following equivalences are obtained, which are a direct consequence of Lemma 1 and Theorems 1 and 3.

Corollary 1. *Let $n \in \mathbb{N}$ and let $F : [0, +\infty]^n \to [0, +\infty]$ be a monotone function such that $F(0_n) = 0$. Then, the following assertions are equivalent:*

(1) *F is a modular relaxed pseudo-metric aggregation function.*
(2) *$F(c) \leq F(a) + F(b)$ for all $a, b, c \in [0, +\infty]^n$ with $c \preceq a + b$.*
(3) *F is a modular pseudo-metric aggregation function.*
(4) *F is subadditive.*
(5) *F transforms n-triangular triplets into 1-triangular triplet.*

4   Conclusions and Future Work

The aggregation problem has become increasingly significant in the field of applied sciences, often involving the use of metrics. This has encouraged several authors to discuss which sort of functions merge different metrics into a single one, preserving their inherent properties. Additionally, in many applications, in order to fully describe the targeted problem, it becomes essential to incorporate a parameter to the distance's definition. In this direction, we have introduced the concept of modular relaxed pseudo-metric extending the known relaxed pseudo-metrics given in [5]. This new concept has been introduced to offer a less restrictive notion of distance than the modular pseudo-metric, with the aim of being able to cover a wider range of applications. Moreover, we have solved the associated aggregation problem. More specifically, a characterization of those functions that aggregate such distances has been obtained. With the presented characterization, it is shown that monotony and $F(0_n) = 0$ are not necessary conditions for functions that aggregate modular relaxed pseudo-metrics. Furthermore, we have shown that, despite modular (pseudo-)metric aggregation functions are also modular relaxed pseudo-metrics, this is not the case in the other direction. Nevertheless, in the event that a function is monotone and at the same time vanishes at 0_n the preceding notions coincide. In addition, some examples reveal that properties such as subadditivity and preservation of triangular triplets are necessary, but not sufficient, conditions for modular relaxed pseudo-metric aggregation functions. This shows a difference with respect to modular (pseudo-)metric aggregation functions. Illustrative examples have been provided.

In future work, we plan on completing the study of the aggregation problem in the modular case. Thus the modular version of relaxed metrics and SSD-relaxed (pseudo-)metrics (see [10]) will be introduced and the associated aggregation problem will be addressed. Additionally, we aim to study the differences between this problem and the aggregation problems associated to modular relaxed pseudo-metrics and, as outlined in [3], to modular quasi-pseudo metrics (for which the symmetry axiom is not hold).

Acknowledgments. This research is part of project PID2022-139248NB-I00 funded by MICIU/AEI/10.13039/501100011033 and ERDF/EU. The authors thank the support from *Programa de Foment de la Recerca i la Innovació de la Universitat de les Illes Balears 2024–2026* and ITS2023-086-Programa de Foment a la recerca.

Disclosure of Interests. The authors have no competing interests to declare that are relevant to the content of this article.

References

1. Abdou, A.: Fixed points of Kannan maps in modular metric spaces. AIMS Math. **5**, 6395–6403 (2020)
2. Bibiloni-Femenias, M.D.M., Miñana, J.J., Valero, O.: Aggregating distances with uncertainty: the modular (pseudo-)metric case. In: Intelligent and Fuzzy Systems, pp. 94–101. Springer, Cham (2023). https://doi.org/10.1007/978-3-031-39774-5_12
3. Bibiloni-Femenias, M.D.M., Valero, O.: Modular quasi-pseudo metrics and the aggregation problem. Mathematics **12**(12) (2024)
4. Borsík, J., Boboš, J.: On a product of metric spaces. Mathematica Slovaca **31**, 193–205 (1981)
5. Bukatin, M., Kopperman, R., Matthews, S.: Some corollaries of the correspondence between partial metrics and mutlivalued equalities. Fuzzy Sets Syst. **256**, 57–72 (2014)
6. Chistyakov, V.V.: Modular metric spaces, I: basic concepts. Nonlinear Anal. Theory Methods Appl. **72**(1), 1–14 (2010)
7. Chistyakov, V.V.: Modular metric spaces, II: application to superposition operators. Nonlinear Anal. Theory Methods Appl. **72**(1), 15–30 (2010)
8. Chistyakov, V.V.: Metric Modular Spaces: Theory and Applications. Springer, Cham (2015). https://doi.org/10.1007/978-3-319-25283-4
9. Ege, M.E., Alaca, C.: Some results for modular b-metric spaces and an application to system of linear equations. Azerbaijan Journal of Mathematics **8**, 3–14 (2018)
10. Fuster-Parra, P., Martín, J., Miñana, J.J., Valero, O.: A study on the relationship between relaxed metrics and indistinguishability operators. Soft. Comput. **23**, 6785–6795 (2019)
11. Gholidahneh, A., Sedghi, S., Ege, O., Mitrovic, Z.D., de la Sen, M.: The Meir-Keeler type contractions in extended modular b-metric spaces with an application. AIMS Math. **6**, 1781–1799 (2021)
12. Miñana, J.J., Valero, O.: On indistinguishability operators, fuzzy metrics and modular metrics. Axioms **6**(4), 34 (2017)
13. Miñana, J.J., Valero, O.: Characterizing quasi-metric aggregation functions. Int. J. Gen Syst **48**(8), 890–909 (2019)
14. Ortiz, A., Valero, O.: Addressing multi-class classification tasks by means of RBFNN-like models using modular indistinguishability operators. In: Kahraman, C., et al. (ed.) Intelligent and Fuzzy Systems. INFUS 2024. LNNS, vol. 1089, pp. 304–312. Springer, Heidelberg (2024). https://doi.org/10.1007/978-3-031-67195-1_36
15. Ortiz, A., Valero, O., Miñana, J.: On the use of modular indistinguishability operators in RBFNN-like models. In: Lesot, MJ., e.a. (ed.) Information Processing and Management of Uncertainty in Knowledge-Based Systems. IPMU 2024. LNNS, vol. 1174, pp. 345–359. Springer, Heidelberg (2024). https://doi.org/10.1007/978-3-031-74003-9_28
16. Otafudu, O.O., Sebogodi, K.: On w-Isbell-convexity. Appl. General Topol. **23**(1), 91–105 (2022)

17. Pradera, A., Trillas, E., Castiñeira, E.: On distances aggregation. In: Proceedings of the Information Processing and Management of Uncertainty in Knowledge-Based Systems International Conference. pp. 693–700. Madrid Consejo Superior de Investigaciones Científicas Press, Madrid (2000)
18. Pradera, A., Trillas, E., Castiñeira, E.: On the aggregation of some classes of fuzzy relations. In: Technologies for Constructing Intelligent Systems, pp. 125–147. Springer, Heidelberg (2002). https://doi.org/10.1007/978-3-7908-1796-6_10
19. Sebogodi, K.: Some topological aspects of modular quasi-metric spaces. Phd thesis, University of the Witwatersrand (2019)
20. Zhu, C.I., Chen, J., Huang, X.J., Chen, J.H.: Fixed point theorems in modular spaces with simulation functions and altering distance functions with applications. J. Nonlinear Convex Anal. **21**, 1403–1424 (2020)

Incomplete Preference Relation Analysis for Multi-granular Group Decision-Making Systems

José Ramón Trillo[1]([✉])(ID), Juan Carlos González-Quesada[1](ID),
Francisco Mata[2](ID), Ignacio Javier Pérez[1](ID),
and Francisco Javier Cabrerizo[1](ID)

[1] Andalusian Research Institute of Data Science and Computational Intelligence
(DASCI), University of Granada, 18071 Granada, Spain
{jrtrillo,juancarlosgq}@ugr.es, {ijperez,cabrerizo}@decsai.ugr.es
[2] University of Jaén, 23071 Jaén, Spain
fmata@ujaen.es

Abstract. Decision-making is a process inherent to everyday life and momentous situations, which is often complicated, especially in group contexts, due to the diversity of opinions and constraints in the available information. A novel multi-granular group decision-making method based on individual similarity is presented in this context. This method is also a consensus model that secures flexibility by allowing individuals to provide information in numerical format and based on their perspective, avoiding the need to fill in the reciprocal preference relationships with information they do not know. Furthermore, the system assigns weights to individuals based on the quality and quantity of their contributions, recognising and rewarding those who provide relevant and valuable information. Ultimately, this approach promotes a more reliable and accurate decision-making process, tailored to the knowledge and experience of the group of individuals involved, thus improving the quality of decisions made as a team.

Keywords: Consensus Model · Reciprocal Preference Relations · Multi-granular Method · Similarities · Group Decision-Making

1 Introduction

Decision-making is an ongoing process in everyday life and business, and group decision-making (GDM) systems [8,25] facilitate group choice among multiple alternatives by leveraging the diversity of perspectives, information gathering, reduction of individual biases, risk/benefit assessment, collaboration among individuals, recording of decisions [14], and adaptation to change [13]. However, they can also present challenges such as conflict and complexity in the process, which makes it essential to manage these dynamics to maximize their benefits effectively [10,23].

M. Baczyński et al. (Eds.): EUSFLAT 2025, LNCS 15883, pp. 66–77, 2025.
https://doi.org/10.1007/978-3-031-97225-6_6

Currently, the literature offers a variety of solutions to address problems in the decision-making domain, as seen in several current articles, including [21] and [22]. These articles focus on a group of individuals making decisions based on information provided by individuals, but notable challenges arise [4]. The first challenge arises when individuals are required to use a common set of assessment expressions, either numerical or linguistic, which can limit their input [3,24]. The second challenge lies in the obligation of individuals to provide complete information, even when they do not possess the necessary knowledge to compare a given pair of alternatives, which may result in incorrect information. Nevertheless, if individuals have the option not to provide information, a third problem arises related to the lack of data to obtain an accurate ranking of alternatives [11,28].

To address these interconnected problems, this article proposes a multi-granular group decision-making method that relies on similarity between individuals. This system allows individuals to contribute the information they deem relevant and use sets of assessments of their choice, thus ensuring the reliability and accuracy of the input data. A consensus process is then carried out to ensure that the agreement between individuals is sufficiently high by setting a threshold that must be met. The individuals' contributions are then standardised to obtain a single scale of information for all. If some individuals cannot provide complete information, their missing data is filled in automatically. Finally, the information is combined in a weighted way, giving more weight to the individuals who have contributed the most, and a ranking of alternatives is calculated. This process is expected to ensure more accurate and reliable decision-making.

The paper is organised in five sections. In Sect. 2, we go into the fundamental concepts associated with the GDM system. Then, in Sect. 3, the proposed GDM system is presented. In Sect. 4, we provide a concrete example illustrating its application to a specific problem. Section 5 is devoted to a comprehensive review of the merits and drawbacks of the system, which are also compared with other systems reported in the current literature. Finally, in Sect. 6, we conclude with a summary of the proposed method.

2   Preliminaries

In this section, we discuss the basic concepts of group decision-making (GDM). The following setting is assumed: a finite set of individuals, to be denoted as $E = \{e_1, \ldots, e_n\}$, is considered which have to choose among a finite set of alternatives, denoted as $X = \{x_1, \ldots, x_m\}$ [9,15,21]. Based on their knowledge, for each pair of alternatives, individuals point out which one they consider "better". Thus, individuals have to provide input, which, e.g., can take the form of numerical arrays [19] or linguistic labels [5,7]. It is assumed that this input takes the form of reciprocal preference relations [16]. Consequently, expressing the reciprocal preference relation denoted as γ_a, where a ranges from 1 to n, an individual compares pairs of alternatives x_i and x_j. The result of such a comparison, carried out by individual $e_a \in E$, is assumed to be expressed as a number, denoted as

$\beta_{ij}^a \in [min^a, max^a]$, where $min^a, max^a \in \mathbb{N}$, i.e., individuals are allowed to employ different intervals of values describing their preferences when comparing pairs of alternatives.

Having established the fundamental concepts, we can now delineate the various components of a GDM method:

- Debate and give opinions and preferences: in the initial phase, individuals engage in a discussion regarding the spectrum of available alternatives at their disposal. Within this discourse, they articulate their thoughts and viewpoints, elucidating the reasons behind their preferences for certain alternatives over others. Upon the conclusion of this deliberation, the individuals consolidate their insights into reciprocal preference relations.
- Consensus analysis using individuals' preferences: within this phase, the reciprocal preference relations provided by the individuals serve as the basis for assessing whether the disparities in viewpoints and ideas warrant a feedback process. To gauge the presence of consensus in opinions, a critical threshold known as the consensus threshold is assumed, and this threshold must be reached by the consensus degree assessment to declare consensus in the group [17,19]. When the consensus threshold is exceeded, the aggregation of reciprocal preference relations is executed. Otherwise, when it is not exceeded, the aforementioned feedback process is initiated, requiring individuals to engage again in deliberations aimed at achieving mutual agreement among them [6,12].
- Aggregation of individual information: using the insights contributed by the individuals, we aggregate the information to produce a unified collective reciprocal preference relation, denoted as m. This reciprocal preference relation is derived by amalgamating the individuals' information with the aid of aggregation operators. An array of operators is available, including the Weighted Average (WA) operator, which is the one we employ in our method.
- Getting the ranking of alternatives: the final step involves leveraging the information consolidated in the collective reciprocal preference relation to ascertain the alternative or set of alternatives preferred among the individuals. This necessitates the application of an operator on the collective reciprocal preference relation [27]. In the existing literature, various operators are employed to establish the ranking of alternatives, and in our method, we utilize the Quantifier-Guided Degree of Dominance (QGDD) operator [18,26].

Within the current literature, one can encounter a diverse array of GDM-related research papers. In the work of [1], a multi-granular GDM model is developed to enhance consensus among individuals. In [14], a multi-criteria GDM approach is introduced, employing fuzzy ontologies to generate a ranking of alternatives. Finally, in [22], a consensus-oriented GDM method is presented, aiming to reveal an alternative ranking while allowing individuals the flexibility to modify their opinions at their discretion.

3   Proposed Consensus Model

In this section, we will describe the proposed multi-granular method of group decision-making. This method is composed of the seven steps that can be seen in Fig. 1 and each of the steps will be developed in detail below.

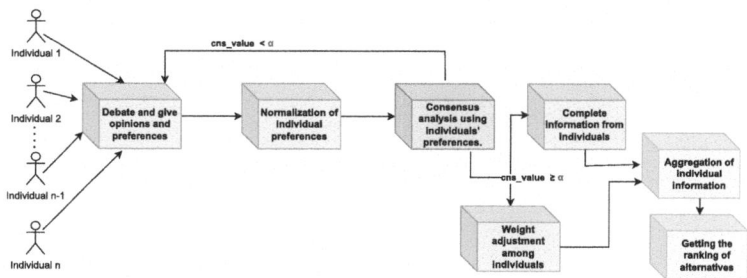

Fig. 1. Diagram of the proposed method

3.1   Debate and Give Opinions and Preferences

During the debate, the individuals, denoted as $e_a \in E$, $E = \{e_1, \ldots, e_n\}$, issue comments on the alternatives (alternative decisions), denoted as $x_i \in X$, $X = \{x_1, \ldots, x_m\}$.

Once the discussion is concluded, each individual expresses his or her opinions and preferences using reciprocal preference relation, which were previously defined in Sect. 2 as γ_a, $e_a \in E$. The individuals are not required to make all comparisons but can compare pairs of alternatives of their choice. These reciprocal preference relations are represented as matrices of dimension $m \times m$, with an empty main diagonal. The individuals express their preferences among the pairs of alternatives using numbers. It is not required that all individuals use the same scale to express their preferences.

3.2   Normalization of Individuals Preferences

In this second step, the diversity of scales used by the individuals to express their preferences is addressed. The selection of information in this process is carried out within a variety of intervals which requires this information to be normalised. Thus, element of the preference matrix, denoted β_{ij}^a is normalized as follows:

$$\zeta_{ij}^a = \frac{\beta_{ij}^a - min^a}{max^a - min^a} \quad (1)$$

And the normalized preference matrix takes the following form: $\gamma_a = (\zeta_{ij}^a; i \neq j = 1, \ldots, m)$.

3.3   Consensus Analysis Using Individuals' Preferences

The primary objective at this stage is to assess whether the disparities among the individuals are substantial enough to warrant initiating a feedback process. To assert the existence of consensus among the individuals, we establish a consensus threshold denoted by the value $\alpha \in [0, 1]$. A maximum number of the feedback rounds is assumed and is denoted as $R \in \mathbb{N}$. Moreover, the consensus degree denoted as $cns\_deg \in [0, 1]$, is calculated as follows:

$$cns\_deg = 1 - \frac{2 \cdot \sum_{a=1}^{n-1} \sum_{a<k}^{n} \frac{\sqrt{2 * \sum_{i=1}^{m} \sum_{i<j;\zeta_{ij}^a,\zeta_{ij}^k \neq \emptyset}^{m} (\zeta_{ij}^a - \zeta_{ij}^k)}}{m \cdot m - m}}{(n-1) \cdot n} \tag{2}$$

3.4   Weight Adjustment Among Individuals

In the previous section, an analysis of the consensus among individuals based on their standardised alternatives comparison, if any, was presented. This comparison has generated a consensus value that must exceed the threshold α for the consensus to be declared. If the consensus degree is greater than α, the weight attributed to each individual is calculated. This weight is determined according to the amount of information each individual provides, which means that those who provide more information will have a higher weight.

The process of calculating the weight of the individuals is divided into two parts. The first is the raw weight, which is assigned individually to each individual and is represented as $w_a \in \mathbb{N}$. This weight is calculated as follows:

$$w_a = \sum_{i=1}^{m-1} \sum_{j=i+1}^{m} \begin{cases} 1 & \zeta_{ij}^a \neq \emptyset \\ 0 & \zeta_{ij}^a = \emptyset \end{cases} \tag{3}$$

where $\emptyset$ denotes a missing entry of the preference matrix, not provided by an individual.

Once the gross weight of each individual has been obtained, its relative weight, denoted as $W_a \in [0, 1]$, is calculated. This weight is meant to be the weight of an individual concerning all the other individuals. For this reason, the sum of all the W_a is equal to 1. Thus, W_a is calculated as follows:

$$W_a = \frac{w_a}{\sum_{k=1}^{n} w_k} \tag{4}$$

3.5   Complete Information from Individuals

Once the weights of the individuals have been calculated, we proceed to complete the information on the reciprocal preference relations of each individual. To achieve it, we first calculate the standard deviation, denoted as S, of the affected individual, i.e. the one who has not completed his information. Following this, we determine which is the closest individual. This is the user who has made the comparison of the specific alternatives that the user has not made and among the group of users who have made that comparison the one with the closest Euclidean distance to the user who has not made the comparison. If no individual meets these requirements, we assign a value of 0.5 to the comparison of this pair of alternatives.

$$
S_a = \frac{\displaystyle\sum_{i=1}^{m-1} \sum_{i<j;\zeta_{ij}^a \neq \emptyset}^{m} |(\zeta_{ij}^a - \bar{\gamma}_a)|}{l_a - 1} \tag{5}
$$

where $\emptyset$, as previously, denotes missing data, $l_a \in \mathbb{N}$ is the number of comparisons made by the individual a, divided by 2 and $\bar{\gamma}_a \in [0, 1]$ is the average of the values of the upper triangular matrix having information. If we find the right individual, two scenarios can be considered:

- if the comparison performed by the found individual exceeds the value of 0.5, then we subtract the standard deviation S_a from the value of the individual and assign the result to the individual with incomplete information,
- If the comparison is less than or equal to 0.5, we add the standard deviation to the value of the individual and assign the result to the individual with incomplete information.

This procedure is carried out to enrich the information of all users, avoiding the exact reproduction of values, given that similarity between two users does not necessarily imply identity. This practice seeks to generate small variations in opinions between two users who share similar views. Furthermore, the values are adjusted accordingly to bring them closer to the middle, thus avoiding deviations from the possible range for these values. This process is formalised as follows:

$$
\zeta_{ij}^a = \begin{cases} \zeta_{ij}^k - S_a & \zeta_{ij}^k \neq \emptyset \wedge \zeta_{ij}^k > 0.5 \\ \zeta_{ij}^k + S_a & \zeta_{ij}^k \neq \emptyset \wedge \zeta_{ij}^k \leq 0.5 \end{cases} \tag{6}
$$

where k is the index of the closest individual.

3.6 Aggregation of Individual Information

Once the weight associated with each individual has been determined and all the information from the individuals has been collected, we proceed to combine this information in a weighted manner to obtain the collective reciprocal preference relation. The collective reciprocal preference relation, denoted as $\Omega = (\delta_{ij}; i \neq j = 1, \ldots, m)$, is represented as a matrix of dimension $m \times m$, with its empty main diagonal, which consolidates all the information generated by the individuals. To achieve this aggregation of data, the use of aggregation operators is required. In this context, we have selected the Weighted Average

(WA) operator, as this operator uses the reciprocal preference relation of each individual together with its respective weight. In this way, each element of the collective reciprocal preference relation is calculated as follows:

$$\delta_{ij} = \sum_{a=1}^{n} \zeta_{ij}^a \cdot W_a \tag{7}$$

3.7 Getting the Ranking of Alternatives

In this final stage, once we have obtained the collective reciprocal preference relationship, we will proceed to generate the ranking of alternatives. To carry out this process, we must apply an operator and, among the variety of options available, we have selected the Quantifier Guided Degree of Dominance (QGDD). This operator is the ideal choice as it allows us to determine how much one alternative is quantitatively preferred over another. In addition, we have opted for the average operator to calculate the value of each alternative relative to the others. Consequently, to determine the degree of dominance of an alternative x_i over the others, we calculate the value $QGDD_{x_i}$ as follows:

$$QGDD_{x_i} = \frac{\sum_{j=1;i\neq j}^{m} \delta_{ij}}{m-1} \tag{8}$$

After obtaining the values for each option, we move on to verify the correctness of the results. This check is carried out using Trillo's theorem [18], which gives us an optimal way to ensure that the process does not contain logical errors. Once we have confirmed the validity of the results, we proceed to calculate the maximum value among the values generated by the previous operation. To formalise this process, we can express it as follows:

$$x_{QGDD} = \{x_i \in x \mid QGDD_{x_i} = \max_{x_j \in X} QGDD_{x_j}\} \tag{9}$$

The option resulting from the maximum value is in line with the individuals' preference, based on the information provided.

4   Illustrative Example

In this section, we will proceed to elaborate an illustrative example to assess the effectiveness of the model. Let us imagine a situation in which three individuals, $e = \{e_1, e_2, e_3\}$ are challenged to make strategic decisions about how to invest financial resources to optimise the energy efficiency of a local settlement. A set of four alternative courses of action are considered, represented by $x = \{x_1, x_2, x_3, x_4\}$, and the individuals are expected to provide their judgement to select the option which best suits specific energy efficiency needs and objectives of their community. Option x_1 is a restructuring of the houses to take advantage of sunlight, option x_2 is an improvement of the floor to avoid heat loss, option x_3 is the replacement of windows with more efficient ones and option x_4 is the investment in solar tubes to transport the light. With this information, the discussion takes place and the first individual decides to evaluate alternatives under consideration using three values, the second five values and the third ten values. In this way, the following preferences were obtained:

$$\gamma_1 = \begin{pmatrix} - & 2.0 & 2.0 & 2.0 \\ 0.0 & - & - & 1.0 \\ 0.0 & - & - & 1.0 \\ 0.0 & 1.0 & 1.0 & - \end{pmatrix} \quad \gamma_2 = \begin{pmatrix} - & 4.0 & 4.0 & 4.0 \\ 0.0 & - & - & 3.0 \\ 0.0 & - & - & 2.0 \\ 0.0 & 1.0 & 2.0 & - \end{pmatrix} \quad \gamma_3 = \begin{pmatrix} - & 0.8 & 0.9 & 0.9 \\ 0.2 & - & 0.7 & 0.6 \\ 0.1 & 0.3 & - & 0.5 \\ 0.1 & 0.4 & 0.5 & - \end{pmatrix}$$

We then normalise the values to be able to make a consensus analysis:

$$\gamma_1 = \begin{pmatrix} - & 1.0 & 1.0 & 1.0 \\ 0.0 & - & - & 0.5 \\ 0.0 & - & - & 0.5 \\ 0.0 & 0.5 & 0.5 & - \end{pmatrix} \quad \gamma_2 = \begin{pmatrix} - & 1.0 & 1.0 & 1.0 \\ 0.0 & - & - & 0.75 \\ 0.0 & - & - & 0.5 \\ 0.0 & 0.25 & 0.5 & - \end{pmatrix} \quad \gamma_3 = \begin{pmatrix} - & 0.8 & 0.9 & 0.9 \\ 0.2 & - & 0.7 & 0.6 \\ 0.1 & 0.3 & - & 0.5 \\ 0.1 & 0.4 & 0.5 & - \end{pmatrix}$$

With this, we perform the consensus analysis using the consensus degree threshold, which for this example has been set to a value of $\alpha = 0.95$. This value has been chosen as the number of individuals is low and therefore it is relevant that they are in strong agreement in their opinions. As the consensus value is equal to 0.9685 we can continue with the process. By which the weight of each individual is calculated, obtaining that $w_1 = \frac{5}{16}$, $w_2 = \frac{5}{16}$ and $w_3 = \frac{3}{8}$. Since the standard deviation of the first preference relation is $S_1 = 0.17$ and the second is $S_2 = 0.18$, we proceed to complete the information:

$$\gamma_1 = \begin{pmatrix} - & 1.00 & 1.00 & 1.00 \\ 0.00 & - & 0.53 & 0.50 \\ 0.00 & 0.47 & - & 0.50 \\ 0.00 & 0.50 & 0.50 & - \end{pmatrix} \quad \gamma_2 = \begin{pmatrix} - & 1.00 & 1.00 & 1.00 \\ 0.00 & - & 0.52 & 0.75 \\ 0.00 & 0.48 & - & 0.50 \\ 0.00 & 0.25 & 0.50 & - \end{pmatrix} \quad \gamma_3 = \begin{pmatrix} - & 0.8 & 0.9 & 0.9 \\ 0.2 & - & 0.7 & 0.6 \\ 0.1 & 0.3 & - & 0.5 \\ 0.1 & 0.4 & 0.5 & - \end{pmatrix}$$

With the weights obtained and the information completed, the collective reciprocal preference relation is calculated.

$$\Omega = \begin{pmatrix} - & 0.9250 & 0.9625 & 0.9625 \\ 0.0750 & - & 0.5926 & 0.6156 \\ 0.0375 & 0.4094 & - & 0.5000 \\ 0.0375 & 0.3844 & 0.5000 & - \end{pmatrix}$$

Finally, we apply the GQDD with the average operator to this matrix to obtain the ranking of alternatives:

Finally, we apply Trillo's theorem [18] to verify that all operations have been carried out correctly. Once these results have been verified, it can be stated that x_1 is the preferred option by the individuals (Table 1).

Table 1. QGDD results

	x_1	x_2	x_3	x_4
QGDD	0.9500	0.4271	0.0316	0.3073

5   Discussion

In this article, a method has been presented that has the remarkable ability to enrich and extend the information provided by other individuals in the field. This unique feature empowers individuals to contribute their opinions in an authentic and informed manner, emphasising information that they have a solid grasp of. Nevertheless, it is not limited to these advantages alone, as this method reveals several additional advantages:

- **Use of different granularities to make comparisons correctly**: in group decision-making methods, a single set of linguistic labels or a single set of numerical labels is generally used. Nonetheless, in this system, users are free to select the set of numerical labels that best suits their needs. In this way, individual opinions can be optimally adjusted to the individual preferences of each user.
- **The additional information from individuals is based on the proximity of opinions**: the method presented in this paper highlights the advantage, mentioned above, that if an individual is not able to contribute certain information, he/she is not obliged to do so. This implies, as mentioned above, that the information obtained is more authentic and closer to reality. Notwithstanding, the method can supplement the individuals' information based on the affinity with the knowledge generated by the closest individual in terms of opinion. In other words, when an individual encounters limitations in his or her knowledge or ability to provide information, the system can call on other individuals whose opinions or knowledge are more closely aligned with the topic in question. This flexibility to adapt to the individual capabilities and affinities of the individuals not only improves the quality of the information gathered but also increases the efficiency of the group decision-making process, allowing each individual to contribute his or her expertise in an optimal way and contribute to more accurate and effective results.
- **The value of an individual's input is adjusted in line with the information he or she provides**: individual opinions represent a valuable resource that deserves recognition. On this premise, the system considers the contribution of each individual, and as an individual generates a greater number of relevant opinions, his or her weight compared to peers increases significantly.

As can be seen, the advantages of this method are considerably significant. Nonetheless, it is relevant to compare it with approaches present in the current literature. In [20], the weight of the individuals is adjusted according to the type of opinions they give, distinguishing between aggressive and non-aggressive opinions. Nevertheless, in the method presented here, the weight of the individuals corresponds to the number of pairs of alternatives they were in a position to compare. This difference concerning [20] is considered an advantage, as our approach does not reward comments per se, but values and adjusts the weight of the individuals according to their preferences and active participation in the process. Finally, in [2], a system is presented that aims to increase the consensus among individuals employing minimal self-tuning adjustments. On the other hand, in the method described in this work, minor modifications are not required, since the comparisons not made by the individuals are completed using the preferences of other participants in the process.

6   Conclusions

This paper presents a multi-granular group decision-making system that enriches individuals' preferences with input from their peers. This capability, combined with the flexibility to use any numerical set of their choice, not only allows people to express their opinions more realistically but also with greater accuracy.

This document represents a starting point towards an ever-expanding field of research. A future direction of study could involve creating a large-scale decision-making process that goes beyond the exclusive consideration of the closest individual. Instead, the idea of incorporating and weighing the opinions of a diverse set of individuals is proposed, to obtain a more comprehensive and robust assessment.

Furthermore, the method presented in this article transcends the mere consideration of the closest individual, unless he or she has completed his or her preferences. Instead, priority is given to the most relative individual who has carried out a detailed comparison between the alternatives in question. This approach not only suggests the potential influence of one individual over another but also opens up the possibility that a group of individuals can exert significant influence on an individual's decision-making. This broader perspective on collaboration and the weighting of multiple individual perspectives promises to improve the quality of decisions in complex, multidisciplinary contexts, providing higher reliability and accuracy in the results obtained.

Acknowledgments. This work has been supported by the grant PID2022-139297OB-I00 funded by MICIU/AEI/10.13039/501100011033 and by ERDF/EU. Moreover, it is part of the project C-ING-165-UGR23, co-funded by the Regional Ministry of University, Research and Innovation and by the European Union under the Andalusia ERDF Program 2021-2027.

References

1. Cabrerizo, F.J., Trillo, J.R., Alonso, S., Morente-Molinera, J.A.: Adaptive multi-criteria group decision-making model based on consistency and consensus with

intuitionistic reciprocal preference relations: a case study in energy storage technology selection. J. Smart Environ. Green Comput. **2**(2), 58–75 (2022)

2. Cabrerizo, F.J., Trillo, J.R., Morente-Molinera, J.A., Alonso, S., Herrera-Viedma, E.: A granular consensus model based on intuitionistic reciprocal preference relations and minimum adjustment for multi-criteria group decision making. In: 19th World Congress of the International Fuzzy Systems Association (IFSA), 12th Conference of the European Society for Fuzzy Logic and Technology (EUSFLAT), and 11th International Summer School on Aggregation Operators (AGOP), pp. 298–305. Atlantis Press (2021)

3. Chen, Z.S., Zhang, X., Rodríguez, R.M., Pedrycz, W., Martínez, L., Skibniewski, M.J.: Expertise-structure and risk-appetite-integrated two-tiered collective opinion generation framework for large-scale group decision making. IEEE Trans. Fuzzy Syst. **30**(12), 5496–5510 (2022)

4. Fedrizzi, M., Kacprzyk, J., Nurmi, H.: Consensus degrees under fuzzy majorities and fuzzy preferences using OWA (ordered weighted average) operators. Control. Cybern. **22**(4), 71–80 (1993)

5. Herrera-Viedma, E., Cabrerizo, F.J., Kacprzyk, J., Pedrycz, W.: A review of soft consensus models in a fuzzy environment. Inf. Fusion **17**, 4–13 (2014)

6. Jiang, Y., Xu, Z., Yu, X.: Compatibility measures and consensus models for group decision making with intuitionistic multiplicative preference relations. Appl. Soft Comput. **13**(4), 2075–2086 (2013)

7. Kabak, Ö., Ervural, B.: Multiple attribute group decision making: a generic conceptual framework and a classification scheme. Knowl.-Based Syst. **123**, 13–30 (2017)

8. Kacprzyk, J.: On some fuzzy cores and "soft" consensus measures in group decision making. Anal. Fuzzy Inf. **2**, 119–130 (1987)

9. Kacprzyk, J., Yager, R.R., Merigo, J.M.: Towards human-centric aggregation via ordered weighted aggregation operators and linguistic data summaries: a new perspective on zadeh's inspirations. IEEE Comput. Intell. Mag. **14**(1), 16–30 (2019)

10. Kacprzyk, J., Zadrożny, S.: Towards a general and unified characterization of individual and collective choice functions under fuzzy and nonfuzzy preferences and majority via the ordered weighted average operators. Int. J. Intell. Syst. **24**(1), 4–26 (2009)

11. Kirişci, M., Demir, I., Şimşek, N.: Fermatean fuzzy electre multi-criteria group decision-making and most suitable biomedical material selection. Artif. Intell. Med. **127**, 102278 (2022)

12. Li, Y., Kou, G., Li, G., Peng, Y.: Consensus reaching process in large-scale group decision making based on bounded confidence and social network. Eur. J. Oper. Res. **303**(2), 790–802 (2022)

13. Morente-Molinera, J., Barragán-Guzmán, M., Trillo, J., Martínez-Sánchez, M., Cabrerizo, F., Herrera-Viedma, E.: Reviving stagnated debates in group decision making environments with high number of alternatives. Procedia Comput. Sci. **221**, 65–72 (2023)

14. Morente-Molinera, J.A., Cabrerizo, F.J., Trillo, J., Pérez, I., Herrera-Viedma, E.: Managing group decision making criteria values using fuzzy ontologies. Procedia Comput. Sci. **199**, 166–173 (2022)

15. Nurmi, H., Kacprzyk, J.: On fuzzy tournaments and their solution concepts in group decision making. Eur. J. Oper. Res. **51**(2), 223–232 (1991)

16. Pramanik, S., Mukhopadhyaya, D.: Grey relational analysis based intuitionistic fuzzy multi-criteria group decision-making approach for teacher selection in higher education. Int. J. Comput. Appl. **34**(10), 21–29 (2011)

17. Qin, J., Li, M., Liang, Y.: Minimum cost consensus model for CRP-driven preference optimization analysis in large-scale group decision making using louvain algorithm. Inf. Fusion **80**, 121–136 (2022)
18. Trillo, J.R., Cabrerizo, F.J., Chiclana, F., Martínez, M.Á., Mata, F., Herrera-Viedma, E.: Theorem verification of the quantifier-guided dominance degree with the mean operator for additive preference relations. Mathematics **10**(12), 2035 (2022)
19. Trillo, J.R., Cabrerizo, F.J., Morente-Molinera, J.A., Herrera-Viedma, E., Zadrożny, S., Kacprzyk, J.: Large-scale group decision-making method based on trust clustering among experts. In: 2022 IEEE 11th International Conference on Intelligent Systems (IS), pp. 1–8. IEEE (2022)
20. Trillo, J.R., Herrera-Viedma, E., Morente-Molinera, J.A., Cabrerizo, F.J.: A group decision-making method based on the experts' behavior during the debate. IEEE Trans. Syst. Man Cybern. Syst. (2023)
21. Trillo, J.R., Herrera-Viedma, E., Morente-Molinera, J.A., Cabrerizo, F.J.: A large scale group decision making system based on sentiment analysis cluster. Inf. Fusion **91**, 633–643 (2023)
22. Trillo, J.R., Pérez, I.J., Herrera-Viedma, E., Morente-Molinera, J.A., Cabrerizo, F.J.: Multi-granular large scale group decision-making method with a new consensus measure based on clustering of alternatives in modifiable scenarios. In: International Conference on Industrial, Engineering and Other Applications of Applied Intelligent Systems, pp. 747–758. Springer (2022)
23. Trillo, J., Cabrerizo, F., Chiclana, F., Martínez, M., Herrera-Viedma, E.: Some trends in fuzzy decision making. In: International Conference on Computers Communications and Control, pp. 320–332. Springer (2022)
24. Wang, S., Wu, J., Chiclana, F., Sun, Q., Herrera-Viedma, E.: Two-stage feedback mechanism with different power structures for consensus in large-scale group decision making. IEEE Trans. Fuzzy Syst. **30**(10), 4177–4189 (2022)
25. Yager, R.R.: On ordered weighted averaging aggregation operators in multicriteria decisionmaking. IEEE Trans. Syst. Man Cybern. **18**(1), 183–190 (1988)
26. Yager, R.R.: Quantifier guided aggregation using OWA operators. Int. J. Intell. Syst. **11**(1), 49–73 (1996)
27. Yager, R.R., Kacprzyk, J.: The Ordered Weighted Averaging Operators: Theory and Applications. Springer (2012)
28. Zhang, H., Wei, G., Chen, X.: SF-GRA method based on cumulative prospect theory for multiple attribute group decision making and its application to emergency supplies supplier selection. Eng. Appl. Artif. Intell. **110**, 104679 (2022)

On Metric Aggregation Functions and Fuzzy Decision-Making

M. A. Serra-Moll[1,2] , O. Martorell-Cunill[3] , C. Mulet-Forteza[3] ,
and O. Valero[1,2(✉)]

[1] Department of Mathematics and Computer Science, Universitat de les Illes Balears,
Ctra. de Valldemossa km. 7.5, 07122 Palma de Mallorca, Illes Balears, Spain
{m.serra,o.valero}@uib.cat
[2] Health Research Institute of the Balearic Islands (IdISBa), Hospital Universitari
Son Espases, 07120 Palma de Mallorca, Illes Balears, Spain
[3] Department of Business Economics, University of the Balearic Islands, Ctra. de
Valldemossa Km 7.5, 07122 Palma de Mallorca, Illes Balears, Spain
{onofre.martorell,carles.mulet}@uib.cat

Abstract. In fuzzy decision-making it is required to aggregate numerical pieces of information that incorporate vagueness and that comes from various sources in order to get a unique numerical value that is incorporated in some decision-making technique and, hence, it allows to select one option between several available. In order to select which alternative is the best one, an ideal profile is defined and the alternative chosen is exactly the one that minimizes the distance to the aforementioned ideal. The Ordered Weighted Averaging (OWA) is an instance of aggregation function which appears to be well-suited to be applied in these type of situations. Concretely, it has been shown to be useful in generating mean distances which are used to evaluate all different strategies and to find the best one according to the interest of the decision-maker. However, in a natural way, the decision process imposes many times that the aggregate information corresponds to an overall distance between alternatives rather than an average distance. In this direction, metric aggregation functions are more useful. In this paper, we introduce a technique to generate this type of functions and we show a few limitations of the OWA for this purpose. Instances of such functions induced by the new technique are provided. Moreover, such examples are used to illustrate the usefulness of this type of functions in fuzzy decision-making. The selection of strategies is compared with those provided by the OWA.

Keywords: OWA · Metric Aggregation Function · Decision-Making · Investment Strategies

1 Introduction

In recent years, we find an important growth in interest in the information aggregation theory. The main reason for this is its high potential in a wide

---

Dedicated to the memory of Professor Alexander Šostak.

M. Baczyński et al. (Eds.): EUSFLAT 2025, LNCS 15883, pp. 78–90, 2025.
https://doi.org/10.1007/978-3-031-97225-6_7

range of applications. In decision-making it is required to aggregate numerical pieces of information that incorporate vagueness and that come from various sources in order to get a unique numerical value that is incorporated in some decision-making technique. Typically such a vagueness is mathematically represented by fuzzy sets. In many problems that arise in a natural way in fuzzy decision-making, in order to select which alternative is the best one, an ideal profile is defined and the alternative chosen is exactly the one that minimizes the distance to the aforementioned ideal. The earlier stated distance is computed between fuzzy vectors that describe the ideal profile and every alternative in such a way that their components determine the level in which each characteristic of the problem is met. This kind of decision-making processes is usual in human resource selections, financial management and sport management (see, for instance, [5,6,8]). Metrics that are commonly used for this type of comparison between fuzzy sets are the so-called Hamming metric, the Euclidean metric and the Minkowsky metric (see [2,9]).

Recently, the Ordered Weighted Averaging (OWA) has been shown to be an instance of aggregation function which appears to be well-suited to be applied in these type of situations. Concretely, it has been used to generate mean distances which are used to evaluate all different strategies and to find the best one according to the interest of the decision-maker. Utilizing the OWA has the advantage that allows to incorporate the optimist/pessimist attitude of the decision-maker towards those aspects of the problem under consideration that generate uncertainty. Motivated by this aspect, J.M. Merigó and A.M. Gil-Lafuente have explored the utility of the OWA in fuzzy decision-making in [11–13]. Thus, they have introduced and studied new metrics obtained through the combination of the OWA and any of the three metrics mentioned above. These new metrics are considered for comparing the characteristics of fuzzy vectors and later, such individual numerical values are merged with the OWA. Concretely, they have defined the so-called Ordered Weighted Averaging Distance (OWAD), the Euclidean Ordered Weighted Averaging Distance (EOWAD) and the Minkowski Ordered Averaging Distance (MOWAD) in [11–13]. Applications of such metrics to several strategy selection problems are also exemplified in the same references.

In a natural way, the decision process imposes many times that the aggregated information corresponds to an overall distance between alternatives rather than an average distance. In this direction, metric aggregation functions are more pertinent because they allow to merge a collection of metrics into a new global one (see [3,14]). However, the literature lacks a large number of instances of this type of functions that would allow us to develop appropriate applications to decision-making. In this paper, we introduce a technique to generate systematically this type of functions and we show a few limitations of the OWA for this purpose. Instances of such functions induced by the new technique are provided. Moreover, such examples are used to illustrate the usefulness of this type of functions in fuzzy decision-making where a generic strategy selection problem is considered. The selection of strategies induced by the use of the metric generated

via the application of the obtained metric aggregation functions are compared
with those provided by the OWA.

The remainder of the paper is organized as follows: Sect. 2 is devoted to the
revision of the key concepts for our study: bounded metrics, metric aggregation
functions, the OWA and the metrics derived from it and considered in [11–13].
In Sect. 3, we introduce the mentioned newly proposed technique for generating
metric aggregation functions and we showcase some examples of such functions.
In Sect. 4, these instances are tested by applying them to a generic hypothetical
case. The results are compared to those obtained by the OWAD, the EOWAD
and the MOWAD. Hence, it is illustrated that metric aggregation functions
could be reasonably useful in fuzzy decision-making problems. Finally, closing
conclusions are provided in Sect. 5.

2 Preliminaires

In the following, we introduce some pertinent notions for a better understanding
of the ensuing study. Particularly, we will review some core concepts such as
bounded metrics and metric aggregation functions. Moreover, we will recall the
OWA, some of its generalizations and the metrics derived from them i.e., the so-
called Ordered Weighted Averaging Distance (OWAD), the Euclidean Ordered
Weighted Averaging Distance (EOWAD) and the Minkowski Ordered Averaging
Distance (MOWAD).

Although the notion of metric is well known, we recall it with the aim of
highlighting more clearly a few limitations of the OWA in order to induce metrics
later. According to [14] (see also [2]), a metric d on a non-empty set I is a function
$d : I \times I \to [0, \infty[$ that fulfills the following properties for all $x, y, z \in I$:

M1. $d(x, y) = 0 \iff x = y$ Identity of indiscernibles.
M2. $d(x, y) = d(y, x)$ Symmetry.
M3. $d(x, z) \leq d(x, y) + d(y, z)$ Triangle Inequality.

If there exists $c \in]0, \infty[$ such that $d(x, y) \leq c$ for all $x, y \in I$, then the metric
d is said to be bounded with c as constant of boundedness (c-metric from now
on).

Typical examples of bounded metrics are the weighted Hamming metric, the
weighted Euclidean metric and the weighted Minkowski metric on $[0, c]^n$. Recall
that, given $a, b \in [0, c]^n$ and $w_1, \ldots, w_n \in]0, 1[$ such that $\sum_{j=1}^{n} w_j = 1$, the
aforementioned metrics are given as follows:

$d_{wH}(a, b) = \sum_{j=1}^{n} w_j |b_j - a_j|$ weighted Hamming metric.

$d_{wE}(a, b) = \left(\sum_{j=1}^{n} w_j |b_j - a_j|^2 \right)^{\frac{1}{2}}$ weighted Euclidean metric.

$d_{wM}(a, b) = \left(\sum_{j=1}^{n} w_j |b_j - a_j|^\lambda \right)^{\frac{1}{\lambda}} \ (\lambda \in [1, \infty[)$ weighted Minkowski metric.

Of course, from the preceding expressions one can retrieve the normalized Hamming metric, normalized Euclidean metric and the normalized Minkowski metric when $w_j = \frac{1}{n}$ for all $j = 1, \ldots, n$.

In some applied problems, such as those arising from decision-making, it is necessary to aggregate a collection of numerical data representing distances so that the merged value can be identified with a global distance and can be used for getting a working decision. Here, metric aggregation functions, functions that are able to fuse a collection of bounded metrics into a new, play a central role. Let us recall such this concept from [14] (see also [3]).

Set $c, r \in]0, \infty[$ and $n \in \mathbb{N}$ ($\mathbb{N}$ denotes the set of positive integer numbers). A function $A : [0, c]^n \to [0, r]$ is a metric aggregation function if $A(d_1, \ldots, d_n)$ is an r-metric on a non-empty set $\prod_{i=1}^n I_i$, provided that d_i is a c-metric on I_i for all $i = 1, \ldots, n$. Observe that the function $A(d_1, \ldots, d_n)$ is given, for all $x, y \in I$, by $A(d_1, \ldots, d_n)(x, y) = A(d_1(x, y), \ldots, d_n(x, y))$.

With the purpose of generating metrics in the spirit of metric aggregation functions and to apply them in fuzzy decision-making problems, the Ordered Weighted Averaging Distance, the Euclidean Ordered Weighted Averaging Distance and the Minkowski Ordered Averaging Distance are introduced in [13], [11] and [12], respectively. All of them are based on the use of the Ordered Weighted Averaging. Next we recall that, given $c \in]0, \infty[$ and $w_1, \ldots, w_n \in [0, 1]$ such that $\sum_{j=1}^n w_j = 1$, the OWA$_w$, as introduced by R. Yager in [16], is a function OWA $: [0, c]^n \to [0, c]$ defined for all $a \in [0, c]^n$ as follows: OWA$(a_1, a_2, ..., a_n) = \sum_{j=1}^n w_j b_j$, where b_j is the j-th largest element of $\{a_1, \ldots, a_n\}$.

In this study, from now on, only the OWAs with the weights arranged in decreasing order are considered. We explain the reason later on.

It is also worth mentioning that OWA is a commutative (invariant under permutations), monotone and averaging function. This latter property means that $\min\{a_1, a_2, ..., a_n\} \leq$ OWA$(a_1, a_2, ..., a_n) \leq \max\{a_1, \ldots, a_n\}$ for all $a \in [0, c]^n$. Recall that, fixed given $c, r \in]0, \infty[$, a function $A : [0, c]^n \to [0, r]$ is said to be monotone provided that $A(a) \leq A(b)$ for all $a, b \in [0, c]^n$ with $a_i \leq b_i$ for all $i = 1, \ldots, n$.

In [13], the notion of normalized Hamming metric was extended combining the OWA and the weighted Hamming metric. Thus, the notion of Ordered Weighted Averaging Distance (OWAD) was introduced and defined as follows. Given $c \in]0, \infty[$ and $w_1, \ldots, w_n \in [0, 1]$ such that $\sum_{j=1}^n w_j = 1$, the OWAD$_w$ is the function OWAD$_w : [0, c]^n \to [0, c]$ given by OWAD$_w(a, b) = \sum_{j=1}^n w_j D_j$, where D_j is the j-th largest element of the $\{|a_1 - b_1|, \ldots, |a_n - b_n|\}$. Observe that the preceding notion recovers the normalized Hamming metric when $w_j = \frac{1}{n}$ for all $j = 1, \ldots, n$.

On the other hand, the notion of Generalized Ordered Weighted Average was introduced in [17]. Let us recall that, given $c \in]0, \infty[$ and $w_1, \ldots, w_n \in [0, 1]$ such that $\sum_{j=1}^n w_j = 1$, the GOWA is a function GOWA$_w : [0, c]^n \to [0, c]$ defined for all $a \in [0, c]^n$ as follows: GOWA$_w^\lambda(a_1, a_2, ..., a_n) = \left(\sum_{j=1}^n w_j b_j^\lambda \right)^{\frac{1}{\lambda}}$, where b_j

is the j-th largest element of $\{a_1, \ldots, a_n\}$ and $\lambda \in]-\infty, \infty[$. Recall that when $\lambda = 0$, the GOWA_w^λ is understood as the ordered weighted geometric mean.

When $w_j = \frac{1}{n}$ for all $j = 1, \ldots, n$ the above notion retrieves as a particular case the notion of Generalized Mean introduced in [4].

Notice that GOWAs do not preserve the averaging character of the OWA in general. A proper analysis of parameter λ allows to obtain special cases which are analyzed in [16] and [11].

Combining the GOWA and the weighted Minkowski metric, the Minkowski Ordered Averaging Distance (MOWAD) was introduced in [12]. Concretely, given $c \in]0, \infty[$ and $w_1, \ldots, w_n \in [0, 1]$ such that $\sum_{j=1}^{n} w_j = 1$, the MOWAD_w^λ is the function $\text{MOWAD}_w^\lambda : [0, c]^n \to [0, c]$ given by $\text{MOWAD}_w^\lambda(a, b) = \left(\sum_{j=1}^{n} w_j D_j^\lambda \right)^{\frac{1}{\lambda}}$, where D_j is the j-th largest element of the $\{|a_1 - b_1|, \ldots, |a_n - b_n|\}$, where $\lambda \in]-\infty, \infty[$. Observe that, when $\lambda = 2$, the above notion gets back the Euclidean Ordered Weighted Averaging Distance as introduced in [11].

Motivated by the utility of the OWA in fuzzy decision-making, the applicability of the OWAD, the MOWAD and the EOWAD was demostrated in [11–13] where examples of strategy decision processes in sport management and finance management were implemented.

In spite of the success of the OWAD, the MOWAD and the EOWAD in the applications, it must be pointed that they have certain limitations. First of all, the values of such distances should be interpreted as an average distance rather than an overall distance between the fuzzy vectors. Although in some cases the averaging character of the OWA is not preserved by the generalizations. Observe that for values of λ very large (for instance) MOWAD_w^λ is not averaging. Moreover, there are other limitations of this type of distances. On the other hand, the OWAD_w, the MOWAD_w^λ and the EOWAD_w are generally not really metrics. It is known that OWAD_w is only a metric when the weights are different from zero and are arranged in decreasing order (see [15]). This is the reason for which we have only considered the OWA with weights arranged in decreasing order at the beginning of this section. On the other hand, the MOWAD_w^λ does not satisfy the triangle inequality when $0 < \lambda < 1$ such as the example below shows.

Example 1. Let $\lambda = \frac{1}{2}$ and $n = 3$. Consider $r = (1, 1, 0)$, $t = (0, 1, 0)$ and $s = (0, 0, 0)$. Set $w_1 = w_2 = w_3 = \frac{1}{3}$. Then, we have that $\text{MOWAD}_w^{\frac{1}{2}}(r, t) \doteq 0.11 \doteq \text{MOWAD}_w^{\frac{1}{2}}(t, s)$. Moreover, $\text{MOWAD}_w^{\frac{1}{2}}(r, s) \doteq 0.44$. It follows that

$$\text{MOWAD}_w^{\frac{1}{2}}(r, s) > \text{MOWAD}_w^{\frac{1}{2}}(r, t) + \text{MOWAD}_w^{\frac{1}{2}}(t, s).$$

So the triangle inequality is not satisfied.

Furthermore, observe that for $\lambda < 0$ another irregularity appears when MOWAD_w^λ is under consideration. Indeed, observe that when $a, b \in [0, c]^n$ is such that there exists $i \in \{1, \ldots, n\}$ with $a_i = b_i$ we have that $\text{MOWAD}_w^\lambda(a, b) = \frac{1}{(\sum_{j=1}^{n} \frac{w_j}{D_j^\lambda})^{\frac{1}{\lambda}}}$. So, a division by zero takes place, resulting in a mathematical inconsistency.

Taking into account the exposed facts and that many fuzzy decision processes impose that the aggregated information corresponds to an overall distance between fuzzy vectors (alternatives) rather than an average distance (see [5,7]), it seems natural to discern whether metric aggregation functions could be useful in order to develop mathematical techniques serviceable for fuzzy decision-making. So, the rest of the paper is devoted to the introduction of a technique to generate systematically this type of functions and to give a few instances. Moreover, such examples are used to illustrate the usefulness of this type of functions in fuzzy decision-making where a generic strategy selection problem is considered.

3   A New Technique for Generating Metric Aggregation Functions

On account of [14], given $c, d \in]0, \infty[$, a function $A : [0, c]^n \to [0, d]$ is said to be subadditive when $A(a + b) \leq A(a) + A(b)$ for all $a, b \in [0, c]^n$ with $a + b \in [0, c]^n$. In the following we denote by $O_{c,d}([0, c]^n)$ the set of functions $A : [0, c]^n \to [0, d]$ which are monotone, subadditive and satisfy that $A(x) = 0 \Leftrightarrow x = 0_n$, where $0_n = (0, \ldots, 0)$.

Notice that, given $w_1, \ldots, w_n \in [0, 1]$ such that $\sum_{j=1}^n w_j = 1$, the OWA$_w$ is a subadditive function provided that $w_i \geq w_j$ for $i < j$ (see [1]).

The following result provides a partial description of metric aggregation functions and its proof can be found in [14]. A full characterization of such functions can be found in [3].

Proposition 1. *Let $c, d \in]0, \infty[$. Every function F belonging to $O_{c,d}([0, c]^n)$ is a metric aggregation function.*

Examples of metric aggregation functions which are immediately provided by the above result are the following.

Example 2. Fix $c \in]0, \infty[$ and let $w_1, \ldots, w_n \in]0, 1[$ with $\sum_{i=1}^n w_i = 1$. Then the functions $A : [0, c]^n \to [0, A(c, \ldots, c)]$ are metric aggregation functions, where:

(1) $A_1(a) = (\sum_{i=1}^n a_i^p)^{\frac{1}{p}}$ for all $a \in [0, c]^n$ and $p \in [1, \infty[$ (l_p-norm).
(2) $A_2(a) = (\sum_{i=1}^n \frac{1}{n} a_i^p)^{\frac{1}{p}}$ for all $a \in [0, c]^n$ and $p \in [1, \infty[$ (p-means).
(3) $A_3(a) = \sum_{i=1}^n w_i a_i$ for all $a \in [0, c]^n$ (weighted sum, which includes the arithmetic mean for which $w_i = \frac{1}{n}$ for all $i = 1, \ldots, n$).
(4) $A_4(a) = \max\{w_1 a_1, \ldots, w_n a_n\}$ for all $a \in [0, c]^n$.
(5) $A_5(a) = \ln\left(1 + \sum_{i=1}^n a_i\right)$ for all $a \in [0, c]^n$.

Although the preceding result provides a way to generate metric aggregation functions, the literature lacks a large number of samples of this type of functions. Motivated by this fact, a new technique, which rests on the previous one, to generate metric aggregation functions is provided by the result below.

Proposition 2. *Let* $c, d \in]0, \infty[$ *and let* $n, m \in \mathbb{N}$ *with* $m < n$. *If* $F_1 \in O_{c,d}([0, c]^m)$, $F_2 \in O_{c,d}([0, c]^{n-m})$ *and* $G \in O_{2d,d}([0, 2d]^2)$, *then the function* $A : [0, c]^n \to [0, d]$, *defined by* $A = G \circ (F_1 \times F_2)$, *satisfies that* $A \in O_{c,d}([0, c]^n)$.

Proof. First of all we show that A is monotone. Consider $a, b \in [0, c]^n$ such that $a_i \leq b_i$ for all $i = 1, \ldots, n$. Since F_1 and F_2 are monotone we have that $F_1(a_1, \ldots, a_n) \leq F_1(b_1, \ldots, b_n)$ and $F_2(a_{m+1}, \ldots, a_n) \leq F_2(b_{m+1}, \ldots, b_n)$. Then

$$A(a) = G\left(F_1(a_1 \ldots, a_m), F_2(a_{m+1}, \ldots, a_n)\right) \leq$$

$$G\left(F_1(b_1 \ldots, b_m), F_2(b_{m+1}, \ldots, b_n)\right) = A(b).$$

Next we show that A is subadditive. Indeed, consider $a, b \in [0, c]^n$ such that $a + b \in [0, c]^n$. Then $F_1(a_1 + b_1, \ldots, a_m + b_m) \leq F_1(a_1, \ldots, a_m) + F_1(b_1, \ldots, b_m)$ and $F_2(a_{m+1} + b_{m+1}, \ldots, a_n + b_n) \leq F_2(a_{m+1}, \ldots, a_n) + F_2(b_{m+1}, \ldots, b_n)$. The facts that G is subadditive and monotone provide that

$$A(a + b) = G\left(F_1(a_1 + b_1, \ldots, a_m + b_m), F_2(a_{m+1} + b_{m+1}, \ldots, a_n + b_n)\right) \leq$$

$$G\left(F_1(a_1, \ldots, a_m) + F_1(b_1, \ldots, b_m), F_2(a_{m+1}, \ldots, a_n) + F_2(b_{m+1}, \ldots, b_n)\right) \leq$$

$$G\left(F_1(a_1, \ldots, a_m), F_2(a_{m+1}, \ldots, a_n)\right) + G\left(F_1(b_1, \ldots, b_m), F_2(b_{m+1}, \ldots, b_n)\right)$$

$$= A(a) + A(b).$$

Finally, we show that $A(a) = 0 \Leftrightarrow x = 0_n$. Assume that $A(a) = 0$ for any $a \in [0, c]^n$. The fact that $G \in O_{2d,d}([0, 2d]^2)$ yields that $F_1(a_1, \ldots, a_m) = 0 = F_2(a_{m+1}, \ldots, a_n)$. Since $F_1 \in O_{c,d}([0, c]^m)$ and $F_2 \in O_{c,d}([0, c]^{n-m})$ we have that $(a_1 \ldots, a_m) = 0_m$ and $(a_{m+1}, \ldots, a_n) = 0_{n-m}$. It follows that $a = 0_n$. Observe that $A(0_n) = 0$. □

Proposition 2 allows us to provide a few examples of metric aggregation functions which are not so evident.

Example 3. Let $c \in]0, \infty[$ and let $w_1, \ldots, w_n \in]0, 1[$ with $\sum_{i=1}^n w_i = 1$. The functions $A : [0, c]^n \to [0, A(c, \ldots, c)]$ below are instances of metric aggregation functions, where:

(6) $A_6(a) = \text{GOWA}_w^\lambda(a)$ for all $a \in [0, c]^n$ with $w_i \geq w_j$ for $i < j$ and $\lambda \in [1, \infty[$.

(7) $A_7(a) = \left(\sum_{i=1}^m a_i^p\right)^{\frac{1}{p}} + \sum_{i=m+1}^n a_i$ with $p \in [1, \infty[$.

(8) $A_8(a) = \max\{\sum_{i \neq j} a_i + v \cdot a_j, \sum_{i \neq k} a_i + t \cdot a_k\}$ for all $v, t \in]0, \infty[$ and where $j \neq k$ with $j, k \in \{1, \ldots, n\}$.

According to [14], every subadditive triangular conorm is a sample of a function G satisfying the conditions in the statement of Proposition 2. Keeping this in mind, we provide a few surprising examples of metric aggregation functions.

Example 4. Let $c \in]0, \infty]$ and let $n, m \in \mathbb{N}$ with $m < n$. If $w_1, \ldots, w_n \in]0, 1[$ with $\sum_{i=1}^n w_i = 1$, then the functions $A : [0, c]^n \to [0, c]$ below are instances of metric aggregation functions, where:

(9) $A_9(a) = \min\{c, \sum_{i=1}^n w_i a_i\}$ for all $a \in [0, c]^n$.

(10) $A_{10}(a) = \min\{c, \sum_{i=1}^n a_i\}$ for all $a \in [0, c]^n$ (bounded sum).

(11) $A_{11}(a) = \min\left\{ \left(\left((\sum_{i=1}^m a_i^p)^{\frac{1}{p}} \right)^\lambda + (\max\{w_{m+1} a_{m+1}, \dots, w_n a_n\})^\lambda \right)^{\frac{1}{\lambda}}, c \right\}$

for all $a \in [0, c]^n$ and $p, \lambda \in [1, \infty[$.

(12) $\qquad A_{12}(a) \qquad = \qquad \min\left\{ \sum_{i=1}^m w_i a_{(i)} \quad + \quad \min\{c, \sum_{i=m+1}^n w_i a_i\} + \right.$

$\left. \lambda \left(\sum_{i=1}^m w_i a_{(i)} \cdot \min\{c, \sum_{i=m+1}^n w_i a_i\} \right), c \right\}$ for all $a \in [0, c]^n$ and $\lambda \in [-1, 0]$

and such that $w_i \geq w_j$ for $i < j$ with $i, j \in \{1, \dots, m\}$ ($a_{(i)}$ is the i-th largest element of $\{a_1, \dots, a_m\}$).

4   Metric Aggregation Functions in the Strategy Selection Problem

One of the main applications of the OWA and its variations, such as OWAD, EOWAD and MOWAD, is in strategy selection problems. For instance, we can find them in human resource management, sport management or finance management [5,6,8,11–13]. Next, we show that metric aggregation functions allow to provide a global distance to compute the dissimilarity between the fuzzy vectors that describe the ideal profile and every alternative and, thus, to select the best alternative that minimizes the distance to the aforementioned ideal. Specifically, we test a few instances of metric aggregation functions induced by Propositions 1 and 2. Finally, we compare the selection of strategies induced by the use of the metric generated via the application of the aforesaid instances and those provided by the weighted Hamming metric (including the normalized one), the weighted Euclidean metric (including the normalized one), the OWAD and the EOWAD.

4.1   General Decision-Making Procedure

Assume a situation where different alternatives are presented and the matter under consideration is selecting the most appropriate one by means of minimizing the distance between an ideal profile and every alternative. In general, the analysis of a general case is performed following the steps (see, for instance, [13]):

1. Identification of the main characteristics for each alternative. The representation is stated as $C = \{C_1, C_2, \dots, C_n\}$ where C_i is the i-th characteristic of the case under consideration. A finite number of characteristics, namely $m \in \mathbb{N}$, is required as displayed in Table 1. Notice that P_k is the k-th alternative being a fuzzy subset and μ_i^k ($\mu_i^k \in [0, 1]$) the level in which the k-characteristic is met, i.e., $P_k(C_i) = \mu_i^k$ for all $i = 1, \dots, n$ and $k = 1, \dots, m$.

2. Identification of the characteristics of the ideal case (even if it is hypothetical). The representation is shown in Table 1. Notice that P is the ideal case or ideal product being a fuzzy subset and μ_i ($\mu_i \in [0,1]$) the value of the i-th characteristic.
3. Comparison of the ideal situation and the different possible alternatives under consideration. It follows the calculation of the distance between them by using a distance (metric).
4. Make the final decision according to the results computed in the previous step and choose the best alternative, as the one that minimizes the distance between the ideal and every alternative.

Table 1. Characteristics considered for the ideal and each alternative strategy, and their compliance level.

	C_1	C_2	...	C_i	...	C_n
$P_1=$	$\mu_1^{(1)}$	$\mu_2^{(1)}$	...	$\mu_i^{(1)}$	...	$\mu_n^{(1)}$
...	...	...	...	...	...	...
$P_m=$	$\mu_1^{(m)}$	$\mu_2^{(m)}$	...	$\mu_i^{(m)}$	...	$\mu_n^{(m)}$
$P=$	μ_1	μ_2	...	μ_i	...	μ_n

4.2 Numerical Example

Now we propose a practical example so that we can apply metric aggregation functions to the decision-making procedure exposed. This application is based on the data and results presented in [12]. The aim is to carry out a comparison analysis between the selection of strategies induced by the use of the metric generated via the application of a few instances of metric aggregation functions and those provided by the weighted Hamming metric WHD (including the normalized one NHD), the weighted Euclidean metric WED (including the normalized one NED), the OWAD and the EOWAD proposed in [12].

Here, a hypothetical example is shown where different strategies have to be analyzed by a decision-maker and thus, he/she has to evaluate which is the best indicated, i.e., that minimizing the distance between the ideal profile and the alternatives, regarding the interests and the current situation of the enterprise. Thus, the main objective is to determine the best alternative by using metric aggregation functions and to confirm that the estimation provided by them is reasonable and could be considered as suitable as the ones provided by those derived from the OWA and given in [12].

Concretely, we are assuming a case where a business is thinking about investing in a new strategy so as to obtain more gains. The different possibilities are five strategies that we denote by S_i ($i = 1, \ldots, 5$).

Table 2 summarizes the values of the different characteristics that describe the strategies in the example. Consider that this hypothetical data is supposed to be obtained after a meticulous research. Five main variables or characteristics are considered and denoted by C_i ($i = 1, \ldots, 5$). Table 2 shows the compliance level ($C_i \in [0, 1]$) of each characteristic associated to each strategy.

Furthermore, the same expert needs to register an ideal strategy based on the interests and objectives of the company. This is also displayed in Table 2.

Next, we make the dissimilarity comparisons between the vector associated to the ideal strategy and those associated to the alternatives using NHD, WHD,WED, OWAD and EOWAD (all particular cases of MOWAD). Note that these computations were made in [12]. Additionally, we use for the same comparisons the following metric aggregation functions (always applied to the vector of distances computed coordinate-by-coordinate with the Euclidean $|\cdot|$): (6) with $\lambda = 4$, (7) with $p = 2$, (5), (11) with $p = 1$, $\lambda = 2$ and $c = 1$, and finally (12) with $c = 1$ and $\lambda = -\frac{1}{2}$. Notice that the vector of weights used is $(0.3, 0.2, 0.2, 0.2, 0.1)$ (Table 3).

Table 4 shows in detail the mentioned results. As it can be seen, the selected strategy will also be in accordance of the particular case of the tested metric. The selection criteria of all the presented strategies is ordered in Table 5.

Table 2. The different strategies and their compliance level of the characteristics.

	C_1	C_2	C_3	C_4	C_5
S_1	0.5	0.7	0.8	0.6	0.5
S_2	0.8	0.9	0.2	0.4	0.5
S_3	0.5	0.7	0.6	0.3	0.7
S_4	0.7	0.9	0.6	0.2	0.6
S_5	0.2	0.7	0.98	0.7	0.5
Ideal	0.9	1	0.9	0.9	0.8

Table 3. Results for the cases of averaged distances considered.

	NHD	NED	WHD	WED	OWAD	EOWAD
S_1	0.28	0.29	0.27	0.28	0.25	0.27
S_2	0.34	0.41	0.36	0.42	0.28	0.349
S_3	0.34	0.37	0.31	0.35	0.29	0.327
S_4	0.3	0.36	0.3	0.36	0.24	0.293
S_5	0.32	0.38	0.28	0.32	0.26	0.309

Table 4. Results for the tested metric aggregation functions.

	(6)	(7)	(5)	(11)	(12)
S_1	0.33	0.59	0.25	0.8	0.28
S_2	0.54	0.81	0.29	0.9	0.3
S_3	0.47	0.69	0.29	1	0.31
S_4	0.52	0.67	0.26	0.61	0.29
S_5	0.52	0.69	0.25	0.92	0.32

Table 5. Strategy ordering.

NHD	$S_1 \succ S_4 \succ S_5 \succ S_2 = S_3$	(6)	$S_1 \succ S_3 \succ S_4 \succ S_5 \succ S_2$
NED	$S_1 \succ S_4 \succ S_3 \succ S_5 \succ S_2$	(7)	$S_1 \succ S_4 \succ S_3 \succ S_5 \succ S_2$
WHD	$S_1 \succ S_5 \succ S_4 \succ S_3 \succ S_2$	(5)	$S_1 \succ S_5 \succ S_4 \succ S_2 = S_3$
WED	$S_1 \succ S_5 \succ S_3 \succ S_4 \succ S_2$	(11)	$S_4 \succ S_1 \succ S_2 \succ S_5 \succ S_3$
$OWAD$	$S_4 \succ S_1 \succ S_5 \succ S_2 \succ S_3$	(12)	$S_1 \succ S_4 \succ S_2 \succ S_3 \succ S_5$
$EOWAD$	$S_1 \succ S_4 \succ S_5 \succ S_3 \succ S_2$		

In the light of the results, we can conclude the following. Depending on the metric aggregation function a different strategy will be selected. Observe that for every tested metric aggregation function the optimal strategy is S_1 as is the case when we use all particular cases of MOWAD with the exception of the OWAD and (11), which yield strategy S_4 as the optimal. Observe that the use of metric aggregation functions does not generally provide the attitude of the decision-maker in the spirit of OWAs, but they give a global metric rather than an average metric. Although the procedure gives an optimal strategy, the decision-maker could be interested in the orderering of the strategies in order to select another one as the most appropriate based on her/his experience or on subjective judgement. As in the case with MOWADs, Table 5 shows that the use of different metric aggregation function generally gives a different ordering of the strategies, which could lead to the decision-maker taking markedly different choices. The obtained results indicate that they could be equally appropriate for the assessment of strategies for enterprises as those induced by the MOWADs.

5   Conclusions

In order to select which alternative is the best one in fuzzy decision-making, an ideal profile is defined and the alternative chosen is exactly the one that minimizes the distance to the aforementioned ideal. The OWA has been shown to be useful in generating mean distances which are used to evaluate all different strategies and to find the best one according to the interest of the decision-maker. However, in a natural way the decision process imposes many times that the aggregate information corresponds to an overall distance between alternatives rather than an average distance. Inspired by this fact, we have introduced a technique to generate metric aggregation functions. Instances of such functions induced by the new technique have been provided. Finally, such examples have been used to illustrate the usefulness of this type of functions in fuzzy decision-making. The selection of strategies have been compared with those provided by the OWA, showing that metric aggregation functions can be considered an appropriate tool as a metric measurement of the dissimilarities between an ideal profile and the alternatives in decision-making procedures. In [13], the dual adequacy coefficient which corresponds to a quasi-metric obtained by aggregation, was introduced. Moreover, an ordered weighted averaging version of such a coefficient has been shown to be useful in fuzzy decision-making in the same reference. As a further work, a study about the utility in fuzzy decision-making of quasi-metric aggregation function, in the sense of [10], will be explored. Moreover, it seems interesting to develop a software tool, which could be incorporated in the expert's control panel with the aim of analyzing various scenarios by simply changing the desired value of characteristics and weights and, thus, giving the expert more support for decision-making.

Acknowledgments. This research is part of project PID2022-139248NB-I00 funded by MICIU/AEI/10.13039/501100011033 and ERDF/EU. The authors thank the support from *Programa de Foment de la Recerca i la Innovació de la Universitat de les Illes Balears 2024-2026* and ITS2023-086-Programa de Foment a la recerca.

Disclosure of Interests. The authors have no competing interests to declare that are relevant to the content of this article.

References

1. Beliakov, G., Bustince, H., Calvo, T.: A Practical Guide to Averaging Functions, Studies of Fuzziness and Soft Computing, vol. 329. Springer, Heidelberg (2015)
2. Deza, M.M., Deza, E.: Encyclopedia of Distances. Springer, Berlin (2016)
3. Dobos, J.: Metric Preserving Functions. Štroffek, Košice (1998)
4. Dujmović, J.J.: Weighted conjunctive and disjunctive means and their application in system evaluation. J. Univ. Belgrade EE Dept. Ser. Math. Phys. **483**, 147–158 (1974)
5. Gil-Aluja, J.: The Interactive Management of Human Resources in Uncertainty. Kluwer Academic Press, Dordrecht (1998)
6. Gil-Lafuente, A.: Fuzzy Logic in Financial Analysis. Springer, Berlin (2005)
7. Gomes, M., Chibeles-Martins, N.: Mathematical Models for Decision Making with Multiple Perspectives. An Introduction. CRC Press, Boca Raton (2022)
8. Kahraman, C., Haktanr, E.: Fuzzy Investment Decisoin Making with Examples. Springer, Cham (2024)
9. Kundu, S., Aggarwal, M.: Metric Spaces and Related Analysis. World Scientific, New Jersey (2024)
10. Mayor, G., Valero, O.: Aggregation of asymmetric distances in computer science. Inf. Sci. **180**, 803–812 (2010)

11. Merigó, J.M., Gil-Lafuente, A.M.: On the use of the OWA operator in the euclidean distance. Int. J. Comput. Sci. Eng. **2**(4), 170–176 (2008)
12. Merigó, J.M., Gil-Lafuente, A.M.: Using the OWA operator in the minkowski distance. Int. J. Econ. Manag. Eng. **2**(9), 1032–1040 (2008)
13. Merigó, J.M., Gil-Lafuente, A.M.: New decision-making techniques and their application in the selection of financial products. Inf. Sci. **180**(11), 2085–2094 (2010)
14. Pradera, A., Trillas, E.: A note on pseudometric aggregation. Int. J. Gen Syst **32**(1), 41–51 (2002)
15. Recasens, J.: Indistinguishability Operators: Modelling Fuzzy Equailities and Fuzzy Eqivalences Relations. Springer, Berlin (2010)
16. Yager, R.: On ordered weighted averaging aggregation operators in multicriteria decision-making. IEEE Trans. Syst. Man Cybern. **18**(1), 183–190 (1988)
17. Yager, R.: Generalized OWA aggregation operators. Fuzzy Optim. Decis. Making **3**, 93–107 (2004)

On Modular Fuzzy Equivalences, Aggregation and Modular Pseudo-metrics

G. Jaume-Martin[1,2]($\boxtimes$) (ID), M. D. M. Bibiloni-Femenias[1,2] (ID), and O. Valero[1,2] (ID)

[1] Department of Mathematics and Computer Science, Universitat de les Illes Balears,
Ctra. de Valldemossa km. 7.5, 07122 Palma de Mallorca, Illes Balears, Spain
`{gabriel.jaume,m.bibiloni}@uib.cat, o.valero@uib.es`
[2] Health Research Institute of the Balearic Islands (IdISBa), Hospital Universitari
Son Espases, 07120 Palma de Mallorca, Illes Balears, Spain

Abstract. Since the introduction of the notion of fuzzy equivalence, many studies have explored theoretical aspects and its applications. In particular, two theoretical aspects have attracted the attention of many researchers. On the one hand, methods for generating from a collection of fuzzy equivalences a new one by means of aggregation have been extensively studied. On the other hand, the relation between fuzzy equivalences and pseudo-metrics has been profusely explored. Moreover, characterizations of those functions that are useful for merging a collection of fuzzy equivalences have been provided in terms of particular constructions of functions that aggregate extended pseudo-metrics in such a way that the construction takes advantage of the aforementioned duality relation. This type of characterizations are yet to be examined in the modular framework. This is why, in this paper, we focus our efforts on obtaining modular versions of the previously mentioned characterizations through the use of the duality relationship. Furthermore, we finally compare our new correspondences to the ones coming from the non modular scenario, pointing out their differences.

Keywords: Modular fuzzy equivalence · Modular pseudo-metric · Aggregation · Additive generator · Pseudo-inverse

1 Introduction

Thanks to its multiple applications in many fields such as Artificial Intelligence or Decision Making, the notion of T-equivalence (also known as indistinguishability operator with respect to a t-norm T) has gained much popularity. This notion was introduced by E. Trillas in 1982 (see [15]). More precisely, in [15] a T-equivalence on a non empty set X was defined as a fuzzy set $E : X \times X \to [0,1]$ satisfying for all $x, y, z \in X$ the following properties:

1. $E(x,x) = 1$.

Dedicated to the memory of Professor Alexander Šostak.

M. Baczyński et al. (Eds.): EUSFLAT 2025, LNCS 15883, pp. 91–103, 2025.
https://doi.org/10.1007/978-3-031-97225-6_8

2. $E(x,y) = E(y,x)$.
3. $T(E(x,z), E(z,y)) \leq E(x,y)$.

In this sense, $E(x,y)$ represents the degree of similarity or indistinguishability between x and y. The higher the value of $E(x,y)$, the harder it is to distinguish elements x and y. So much so, that $E(x,y) = 1$ can be interpreted as x and y are indistinguishable. From now on, we will consider that the reader is acquainted with the basics of T-norms and we refer the reader to [9] otherwise.

Since the introduction of such notion to the literature, many studies exploring its theoretical properties and applications have flourished. In particular, many authors have targeted the problem of generating new T-equivalences through two possible ways: either by means of the aggregation of a collection of T-equivalences, or via the transformation of extended pseudo-metrics. Next we recall briefly both approaches.

With regard to the second stated way to target the aforementioned problem, it is worth mentioning that in [1] it was shown that a T-equivalence can be generated from an extended pseudo-metric on a non empty set X and a continuous Archimedean t-norm T, and reciprocally. For the purpose of recalling such a technique, let us remind that, according to [6], an extended pseudo-metric on a non empty set X is a function $d: X \times X \rightarrow [0, \infty]$ satisfying for each $x, y, z \in X$:

1. $d(x,x) = 0$.
2. $d(x,y) = d(y,x)$.
3. $d(x,z) + d(z,y) \geq d(x,y)$.

In the light of the preceding notion and following [1], given a continuous Archimedean T-norm with additive generator f_T, then a fuzzy equivalence E_{d,f_T} can be induced from an extended pseudo-metric d on X assigning, for each $x, y \in X$: $E_{d,f_T}(x,y) = f_T^{(-1)}(d(x,y))$, where $f_T^{(-1)}$ denotes the pseudo-inverse of f_T (see [9] for details about additive generators and their associated pseudo-inverses). Conversely, an extended pseudo-metric d_{E,f_T} on X can be generated from a fuzzy equivalence E with respect to T on X, for each $x, y \in X$ by $d_{E,f_T}(x,y) = f_T(E(x,y))$.

Regarding the first way of generating T-equivalences, in [14] Pradera, Trillas and Castiñeira, taking advantage of the transformation approach, were able to provide a characterization of those functions that aggregate collections of fuzzy equivalences into a single fuzzy equivalence by means of a specific construction of functions that merge collections of extended pseudo-metrics. With the aim of introducing such a characterization, next we recall according to [14] that, given a collection of t-norms $\mathcal{T} = \{T_i\}_{i=1}^n$, a collection of fuzzy binary relations $\{E_i\}_{i=1}^n$ ($n \in \mathbb{N}$) is said to be a collection of $\mathcal{T}$-equivalences when each E_i is a T_i-equivalence on a non empty set X for all $i \in \{1, \ldots, n\}$. Besides, given a t-norm T, a function $F: [0,1]^n \rightarrow [0,1]$ is said to aggregate $\mathcal{T}$-equivalences into a T-equivalence provided that $F(E_1, \ldots, E_n)$ is a T-equivalence on a non empty set X when $\{E_i\}_{i=1}^n$ is a collection of $\mathcal{T}$-equivalences on X. In addition, a function $G: [0, \infty]^n \rightarrow [0, \infty]$ aggregates extended pseudo-metrics into an extended pseudo-metric given that $G(d_1, \ldots, d_n)$ is an extended pseudo-metric on a non-empty set Y, provided that $\{d_i\}_{i=1}^n$ is a collection of extended pseudo-metrics on Y. Observe that the function $G(d_1, \ldots, d_n)$ is given, for all $x, y \in Y$, by $G(d_1, \ldots, d_n)(x, y) = G(d_1(x, y), \ldots, d_n(x, y))$.

Following [5], an extended pseudo-metric d on X will be called a b-bounded pseudo-metric whenever $d(x, y) \leq b$ for all $x, y \in X$ and for any $b \in]0, \infty]$. It is clear that extended pseudo-metrics are ∞-bounded pseudo-metrics.

When extended pseudo-metrics are exactly bounded, a function $H: [0, b_i]^n \to [0, c]$, with $c \in]0, \infty]$ aggregates a collection of $(b_i)_{i=1}^n$-bounded pseudo-metrics $\{d_i\}_{i=1}^n$ on Y provided that $H(d_1, \ldots, d_n)$ is a c-bounded pseudo-metric on Y whenever each d_i is a b_i-bounded pseudo-metric on Y for all $i = \{1, \ldots, n\}$ (see [7]).

In the light of the concepts introduced above, the characterization can be formulated in the following way.

Theorem 1. *Let $n \in \mathbb{N}$ and let $\mathcal{T} = \{T_i\}_{i=1}^n$ be a collection of continuous Archimedean t-norms. If T is a continuous Archimedean t-norm and $F : [0, 1]^n \to [0, 1]$ is a function, then the following assertions are equivalent:*

1. *F aggregates $\mathcal{T}$-equivalences into a T-equivalence.*
2. *The function $H : \prod_{i=1}^n [0, f_{T_i}(0)]^n \to [0, f_T(0)]$, where $H = f_T \circ F \circ (f_{T_1}^{(-1)} \times \ldots \times f_{T_n}^{(-1)})$, aggregates every collection of $(f_{T_i}(0))_{i=1}^n$-bounded pseudo-metrics $\{d_i\}_{i=1}^n$ into a $f_T(0)$-bounded pseudo-metric.*

Notice that the second statement of Theorem 1 makes use of the transformation technique based on the additive generators and their associated pseudo-inverses exposed above.

It is worth noting that, in the particularly case in which all continuous Archimedean t-norms are strict, we retrieve from Theorem 1 the next result.

Corollary 1. *Let $n \in \mathbb{N}$ and let $\mathcal{T} = \{T_i\}_{i=1}^n$ be a collection of strict continuous Archimedean t-norms. If T is a strict continuous Archimedean t-norm and $F: [0, 1]^n \to [0, 1]$ is a function, then the following assertions are equivalent:*

1. *F aggregates $\mathcal{T}$-equivalences into a T-equivalence.*
2. *The function $H : [0, \infty]^n \to [0, \infty]$, where $H = f_T \circ F \circ (f_{T_1}^{-1} \times \ldots \times f_{T_n}^{-1})$, aggregates every collection of extended pseudo-metrics $\{d_i\}_{i=1}^n$ into an extended pseudo-metric.*

Later on, in [7], González-Hedström, Miñana and Valero further extended the result from Theorem 1, but making use of the characterization for the T-equivalence aggregation functions in terms of triangular triplets. Let us recall the notion of triangular triplet. On account of [7,13], a triplet (a, b, c), with $a, b, c \in \prod_{i=1}^n [0, s_i]$ ($n \in \mathbb{N}$) and $s_i \in]0, \infty]$ for each $i \in \{1, \ldots, n\}$, is a n-dimensional triangular triplet in $\prod_{i=1}^n [0, s_i]$ provided that $a_i \leq b_i + c_i$, $b_i \leq a_i + c_i$ and $c_i \leq a_i + b_i$ for all $i \in \{1, \ldots, n\}$. If $s_i = \infty$ for all $i \in \{1, ..., n\}$ and $a, b, c \in [0, \infty]^n$ forms a n-dimensional triangular triplet in $[0, \infty]^n$, then we will simply say that $a, b, c \in [0, \infty]^n$ is a n-dimensional triangular triplet.

The aforesaid extension of Theorem 1 was stated as follows:

Theorem 2. *Let $n \in \mathbb{N}$, let $\mathcal{T} = \{T_I\}_{i=1}^n$ be a collection of continuous Archimedean t-norms, and let $\{f_{T_i}\}_{i=1}^n$ be a collection of additive generators of $\mathcal{T}$. If T is a continuous Archimedean t-norm and $F : [0,1]^n \to [0,1]$ is a function, then the following assertions are equivalent:*

1. *F aggregates $\mathcal{T}$-equivalences into a T-equivalence.*
2. *The function $G : [0,\infty]^n \to [0, f_T(0)]$, where $G = f_T \circ F \circ (f_{T_1}^{(-1)} \times ... \times f_{T_n}^{(-1)})$, satisfies:*
    (a) *$G(0_n) = 0$, where $0_n = (0, \ldots, 0)$.*
    (b) *G transforms n-dimensional triangular triplets into a one-dimensional triangular triplet in $[0, f_T(0)]$.*
3. *The function $G : [0,\infty]^n \to [0, f_T(0)]$, where $G = f_T \circ F \circ (f_{T_1}^{(-1)} \times ... \times f_{T_n}^{(-1)})$, aggregates every collection of extended pseudo-metrics $\{d_i\}_{i=1}^n$ into a $f_T(0)$-bounded pseudo-metric.*
4. *The function $H : \prod_{i=1}^n [0, f_{T_i}(0)] \to [0, f_T(0)]$, where $H = f_T \circ F \circ (f_{T_1}^{(-1)} \times ... \times f_{T_n}^{(-1)})$, satisfies:*
    (a) *$H(0_n) = 0$.*
    (b) *H transforms n-dimensional triangular triplets in $\prod_{i=1}^n [0, f_{T_i}(0)]$ into a one-dimensional triangular triplet in $[0, f_T(0)]$.*

In the particular case in which the involved t-norms are all strict we get the next result as a consequence of Theorem 2.

Corollary 2. *Let $n \in \mathbb{N}$, let $\mathcal{T} = \{T_i\}_{i=1}^n$ be a collection of strict continuous Archimedean t-norms, and let $\{f_{T_i}\}_{i=1}^n$ be a collection of additive generators of $\mathcal{T}$. If T is a strict continuous Archimedean t-norm and $F : [0,1]^n \to [0,1]$ is a function, then the following assertions are equivalent:*

1. *F aggregates $\mathcal{T}$-equivalences into a T-equivalence.*
2. *The function $G : [0,\infty]^n \to [0,\infty]$, where $G = f_T \circ F \circ (f_{T_1}^{-1} \times ... \times f_{T_n}^{-1})$, satisfies:*
    (a) *$G(0_n) = 0$.*
    (b) *G transforms n-dimensional triangular triplets into a one-dimensional triangular triplet.*
3. *The function $G : [0,\infty]^n \to [0,\infty]$, where $G = f_T \circ F \circ (f_{T_1}^{-1} \times ... \times f_{T_n}^{-1})$, aggregates every collection of extended pseudo-metrics $\{d_i\}_{i=1}^n$ into an extended pseudo-metric.*

Nevertheless, in many situations, the degree of similarity between two objects can depend on a certain parameter. This behavior is too complex in order to be described by a classical T-equivalence. This is why, in [10], Miñana and Valero introduced the notion of modular indistinguishability operator. More precisely, a modular indistinguishability operator (or modular T-equivalence) for a t-norm T on a non empty set X is a fuzzy set $E : X \times X \times]0, \infty[\to [0, 1]$ satisfying, for each $x, y, z \in X$, the following conditions:

1. $E(x, x, t) = 1$ for all $t \in]0, \infty[$.
2. $E(x, y, t) = E(y, x, t)$ for all $t \in]0, \infty[$.
3. $T(E(x, z, t), E(z, y, s)) \leq E(x, y, t + s)$ for all $t, s \in]0, \infty[$.

Observe that this definition preserves the essence of fuzzy equivalences and can be understood as the degree of indistinguishability between two elements for a certain value of the parameter t.

As is the case with pseudo-metrics, there is a dual concept of modular indistinguishability operator. Such a notion was introduced in [4] and it is known as modular pseudo-metric. Recall that a modular pseudo-metric on a non empty set X, is a function $m : X \times X \times]0, \infty[\to [0, \infty]$ which fulfills the conditions below for all $x, y, z \in X,$:

1. $m(x, x, t) = 0$ for all $t \in]0, \infty[$.
2. $m(x, y, t) = m(y, x, t)$ for all $t \in]0, \infty[$.
3. $m(x, z, t + s) \leq m(x, y, t) + m(y, z, s)$ for all $t, s \in]0, \infty[$.

Recent applications of modular equivalences and modular pseudo-metrics can be found in [8, 11, 12].

In [10], analogous results to those offered in [1] were proposed (see Sect. 1), regarding the construction of modular equivalences from modular pseudo-metrics, and reciprocally. More details about the outcomes of the aforementioned study can be found in the following:

If X is a non empty set and T is a continuous t-norm with additive generator $f_T : [0, 1] \to [0, \infty]$, then the following assertions hold:

– For any modular indistinguishability operator E on X for T, the function $d^{E, f_T} :]0, \infty[\times X \times X \to [0, \infty]$, defined by $d^{E, f_T}(x, y, t) = f_T(E(x, y, t))$ for each $x, y \in X$ and $t \in]0, \infty[$, is a modular pseudo-metric on X.

– The function $E^{d, f_T} : X \times X \times]0, \infty[\to [0, 1]$ defined by $E^{d, f_T}(x, y, t) = f_T^{(-1)}(d_t(x, y))$ for all $x, y \in X$ and $t \in]0, \infty[$, is a modular indistinguishability operator for T.

Due to the wide number of potential applications for modular equivalences, many theoretical studies have been carried out. Similarly to fuzzy equivalences, one of the main problems regarding modular equivalences is their generation. In particular, the aggregation problem of such fuzzy relations was solved in [2], as Theorem 3 shows. Notice that the notion of $\mathcal{T}$-equivalences and function that aggregates $\mathcal{T}$-equivalences into a T-equivalence can be adapted to the modular context in a way analogous to the non modular case.

Theorem 3. *Let $n \in \mathbb{N}$, let $\mathcal{T} = \{T_i\}_{i=1}^n$ be a collection of t-norms and let T be a t-norm. If $F : [0, 1]^n \to [0, 1]$ is a function, then the following statements are equivalent:*

1. *F aggregates modular $\mathcal{T}$-equivalences into a modular T-equivalence.*

2. $F(1_n) = 1$ and $T(F(a), F(b)) \leq F(c)$ whenever $a, b, c \in [0, 1]^n$ such that $T_i(a_i, b_i) \leq c_i$ for all $i \in \{1, ..., n\}$, where $1_n = (1, \ldots, 1)$.

Observe that the following characterization of functions that aggregate $\mathcal{T}$-equivalences into a T-equivalence was given in [3].

Theorem 4. Let $n \in \mathbb{N}$, let $\mathcal{T} = \{T_i\}_{i=1}^n$ be a collection of t-norms, and let $\{f_{T_i}\}_{i=1}^n$ be a collection of additive generators of $\mathcal{T}$. If T is a t-norm and $F : [0, 1]^n \to [0, 1]$ is a function, then the assertions below are equivalent:

1. F aggregates $\mathcal{T}$-equivalences into a T-equivalence.
2. F holds the following conditions:
   (a) $F(1_n) = 1$.
   (b) F transforms n-dimensional $\mathcal{T}$-triangular triplets into 1-dimensional T-triangular triplets.

Besides, according to [2], the functions that aggregate modular $\mathcal{T}$-equivalences into a modular T-equivalence are also useful to aggregate $\mathcal{T}$-equivalences into a T-equivalence.

Proposition 1. Let $n \in \mathbb{N}$, let $\mathcal{T} = \{T_i\}_{i=1}^n$ be a collection of t-norms, and let $\{f_{T_i}\}_{i=1}^n$ be a collection of additive generators of $\mathcal{T}$. If T is a t-norm and $F : [0, 1]^n \to [0, 1]$ is a function, then among the following assertions (1) $\Rightarrow$ (2):

1. F aggregates modular $\mathcal{T}$-equivalences into a modular T-equivalence.
2. F aggregates $\mathcal{T}$-equivalences into a T-equivalence.

However, the next result shows that assertion (2) does not imply assertion (1) in general.

Example 1. Consider the function $F : [0, 1]^2 \to [0, 1]$ defined by

$$
F(a) = \begin{cases} \frac{1}{4}, & \text{if } a = (\frac{1}{4}, \frac{1}{4}) \\ 1, & \text{if } a = (1, 1) \\ \frac{1}{3}, & \text{otherwise} \end{cases}
$$

It is a simple matter to check that F transforms n-dimensional $\mathcal{T}$-triangular triplets into 1-dimensional T_P-triangular triplets, where T_P denotes the Product t-norm and $\mathcal{T} = \{T_i\}_{i=1}^2$ with $T_i = T_P$ for $i \in \{1, 2\}$. Thus by Proposition 1, F aggregates $\mathcal{T}$-equivalences into a T-equivalence. Nevertheless, F is not monotonic and, hence, it does not aggregate modular $\mathcal{T}$-equivalences into a modular T-equivalence. Observe that condition (2) in Theorem 3 yields the monotony for those functions aggregating modular $\mathcal{T}$-equivalences into a modular T-equivalence.

Motivated by the fact that the equivalences provided by Theorem 2 and Corollary 2 are not yet explored in the modular framework, the goal of this paper is to provide an extension of such results in such a way that a description of those functions that aggregate modular fuzzy equivalences can be obtained in terms of a particular type of functions that aggregate modular pseudo-metrics.

The remainder of the paper is organized as follows. In Sect. 2, the modular versions of Theorem 2 and Corollary 2 are obtained. Hence, the equivalence between the functions that merge modular fuzzy equivalences and a concrete kind of functions merging modular pseudo-metrics is proved. Also in this section, some consequences are derived from the fact that those functions aggregating modular equivalences belong to the class of functions that aggregate fuzzy equivalences and that the reciprocal is not verified in general. Finally, in Sect. 3, we expose the conclusions obtained and some ideas for future work.

2 Aggregation of Modular Equivalences and Modular Pseudo-metrics: the Equivalence

In this section we are going to tackle the modular version of the problem solved in [7], i.e., we are going to present an extension of Theorem 2 and Corollary 2 to the modular context. In order to do so, we first recall that the pseudo-inverse $f_T^{(-1)}$ of an additive generator f_T of a continuous Archimedean t-norm T is given by $f_T^{(-1)}(y) = f_T^{-1}(\min\{f_T(0), y\})$ for all $y \in [0, \infty]$ (see [9]). From now on, a modular pseudo-metric m on X will be called a b-bounded pseudo-metric whenever $m(x, y, t) \leq b$ for all $x, y \in X$, for all $t \in]0, \infty[$ and for any $b \in]0, \infty]$. Of course, ∞-bounded modular pseudo-metrics matches up with modular pseudo-metrics. Notice that the notion of function that aggregates a collection of bounded modular pseudo-metrics into a bounded modular pseudo-metric can be defined in a similar way as in the non modular case.

Now we are ready to provide the solution to the aforementioned problem.

Theorem 5. *Let $n \in \mathbb{N}$, let $\mathcal{T} = \{T_i\}_{i=1}^n$ be a collection of continuous Archimedean t-norms, and let $\{f_{T_i}\}_{i=1}^n$ be a collection of additive generators of $\mathcal{T}$. If T is a continuous Archimedean t-norm and $F : [0, 1]^n \rightarrow [0, 1]$ is a function, then the following assertions are equivalent:*

1. *F aggregates modular $\mathcal{T}$-equivalences into a modular T-equivalence.*
2. *$F(1_n) = 1$ and $T(F(a), F(b)) \leq F(c)$ whenever $a, b, c \in [0, 1]^n$ such that $T_i(a_i, b_i) \leq c_i$ for all $i \in \{1, ..., n\}$.*
3. *The function $G : [0, \infty]^n \rightarrow [0, f_T(0)]$, where $G = f_T \circ F \circ (f_{T_1}^{(-1)} \times ... \times f_{T_n}^{(-1)})$, satisfies:*
   (a) *$G(0_n) = 0$.*
   (b) *$G(c) \leq G(a) + G(b)$ for all $a, b, c \in [0, \infty]^n$ such that $c_i \leq a_i + b_i$ for all $i \in \{1, ..., n\}$.*
4. *The function $G : [0, \infty]^n \rightarrow [0, f_T(0)]$, where $G = f_T \circ F \circ (f_{T_1}^{(-1)} \times ... \times f_{T_n}^{(-1)})$, aggregates every collection of modular pseudo-metrics $\{d_i\}_{i=1}^n$ into a $f_T(0)$-bounded modular pseudo-metric.*

5. *The function $H : \prod_{i=1}^{n}[0, f_{T_i}(0)] \to [0, f_T(0)]$, where $H = f_T \circ F \circ (f_{T_1}^{(-1)} \times$*
   $... \times f_{T_n}^{(-1)})$, aggregates every collection of $(f_{T_i}(0))_{i=1}^{n}$-bounded modular pseudo-
   metrics $\{d_i\}_{i=1}^{n}$ into a $f_T(0)$-bounded modular pseudo-metric.
6. *The function $H : \prod_{i=1}^{n}[0, f_{T_i}(0)] \to [0, f_T(0)]$, where $H = f_T \circ F \circ (f_{T_1}^{(-1)} \times$*
   $... \times f_{T_n}^{(-1)})$, satisfies:
   (a) $H(\mathbf{0}_n) = 0$.
   (b) $H(c) \leq H(a) + H(b)$ for all $a, b, c \in \prod_{i=1}^{n}[0, f_{T_i}(0)]$ such that $c_i \leq a_i + b_i$
   for all $i \in \{1, ..., n\}$.

Proof. $(1) \Rightarrow (2)$. It is proven in Theorem 3.

$(2) \Rightarrow (3)$. We will begin by proving that 3(a) is satisfied. From the fact that $\{f_{T_i}\}_{i=1}^{n}$ is a collection of additive generators of T, we have that $f_{T_i}^{(-1)}(y) = f_{T_i}^{-1}(\min\{f_{T_i}(0), y\})$ for all $y \in [0, \infty]$. Therefore, $f_{T_i}^{(-1)}(0) = 1$. Provided that $F(\mathbf{1}_n) = 1$ and that $f_T(1) = 0$, we get

$$G(\mathbf{0}_n) = f_T \circ F \circ (f_{T_1}^{(-1)}(0) \times ... \times f_{T_n}^{(-1)}(0)) = f_T \circ F(\mathbf{1}_n) = f_T(1) = 0.$$

We continue with 3(b). Consider $a, b, c \in [0, \infty]^n$ such that $c_i \leq a_i + b_i$ for all $i \in \{1, ..., n\}$. The fact that the pseudo-inverse of any additive generator must be a decreasing function and that T is continuous and Archimedean, ensure that for all $i \in \{1, ..., n\}$ we have the following:

$$f_{T_i}^{(-1)}(c_i) \geq f_{T_i}^{(-1)}(a_i + b_i) \geq f_{T_i}^{(-1)}\left(f_{T_i}(f_{T_i}^{(-1)}(a_i)) + f_{T_i}(f_{T_i}^{(-1)}(b_i))\right)$$

$$= T_i(f_{T_i}^{(-1)}(a_i), f_{T_i}^{(-1)}(b_i)).$$

Consequently, from condition 2) we can ensure that

$$T(F(f_{T_1}^{(-1)}(a_1) \times ... \times f_{T_n}^{(-1)}(a_n)), F(f_{T_1}^{(-1)}(b_1) \times ... \times f_{T_n}^{(-1)}(b_n)))$$
$$\leq F(f_{T_1}^{(-1)}(c_1) \times ... \times f_{T_n}^{(-1)}(c_n)).$$

Since T is continuous and Archimedean we know that

$$T(F(f_{T_1}^{(-1)}(a_1) \times ... \times f_{T_n}^{(-1)}(a_n)), F(f_{T_1}^{(-1)}(b_1) \times ... \times f_{T_n}^{(-1)}(b_n))) =$$
$$f_T^{(-1)}(f_T \circ F(f_{T_1}^{(-1)}(a_1) \times ... \times f_{T_n}^{(-1)}(a_n)) + f_T \circ F(f_{T_1}^{(-1)}(b_1) \times ... \times f_{T_n}^{(-1)}(b_n))).$$

From the previous expressions, and recalling that f_T is decreasing, we finally get

$$f_T \circ F(f_{T_1}^{(-1)}(a_1) \times ... \times f_{T_n}^{(-1)}(a_n))) + f_T \circ F(f_{T_1}^{(-1)}(b_1) \times ... \times f_{T_n}^{(-1)}(b_n)) \geq$$
$$f_T \circ F(f_{T_1}^{(-1)}(c_1) \times ... \times f_{T_n}^{(-1)}(c_n)).$$

It follows that $G(a) + G(b) \geq G(c)$.

$(3) \Rightarrow (4)$. Consider a collection of $\{d_i\}_{i=1}^{n}$ modular pseudo-metrics on a non empty set X. It is direct to prove that $G(d_1, ..., d_n)(x, y, t) = G(d_1, ..., d_n)(y, x, t)$, because modular pseudo-metrics are symmetric. Moreover, from the fact that, for all $i \in \{1, \ldots, n\}$, $d_i(x, x, t) = 0$ for all $t \in]0, \infty[$ and condition 3(a) we get that $G(d_1, \ldots, d_n) = G(0_n) = 0$. Finally, as $d_i(x, y, t) + d_i(y, z, s) \geq d_i(x, z, t + s)$ for all $x, y, z \in X$ and $t, s \in]0, \infty[$, condition 3(b) warrants that

$$G(d_1, \ldots, d_n)(x, y, t) + G(d_1, \ldots, d_n)(y, z, t) \geq G(d_1, \ldots, d_n)(x, z, t + s),$$

for all $x, y, z \in X$ and $t, s \in]0, \infty[$.

We have seen that G is a modular pseudo-metric aggregation function on X. Also notice that for all $x, y \in X$ and $t \in]0, \infty[$ we have that $G(d_1, \ldots, d_n)(x, y, t) \leq f_T(0)$, so $G(d_1, \ldots, d_n)$ is $f_T(0)$-bounded.

(4) $\Rightarrow$ (5). It is direct to prove.

(5) $\Rightarrow$ (6). Consider $a, b, c \in \prod_{i=1}^{n}[0, f_{T_i}(0)]$ such that $c_i \leq a_i + b_i$ for all $i \in \{1, \ldots, n\}$. Define a collection $\{d_i\}_{i=1}^{n}$ of $(f_{T_i}(0))_{i=1}^{n}$-bounded modular pseudo-metrics on a non empty set $X = \{x, y, z\}$, on the one hand by $d_i(x, x, t) = d_i(y, y, t) = d_i(z, z, t) = 0$ for all $t \in]0, \infty[$ and, on the other hand by

$$d_i(x, y, t) = d_i(y, x, t) = \begin{cases} \min\{a_i + b_i, f_{T_i}(0)\}, & \text{if } 0 < t \leq 1 \\ c_i, & \text{if } t > 1 \end{cases},$$

$$d_i(x, z, t) = d_i(z, x, t) = \begin{cases} b_i, & \text{if } 0 < t \leq 1 \\ \min\{c_i, b_i\}, & \text{if } t > 1 \end{cases},$$

$$d_i(y, z, t) = d_i(z, y, t) = \begin{cases} a_i, & \text{if } 0 < t \leq 1 \\ \min\{c_i, a_i\}, & \text{if } t > 1 \end{cases}.$$

In order to verify that this is indeed a collection of $(f_{T_i}(0))_{i=1}^{n}$-bounded modular pseudo-metrics, we only need to ascertain that, for all $x, y, z \in X$ and for all $t, s \in]0, \infty[$ the following inequalities are fulfilled for all $i \in \{1, \ldots, n\}$:

$$d_i(x, y, t) + d_i(y, z, s) \geq d_i(x, z, t + s).$$

Notice that for all $i \in \{1, \ldots, n\}$, $d_i(u, v, t)$ is a decreasing function for all $u, v \in X$ with respect to t. Therefore we obtain that

$$d_i(u, u, t) + d_i(u, v, s) \geq d_i(u, v, t + s) \quad \text{and} \quad d_i(u, v, t) + d_i(v, v, s) \geq d_i(u, v, t + s).$$

Consequently, it is enough to study the cases where $u, v, w \in X$ are all different from each other.

Case 1: $0 < t, s \leq 1$. Then $d_i(u, w, t) + d_i(w, v, s) \geq a_i + b_i \geq d_i(u, v, t + s)$ for all $u, v, w \in X$, being all different from each other.

Case 2: $0 < t \leq 1$ and $s > 1$ (the reasoning is analogous if $0 < s \leq 1$ and $t > 1$). Then we obtain that $d_i(u, w, t) + d_i(w, v, s) \geq c_i \geq d_i(u, v, t + s)$ for all $u, v, w \in X$, being all different from each other.

Case 3: $t, s > 1$. Then we have that $d_i(u, w, t) + d_i(w, v, s)) \geq \min\{c_i, a_i\} + \min\{c_i, b_i\} \geq c_i \geq d_i(u, v, t + s)$ for all $u, v, w \in X$, being all different from each other.

Now that we have shown that this is indeed a collection of $(f_{T_i}(0))_{i=1}^n$-bounded modular pseudo-metrics, we can prove the desired assertions.

From 5), it is obvious that $H(d_1, ..., d_n)$ is a $f_T(0)$-bounded modular pseudo-metric. Hence, for any $x, y, z \in X$ and any $t, s \in]0, \infty[$ we have that

$$H(0_n) = H(d_1(x, x, t), ..., d_n(x, x, t)) = H(d_1, ..., d_n)(x, x, t) = 0$$

and, additionally, that

$$H(d_1, ..., d_n)(x, y, t) + H(d_1, ..., d_n)(y, z, s) \geq H(d_1, ..., d_n)(x, z, t + s).$$

Then, $H(c) \leq H(a) + H(b)$ for all $a, b, c \in \prod_{i=1}^n [0, f_{T_i}(0)]$ such that $c_i \leq a_i + b_i$ for all $i \in \{1, ..., n\}$, as we wanted.

(6) $\Rightarrow$ (1). Consider a collection $\{E_i\}_{i=1}^n$ of modular $\mathcal{T}$-equivalences on a non empty set X. Our goal is to prove that $F(E_1, ..., E_n)$ is also a modular $\mathcal{T}$-equivalence on X. First, notice that $E_i(x, x, t) = 1$ for all $x \in X$ and for all $t \in]0, \infty[$. Then, $f_{T_i}(E_i(x, x, t)) = 0$. Hence:

$$
\begin{aligned}
0 = H(0_n) &= H(f_{T_1}(E_1(x, x, t)), ..., f_{T_n}(E_n(x, x, t))) \\
&= f_T \circ F \circ (f_{T_1}^{(-1)} \times ... \times f_{T_n}^{(-1)})(f_{T_1}(E_1(x, x, t)), ..., f_{T_n}(E_n(x, x, t))) \\
&= f_T \circ F(E_1, ..., E_n)(x, x, t)
\end{aligned}
$$

Consequently, $F(E_1, ..., E_n)(x, x, t) = 1$. Since modular equivalences are symmetric, it is clear that $F(E_1, ..., E_n)(x, y, t) = F(E_1, ..., E_n)(y, x, t)$ for all $x, y \in X$ and for all $t \in]0, \infty[$. It only rests to prove that

$$T(F(E_1, ..., E_n)(x, y, t), F(E_1, ..., E_n)(y, z, s)) \leq F(E_1, ..., E_n)(x, z, t + s),$$

for all $x, y, z \in X$ and for all $t, s \in]0, \infty[$. We know that $d^{E_i, f_{T_i}}$ is a modular metric on X for all $i \in \{1, ..., n\}$ (see Sect. 1), where $d^{E_i, f_{T_i}}(x, y, t) = f_{T_i}(E_i(x, y, t))$ for all $x, y \in X$ and for all $t \in]0, \infty[$. Then, for all $i \in \{1, ..., n\}$, it is satisfied that $d^{E_i, f_{T_i}}(x, z, t + s) \leq d^{E_i, f_{T_i}}(x, y, t) + d^{E_i, f_{T_i}}(y, z, s)$ for all $x, y, z \in X$ and for all $t, s \in]0, \infty[$. So we have, for all $i \in \{1, ..., n\}$, that

$$f_{T_i}(E(x, z, t + s)) \leq f_{T_i}(E(x, y, t)) + f_{T_i}(E(y, z, s)),$$

for all $x, y, z \in X$ and for all $t, s \in]0, \infty[$. Moreover, for all $i \in \{1, ..., n\}$, it is clear that $f_{T_i}(E(x, y, t)) \in [0, f_{T_i}(0)]$ for all $x, y \in X$ and for all $t \in]0, \infty[$. Using condition 6(b), we get

$$
\begin{aligned}
&H(f_{T_1}(E_1(x, z, t + s)), ... f_{T_n}(E_n(x, z, t + s))) \leq \\
&H(f_{T_1}(E_1(x, y, t)), ..., f_{T_n}(E_n)(x, y, t)) + H(f_{T_1}(E_1(y, z, s)), ..., f_{T_n}(E_n(y, z, s))).
\end{aligned}
$$

As $H(f_{T_1}(E_1)(x, y, t)), ..., f_{T_n}(E_n)(x, y, t)) \in [0, f_T(0)]$ for all $x, y \in X$ and for all $t \in]0, \infty[$, we deduce that

$$f_T^{-1} \circ H(f_{T_1}(E_1(x, z, t + s)), ..., f_{T_n}(E_n(x, z, t + s))) = F(E_1, ..., E_n)(x, z, t + s),$$

and, using that T is continuous and Archimedean, we obtain that

$$f_T^{(-1)}(H(f_{T_1}(E_1(x,y,t)), \ldots, f_{T_n}(E_n(x,y,t)))+$$
$$H(f_{T_1}(E_1(y,z,s)), \ldots, f_{T_n}(E_n(y,z,s))))=$$

$$= f_T^{(-1)}(f_T \circ F(E_1, \ldots, E_n)(x,y,t) + f_T \circ F(E_1, \ldots, E_n)(y,z,s))$$
$$= T(F(E_1, \ldots, E_n)(x,y,t), F(E_1, \ldots, E_n)(y,z,s)).$$

Combining all equalities and inequalities above, and remembering that $f_T^{(-1)}$ is a decreasing function, we finally obtain

$$F(E_1, \ldots, E_n)(x,z,t+s) \geq T(F(E_1, \ldots, E_n)(x,y,t), F(E_1, \ldots, E_n)(y,z,s)).$$

Therefore, F aggregates modular $\mathcal{T}$-equivalences into a modular T-equivalence.

When all involved t-norms are strict we get the next result as a consequence of Theorem 5.

Corollary 3. *Let $n \in \mathbb{N}$, let $\mathcal{T} = \{T_i\}_{i=1}^n$ be a collection of strict continuous Archimedean t-norms, and let $\{f_{T_i}\}_{i=1}^n$ be a collection of additive generators of $\mathcal{T}$. If T is a strict continuous Archimedean t-norm and $F : [0,1]^n \rightarrow [0,1]$ is a function, then the following assertions are equivalent:*

1. *F aggregates modular $\mathcal{T}$-equivalences into a modular T-equivalence.*
2. *$F(1_n) = 1$ and $T(F(a), F(b)) \leq F(c)$ whenever $a, b, c \in [0,1]^n$ such that $T_i(a_i, b_i) \leq c_i$ for all $i \in \{1, \ldots, n\}$.*
3. *The function $G : [0, \infty]^n \rightarrow [0, \infty]$, where $G = f_T \circ F \circ (f_{T_1}^{(-1)} \times \ldots \times f_{T_n}^{(-1)})$, satisfies:*
   (a) *$G(0_n) = 0$.*
   (b) *$G(c) \leq G(a) + G(b)$ for all $a, b, c \in [0, \infty]^n$ such that $c_i \leq a_i + b_i$ for all $i \in \{1, \ldots, n\}$.*
4. *The function $G : [0, \infty]^n \rightarrow [0, \infty]$, where $G = f_T \circ F \circ (f_{T_1}^{(-1)} \times \ldots \times f_{T_n}^{(-1)})$, aggregates every collection of modular pseudo-metrics $\{d_i\}_{i=1}^n$ into a modular pseudo-metric.*

According to Proposition 1, the functions that aggregate modular $\mathcal{T}$-equivalences into a modular T-equivalence are also useful to aggregate $\mathcal{T}$-equivalences into a T-equivalence. From the preceding fact, we can derive that the former class of functions also satisfies all assertions in the statement of Theorem 2, which complements the information that describes them provided by Theorem 5. However, Example 1 shows that there are functions belonging to the second class (the non modular) that does not belong to the first one.

3 Conclusions and Future Work

The duality between functions that aggregate fuzzy equivalences and those that merge collections of pseudo-metrics has been profusely studied by many authors. Theorems 1 and 2 are some of the results that stand out from this research line. Inspired by them, and the increasing use of the modular version of the aforementioned functions, we have provided a characterization of those functions that aggregate modular fuzzy equivalences trough a particular construction of functions that aggregate modular pseudo-metrics. In addition, we have discussed the relationship between the class of functions that aggregate modular fuzzy equivalences and the class of those functions that merge fuzzy equivalences, showing that the latter is contained in the former but they are not the same. As for future work, we plan on extending the study of this problem to the entire modular framework. Particularly, we plan to approach the asymmetric scenario and explore the connections with the non modular case.

Acknowledgments. This research is part of project PID2022-139248NB-I00 funded by MICIU/AEI/10.13039/501100011033 and ERDF/EU. The authors thank the support from *Programa de Foment de la Recerca i la Innovació de la Universitat de les Illes Balears 2024-2026* and ITS2023-086-Programa de Foment a la recerca.

Disclosure of Interests. The authors have no competing interests to declare that are relevant to the content of this article.

References

1. Baets, B.D., Mesiar, R.: Pseudo-metrics and t-equivalences. J. Fuzzy Math. **5**(2), 471–481 (1997)
2. Bibiloni-Femenias, M.: A Study on Modular Indistinguishability Operators with Applications. Doctoral thesis, University of Balearic Islands, Palma, Illes Balears (2024). https://dspace.uib.es/xmlui/handle/11201/166179
3. Calvo-Sánchez, T., Fuster-Parra, P., Valero, O.: The aggregation of transitive fuzzy relations revisited. Fuzzy Sets Syst. **446**, 243–260 (2022)
4. Chistyakov, V.: Metric Modular Spaces: Theory and Applications. Springer, Cham (2015)
5. Copson, E.: Metric Spaces. Cambridge University Press, London (1968)
6. Deza, M., Deza, E.: Encyclopedia of Distances. Springer, Heidelberg (2009)
7. González-Hedström, J.D.D., Miñana, J.J., Valero, O.: Aggregation of indistinguishability fuzzy relations revisited. Mathematics **9**(12) (2021)
8. Guerrero, J., Jaume-Martin, G., Bibiloni-Femenias, M., Valero, O.: On the use of modular quasi-metrics and possibility theory for heterogeneous multi-robot systems. In: Alsinet, T., et al. (ed.) Artificial Intelligence Research and Development. Proceedings of the 26th International Conference of the Catalan Association for Artificial Intelligence. CCIA 2024. Frontiers in Artificial Intelligence and Applications, vol. 390, pp. 213–222 (2024)
9. Klement, E.P., Mesiar, R., Pap, E.: Triangular Norms, vol. 8. Springer, Dordrecht (2000)
10. Miñana, J.J., Valero, O.: On indistinguishability operators, fuzzy metrics and modular metrics. Axioms **6**(4) (2017)
11. Ortiz, A., Valero, O.: Addressing multi-class classification tasks by means of RBFNN-like models using modular indistinguishability operators. In: Kahraman, C., et al. (ed.) Intelligent and Fuzzy Systems. INFUS 2024. Lecture Notes in Networks and Systems, vol. 1089, pp. 304–312 (2024)

12. Ortiz, A., Valero, O., Miñana, J.: On the use of modular indistinguishability operators in RBFNN-like models. In: Lesot, MJ., et al. (ed.) Information Processing and Management of Uncertainty in Knowledge-Based Systems. IPMU 2024. Lecture Notes in Networks and Systems, vol. 1174, pp. 345–359 (2024)
13. Pradera, A., Trillas, E.: A note on pseudo-metrics aggregation. Int. J. Gen. Syst. **31**, 41–51 (2002)
14. Pradera, A., Trillas, E., Castiñeira, E.: On the Aggregation of Some Classes of Fuzzy Relations, pp. 125–136. Physica-Verlag HD, Heidelberg (2002)
15. Trillas, E.: Assaig sobre les relacions d'indistingibilitat. In: Actes del Primer Congress Catala de Logica Matematica, Barcelona, pp. 51–59 (1982)

On the Impossibility of Universally Transforming Similarity Metrics into Partial Metrics

A. Mir-Fuentes[1,2]($\boxtimes$) (iD) and O. Valero[1,2] (iD)

[1] Department of Mathematics and Computer Science, Universitat de les Illes Balears,
Ctra. de Valldemossa km. 7.5, 07122 Palma de Mallorca, Illes Balears, Spain
`a.mir@uib.cat`, `o.valero@uib.es`
[2] Health Research Institute of the Balearic Islands (IdISBa), Hospital Universitari
Son Espases, 07120 Palma de Mallorca, Illes Balears, Spain

Abstract. Partial metrics generalize traditional metrics by allowing non-zero self-distances. This distinguished property makes them suitable for the development of many applications to computer science, artificial intelligence and applied mathematics. Such distances are interpreted as a dissimilarity measure. However, in cases where the measurement method must quantify the degree of common information between two objects, rather than quantifying the level of difference between them, it is required to handle the notion of similarity. This paper studies a duality relationship between the so-called similarity metrics and partial metrics. In particular, we focus on the search of a characterization of those functions that transform every similarity metric into a partial metric. While transformations can exist for specific similarity metrics, we prove the non-existence of a function that can universally transform any similarity metric into a partial metric.

Keywords: Metric · Partial Metric · Similarity Metric · Duality

1 Introduction

The concept of dissimilarity plays a fundamental role in mathematics and its applications. Despite the usefulness and extensive use of the notion of metric as dissimilarity, the rigidity of some of its axioms makes it impossible to obtain certain applications of interest. To address these limitations, *partial metrics* were introduced in 1994 by Mathews [8], which generalize the notion of metric in such a way that the distance between a point and itself may be non-zero. However, in cases where the measurement method must quantify the degree of common information between two objects, rather than quantifying the level of difference between them, it is required to handle the notion of *similarity*.

Dedicated to the memory of Professor Alexander Šostak.

At present, the axiomatics of similarities has not been fully formalized. In fact, various notions of similarity can be found in the literature in such a way that notable disparity in their axiomatics can be evidenced (see, for instance, [2,3,10, 15,20]). In the following we focus our attention on the notion of similarity metric in the sense of [15] (see also [4,14]). Recently, a few works have been devoted to discern what is really the relationship that they have with the dissimilarities. Concretely, in [1,14,21] it has been argued that they are very closely related in such a way that they are dual notions. This duality arises from the relaxed axioms of partial metrics, which better align with those of similarity metrics. This makes that a perfect duality between traditional metrics and similarity metrics cannot be attainable due to the inherent differences in their axioms.

In spite of the apparent equivalence linking both concepts, a mathematical methodology for transforming in a systematic way a similarity metric into a partial metric remains largely unexplored so far. Motivated by this fact, we try to clarify the duality relationship between partial metrics defined as in [8] and similarity metrics in the sense of [15]. Specifically, we seek to characterize the functions that transform similarity metrics into partial metrics in a universal way. Thus, we provide the exact properties that a function must fulfill in order to be able to generate from any similarity metric a partial metric. Moreover, we show that such a function does not exist. So, while specific transformations may exist for particular instances of similarity metrics, no single function can ensure the universal transformation of any similarity metric into a partial metric.

The remainder of the paper is organized as follows: Sect. 2 is devoted to fix the pertinent notions which will play a central role in our subsequent work, partial metrics and similarity metrics. Illustrative examples of both are introduced. In Sect. 3, we provide a characterizations of those functions, that we have called SM-partializer functions, that are able to transform any similarity metric into a partial metric. Besides, in the same section we show that the set of SM-partializer functions is empty. Finally, Sect. 4 is devoted to conclusions and ideas for future work.

2   Preliminaries

In this section, we introduce the fundamental concepts that will be used in the rest of sections.

Although the notion of metrics is well known, we recall it in order to highlight more clearly the differences between its axiomatics and that of partial metrics. To this aim, we denote by $\mathbb{R}$ the set of real numbers. According to [3], a *metric d* on a non-empty set X is a function $d : X \times X \to \mathbb{R}$ which satisfies the following properties for all $x, y, z \in X$:

M1. $d(x,y) \geq 0$ **(Non-negativity)**.
M2. $d(x,y) = 0$ if and only if $x = y$ **(Identity of indiscernibles)**.
M3. $d(x,y) = d(y,x)$ **(Symmetry)**.
M4. $d(x,z) \leq d(x,y) + d(y,z)$ **(Triangle inequality)**.

In [8], S.G. Matthews extended the concept of metric by introducing the notion of *partial metric*. This generalization allows for the distance between a point and itself to be non-zero, providing a more flexible axiomatisation which is appropriate for certain problems that arise in a natural way in computer science and artificial intelligence ([5,6,9,12,16–19]). Thus, given a non-empty set X, a *partial metric* on X is a function $p : X \times X \to \mathbb{R}$ which satisfies the following properties for all $x, y, z \in X$:

PM1. $p(x, x) \geq 0$ (**Non-negativity**).
PM2. $p(x, y) = p(x, x) = p(y, y) \iff x = y$ (**Identity of indiscernibles**).
PM3. $p(x, y) = p(y, x)$ (**Symmetry**).
PM4. $p(x, x) \leq p(x, y)$ (**Small self-distances**).
PM5. $p(x, z) \leq p(x, y) + p(y, z) - p(y, y)$ (**Triangular inequality**).

With the aim of illustrating the previous notion, we provide an instance of partial metric in the example below, which has been shown to be useful in parallel computing ([8]).

Example 1. Denote by $\mathbb{N}$ the set of positive integer numbers. Consider the set of all finite and infinite sequences (strings) Σ^∞ over a nonempty alphabet Σ. If $s \in \Sigma^\infty$ then we denote by $l(s)$ the length of s. So $l(s) \in \mathbb{N} \cup \{\infty\}$ for all $s \in \Sigma^\infty$. Let $\Sigma_F = \{v \in \Sigma^\infty : l(v) \in \mathbb{N}\}$ and $\Sigma_\infty = \{v \in \Sigma^\infty : l(v) = \infty\}$. Then $\Sigma^\infty = \Sigma_F \cup \Sigma_\infty$. Consider the function $p_\Sigma : \Sigma^\infty \times \Sigma^\infty \to \mathbb{R}$ given by $p_\Sigma(s, t) = 2^{-lcp(s,t)}$ for all $s, t \in \Sigma^\infty$, where $lcp(s, t)$ denotes the longest common prefix of s and t ($lcp(s, t) = 0$ when s and t have no common prefix). Of course, we adopt the arrangement that $2^{-\infty} = 0$. It is not hard to check that p_Σ is a partial metric on Σ^∞.

Observe that every metric is a partial metric such that self-distance of a point is always zero. However, in a partial metric space, the self-distance $p(x, x)$ of a point x may be greater than zero. In fact, in Example 1 we have that $p_\Sigma(s, s) = 2^{-l(s)} > 0$ for all string s. It is clear that we do not consider the empty string.

We now introduce the concept of a *similarity metric*, which measure how close elements of a set are. Hence, in this case, the measurement quantifies the degree of common information between two objects, rather than the level of difference between them. On account of [15], (compare with [2,14]), given a non-empty set X, a function $s : X \times X \to \mathbb{R}$ is called a *similarity metric* on X provided that it satisfies the following properties for all $x, y, z \in X$:

SM1. $s(x, y) \geq 0$ (**Non-negativity**).
SM2. $s(x, y) = s(x, x) = s(y, y) \iff x = y$ (**Identity of indescernibles**).
SM3. $s(x, y) = s(y, x)$ (**Symmetry**).
SM4. $s(x, x) \geq s(x, y)$ (**Bounded self-similarities**).
SM5. $s(x, z) \geq s(x, y) + s(y, z) - s(y, y)$ (**Reverse triangle inequality**).

Notice that the preceding notion presents eminent differences from those notions of similarity that can be found in [10,13] and in [20].

The following example provides a sample of similarity metric with the aim of exemplifying the previous notion.

Example 2. Consider a non-empty set and a partial metric on X. Define the function $s_p : X \times X \to [0, 1]$, for all $x, y \in X$, as follows:

$$s_p(x, y) = e^{-p(x,y)}.$$

Next we show that s_p is a similarity metric.

Since $p(x, y) = p(y, x)$ for all $x, y \in X$ we have that

$$s_p(x, y) = e^{-p(x,y)} = e^{-p(y,x)} = s_p(y, x).$$

So s_p satisfies **SM3**.

The fact that the exponential function e^{-z} is always non-negative for any $z \geq 0$ and $p(x, y) \geq 0$ for all $x, y \in X$ we deduce that $s_p(x, y) = e^{-p(x,y)} \geq 0$. Hence, s_p fulfills **SM1**. Moreover, notice that $e^{-p(x,y)} \leq 1$ for all all $x, y \in X$.

Now we show that s_p satisfies **SM2**. Assume that $x = y$. Then $p(x, y) = p(x, x) = p(y, y)$ and, thus, we have that $s_p(x, y) = s_p(x, x) = s_p(y, y)$. Conversely, if $s_p(x, y) = s_p(x, x) = s_p(y, y)$, then $e^{-p(x,y)} = e^{-p(x,x)} = e^{-p(y,y)}$, which implies $p(x, y) = p(x, x) = p(y, y)$. Since p is a partial metric we obtain that $x = y$.

Next we show that **SM4** is held by s_p. The fact that $p(x, x) \leq p(x, y)$ provides that

$$s_p(x, x) = e^{-p(x,x)} \geq e^{-p(x,y)} = s_p(x, y).$$

It remains to show that s_p satisfies **SM5**. Consider $x, y, z \in X$. We can assume that $p(x, z) < p(x, y)$ and $p(y, z) < p(x, y)$. Otherwise the reverse triangle inequality is trivial. Indeed, we only show the case in which $p(x, z) = p(x, y)$, since the proof when $p(y, z) = p(x, y)$ runs following the same arguments.

Assuming that $p(x, z) = p(x, y)$ we have that $e^{-p(x,z)} = e^{-p(x,y)}$. Thus we obtain that the following inequality holds:

$$e^{-p(x,z)} \geq e^{-p(x,y)} + e^{-p(y,z)} - e^{-p(y,y)},$$

since it is equivalent to the next one

$$e^{-p(y,y)} \geq e^{-p(y,z)},$$

and this one is true because $p(y, y) \leq p(y, z)$.

The fact that the inequality

$$e^{-p(x,z)} \geq e^{-p(x,y)} + e^{-p(y,z)} - e^{-p(y,y)}$$

is equivalent to $s_p(x, z) \geq s_p(x, y) + s_p(y, z) - s_p(y, y)$ provides that **SM5** is fulfilled.

Next we focus on the case in which $p(x, z) < p(x, y)$ and $p(y, z) < p(x, y)$. Observe that the preceding assumption implies that x, y, z are all different from one another. Then we consider the intervals:

$$[p(z,z), \min\{p(x,z), p(y,z)\}] \quad \text{and} \quad [\max\{p(x,z), p(y,z)\}, p(x,y)].$$

Observe that $p(z,z) < p(x,y)$. Without restriction of generality we can assume that $\max\{p(x,z), p(y,z)\} = p(x,z)$. Since e^{-z} is a continuous function on the both intervals and differentiable on the both open intervals we can apply the Mean-Value theorem (see, for instance, [7]). Hence we have the existence of $c \in]p(x,z), p(x,y)[$ and $d \in]p(z,z), p(z,y)[$ such that

$$e^{-p(x,y)} - e^{-p(x,z)} = -e^{-c}(p(x,y) - p(x,z))$$

and

$$e^{-p(z,y)} - e^{-p(z,z)} = -e^{-d}(p(z,y) - p(z,z)).$$

Moreover, we have that

$$-e^{-c}(p(x,y) - p(x,z)) = e^{-c}(p(x,z) - p(x,y)) \geq$$

$$e^{-c}(p(x,z) - p(x,z) - p(z,y) + p(z,z)) =$$

$$e^{-c}(p(z,z) - p(z,y)) =$$

$$-e^{-c}(p(z,y) - p(z,z)) \geq -e^{-d}(p(z,y) - p(z,z))$$

as we claim. Notice that $d \leq c$ because $p(y,z) \leq p(x,z)$ and $p(z,z) < p(x,y)$, and that the function $-e^{-z}$ is increasing on the considered intervals.

It must be pointed out that in the light of the presented notions, it is clear that similarity metrics are closer to partial metrics than metrics as argued in [1,14,21]. It is clear that, given a partial metric p, the numerical value $p(x,y)$ measures a generalized dissimilarity, allowing $p(x,x)$ to represent a non-zero self-distance. Moreover, provided a similarity metric s, the numerical value $s(x,y)$ quantifies how similar x and y are, with $s(x,x)$ representing the maximum self-similarity. This suggests that both notions provide complementary perspectives on measuring relationships between elements in a set. The fact that the conditions **PM5** and **PM4** are dual to conditions **SM5** and **SM4** respectively, reforces the interpretation of one as the counterpart of the other.

3   Transforming Similarity Metrics into Partial Metrics

Example 1 provides a sample of partial metric which is obtained by means of a transformation of a similarity metric through the function $f : \mathbb{R}^+ \to \mathbb{R}^+$ given by $f(z) = 2^{-z}$, where $\mathbb{R}_+$ stands for the set of non-negative real numbers. Observe that a straightforward verification shows that l is a similarity metric on the set of strings Σ^∞. Motivated by this fact, we try to clarify the duality relationship between partial metrics in the sense of [8] and similarity metrics in the spirit of [15]. Thus we yield a characterization of those functions that transform similarity metrics into partial metrics in a universal way. We provide the exact properties that a function must fulfill in order to be able to generate from any similarity metric into a partial metric. We have called such functions SM-partializers. Regrettably, we show that such functions do not exist. So, while specific transformations may exist for particular instances of similarity metrics, such as that given in Example 1, no single function can ensure the universal transformation of any similarity metric into a partial metric.

The next notion is crucial for our subsequent discussion.

Definition 1. *A function* $f : \mathbb{R}^+ \to \mathbb{R}^+$ *is an SM-partializer function provided that* $f \circ s$ *is a partial metric on a set* X *when* s *is a similarity metric on* X.

The following result will be extremely useful in Theorem 1.

Lemma 1. *Let* $a, b, c, d \in \mathbb{R}^+$ *with* $b > c$, $b > d$ *such that* $a + b \geq c + d$ *and, in addition,* $\{x,y,z\}$ *a set such that all elements are different from one to another. Then, a similarity metric* $s : \{x, y, z\} \times \{x, y, z\} \to \mathbb{R}^+$ *can be induced in the following way:* $s(x, x) = \max\{a, c, d\} + b$, $s(y, y) = \max\{a, c, d\} + b$, $s(z, z) = b$, $s(x, y) = s(y, x) = a$, $s(x, z) = s(z, x) = c$ *and* $s(y, z) = s(z, y) = d$.

Proof. Let us check that s fulfills the axioms of a similarity metric. Clearly condition **SM3** is held, i.e., $s(u, v) = s(v, u)$ for all $u, v \in \{x, y, z\}$. Regarding to the condition **SM2** we have that

$$s(x, x) = \max\{a, c, d\} + b \geq \max\{a, c\} = \max\{s(x, y), s(x, z)\},$$

$$s(y, y) = \max\{a, c, d\} + b \geq \max\{a, d\} = \max\{s(x, y), s(y, z)\},$$

$$s(z, z) = b \geq \max\{c, d\} = \max\{s(y, z), s(x, z)\}.$$

Moreover, we have that s fulfills condition **SM4**. Indeed,

$$s(x, x) = \max\{a, c, d\} + b > \max\{a, c\} = \max\{s(x, y), s(x, z)\},$$

$$s(y, y) = \max\{a, c, d\} + b > \max\{a, d\} = \max\{s(x, y), s(y, z)\},$$

and

$$s(z, z) = b > \max\{c, d\} = \max\{s(y, z), s(x, z)\}.$$

Since $a, b, c, d \in \mathbb{R}^+$ we have that $s(x, y), s(x, z), s(y, z), s(x, x), s(y, y), s(z, z) \geq 0$ and, hence, that condition **SM1** is held.

Finally, we show that s satisfies condition **SM5**. Certainly all possible inequalities are the following:

$$s(x, y) + s(z, z) = a + b \geq c + d = s(x, z) + s(z, y),$$

$$s(x, z) + s(y, y) = c + \max\{a, c, d\} + b \geq a + d = s(x, y) + s(y, z),$$

and

$$s(y, z) + s(x, x) = d + \max\{a, c, d\} + b \geq a + c = s(y, x) + s(x, z).$$

The following result provides the description of SM-partializer functions.

Theorem 1. *Let $f : \mathbb{R}^+ \to \mathbb{R}^+$ be a function. Then the following assertions are equivalent:*

(1) f is an SM-partializer function.
(2) f satisfies the following assertions:
  (2.1) f is strictly decreasing ($f(x) > f(y)$ when $x < y$).
  (2.2) $f(a) + f(b) \le f(c) + f(d)$ provided that $a, b, c, d \in \mathbb{R}^+$ with $b > c$, $b > d$ and $a + b \ge c + d$.

Proof. $(1) \Rightarrow (2)$. Let $a, b \in \mathbb{R}^+$ with $a < b$. Consider the set $\{x, y\}$ with $x \ne y$. Define the function $s : \{x, y\} \times \{x, y\} \to \mathbb{R}^+$ by $s(x, x) = s(y, y) = b$ and $s(x, y) = s(y, x) = a$. It follows immediately that s is a similarity metric. Since f is an SM-partializer function, we have that $f \circ s$ is a partial metric on $\{x, y\}$. Therefore, $f(s(x, x)) < f(s(x, y))$ because otherwise we obtain that $f(s(y, y)) = f(s(x, x)) = f(s(x, y))$ and, hence, that $x = y$ which is impossible. The fact that $f(s(x, x)) < f(s(x, y))$ gives that $f(b) < f(a)$ proving that f is strictly decreasing.

Now, let $a, b, c, d \in \mathbb{R}^+$ with $b > c$, $b > d$ and $a + b \ge c + d$. Consider the similarity metric constructed in Lemma 1. Since f is an SM-partializer function we get that $f \circ s$ is a partial metric on $\{x, y, z\}$. Whence we deduce from **PM5** that $f(s(x, y)) + f(s(z, z)) \le f(s(x, z)) + f(s(y, z))$. So $f(a) + f(b) \le f(c) + f(d)$.

$(2) \Rightarrow (1)$. Let s be an arbitrary similarity metric on a non-empty set X, and let us verify that $f \circ s$ is a partial metric on X. Conditions **PM1** and **PM3** clearly hold. Next we show **PM4**. We know that s is a similarity metric and, thus, that $s(x, y) \le s(x, x)$ for all $x, y \in X$. We can assume that $s(x, y) < s(x, x)$ because $s(x, y) = s(x, x)$ immediately gives that $f(s(x, y)) = f(s(x, x))$. Since f is a strictly decreasing function we obtain that

$$f(s(x, y)) > f(s(x, x))$$

for all $x, y \in X$. In order to show that $f \circ s$ fulfills condition **PM2** we assume that there exists $x, y, z \in X$ such that $f \circ s(x, y) = f \circ s(x, x) = f \circ s(y, y)$. The fact that f is strictly decreasing yields that it is injective. It follows that $s(x, y) = s(x, x) = s(y, y)$. Since s is a similarity metric we deduce that $x = y$. We end the proof showing that condition **PM5** also holds. With this aim we can consider $x, y, z \in X$ which are all different from one to another. Otherwise the triangle inequality is trivially satisfied. We have that

$$s(u, v) + s(w, w) \ge s(u, w) + s(v, w)$$

for all $u, v, w \in \{x, y, z\}$. Next we want to prove that

$$f(s(u, v)) + f(s(w, w)) \le f(s(u, w)) + f(s(w, v)).$$

With this aim we can suppose that $s(w,v) < s(w,w)$ and $s(u,w) < s(w,w)$ for all $u,v,w \in \{x,y,z\}$ with all different from each other, since otherwise the desired inequality is satisfied. But under the assumed hypothesis, (2.2) guarantees that

$$f(s(u,v)) + f(s(w,w)) \leq f(s(u,w)) + f(s(w,v)).$$

Finally, we prove that no single function can transform every similarity metric into a partial metric.

Theorem 2. *The set of SM-partializer functions is the empty set.*

Proof. With the purpose of contradiction we suppose that there exists a strictly decreasing function f satisfying condition (2.2). Now consider the sequence $\{x_n\}$ given by $x_n = n$ for all $n \in \mathbb{N}$. Such a sequence is strictly increasing. Since f is strictly decreasing we obtain that the sequence $\{f(x_n)\}$ is strictly decreasing and bounded below by 0. Therefore there exists $L \in \mathbb{R}_+$ such that $\lim_{n\to\infty} f(x_n) = L$. Now set $a = x_1 = 1$ and $r = f(a) - L$. Notice that $r > 0$ because f is strictly decreasing. Let $\epsilon = \frac{r}{2}$, there exists $n_0 \in \mathbb{N}$ such that $|f(x_n) - L| < \epsilon$ for all $n \geq n_0$. Observe that $n_0 \neq 1$ because otherwise we have that $r = f(a) - L = |f(x_1) - L| < \epsilon = \frac{r}{2}$, which is impossible. Since f is strictly decreasing we have that $0 < f(x_n) - L < \epsilon$ for all $n \geq n_0$. On the other hand, $\{f(x_n)\}$ is a Cauchy sequence and it provides the existence of $n_1 \in \mathbb{N}$ such that $f(x_m) - f(x_n) < \epsilon$ for all $n_1 \leq n < m$.

Next set $b = x_{2max(n_0,n_1)} = 2max(n_0,n_1)$, $c = d = x_{max(n_0,n_1)} = max(n_0,n_1)$. Then $b > c$, $b > d$ and $a + b \geq c + d$. Since f is an SM-partializer function we obtain from Theorem 1 that $f(a) + f(b) \leq f(c) + f(d)$. Moreover,

$$f(a) + f(b) = r + L + f(x_{2max(n_0,n_1)}) =$$

$$r + L + f(x_{2max(n_0,n_1)}) + 2f(x_{max(n_0,n_1)}) - 2f(x_{max(n_0,n_1)}) =$$

$$r + L - f(x_{max(n_0,n_1)}) + f(x_{2max(n_0,n_1)}) - f(x_{max(n_0,n_1)}) + 2f(x_{max(n_0,n_1)}) >$$

$$r - \epsilon - \epsilon + 2f(x_{max(n_0,n_1)}) = 2f(x_{max(n_0,n_1)}) =$$

$$f(c) + f(d).$$

It follows that

$$f(c) + f(d) < f(a) + f(b) \leq f(c) + f(d),$$

which is a contradiction.

4 Conclusions

Similarity metrics and partial metrics are dual concepts as argued in [1,14,21]. Nevertheless, a mathematical methodology for transforming in a systematic way a similarity metric into a partial metric has not been thoroughly explored. Motivated by this fact, we have studied the duality relationship between partial metrics defined as in [8] (non-negative partial metrics) and similarity metrics in the sense of [15] (non-negative similarity metrics). Concretely, we have provided a complete description of those functions that transform non-negative similarity metrics into non-negative partial metrics in a universal way. Surprisingly, we have proved that there is no function simultaneously fulfilling all the necessary characteristics to be able to achieve the aforementioned target. On the other hand, Example 2 gives an instance of non-negative similarity metric obtained via the transformation of a non-negative partial metric by means of a specific function. So this inspires us to explore the possibility of developing a systematic methodology based on the use of functions that allow to transform any instance of non-negative partial metric into a non-negative similarity metric. Moreover, specific instances of transformations of similarity metrics in the sense of [2] into partial metrics in the spirit of [11], and vice versa, have been provided in the literature. Stimulated by the preceding fact we will also focus our efforts on developing a mathematical methodology for transforming in a systematic way both notions into each other.

Acknowledgments. This research is part of project PID2022-139248NB-I00 funded by MICIU/AEI/10.13039/501100011033 and ERDF/EU. The authors thank the support from *Programa de Foment de la Recerca i la Innovació de la Universitat de les Illes Balears 2024-2026* and ITS2023-086-Programa de Foment a la recerca.

Disclosure of Interests. The authors have no competing interests to declare that are relevant to the content of this article.

References

1. Alhajjar, E., Lefèvre, C.: On the similarity metric. Mathematica Militaris **24**(1), Article 4 (2019)
2. Chen, S., Ma, B., Zhang, K.: On the similarity metric and the distance metric. Theoret. Comput. Sci. **410**(24), 2365–2376 (2009)
3. Deza, M., Deza, E.: Encyclopedia of Distances. Springer, Heidelberg (2009)
4. Elzinga, C., Studer, M.: Normalization of distance and similarity in sequence analysis. Sociol. Methods Res. **48**(4), 877–904 (2019)
5. Seda, A.K., Hitzler, P.: Generalized distance functions in the theory of computation. Comput. J. **53**(4), 443–464 (2010)
6. Hitzler, P., Seda, A.: Mathematical Aspects of Logic Programming Semantics. CRC Press, Boca Raton (2011)
7. Little, C., Teo, K., Brunt, B.: Real Analysis via Sequences and Series. Springer, New York (2015)
8. Matthews, S.G.: Partial metric topology. Ann. N. Y. Acad. Sci. **728**(1), 183–197 (1994)
9. Matthews, S.G.: An extensional treatment of lazy data flow dedlock. Theoret. Comput. Sci. **151**(1), 195–205 (1995)
10. Montes, S., Montes, I., Iglesias, T.: Fuzzy Relations: Past, Present, and Future, pp. 171–181. Wiley (2015)
11. O' Neill, S.: Two topologies are better than one. Technical report, University of Warwick. Department of Computer Science (1995)

12. O' Neill, S.: A fundamental study into the theory and application of the partial metric space. Ph.D. thesis, Univerity of Warwick (1998)
13. Recasens, J.: Indistinguishability Operators: Modelling Fuzzy Equalities and Fuzzy Equivalences Realtions. Studies in Fuzziness and Soft Computing. Springer, Heidelberg (2010)
14. Rozinek, O., Mareš, J.: The duality of similarity and metric spaces. Appl. Sci. **11**(4), 1910 (2021)
15. Rozinek, O., Mareš, J.: Theorems for Boyd-Wong contraction mappings on similarity spaces. Mathematics **11**(20), 4359 (2023)
16. Shahzad, N., Valero, O.: On 0-complete partial metric spaces and quantitative fixed point techniques in denotational semantics. Abstract Appl. Anal. **2013**, Article ID 985095, 11 p (2013)
17. Shahzad, N., Valero, O., Alghamdi, M., Alghamdi, M.: A fixed point theorem in partial metric quasi-metric spaces and an application to software engineering. Appl. Math. Comput. **268**, 1292–1301 (2015)
18. Stojmirović, A.: Quasi-metrics, similarities and searches: aspects of geometry of protein datasets. Ph.D. thesis, Victoria University of Wellington (2005)
19. Stojmirović, A., Yu, Y.: Geometric aspects of biological sequence comparison. J. Comput. Biol. **16**(4), 579–610 (2009)
20. Theodoridis, S., Koutroumbas, K.: Patter Recognition. Academic Press, San Diego (2009)
21. Znamenskij, S.: From similarity to distance: axiom set, monotonic transformations and metric determinacy. J. Siberian Federal Univ. Math. Phys. **11**, 331–341 (2018)

Fuzzy Transforms

A Natural Extension of F-Transform to Triangular and Triangulated Domains Necessitates the Use of Triangular Membership Functions

Hana Zámečniková[1], Irina Perfilieva[1], Olga Kosheleva[2],
and Vladik Kreinovich[3]([✉])

[1] IRAFM, University of Ostrava, 30. dubna 22, 701 03 Ostrava, Czech Republic
{hana.zamecnikova,irina.perfilieva}@osu.cz
[2] Department of Teacher Education, University of Texas at El Paso,
500 W. University, El Paso, TX 79968, USA
olgak@utep.edu
[3] Department of Computer Science, University of Texas at El Paso,
500 W. University, El Paso, TX 79968, USA
vladik@utep.edu

Abstract. In many practical situations when we process 1-D data, the method of F-transform turned out to be very useful. In this method, we can use either triangular membership functions or more complex ones. Because this method has been so successful in 1-D applications, a natural idea is to extend it to functions defined on 2-D and higher-dimensional domains – e.g., to images. This method allows natural generalization to rectangular domains, where it indeed turned out to be very effective. A recent paper showed that it can be extended to more general domains – e.g., to triangular domains and to more general domains that are divided into triangular domains by triangulation. Interestingly, while all 1-D membership functions can be extended to the rectangular domains, the current extension to triangular and more general domains was produced only for triangular membership functions. In this paper, we show that this restriction is not accidental: a natural extension of F-transform to triangular domains is only possible for triangular membership functions. This may explain why such membership functions are often very effective.

Keywords: F-transform · Triangular and triangulated domains · Triangular membership functions

1 Introduction

1-D and Multi-D F-Transform: Outline. In many practical situations when we process 1-D data, the method of F-transform turned out to be very useful; see, e.g., [3,4].

M. Baczyński et al. (Eds.): EUSFLAT 2025, LNCS 15883, pp. 117–126, 2025.
https://doi.org/10.1007/978-3-031-97225-6_10

In this method, we can use both piecewise-linear (e.g., triangular) membership functions, as well as more complex ones. Because this method has been so successful in 1-D applications, a natural idea is to extend it to functions defined on 2-D and higher-dimensional domains – e.g., to images.

This method allows natural generalization to rectangular domains, where it indeed turned out to be very effective; see, e.g., [2,6]. A recent paper [5] showed that it can extended to more general domains – e.g., to triangular domains and to more general domains that are divided into triangular domains by triangulation.

F-Transform for Triangular Domains: Challenge. Interestingly:

- while all 1-D membership functions can be extended to the rectangular domains,
- the current extension to triangular and more general domains was produced only for triangular membership functions.

What we do in this Paper. In this paper, we show that this restriction is not accidental: a natural extension of F-transform to triangular domains is only possible for triangular membership functions.

This may explain why such membership functions are often very effective.

How this Paper is Structured. In Sect. 2, we briefly remind the readers about 1-D F-transform. In Sect. 3, we explain the main ideas behind extending 1-D F-transform to triangular domains. In Sect. 4, we explain our main result: that extension to triangular domains is only possible for triangular membership functions. The paper ends with the Conclusions section.

2   1-D F-Transform: A Brief Reminder

In many practical situations when we process 1-D data $x(t)$, $t \in [0, T]$, the method of F-transforms turned out to be very useful.

In this method, we divide the interval $[0, T]$ into several subintervals $[t_0, t_1]$, ..., $[t_{n-1}, t_n]$ of equal length, and select continuous membership functions $A_0(t)$, $A_1(t)$, ..., $A_{n-1}(t), A_n(t)$ each of which $A_i(t)$ is equal to 0 outside the interval $[t_{i-1}, t_{i+1}]$ and whose sum is equal to 1 for all t. These functions may be triangular, or they may be more complex. Usually, with the exception of the first and the last of these functions $A_0(t)$ and $A_n(t)$, all these functions can be obtained from each other by shift: $A_i(t - t_i) = A_j(t - t_j)$.

Then, we replace the original signal $x(t)$ with the values

$$F_i = \frac{\int_0^T A_i(t) \cdot x(t) \, dt}{\int_0^T A_i(t) \, dt}.$$

These values $F_0, \ldots, F_n$ form what is known as *F-transform* of the original signal. To form these values, we take the weighted average of the original signal – and thus, drastically decrease the random noise component of the measured signal.

Based on the F-transform, we can reasonably accurately reconstruct the original signal by applying the inverse transform:

$$\bar{x}(t) = \sum_{i=0}^{n} F_i \cdot A_i(t).$$

3 Main Idea Behind Extending 1-D F-Transform to Triangular Domains

To Describe the Desired Extension, Let us First Reformulate 1-D Transform in a More General Form. On the local level, when we only consider the functions on a single subinterval $[t_i, t_{i+1}]$, the above description of 1-D transform becomes simplified. Namely, on each such subinterval, we have only two non-zero membership functions $A_i(t)$ and $A_{i+1}(t)$ (that add up to 1):

- the function $A_i(t)$ that is equal to 1 at one of the endpoints of the subinterval, when $t = t_i$ and to 0 at the other endpoint, when $t = t_{i+1}$, and
- the function $A_{i+1}(t)$ that is equal to 1 at the endpoint $t = t_{i+1}$ and to 0 at the endpoint $t = t_i$.

Since all the functions $A_i(t)$ are obtained from each other by a shift, to describe all the functions $A_i(t)$, it is sufficient to describe two basic functions $a : [0,1] \mapsto [0,1]$ and $b : [0,1] \mapsto [0,1]$ that transform interval $[0,1]$ into itself, and that transform 0 into 0 and 1 into 1. For this purpose, we can take $a(s) \stackrel{\text{def}}{=} A_{i+1}(t_i + s \cdot (t_{i+1} - t_i))$ and $b(s) \stackrel{\text{def}}{=} A_i(t_{i+1} - s \cdot (t_{i+1} - t_i))$. In terms of these functions, the functions $A_{i+1}(t)$ and $A_i(t)$ can be obtained by applying a linear transformation from $[0,1]$, correspondingly, to the interval $[t_i, t_{i+1}]$ and to the same interval with the opposite direction – which we will denote by $[t_{i+1}, t_i]$. Namely we have

$$A_{i+1}(t) = a\left(\frac{t - t_i}{t_{i+1} - t_i}\right)$$

and

$$A_i(t) = b\left(\frac{t_{i+1} - t}{t_{i+1} - t_i}\right).$$

In particular, triangular membership function corresponds to $a(s) = b(s) = s$.

In terms of these basic functions, the condition $A_i(t) + A_{i+1}(t) = 1$ takes the following simplified form:

$$a(s) + b(1 - s) = 1. \tag{1}$$

This condition is, of course, always satisfied in the case of triangular membership functions, when $a(s) = b(s) = s$.

The Above Reformulation Leads to a Natural Extension of 1-D F-Transform to a Triangular Domain. The above reformulation uses the fact that an interval has two endpoints. For each of these two endpoints, we formed a membership function that is equal to 1 in the selected endpoint and equal to 0 at the other endpoint. This provides the values of these two membership functions at both endpoints of the interval. To get the values of each of the two membership functions at a point P inside the interval, we use two basic functions $a(s)$ and $b(s)$ defined on the basic interval $[0, 1]$ for which $a(0) = b(0) = 0$ and $a(1) = b(1) = 1$.

For each of the two desired membership functions m and for each point P, we take $m(P) = a(s)$ (or, correspondingly, $m(P) = b(s)$), where $s = L(P)$ for a linear transformation L that:

- maps the point $s = 0$ (where the basic function has value 0) into the point where the desired membership function has the value 0, and
- maps the point $s = 1$ (where the basic function has value 1) into the point where the desired membership function has the value 1.

Of course, a linear transformation L from an interval to an interval is uniquely determined by the values $L(e)$ for both endpoints e, so this transformation – and thus, the resulting membership functions – are uniquely defined.

A triangular domain has *three* vertices. We will denote them by A, B, and C. It is therefore reasonable to come up with *three* membership functions $m_a(x, y)$, $m_b(x, y)$, and $m_c(x, y)$, for which:

- the function $m_a(x, y)$ is equal to 1 at the point A and is equal to 0 at the two other vertices B and C – and on the whole segment BC;
- the function $m_b(x, y)$ is equal to 1 at the point B and is equal to 0 at the two other vertices A and C – and on the whole segment AC; and
- the function $m_c(x, y)$ is equal to 1 at the point C and is equal to 0 at the two other vertices A and B – and on the whole segment AB.

To describe the values of these three membership functions at a point P inside the triangular domain, we select three basic functions $a(s)$, $b(s)$, and $c(s)$ from $[0, 1]$ to $[0, 1]$, for which $a(0) = b(0) = c(0) = 0$ and $a(1) = b(1) = c(1) = 1$.

Then, to find the value $m_a(P)$, we take a straight line segment AQ starting with A and going through P until it reaches the segment BC at some point $Q \in BC$. We know that $m_a(Q) = 0$ and that $m_a(A) = 1$. So, to find the value $m_a(P)$, we use the value $a(s)$, where $s = L(P)$ is obtained by a linear transformation L from the interval QA to the interval $[0, 1]$ – a linear transformation L for which:

- the point Q at which $m_a(Q) = 0$ maps into the value $s = 0$ for which $a(s) = 0$, and
- the point A at which $m_a(A) = 1$ maps into the value $s = 1$ for which $a(s) = 1$.

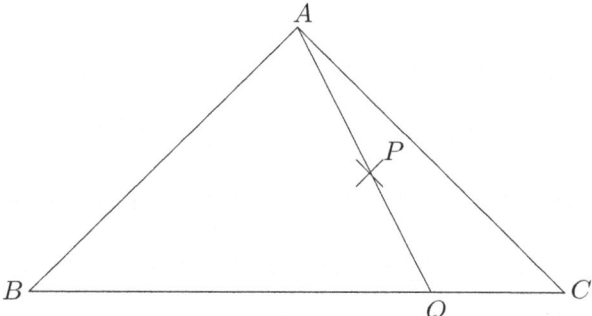

Similarly, to find the value $m_b(P)$, we take a straight line segment BQ starting with B and going through P until it reaches the segment AC at some point $Q \in AC$. We know that $m_b(Q) = 0$ and that $m_b(B) = 1$. So, to find the value $m_b(P)$, we use the value $b(s)$, where $s = L(P)$ is obtained by a linear transformation L from the interval QB to the interval $[0, 1]$ – a linear transformation L for which:

– the point Q at which $m_b(Q) = 0$ maps into the value $s = 0$ for which $b(s) = 0$, and
– the point B at which $m_b(B) = 1$ maps into the value $s = 1$ for which $b(s) = 1$.

Finally, to find the value $m_c(P)$, we take a straight line segment CQ starting with C and going through P until it reaches the segment AB at some point $Q \in AB$. We know that $m_c(Q) = 0$ and that $m_c(C) = 1$. So, to find the value $m_c(P)$, we use the value $c(s)$, where $s = L(P)$ is obtained by a linear transformation L from the interval QC to the interval $[0, 1]$ – a linear transformation L for which:

– the point Q at which $m_c(Q) = 0$ maps into the value $s = 0$ for which $c(s) = 0$, and
– the point C at which $m_c(C) = 1$ maps into the value $s = 1$ for which $c(s) = 1$.

The three functions $m_a(P)$, $m_b(P)$, and $m_c(P)$ should add up to 1 for all P.

This is how the Extension was Done. This is how an extension was done in [5] – with $a(s) = b(s) = c(s) = s$.

Remaining Challenge. Remaining challenge is to check if we can extend it to more general membership functions – i.e., to more general basic functions. As promised, in the following (last) section, we prove that this is not possible: that only for triangular membership functions, we can have an extension to a triangular domain.

4 Main Result: Extension to Triangular Domains Is Only Possible for Triangular Membership Functions

All Triangular Domains are Equivalent (in Some Reasonable Sense). As we have mentioned earlier, for every pair of intervals – for each of which we mark every endpoint by a number (1 or 2), there exists exactly one linear transformation that:

- transforms the first interval into the second one,
- maps endpoint 1 of the first interval into endpoint 1 of the second interval, and
- maps endpoint 2 of the first interval into endpoint 2 of the second interval.

Similarly, for every two triangles – for each of which we mark each vertex by a number (1, 2, or 3), there exists exactly one linear (= affine) transformation that maps each vertex of the first triangle into a similar vertex of the second triangle – and that therefore maps the first triangle into the second one. In this sense, all triangular domains are equivalent modulo an appropriate linear transformation.

A linear transformation changes the locations of the points, but it does not change the values of the membership functions. Thus, the condition that the sum of the membership functions is equal to 1 at all the points is preserved under a linear transformation. The above construction of a membership function is also preserved under a linear transformation. Thus, if for one triangular domain, we have a set of three membership function for which the sum is 1, then by applying an appropriate linear transformation we can get a set of three membership functions for any other triangular domain.

Specific Case. Because of the above equivalence, without losing generality, it is sufficient to consider a specific example of a triangular domain. As this example, let us take a right equilateral triangle with sides of length 1:

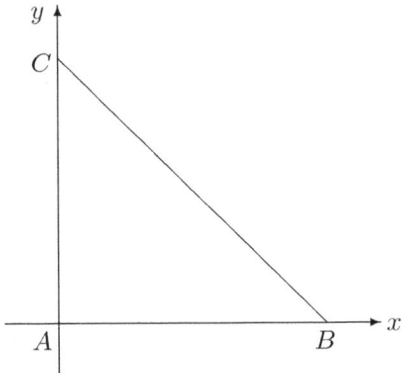

Corresponding Membership Functions. One can check that for $m_a(P)$, the above procedure leads to

$$m_a(x, y) = a(1 - (x + y)) :$$

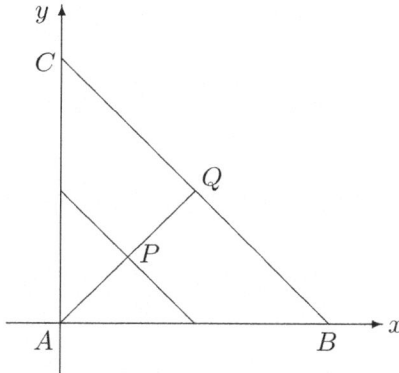

For $m_b(P)$, we get $m_b(x, y) = b(x)$:

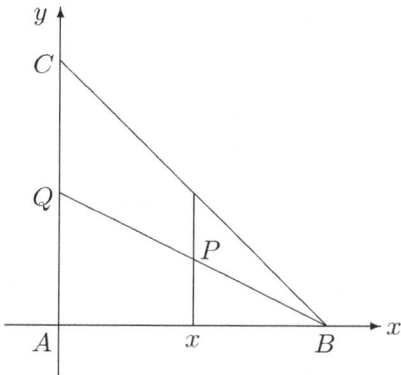

Finally, for $m_c(P)$, we get $m_c(x, y) = c(y)$:

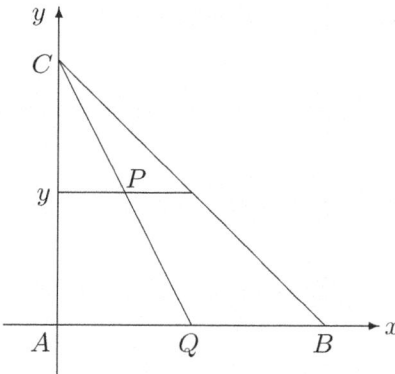

The Functional Equation Describing the Requirement that the Membership Functions Should Add to 1. Now that we have explicit expressions for all three membership functions in terms of the basic functions, the requirement $m_a(P) + m_b(P) + m_c(P) = 1$ (that the sum of the three membership functions be equal to 1) takes the following form:

$$a(1 - (x + y)) + b(x) + c(y) = 1. \tag{2}$$

Let us find all possible triples of functions that satisfy this functional equation.

Let us Solve the Resulting Functional Equation. For $y = 0$, we have $c(y) = c(0) = 0$ and thus, the equation (2) takes the following simplified form:

$$a(1 - x) + b(x) = 1. \tag{3}$$

Thus, for all x, we have

$$a(1 - x) = 1 - b(x). \tag{4}$$

Similarly, for $x = 0$, we have $b(x) = b(0) = 0$ and thus, the equation (2) takes the following simplified form:

$$a(1 - y) + c(y) = 1. \tag{5}$$

Thus, for all y, we have

$$a(1 - y) = 1 - c(y). \tag{6}$$

For $x = y$, from (4) and (6), we can conclude that $1 - b(y) = 1 - c(y)$, so

$$c(y) = b(y). \tag{7}$$

Now, from (4), we can conclude that

$$a(1 - (x + y)) = 1 - b(x + y). \tag{8}$$

Substituting the expressions (7) and (8) into the equality (2), we conclude that

$$1 - b(x + y) + b(x) + b(y) = 1. \tag{9}$$

Subtracting 1 from both sides and adding $b(x + y)$ to both sides, we conclude that

$$b(x + y) = b(x) + b(y). \tag{10}$$

It is known (see, e.g., [1]) that every continuous solution of the equation (10) has the form $b(x) = c \cdot x$ for some c. Since $b(1) = 1$, we get $c = 1$ and $b(x) = x$. From the formulas (7) and (8), we can now conclude that $c(x) = a(x) = x$, i.e., that indeed $a(s) = b(s) = c(s) = s$ for all s.

In other words, the only case when the three above-defined membership functions $m_a(P)$, $m_b(P)$, and $m_c(P)$ add up to 1 is when all these functions are triangular. The result is thus proven.

5   Conclusions and Future Work

Conclusions. Because of numerous successful applications of 1-D F-transform and its generalization to rectangular domains, it is desirable to extend F-transform techniques to other types of domains – e.g., to triangular ones (and, as a result, to general polygonal domains – since these domains can be represented as a union of finitely many triangular ones). Such a generalization has indeed been recently proposed. Interesting, in contrast to the cases of 1-D domains and 2-D rectangular domains, where we can use generic membership functions, the extension to triangular domains was only described for triangular membership functions.

In this paper, we provide a theoretical explanation for this restriction. Namely, we prove that under the usual assumptions – e.g., that all membership functions are of the same shape, and that the sum of all the used membership functions is equal to 1 – the extension to triangular domains is only possible for triangular membership functions.

Future Work. Our result is based on the usual assumptions. However, it is known that F-transforms ideas work in more general situations as well, when the above assumptions are not always satisfied: e.g., where the sum of membership functions is, in general, different from 1.

It is therefore desirable to analyze what happens if we generalize such more general F-transform setting to triangular domains – maybe this way, we will be able to use membership functions of more general shape.

Acknowledgments. This work was supported in part by the National Science Foundation grants 1623190 (A Model of Change for Preparing a New Generation for Professional Practice in Computer Science), HRD-1834620 and HRD-2034030 (CAHSI Includes), EAR-2225395 (Center for Collective Impact in Earthquake Science C-CIES), and by the AT&T Fellowship in Information Technology.

It was also supported by a grant from the Hungarian National Research, Development and Innovation Office (NRDI), and by the Institute for Risk and Reliability, Leibniz Universitaet Hannover, Germany.

The users are thankful to the anonymous referees for valuable suggestions.

References

1. Aczél, J., Dhombres, J.: Functional Equations in Several Variables. Cambridge University Press, Cambridge (2008)
2. Di Martino, F., et al.: A color image reduction based on fuzzy transforms. Inf. Sci. **266**, 101–111 (2014)
3. Perfilieva, I.: F-transform. In: Springer Handbook of Computational Intelligence, pp. 113–130. Springer, Heidelberg (2015)
4. Pham, T.M.T., Janeček, J., Perfilieva, I.: Fuzzy transform on 1-D manifolds. In: Biomedical and Other Applications of Soft Computing, pp. 13–24. Springer, Cham (2022)

5. Zámečniková, H., Perfilieva, I.: F-transform on triangulated domain. In: Lesot, M.-J., et al. (eds.) Information Processing and Management of Uncertainty in Knowledge-Based Systems, Abstracts of the 20th International Conference IPMU 2024, Portugal, Lisbon, 22–26 July 2024 (2024)
6. Zámečniková, H., Perfilieva, I., Valášek, R.: Nonlocal Laplace operator in image processing. In: Developments of Artificial Intelligence Technologies in Computations and Robotics: Proceedings of the 14th International FLINS Conference, pp. 956–963 (2020)

Locally Modified Multivariate F^m-Transform: Theoretical Background and Possible Applications

Martins Kokainis[1]([✉])[iD] and Svetlana Asmuss[1,2][iD]

[1] Department of Mathematics, University of Latvia, Jelgavas 3, Riga 1004, Latvia
{martins.kokainis,svetlana.asmuss}@lu.lv
[2] Institute of Mathematics and Computer Science, University of Latvia,
Raina bulvaris 29, Riga 1459, Latvia

Abstract. This contribution considers approximating smooth multivariate functions via a local modification of the higher degree multivariate fuzzy transform (F^m-transform), when the fuzzy partition is constructed via B-splines. The modification seeks to extend the improved approximation properties on the whole domain of the initial function, rather than just a smaller subset where the Ruspini condition is satisfied. The aim of this paper is to provide a practical and computationally efficient implementation of such modification, enabling a wider scope of applications. In particular, we discuss how to apply the proposed approximation scheme for solving partial differential equations and provide some numerical examples of the proposed method. The proposal utilizes the collocation method, with the numerical solution sought as the F^m-transform of a discrete function.

Keywords: Multivariate fuzzy transform · B-spline · extrapolation · approximation error · collocation method

1 Introduction

The notion of ordinary F-transforms, introduced by I. Perfilieva [10,13], was expanded [12] to include higher-degree F^m-transforms. It was further adapted to multivariate contexts [3,14,17]. The selection of basic functions for forming a fuzzy partition considerably affects the F-transforms' characteristics. This contribution examines F^m-transforms built on a spline-based fuzzy partition proposed in [5] and extended to multivariate applications in [6]. B-splines can improve the approximation properties of F^m-transforms for smooth functions in both settings; however, the improved approximation is confined to a strictly smaller region where the Ruspini condition is satisfied. To overcome this limitation and widen the applicability of the F^m-transform technique, a modified version of the spline-based F^m-transform was suggested. This modification was initially proposed for the univariate case [8] and subsequently extended to the multivariate setting [9].

M. Baczyński et al. (Eds.): EUSFLAT 2025, LNCS 15883, pp. 127–138, 2025.
https://doi.org/10.1007/978-3-031-97225-6_11

However, the method proposed in [9] faces limitations influencing its utility. It depends on globally defined extrapolation operators with specific locality properties; obtaining explicit constructions of such extrapolators is challenging. The suggested approach poorly generalizes to higher-dimensional cases in part due to instability and increased computational costs, resulting in impractical runtimes for even moderately-sized problems.

This contribution seeks to overcome the outlined limitations by handling the missing data in a manner that is inherently local, maintaining the conceptual advantage of the fuzzy transform. The proposed method is designed to be both straightforward to implement and computationally efficient, making it more practical for applications. Specifically, we illustrate how the proposal can be used for a fuzzy transform collocation technique for solving partial differential equations. This idea builds upon a body of previous work on utilizing fuzzy transforms for solving numerically ordinary and partial differential equations, see, e.g. [4, 16].

The structure of the paper is as follows. Section 2 provides preliminaries on spline-based fuzzy partitions and F^m-transforms; Sect. 3 presents our approach of dealing with the missing data and examines the approximation properties of the resulting F^m-transform. Section 4 considers numerical results when the approach is used for a collocation scheme for partial differential equations.

2   Preliminaries

Let $\mathbb{N}$ stand for the set of positive integers and $\mathbb{N}_0 := \mathbb{N} \cup \{0\}$. By $[n]$, for a positive integer n, we will denote the set $\{1, 2, ..., n\}$.

2.1   Fuzzy Partitions

Univariate Uniform Fuzzy Partition. We recall the definition of a generalized (h, h')-uniform fuzzy partition.

Let $[a, b] \subset \mathbb{R}$ be a fixed interval. Suppose that $N \in \mathbb{N}$ and h, h' are positive reals satisfying $h' > h/2$. Let $t_0 < \ldots < t_N$ be h-equidistant nodes in the interior of (a, b). Also assume that $\bigcup_{j=0}^{N}[t_i - h', t_i + h'] = [a, b]$.

Definition 1 ([11]). *Fuzzy sets $A_0, \ldots, A_N \in C[a, b]$ are said to constitute a generalized (h, h')-uniform fuzzy partition of $[a, b]$ if the following conditions are satisfied: for all $j \in \{0, \ldots, N\}$,*

- *$A_j(t) \in (0, 1]$ if $t \in (t_j - h', t_j + h')$, and $A_j(t) = 0$ otherwise;*
- *$A_j(t_j - t) = A_j(t_j + t)$ for all $t \in [0, h']$;*
- *$\sum_{j=0}^{N} A_j(t) > 0$ for all $t \in (a, b)$;*
- *$A_j(t) = A_{j+1}(t + h)$ for all $t \in [t_j - h', t_j + h']$, if $j \neq N$.*

Then there is a function $A : [-H, H] \to \mathbb{R}$ (called the generating function of the partition), where $H = h'/h$, s.t. for all $j \in \{0, \ldots, N\}$ and $t \in [t_j - h', t_j + h']$,

$$A_j(t) = A\left(\frac{t - t_j}{h}\right). \tag{1}$$

We will also say that each fuzzy set A_j is associated with the basic node t_j, $j = 0, 1, \ldots, N$. Furthermore, the fuzzy partition is said to fulfill the Ruspini condition on an interval $I \subset [a, b]$ if $\sum_{j=0}^{N} A_j(t) = 1$ for all $t \in I$.

Fuzzy Partition Based on B-Splines. One particular choice of the generating function A is that of the central B-spline (of degree $2k - 1$ for an integer $k \geq 1$), which is [15] an even B-spline with 1-equidistant knots:

Definition 2. *The central B-spline of degree $2k - 1$, denoted by ϕ_{2k-1}, is the unique piecewise polynomial function satisfying the following requirements: 1) for each $j \in \{-k, \ldots, k - 1\}$ the restriction of ϕ_{2k-1} to $[i, i + 1]$ is a polynomial of degree at most $2k - 1$; 2) $\phi_{2k-1} \in C^{2k-2}(\mathbb{R})$; 3) $\phi_{2k-1}(t) = 0$ if $t \notin (-k, k)$; 4) $\int_{\mathbb{R}} \phi_{2k-1}(t)\, dt = 1$.*

For more properties of B-splines in the context of constructing a fuzzy partition we refer to [6]. Every central B-spline is a nonnegative function and can be viewed as membership functions of a fuzzy set. In particular, $k = 1$ recovers the commonly used triangular generating function $A(t) = 1 - |t|$, $t \in [-1, 1]$.

Fuzzy sets constructed via (1) consist of $2k$ consecutive basic intervals and form a (h, hk)-uniform fuzzy partition. For the sake of convenience we let the interval $[a, b]$ be partitioned into N parts by h-equidistant nodes $t_j = a + jh$, $j = 0, 1, \ldots, N$, where $h = (b - a)/N$; however, that implies that the basis functions are indexed as A_k, ..., A_{N-k}, with, e.g. A_k being supported on (t_0, t_{2k}). We refer to this fuzzy partition to as FPB (fuzzy partition based on B-splines).

It can be shown that the Ruspini condition is fulfilled on the $[t_{2k-1}, t_{N-2k+1}]$; we require $N \geq 4k - 1$ to ensure that this set includes at least one basic interval.

Extended FPB. A straightforward way of ensuring that the Ruspini condition is fulfilled on the whole $[a, b]$ is to add more basic functions (with support extending outside $[a, b]$) and restricting them to the $[a, b]$, resulting in a fuzzy partition that is not uniform in the strict sense of Definition 1.

Indeed, this has been the approach with other generating functions, e.g., the triangular basis functions or the raised cosine basis. In the mentioned cases, however, the fuzzy sets are supported on two basic intervals, thus only one restricted fuzzy set on each end of the interval is necessary. In the case of B-splines, however, since each A_j covers exactly $2k$ basic intervals, we have to introduce $2k - 1$ additional fuzzy sets on each end of the interval. We refer to this as the extended FPB (eFPB). It is helpful to think of this construction as the FPB of a wider interval (specifically, of $[\tilde{a}, \tilde{b}]$, where $\tilde{a} = a - (2k - 1)h$, $\tilde{b} = b + (2k - 1)h$) such that the Ruspini condition for this partition is fulfilled precisely on the initial interval $[a, b]$.

Formally, we will say that the (k, N)-eFPB of $[a, b]$ is the fuzzy partition consisting of the fuzzy sets A_j, $j = -k + 1, \ldots, N + k - 1$, given by $A_j(t) = A\left(\frac{t - t_j}{h}\right)\Big|_{t \in [a,b]}$ where $t_j = a + hj$ for all j and $A = \phi_{2k-1}$ is the central B-spline of degree $2k - 1$.

Finally, we note in the case $k = 1$ the eFPB coincides precisely with the well-known uniform fuzzy partition with triangular shaped membership functions.

Multivariate Fuzzy Partition. The fuzzy partition of the Cartesian product $[a_1, b_1] \times \ldots \times [a_d, b_d] =: \prod_{i=1}^{d}[a_i, b_i]$ can [14,17] be obtained from the tensor product of the univariate membership functions. Formally, if $A_{i,0}, \ldots, A_{i,N_i}$ is a fuzzy partition of $[a_i, b_i]$ for all $i \in [d]$, then the collection of functions

$$A_{\mathbf{j}}(\mathbf{t}) := \prod_{i=1}^{d} A_{i,j_i}(t_i), \quad \mathbf{t} = (t_1, \ldots, t_d) \in \prod_{i=1}^{d}[a_i, b_i],$$

with $\mathbf{j} = (j_1, \ldots, j_d)$ s.t. $0 \leq j_i \leq N_i$ (the set of such multi-indices $\mathbf{j}$ will be compactly denoted as $\{\mathbf{j} : 0 \leq \mathbf{j} \leq \mathbf{N}\}$ where $\mathbf{N} := (N_1, \ldots, N_d)$), is called a fuzzy partition of the set $\prod_{i=1}^{d}[a_i, b_i]$. Let the univariate fuzzy sets $A_{i,j}$ be associated with the basic nodes $t_{i,j}$, then we say that each multivariate membership function $A_{\mathbf{j}}$ is associated with the (multivariate) basic node $\mathbf{t_j} = (t_{1,j_1}, t_{2,j_2}, \ldots, t_{d,j_d})$.

Moreover, if for the i-th univariate fuzzy partition the Ruspini condition is fulfilled on $[\hat{a}_i, \hat{b}_i] \subset [a_i, b_i]$, then for the multivariate partition the Ruspini condition is fulfilled on the respective Cartesian product $\prod_{i=1}^{d}[\hat{a}_i, \hat{b}_i]$.

In particular, we will speak of the multivariate (k, N)-eFPB to refer to the resulting partition in the case when the i-th univariate fuzzy partition is the (k, N)-eFPB of $[a_i, b_i]$.[1]

2.2   Discrete F^m-Transform

Here we recall the following form of the discrete F^m-transform (see, e.g. [3]).

Let $I = \prod_{i=1}^{d}[a_i, b_i]$. We assume that we are given a discrete function, defined at L points of I. More formally, let $\Delta = \{\mathbf{z}_1, \ldots, \mathbf{z}_L\} \subset I$ be given and let $f : \Delta \to \mathbb{R}$. Denote $y_l = f(\mathbf{z}_l)$, for each $l \in [L]$, and let $\mathbf{y}$ be the column vector containing the values of the function f. Let $\mathbb{A} = \{A_{\mathbf{j}} : 0 \leq \mathbf{j} \leq \mathbf{N}\}$ be a fixed fuzzy partition of I.

We enumerate all d-variate polynomials of total degree at most m in the following way. Fix any ordering of the index set $\{\mathbf{l} \in \mathbb{N}_0^d : 0 \leq |\mathbf{l}| \leq m\}$ and suppose that it is given using the following notation: $\mathbf{l}_r$, $r \in [m']$, where $m' := \binom{m+d}{d}$ is the number of elements of this set.

For any fuzzy set $A_{\mathbf{j}} \in \mathbb{A}$, associated the basic node $\mathbf{t_j}$, we define the following $L \times m'$ matrix $\mathbf{X_j}$ and the $L \times L$ diagonal matrix $\mathbf{A_j}$:

$$\mathbf{X_j} = \begin{pmatrix} P_{\mathbf{l}_1}(\mathbf{z}_1 - \mathbf{t_j}) & \ldots & P_{\mathbf{l}_{m'}}(\mathbf{z}_1 - \mathbf{t_j}) \\ P_{\mathbf{l}_1}(\mathbf{z}_2 - \mathbf{t_j}) & \ldots & P_{\mathbf{l}_{m'}}(\mathbf{z}_2 - \mathbf{t_j}) \\ & \ddots & \\ P_{\mathbf{l}_1}(\mathbf{z}_L - \mathbf{t_j}) & \ldots & P_{\mathbf{l}_{m'}}(\mathbf{z}_L - \mathbf{t_j}) \end{pmatrix},$$

$$\mathbf{A_j} = \mathrm{diag}\left(A_{\mathbf{j}}(\mathbf{z}_1), \ldots, A_{\mathbf{j}}(\mathbf{z}_L)\right),$$

where $P_{\mathbf{l}}(\mathbf{x}) := \mathbf{x}^{\mathbf{l}} = x_1^{l_1} x_2^{l_2} \ldots x_d^{l_d}$.

---

[1] It is possible to consider the case when k_i and N_i are different for each i; for the sake of presentation, we do not consider the fully general case in this contribution.

Definition 3. *We say that the set Δ is sufficiently dense in the fuzzy partition $\mathbb{A}$ w.r.t. m if for each $\mathbf{j}$ the matrix $\mathbf{X}_{\mathbf{j}}^{\top} \mathbf{A}_{\mathbf{j}} \mathbf{X}_{\mathbf{j}}$ is invertible.*

Definition 4. *Let $\mathbf{p} = (p_{\mathbf{j}} : 0 \leq \mathbf{j} \leq \mathbf{N})$ be a collection of polynomials of the total degree at most m in d variables. Then the function*

$$F_m^{\leftarrow}[\mathbf{p}](\mathbf{t}) = \frac{\sum_{0 \leq \mathbf{j} \leq \mathbf{N}} p_{\mathbf{j}}(\mathbf{t})\, A_{\mathbf{j}}(\mathbf{t})}{\sum_{0 \leq \mathbf{j} \leq \mathbf{N}} A_{\mathbf{j}}(\mathbf{t})} \tag{2}$$

is called the inverse F^m-transform *of $\mathbf{p}$.*

Definition 5. *Let $\Delta = \{\mathbf{z}_1, \dots, \mathbf{z}_L\} \subset I$ be sufficiently dense in the FP $\mathbb{A}$ w.r.t. m and let $f : \Delta \to \mathbb{R}$ and $\mathbf{y}$ be the column vector containing the values of the function f. Then the collection $F_m^{\rightarrow}[f] = (F_{m,\mathbf{j}}^{\rightarrow} : 0 \leq \mathbf{j} \leq \mathbf{N})$ of polynomials $F_{m,\mathbf{j}}^{\rightarrow}$ defined by*

$$F_{m,\mathbf{j}}^{\rightarrow}(\mathbf{t}) = \sum_{r=1}^{m'} \beta_r^{(\mathbf{j})} P_{1_r}(\mathbf{t} - \mathbf{t}_{\mathbf{j}}),$$

where

$$\beta^{(\mathbf{j})} = \left(\mathbf{X}_{\mathbf{j}}^{\top} \mathbf{A}_{\mathbf{j}} \mathbf{X}_{\mathbf{j}}\right)^{-1} \mathbf{X}_{\mathbf{j}}^{\top} \mathbf{A}_{\mathbf{j}} \mathbf{y}, \tag{3}$$

is said to be the direct discrete F^m-transform *of f w.r.t. the fuzzy partition $\mathbb{A}$. The inverse F^m-transform of this collection, i.e., the function*

$$F_m[f](\mathbf{t}) = \frac{\sum_{0 \leq \mathbf{j} \leq \mathbf{N}} F_{m,\mathbf{j}}^{\rightarrow}(\mathbf{t})\, A_{\mathbf{j}}(\mathbf{t})}{\sum_{0 \leq \mathbf{j} \leq \mathbf{N}} A_{\mathbf{j}}(\mathbf{t})}, \tag{4}$$

is called the (composite) F^m-transform *of f.*

A well-known important property of the F^m-transform is that it is exact for polynomials of total degree at most m, i.e., $F_m[p] \equiv p$ for such polynomials. Using B-splines to generate the fuzzy partition improves this property, making $F_m[p]$ exact for all polynomials of total degree up to $2m+1$, provided that $2m+1$ does not exceed the spline degrees, in the subset where the Ruspini condition holds.

More precisely, the fuzzy partition $\mathbb{A}$ is generated by B-splines with parameters k, N, and the discrete set Δ consists of all the basic nodes $\mathbf{t}_{\mathbf{j}}, 0 \leq \mathbf{j} \leq \mathbf{N}$ (one can also allow Δ to be a uniform refinement of the grid formed by the basic nodes $\mathbf{t}_{\mathbf{j}}$, i.e., by subdividing each grid cell evenly into smaller cells, see [6] for details); then Δ is sufficiently dense for[2] $m \leq 2k - 2$. In that case, the (composite) F^m-transform satisfies [6, Theorem 1] the following:

Theorem 1. *Let non-negative integers r, m satisfy $r \leq \min\{2m + 1, 2k - 1\}$ and $m \leq 2k - 2$. Then for all d-variate polynomials p of total degree r,*

$$F_m[p](\mathbf{t}) = p(\mathbf{t}) \quad \text{for all } \mathbf{t} \in \prod_{i=1}^{d} [t_{i,2k-1}, t_{i,N-2k+1}].$$

---

[2] Taking Δ as a refinement of the basic nodes' grid increases the allowed values of m, see [6] for a precise statement.

3 Locally Modified F^m-Transform and Smooth Function Approximation

In many applications the approximation provided by the F^m-transform is necessary on the whole domain I, something that Theorem 1 does not achieve. Merely using the extending the fuzzy partition (so that the Ruspini condition is fulfilled on the whole I), i.e., using the eFPB, does not alleviate that. In fact, the F^m-transform will be even undefined for such an extended partition, because the discrete set Δ will not be sufficiently dense (since the fuzzy sets near the boundary of I will contain too few discrete points).

By treating the eFPB as a fuzzy partition of a wider domain (with the unrestricted membership functions), this obstacle can be viewed as that of the missing data: one might extend Δ outside the initial cuboid I as well, but the function's values at the respective points are not accessible. A similar scenario could be envisioned when some of the f values *inside* I are missing, e.g. due to errors during the data acquiring process (or, when the requirements on the basic nodes are incompatible with the discrete set associated with the input data). In all these cases, the assumptions of Theorem 1 fail.

A natural approach to handle (a few) missing data is to extrapolate the nearby values; in the univariate case this approach can [8] also deal with, e.g. the missing data on the $2k - 1$ basic intervals to the left of the node t_0, required for the additional basic functions of the eFPB. In the multivariate case, however, trying to define a global function $\tilde{f}$, defined on a wider set $\prod_{i=1}^{d}[a_i - \epsilon, b_i + \epsilon]$, to which the F^m-transform is applied, leads [9] to introducing a family of extrapolation operators with rather restrictive properties, which results in the aforementioned issues. Instead, what works well in practice, is to perform extrapolation separately for each fuzzy set depending on data that are missing.

3.1 Extrapolation Method

For the sake of simplicity, in the following we will assume that extrapolation parameters (input and output points) are the same in each dimension.

Univariate Case. Let $E_{n,n_{\mathrm{L}},n_{\mathrm{R}},S} : \mathbb{R}^n \to \mathbb{R}^{n_{\mathrm{L}}+n+n_{\mathrm{R}}}$ be a linear operator that, upon receiving n values of a function f defined at n equispaced nodes x_0, x_1, ..., x_{n-1}, where $x_j = x_0 + jh$ for any $x_0 \in \mathbb{R}$ and $h > 0$, outputs $n_{\mathrm{L}} + n + n_{\mathrm{R}}$ values $y_{-n_{\mathrm{L}}}$, ..., $y_{n+n_{\mathrm{R}}-1}$ with the following property: if f is a polynomial of degree at most S, then $y_j = f(x_0 + jh)$ for all $j \in \{-n_{\mathrm{L}}, \ldots, n + n_{\mathrm{R}} - 1\}$. This imposes the requirement $S \leq n - 1$ (i.e., the parameters for polynomials for which the extrapolation is exact cannot exceed the total number of input values); in practice it is beneficial to take $S \ll n$.

Since the nodes are equispaced, an implementation of the extrapolation operator might benefit [1] from using Chebyshev polynomial basis. For that reason, we set $x_0 = 0$ and $h = 2/(n - 1)$, so that the input data are values at the equispaced on the interval $[-1, 1]$. Let $\mathbf{V}$ be a pseudo-Vandermonde matrix of size $(n_L + n + n_R) \times (S + 1)$, containing the values $V_{jl} = T_l(x_j)$, where T_l is the l-th Chebyshev polynomial of the first kind. We note that, e.g. in Numpy [2] this is the matrix returned by the `np.polynomial.chebyshev.chebvander` method. Let $\mathbf{V}_0$ be the $n \times (S + 1)$ submatrix of $\mathbf{V}$, corresponding to the rows indexed by $x_0, \ldots, x_{n-1}$. Then $E_{n,n_L,n_R,S}$ is the linear operator associated with the $(n_L + n + n_R) \times n$ matrix $\mathbf{V}(\mathbf{V}_0^\top \mathbf{V}_0)^{-1} \mathbf{V}_0^\top$. Notice that, even if $x_0 = 0$, $h = 2/(n-1)$ was used for the construction of this matrix, the operator acts only on the values of the discrete function, irregardless of the particular placement of its nodes.

Multivariate Case. By $E_{n,n_L,n_R,S} : \mathbb{R}^{n^d} \to \mathbb{R}^{(n_L+n+n_R)^d}$ we denote a linear operator that acts the following way:

- upon receiving n^d values of a function f defined at a uniform grid consisting of n equispaced nodes $x_{i,0}, \ldots, x_{i,n-1}$, at each dimension, $x_{i,j} = x_{i,0} + jh$ for any $x_{i,0} \in \mathbb{R}$ and $h > 0$,
- outputs $(n_L + n + n_R)^d$ values $y_{\mathbf{j}}$, $-n_L \leq \mathbf{j} \leq n + n_R - 1$, with the following property: if f is a d-variate polynomial of the total degree at most S, then $y_{\mathbf{j}} = f(\mathbf{x_j})$ for all $\mathbf{j}$ s.t. $-n_L \leq \mathbf{j} \leq n + n_R - 1$, where $\mathbf{x_j} = (x_{1,j_1}, \ldots, x_{d,j_d})$.

We note that operator $E_{n,n_L,n_R,S}$ can be constructed from the univariate operators, essentially by taking the tensor powers of the previously introduced matrix $\mathbf{V}$, but discarding columns corresponding to polynomials of total degree exceeding S.

We will use such operators with parameters $S = \max\{2m + 1, 2k - 1\}$ and $n = 2k + 1$, assuming[3] $m \leq k - 1$. We set[4] $n_L = n_R = (2k - 1) - 1$.

3.2   Locally Modified Fuzzy Transform

Let a (k, N)-eFPB $\mathbb{A}$ of $I = \prod_{i=1}^d [a_i, b_i]$ and the operator $E_{n,n_L,n_R,S}$ be fixed, with parameters and assumptions as before.

We note that one can (and in practice, does) use a slightly different version of the matrices and vectors described in Sect. 2.2: since only a subset of all L discrete points belongs to the fuzzy set $A_\mathbf{j}$ with nonzero degree, one can reduce the size of the matrices $\mathbf{X_j}$ and $\mathbf{A_j}$ by considering only those points (instead of all L of them) and taking the respective part of the vector $\mathbf{y}$, corresponding to those points.

In our case, $L = (N + 1)^d$, but each (unrestricted) basic function contains only $L' := (2k - 1)^d$ of them with nonzero degree. In the following we will assume that $\mathbf{X_j}$ and $\mathbf{A_j}$ are matrices of size $L' \times m'$ and $L' \times L'$, respectively, corresponding to those points. Then the vector $\beta^{(\mathbf{j})}$, generally given by (3), can be computed as

$$\beta^{(\mathbf{j})} = \left(\mathbf{X_j}^\top \mathbf{A_j} \mathbf{X_j}\right)^{-1} \mathbf{X_j}^\top \mathbf{A_j} \mathbf{y}(\mathbf{j}), \tag{5}$$

---

[3] Taking Δ as a refinement of the basic nodes' grid allows to increase the maximal m.
[4] Choosing $n_L \neq n_R$ allows to deal with a more irregular discrete set Δ.

where $\mathbf{y}(\mathbf{j})$ is the part of $\mathbf{y}$ corresponding to the selected discrete points (it can also be easily shown that $\mathbf{X_j} = \mathbf{X}$ and $\mathbf{A_j} = \mathbf{A}$ do not depend on $\mathbf{j}$ under an appropriate ordering of the discrete set, which allows to precompute the matrix $\left(\mathbf{X}^\top \mathbf{A} \mathbf{X}\right)^{-1} \mathbf{X}^\top \mathbf{A}$).

For the unrestricted membership functions in $\mathbb{A}$, i.e., those with $k \leq \mathbf{j} \leq N - k + 1$, we use the (5) as is, resulting in the usual direct F^m-transform of f. For the additional membership functions, however, we modify (5) by replacing $\mathbf{y}(\mathbf{j})$ by $\tilde{\mathbf{y}}(\mathbf{j})$; the values $\tilde{\mathbf{y}}(\mathbf{j})$ correspond to a (subvector of) the values returned by the operator $\mathrm{E}_{n,n_\mathrm{L},n_\mathrm{R},S}$ applied to the n^d values that are closest to the $\mathbf{t_j}$.

More precisely, for any $\mathbf{j}$ failing the constraint $k \leq \mathbf{j} \leq N - k + 1$, the input to $\mathrm{E}_{n,n_\mathrm{L},n_\mathrm{R},S}$ consists of all the nodes $\mathbf{t}_{j'}$ such that for each dimension $i \in [d]$,

- if $k \leq j_i \leq N - k$, let j_i' range over the set $\{j_i - k, \ldots, j_i + k\}$, i.e., the nodes in the closure of the support of the membership function A_{i,j_i};
- if $j_i < k$, let j_i' range over the first $n = 2k + 1$ available nodes for the i-th dimension: $j_i' \in \{0, 1, \ldots, 2k\}$;
- if $j_i > N - k$, let j_i' range over the last n available nodes for the i-th dimension: $j_i' \in \{N - 2k, \ldots, N - 1, N\}$.

Similarly we choose only a part of the output of the operator $\mathrm{E}_{n,n_\mathrm{L},n_\mathrm{R},S}$ for the $L' = (2k - 1)^d$ components of $\tilde{\mathbf{y}}(\mathbf{j})$. By interpreting the output as $(n_\mathrm{L} + n + n_\mathrm{R})^d$ values $\tilde{y}_{\mathbf{j}'}$, $-(2k - 2) \leq \mathbf{j}' \leq 4k - 2$, we let $\tilde{\mathbf{y}}(\mathbf{j})$ consist of those values for which $\mathbf{j}'$ is as follows:

- if $k \leq j_i \leq N - k$, let j_i' range over the set $\{1, \ldots, 2k - 1\}$, i.e., the "inner part" of the extrapolated values in the i-th dimension;
- if $j_i < k$, let j_i' range over the set $\{j_i - k + 1, \ldots, j_i + k - 1\}$, i.e., we take as many nodes to the left of $t_{i,0}$ as there are in the support of the unrestricted version of the membership function A_{i,j_i};
- if $j_i > N - k$, we take all j_i' in the set $\{j_i - (N - k) + 1, \ldots, j_i - (N - k) + 2k - 1\}$.

We note that each j_i ranges from $-k + 1$ to $N + k - 1$ in the case of (k, N)-eFPB, thus the described indexing scheme utilizes all (and only those) values returned by the operator $\mathrm{E}_{n,n_\mathrm{L},n_\mathrm{R},S}$ with $n = 2k + 1$ and $n_\mathrm{L} = n_\mathrm{R} = 2k - 2$.

The described algorithm computes

$$\beta^{(\mathbf{j})} = \left(\mathbf{X_j}^\top \mathbf{A_j} \mathbf{X_j}\right)^{-1} \mathbf{X_j}^\top \mathbf{A_j} \tilde{\mathbf{y}}(\mathbf{j}),$$

where $\tilde{\mathbf{y}}(\mathbf{j})$ is essentially the vector of values of a local extrapolation of the function f; moreover, by construction, $\tilde{\mathbf{y}}$ coincides with the actual values of f in case f is a polynomial of total degree at most S. One can view this two-step process (extrapolate f; compute its fuzzy transform) as a single-step *modification* of the fuzzy transform of the function f when there are missing data, hence we refer to this method as the (locally) modified F^m-transform and denote it('s composition with the inverse transform) by $\tilde{F}_m[f]$.

The choice $S = \max\{2m + 1, 2k - 1\}$ and Theorem 1 immediately imply:

Theorem 2. *Let $m \in \{0, 1, \ldots, k - 1\}$; then $\tilde{F}_m[p] \equiv p$ on I for all d-variate polynomials p of total degree at most $2m + 1$.*

We also recover approximation of smooth function on the whole domain:

Theorem 3. *Let m, r be nonnegative integers satisfying $m \leq k - 1$ and $r \leq 2m + 1$. Then*

$$\left\| f - \tilde{F}_m[f] \right\| = O(h^{r+1}) \quad \text{for all} \quad f \in C^{r+1}(I).$$

The proof contains mostly technical arguments and is omitted here for the sake of brevity.

4 Application: Collocation Method for PDEs

As a potential application, we numerically investigate a fuzzy transform-based collocation method; in the following we will focus on solving second order partial differential equations (PDEs) in two variables.

Similarly as in the univariate case [7], we aim for constructing a numerical solution as a (composite) modified F^m-transform of some function f, in the sense that $\tilde{F}_m[f]$ must satisfy the given equation at the collocation nodes.

In this section, let[5] $\Omega = (a, b) \times (c, d) \subset \mathbb{R}^2$. For a linear PDE problem, consider the standard form of the Poisson's equation, $\frac{\partial^2 u}{\partial x^2}(x, y) + \frac{\partial^2 u}{\partial y^2}(x, y) = f(x, y)$, $(x, y) \in \Omega$, with Dirichlet boundary conditions: $u(x, y) = g(x, y)$ for $(x, y) \in \partial\Omega$ (where $\partial\Omega$ stands for the boundary of the set Ω).

Let $\mathbb{A}$ be a (k, N)-eFPB of (the closure of) Ω; let Δ be the respective discrete set consisting of the basic nodes $\mathbf{t_j}$ associated with $\mathbb{A}$. Partition $\Delta = \Delta_{\text{int}} \cup \Delta_{\text{bdy}}$ where $\Delta_{\text{int}} := \Delta \cap \Omega$ and $\Delta_{\text{bdy}} := \Delta \cap \partial\Omega$. Let the space of the trial functions be the space of all (locally modified, composite) F^m-transforms w.r.t. the fixed (k, N)-eFPB: $\mathbb{U}_{m,k,N} = \{\tilde{F}_m[\phi] : \phi : \Delta \to \mathbb{R}\}$.

We consider the problem of finding $\phi : \Delta \to \mathbb{R}$ such that its modified F^m-transform, $\tilde{F}^m[\phi] =: u_{m,k,N} \in \mathbb{U}_{m,k,N}$, satisfies the differential equation at the collocation points Δ_{int}, and the boundary conditions at the points Δ_{bdy}:

$$\frac{\partial^2 u_{m,k,N}}{\partial x^2}(x, y) + \frac{\partial^2 u_{m,k,N}}{\partial y^2}(x, y) = f(x, y), \qquad (x, y) \in \Delta_{\text{int}}, \qquad (6)$$

$$u_{m,k,N}(x, y) = g(x, y), \qquad (x, y) \in \Delta_{\text{bdy}}. \qquad (7)$$

For the linear PDE problem this system of equations becomes a linear system of equations w.r.t. the values of the discrete function ϕ.

Instead of the linear PDE problem, one can also consider a nonlinear differential operator. Discretizing it similarly leads to a nonlinear system of equations that is iteratively solved in the least squares sense (i.e., only approximately satisfied).

While the questions of existence/uniqueness of the solution $u_{m,k,N}$ and convergence to the true solution remain open, we consider numerically the behavior of the proposed scheme. In the following we present a few numerical examples, both considered in a recent paper [4] dealing with solving two-dimensional nonlinear elliptic PDEs using fuzzy transform.

---

[5] For the sake of brevity, we will use (a, b), (c, d) instead of (a_1, b_1), (a_2, b_2).

4.1 Numerical Examples

Example 1. We consider a simple Poisson's equation, examined in [4, Example 6b]:

$$\frac{\partial^2 u}{\partial x^2}(x,y) + \frac{\partial^2 u}{\partial y^2}(x,y) = \mathrm{e}^{-x}(x + y^3 + 6y - 2), \quad x, y \in (0,1),$$

with the boundary conditions given by the true solution $u(x,y) = (y^3 + x)\mathrm{e}^{-x}$.

In Fig. 1 we depict the collocation solution $u_{0,2,10}$ when $k = 2$ (cubic B-splines) and $N = 10$; also the true solution and the approximation error is shown.

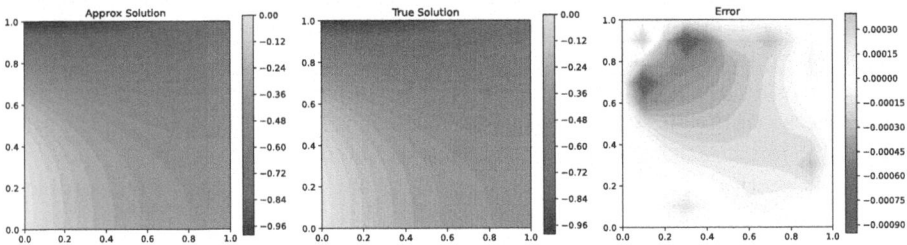

Fig. 1. Example 1: the collocation solution based on $(2, 10)$-eFPB, the true solution and the approximation error

In Table 1 we show the maximal approximation error (evaluated at the nodes Δ) $|u - u_{0,k,N}|$ for $k = 2$ and $k = 3$, respectively, and various N. Similarly as in the univariate case [7], already the $\tilde{F}$-transform ($m = 0$) appears to provide $O(h^{2k-2})$ accuracy of the numerical solution.

Table 1. Example 1: step-size h and ℓ_∞-norm of approximation error: ϵ_2 (for cubic splines, $k = 2$) and ϵ_3 (for quintic splines, $k = 3$), for various values of N

N	30	40	50	60	70	80
h	3.333e-02	2.500e-02	2.000e-02	1.667e-02	1.429e-02	1.250e-02
ϵ_2	1.510e-05	8.330e-06	5.292e-06	3.672e-06	2.693e-06	2.059e-06
ϵ_3	5.344e-08	1.954e-08	3.642e-09	8.141e-10	3.593e-10	1.405e-10

Example 2. We also consider the following nonlinear PDE, also found in [4, Example 4]:

$$\frac{1}{10}\left(\frac{\partial^2 u}{\partial x^2}(x,y) + \frac{\partial^2 u}{\partial y^2}(x,y)\right) - u(x,y)\left(\frac{\partial u}{\partial x}(x,y) + \frac{\partial u}{\partial y}(x,y)\right) = f(x,y),$$

for $x, y \in (-2, 2)$, where f and the boundary conditions are given by the true solution $u(x,y) = xy\mathrm{e}^{-10(x^2+y^2)}$. As discussed earlier, the induced nonlinear system of collocation equations is iteratively solved in the least squares sense.

We again consider (Table 2) the maximal approximation error (evaluated at the nodes Δ) $|u - u_{0,k,N}|$ for $k = 2$ and $k = 3$, respectively, and various N. The error appears consistent with the estimates $O(h^2)$ and $O(h^4)$ (for $k = 2$ and $k = 3$, respectively); for values $m > 0$ the error dependence on h remains unclear.

Table 2. Example 2: step-size h and ℓ_∞-norm of approximation error: ϵ_2 (for cubic splines, $k = 2$) and ϵ_3 (for quintic splines, $k = 3$), for various values of N

N	30	40	50	60	70	80
h	1.333e-01	1.000e-01	8.000e-02	6.667e-02	5.714e-02	5.000e-02
ϵ_2	1.114e-03	7.931e-04	4.949e-04	3.597e-04	2.641e-04	2.037e-04
ϵ_3	5.307e-05	1.283e-05	5.783e-06	2.492e-06	1.381e-06	7.948e-07

5   Conclusions and Outlook

In this contribution we investigated a modified version of the higher degree multivariate fuzzy transform, when the fuzzy partition is constructed via B-splines. Eliminating the artificial global constraints implicitly imposed in an earlier proposal [9] permits a wider range of extrapolation techniques and facilitates problem-specific explicit constructions. In particular, the ability to deal with missing data permits recovering the improved approximation properties in scenarios when (in case of the discrete transform) the discrete input data do not conform to the restrictive requirements of the usual B-spline based F^m-transform.

Based on the locally modified F^m-transform, we considered a fuzzy transform-based collocation technique for solving numerically PDEs. While the theoretical properties of the proposed method are yet to be investigated, the numerical results suggest a potential for such applications of fuzzy transforms with sufficiently smooth basic functions.

Besides developing theoretical analysis for the suggested fuzzy transform-based numerical methods and possibly extensions to non-rectangular domains, our future work will include developing an open-source Python package implementing the various variants of B-spline based fuzzy partitions and the fuzzy transforms based on them.

Disclosure of Interests. The authors have no competing interests to declare that are relevant to the content of this article.

References

1. Demanet, L., Townsend, A.: Stable extrapolation of analytic functions. arXiv preprint (2016). arXiv:1605.09601
2. Harris, C.R., et al.: Array programming with NumPy. Nature **585**(7825), 357–362 (2020). https://doi.org/10.1038/s41586-020-2649-2
3. Holčapek, M., Tichý, T.: Discrete multivariate F-transform of higher degree. In: IEEE International Conference on Fuzzy Systems, FUZZ-IEEE 2015, Istanbul, Turkey, 2–5 August 2015. IEEE (2015)
4. Jha, N., Perfilieva, I., Kritika: A high-resolution fuzzy transform combined compact scheme for 2D nonlinear elliptic partial differential equations. MethodsX **10**, 102206 (2023)
5. Kokainis, M., Asmuss, S.: Approximation properties of higher degree F-transforms based on B-splines. In: IEEE International Conference on Fuzzy Systems, FUZZ-IEEE 2015, Istanbul, Turkey, 2–5 August 2015. IEEE (2015)
6. Kokainis, M., Asmuss, S.: Approximation by multivariate higher degree F-transform based on B-splines. Soft. Comput. **21**(13), 3587–3614 (2017)
7. Kokainis, M., Asmuss, S.: Collocation method for linear BVPs via B-spline based fuzzy transform. In: Medina, J., Ojeda-Aciego, M., Verdegay, J.L., Pelta, D.A., Cabrera, I.P., Bouchon-Meunier, B., Yager, R.R. (eds.) Information Processing and Management of Uncertainty in Knowledge-Based Systems. Theory and Foundations, pp. 187–198. Springer, Cham (2018)
8. Kokainis, M., Asmuss, S.: Modified F-transform based on B-splines. In: Information Processing and Management of Uncertainty in Knowledge-Based Systems. Theory and Foundations. 17th International Conference, IPMU 2018, Cádiz, Spain, 11–15 June 2018, pp. 175–186. Springer, Cham (2018)
9. Kokainis, M., Asmuss, S.: Modified multivariate F-transform based on B-splines. In: Proceedings of the 11th Conference of the European Society for Fuzzy Logic and Technology (EUSFLAT 2019), pp. 740–747. Atlantis Press (2019). https://doi.org/10.2991/eusflat-19.2019.101
10. Perfilieva, I.: Fuzzy transforms: theory and applications. Fuzzy Sets Syst. **157**(8), 993–1023 (2006)
11. Perfilieva, I.: F-transform. In: Kacprzyk, J., Pedrycz, W. (eds.) Springer Handbook of Computational Intelligence, pp. 113–130. Springer, Heidelberg (2015)
12. Perfilieva, I., Daňková, M., Bede, B.: Towards a higher degree F-transform. Fuzzy Sets Syst. **180**(1), 3–19 (2011)
13. Perfilieva, I., Haldeeva, E.: Fuzzy transformation and its applications. In: Proceedings of the 4th Czech-Japan Seminar on Data Analysis and Decision Making under Uncertainty, Czech Republic, pp. 116–124 (2001)
14. Perfilieva, I., Hodáková, P.: F^1-transform of functions of two variables. In: Montero, J., Pasi, G., Ciucci, D. (eds.) Proceedings of EUSFLAT 2013, Milan, Italy, Advances in Intelligent Systems Research, vol. 32, pp. 547–553. Atlantis Press (2013)
15. Schoenberg, I.J.: Cardinal Spline Interpolation, CBMS, vol. 12. SIAM (1973)
16. Štěpnička, M., Valášek, R.: Numerical solution of partial differential equations with help of fuzzy transform. In: Proceedings of the 14th IEEE International Conference on Fuzzy Systems, pp. 1104–1109 (2005)
17. Štěpnička, M., Valašek, R.: Fuzzy transforms for functions with two variables. In: Proceedings of the 6th Czech-Japan Seminar on Data Analysis and Decision Making under Uncertainity, pp. 100–107 (2003)

Generalized Quantifiers, Logical Syllogisms and Applications

Using Intermediate Quantifiers to Reduce the Number of Linguistic Rules for Diagnosing Mood Disorders from Incomplete Data

Lucas Dantas de Oliveira and Peter Sussner(✉)

Universidade de Campinas, Campinas, SP 08544, Brazil
1201848@dac.unicamp.br, sussner@unicamp.br

Abstract. This paper aims to establish a method for detecting major depressive episodes experienced by people with bipolar or major depressive disorder. The method only considers motor activity and total sleep time per day. Both symptoms were measured using actigraphy. Motor activity and total sleep time are usually evaluated subjectively according to the patient's statements or a professional's perception. However, it is better to use a linguistic description of the patient's situation based on objective measurements. As a test bed, we used a public domain database concerning actigraphy data of merely 55 participants that either have or do not have one of the two aforementioned mood disorders.

We resorted to fuzzy natural logic (FNL) since this theory takes linguistic expressions and human reasoning into account and seeks logical conclusions that are applicable to complicated and real situations, thus being a resource that helps to develop diagnostic reasoning and not replace it.

Initially, we created implicative rules based on already established knowledge about mood disorders and designed fuzzy sets that describe the total sleep time and motor activity of each participant in terms of evaluative linguistic expressions (ELE). Using intermediate quantifiers, we were able to reduce the number of linguistic rules from fifteen to three.

Keywords: Fuzzy natural logic · mood disorder · medical diagnostic support · actigraphy · motor activity · sleep time

1 Introduction

Psychiatric diagnosis is largely based on interviewing the patient [16]. The vagueness in language used to identify a symptom increases as the subjectivity of its description increases, which in turn results in greater uncertainty surrounding the diagnosis. Especially in the public sector and some private medical insurance plans, the main difficulties faced by mental health professionals are the excessive

© The Author(s), under exclusive license to Springer Nature Switzerland AG 2025
M. Baczyński et al. (Eds.): EUSFLAT 2025, LNCS 15883, pp. 141–152, 2025.
https://doi.org/10.1007/978-3-031-97225-6_12

workload and the lack of time required to conduct consultations [16]. The latter is one of the main causes of erroneous diagnoses [1].

The main goal of our investigations is to develop a method that helps detect a major depressive episode, present in both major depressive disorder (MDD) and bipolar disorder (BD), and whose findings can be interpreted by professionals in psychiatry and psychology. This paper is meant to be a first step toward achieving this goal.

Two symptoms of a major depressive episode are an abnormal psychomotor activity and amount of sleep that are most often detected using the perceptions and subjective accounts of the patient him/herself, people close to the patient, or a health professional [2]. A more objective way of estimating a person's motor activity and total sleep time over a number of days is a non-invasive test known as actigraphy. In this paper, we used a small publicly available database called Depresjon database that comprises actigraphy data stemming from 55 participants, 23 of whom have one of the two aforementioned mood disorders [6]. To the best of our knowledge, there is a *lack of large publicly available databases consisting of actigraphy signals.*

The methods described in this paper are based on FNL. Since this theory takes linguistic expressions [14] and human reasoning into account and seeks logical conclusions that are applicable to complicated and real situations, we believe that FNL can serve as a valuable aid in diagnostic reasoning without replacing it. Specifically, we took advantage of the facts that FNL permits formulating linguistic rules that involve intermediate quantifiers and drawing linguistic conclusions by means of "Perception-Based Logical Deduction" (PbDL) [13].

The paper is organized as follows: Sect. 2 reviews some basic concepts of FNL. Section 3 describes two approaches toward computer-aided diagnosis of mood disorders and presents some experimental results. We finish with some concluding remarks in Sect. 4.

2   Basic Concepts of Fuzzy Natural Logic

Two of the features that characterize imprecision are the presence of borderline cases and ill-defined borders. Since psychiatry is unable to firmly define the borders of mental disorders [17], we may conclude that the imprecision in this field is an interesting topic for investigation. Furthermore, much of this imprecision stems from the vagueness of language, as diagnoses are primarily based on the interviews with patients [16]. While a fuzzy set is a quantitative model of imprecision that aims to generalize the classical set model [21], fuzzy logic provides a framework for logical reasoning with vagueness. FNL is a field of study that seeks to model ELEs of *natural language* mathematically, regardless of the language, using semantic concepts together with the structure of fuzzy logic [15].

Recall that the Łukasiewicz logic is one of the most important mathematical fuzzy logics [4]. Every continuous t-norm can be approximated by a combination of the minimum, product, and Łukasiewicz t-norms by means of an ordinal sum [10]. The Łukasiewicz t-norm is the only one of the three having a continous residual implication. In this paper, we use the symbols $\otimes$, $\oplus$, $\rightarrow$, and $\leftrightarrow$ to denote the *Łukasiewicz* t-norm, t-conorm, implication, and bi-implication, respectively. Moreover, given a fuzzy set A on a universe U, let us use the symbol $A(u)$ to refer to the membership degree of u in A. The class of all fuzzy sets on U is denoted $\mathcal{F}(U)$. The complement of $A \in \mathcal{F}(U)$ is given by $A^c(u) = 1 - A(u)$. Note that a crisp set $B \subseteq U$ can be viewed as an element of $\mathcal{F}(U)$. For $A, B \in \mathcal{F}(U)$, one writes $A \subseteq B$ if and only if $A(u) \leq B(u)$ for every $u \in U$.

The theory of FNL makes use of the notion of a linguistic variable, originally defined as a quintuple [22]. In this paper, we employ the following definition:

Definition 1. *[15] A* linguistic variable *is a* sextuplet $(X, T(X), U, G, W, M)$, *such that*

- *X is the name of the variable,*
- *$T(X)$ is the set of linguistic expressions that describes this variable,*
- *U is the universal set,*
- *G is the syntactic rule by which linguistic expressions are formed,*
- *W is the set of all possible contexts,*
- *M is the semantic rule in which each linguistic expression is assigned its meanings.*

An object can be described in terms of linguistic expressions. If the information provided by a linguistic expression can be evaluated and classified on an ordered scale, then the expression is called an *Evaluative Linguistic Expression* (ELE) [14]. To model a linguistic expression as a fuzzy set, the concepts of extension and intension will be used. While the *extension* is a fuzzy set that encompasses all objects that an expression can describe, the *intension* relates an expression in all possible contexts to all fuzzy subsets of the universal set. Our focus is on ELEs, given by a *linguistic hedge* [23] followed by a *TE-adjective*[1].

TE-adjectives are evaluative and gradual adjectives that participate in a *fundamental evaluative trichotomy* consisting of a pair of non-complementary antonyms and an adjective that lies between them on the scale of the universe in which the discourse is inserted [14]. The adjectives "Small", "Medium" and "Big" are called *canonical TE-adjectives* and they form the basic evaluative trichotomy. The TE-adjective (from a fundamental evaluative trichotomy) on the left of linearly ordered scale will be associated with the TE-adjective "small". Likewise, the one in the middle and the one on the right of the linearly ordered scale will be associated with the TE-adjectives "middle" and "big", respectively.

Lakoff defined hedges as "words whose job is to make things fuzzier or less fuzzy" [9]. In this paper, we only consider *linguistic hedges, aka linguistic modifiers* [7], for ELEs given by intensifying adverbs such as "very" and "somewhat" that have the effect of narrowing or widening the meaning of a TE-adjective, that is, decreasing or increasing the extension of the expression, respectively [14]. The grammatical structure of a pure ELE is of the following form:

$$\mathcal{A} = \text{<linguistic hedge><TE-adjective>}.$$

---

[1] "TE-adjective" is an abbreviation of "trichotomous evaluative adjective".

Alternatively, a pure evaluative linguistic predication (ELP) is of the form "X is $\mathcal{A}$". Throughout this text, any mention of ELEs or ELPs refers exclusively to pure ELEs or ELPs, respectively. Furthermore, the set of all ELEs and all ELPs is denoted by $EvExpr$.

Definition 2. *[15] Let v_L, v_S and $v_R \in \mathbb{R}$ be distinct numerical points with appropriate units of measurement of the universal set (associated with a pure ELE) such that $v_L < v_S < v_R$. Here, v_L is the least value that makes sense in the context under consideration, v_R is the greatest value that makes sense in this context, and v_S is a value in between, which is usually the most common value. A* linguistic context *is a strictly increasing bijection*

$$w : [0, 1] \to [v_L, v_S] \cup [v_S, v_R] = [v_L, v_R],$$

where $w(0) = v_L, w(0.5) = v_S$ and $w(1) = v_R$. A context is denoted using the symbol $w = <v_L, v_S, v_R>$.

Although w is a function, the notation $u \in w$ will be used to indicate that $u \in U$ in the context of w.

Definition 3. *[15] Let W be a set of contexts and U be a universal set. The* intension *of $\mathcal{A} \in EvExpr$ (and "X is $\mathcal{A}$" $\in EvExpr$) is a function*

$$Int(\mathcal{A}) : W \to \mathcal{F}(U) \tag{1}$$

which assigns to each context $w \in W$ a fuzzy set contained in U. This fuzzy set is called the extension *of the expression $\mathcal{A}$ (and "X is $\mathcal{A}$") in a context $w \in W$:*

$$Ext_w(\mathcal{A}) = Int(\mathcal{A})(w) \in \mathcal{F}(U). \tag{2}$$

One way to order the pure ELEs (and ELPs) of a fundamental evaluative trichotomy is to first compare the TE-adjectives and then the linguistic hedges (lexicographical order) [15]. The canonical TE-adjectives are ordered as follows:

$$\text{small} \ll \text{medium} \ll \text{big}$$

If hedge$_1$ has a greater narrowing effect than hedge$_2$, then the linguistic hedges are ordered as follows:

$$\text{hedge}_1 \ll \text{hedge}_2$$

Definition 4 presents the concept of a horizon, which will be used to model TE-Adjectives.

Definition 4. *[15] Given a context $w = <v_L, v_S, v_R>$, the* left *and the* right horizons *are the fuzzy sets associated with the adjective "small" and "big", respectively. Their membership functions are $LH, RH : w \to [0, 1]$ given by*

$$LH(x) = \left(\frac{v_S - x}{v_S - v_L} \right)^*, \quad RH(x) = \left(\frac{x - v_S}{v_R - v_S} \right)^*, \tag{3}$$

where $x \in w$ and $f^*(x) = min\{1, max\{f(x), 0\}\}$. Furthermore, the middle *hori-*
zon $MH : w \to [0,1]$ is defined as the fuzzy set that is neither small nor big and whose membership function is given by

$$MH(x) = [1 - LH(x)] \otimes [1 - RH(x)]. \tag{4}$$

A *shift and/or deformation of the horizon caused by a linguistic hedge* can be effected using a certain type of parametrized function $\nu_{a,b,c} : [0,1] \to [0,1]$, where $0 < a < b < c < 1$. We used the same type of parameterized function as well as the same triples (a, b, c) to model the empty hedge, "somewhat"[2], and "very" as Novak et al. (cf. Equation 5.17 and Table 5.1 of [15]).

Let $\mathcal{A} = <$ linguistic hedge $><$ TE-adjective $> \in EvExpr$. In context $w = <\upsilon_L, \upsilon_S, \upsilon_R >$, the extension of $\mathcal{A}$ is the function $\nu_{a,b,c}$ associated with a linguistic hedge, applied to the horizon of the respective TE-adjective, at a certain point in the context. Considering the canonical TE-adjectives, the extension of $\mathcal{A}$ in w is of the form

$$Ext_w(< \text{linguistic hedge} > \text{small})(x) = \nu_{a,b,c}(LH(x)), \tag{5}$$

$$Ext_w(< \text{linguistic hedge} > \text{medium})(x) = \nu_{a,b,c}(MH(x)), \tag{6}$$

$$Ext_w(< \text{linguistic hedge} > \text{big})(x) = \nu_{a,b,c}(RH(x)), \tag{7}$$

$$\forall x \in w.$$

An If-Then rule $\mathcal{R}$ is a conditional proposition formed by n ELPs in the antecedent and another ELP in the consequent. In the case of this paper, the only logical connective used is 'and'. The rules, their intension and extension are

$$\mathcal{R} : \text{If } X_1 \text{ is } \mathcal{A}^1 \text{ and } X_2 \text{ is } \mathcal{A}^2 \text{ and } ... \text{ and } X_n \text{ is } \mathcal{A}^n, \text{ then Y is } \mathcal{B}. \tag{8}$$

$$Int(\mathcal{R}) := \underbrace{W \times ... \times W}_{n+1} \to \underbrace{\mathcal{F}(\mathbb{R}) \times ... \times \mathcal{F}(\mathbb{R})}_{n+1}. \tag{9}$$

$$Ext_{<w_1,..,w_n,w'>}(\mathcal{R})(x_1, ..., x_n, y) = \left[\bigotimes_{i=1}^{n} Ext_{w_i}(\mathcal{A}^i)(x_i) \right] \to Ext_{w'}(\mathcal{B})(y). \tag{10}$$

A *linguistic description* of an object or situation is the set of rules $LD = \{\mathcal{R}_1, ..., \mathcal{R}_m\}$, such that

$$\mathcal{R}_i : \text{If } X_1 \text{ is } \mathcal{A}_i^1 \text{ and } X_2 \text{ is } \mathcal{A}_i^2 \text{ and } ... \text{ and } X_n \text{ is } \mathcal{A}_i^n, \text{ then Y is } \mathcal{B}_i \tag{11}$$

for $i \in \{1, 2, ..., m\}$, where $m, n \in \mathbb{N}$.

Definition 5 introduces the Local Perception Function, which is used to choose a rule from a linguistic description to be fired. This function is applied to the set of ELPs in the antecedents of the rules of a linguistic description. While Definition 5 is used for rules with $n = 1$, Definition 6 is used for rules with $n \geq 1$.

---

[2] "Somewhat" corresponds to "roughly" in "Insight into Fuzzy Modeling" [15].

Definition 5. *[15] Let W be a set of contexts and $x \in \mathbb{R}$. Let $K \subset EvExpr$ be a finite set of ELPs such that $K, \ll)$ is a chain. Let P be the set*

$$P = \{ \text{"X is } \mathcal{B}\text{"} \in K | Ext_w(\text{"X is } \mathcal{B}\text{"})(x) > 0 \}$$

and $P' \subseteq P$ be such that "X is $\mathcal{B}$" $\in P'$ if and only if $Ext_w(\text{"X is } \mathcal{B}\text{"})(x)$ is maximal in P. Lastly, let[3]

$$P'' = \{ \text{"X is } \mathcal{B}\text{"} \in K \,|\, Ext_w(\text{"X is } \mathcal{B}\text{"})(x) \geq a_0 \},$$

Finally, the local perception function *$LPerc^K : \mathbb{R} \times W \to K$ satisfies*

$$LPerc^K(x, w) = \text{"X is } \mathcal{A}\text{"} = \begin{cases} \min P'', & \text{if } P'' \neq \emptyset \\ \min P', & \text{if } P'' = \emptyset \text{ and } P \neq \emptyset \\ \text{Undefined otherwise.} \end{cases} \quad (12)$$

Definition 6. *Let LD be a linguistic description. To compute the local perception function for an antecedents with n predications, one defines $LPerc^{LD}$: $\mathbb{R}^n \times W^n \to K_1 \times K_2 \times ... \times K_n$ as follows:*

$$LPerc^{LD}((x_1, ..., x_n), (w_1, ..., w_n)) = (LPerc^{K_1}(x_1, w_1), ..., LPerc^{K_n}(x_n, w_n)).$$

Classical logic is equipped with the universal ($\forall$) and the existential ($\exists$) quantifier. In natural language there are quantifiers that generate imprecision. Such quantifiers are called fuzzy quantifiers [24]. Fuzzy quantifiers are classified as absolute or relative. While the former convey complete meaning, the latter require an implicit comparison between sets [24]. In this text, we will focus exclusively on relative fuzzy quantifiers, aka *intermediate quantifiers* [12], since they stand for quantities that lie between "none" ($\nexists$) and "all" ($\forall$).

Let U be a finite universe, $A \subseteq B \subseteq U$, and $F_R : \mathcal{P}(U) \setminus \{\emptyset\} \times \mathcal{F}(U) \to [0,1]$ be as follows:

$$F_R(B, A) = \frac{1}{|B|} \sum_{u \in B} 1 \leftrightarrow A(u). \quad (13)$$

Note that $F_R(B, A)$ represents a degree of subsethood of A in B, which can be used to calculate the extension of a sentence of the form "$\mathcal{Q}B$ is A", where B is a crisp set, $A \subseteq B$ and $\mathcal{Q}$ is an intermediate quantifier.

The symbols $Q^{\forall}_{ExBi}(B, A)$ and $Q^{\forall}_{VeBi}(B, A)$ denote respectively the truth degrees of propositions of the type "Almost all B are A" and "Most B are A" that are determined by the following expressions [12]:

$$Q^{\forall}_{ExBi}(B, A) \equiv Ext_w(\text{"Extremely Big"})(F_R(B, A)), \quad (14)$$
$$Q^{\forall}_{VeBi}(B, A) \equiv Ext_w(\text{"Very Big"})(F_R(B, A)), \quad (15)$$

where $w = < 0, 0.5, 1 >$. In this paper, the parameters $a, b,$ and c of "Extremely" and "Very" were taken from [11].

---

[3] In this paper, we used the same parameter $a_0 = 0.9$ as Novák et al. in [15].

3   Two Approaches Toward Computer-Aided Diagnosis of Mood Disorders

3.1   Description of the Database and Experimental Setup

The Depresjon dataset [6] comprises 55 signals obtained using actigraphy that correspond to 55 participants, with 32 belonging to the control group and 23 to the condition group. The condition group includes 15, 1, and 7 participants with major depressive disorder (MDD), bipolar I disorder (BD I), and bipolar II disorder (BD II), respectively, previously diagnosed as such by psychiatrists. The datum of each participant consists of a vector in which each entry refers to the motor activity per minute. Entries are measured in counts. Each research participant used the device for a different number of days.

To calculate the total motor activity (TMA) of a day, we first determined the 240-minute interval with the highest number of activity counts per day. Then this interval was discarded. The TMA of a day is the sum of activity (in counts) of the remaining minutes of the day. The total sleep time (TST) was determined by implementing the sleep scoring algorithm according to the Actiwatch manual [3]. The algorithm identifies when the individual is asleep and when (s)he is awake. The TST is the number of minutes that the person was considered to be asleep in a day.

The chosen context for TST was $w_Y =< 225, 340, 510 >$ (in minutes) and for TMA was $w_X =< 130, 190, 280 >$ (in kilocounts). The sets of ELEs that describe each variable were the following:

1. For the linguistic variable X that stands for TMA, we used

$$K_X = \{\text{"low"}, \text{"medium"}, \text{"high"}\};$$

2. For the linguistic variable Y that stands for TST, we used

$$K_Y = \{\text{"low"}, \text{"somewhat low"}, \text{"medium"}, \text{"high"}, \text{"somewhat high"}\};$$

3. For the linguistic variable Z that stands for state of health, we used

$$K_Z = \{\text{"very well"}, \text{"well"}, \text{"borderline"}, \text{"very unwell"}, \text{"unwell"}\}.$$

Figures 1 and 2 show the extensions of the ELEs of K_X and K_Y, respectively. We used the first 7200 entries for each participant, as all participants wore the device for at least five days, creating five 1440-dimensional vectors to analyze each participant's day. To avoid discrepant values, we discarded the days with the highest and lowest TST (and TMA) values, retaining the TST (and TMA) scores from the remaining three days. The arithmetic average of these three days was calculated and used to determine the best expression for TST (and TMA) based on the local perception function.

The decision to evaluate an individual's state of health comes from the understanding that a mood disorder cannot be reliably diagnosed based only on two out of the nine criteria for a major depressive episode [2]. For this reason, we refer to the work of Sadegh-Zadeh, who conceptualized the idea of illness using a fuzzy-theoretic approach with linguistic terms [18].

3.2   Method 1

Several articles [5, 19] and the Fifth Edition of the Diagnostic and Statistical Manual of Mental Disorders (DSM-5-TR) [2] indicate that TST is often greater or less in patients with MDD or BD than in healthy individuals. Generally, in depressive episodes or euthymic periods of patients with MDD or BD, TMA is significantly lower when compared to healthy individuals. Furthermore, considering the total life span of a person with BD, a depressive episode or an euthymic period will be present for longer.

In Method 1, we created fifteen implicative rules and designed fuzzy sets that describe the TST and TMA of each participant in terms of ELEs [14, 15]. Taking only TMA and TST into account, we formulated the following linguistic rules to determine the state of health of a person:

$$\mathcal{R}_i = \text{"If } X \text{ is } \mathcal{A} \text{ and } Y \text{ is } \mathcal{B}, \text{ then } Z \text{ is } \mathcal{C}\text{"},$$

where $\mathcal{A} \in K_X$, $\mathcal{B} \in K_Y$, and $\mathcal{C} \in K_Z$ are given by Table 1.

Table 1. Implicative Rules.

$\mathcal{A}$	L	L	L	L	M	M	M	M	M	H	H	H	H	H
$\mathcal{B}$	L	SL	M	SH	H	L	SL	M	SH	H	L	SL	M	SH	H
$\mathcal{C}$	VU	VU	U	VU	VU	U	BC	BC	U	VU	W	VW	VW	W	BC

Abbreviations: L = low, SL = somewhat low, M = medium, SH = somewhat high, H = high, VU = very unwell, U = unwell, BC = borderline case, VW = very well, W = well.

Therefore, $Ext_{<w_X, w_Y, w_Z>}(\mathcal{R})(x, y, z) = (Ext_{w_X}(\mathcal{A})(x) \otimes Ext_{w_Y}(\mathcal{B})(y)) \rightarrow Ext_{w_Z}(\mathcal{C})(z)$ which implies that $Ext_{w_Z}(\mathcal{C})(z) = Ext_{w_X}(\mathcal{A})(x) \otimes Ext_{w_Y}(\mathcal{B})(y)$.

3.3   Method 2

In order to reduce the number of rules, we resorted to the theory of intermediate quantifiers [12] and generated three implicative rules, based on the DSM-5-TR [2], that evaluate if the patient is unwell or very unwell over a time frame of 5–14 days, depending on data availability. When formulating these rules, we took the following fact into account: The evaluation of TMA by means of an actigraph is more reliable than the one of TST.

- $\mathcal{R}_1$: If motor activity is **not high almost every day** AND total sleep time is **high or very low most days**, then the participant is **very unwell**.
- $\mathcal{R}_2$: If motor activity is **low most days**, then the participant is **very unwell**.
- $\mathcal{R}_3$: If motor activity is **not high almost every day** OR total sleep time is **high or very low most days**, then the participant is **unwell**.

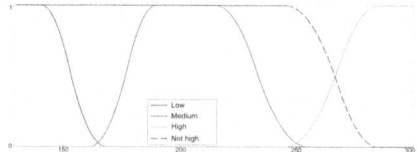

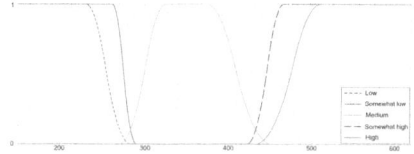

Fig. 1. Extensions of the elements of K_X and "not high" in the context w_X.

Fig. 2. Extensions of the elements of K_Y in the context w_Y.

Let $A_{\neg High}^X(\mathbf{x})$, $A_{Low}^X(\mathbf{x})$, $A_{Low}^Y(\mathbf{y})$, and $A_{SoHigh}^Y(\mathbf{y})$ be given as follows:

- $A_{Low}^X(\mathbf{x})(i) = Ext_{w_X}(\text{"TMA is low"})(x_i)$;
- $A_{\neg High}^X(\mathbf{x})(i) = Ext_{w_X}(\text{"TMA is not high"})(x_i)$;
- $A_{Low}^Y(\mathbf{y})(i) = Ext_{w_Y}(\text{"TST is low"})(y_i)$;
- $A_{SoHigh}^Y(\mathbf{y})(i) = Ext_{w_Y}(\text{"TST is somewhat high"})(y_i)$.

Where $\mathbf{x} = (x_1, x_2, .., x_n)$, $\mathbf{y} = (y_1, y_2, .., y_n)$, x_i is the TMA value on the i-th day, y_i is the TST value on the i-th day and n is the number of days under consideration. Moreover, let $B^X = B^Y = \{1, \ldots, n\}$ be crisp sets with n elements.

The extension of the first rule $Ext_{<w_X,w_Y,w_Z>}(\mathcal{R}_1)(\mathbf{x}, \mathbf{y}, \mathbf{z})$ equals

$$(Q_{ExBi}^\forall \mathbf{x})(B^X, A_{\neg High}^X) \otimes (Q_{VeBi}^\forall \mathbf{y})(B_Y, A_{Low}^Y \oplus A_{SoHigh}^Y)]$$

$$\rightarrow Ext_{w_Z}(\text{"Z is very unwell"})(\mathbf{z}).$$

Therefore, the truth degree for the a person being very unwell, for $\mathbf{x}^*$ and $\mathbf{y}^*$ given, is $Ext_{w_Z}(\text{"Z is very unwell"})(\mathbf{z}^*)$ which equals[4]

$$(Q_{ExBi}^\forall \mathbf{x})(B^X, A_{\neg High}^X) \otimes (Q_{VeBi}^\forall \mathbf{y})(B_Y, A_{Low}^Y \oplus A_{SoHigh}^Y).$$

In this method, we first fire the three rules, and then we choose the expression that best describes the person's state of health, as follows:

1. If $Ext_{w_Z}(\text{"Z is very unwell"})(\mathbf{z}^*) > 0.25$ from the first rule or second rule, we say that the person is very unwell.
2. if $Ext_{w_Z}(\text{"Z is unwell"})(\mathbf{z}^*) > 0.25$ from third rule, we say that the person is unwell.
3. If the person is not very unwell nor unwell, we say that the state of health is undefined.

Given that Method 2 involves more sophisticated rules, it was challenging to determine linguistic expressions that cover all possible situations. Therefore, we decided to formulate of the rules solely based on the symptom descriptions provided in the DSM-5-TR [2]. As a result, Method 2 only classifies participants that are considered 'unwell' or 'very unwell'.

---

[4] For $\mathbf{x}$ and $\mathbf{y}$ given, that is the minimum value of $Ext_{w_Z}(\text{"Z is very unwell"})$ that makes $Ext_{<w_X,w_Y,w_Z>}(\mathcal{R}_1)(\mathbf{x}, \mathbf{y}, \mathbf{z}) = 1$.

4   Experimental Results

Tables 2 and 3 show the linguistic labels obtained using Methods 1 and 2, respectively. On the one hand, the fact that the Method 1 associated a higher percentage of condition group participants with the linguistic labels "unwell" or "very unwell" reveals an advantage compared to Method 2. On the other hand, Method 2 outperformed the Method 1 by associating a smaller percentage of control group participants with the ELEs "unwell" or "very unwell". Note that the percentages in each line of Tables 2 and 3 do not add up to 100% because anyone classified as "very unwell" or "very well" is also considered "unwell" or "well", respectively. Note that all elements of K_Z, K_X, and K_Y are ELEs that differ from fuzzy categories [14], commonly used in fuzzy inference systems.

Table 2. Classification of participants' state of health according to Method 1 that employs the rules in Table 1.

Group	Very Unwell	Unwell	Borderline	Well	Very Well
Condition	56.52%	69.56%	26.08%	4.34%	4.34%
Control	6.25%	18.75%	15.62%	65.63%	56.25%

Table 3. Classification of participants' state of health according to Method 2 that is based on merely three linguistic rules that involve intermediate quantifiers.

Group	Very Unwell	Unwell	Undefined
Condition	26.08%	60.87%	39.13%
Control	3.12%	12.5%	87.5%

To summarize, using intermediate quantifiers, only three implicative rules that depend on two of the nine symptoms of a major depressive episode were sufficient to classify more than 60% of the condition group as unwell. At the same time, 87.5% of the control group were not associated with the ELE "unwell". In light of the fact that we generated merely three rules, taking only two out of the nine symptoms of a major depressive episode into account, our results can be considered satisfactory and our methodology is highly interpretable compared to Kumar et al.'s previous investigations using the same dataset [8].

Specifically, Kumar et al. applied a hybrid approach that combines convolutional neural networks with an adaptive neuro-fuzzy inference system to the same dataset for binary classification, achieving an accuracy of 85.1%. To this end, these authors increased the number of instances to train their model by partitioning each participant's actigraphy data into 48-hour periods of time. Possibly, data from the same person was used for both training and testing which may lead to biased results due to the ongoing nature of the symptoms of BD and MDD.

5   Concluding Remarks

In this paper, we investigated how techniques of FNL can be applied as an assistance for diagnosing mood disorders. To this end, we used linguistic rules involving intermediate quantifiers and PbDL in order to formulate linguistic rules and arrived at conclusions that a health care professional is able to understand. This said, our investigations were conducted using a very small database and the results are preliminary.

Additional research is needed to present a fair comparison of our FNL-based methodology with one that is based on fuzzy linguistic summaries [20]. We also envision further improvements, e.g., by using a larger and more expressive database that allows for extracting more than two symptoms and by optimizing the parameters.

Acknowledgements. This research was partially supported by FAPESP and CNPq under grants nos. 2020/09838-0 (Brazilian Institute of Data Science) and 165441/2021-6, respectively, as well as CAPES.

Disclosure of Interests. The authors have no competing interests to declare that are relevant to the content of this article.

References

1. Ahmadi, H., et al.: Diseases diagnosis using fuzzy logic methods: a systematic and meta-analysis review. Comput. Methods Programs Biomed. **161**, 145–172 (2018). https://doi.org/10.1016/j.cmpb.2018.04.013
2. American Psychiatric Association: Diagnostic and Statistical Manual of Mental Disorders, 5th edn. Text Revision. American Psychiatric Publishing, Washington, DC (2022)
3. CamNtech. The Actiwatch User Manual. Cambridge (2008)
4. Cintula, P., Hájek, P. and Noguera, C.: Handbook of Mathematical Fuzzy Logic, vols. 1–3. College Publications, London (2011)
5. De Crescenzo, F., et al.: Actigraphic features of bipolar disorder: a systematic review and meta-analysis. Sleep Med. Rev. **33**, 58–69 (2017). https://doi.org/10.1016/j.smrv.2016.05.003
6. Garcia-Ceja, E., et al.: Depresjon: a motor activity database of depression episodes in unipolar and bipolar patients. In: Proceedings of 9th ACM Multimedia Systems Conference, Amsterdam, Netherlands (MMSys 2018) (2018). https://doi.org/10.1145/3204949.3208125
7. Kerre, E.E., De Cock, M.: Linguistic modifiers: an overview. In: Chen, G., Ying, M., Cai, K.Y. (eds.) Fuzzy Logic and Soft Computing. The International Series on Asian Studies in Computer and Information Science, vol. 6. Springer (1999). https://doi.org/10.1007/978-1-4615-5261-1_5
8. Kumar, A., Sangwan, S., Arora, A., Menon, V.: Depress-DCNF: a deep convolutional neuro-fuzzy model for detection of depression episodes using IoMT. Appl. Soft Comput. **122**(5) (2022). https://doi.org/10.1016/j.asoc.2022.108863
9. Lakoff, G.: Hedges: a study in meaning criteria and the logic of fuzzy concepts. J. Philos. Log. **2**, 458–508 (1973). https://doi.org/10.1007/BF00262952

10. Mostert, P., Shields, A.: On the structure of semigroups on a compact manifold with boundary. Ann. Math. **65**(1), 117–143 (1957). https://doi.org/10.2307/1969668
11. Murinová, P., Novák, V.: Analysis of the intermediate quantifier "many" in fuzzy natural logic. In: Proceedings of the 2015 Conference of the International Fuzzy Systems Association and the European Society for Fuzzy Logic and Technology, Gijón, Spain (2015). https://doi.org/10.2991/ifsa-eusflat-15.2015.162
12. Novák, V.: A formal theory of intermediate quantifiers. Fuzzy Sets Syst. **159**(10), 1229–1246 (2008). https://doi.org/10.1016/j.fss.2007.12.008
13. Novák, V.: Perception-based logical deduction as alternative approximate reasoning method. In: The 14th IEEE International Conference on Fuzzy Systems, FUZZ 2005, Reno, NV, USA, pp. 1032–1037 (2005). https://doi.org/10.1109/FUZZY.2005.1452536
14. Novák, V.: Evaluative linguistic expressions vs. fuzzy categories. Fuzzy Sets Syst. **28**, 73–87 (2015). https://doi.org/10.1016/j.fss.2015.08.022
15. Novák, V., Perfilieva, I., Dvořák, A.: Fuzzy natural logic and approximate reasoning. In: Insight into Fuzzy Modeling (2016). https://doi.org/10.1002/9781119193210.ch5
16. Oda, A., Dalgalarrondo, P., Banzato, C.: Introdução à Avaliação Psiquiátrica [Introduction to Psychiatric Assessment]. Artmed, Porto Alegre (2022)
17. Pierre, J.M., Frances, A.: Language in psychiatry: a bedevilling dictionary. BJPsych Adv. **22**(5), 313–315 (2016). https://doi.org/10.1192/apt.bp.116.016238
18. Sadegh-Zadeh, K.: Fuzzy health, illness, and disease. J. Med. Philos. **25**(5), 605–638 (2000). https://doi.org/10.1076/0360-5310
19. Wüthrich, F., et al.: Actigraphically measured psychomotor slowing in depression: systematic review and meta-analysis. Psychol. Med. **52**(7), 1208–1221 (2022). https://doi.org/10.1017/S0033291722000903
20. Yager, R.: A new approach to the summarization of data. Inf. Sci. **28**(1), 69–86 (1982). https://doi.org/10.1016/0020-0255(82)90033-0
21. Zadeh, L.: Fuzzy sets. Inf. Control **8**(3), 338–353 (1965). https://doi.org/10.1016/S0019-9958(65)90241-X
22. Zadeh, L.: The concept of a linguistic variable and its application to approximate reasoning - I. Inf. Sci. **8**(3), 199–249 (1975). https://doi.org/10.1016/0020-0255(75)90036-5
23. Zadeh, L.: A fuzzy-set-theoretic interpretation of linguistic hedges. J. Cybern. **3**, 4–34 (1972). https://doi.org/10.1080/01969727208542910
24. Zadeh, L.: A computational approach to fuzzy quantifiers in natural languages. Comput. Math. Appl. **9**(1), 149–184 (1983). https://doi.org/10.1016/0898-1221(83)90013-5

Verification of Validity of Generalized Logical Syllogisms Applying the Contraposition

Karel Fiala$^{(\boxtimes)}$ and Petra Murinová

Institute for Research and Applications of Fuzzy Modeling NSC IT4Innovations,
University of Ostrava, 30. dubna 22, 701 03 Ostrava 1, Czech Republic
{karel.fiala,petra.murinova}@osu.cz

Abstract. This publication closely follows previous results concerning verifying the validity and invalidity of logical syllogisms with intermediate quantifiers that form selected logical structures of opposites. The goal of this publication is to use the property of contraposition to show that from selected valid forms of logical syllogisms related to graded Peterson's square, we are able to prove valid logical syllogisms related to graded Peterson's cube of opposition. By this procedure we are able to search for valid syllogisms systematically. We also use property of monotonicity of quantifiers to prove other valid syllogisms and order obtained syllogisms. Last but not least we discuss the relationship between valid logical syllogisms obtained by contraposition.

Keywords: Graded Peterson's cube of opposition · Contraposition · Generalized quantifiers · Logical syllogism with intermediate quantifiers

1 Introduction

In previous publications, we focused mainly on syntactic proof of logical syllogisms related to graded Peterson's square and cube of opposition, which are formed using generalized intermediate quantifiers (see [5,10,13]). In this publication, we turn attention to the property of contraposition, with the help of which we show that it is enough to formally prove selected forms of logical syllogisms and other related ones will also be valid.

In general, if we only consider Aristotle's syllogisms, we only work with classical quantifiers *All* and *Some*, we essentially have four different quantifiers, as both *All* and *Some* have affirmative and negative forms. From these four quantifiers, we can construct 256 possible forms of logical syllogisms, of which 24 are valid. If we add the quantifiers *Almost all*, *Most* and *Many* (each has affirmative and negative form) to the classical quantifiers, we obtain ten quantifiers. These quantifiers form graded Peterson's square of opposition [14] and it is possible to construct 4000 possible forms of syllogisms, of which 105 syllogisms are valid. Recall that formal proofs of these forms can be found in [12].

© The Author(s), under exclusive license to Springer Nature Switzerland AG 2025
M. Baczyński et al. (Eds.): EUSFLAT 2025, LNCS 15883, pp. 153–165, 2025.
https://doi.org/10.1007/978-3-031-97225-6_13

The goal of this publication is to focus on logical syllogisms that are constructed using twenty forms of intermediate quantifiers that form graded Peterson's cube of opposition from which it is possible to construct 32000 possible forms of logical syllogisms. The main question is which syllogisms are valid and invalid. If a syllogism is valid, we must find a formal proof; if it is invalid, we must provide a counterexample. Since there is a large number of syllogisms, it is difficult to do it for each syllogism. An example of syllogism that is related to graded Peterson's cube of opposition is as follows:

P_1 : *Most people who don't sport don't suffer from lung diseases.*
P_2 : *Most people who don't sport don't have hobby.*
C : *Some people who don't have hobby don't suffer lung diseases.*

The aim of this publication is to take advantage of knowledge of valid syllogisms with respect to quantifiers which form graded Peterson's square of opposition, logical operation contraposition and properties of quantifiers to find some valid syllogisms from quantifiers which form the graded Peterson's cube of the opposition, without the need to prove each valid syllogism individually.

The paper is structured as follows: In Sect. 1.1, we recall the motivation for using intermediate quantifiers and mention the related work. In Sect. 2, we briefly recall the Łukasiewicz fuzzy type theory, evaluative linguistic expressions, and the definition of intermediate quantifiers and syllogisms. In Sect. 3, we present verification of valid syllogisms using contraposition, and we also discuss the relationships between proven valid syllogisms. In Sect. 4, we summarize the results achieved, mention the limitations of the presented approach, and describe future work on this topic.

1.1   Motivation and Related Works

In previous publications, we focused on formal proof, semantic verification and interpretation of natural data using forms of generalized intermediate quantifiers (see [11]), which offers us the possibility to consider affirmative or negative intermediate quantifiers. Typical examples are "Most politicians have high self-esteem" or "Almost all politicians are not telling the truth". The possibility to consider all forms related to the cube of opposition offers to work also with expressions such as, e.g. "Several people who are not vaccinated against the flu later develop asthma". These new forms can be used especially for the interpretation of natural data and for using logical syllogisms to derive new conclusions in the areas of processing time series, linguistic summarization, etc.

Intermediate quantifiers, which are a subclass of generalized quantifiers were introduced by Thompson and Peterson in [19, 20]. Their mathematical definition was proposed by Novák in [17]. Fuzzy quantifiers and related fuzzy syllogisms were studied by several authors Zadeh [23], Holčapek a Dvořák [4], Dubois and Prade [3], Farina et al. [18].

Time series analysis was also explored by a group of authors in [6]. Additionally, publications are focusing on the linguistic summarization of data. For instance, in [9], the authors demonstrated the use of linguistic database summaries natural data (see [22]). These methods were later refined in [7] and implemented by Kacprzyk and Zadrozny [8]. Another approach to linguistic summarization for process data was introduced in [21].

2 Preliminaries

2.1 Łukasiewicz Fuzzy Type Theory

Łukasiewicz fuzzy type theory (Ł-FTT) [16] is a logic of higher order. The basic syntactic object of Ł-FTT are classical, namely concepts of *type* and *formula* (see [1]). Let us recall the following property:

Theorem 1 ([16]). *Let* $S, P \in Form_{o\alpha}$ *be formulas. Then the following formula is provable in Ł-FTT:*

$$\text{Ł-FTT} \vdash (\neg S \Rightarrow \neg P) \Rightarrow (P \Rightarrow S)$$

This property is called contraposition. Below we present a property that will be used in the main syntactic proofs later.

Theorem 2. *Let* $S, P \in Form_{o\alpha}$ *be formulas and* $x \in Form_{\alpha}$ *be variable. Then the following formulas are provable in Ł-FTT:*

$$\text{Ł-FTT} \vdash (\forall x)(Sx \Rightarrow Px) \Leftrightarrow (\forall x)(\neg Px \Rightarrow \neg Sx) \tag{2.1}$$

$$\text{Ł-FTT} \vdash (\forall x)(Sx \Rightarrow \neg Px) \Leftrightarrow (\forall x)(Px \Rightarrow \neg Sx) \tag{2.2}$$

Proof. From contraposition, rule of the generalization and double negation.

We will use these formulas (in particular (2.1)) in this paper to obtain new valid syllogisms. The proofs of these formulas are strongly based on contraposition and preserve its main idea. In what follows, we will refer to the these formulas as contraposition.

2.2 Evaluative Linguistic Expressions and Intermediate Quantifiers

Intermediate quantifiers are expressed through specific formulas within the formal framework of Ł-FTT of the theory of intermediate quantifiers (T^{IQ} for detail see [14]). These formulas represent quantification over a universe defined by a fuzzy set, with its size determined by a formally established measure [14]. The theory of evaluative linguistic expressions enables the use of particular natural language constructs to assess the magnitude of a given measure. To define intermediate quantifiers, we use the following evaluation expressions: *utmost big* (*Bi* $\mathbf{\Delta}$), *extremely big* (*Bi Ex*), *very big* (*Bi Ve*) and *not small* (¬ *Sm*).

Definition 1 ([14]). *Let $Ev \in Form_{oo}$ be an intension of some evaluative expression, $x \in Form_\alpha$ be variable and $A, B, z \in Form_{o\alpha}$ be formulas. Then either of the formulas*[1]

$$(Q_{Ev}^\forall x)(B, A) \equiv (\exists z)[(\forall x)((B|z)\, x \Rightarrow Ax) \wedge Ev((\mu B)(B|z))], \tag{2.3}$$

$$(Q_{Ev}^\exists x)(B, A) \equiv (\exists z)[(\exists x)((B|z)x \wedge Ax) \wedge Ev((\mu B)(B|z))]. \tag{2.4}$$

construes the sentence "⟨Quantifier⟩ B's are A".

A: All B's are $A := (Q_{Bi\Delta}^\forall x)(B, A) \equiv (\forall x)(Bx \Rightarrow Ax),$

E: No B's are $A := (Q_{Bi\Delta}^\forall x)(B, \neg A) \equiv (\forall x)(Bx \Rightarrow \neg Ax),$

P: Almost all B's are $A := (Q_{Bi\ Ex}^\forall x)(B, A)$

B: Almost all B's are not $A := (Q_{Bi\ Ex}^\forall x)(B, \neg A)$

T: Most B's are $A := (Q_{Bi\ Ve}^\forall x)(B, A)$

D: Most B's are not $A := (Q_{Bi\ Ve}^\forall x)(B, \neg A)$

K: Many B's are $A := (Q_{\neg\ Sm}^\forall x)(B, A)$

G: Many B's are not $A := (Q_{\neg\ Sm}^\forall x)(B, \neg A)$

I: Some B's are $A := (Q_{Bi\Delta}^\exists x)(B, A) \equiv (\exists x)(Bx \wedge Ax),$

O: Some B's are not $A := (Q_{Bi\Delta}^\exists x)(B, \neg A) \equiv (\exists x)(Bx \wedge \neg Ax).$

We can extend this definition by a formula that secures the non-emptiness of the antecedent by adding presupposition to the formulas (see [10]). The corresponding quantifiers with the presupposition are denoted by ***A, *E, *P, *B, *T, *D, *K, *G, *I, *O.**

Definition 2 ([15], **Negative forms of fuzzy intermediate quantifiers**). *Let $Ev \in Form_{oo}$ be an intension of some evaluative expression, $x \in Form_\alpha$ be variable and $A, B, z \in Form_{o\alpha}$ be formulas. Then either of the formulas*

$$(Q_{Ev}^\forall x)(\neg B, \neg A) \equiv (\exists z)[(\forall x)((\neg B|z)\, x \Rightarrow \neg Ax) \wedge Ev((\mu(\neg B))(\neg B|z))], \tag{2.5}$$

$$(Q_{Ev}^\exists x)(\neg B, \neg A) \equiv (\exists z)[(\exists x)((\neg B|z)x \wedge \neg Ax) \wedge Ev((\mu(\neg B))(\neg B|z))] \tag{2.6}$$

construes the sentence "⟨Quantifier⟩ not B's are not A".

---

[1] If B, z are fuzzy sets then a *cut* $B|z$ *of a fuzzy set* B *w.r.t.* z is obtained by setting $(B|z)(u) = B(u)$ for $u \in N$ such that $B(u) = z(u)$ and $(B|z)(u) = 0$ otherwise.

Below we introduce the list of several forms of fuzzy intermediate quantifiers.

a: All $\neg B$'s are not $A := (Q^\forall_{Bi\Delta}x)(\neg B, \neg A) \equiv (\forall x)(\neg Bx \Rightarrow \neg Ax)$,

e: No $\neg B$'s are not $A := (Q^\forall_{Bi\Delta}x)(\neg B, A) \equiv (\forall x)(\neg Bx \Rightarrow Ax)$,

p: Almost all $\neg B$'s are not $A := (Q^\forall_{Bi\ Ex}x)(\neg B, \neg A)$

b: Almost all $\neg B$'s are $A := (Q^\forall_{Bi\ Ex}x)(\neg B, A)$

t: Most $\neg B$'s are not $A := (Q^\forall_{Bi\ Ve}x)(\neg B, \neg A)$

d: Most $\neg B$'s are $A := (Q^\forall_{Bi\ Ve}x)(\neg B, A)$

k: Many $\neg B$'s are not $A := (Q^\forall_{\neg\ Sm}x)(\neg B, \neg A)$

g: Many $\neg B$'s are $A := (Q^\forall_{\neg\ Sm}x)(\neg B, A)$

i: Some $\neg B$'s are not $A := (Q^\exists_{Bi\Delta}x)(\neg B, \neg A) \equiv (\exists x)(\neg Bx \wedge \neg Ax)$,

o: Some $\neg B$'s are $A := (Q^\exists_{Bi\Delta}x)(\neg B, A) \equiv (\exists x)(\neg Bx \wedge Ax)$.

If the presupposition is needed we will denote the corresponding quantifiers by ***a, *e, *p, *b, *t, *d, *k, *g, *i, *o.**

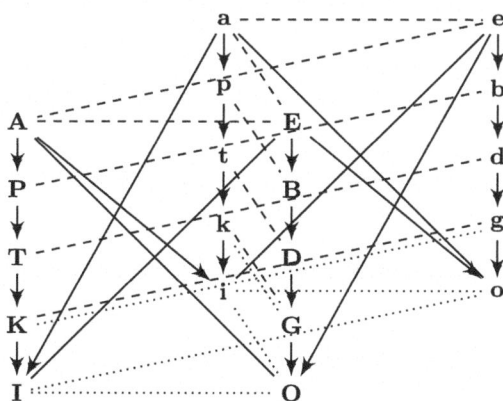

Fig. 1. Graded Peterson's cube of opposition.

We are able to construct the graded Peterson's cube of the opposition (see Fig. 1) from the defined quantifiers. Let us note that the first face of the graded Peterson's cube of the opposition is in fact graded Peterson's square of opposition. The graded Peterson's cube of the opposition describes properties of contrary (dashed line), contradictory (straight line), sub-contrary (dotted line), subaltern and superaltern (arrow). The subaltern and superaltern describes monotonicity of the quantifiers therefore we are able to order quantifiers by size using these properties. Since we will use the property of monotonicity in this publication we will present respective theorems.

Theorem 3 ([17]). *Let T^{IQ} be a consistent extension of T^{Ev}. Then the following implications are provable:*

(a) $T^{IQ} \vdash (\boldsymbol{A}) \Rightarrow (\boldsymbol{P})$, $T^{IQ} \vdash (\boldsymbol{P}) \Rightarrow (\boldsymbol{T})$, $T^{IQ} \vdash (\boldsymbol{T}) \Rightarrow (\boldsymbol{K})$.

(b) $T^{IQ} \vdash (^*\boldsymbol{A}) \Rightarrow (\boldsymbol{I})$, $T^{IQ} \vdash (^*\boldsymbol{P}) \Rightarrow (\boldsymbol{I})$, $T^{IQ} \vdash (^*\boldsymbol{T}) \Rightarrow (\boldsymbol{I})$, $T^{IQ} \vdash (^*\boldsymbol{K}) \Rightarrow (\boldsymbol{I})$.

(c) $T^{IQ} \vdash (\boldsymbol{E}) \Rightarrow (\boldsymbol{B})$, $T^{IQ} \vdash (\boldsymbol{B}) \Rightarrow (\boldsymbol{D})$, $T^{IQ} \vdash (\boldsymbol{D}) \Rightarrow (\boldsymbol{G})$.

(d) $T^{IQ} \vdash (^*\boldsymbol{E}) \Rightarrow (\boldsymbol{O})$, $T^{IQ} \vdash (^*\boldsymbol{B}) \Rightarrow (\boldsymbol{O})$, $T^{IQ} \vdash (^*\boldsymbol{D}) \Rightarrow (\boldsymbol{O})$, $T^{IQ} \vdash (^*\boldsymbol{G}) \Rightarrow (\boldsymbol{O})$.

Theorem 4 ([15]). *Let T^{IQ} be a consistent extension of T^{Ev}. Then the following implications are provable:*

(a) $T^{IQ} \vdash (\boldsymbol{a}) \Rightarrow (\boldsymbol{p})$, $T^{IQ} \vdash (\boldsymbol{p}) \Rightarrow (\boldsymbol{t})$, $T^{IQ} \vdash (\boldsymbol{t}) \Rightarrow (\boldsymbol{k})$.

(b) $T^{IQ} \vdash (^*\boldsymbol{a}) \Rightarrow (\boldsymbol{i})$, $T^{IQ} \vdash (^*\boldsymbol{p}) \Rightarrow (\boldsymbol{i})$, $T^{IQ} \vdash (^*\boldsymbol{t}) \Rightarrow (\boldsymbol{i})$, $T^{IQ} \vdash (^*\boldsymbol{k}) \Rightarrow (\boldsymbol{i})$.

(c) $T^{IQ} \vdash (\boldsymbol{e}) \Rightarrow (\boldsymbol{b})$, $T^{IQ} \vdash (\boldsymbol{b}) \Rightarrow (\boldsymbol{d})$, $T^{IQ} \vdash (\boldsymbol{d}) \Rightarrow (\boldsymbol{g})$.

(d) $T^{IQ} \vdash (^*\boldsymbol{e}) \Rightarrow (\boldsymbol{o})$, $T^{IQ} \vdash (^*\boldsymbol{b}) \Rightarrow (\boldsymbol{o})$, $T^{IQ} \vdash (^*\boldsymbol{d}) \Rightarrow (\boldsymbol{o})$, $T^{IQ} \vdash (^*\boldsymbol{g}) \Rightarrow (\boldsymbol{o})$.

2.3   Syllogisms

Definition 3 (Syllogism). *A sylogism consists of three statements P_1, P_2, C. Premises are denoted by P_1, P_2 where P_1 represents major premise, P_2 represents minor premise. By C we denote conclusion. Subject S occurs in P_2 and is also first formula in C. Predicate P occurs in P_1 and is second formula in C. Middle formula occurs in the both premises P_1, P_2.*

Definition 4 *Syllogism $\langle P_1, P_2, C \rangle$ is valid in T^{IQ} if $T^{IQ} \vdash (P_1 \& P_2) \Rightarrow C$ or equivalently if $T^{IQ} \vdash P_1 \Rightarrow (P_2 \Rightarrow C)$.*

We distinguish four possible formula which are different in position of the middle formula M.

Definition 5. *Let Q_1, Q_2, Q_3 be fuzzy quantifiers and M, P, S be formulas. Let M be a middle formula, S be a subject and P be a predicate. Then we distinguish four corresponding figures:*

Figure-I	**Figure-II**	**Figure-III**	**Figure-IV**
Q_1 M are P	Q_1 P are M	Q_1 M are P	Q_1 P are M
Q_2 S are M	Q_2 S are M	Q_2 M are S	Q_2 M are S
Q_3 S are P	Q_3 S are P	Q_3 S are P	Q_3 S are P

3   Verification of Syllogisms Based on Contraposition

In this section, we will show some valid syllogisms concerning 20 quantifiers defined in the previous sections. The goal is to show that we are capable of proving valid syllogisms based on knowledge of other valid syllogisms and by using logical operations (mainly contraposition) and the properties of quantifiers.

We want to present the validity of these syllogisms without the need for their syntactic proofs.

In this article, we will focus on contraposition from formula (2.1), which describes the equivalent relationship between two quantifiers, where the first is the quantifier **A** and the second is the quantifier **a**. Let us note, that it does not mean that the quantifier **A** and **a** are equivalent in the graded Peterson's cube of opposition because that is not true. The formula tells us if we from the quantifier **A** take negation of S, P and interchange them, the obtained quantifier is equivalent and has form of the quantifier **a** and vice versa. This formula therefore describes an equivalent relationship between two quantifiers, **A** and **a**, each originating from a different graded Peterson's cube of opposition. In one cube, the antecedent position is occupied by S or $\neg S$, and the consequent position by P or $\neg P$, while in the other cube, this arrangement of S,P is reversed.

We will base our approach on the knowledge of valid syllogisms which we present in Theorem 5, which are valid syllogisms related to the graded Peterson's square of opposition.

Theorem 5 ([12]). *The following syllogisms are valid in T^{IQ} in the Figure-I:*

$$AAA$$
$$AAP \quad APP$$
$$AAT \quad APT \quad ATT$$
$$AAK \quad APK \quad ATK \quad AKK$$
$$A(*A)I\ A(*P)I\ A(*T)I\ A(*K)I\ AII$$

Then we will apply contraposition on the first, second or both premise of valid syllogisms in this section. To be able to apply contraposition (Theorem 2) on the syllogism, the premise has to be a universal quantifier. The universal quantifiers with respect to graded Peterson's cube of opposition are quantifiers which we denote by **A, E, a, e**. As we mentioned before we will focus on contraposition from formula (2.1).

We will show how this approach works in the proof of the following theorem.

Theorem 6. *The syllogisms aAA-II,AaA-III,aaA-IV are valid in T^{IQ}.*

Proof. We know that syllogisms **AAA**-I is valid from Theorem 5.

$$T^{IQ} \vdash [(\forall x)(Mx \Rightarrow Px) \& (\forall x)(Sx \Rightarrow Mx)] \Rightarrow (\forall x)(Sx \Rightarrow Px)$$

By adjunction we obtain

$$T^{IQ} \vdash (\forall x)(Mx \Rightarrow Px) \Rightarrow [(\forall x)(Sx \Rightarrow Mx) \Rightarrow (\forall x)(Sx \Rightarrow Px)] \qquad (3.1)$$

From formula (2.1) we know that

$$T^{IQ} \vdash (\forall x)(\neg Px \Rightarrow \neg Mx) \Rightarrow (\forall x)(Mx \Rightarrow Px) \qquad (3.2)$$

By application transitivity we obtain

$$T^{IQ} \vdash (\forall x)(\neg Px \Rightarrow \neg Mx)) \Rightarrow [(\forall x)(Sx \Rightarrow Mx) \Rightarrow (\forall x)(Sx \Rightarrow Px)] \qquad (3.3)$$

Based on the position of middle formulas, this proved syllogism is in Figure II. Based on the quantifiers in the respective premises, we write this syllogism as **aAA**. We have proven the validity of syllogism **aAA**-II by application contraposition on the first premise of valid syllogism **AAA**-I. As the formula (2.1) describes equivalence, similarly, we are able to prove validity **AAA-I** from valid syllogism **aAA-II**. Similarly, we can apply contraposition on the second premise to obtain valid syllogism **AaA**-III. If we apply contraposition on both premises, we obtain valid syllogism **aaA**-IV.

We present these four valid syllogisms as follows:

AAA-I

$$(\forall x)(Mx \implies Px)$$
$$(\forall x)(Sx \implies Mx)$$
$$\overline{(\forall x)(Sx \implies Px)}$$

aAA-II

$$(\forall x)(\neg Px \implies \neg Mx)$$
$$(\forall x)(Sx \implies Mx)$$
$$\overline{(\forall x)(Sx \implies Px)}$$

AaA-III

$$(\forall x)(Mx \implies Px)$$
$$(\forall x)(\neg Mx \implies \neg Sx)$$
$$\overline{(\forall x)(Sx \implies Px)}$$

aaA-IV

$$(\forall x)(\neg Px \implies \neg Mx)$$
$$(\forall x)(\neg Mx \implies \neg Sx)$$
$$\overline{(\forall x)(Sx \implies Px)}$$

We can see that if we apply contraposition on the first premise of a syllogism from Figure I we obtain syllogism from Figure II, if we apply it on the second premise we obtain syllogisms from Figure III and if we apply it on both premises we obtain syllogism on the Figure IV. This relationship is not surprising since the Figures (see Definition 5) differ in the position of formulas S,P,M in respective premises and we "interchange" their position using contraposition. We can see that newly obtained syllogisms **aAA-II**, **AaA-III**, **aaA-IV** correspond to the graded Peterson's cube of opposition.

Let us note that the use of the formula 2.2 is not that useful, since it describes equivalence between two quantifiers but both are negative forms of universal quantifier (**E**). Then apply (2.2) on valid syllogism **EAE-I** we obtain valid syllogism **EAE-II**. We can see that we again obtain syllogism from other Figure, but the syllogism is still related to the graded Peterson's square of opposition, which syllogisms are already proved. Both formulas rely on the contraposition in their proof, but from a philosophical point of view formula (2.1) is a valid contraposition and formula (2.2) is a valid conversion (see [2]).

3.1   Valid Syllogisms of Figure II

Let us focus on the application of contraposition on the first premise on valid quantifiers from Theorem 5. We can apply contraposition on every syllogism from this Theorem which has quantifier **A** in the first premise similarly as we did previously.

Alternatively, we can apply contraposition on a few valid syllogisms and the rest prove by monotonicity. We will show this in the following part. Firstly, we prove validity of syllogisms **aAA-II**, **aPP-II**, **aTT-II**, **aKK-II**, **aII-II**.

Theorem 7. *The following syllogisms are valid in Figure II: **aAA-II**, **aPP-II**, **aTT-II**, **aKK-II**, **aII-II**.*

Proof. Similarly as in Theorem 6.

From these valid syllogisms, we are able to prove the validity of the following syllogisms using monotonicity.

Theorem 8. *The following syllogisms are strongly valid in T^{IQ} in Figure-II:*

$$aAA$$
$$aAP \quad aPP$$
$$aAT \quad aPT \quad aTT$$
$$aAK \quad aPK \quad aTK \quad AKK$$
$$a(*A)I \ a(*P)I \ a(*T)I \ a(*K)I \ aII$$

Proof. We know validity of **aAA-II**, **aPP-II**, **aTT-II**, **aKK-II**, **aII-II** from Theorem 7. From validity of syllogism **aII-II** we know that

$$T^{IQ} \vdash (\forall x)(\neg Px \Rightarrow \neg Mx) \Rightarrow \big((\exists x)(Sx \wedge Mx) \Rightarrow (\exists x)(Sx \wedge Px)\big) \qquad (3.4)$$

From Theorem 3 (monotonicity) we know that $T^{IQ} \vdash (^*\mathbf{K}) \Rightarrow (\mathbf{I})$

$$T^{IQ} \vdash (\exists z)[(\forall x)((S|z)\, x \Rightarrow Mx)\&(\exists x)(S|z)x \wedge \neg\, Sm((\mu S)(S|z))] \Rightarrow$$
$$(\exists x)(Sx \wedge Mx) \quad (3.5)$$

Using adjunction and transitivity on 3.4 and 3.5 we obtain

$$T^{IQ} \vdash (\forall x)(\neg Px \Rightarrow \neg Mx) \Rightarrow$$
$$\big((\exists z)[(\forall x)((S|z)\, x \Rightarrow Mx)\&(\exists x)(S|z)x \wedge \neg\, Sm((\mu S)(S|z))] \Rightarrow (\exists x)(Sx \wedge Px)\big)$$

We proved the validity of syllogism **a(*K)I-II** using knowledge of validity **aII-II** and monotonicity. Similarly, we prove the rest of the valid syllogisms in the first row. We prove the validity of the remaining syllogisms in the first column using valid syllogism **aAA-II** and monotonicity. Similarly, we prove the validity of other remaining syllogisms.

3.2   Valid Syllogisms of Figure III

Let us move to Figure III. We obtain valid syllogism in Figure III by application contraposition on the second premise. We can see that only syllogisms from the first column contain universal quantifiers on the second premise in Theorem 5. We can apply our approach to all syllogisms in the first column or we can prove syllogism **AaA-III** and use monotonicity to prove others (except for **A(*a)I**).

Theorem 9. *The following syllogism of Figure III are valid in T^{IQ}.*

$$AaA$$
$$AaP$$
$$AaT$$
$$AaK$$

Proof. Syllogism **AaA-III** is valid (Theorem 6). Applying monotonicity to valid syllogism **AaA-III** we prove the validity of other syllogisms.

Special case can occur when we apply contraposition on the premise which contains presupposition. In our case, only syllogism **A(*A)I-I** contains a universal quantifier with presupposition.

Theorem 10. *The syllogism A(*a)I of Figure III is valid in T^{IQ}.*

Proof. We know that syllogism A(*A)I-I is valid

$$T^{IQ} \vdash ((\forall x)(Mx \Rightarrow Px) \& (\forall x)(Sx \Rightarrow Mx) \& (\exists x)(Sx)) \Rightarrow (\exists x)(Sx \wedge Px)$$

Using adjunction we obtain

$$T^{IQ} \vdash (\forall x)(Sx \Rightarrow Mx) \Rightarrow \left(((\forall x)(Mx \Rightarrow Px) \& (\exists x)(Sx)) \Rightarrow (\exists x)(Sx \wedge Px) \right) \tag{3.6}$$

From formula (2.1) we know that

$$T^{IQ} \vdash (\forall x)(\neg Mx \Rightarrow \neg Sx) \Rightarrow (\forall x)(Sx \Rightarrow Mx) \tag{3.7}$$

Using transitivity we obtain

$$T^{IQ} \vdash (\forall x)(\neg Mx \Rightarrow \neg Sx) \Rightarrow \left(((\forall x)(Mx \Rightarrow Px) \& (\exists x)(Sx)) \Rightarrow (\exists x)(Sx \wedge Px) \right)$$

By adjunction we obtain

$$T^{IQ} \vdash ((\forall x)(Mx \Rightarrow Px) \& (\forall x)(\neg Mx \Rightarrow \neg Sx) \& (\exists x)(Sx)) \Rightarrow (\exists x)(Sx \wedge Px)$$

Remark 1. Notice that the presupposition remains the same as in the original syllogism. Thus, we consider presupposition $(\exists x)(Sx)$, even though the syllogism contains in the premise $\neg Sx$. This situation also occurs for classical syllogisms, where syllogism **A(*E)O-IV** likewise contains the presupposition $(\exists x)(Sx)$ in the premise, even though the syllogism includes $\neg Sx$. This is also due to the use of contraposition in the proof.

3.3   Valid Syllogisms of Figure IV

When we apply contraposition on the first and the second premise we obtain syllogism in Figure IV. Only syllogisms in the first column have universal quantifiers in both premises in Theorem 5.

Theorem 11. *The following syllogisms of Figure IV are valid in T^{IQ}.*

$$aaA$$
$$aaP$$
$$aaT$$
$$aaK$$
$$a(*a)I$$

Proof. Syllogism **aaA** is valid (Theorem 6). Using valid syllogism **aaA** and monotonicity we prove the validity of syllogisms **aaP**, **aaT**, **aaK**. We can prove **a(*a)I** similarly as in Theorem 10.

3.4   Relationship Between Syllogisms Obtained by Contraposition

It follows that the syllogisms obtained by contraposition are logically equivalent, hence the individual premises are equivalent. In the previous section, we showed that applying the contraposition to a valid syllogism **AAA-I**, we obtain valid syllogisms **aAA-II, AaA-III** and **aaA-IV**. Thus, these syllogisms are logically equivalent, and we derive the conclusion based on logically equivalent premises, with the premises expressed using different but equivalent quantifiers. We will show it in the following illustrative example:

AAA-I	**aAA-II**
All people, who do sport are healthy.	All non-healthy people do not sport.
All young people do sport.	All young people do sport.
All young people are healthy.	All young people are healthy.

We can see that both syllogisms differs in the first premise, but these premises are equivalent, so the both syllogisms are equivalent and describe same information.

4   Conclusion and Future Work

In conclusion, we presented a systematic approach to the analysis of syllogisms in this article, avoiding the blind search for valid syllogisms. We utilized the knowledge of valid syllogisms with respect to graded Peterson's square of opposition and a simple property of contraposition, which allowed us to identify valid syllogisms within the graded Peterson's cube of opposition.

Due to the scope of the article, we naturally did not apply this approach to all valid syllogisms within graded Peterson's square of opposition. However, the procedure would be analogous to what we have presented in this article. Obtained valid syllogisms were further organized based on their monotonicity. Additionally, by using contraposition, we discovered relationships between syllogisms, as syllogisms obtained through contraposition are mutually equivalent.

It is important to highlight a few limitations. Using this approach, we are not able to identify all valid syllogisms within the graded Peterson's cube of opposition. For instance, we cannot determine the validity of the syllogism aaa-I. Furthermore, we are unable to work with syllogisms that do not contain a universal quantifier in one of their premises.

In further research, we will build on the findings of this article and apply contraposition to invalid syllogisms. We also aim to focus on other properties and methods that would allow us to determine the validity or invalidity of the remaining unresolved syllogisms. This expanded approach could contribute to a deeper understanding of syllogistic logic and broaden the possibilities for its analysis.

Acknowledgements. This article has been produced with the financial support of the European Union under the: Biography of Fake News with a Touch of AI: Dangerous Phenomenon through the Prism of Modern Human Sciences project no.: CZ.02.01.01/00/23_025/0008724 via the Operational Programme Jan Ámos Komenský.

Disclosure of Interests. Authors have no competing interests.

References

1. Andrews, P.: An Introduction to Mathematical Logic and Type Theory: To Truth Through Proof. Kluwer, Dordrecht (2002)
2. Copi, I.M., Cohen, C., McMahon, K.: Introduction to logic. Pearson Education Limited, Harlow (2014)
3. Dubois, D., Prade, H.: On fuzzy syllogisms. Comput. Intell. **4**, 171–179 (1988)
4. Dvořák, A., Holčapek, M.: Type ⟨1, 1⟩ fuzzy quantifiers determined by fuzzy measures on residuated lattices. Part I. basic definitions and examples. Fuzzy Sets Syst. **242**, 31–55 (20014)
5. Fiala, K., Murinová, P.: A formal analysis of generalized Peterson's syllogisms related to graded Peterson's cube. Mathematics **10**(6) (2022)
6. Kacprzyk, J., Wilbik, A., Zadrozny, S.: Linguistic summarization of time series using a fuzzy quantifier driven aggregation. Fuzzy Sets Syst. **159**, 1485–1499 (2008)
7. Kacprzyk, J., Yager, R.: Linguistic summaries of data using fuzzy logic. Int. J. Gen Syst **30**, 133–154 (2001)
8. Kacprzyk, J., Zadrożny, S.: Linguistic summarization of data sets using association rules. In: Proceedings of FUZZ-IEE 2003, St. Louis, USA, pp. 702–707 (2003)
9. Kacprzyk, J., Zadrożny, S.: Linguistic database summaries and their protoforms: towards natural language based knowledge discovery tools. Inf. Sci. **173**, 281–304 (2005)
10. Murinová, P.: Graded structures of opposition in fuzzy natural logic. Log. Univers. **265**, 495–522 (2020)
11. Murinová, P., Burda, M., Pavliska, V.: An algorithm for intermediate quantifiers and the graded square of opposition towards linguistic description of data. In: Advances in Fuzzy Logic and Technology, pp. 592–603 (2017)
12. Murinová, P., Novák, V.: A formal theory of generalized intermediate syllogisms. Fuzzy Sets Syst. **186**, 47–80 (2013)
13. Murinová, P., Novák, V.: The structure of generalized intermediate syllogisms. Fuzzy Sets Syst. **247**, 18–37 (2014)
14. Murinová, P., Novák, V.: The theory of intermediate quantifiers in fuzzy natural logic revisited and the model of "many". Fuzzy Sets Syst. **388**, 56–89 (2020)
15. Murinová, P., Novák, V.: Graded cube of opposition with intermediate quantifiers in fuzzy natural logic. In: Lesot, M.-J., et al. (eds.) IPMU 2020. CCIS, vol. 1239, pp. 145–158. Springer, Cham (2020). https://doi.org/10.1007/978-3-030-50153-2_11
16. Novák, V.: On fuzzy type theory. Fuzzy Sets Syst. **149**, 235–273 (2005)
17. Novák, V.: A formal theory of intermediate quantifiers. Fuzzy Sets Syst. **159**(10), 1229–1246 (2008)
18. Pereira-Fariña, M., Vidal, J.C., Díaz-Hermida, F., Bugarín, A.: A fuzzy syllogistic reasoning schema for generalized quantifiers. Fuzzy Sets Syst. **234**, 79–96 (2014)

19. Peterson, P.: Intermediate Quantifiers. Logic, linguistics, and Aristotelian semantics. Ashgate, Aldershot (2000)
20. Thompson, B.E.: Syllogisms using "few","many" and "most". Notre Dame J. Formal Logic **23**, 75–84 (1982)
21. Wilbik, A., Kaymak, U.: Linguistic summarization of processes – a research agenda. In: Proceedings of the 2015 Conference of the International Fuzzy Systems Association and the European Society for Fuzzy Logic and Technology, pp. 136–143 (2015)
22. Yager, R.: Linguistic summaries as a tool for database discovery. In: Proceedings of FUZZIEEE 1995 Workshop on Fuzzy Database Systems and Information Retrieval, Yokohama, pp. 79–82 (1995)
23. Zadeh, L.A.: A computational approach to fuzzy quantifiers in natural languages. Comput. Math. **9**, 149–184 (1983)

Verification of Validity of Logical Syllogisms Generated by Cube of Opposition Using Extended Peterson's Rules

Petra Murinová$^{(\boxtimes)}$ (iD) and Vilém Novák

Institute for Research and Applications of Fuzzy Modeling, NSC IT4Innovations, University of Ostrava, 30. dubna 22, 701 03 Ostrava 1, Czech Republic
{petra.murinova,vilem.novak}@osu.cz

Abstract. In this paper, we first advocate for mathematical logic as an indispensable tool for the development of AI. Then we will introduce the concept of intermediate quantifiers and syllogisms with them. Furthermore, we will introduce the graded cube of opposition and suggest extended Peterson's rules for verification of validity of syllogisms with negations. We will prove that all valid syllogisms with negations verify the extended Peterson's rules.

Keywords: Fuzzy natural logic · Intermediate quantifiers · Intermediate syllogisms · Graded cube of opposition · Extended Peterson's rules · Evaluative linguistic expressions

1 Introduction

1.1 The Role of Logic in Reasoning Using AI

We now witness the boom of artificial intelligence (AI). The problem is that society only identifies AI with neural networks. But AI covers much more areas than only the latter. We argue that formal logic cannot be avoided in AI and demonstrate our arguments on two widely used systems of AI, namely ChatGPT and DeepThink. Both systems can generate human-like conversational responses and enable users to refine and steer a conversation towards a desired length, format, style, and level of detail, generate articles, and poems, provide information about people, answer various kinds of questions, and other sometimes astonishing abilities.

The problem with such systems consists of the unreliability of the provided information and conclusions because we do not know all the sources that were used. More significant is the fact that the answer is generated based on the highest probability of occurrence of subsequent words which is derived from the elaborated sources of the input information. The latter, however, does not provide a clue for verification of the logical validity of the suggested conclusion. The only way such systems can provide is by finding some model in which

M. Baczyński et al. (Eds.): EUSFLAT 2025, LNCS 15883, pp. 166–177, 2025.
https://doi.org/10.1007/978-3-031-97225-6_14

the conclusion may be true. Mathematical logic, however, provides much more. Among others, it suggests formal methods how to verify that a given conclusion is generally valid, i.e., that it is true in all models.

However, even finding a model may be very unsafe leading to wrong conclusion. We will demonstrate this on the following example of syllogism:

$$\mathscr{P}_1 : Almost\ all\ M\ are\ P.$$
$$\mathscr{P}_2 : Most\ S\ are\ M.$$
$$\mathscr{C} : Some\ S\ are\ P.$$

We know that this syllogism is invalid because there is a model in which it is not true. Such a model is schematically depicted in Fig. 1 where one can see that sizes of the extensions of the respective properties must be taken into account.

Most S are M Almost all M are P

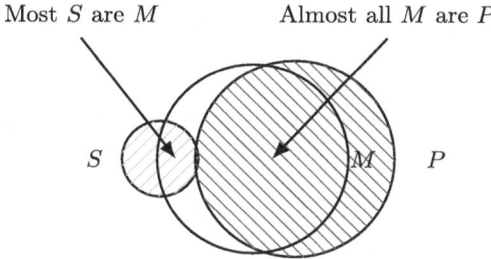

Fig. 1. Venn diagram demonstrating invalidity of the given syllogism.

Now we will present the answer of two widely used AI systems, namely Chat-GPT and DeepThink that is a part of DeepSeek.

1.2 ChatGPT

We asked the following question to ChatGPT (https://chat.chatbotapp.ai/):

> Verify the validity of the logical syllogism if you know that *"Almost all M are P"* and *"Most S are M"*. Is it true that *"Some S are P"*?

The system gave the following answer:

- Since "Most S are M", this means that a significant portion of S are inside M, but not necessarily all.
- Since "Almost all M are P", this means that nearly every M is inside P, but there may be a few exceptions.
- We need to determine whether this guarantees that at least one S is also in P.

Probability-Based Reasoning: Suppose M is a large set, and "almost all M are P means that nearly every element of M is in P, leaving only a small fraction outside. If "most S are M", then at least half (more than 50%) of S are inside M. Given that nearly all M are in P, it is highly likely that at least some of the S that belong to M also belong to P. While not an absolute logical certainty, in standard reasoning and probabilistic terms, this strongly suggests that "Some S are P" is true.

Conclusion: Yes, it is very likely that some S are P, though the argument is not 100% logically airtight (since "almost all" allows for a few exceptions). In practical reasoning, the conclusion "Some S are P" is valid based on high probability.

We see that ChatGPT incorrectly concluded that the syllogism is valid though it admits that this is not absolute logical certainty. The arguments that "it is very likely that some S are P" and that it holds in practical reasoning with high probability are untenable. They could make some sense if a well-prepared experiment with specific S, P, M and with known probability distribution was carried out. But this has no place in logic, even if used in commonsense reasoning and we argue that in practice, such a conclusion is pointless.

1.3 DeepThink

We asked the same question also to DeepSeek (https://chat.deepseek.com/) (it was transfered to DeepThink assistant). The answer is the following: **The syllogism is valid**.

Analysis:

- Premise 1: "Almost all M are P". This means the vast majority of M are in P, with only a small fraction (10% or less) of M not in P.
- Premise 2: "Most S are M". This implies more than half of S are in M (e.g., 51% or more).
- Overlap Analysis: Since "most S are M", at least a majority of S must overlap with M. But "almost all M are P", so the non-P portion of M is very small.

Contradiction Approach:

- Assume the conclusion "Some S are P" is false (i.e., no S are P).
- If no S are P, then all S (including those that are M) must be in the non-P part of M.
- However, the non-P part of M is too small (by Premise 1) to accommodate "most S" (from Premise 2).
  This creates a contradiction because the number of S in M (majority of S) exceeds the capacity of the non-P portion of M.

– Conclusion: The assumption fails, so some S must be P. *Thus, the syllogism is valid.*

The arguments provided by DeepThink seem to be more logical. But still, they are incorrect. As can be seen from the analysis as well as from the attempt to find a contradiction, the system does not take into account that the size of S can be sufficiently small so that its majority can well be included in the rest of M not covered by P (cf. Fig. 1). Therefore, we can find a model in which this syllogism is not true and so, it is not valid.

Both examples support the claim that *formal logic is a necessary tool for the development of AI.* Moreover, it also makes it possible to express general rules based on which we can reduce the number of examples on which the deep networks must be trained.

1.4   The Main Goals

The main objective of this paper is to propose generalized Peterson rules for logical syllogisms with intermediate quantifiers related to the graded Peterson cube of opposites. Note that there are other related works on other kinds of generalized logical syllogisms. From the point of view of fuzzy quantifiers, which are represented as intervals in Didier Dubois's approach in [1,2], Zadeh's special syllogism is compared by M. Pereira-Fariña in [3]. In the publications, Dubois et al. works with quantifiers represented as crisp closed intervals (*more than a half* $= [0.5, 1]$, *around five* $= [4, 6]$).

2   Preliminaries

2.1   Basic Concepts

The theory of intermediate quantifiers has been formulated using the tools of higher-order fuzzy logic (fuzzy type theory; L-FTT) that was in detail elaborated in [4]. We will assume that the algebra of truth values is an MV_Δ-algebra $\mathscr{E} = \langle E, \vee, \wedge, \otimes, \rightarrow, \mathbf{0}, \mathbf{1}, \Delta \rangle$ where $\mathbf{0}$ is the least and $\mathbf{1}$ is the greatest element, respectively. We will usually consider the standard Łukasiewicz MV_Δ-algebra with the support $E = [0, 1]$.

The fundamental syntactical entities in L-FTT are classical and revolve around the concepts of *type* and *formula* (see [5]). Atomic types include ϵ (elements) and o (truth values). More general types are defined as follows: if α and β are types, then $(\beta\alpha)$ is a type. We represent types using Greek letters, and the collective set of all types is denoted by *Types*.

The types in a model correspond to specific objects. Namely, if $\mathscr{M}$ is a model then $\mathscr{M}(A_o) \in E$, $\mathscr{M}(A_\epsilon) \in M_\epsilon$ is some element and $\mathscr{M}(A_{\beta\alpha}) : M_\alpha \longrightarrow M_\beta$ is a function.

2.2   Evaluative Linguistic Expressions

Evaluative linguistic expressions are special expressions of natural language using which we evaluate sizes of objects. Examples of these expressions are "roughly large, extremely tall, very thin, medium tall", etc. The logical theory of evaluative expressions is presented in [6].

The evaluative expressions are modeled as formulas of type oo. Selected ones are *small* $(Sm\bar{\nu})$[1], *not small* $(\neg Sm)$, *very big* $(Bi\,Ve)$, *extremely big* $(Bi\,Ex)$ and *utmost big*, i.e., the biggest $(Bi\Delta)$. Recall that *very* (Ve), *extremely* (Ex) and *utmost* (Δ) are linguistic hedges that are modeled using special unary functions on $[0,1]$ which are ordered according to their precision as follows:

$$Ex \preceq Si \preceq Ve \preceq \bar{\nu} \preceq ML \preceq Ro \preceq QR \preceq VR. \tag{1}$$

The relation $\preceq$ means that the hedge on the left is more precise than the hedge on the right.

Lemma 1. *The following system of inequalities holds for extensions of evaluative expressions in the standard context:*

$$\inf \mathrm{Supp}(\neg Sm\,Si) \leq \inf \mathrm{Supp}(\neg Sm\,Ve) \leq a_{\neg Sm\bar{\nu}} = \inf \mathrm{Supp}(\neg Sm\bar{\nu}) < 0.5$$
$$< a_{BiVe} = \inf \mathrm{Supp}(BiVe) \leq a_{BiEx} = \inf \mathrm{Supp}(BiEx) \leq \inf \mathrm{Supp}(Bi\Delta) = 1.$$

Proof. The lemma follows from the general definitions of the semantics of evaluative expressions [6,7]. □

2.3   Intermediate Quantifiers Related to Peterson's Cube

Intermediate quantifiers are represented by specific formulas in a special formal theory T^{IQ} of L-FTT. These formulas capture quantification over a universe represented by a fuzzy set, with its size characterized by a measure (cf. [7]). Recall that intermediate quantifiers belong among a wider class of fuzzy and generalized ones [8,9]. Below we introduce mathematical definitions of intermediate quantifiers which form a graded Peterson's cube of opposition (the second face). Let us recall that the first face and the corresponding rules were introduced in [10].

Definition 1 (New forms of fuzzy intermediate quantifiers). *Let Ev be a formula representing an evaluative expression, x be variables and A, B, z be formulas. Then either of the formulas*

$$(Q_{Ev}^{\forall} x)(\neg B, \neg A) \equiv (\exists z)[(\forall x)((\neg B|z)\,x \Rightarrow \neg Ax) \wedge Ev((\mu(\neg B))(\neg B|z))], \tag{2}$$
$$(Q_{Ev}^{\exists} x)(\neg B, \neg A) \equiv (\exists z)[(\exists x)((\neg B|z)x \wedge \neg Ax) \wedge Ev((\mu(\neg B))(\neg B|z))]. \tag{3}$$

construes the sentence "⟨Quantifier⟩ not B's are not A".

---

[1] There are good reasons to take the expression "small" formally as $Sm\bar{\nu}$ where $\bar{\nu}$ is an empty modifier. This enables us to treat all simple evaluative expressions in a unique way as "linguistic hedge—adjective".

Below we introduce the list of several forms of fuzzy intermediate quantifiers.

$$\mathbf{a} : \text{All } \neg B\text{'s are not } A := (Q^{\forall}_{Bi\Delta}x)(\neg B, \neg A) \equiv (\forall x)(\neg Bx \Rightarrow \neg Ax),$$

$$\mathbf{e} : \text{No } \neg B\text{'s are not } A := (Q^{\forall}_{Bi\Delta}x)(\neg B, A) \equiv (\forall x)(\neg Bx \Rightarrow Ax),$$

$$\mathbf{p} : \text{Almost all } \neg B\text{'s are not } A := (Q^{\forall}_{BiEx}x)(\neg B, \neg A)$$

$$\mathbf{b} : \text{Almost all } \neg B\text{'s are } A := (Q^{\forall}_{BiEx}x)(\neg B, A)$$

$$\mathbf{t} : \text{Most } \neg B\text{'s are not } A := (Q^{\forall}_{BiVe}x)(\neg B, \neg A)$$

$$\mathbf{d} : \text{Most } \neg B\text{'s are A} := (Q^{\forall}_{BiVe}x)(\neg B, A)$$

$$\mathbf{k} : \text{Many } \neg B\text{'s are not } A := (Q^{\forall}_{\neg Sm}x)(\neg B, \neg A)$$

$$\mathbf{g} : \text{Many } \neg B\text{'s are } A := (Q^{\forall}_{\neg Sm}x)(\neg B, A)$$

$$\mathbf{f} : \text{A few (A little) } \neg B\text{'s are not } A := (Q^{\forall}_{\neg SmVe}x)(\neg B, \neg A)$$

$$\mathbf{v} : \text{A few (A little) } \neg B\text{'s are } A := (Q^{\forall}_{\neg SmVe}x)(\neg B, A)$$

$$\mathbf{s} : \text{Several } \neg B\text{'s are not } A := (Q^{\forall}_{\neg SmSi}x)(\neg B, \neg A)$$

$$\mathbf{z} : \text{Several } \neg B\text{'s are } A := (Q^{\forall}_{\neg SmSi}x)(\neg B, A)$$

$$\mathbf{i} : \text{Some } \neg B\text{'s are not } A := (Q^{\exists}_{Bi\Delta}x)(\neg B, \neg A) \equiv (\exists x)(\neg Bx \wedge \neg Ax),$$

$$\mathbf{o} : \text{Some } \neg B\text{'s are } A := (Q^{\exists}_{Bi\Delta}x)(\neg B, A) \equiv (\exists x)(\neg Bx \wedge Ax).$$

2.4 Graded Cube of Opposition and Related Syllogisms

Graded Peterson's square of opposition (cf. [11]) suggests us to work with *negative information in the consequent only*. In Peterson's *cube of opposition*, we can consider other negated expressions, for example:

– Most people who do not do sports have a problem with their spine,
– Most people who don't smoke don't suffer from asthma.

By combining various forms of quantifiers contained in the cube of opposition we arrive at related logical syllogisms. We focused on selected forms and syntactic verification of their validity in [12]. A *syllogism* is a triple of formulas $\mathscr{P}_1, \mathscr{P}_2, \mathscr{C}$ of the theory T^{IQ} where $\mathscr{P}_1$ is a *major premise*, $\mathscr{P}_2$ a *minor premise* and $\mathscr{C}$ is a *conclusion*. Let $Q_{\mathscr{P}_1}, Q_{\mathscr{P}_2}, Q_{\mathscr{C}}$ be quantifier symbols occurring in both premises and conclusion, respectively, and S (*subject*), P (*predicate*) and M (*middle formula*).

Figure I	**Figure II**	**Figure III**	**Figure IV**
$Q_{\mathscr{P}_1} M$ are P	$Q_{\mathscr{P}_1} P$ are M	$Q_{\mathscr{P}_1} M$ are P	$Q_{\mathscr{P}_1} P$ are M
$Q_{\mathscr{P}_2} S$ are M	$Q_{\mathscr{P}_2} S$ are M	$Q_{\mathscr{P}_2} M$ are S	$Q_{\mathscr{P}_2} M$ are S
$Q_{\mathscr{C}} S$ are P	$Q_{\mathscr{C}} S$ are P	$Q_{\mathscr{C}} S$ are P	$Q_{\mathscr{C}} S$ are P

The following is an example of intermediate syllogisms related to the graded cube of opposition (Fig. 2).

P_1 : *Most people who don't smoke don't suffer from asthma.*
P_2 : *Most people who don't smoke don't have yellow teeth.*

C : *Some people who don't have yellow teeth don't suffer from asthma.*

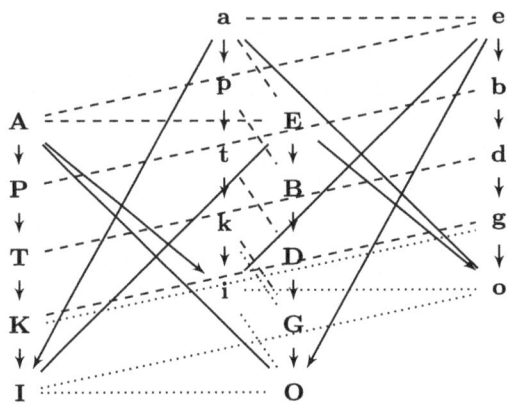

Fig. 2. Graded Peterson's cube of opposition.

3   Extended Peterson's Rules for Graded Peterson's Cube of Opposition

The main goal of this section is to give a mathematical definition of the extended Peterson rules for verifying the validity of logical syllogisms related to the graded Peterson cube of opposition. In a previous publication (see [10]), we proposed rules for logical syllogisms related to Peterson's square of opposites [13]. In this publication, we will focus on the back square of the Peterson cube.

Let us first recall the mathematical definition of the distribution of a given formula in another one.

Definition 2 ([10]). *Let $S \in \text{Form}_o$ and $Z \in \text{Form}_{o\alpha}$ be formulas. Then formulas $A_1, \ldots, A_n \in \text{Form}_{o\alpha}$ are distributed in S if there is a formula $T \in \text{Form}_o$ such that:*

(i) $\vdash S \equiv T$,
(ii) *T contains a subformula $(\forall x_\alpha)(A_1 x \& \cdots \& A_n x \Rightarrow Z x)$.*

Lemma 2 ([10]). *Let $A \in \text{Form}_o$, $S, P \in \text{Form}_{o\alpha}$ be formulas and $x \in \text{Form}_\alpha$ be a variable.*

(a) *Let $A \equiv (\forall x)(Sx \Rightarrow Px)$. Then S is* distributed *in A.*
(b) *Let $A \equiv (\forall x)(Sx \Rightarrow \neg Px)$. Then both S, P are* distributed *in A.*
(c) *Let $A \equiv (\exists x)(Sx \wedge \neg Px)$. Then P is* distributed *in A.*

A slight modification of this lemma works also for negation.

Lemma 3. *Let $A \in Form_o$, $S, P \in Form_{o\alpha}$ be formulas and $x \in Form_\alpha$ be a variable.*

(a) *Let $A \equiv (\forall x)(\neg Sx \Rightarrow \neg Px)$. Then $\neg S$ is* distributed *in A.*
(b) *Let $A \equiv (\forall x)(\neg Sx \Rightarrow Px)$. Then both $\neg S, \neg P$ are* distributed *in A.*
(c) *Let $A \equiv (\exists x)(Sx \wedge Px)$. Then $\neg P$ is* distributed *in A.*

Proof. Due to the double negation property, we have $\vdash (\neg Sx \Rightarrow Px) \equiv (\neg Sx \Rightarrow (\neg P \Rightarrow \bot))$ which implies (b). Similar argument holds also for (c). ☐

Definition 3 (Distribution index-second face). *Let N be a set, $A, B \in \mathscr{F}(N)$. Let $Q_{Ev}^K(\neg B, \neg A)$, $K \in \{\forall, \exists\}$ be an intermediate quantifier determined by the evaluative expression Ev. The distribution index $\mathrm{DI}(X, Q_{Ev}^K(\neg B, \neg A))$ (or shortly, $\mathrm{DI}(X, Q^K)$) of the fuzzy set $X \in \mathscr{F}(N)$ is:*

$$\mathrm{DI}(X, Q_{Ev}^K(\neg B, \neg A)) = \begin{cases} \inf \mathrm{Supp}(Ev) & \text{if } K = \forall \text{ and } X = \neg B, \\ 0 & \text{if } K = \forall \text{ and } X = \neg A, \\ 0 & \text{if } K = \exists \text{ and } X \in \{\neg A, \neg B\}, \end{cases}$$

$$\mathrm{DI}(X, Q_{Ev}^K) = \neg \mathrm{DI}(\neg X, Q_{Ev}^K).$$

1. *Rules of Distribution*
   Let $K, L \in \{\forall, \exists\}$.
   (fER1) $\mathrm{DI}(X, Q_{\mathscr{P}_1}^K) \oplus \mathrm{DI}(X, Q_{\mathscr{P}_2}^L) = 1$ where $X \in \{M, \neg M\}$.
   (fER2a) $\mathrm{DI}(X, Q_{\mathscr{C}}^K) \leq \mathrm{DI}(Y, Q_{\mathscr{P}_2}^L)$ where $X, Y \in \{S, \neg S\}$.
   (fER2b) $\mathrm{DI}(X, Q_{\mathscr{C}}^K) \leq \mathrm{DI}(Y, Q_{\mathscr{P}_1}^L)$ where $X, Y \in \{P, \neg P\}$.
2. *Rules of Quality second face*
   (fER3) Let $X, Y \in \{S, P, M\}$, $X \neq Y$ and $K \in \{\forall, \exists\}$. Then at least one of the following must hold: $\mathscr{P}_1 = Q_{Ev}^K(\neg Y, \neg X)$ or $\mathscr{P}_2 = Q_{Ev}^K(\neg Y, \neg X)$.
   (fER4) Let $X, Y \in \{S, P, M\}$, $X \neq Y$ and $K, L \in \{\forall, \exists\}$. Then

$$\mathscr{C} = Q_{Ev}^K(\neg S, P) \quad \text{iff} \quad \mathscr{P} = Q_{Ev}^L(\neg Y, X)$$

   where $\mathscr{P} \in \{\mathscr{P}_1, \mathscr{P}_2\}$.
3. *Rules of Quantity*
   (fER5) $0.5 < \inf \mathrm{Supp}(Ev_{\mathscr{P}_1}) \vee \inf \mathrm{Supp}(Ev_{\mathscr{P}_2})$.
   (fER6) $\inf \mathrm{Supp}(Ev_{\mathscr{C}}) \leq \inf \mathrm{Supp}(Ev_{\mathscr{P}_1}) \wedge \inf \mathrm{Supp}(Ev_{\mathscr{P}_2})$.

Recall, that we proved in [10] that rules (fER1)–(fER4) imply (fER5) and (fER6) and, therefore, they are sufficient.

Below we explain the definition of the distribution index for the second face. Let us consider the following syllogism **aai**-III:

$$\mathscr{P}_1: \text{All } \neg M \text{ are } \neg P : (\forall x)(\neg Mx \Rightarrow \neg Px).$$
$$\mathscr{P}_2: \text{All } \neg M \text{ are } \neg S : (\forall x)(\neg Mx \Rightarrow \neg Sx).$$
$$\mathscr{C}: \text{Some } \neg S \text{ are } \neg P : (\exists x)(\neg Sx \wedge \neg Px)$$

We know that this syllogism is valid. The formal proof is based on the provable formula

$$T^{\mathrm{IQ}}(\forall x)(\neg Mx \Rightarrow \neg Px)\&\forall x)(\neg Mx \Rightarrow \neg Sx)\&(\exists x)(\neg Mx) \Rightarrow (\exists x)(\neg Sx \wedge \neg Px).$$

It follows that the distribution index of the middle formula in the antecedent must be equal to one to guarantee (fER1). So it means that $\mathrm{DI}(\neg M, Q^{\forall}_{Bi\Delta}(\neg M, \neg P)) = 1$ as well as well as $\mathrm{DI}(\neg M, Q^{\forall}_{Bi\Delta}(\neg M, \neg S)) = 1$. Next, let's show and justify other definitions of the other formulas.

Let us consider **invalid** syllogism **aee**-I (its invalidity can be verified, e.g., using Venn's diagram).

$$\mathscr{P}_1: \text{All } \neg M \text{ are } \neg P : (\forall x)(\neg Mx \Rightarrow \neg Px)$$
$$\mathscr{P}_2: \text{All } \neg S \text{ are } M : \ (\forall x)(\neg Sx \Rightarrow Mx)$$
$$\mathscr{C}: \ \text{All } \neg S \text{ are } P : \ (\forall x)(\neg Sx \Rightarrow Px)$$

By Definition 3 we know that $\mathrm{DI}(\neg M, Q^{\forall}_{Bi\Delta}(\neg M, \neg P)) = 1$. It means that the Rule (fER1) holds. Furthermore, we know that $\mathrm{DI}(\neg S, Q^{\forall}_{Bi\Delta}(\neg S, \neg M)) = 1$ as well as $\mathrm{DI}(\neg S, Q^{\forall}_{Bi\Delta}(\neg S, P)) = 1$. It means that the Rule (fER2a) is fulfilled. Rules (fER3) and (fER4) are trivially fulfilled.

Now let's discuss Rule (fER2b). Using Definition 3 we obtain $\mathrm{DI}(\neg P, Q^{\forall}_{Bi\Delta}(\neg M, \neg P)) = 0$. By the property

$$\neg\mathrm{DI}(\neg P, Q^{\forall}(\neg M, \neg P)) = \mathrm{DI}(P, Q^{\forall}(\neg S, P)) = 1.$$

We conclude that

$$1 = \mathrm{DI}(P, Q^{\forall}_{Bi\Delta}(\neg S, P)) \not\leq \mathrm{DI}(\neg P, Q^{\forall}_{Bi\Delta}(\neg M, \neg P)) = 0$$

which means that Rule (fER2b) is not fulfilled.

The definition of the distribution index for particular quantifiers is demonstrated in the last section of this paper.

3.1   Verifying Valid Generalized Syllogisms Generated by Graded Peterson's Cube

The first main goal of this publication is to verify a group of selected logical syllogisms that are generated from Peterson's cube of opposition. This group of syllogisms is created by using new forms of intermediate quantifiers and four figures. This requires proving two implications:

(i) If a given syllogism is valid then it satisfies Rules (fER1)–(fER4).
(ii) If a syllogism satisfies Rules (fER1)–(fER4) then it is valid.

Implication (i) is proved in this section, implication (ii) in will be proved in another publication. Syntactical proofs of the validity of the mentioned syllogisms can be found in [12].

Lemma 4. *Let us consider Figure-I. Then the following valid negative syllogisms satisfy Rules (fER1)–(fER4):*

(a) **aaa, aap, aat, aak, aaf, aas, aai, aii,**
(b) **eae, eab, ead, eag, eav, eaz, eao, eio.**

Proof. (a) Let us consider syllogism **aaa**-I. Then $\mathscr{P}_1 = Q_{Bi\Delta}^{\forall}(\neg M, \neg P)$, $\mathscr{P}_2 = Q_{Bi\Delta}^{\forall}(\neg S, \neg M)$ and $\mathscr{C} = Q_{Bi\Delta}^{\forall}(\neg S, \neg P)$. From it, we conclude that $\mathrm{DI}(\neg M, Q_{Bi\Delta}^{\forall}(\neg M, \neg P)) = 1$ and $\mathrm{DI}(\neg M, Q_{Bi\Delta}^{\forall}(\neg S, \neg M)) = 0$ which means that Rule (fER1) is satisfied. The same argument can be applied also to syllogisms **aap**-I, **aat**-I, **aak**-I, **aaf**-I,**aas**-I, **aai**-I and **aii**-I.

As for Rule (fER2a), note that $\mathrm{DI}(\neg S, Q_{Bi\Delta}^{\forall}(\neg S, \neg M)) = 1$ and for the conclusion $\mathrm{DI}(\neg S, Q_{Bi\Delta}^{\forall}(\neg S, \neg P)) = 1$ which means that this rule is satisfied by **aaa**-I, and also by syllogisms **aap**-I, **aat**-I, **aak**-I, **aaf**-I, **aas**-I because

$$\mathrm{DI}(\neg S, Q_{\neg Sm Si}^{\forall}(\neg S, \neg P)) \leq \mathrm{DI}(\neg S, Q_{\neg Sm Ve}^{\forall}(\neg S, \neg P)) \leq$$
$$\mathrm{DI}(\neg S, Q_{Bi Ve}^{\forall}(\neg S, \neg P)) \leq \mathrm{DI}(\neg S, Q_{Bi Ex}^{\forall}(\neg S, \neg P)) \leq$$
$$\mathrm{DI}(\neg S, Q_{Bi\Delta}^{\forall}(\neg S, \neg M)) = 1.$$

Rule (fER2a) is trivially satisfied also by the syllogisms **aai**-I and **aii**-I because using Definition 3 we have

$$\mathrm{DI}(\neg S, Q_{Bi\Delta}^{\exists}(\neg S, \neg P)) = 0.$$

Let $K \in \{\forall, \exists\}$. In case of the Rule (FER2b) we have

$$\mathrm{DI}(\neg P, Q_{Bi\Delta}^{K}(\neg S, \neg P)) = \mathrm{DI}(\neg P, Q_{Bi\Delta}^{\forall}(\neg M, \neg P)) = 0$$

and the same equality holds for **aap**-I, **aat**-I, **aak**-I, **aaf**-I, **aas**-I, **aai**-I, **aii**-I. Hence, all these syllogisms satisfy Rule (fER2b).

All syllogisms from (a) satisfy Rules (fER3) and (fER4).

(b) Let us consider syllogism **eae**-I. Then $\mathscr{P}_1 = Q_{Bi\Delta}^{\forall}(\neg M, P)$, $\mathscr{P}_2 = Q_{Bi\Delta}^{\forall}(\neg S, \neg M)$, $\mathscr{C} = Q_{Bi\Delta}^{\forall}(\neg S, P)$.
From
it follows that $\mathrm{DI}(\neg M, Q_{Bi\Delta}^{\forall}(\neg M, P)) = 1$ and $\mathrm{DI}(\neg M, Q_{Bi\Delta}^{\forall}(\neg S, \neg M)) = 0$ and so, Rule (fER1) is satisfied by this and also by syllogisms **eae**-I, **eab**-I, **ead**-I, **eag**-I, **eav**-I, **eaz**-I, **eao**-I and **eio**-I.

As for Rule (fER2a), note that $\mathrm{DI}(\neg S, Q_{Bi\Delta}^{\forall}(\neg S, \neg M)) = 1$ and for the conclusion $\mathrm{DI}(\neg S, Q_{Bi\Delta}^{\forall}(\neg S, P)) = 1$ which means that this rule is satisfied by **eae**-I, and also by syllogisms **eab**-I, **ead**-I, **eag**-I, **eav**-I, **eaz**-I because

$$\mathrm{DI}(\neg S, Q_{\neg Sm Si}^{\forall}(\neg S, P)) \leq \mathrm{DI}(\neg S, Q_{\neg Sm Ve}^{\forall}(\neg S, P)) \leq$$
$$\mathrm{DI}(\neg S, Q_{Bi Ve}^{\forall}(\neg S, P)) \leq \mathrm{DI}(\neg S, Q_{Bi Ex}^{\forall}(\neg S, P)) \leq$$
$$\mathrm{DI}(\neg S, Q_{Bi\Delta}^{\forall}(\neg S, \neg M)) = 1.$$

Rule (fER2a) is satisfied by **eao**-I, because $\mathrm{DI}(\neg S, Q^{\exists}_{Bi\Delta}(\neg S, P)) = 0$.

Let $K \in \{\forall, \exists\}$ Rule (fER2b) is satisfied by all the syllogisms from (b) because

$$\neg\mathrm{DI}(\neg P, Q^{K}_{Ev}(\neg S, \neg P)) = 1 = \mathrm{DI}(P, Q^{K}_{Ev}(\neg S, P)) = 0 \qquad (4)$$

as well as

$$\neg\mathrm{DI}(\neg P, Q^{K}_{Ev}(\neg M, \neg P)) = 1 = \mathrm{DI}(P, Q^{K}_{Ev}(\neg M, P)) = 0 \qquad (5)$$

From (4) and (5) we conclude that

$$DI(P, Q^{K}_{Ev}(\neg S, P)) \leq DI(P, Q^{K}_{Ev}(\neg M, P)).$$

Rules (fER3) and (fER4) are obviously satisfied by all syllogisms from (b).   □

3.2   Example of Invalid Syllogisms

Below we introduce an example of forms of logical syllogisms which do not satisfy all rules (fER1)–(fER4) .

Lemma 5. *The syllogism*

(a) ***eae-III,***

does not satisfy all rules (fER1)–(fER4).

Proof. (a) $\mathscr{P}_1 = Q^{\forall}_{Bi\Delta}(\neg M, P)$, $\mathscr{P}_2 = Q^{\forall}_{BiEx}(\neg M, \neg S)$, $\mathscr{C} = Q^{\forall}_{BiEx}(\neg S, P)$. Then $\mathrm{DI}(\neg M, Q^{\forall}_{Bi\Delta}(\neg M, P)) = 1$ and $\mathrm{DI}(\neg M, Q^{\forall}_{BiEx}(\neg M, \neg S)) = 1$. Rule (fER1) is satisfied.

Rule (fER2a) says that $\mathrm{DI}(\neg S, Q^{\forall}_{Bi\Delta}(\neg S, P)) = 1$ and $\mathrm{DI}(\neg S, Q^{\forall}_{Bi\Delta}(\neg M, \neg S)) = 0$, that means that the Rule (fER2a) is not satisfied because

$$1 = \mathrm{DI}(\neg S, Q^{\forall}_{Bi\Delta}(\neg S, P)) \not\leq \mathrm{DI}(\neg S, Q^{\forall}_{Bi\Delta}(\neg M, \neg S)) = 0.$$

□

4   Conclusion

In this paper, we discussed the necessity of mathematical logic for the development of AI. Then we recalled our model of the meaning of intermediate quantifiers and syllogisms with them. The main goal was to introduce the graded cube of opposition and suggest extending Peterson's rules for verification of the validity of syllogisms with negations. We proved that indeed, all valid syllogisms with negations verify the extended Peterson's rules.

Further work will focus on two tasks: first, prove the opposite implication, i.e., that any syllogism with negations is valid, if it satisfies the extended rules. Second, we will introduce similar rules also for the other quantifiers occurring in the graded cube of opposition and prove that all syllogisms from it are valid iff they satisfy the extended Peterson's rules.

Acknowledgments. This article has been prepared with the financial support of the European Union under the REFRESH "Research Excellence For REgion Sustainability and High-tech Industries" project number CZ.10.03.01/00/22_003/0000048 via the Operational Programme Just Transition.

This article has been produced with the financial support of the European Union under the: Biography of Fake News with a Touch of AI: Dangerous Phenomenon through the Prism of Modern Human Sciences project no.: CZ.02.01.01/00/23_025/0008724 via the Operational Programme Jan Ámos Komenský.

References

1. Dubois, D., Prade, H.: On fuzzy syllogisms. Comput. Intell. **4**, 171–179 (1988)
2. Dubois, D., Godo, L., López de Mántaras, H., Prade, R.: Qualitative reasoning with imprecise probabilities. J. Intell. Inf. Syst. **2**, 319–363 (1993)
3. Pereira-Fariña, M., Díaz-Hermida, F., Bugarín, A.: On the analysis of set-based fuzzy quantified reasoning using classical syllogistics. Fuzzy Sets Syst. **214**, 83–94 (2013)
4. Novák, V.: On fuzzy type theory. Fuzzy Sets Syst. **149**, 235–273 (2005)
5. Andrews, P.: An Introduction to Mathematical Logic and Type Theory: To Truth Through Proof. Kluwer, Dordrecht (2002)
6. Novák, V.: A comprehensive theory of trichotomous evaluative linguistic expressions. Fuzzy Sets Syst. **159**(22), 2939–2969 (2008)
7. Murinová, P., Novák, V.: The theory of intermediate quantifiers in fuzzy natural logic revisited and the model of "many". Fuzzy Sets Syst. **388**, 56–89 (2020)
8. Peters, S., Westerståhl, D.: Quantifiers in Language and Logic. Clarendon Press, Oxford (2006)
9. Zadeh, L.A.: A computational approach to fuzzy quantifiers in natural languages. Comput. Math. **9**, 149–184 (1983)
10. Novák, V., Murinová, P., Ferbas, P.: Formal analysis of Peterson's rules for checking validity of syllogisms with intermediate quantifiers. Int. J. Aprox. Reason. **150**, 122–138 (2022)
11. Murinová, P., Novák, V.: Analysis of generalized square of opposition with intermediate quantifiers. Fuzzy Sets Syst. **242**, 89–113 (2014)
12. Fiala, K., Murinová, P.: A formal analysis of generalized Peterson's syllogisms related to graded Peterson's cube. Mathematics **10**(6) (2022)
13. Peterson, P.: Intermediate Quantifiers. Logic, linguistics, and Aristotelian semantics, Ashgate, Aldershot (2000)

Fuzzy Entropy

A Study of the Fuzzy Differential Entropy

Zuzana Ontkovičová[1,2]([✉])[iD] and Vicenç Torra[1][iD]

[1] Department of Computing Science, Umeå University, Umeå, Sweden
{zuzanao,vtorra}@cs.umu.se
[2] Institute of Information Engineering, Automation and Mathematics,
Faculty of Chemical and Food Technology, Slovak University of Technology
in Bratislava, Bratislava, Slovakia

Abstract. Entropy is a fundamental concept in information theory but also in some AI algorithms, used for comparison of two distribution functions or measures that describe one specific event. When focusing on the differential (continuous) version of the entropy within the fuzzy measure framework, it is necessary to generalise all the essential concepts from the additive case to the fuzzy setup. This involves shifting from probability to fuzzy measures, from Lebesgue to Choquet integral and from Radon-Nikodym to Choquet-Radon-Nikodym derivatives. In the paper, two formulas for defining fuzzy entropy are proposed with the use of extended versions of the Choquet integral. Their basic properties are examined and compared with the additive case, and a relation with the fuzzy Kullback-Leibler divergence is derived. Using a novel insight into derivatives known as the resulting measure approach, some computations are presented to determine the final entropy value for two given measures.

Keywords: Fuzzy measures · Differential entropy ·
Choquet-Radon-Nikodym derivatives · Resulting measure approach

1 Introduction and Preliminaries

Entropy originated in the 1870s in thermodynamics and statistical physics, derived from thermodynamical considerations based upon the second law of thermodynamics [16]. Hartley applied entropy in his study of random signals, and later, it also served as one of the core ideas in the information theory developed by Shannon [13] in the 1940s. Since then, it has become a fundamental concept across various scientific disciplines and is widely used in diverse applications, including engineering, finance, decision making, optimisation, system modelling, and image processing.

This article focuses on the original mathematical insight into entropy within information theory. Our aim is to make an analogy between the already introduced differential (continuous) entropy in the additive (probability) context and the fuzzy setup. The main difference lies in replacing classic probability with fuzzy measure, which does not require the key property of additivity. This

© The Author(s), under exclusive license to Springer Nature Switzerland AG 2025
M. Baczyński et al. (Eds.): EUSFLAT 2025, LNCS 15883, pp. 181–192, 2025.
https://doi.org/10.1007/978-3-031-97225-6_15

replacement leads to significant changes, particularly in the integral, derivatives, and even the formula itself, all of which we explore in detail in the article. To the best of our knowledge, the only article addressing differential entropy for fuzzy measures, as we do here, is [10] with a primary focus on Kullback-Leibler divergence.

Since information theory can be considered a branch of applied probability theory, let us recall some basic probabilistic concepts necessary for this paper. Consider a probability space $(\Omega, \mathcal{A}, \mathrm{P})$. A mapping $\xi : \Omega \to [-\infty, +\infty]$ is referred to as a random variable (RV) if $\{\omega \in \Omega : \xi(\omega) < t\} \in \mathcal{A}$ for all $t \in \mathbb{R}$. To describe RV ξ, cumulative distribution function (cdf) $\mathcal{H}_\xi : \mathbb{R} \to \mathbb{R}^+$ is commonly used, having the form

$$\mathcal{H}_\xi(t) = \mathrm{P}\left(\{\omega \in \Omega : \xi(\omega) \le t\}\right), \quad t \in \mathbb{R}.$$

The cdf is said to be absolutely continuous if there exists a function $h : \mathbb{R} \to \mathbb{R}_0^+$ such that $\int_{-\infty}^{\infty} h(t)\, \mathrm{d}t = 1$ and $\mathcal{H}_\xi(t) = \int_{-\infty}^{t} h(x)\, \mathrm{d}x$. Then h is called probability density function (pdf), and it holds $h(t) = \dfrac{\mathrm{d}\mathcal{H}_\xi(t)}{\mathrm{d}t} = \mathcal{H}'_\xi(t)$ if the derivative exists.

It is evident that probability measure, cdf and pdf are closely interconnected, so a direct link between the probability and pdf also exists. It is described through the Radon-Nikodym theorem, where assuming two σ-finite[1] measures μ, ν with absolute continuity $\nu \ll \mu$[2], there exists a measurable function $f : \Omega \to \mathbb{R}_0^+$, such that for any measurable set $A \in \mathcal{A}$ it holds

$$\nu(A) = \int_A f \, \mathrm{d}\mu. \tag{1}$$

The function f is then called the Radon-Nikodym (RN) derivative, commonly denoted as $f = \dfrac{\mathrm{d}\nu}{\mathrm{d}\mu}$. In this context, pdf can be represented as RN derivative $h = \dfrac{\mathrm{d}\mathrm{P}}{\mathrm{d}\lambda}$, with λ being Lebesgue measure.

From the information theory perspective [12] inspired by Shannon, the entropy of an event described by a RV ξ associated with pdf h is connected to its gain in information. Intuitively, the information gain is inversely related to its probability of occurrence $\mathsf{IG}(\xi) = \ln\left(\frac{1}{h}\right) = -\ln h$, and the resulting entropy is then taken as its expected value $\mathsf{Ent}(\xi) = \mathbb{E}[\mathsf{IG}(\xi)]$. The corresponding differential entropy is hence defined as

$$\mathsf{Ent}(\xi) = -\int h \ln h \, \mathrm{d}\lambda,$$

with a convention $0 \cdot \ln 0 = 0$. In case the RN derivative is used instead of the pdf, the formula is revised as

$$\mathsf{Ent}(\mathrm{P}) = -\int \frac{\mathrm{d}\mathrm{P}}{\mathrm{d}\lambda} \ln\left(\frac{\mathrm{d}\mathrm{P}}{\mathrm{d}\lambda}\right) \mathrm{d}\lambda. \tag{2}$$

---

[1] μ is σ-finite if $(\forall (A_n)_{n \in \mathbb{N}} \in \mathcal{A} : A_i \cap A_j = \emptyset \; i \ne j, \Omega = \bigcup_{n \in \mathbb{N}} A_n) \; \mu(A_n) < \infty.$
[2] $\nu \ll \mu$ if $(\forall A \in \mathcal{A}) \; \mu(A) = 0 \Rightarrow \nu(A) = 0.$

After modification resulting from (change of variables) property of RN derivatives, it can be shortened to

$$\mathsf{Ent}(\mathrm{P}) = -\int \ln\left(\frac{\mathrm{dP}}{\mathrm{d}\lambda}\right)\mathrm{dP}. \tag{3}$$

The notation for entropy has changed to focus on the measure in the argument
rather than the RV, which does not explicitly appear in the formula. The two formulas (2) and (3) are our starting point for fuzzy generalisation of the definition
of differential entropy.

It is important to highlight significant differences between discrete and differential entropy. One is that the final value of differential entropy cannot be directly
interpreted. It is only interpretable when comparing values or after being divided
by a pre-agreed reference entropy. Another distinction is that the final value of
differential entropy can be any real number, even a negative one, as illustrated
in Example 1. This is not true in the discrete case with only nonnegative values
possible.

Example 1. Let ξ be a RV characterised by Laplace distribution $h_\theta(t) = \frac{\theta}{2}e^{-\theta t}$,
$\theta > 0$. Its differential entropy is given as

$$\mathsf{Ent}(\xi) = -2\int_0^\infty \frac{\theta}{2}e^{-\theta t}\ln\left(\frac{\theta}{2}e^{-\theta t}\right)\mathrm{d}t = \ln\left(\frac{2e}{\theta}\right).$$

Taking e.g. $\theta = 10$, the resulting entropy value is negative $\mathsf{Ent}(\xi) \doteq -0.6094$.

2   Main Fuzzy Results

For the rest of the paper, let us shift to the fuzzy framework. On a measurable
space $(\Omega, \mathcal{A})$, a fuzzy measure $\mu : \mathcal{A} \to [0,1]$ is a set function satisfying the
following properties:

  ○ (groundedness) $\mu(\emptyset) = 0$
  ○ (normalisation) $\mu(\Omega) = 1$
  ○ (monotonicity) $(\forall A, B \in \mathcal{A} : A \subseteq B)\ \mu(A) \leq \mu(B)$.

Using fuzzy measures in integration leads to a transition from the additive
Lebesgue integral to its fuzzy equivalent, the Choquet integral. For a nonnegative RV ξ and a fuzzy measure μ, it is defined as the indefinite Riemann integral
[2,3] in the form

$$(C)\int \xi\,\mathrm{d}\mu = \int_0^\infty \mathcal{S}_{\mu,\xi}(t)\,\mathrm{d}t,$$

with the corresponding survival function given by

$$\mathcal{S}_{\mu,\xi}(t) = \mu(\{\omega \in \Omega : \mu(\omega) > t\}), \quad t \in \mathbb{R},$$

emphasising the use of the fuzzy measure in the lower index. When considering a
general RV with both positive and negative values, there are two different ways

to extend the Choquet integral, namely symmetric (C_s) and asymmetric (C_a) versions given as

$$(C_a) \int \xi \, \mathrm{d}\mu = (C) \int \xi^+ \, \mathrm{d}\mu - (C) \int \xi^- \, \mathrm{d}\overline{\mu}$$

$$(C_s) \int \xi \, \mathrm{d}\mu = (C) \int \xi^+ \, \mathrm{d}\mu - (C) \int \xi^- \, \mathrm{d}\mu.$$

The two Choquet integrals differ in the formula only for the nonpositive part, where the crucial aspect is the dual measure[3] that appears in the asymmetric version. This distinction also influences the properties of the integrals, which can be found in [2] for nonnegative and in [8] for general RV.

2.1 Choquet-Radon-Nikodym Derivatives

The concept of RN derivatives should also be revised for fuzzy measures, using the introduced Choquet integral, as in [7].

Definition 1. *On a measurable space $(\Omega, \mathcal{A})$, consider two σ-finite fuzzy measures μ, ν and the Choquet integral of nonnegative function g given as*

$$\nu(A) = (C) \int_A g \, \mathrm{d}\mu$$

for any $A \in \mathcal{A}$. Then, g is referred to as a Choquet-Radon-Nikodym (CRN) derivative with notation $g = \frac{\partial \nu}{\partial \mu}$ distinguished from the additive RN derivatives.

CRN derivatives are always nonnegative functions, so there is no need to use extended Choquet integrals. In what follows, some properties of the derivatives adopted from [7] are mentioned, namely change of variables for the Choquet integral and basic computational calculus.

Lemma 1. *Assume RV ξ, fuzzy measures μ, ν, and the existence of the corresponding CRN derivative $\frac{\partial \nu}{\partial \mu}$. For a nonnegative ξ, it holds*

$$(C) \int \xi \frac{\partial \nu}{\partial \mu} \, \mathrm{d}\mu = (C) \int \xi \, \mathrm{d}\nu.$$

For a general ξ with positive and negative values, the equality holds only for symmetric, but not for asymmetric Choquet integral.

Lemma 2. *Let μ, ν, τ be fuzzy measures and assume existence of all the necessary CRN derivatives. Then it holds*

i) (homogeneity) $\frac{\partial(k\nu)}{\partial(c\mu)} = \frac{k}{c} \frac{\partial \nu}{\partial \mu}$ μ-a.e. for $c, k \geq 0$

ii) (chain rule) $\frac{\partial \nu}{\partial \tau} \frac{\partial \tau}{\partial \mu} = \frac{\partial \nu}{\partial \mu}$ μ-a.e.

---

[3] $\overline{\mu}$ is dual measure to μ if $(\forall A \in \mathcal{A}) \; \overline{\mu}(A) = \mu(\Omega) - \mu(A^c)$.

iii) (inverse) $\frac{\partial \nu}{\partial \mu} = \left(\frac{\partial \mu}{\partial \nu}\right)^{-1}$

iv) (duality) $\frac{\partial \nu}{\partial \mu} \leq \frac{\partial \nu}{\partial \overline{\mu}} \left[\frac{\partial \nu}{\partial \mu} \geq \frac{\partial \nu}{\partial \overline{\mu}}\right]$ μ-*a.e. for subadditive [superadditive]* μ^4.

Unlike the additive Radon-Nikodym theorem, Definition 1 concerning CRN derivatives does not provide any hint for either theoretical or computational aspects of these derivatives. Just assuming existence, absolute continuity between measures still applies as in the additive case, but additional conditions are required. In [5], the requirement is the submodularity of both measures. A less strict condition but more complex to verify, is given in [4], where both measures are subadditive with a strong decomposition property. This property, derived from the Hahn decomposition of measures, is also studied in [6,11] and [1], where the authors proposed its modified versions.

2.2 Definitions

All the necessary modifications to adapt originally additive concepts to the fuzzy framework have been proposed, specifically the transition from probability to fuzzy measure, from Lebesgue to Choquet integral, and from RN to CRN derivatives. We can now generalise the differential entropy formula itself, which is derived from the additive formulas (2) and (3).

Definition 2 (Fuzzy differential entropy). *On a measurable space* $(\Omega, \mathcal{A})$, *consider two fuzzy measures* μ, ν *such that their corresponding CRN derivative* $\frac{\partial \nu}{\partial \mu}$ *exist. Then, fuzzy differential entropy of* ν *with respect to* μ *is given as*

$$\mathsf{Ent}^a_\mu(\nu) = -(C_a) \int \frac{\partial \nu}{\partial \mu} \ln \left(\frac{\partial \nu}{\partial \mu}\right) \mathrm{d}\mu \tag{4}$$

$$\mathsf{Ent}^s_\mu(\nu) = -(C_s) \int \ln \left(\frac{\partial \nu}{\partial \mu}\right) \mathrm{d}\nu \tag{5}$$

with asymmetric and symmetric Choquet integrals, respectively.

The notation is adapted to the fuzzy context, with the reference measure in the lower index and the type of Choquet integral in the upper index. The two proposed definitions (4) and (5) differ in the type of Choquet integral used, leading to their different forms. The first one with the asymmetric integral is a direct analogy to the longer additive formula (2). The second definition with the symmetric integral is shortened according to Lemma 1, resulting in the change of the integration measure. It is also a direct analogy to the shorter additive formula (3).

---

[4] Subadditivity $(\forall A, B \in \mathcal{A})$ $\mu(A) + \mu(B) \geq \mu(A \cup B)$, superadditivity with $\leq$ instead.

2.3   Properties

An interesting objective is to study some basic properties of fuzzy differential entropy and compare them with the additive case. Next two properties can be viewed as variations of positive homogeneity. The first one, with respect to the reference measure, is additively expressed as $\mathsf{Ent}_{k\lambda}(\mathrm{P}) = \ln k + \mathsf{Ent}_\lambda(\mathrm{P})$ for all $k > 0$, $k \neq 1$. Dealing with fuzzy measures, the corresponding holds.

Theorem 1. *Let μ, ν be fuzzy measures and all the necessary CRN derivatives exist. Then for both extended Choquet integrals*

- $\mathsf{Ent}_{k\mu}(\nu) \leq \mathsf{Ent}_\mu(\nu)$ *for $k \in (0,1)$*
- $\mathsf{Ent}_{k\mu}(\nu) \geq \mathsf{Ent}_\mu(\nu)$ *for $k > 1$.*

Additional inequalities can be obtained using asymmetric Choquet integral

- $\mathsf{Ent}_{k\mu}^a(\nu) \geq \ln k + \mathsf{Ent}_\mu^a(\nu)$ *for $k \in (0,1)$ and submodular μ*
- $\mathsf{Ent}_{k\mu}^a(\nu) \leq \ln k + \mathsf{Ent}_\mu^a(\nu)$ *for $k \in (0,1)$ and supermodular μ.*

Proof. Initially, only the entropy formula (4) with asymmetric Choquet integral is assumed. From the positive homogeneity of derivatives in Lemma 2 i) we have

$$\mathsf{Ent}_{k\mu}^a(\nu) = -(C_a) \int \frac{\partial\nu}{\partial(k\mu)} \ln\left(\frac{\partial\nu}{\partial(k\mu)}\right) \mathrm{d}(k\mu) = -(C_a) \int \frac{\partial\nu}{\partial\mu} \ln\left(\frac{1}{k}\frac{\partial\nu}{\partial\mu}\right) \mathrm{d}\mu.$$

The first two results in the theorem are derived by estimating $1/k$ in the logarithm argument. The next two follow when rewriting logarithm in the form of sum and using weaker integral linearity (additivity). With further condition of sub/supermodularity of the measure, it results in the corresponding inequality (submodular measure is taken in derivation)

$$\ldots \quad \geq -(C_a) \int \frac{\partial\nu}{\partial\mu} (-\ln k) \, \mathrm{d}\mu - (C_a) \int \frac{\partial\nu}{\partial\mu} \ln\left(\frac{\partial\nu}{\partial\mu}\right) \mathrm{d}\mu$$

$$= \ln k \, (C_a) \int \frac{\partial\nu}{\partial\mu} \, \mathrm{d}\mu + \mathsf{Ent}_\mu^a(\nu) = \ln k + \mathsf{Ent}_\mu^a(\nu).$$

In the last line, positive homogeneity of the integral is used, which is valid for $\ln k < 0$, so $k \in (0,1)$. Otherwise, a dual measure is necessary and further inequality comparison between the original and dual measure leads to the additive case. If formula (5) is used with the symmetric Choquet integral, weaker linearity cannot be applied since it requires stricter conditions not satisfied in this case. Thus only the first two results are considered.   □

The second variation of the homogeneity property is done regarding the measure in the argument. Its additive form is given by $\mathsf{Ent}(k\mathrm{P}) = -k\ln k + k\mathsf{Ent}(\mathrm{P})$ for $k > 0$, $k \neq 1$. For fuzzy measures, results are summarised as follows.

Theorem 2. *Let μ, ν be fuzzy measures and all the necessary CRN derivatives exist. Then for both extended Choquet integrals*

○ $\mathsf{Ent}_\mu(k\nu) \geq k\,\mathsf{Ent}_\mu(\nu)$ *for* $k \in (0,1)$
○ $\mathsf{Ent}_\mu(k\nu) \leq k\,\mathsf{Ent}_\mu(\nu)$ *for* $k > 1$.

Closer boundaries can be obtained for asymmetric Choquet integral

○ $\mathsf{Ent}_\mu^a(k\nu) \leq -k\ln k + k\,\mathsf{Ent}_\mu^a(\nu)$ *for* $k > 1$ *and supermodular* μ
○ $\mathsf{Ent}_\mu^a(k\nu) \geq -k\ln k + k\,\mathsf{Ent}_\mu^a(\nu)$ *for* $k > 1$ *and submodular* μ.

The proof follows a similar structure to that of the previous theorem. The next property describes a situation where the reference measure is replaced with its dual.

Theorem 3. *Let* μ, ν *be fuzzy measures,* $\overline{\mu}$ *the dual measure to* μ *(also fuzzy) and all the necessary CRN derivatives exist.*

○ *If* μ *is subadditive, then* $\mathsf{Ent}_{\overline{\mu}}^s(\nu) \leq \mathsf{Ent}_\mu^s(\nu)$.
○ *If* μ *is superadditive, then* $\mathsf{Ent}_{\overline{\mu}}^s(\nu) \geq \mathsf{Ent}_\mu^s(\nu)$.

Proof. Lemma 2 iv) for CRN derivatives is used together with increasingness of logarithm and monotonicity of symmetric Choquet integral, resulting in (assuming subadditive measure in the derivation)

$$\mathsf{Ent}_{\overline{\mu}}^s(\nu) = -(C_s) \int \ln\left(\frac{\partial\nu}{\partial\overline{\mu}}\right) d\nu \leq -(C_s) \int \ln\left(\frac{\partial\nu}{\partial\mu}\right) d\nu = \mathsf{Ent}_\mu^s(\nu).$$

For the asymmetric Choquet integral, an estimation for $\overline{\mu}$ is needed in the CRN derivative and the integral measure, leading to the additive case.   □

The formula for differential entropy can also be deduced from Kullback-Leibler (KL) divergence as a particular case of ϕ-divergence, which is a special class of information divergences. To present this derivation step by step, assume the general fuzzy ϕ-divergence formula proposed in [7]

$$\mathsf{D}_\phi^a(\nu_1, \nu_2 : \mu) = (C_a) \int \frac{\partial\nu_2}{\partial\mu} \phi\left(\frac{\partial\nu_1/\partial\mu}{\partial\nu_2/\partial\mu}\right) d\mu$$

with the asymmetric Choquet integral indicated in the upper index. With Lemma 2 ii) and iii), $\dfrac{\partial\nu_1/\partial\mu}{\partial\nu_2/\partial\mu} = \dfrac{\partial\nu_1}{\partial\mu}\dfrac{\partial\mu}{\partial\nu_2} = \dfrac{\partial\nu_1}{\partial\nu_2}$, resulting in the modified formula

$$\mathsf{D}_\phi^a(\nu_1, \nu_2 : \mu) = (C_a) \int \frac{\partial\nu_2}{\partial\mu} \phi\left(\frac{\partial\nu_1}{\partial\nu_2}\right) d\mu.$$

Moving from the general to the particular case, $\phi(t) = t\ln t$ for KL divergence,

$$\mathsf{D}_{KL}^a(\nu_1, \nu_2 : \mu) = (C_a) \int \frac{\partial\nu_1}{\partial\mu} \ln\left(\frac{\partial\nu_1}{\partial\nu_2}\right) d\mu$$

with the modification $\dfrac{\partial \nu_2}{\partial \mu}\dfrac{\partial \nu_1}{\partial \nu_2} = \dfrac{\partial \nu_1}{\partial \mu}$ according to Lemma 2 ii). For the symmetric Choquet integral, Lemma 1 is used to shorten the form

$$D^s_{KL}(\nu_1, \nu_2) = (C_s)\int \ln\left(\frac{\partial \nu_1}{\partial \nu_2}\right) d\nu_1,$$

with no need for a reference measure. Comparing the last two integrals as the final forms for KL divergence with the fuzzy entropy formulas (4) and (5), it is easily seen that entropy is obtained as their special case.

Lemma 3. *Assume fuzzy measures μ, ν and existence of all the necessary CRN derivatives. Then, the relation between entropy and KL divergence is given as*

$$\mathsf{Ent}^a_\mu(\nu) = -\mathsf{D}^a_{KL}(\nu, \mu : \mu)$$
$$\mathsf{Ent}^s_\mu(\nu) = -\mathsf{D}^s_{KL}(\nu, \mu).$$

2.4   Computation

Computing the entropy value for two given fuzzy measures involves several difficulties. The first problem is calculation of the Choquet integral itself. While definition works well for discrete measures, it can be cumbersome in general for continuous ones. Alternative computational formulas exist [9,14], however, they are limited to only distorted Lebesgue measures and distorted probabilities. An even bigger challenge lies in the computation of the derivatives. Regardless of the additive or fuzzy case, there are no insights on how to compute them in general. The only available approach is through Laplace transforms [14], but it does not take into account whether the derivative actually exists.

A more promising alternative approach to analysing derivatives is proposed in [10]. The authors consider the Choquet integral for an arbitrary nonnegative function g with respect to a fixed class of measures μ and aim to classify the resulting measure $\nu_{g,\mu}$ represented as

$$\nu_{g,\mu}(A) = (C)\int_A g\, d\mu.$$

Thanks to the constructive proof provided, this insight addresses both the existence and computation problems for the studied pairs of integration-resulting measures. Assuming additive case, the resulting measure for both Lebesgue and probability integration measure is probability with the corresponding pdf

$$\nu_{g,\lambda} \equiv \mathrm{P} \quad (p \equiv g) \qquad\qquad \nu_{g,\mathrm{P}'} \equiv \mathrm{P} \quad (p \equiv g\,p'). \qquad (6)$$

In the fuzzy setup, we highlight two discrete results

$$\nu_{g,\mu_{min}} \equiv \mu_{\Omega,k} \quad (k = \min_{\omega \in \Omega} g(\omega)) \qquad\qquad \nu_{g,\mu_{max}} \equiv \mu_\pi \quad (\pi \equiv g), \qquad (7)$$

where $\mu_{\Omega,k}(A) = \begin{cases} k, & A = \Omega \\ 0, & A \neq \Omega \end{cases}$ is the generalised unanimity measure with a special case of the minimal (smallest) measure $\mu_{min} = \mu_{\Omega,1}$. The maximal (greatest) measure is given as $\mu_{max}(A) = \begin{cases} 1, & A \neq \emptyset \\ 0, & A = \emptyset \end{cases}$ and $\mu_{\pi}(A) = \max_{x \in A} \pi(x)$ represents the possibility measure with an arbitrary function $\pi : \Omega \to \mathbb{R}_0^+$.

These results can be applied in a reverse manner to find derivatives. Knowing both integration and resulting measures, hence also their formulas, it is easy to see just by comparison what the final derivative form should be. In the following computation, only two pairs are conveniently taken into account, namely the probability-probability pair from (6) and the maximal-possibility measures pair from (7). The corresponding derivatives are given as

$$\frac{\mathrm{d}P}{\mathrm{d}P'} = g \equiv \frac{p}{p'} \qquad\qquad \frac{\partial \mu_{\pi}}{\partial \mu_{max}} = g \equiv \pi. \tag{8}$$

The following examples serve as a completion of the paper, summarising everything that has been presented and discussed regarding the entropy computation. The first example deals with the additive case, finding the entropy between two particular probability measures. The symmetric version of the definition is used, even though the result with the asymmetric one would be the same because of the additivity.

Example 2. On a bounded interval $[a,b] = [1,3]$, assume probability with uniform distribution P_{uni} with pdf $p_{uni}(x) = \frac{1}{b-a}$ and probability with reciprocal distribution P_{rec} where $p_{rec}(x) = \frac{1}{x \ln\left(\frac{b}{a}\right)}$. The aim is to find the entropy of P_{rec} with respect to P_{uni}, so $\mathsf{Ent}_{\mathrm{P}_{uni}}(\mathrm{P}_{rec})$.
From (8), we obtain the corresponding derivative in the form

$$\frac{\mathrm{d}P_{rec}}{\mathrm{d}P_{uni}} = \frac{\frac{1}{b-a}}{\frac{1}{x \ln\left(\frac{b}{a}\right)}} = \frac{\ln\left(\frac{b}{a}\right)}{b-a} x,$$

which is next used in the entropy definition (5). Due to the additivity, it reduces to the Lebesgue integral, and we calculate the result as follows

$$\mathsf{Ent}_{\mathrm{P}_{uni}}(\mathrm{P}_{rec}) = -\int_{[a,b]} \ln\left(\frac{\mathrm{d}P_{rec}}{\mathrm{d}P_{uni}}\right) \mathrm{d}P_{rec} = -\int_a^b \ln\left(\frac{\mathrm{d}P_{rec}}{\mathrm{d}P_{uni}}(x)\right) p_{rec}(x)\, \mathrm{d}x$$

$$= -\int_a^b \ln\left(\frac{\ln\left(\frac{b}{a}\right)}{b-a} x\right) \frac{1}{x \ln\left(\frac{b}{a}\right)}\, \mathrm{d}x = \ln\left(\frac{b-a}{\ln\left(\frac{b}{a}\right)}\right) - \frac{\ln^2 b - \ln^2 a}{2\ln\left(\frac{b}{a}\right)}$$

$$= \ln\left(\frac{2}{\ln 3}\right) - \frac{\ln 3}{2} \approx 0.04979 \quad \text{for } [a,b] = [1,3].$$

The second example addresses the non-additive case, considering maximal and possibility measures. Since both are discrete, the generally complex integral computation reduces to more manageable summation. For further simplification, function π in the possibility measure has all the values at least equal to 1. That leads to the nonnegative argument and subsequently both versions of the entropy definition give the same result. For this example, let us take the asymmetric version.

Example 3. The task is to compute the entropy of the possibility measure with respect to the maximal measure using the asymmetric Choquet integral, so $\mathsf{Ent}^a_{\mu_{max}}(\mu_\pi)$.

We know that $\frac{\partial \mu_\pi}{\partial \mu_{max}} = \pi$ resulting from (8) and then, the computation of the final entropy value is done as

$$\mathsf{Ent}^a_{\mu_{max}}(\mu_\pi) = -(C_a) \int_\Omega \frac{\partial \mu_\pi}{\partial \mu_{max}} \ln \left(\frac{\partial \mu_\pi}{\partial \mu_{max}} \right) d\mu_{max} = -(C_a) \int_\Omega \pi \ln \pi \, d\mu_{max}$$

$$= - \sum_{i=1}^{n} (\pi \ln \pi)_{(i)} \left[\mu_{max}(\{(i), \dots, (n)\}) - \mu_{max}(\{(i+1), \dots, (n)\}) \right]$$

$$= - \max_{\omega \in \Omega} \left[\pi(\omega) \ln \pi(\omega) \right].$$

The notation (i) in the lower index signifies the nondecreasing order of the elements, while in the measure argument, it refers to the set corresponding to the i-th value after the ordering, as is common in the discrete definition of the Choquet integral. Interesting in this example is the fact that regardless of the specific values of π, even its monotonicity, the result remains unchanged. The reason is that both π and $\ln \pi$ have the same monotonicity, and using the maximal measure leads to the focus only on the largest corresponding element.

Remark 1. Using the computation of entropy $\mathsf{Ent}^a_{\mu_{max}(\mu_\pi)}$ from Example 3, let us verify the results proposed in Theorems 1 and 2. Observe that measure μ_{max} is submodular, and max function is subadditive.

Assuming homogeneity property with respect to the reference measure, we have

$$\mathsf{Ent}^a_{k\mu_{max}}(\mu_\pi) = - \max_{\omega \in \Omega} \left[\pi(\omega) \ln \left(\frac{\pi(\omega)}{k} \right) \right].$$

which for $k \in (0, 1)$ yields higher values and for $k > 1$ smaller values than the original $\mathsf{Ent}^a_{\mu_{max}}(\mu_\pi)$. Continuing with the estimations

$$\dots \quad = - \max_{\omega \in \Omega} \left[\pi(\omega) \ln \pi(\omega) - \ln k \, \pi(\omega) \right] \geq \mathsf{Ent}^a_{\mu_{max}}(\mu_\pi) + \ln k \max_{\omega \in \Omega} \pi(\omega).$$

Since π is always greater than one, we obtain the same result as in Theorem 1 for submodular measures. Looking at homogeneity with respect to measure in the argument, it holds

$$\mathsf{Ent}^a_{\mu_{max}}(k\mu_\pi) = -k \max_{\omega \in \Omega} \left[\pi(\omega) \ln \left(k \, \pi(\omega) \right) \right],$$

thus taking $k \in (0,1)$ leads to smaller values and taking $k > 1$ greater values compared to the original $\mathsf{Ent}^a_{\mu_{max}}(\mu_\pi)$. Also, with further estimations

$$\ldots \quad = -k \max_{\omega \in \Omega} [\ln k\, \pi(\omega) + \pi(\omega) \ln \pi(\omega)] \geq -k \ln k \max_{\omega \in \Omega} \pi(\omega) + k\, \mathsf{Ent}^a_{\mu_{max}(\mu_\pi)},$$

where again π is always greater than one, therefore the result is consistent with the one in Theorem 2 for submodular measures.

3   Conclusions and Future Work

The key concept of the paper was differential entropy and a generalisation of its well-studied additive case for the fuzzy measures. With the use of CRN derivatives, we proposed two entropy definitions with symmetric and asymmetric versions of the Choquet integral. The definitions coincide for nonnegative arguments but differ in general because of the change of variables property of the derivatives valid only in case of the symmetric Choquet integral. Based on the properties of integrals and derivatives, we proved some basic entropy properties, including homogeneities with respect to both reference and argument measures as well as a connection with the dual reference measure. Additionally, we aimed to compute the entropy value for two given measures. The most convenient method for this task appeared to be the resulting measure approach, which is currently the only one addressing both existence and computation issue for the CRN derivatives as the biggest problem here. This novel approach can also be promising for future research, as now it only provides some preliminary results.

Additional efforts may be directed toward potential applications of the proposed fuzzy entropy. This includes both straightforward generalizations of traditionally additive concepts, such as determining the distance between fuzzy measures within machine learning and statistical frameworks, as well as more theoretical investigations, e.g., exploring the use of the maximum entropy principle [15] to derive fuzzy distribution functions.

Acknowledgments. This work was partially supported by the KEMPE foundation. Support from the Wallenberg AI, Autonomous Systems and Software Program (WASP) funded by the Knut and Alice Wallenberg Foundation is also gratefully acknowledged.

Disclosure of Interests. The authors have no competing interests to declare that are relevant to the content of this article.

References

1. Candeloro, D., Volcic, A.: Radon-Nikodym theorems. Handbook of Measure Theory: In Two Volumes. Elsevier (2002)
2. Denneberg, D.: Non-additive measure and integral, vol. 27. Springer (2013)
3. Grabisch, M.: Set Functions, Games and Capacities in Decision Making, vol. 46. Springer, Berlin (2016)

4. Graf, S.: A Radon-Nikodym theorem for capacities. Journal für die reine und ange-wandte Mathematik **1980**(320), 192–214 (1980)
5. Huber, P., Strassen, V.: Minimax tests and the Neyman-Pearson lemma for capac-ities. Ann. Stat. 251–263 (1973)
6. Nguyen, H.T.: An Introduction to Random Sets. Chapman and Hall/CRC Press (2006)
7. Ontkovičová, Z., Kisel'ák, J.: A way to proper generalization of ϕ-divergence based on Choquet derivatives. Soft. Comput. **26**(21), 11295–11314 (2022)
8. Ontkovičová, Z., Kisel'ák, J., Hutník, O.: On quadruplets of nonadditive integrals. Fuzzy Sets Syst. **451**, 297–319 (2022)
9. Ontkovičová, Z., Torra, V.: Computation of Choquet integrals: analytical approach for continuous functions. Inf. Sci. **679**, 121105 (2024)
10. Ontkovičová, Z., Torra, V.: On measures resulting from the Choquet integration. In: Information Processing and Management of Uncertainty in Knowledge-Based Systems: IPMU 2024, Lecture Notes in Networks and Systems **1175**, 3–11 (2025)
11. Ouyang, Y., Li, J.: A Radon-Nikodym theorem for monotone measures. Fuzzy Sets Syst. **487**, 108995 (2024)
12. Pal, N.R., Pal, S.K.: Entropy: a new definition and its applications. IEEE Trans. Syst. Man Cybern. **21**(5), 1260–1270 (1991)
13. Shannon, C.: A mathematical theory of communication. Bell Syst. Tech. J. **27**(3), 379–423 (1948)
14. Sugeno, M.: A way to Choquet calculus. IEEE Trans. Fuzzy Syst. **23**, 1439–1457 (2014)
15. Torra, V.: Entropy for non-additive measures in continuous domains. Fuzzy Sets Syst. **324**, 49–59 (2017)
16. Wehrl, A.: General properties of entropy. Rev. Mod. Phys. **50**(2), 221–260 (1978)

Towards Probabilistic Entropies
for Interval Valued Fuzzy Sets

Christophe Marsala$^{(\boxtimes)}$ and Bernadette Bouchon-Meunier

Sorbonne Université, CNRS, LIP6, 75005 Paris, France
{Bernadette.Bouchon-Meunier,Christophe.Marsala}@lip6.fr

Abstract. Measures of information are a key concept and in the heart in Artificial Intelligence. The well-known measure of information, the Shannon entropy, is commonly used in several domains to value the information associated with a set of probabilistic events. By extension, it is also used to provide information on a distribution of values. This aim of measuring information has been extended to the fuzzy sets theory and to its extension. Indeed, several entropies of interval-valued fuzzy sets (IVFS), or, equivalently, entropies of Atanassov intuitionistic fuzzy sets, have been proposed. However, all these entropies takes only into account the form of the set rather than a probabilistic information that could be associated to it. In this paper, we state the requirements that a probabilistic entropy of IVFS should fulfilled.

Keywords: Measure of information · Entropy · Interval-valued fuzzy sets

1 Introduction

Measuring information is a very crucial task in Artificial intelligence. First of all, one main challenge is to define what is information, as what has been proposed by Lotfi Zadeh [33] who considers two aspects of information: probabilistic information and possibilistic information and their combination.

In this paper, we do not focus on defining information but we discuss on the measurement of information and the evaluation of a measure of information in the particular case of Interval Valued Fuzzy Sets (IVFS) [10,31], closely related to Atanassov intuitionistic fuzzy sets (IFS) [4,28].

After the introduction of an entropy for fuzzy sets [32] and proposals to define it [9,29], various works have proposed definitions of the entropy of IFS [22,24–27] and type-2 fuzzy sets [19,30]. Many so-called entropies have been introduced to evaluate the information provided by IVFS [7,13,14,23,34].

Like the seminal work by De Luca and Termini [9], all of them consider the information associated with the intervals defining their membership functions. They are only regarded from the point of view of the possibilistic information and no probability of event is involved. We propose a more general approach, in line with Zadeh's [32], taking into account both aspects of the imperfection in

© The Author(s), under exclusive license to Springer Nature Switzerland AG 2025
M. Baczyński et al. (Eds.): EUSFLAT 2025, LNCS 15883, pp. 193–204, 2025.
https://doi.org/10.1007/978-3-031-97225-6_16

the observation of events or objects, the imprecise definition of their membership function and their probability.

An instance of application where there exists a need for a combination of probabilistic and possibilistic information is the prediction of the outside temperature for a day (for instance, to predict the temperature in Paris on May 1st). A distribution of probability is known on the set of values for the temperature, defined by previous experiments (the observed temperatures in the past on the same place and on the same day of the year and those observed in the days before). Moreover, the knowledge on the temperature for May 1st in Paris is "average temperature", defined on the universe of temperatures. The question is what is the information brought out by the knowledge of these two kinds of information? How can we evaluate this information by means of an appropriate information measure such as, for instance, an entropy? In [32], such a measure has been defined in the case of fuzzy sets. In the case of IVFS or IFS, it appears that such an extension should also be of great interest.

This paper is composed as follows. In Sect. 2, the context of our work is presented. In Sect. 3, we recall basic definitions of entropies in the probabilistic or fuzzy setting and their possible interpretation. Section 4 introduces probabilistic entropies of interval-valued fuzzy sets on the basis of desirable properties. Section 5 concludes the paper and introduces some future work.

2   Context

In this section, we first recall the notations [6] that are used in the paper, then we recall the IVFS and IFS setting.

2.1   Notations

Let B be a σ-algebra defined on a finite universe $\mathcal{U}$. For any integer $n > 0$, we use the following notations:

- $X_n = \{(x_1, \ldots, x_n) \mid x_i \in B, \forall i = 1, \ldots, n\}$,
- $P_n = \{(p_1, \ldots, p_n) \mid p_i \in [0,1]\}$, p_i being associated with x_i through a function $p : B \to [0,1]$, a particular case being a probability distribution defined on $\mathcal{U}$,
- $W_n = \{(w_{x_1}, \ldots, w_{x_n}) \mid w_{x_i} \in \mathcal{W}, \forall i = 1, \ldots, n\}$, a family of n-tuples of weights, where $\mathcal{W}$ is either a subset of $\mathbb{R}^+$, or, in our setting, a subset of $\mathbb{R}^+ \times \mathbb{R}^+$. In the following, for the sake of simplicity, w_{x_i} is denoted w_i when the meaning of i is clear. Each weight W_n is associated with n-tuples of B through a function $f : B \to \mathbb{R}^{+n}$, such that $f(x_1, \ldots, x_n) = (w_{x_1}, \ldots, w_{x_n})$.

Similarly to the definition of the inset entropy [2], we introduce an **entropy measure** as a sequence of mappings $E_n : X_n \times P_n \times W_n \to \mathbb{R}^+$ satisfying several properties among a long list, available for instance in [1] or in [18]. In our case, the weights define the fuzzy sets or their extensions.

2.2   Intuitionistic and Interval-Valued Fuzzy Sets

Atanassov's *Intuitionistic fuzzy sets* (IFS) [4] and *interval-valued fuzzy sets* (IVFS) [31] are two representations of the imprecision that point out two different ways of representing the same knowledge about the membership of an element $x \in X$ to a subset $A \subseteq X$.

As it has already been shown in the literature, these two models of representation are theoretically close and are two approaches to represent a lack of knowledge about the membership of an element to a set. As such, each of them highlights a particular approach to define A and may be particularly suited to specific applications.

Intuitionistic Fuzzy Sets (IFS). An IFS A of X is a subset of X defined by the memberships of its elements as follows:

$$A = \{(x, \mu_A(x), \nu_A(x)) \mid x \in X\}$$

with $\mu_A : X \rightarrow [0,1]$ and $\nu_A : X \rightarrow [0,1]$ such that for all $x \in X$, $0 \leq \mu_A(x) + \nu_A(x) \leq 1$. The values $\mu_A(x)$ and $\nu_A(x)$ are respectively the membership degree and the non-membership degree of x to A.

The lack of knowledge is represented by $\pi_A(x) = 1 - (\mu_A(x) + \nu_A(x))$, the so-called margin of hesitancy of the membership of x to A: the greater π, the more important the lack of knowledge.

Interval-Valued Fuzzy Sets (IVFS). With the notations classically used in the literature [8,10], an IVFS A of X is defined by a function F_A from X to $\mathbb{I}([0,1])$, the set of all closed intervals of $[0,1]$, such that for every $x \in X$, $F_A(x) = [\underline{\mu}_A(x), \overline{\mu}_A(x)]$ with $\underline{\mu}_A(x) \leq \overline{\mu}_A(x)$. This interval represents a framing of the degree of membership of x to A: $\underline{\mu}_A(x)$ represents the minimum value that can be given to the degree of membership of x to A, and $\overline{\mu}_A(x)$ the maximum value that can be given to this degree. The bigger this interval, the less knowledge or reliable information we have on the belonging of x to A.

In the following, when $X = \{x_1, \ldots, x_n\}$, for the sake of simplicity such an IVFS is denoted $A = \{(\underline{\mu}_i, \overline{\mu}_i), i = 1, \ldots, n\}$ considering $\underline{\mu}_i = \underline{\mu}_A(x_i)$ and $\overline{\mu}_i = \overline{\mu}_A(x_i)$.

The set of all interval-valued fuzzy sets on X is denoted IVFS(X) [11].

3   Information and Measure of Information

In Kampé de Feriet's work, views are *observers* of the objects [15–17]. In our approach, a view is a *measure that reports some information on the objects* of B. Such a view depends on the particular objective that should be fulfilled or the aim of the user. Typically:

Definition 1 (View). *A view is a mapping from 2^X to $\mathbb{R}^+$.*

For instance, in order to make a prediction, it is always interesting to gain some information about the occurrence of the objects and a view is a probability of the occurrence of each object x of X in classic settings. Another example corresponds to the case where we need to define a vague category composed of objects, a useful view is a membership function that defines this category as a fuzzy set of X.

In fuzzy set theory, a fuzzy measure is a view:

Definition 2 (Fuzzy measure). *A fuzzy measure is a mapping* $f : 2^X \to [0, 1]$ *such that*

1. $f(\emptyset) = 0$,
2. $f(X) = 1$,
3. $\forall A, B \in 2^X$, *if* $A \subseteq B$ *then* $f(A) \leq f(B)$.

In other cases, a view on X could be defined as the association of a weight to each element of X. In Evidence theory, mass assignment is an example of such an association. But weights could be of any nature (the age of each element x_i, a given price, a duration, etc.).

Usually, a view enables us to help the *ranking* of elements of X in order to select one, for instance, the most probable event from X, or the most representative element of a fuzzy subset of X.

A *measure of information* enables the aggregation of all the values of a view to gain more knowledge. Depending on the information that should be handled through the view, a measure of information is associated with specific properties: monotonicity, maximality, minimality, etc. In the literature, measures of information take various forms (probabilistic, fuzzy,...), the most basic ones are presented hereunder.

Probabilistic Case. There exist several measures of information to evaluate the global information provided by a view which is a probability distribution. More formally, let $X = \{x_1, \ldots, x_n\}$ for $n \in \mathbb{N}$, $x_i \in B$, and let $p : 2^X \to [0, 1]$, be a probability distribution over X, p_i being associated with x_i. The measure p provides a view of X.

In this setting, the measure of the information brought by the event x_i of probability $p_i > 0$ is evaluated by means of a function I fulfilling the following properties [1]:

1. $I(p_i) \geq 0$ *(non-negativity)*
2. $I(p_i \, p_j) = I(p_i) + I(p_j)$ for any p_i and p_j independent events *(additivity)*

Given that, the measure of the information of the whole set of events (and thus, of the view provided by the probability distribution p) is the aggregation of the measure of information of all the events. Usually, this aggregation is a weighted mean.

The well-known Shannon entropy is such a measure of information, enabling the evaluation of a particular view. It is usually referred to as a measure of the probabilistic disorder of the set X.

Definition 3 (Shannon entropy). *Let a σ-algebra B be defined on a finite universe $\mathcal{U}$, and let $X = \{x_1, \ldots, x_n\}$ for $n \in \mathbb{N}$, $x_i \in B$. Let $p : 2^X \to [0,1]$, be a probability distribution over X, p_i being associated with x_i. The* Shannon entropy *of p is defined as:*

$$H_S(p) = -\sum_{i=1}^{n} p_i \log p_i \tag{1}$$

This entropy can be interpreted as follows. First of all, it is clear that p_i, the probability of the event x_i is an *a priori* measure giving us some information about the expected occurrence of x_i. Thus, $-\log p_i$ can be interpreted as a measure of the surprise that one can have if the event x_i occurs. Considering this, the entropy is the expectation of the surprise caused by the occurrence of one element from X.

It is clear that this kind of evaluation of the view is based on the probabilistic information on X. In particular, the additivity property is a strong commitment for the evaluation of the view. In his work, J. Kampé de Fériet introduced a new way of aggregating information by considering any operation of composition to construct $H(pq)$ from $H(p)$ and $H(q)$ [16].

Fuzzy Case. When the view is not based on a probability, another measure of information can be used. For instance, if the view is a membership function defining a fuzzy set, De Luca and Termini have proposed to define *entropy measures of a fuzzy set* with a membership function $\mu : X \to [0,1]$ as follows [9]:

1. $H(\mu) = 0$ if and only if μ takes values 0 or 1
2. $H(\mu)$ is maximum if and only if μ assumes always the value $\frac{1}{2}$
3. $H(\mu) \geq H(\mu^*)$ for any sharpened version μ^* of μ, i.e. any fuzzy set such that $\mu(x) \leq \mu^*(x)$ if $\mu(x) \geq \frac{1}{2}$ and $\mu(x) \geq \mu^*(x)$ if $\mu(x) \leq \frac{1}{2}$

Another definition of entropy in the fuzzy case has been introduced by [32]. This *entropy of fuzzy events* mixes both fuzzy and probabilistic information. In this setting, $A \subseteq X$ is considered as a fuzzy event with the entropy:

$$H_Z(A) = -\sum_{i=1}^{n} \mu_A(x_i) p_i \log p_i \tag{2}$$

Entropies of IFS (and IVFS). In the literature, there exist several definitions of the entropy of an intuitionistic fuzzy set and several works proposed different ways to define such an entropy, for instance from divergence measures [21]. Hereafter we recall three classical IFS entropies.

In [25], the entropy of the IFS A is defined as:

$$E_{SK}(A) = 1 - \frac{1}{2n} \sum_{i=1}^{n} |\mu_A(x_i) - \nu_A(x_i)|. \tag{3}$$

Other definitions are introduced in [7] based on extensions of the Hamming distance and the Euclidean distance to intuitionistic fuzzy sets. For instance, the following entropy is proposed:

$$E_B(A) = \sum_{i=1}^{n} \pi_A(x_i) = n - \sum_{i=1}^{n} (\mu_A(x_i) + \nu_A(x_i)). \tag{4}$$

In [12], another entropy is introduced:

$$E_G(A) = \frac{1}{2n} \sum_{i=1}^{n} \left(1 - |\mu_A(x_i) - \nu_A(x_i)|\right)(1 + \pi_A(x_i)). \tag{5}$$

As already said, these entropies can also be considered as IVFS entropies by changing the representation as recalled in Sect. 2.2.

Disorder and Homogeneity. Similarities between properties of measures of information in the probabilistic case and the fuzzy case are evident as they both enable the aggregation of a view on X.

As previously said, Shannon entropy is usually considered as a measure of the disorder existing when a prediction of the occurrence of one element of X should be done. The higher the entropy, the less predictable the event x from X to occur. However, another interpretation could be used, that refers to the physical interpretation of the Bolztmann entropy. In physics and thermodynamics, the entropy of a system grows over time and is maximum when all the studied particles have the same temperature.

Thus, an entropy can be considered as *a measure of homogeneity* of the set X through the considered view.

It is easy to see that existing measures for both the probabilistic case or the fuzzy case aim at evaluating homogeneity:

– Shannon entropy is maximum when all probabilities are equal;
– De Luca & Termini entropy is maximum when all the elements of X have the same membership degree $\frac{1}{2}$, which refers to an incomplete membership to the fuzzy set.

All these kinds of entropies are measures of (a particular kind of) information and, depending on what kind of information they are made for, they satisfy common properties [5,6]. In the following, we denote by "entropy measure", or "entropy", all these measures.

4   Probabilistic Entropy of Interval-Valued Fuzzy Sets

In the literature of fuzzy set theory (including both IVFS and IFS) as recalled in Sect. 3, if entropy measures related to the fuzziness of a set are common, the definition of probabilistic entropy for IVFS (or IFS) has not been introduced.

As a consequence, it is clear that these existing definitions measure the homogeneity of a set (fuzzy, IVFS, IFS,...), but they do not capture the same kind of information as the Shannon entropy does. These entropy measures for fuzzy sets and extension (IFS, IVFS) are the descendants of the entropy of fuzzy sets introduced by de Luca & Termini [9].

In several fields of application, and in particular in machine learning, measures that take into account probabilistic information about the data play a predominant role. The need in these fields is a Shannon-like entropy measure that can take into account a probability distribution on the set of training examples. It is therefore of great interest to introduce such a measure for fuzzy sets (as Lotfi Zadeh did) and their extension. In particular, IVFS and IFS can be of great interest in Machine learning due to their capacity to handle a lack of knowledge on the data [20].

With this aim, in the following, we introduce probabilistic entropies for IVFS, we propose a definition and the properties, adapted to IVFS, that should be fulfilled for this kind of measures.

Definition 4. *Let* $A = \{(\underline{\mu}_i, \overline{\mu}_i), i = 1, \ldots, n\}$ *an IVFS defined on* $X = \{x_1, \ldots, x_n\}$, *and* $p = \{p_1, \ldots, p_n\}$ *a probability distribution on* X. *A proba-bilistic entropy is a measure* H *from* $IVFS(X) \times P \rightarrow \mathbb{R}^+$.

Thus, $H(A, p)$ is the probabilistic entropy of IVFS A related to the probability distribution p on the universe X. In the particular case of fuzzy sets, we get the Zadeh entropy $H_Z(A, p)$ defined in Eq. 2.

4.1 Properties of Probabilistic Entropies

According to the literature (see, for instance, Chapter 2 in [1]), classical measures of information, such as Shannon's entropy, must respect the following properties (see also Sect. 3 (probabilistic case)). These properties can be expressed in our setting as follows.

Let $A = \{(\underline{\mu}_i, \overline{\mu}_i), i = 1, \ldots, n\}$ be an IVFS defined on X, and $p : 2^X \rightarrow [0, 1]$, be a probability distribution over X:

P1) $H(A, p) \geq 0$ for any p (non-negativity).
P2) $H(A, p) = 0$ if $\exists k \in \{1, \ldots, n\}$, $p_k = 1$ and $\forall i \neq k, p_i = 0$ (minimality).
P3) $H(A, p)$ is maximal when $p = \{\frac{1}{n}, \ldots, \frac{1}{n}\}$ (maximality).

An important property characterizing a measure of information in the probabilistic case, such as the Shannon entropy, is the additivity that reflects how the measure takes into account the composition of the information [1]. This property can be relaxed into the sub-additivity property.

Let $p = \{p_1 = p(x_1), \ldots, p_n = p(x_n)\}$, be a probability distribution over X, $q = \{q_1 = q(y_1), \ldots, q_m = q(y_m)\}$, be a probability distribution over Y, $A = \{(\underline{\mu}_i, \overline{\mu}_i), i = 1, \ldots, n\}$ be an IVFS defined on X, and $B = \{(\underline{\nu}_i, \overline{\nu}_i), i = 1, \ldots, m\}$ be an IVFS defined on Y:

P4) $H(A \times B, r) \leq H(A, p) + H(B, q)$ (sub-additivity).

with the IVFS $A \times B$ defined on the Cartesian product $X \times Y$ from A and B, and the probability distribution r on $X \times Y$ defined as $r = \{r(x_1, y_1), \ldots, r(x_i, y_j), \ldots, r(x_n, y_m)\}$.

In the classical case, the sub-additivity becomes an additivity when the 2 experiments are independent (i.e. $r(x_i, y_j) = p(x_i)q(y_j)$ for all i, j) [3].

In the IVFS setting, the first step is to define the IVFS $A \times B$ on the Cartesian product $X \times Y$ from A and B. A common definition [10] is: $A \times B = \{\min(\underline{\mu}_A(x_i), \underline{\nu}_B(y_j)), \min(\overline{\mu}_A(x_i), \overline{\nu}_B(y_j)), \forall i = 1, \ldots, n, \text{ and } j = 1, \ldots, m\}$

In this IVFS setting, in relation with the definition of the Cartesian product, it becomes difficult to ask for the additivity when the experiments are independent, thus, we have to extend P4 to any case, even when the experiments are not independent.

In the following, a new probabilistic entropy for IVFS is introduced and its properties are studied.

4.2 A New Probabilistic Entropy for IVFS

There are several ways to define a probabilistic entropy for IVFS, in the following we propose a definition and we study its properties.

Definition 5. *Let* $p : 2^X \rightarrow [0, 1]$, *be a probability distribution over* X, *and* $A = \{(\underline{\mu}_i, \overline{\mu}_i), i = 1, \ldots, n\}$ *be an IVFS defined on* X, *the* probabilistic entropy *of* A *related to* p *is defined as:*

$$H_I(A, p) = -\frac{1}{2} \sum_{i=1}^{n} (\underline{\mu}_i + \overline{\mu}_i) p_i \log p_i \qquad (6)$$

This definition is based on the definition of the entropy of fuzzy events proposed by Lotfi Zadeh (Eq. 2): indeed, if A is a fuzzy set, and thus if $\underline{\mu}_A(x) = \overline{\mu}_A(x)$ for any $x \in X$, then $H_I(A, p) = H_Z(A, p)$.

Considering that an IVFS A gives the boundaries that surround the unknown membership function of a fuzzy set $\tilde{A}$, let $\underline{A}$ and $\overline{A}$ be the fuzzy sets that surround $\tilde{A}$, and let $\underline{\mu}_A$, $\overline{\mu}_A$ and $\mu_{\tilde{A}}$ be the membership functions of these sets. As the Zadeh entropy is monotone[1], it is plausible to consider that $H_I(\underline{A}, p) \leq H_I(\tilde{A}, p) \leq H_I(\overline{A}, p)$. When there is a least one x such that $\underline{\mu}_A(x) \neq \overline{\mu}_A(x)$, there is an infinity of solutions for $\tilde{A}$ and one solution can be to define the entropy of A as the mean value between $H_I(\underline{A}, p)$ and $H_I(\overline{A}, p)$.

---

[1] i.e. for any fuzzy sets $A \subseteq X$ and $B \subseteq X$, if $A \leq B$ then $H_Z(A) \leq H_Z(B)$ with the classic inclusion of fuzzy sets.

4.3   Properties of H_I

The proposed entropy H_I satisfies the properties recalled in Sect. 4.1. We use in this part the notations introduced previously. Let $p = \{p_1,\ldots,p_n\}$, be a probability distribution over X, $q = \{q_1,\ldots,q_m\}$, be a probability distribution over Y, $A = \{(\underline{\mu}_i,\overline{\mu}_i),\ i = 1,\ \ldots,\ n\}$ be an IVFS defined on X, and $B = \{(\underline{\nu}_j,\overline{\nu}_j),\ j = 1,\ \ldots,\ m\}$ be an IVFS defined on Y:

The proof of the non-negativity (property **P1**) of H_I is trivial.

The minimality (property **P2**) of H_I is also easy to prove: when $\exists k \in \{1,\ldots,n\}$ such that $p_k = 1$ and $\forall i \neq k, p_i = 0$, we have $H_I(A,p) = -\frac{1}{2}((\underline{\mu}_k + \overline{\mu}_k)\log 1 = 0$.

To prove the sub-additivity property (**P4**), as explained, we have to set the Cartesian product of the IVFS $A \times B$ on $X \times Y$.

For instance, we consider the classic definition: $A \times B = \{(\min(\underline{\mu}_i,\underline{\nu}_j), \min(\overline{\mu}_i,\overline{\nu}_j)),\ \forall i = 1,\ldots,n,\ \text{and}\ j = 1,\ldots,m\}$, and we suppose that A and B are independent. We have

$$H_I(A \times B, pq) = -\frac{1}{2}\sum_{i=1}^{n}\sum_{j=1}^{m}(\min(\underline{\mu}_i,\underline{\nu}_j) + \min(\overline{\mu}_i,\overline{\nu}_j))p_i q_j \log(p_i q_j)$$

$$= -\frac{1}{2}\sum_{i=1}^{n}\sum_{j=1}^{m}\min(\underline{\mu}_i,\underline{\nu}_j)p_i q_j \log p_i - \frac{1}{2}\sum_{i=1}^{n}\sum_{j=1}^{m}\min(\underline{\mu}_i,\underline{\nu}_j)p_i q_j \log q_j$$

$$-\frac{1}{2}\sum_{i=1}^{n}\sum_{j=1}^{m}\min(\overline{\mu}_i,\overline{\nu}_j)p_i q_j \log p_i - \frac{1}{2}\sum_{i=1}^{n}\sum_{j=1}^{m}\min(\overline{\mu}_i,\overline{\nu}_j)p_i q_j \log q_j$$

$$\leq -\frac{1}{2}\sum_{i=1}^{n}\underline{\mu}_i p_i \log p_i \sum_{j=1}^{m}q_j - \frac{1}{2}\sum_{j=1}^{m}\underline{\nu}_j q_j \log q_j \sum_{i=1}^{n}p_i$$

$$-\frac{1}{2}\sum_{i=1}^{n}\overline{\mu}_i p_i \log p_i \sum_{j=1}^{m}q_j - \frac{1}{2}\sum_{j=1}^{m}\overline{\nu}_j q_j \log q_j \sum_{i=1}^{n}p_i$$

and thus $H_I(A \times B, pq) \leq H_I(A,p) + H_I(B,q)$.

A second possibility is to consider: $A \times B = \{(\underline{\mu}_i\underline{\nu}_j, \overline{\mu}_i\overline{\nu}_j),\ \forall i = 1,\ldots,n,\ \text{and}\ j = 1,\ldots,m\}$, in this case we have:

$$H_I(A \times B, pq) = -\frac{1}{2}\sum_{i=1}^{n}\sum_{j=1}^{m}(\underline{\mu}_i\underline{\nu}_j + \overline{\mu}_i\overline{\nu}_j)p_i q_j \log(p_i q_j)$$

$$= -\frac{1}{2}\sum_{i=1}^{n}\sum_{j=1}^{m}(\underline{\mu}_i\underline{\nu}_j + \overline{\mu}_i\overline{\nu}_j)p_i q_j \log p_i - \frac{1}{2}\sum_{i=1}^{n}\sum_{j=1}^{m}(\underline{\mu}_i\underline{\nu}_j + \overline{\mu}_i\overline{\nu}_j)p_i q_j \log q_j$$

$$= -\frac{1}{2}\sum_{i=1}^{n}p_i \log p_i \sum_{j=1}^{m}(\underline{\mu}_i\underline{\nu}_j + \overline{\mu}_i\overline{\nu}_j)q_j - \frac{1}{2}\sum_{j=1}^{m}q_j \log q_j \sum_{i=1}^{n}(\underline{\mu}_i\underline{\nu}_j + \overline{\mu}_i\overline{\nu}_j)p_i$$

and as $(\underline{\mu}_i \underline{\nu}_j + \overline{\mu}_i \overline{\nu}_j) \leq (\underline{\mu}_i + \overline{\mu}_i)$ for any i and $(\underline{\mu}_i \underline{\nu}_j + \overline{\mu}_i \overline{\nu}_j) \leq (\underline{\nu}_j + \overline{\nu}_j)$ for any j, we have:

$$H_I(A \times B, pq) \leq -\frac{1}{2} \sum_{i=1}^{n} p_i \log p_i \sum_{j=1}^{m} (\underline{\mu}_i + \overline{\mu}_i) q_j - \frac{1}{2} \sum_{j=1}^{m} q_j \log q_j \sum_{i=1}^{n} (\underline{\nu}_j + \overline{\nu}_j) p_i$$

$$\leq -\frac{1}{2} \sum_{i=1}^{n} (\underline{\mu}_i + \overline{\mu}_i) p_i \log p_i \sum_{j=1}^{m} q_j - \frac{1}{2} \sum_{j=1}^{m} (\underline{\nu}_j + \overline{\nu}_j) q_j \log q_j \sum_{i=1}^{n} p_i$$

$$\leq -\frac{1}{2} \sum_{i=1}^{n} (\underline{\mu}_i + \overline{\mu}_i) p_i \log p_i - \frac{1}{2} \sum_{j=1}^{m} (\underline{\nu}_j + \overline{\nu}_j) q_j \log q_j$$

as we know that p and q are distributions of probabilities on X and thus $\sum_{i=1}^{n} p_i = 1$ and $\sum_{j=1}^{m} q_j = 1$.

5 Conclusion

In this paper, a study on probabilistic entropies for interval-valued fuzzy sets is carried out, and a first form on such a probabilistic entropy for IVFS is introduced. This brings out the need for a measure of information able to take into account both a probabilistic information and a possibilistic information on a set of values, in the step of the work done by [32] for fuzzy sets. In order to define such a measure, it is necessary to highlight the properties from Information theory necessary to measure probabilistic information.

In future work, we plan to increase the number of properties to study in such a case, following the seminal work by Aczél and Daróczy [1]. Moreover, the definition of probabilistic entropy we propose opens the way to many perspectives for defining such measures, a point that will be studied deeper.

Furthermore, the aim of this work is to be applied in a machine learning context, in the presence of such kind of information, and to extend the preliminary work introduced in [20].

References

1. Aczél, J., Daróczy, Z.: On Measures of Information and their Characterizations, Mathematics in Science and Engineering, vol. 115. Academic Press, New York (1975)
2. Aczél, J., Daróczy, Z.: A mixed theory of information. I: symmetric, recursive and measurable entropies of randomized systems of events. R.A.I.R.O. Informatique théorique/Theor. Comput. Sci. 12(2), 149–155 (1978)
3. Aczél, J.: Measuring information beyond communication theory: some probably useful and some almost certainly useless generalizations. Inf. Process. Manag. 20(3), 383–395 (1984)
4. Atanassov, K.T.: Intuitionistic fuzzy sets. Fuzzy Sets Syst. 20, 87–96 (1986)

5. Bouchon-Meunier, B., Marsala, C.: Entropy measures and views of information. In: Kacprzyk, J., Filev, D., Beliakov, G. (eds.) Granular, Soft and Fuzzy Approaches for Intelligent Systems: Dedicated to Professor R.R. Yager, pp. 47–63. Springer, Cham (2017)
6. Bouchon-Meunier, B., Marsala, C.: Entropy and monotonicity in artificial intelligence. Int. J. Approx. Reason. **124**, 111–122 (2020)
7. Burillo, P., Bustince, H.: Entropy on intuitionistic fuzzy sets and on interval-valued fuzzy sets. Fuzzy Sets Syst. **78**, 305–316 (1996)
8. Couso, I., Bustince, H.: From fuzzy sets to interval-valued and Atanassov intuitionistic fuzzy sets: a unified view of different axiomatic measures. IEEE Trans. Fuzzy Syst. **27**(2), 362–371 (2019)
9. De Luca, A., Termini, S.: A definition of a nonprobabilistic entropy in the setting of fuzzy sets theory. Inf. Control **20**, 301–312 (1972)
10. Dubois, D., Prade, H.: Internal-valued fuzzy sets, possibility theory and imprecise probability. In: Montseny, E., Sobrevilla, P. (eds.) International Conference in Fuzzy Logic and Technology (EUSFLAT 2005), pp. 314–319. Univ. Poly. de Catalunya, Spain (2005)
11. Grzegorzewski, P., Pekala, B., Dyczkowski, K., Kosior, D.: A new look at the entropy of interval-valued fuzzy sets - theory and applications. In: 2023 IEEE International Conference on Fuzzy Systems (FUZZ), pp. 1–7 (2023)
12. Guo, K., Song, Q.: On the entropy for Atanassov's intuitionistic fuzzy sets: an interpretation from the perspective of amount of knowledge. Appl. Soft Comput. **24**, 328–340 (2014)
13. Hu, C., Hu, Z.: A Computational Study on the Entropy of Interval-Valued Datasets from the Stock Market, pp. 422–435 (2020)
14. Hu, C., Hu, Z.: On statistics, probability, and entropy of interval-valued datasets. In: Information Processing and Management of Uncertainty in Knowledge-Based Systems 2020, vol. 1239, pp. 407–421 (2020)
15. Kampé de Fériet, J.: Mesures de l'information par un ensemble d'observateurs. In: Gauthier-Villars (ed.) Comptes Rendus des Scéances de l'Académie des Sciences. série A, vol. 269, pp. 1081–1085. Paris (Décembre 1969)
16. Kampé de Fériet, J.: Mesure de l'information fournie par un événement, séminaire sur les questionnaires (1971)
17. Kampé de Fériet, J.: Mesure de l'information par un ensemble d'observateurs indépendants. In: Transactions of the Sixth Prague Conference on Information Theory, Statistical Decision Functions, Random Processes - Prague, 1971, pp. 315–329 (1973)
18. Klir, G., Wierman, M.J.: Uncertainty-Based Information. Elements of Generalized Information Theory. Studies in Fuzziness and Soft Computing, Springer-Verlag (1998)
19. Magdalena, L., Torres-Blanc, C., Cubillo, S., Martinez-Mateo, J.: Different types of entropy measures for type-2 fuzzy sets. Axioms **13**(8) (2024)
20. Marsala, C.: Attribute ranking with bipolar information. In: Ciucci, D., Couso, I., Medina, J., Ślezak, D., Petturiti, D., Bouchon-Meunier, B., Yager, R.R. (eds.) Information Processing and Management of Uncertainty in Knowledge-Based Systems, pp. 345–356. Springer, Cham (2022)
21. Montes, I., Pal, N.R., Montes, S.: Entropy measures for Atanassov intuitionistic fuzzy sets based on divergence. Soft. Comput. **22**(15), 5051–5071 (2018). https://doi.org/10.1007/s00500-018-3318-3

22. Montes Gutiérrez, I., Pal, N.R., Montes Rodríguez, S.: Entropy measures for atanassov intuitionistic fuzzy sets based on divergence. Soft. Comput. **22**, 5051–5071 (2018)
23. Suo, C., Li, X., Li, Y.: Distance-based knowledge measure and entropy for interval-valued intuitionistic fuzzy sets. Mathematics **11**(16) (2023)
24. Szmidt, E., Kacprzyk, J.: Entropy for intuitionistic fuzzy sets. Fuzzy Sets Syst. **118**(3), 467–477 (2001)
25. Szmidt, E., Kacprzyk, J.: New measures of entropy for intuitionistic fuzzy sets. In: Proceedings of the Ninth International Conference on Intuitionistic Fuzzy Sets (NIFS), Sofia, Bulgaria, vol. 11, pp. 12–20 (2005)
26. Szmidt, E., Kacprzyk, J.: Entropy and similarity of intuitionistic fuzzy sets. In: Information Processing and Management of Uncertainty in Knowledge-Based Systems (2006)
27. Szmidt, E., Kacprzyk, J.: Some problems with entropy measures for the atanassov intuitionistic fuzzy sets. In: Masulli, F., Mitra, S., Pasi, G. (eds.) Applications of Fuzzy Sets Theory, pp. 291–297. Springer, Heidelberg (2007)
28. Szmidt, E., Kacprzyk, J.: Atanassov's intuitionistic fuzzy sets demystified. In: Ciucci, D., et al. (eds.) Information Processing and Management of Uncertainty in Knowledge-Based Systems, pp. 517–527. Springer, Cham (2022)
29. Trillas, E., Riera, T.: Entropies in finite fuzzy sets. Inf. Sci. **15**(2), 159–168 (1978)
30. Wu, D., Mendel, J.M.: Uncertainty measures for interval type-2 fuzzy sets. Inf. Sci. **177**(23), 5378–5393 (2007)
31. Zadeh, L.: The concept of a linguistic variable and its application to approximate reasoning—i. Inf. Sci. **8**(3), 199–249 (1975)
32. Zadeh, L.A.: Probability measures of fuzzy events. J. Math. Anal. Appl. **23**, 421–427 (1968)
33. Zadeh, L.A.: The information principle. Inf. Sci. **294**, 540–549 (2015)
34. Zhang, H., Zhang, W., Mei, C.: Entropy of interval-valued fuzzy sets based on distance and its relationship with similarity measure. Knowl.-Based Syst. **22**(6), 449–454 (2009)

Fuzzy Metric Spaces and Their Generalizations

Fuzzy Equivalence Based Metrizable Space

Reinis Isaks$^{(\boxtimes)}$ ⓘ and Olga Grigorenko ⓘ

Department of Mathematics, University of Latvia,
3 Jelgavas Street, Riga 1004, Latvia
ri19002@edu.lu.lv

Abstract. In this paper, we introduce and analyze the concept of T-equivalence spaces, which are defined as pairs (X, E), where X is a set and E is a T-equivalence relation on X. Our primary focus is on the structure of balls in these spaces and their topological properties. Specifically, we define balls as α-cuts of a T-equivalence and prove that thus defined balls are open sets. In the metrizable case, we investigate how these relations can be expressed through a metric and an additive generator.

Keywords: Metric · Fuzzy metric space · Fuzzy relation · Fuzzy equivalence · Topology

1 Introduction

The notion of metric spaces emerged in the late 19th and early 20th centuries as mathematicians sought to generalize ideas from Euclidean and non-Euclidean geometries. Arthur Cayley, in his paper "A sixth Memoir upon Quantics" (1859), extended metric concepts beyond Euclidean geometry into domains bounded by a conic in a projective space [2]. The idea of an abstract space with metric properties was addressed in 1906 by René Maurice Fréchet, who laid the foundation for understanding convergence, continuity, and other key concepts in nongeometric spaces. The ideas are discussed in [1]. In 1914, Felix Hausdorff defined the term metric space and introduced topological spaces as a generalization of metric spaces [15]. Stefan Banach further refined and expanded the framework of metric spaces in the 1920s, making substantial contributions to functional analysis, which heavily relied on the metric structure.

In the mid-20th century, Ryszard Engelking emerged as a leading figure in topology. His 1989 book "General Topology" offers a comprehensive introduction to the subject, covering fundamental concepts and theorems, and remains a standard reference in the field [5].

This research is funded by the Latvian Council of Science, project "A fuzzy logic based approach to the value of information estimation in optimal control problems under uncertainty with applications to ecological management", project No. lzp-2024/1-0188.

M. Baczyński et al. (Eds.): EUSFLAT 2025, LNCS 15883, pp. 207–218, 2025.
https://doi.org/10.1007/978-3-031-97225-6_17

Since L.A. Zadeh introduced fuzzy sets in 1965 [19], researchers have been actively exploring ways to integrate different mathematical concepts within the context of fuzzy sets. Among the key developments was the introduction of fuzzy metrics and fuzzy metric spaces. Notable contributions to the field were made by A. George and P. Veeramani [6], Z. Deng [4], and O. Kaleva and S. Seikkala [16]. Currently, there is an interest in the topological properties of fuzzy metrics. Topological properties have been studied in [7–12,14], and [18].

This work is inspired by [6] and [13]. In the paper, we explore the concept of T-equivalence spaces, defined as pairs (X, E), where X is a set and E is a T-equivalence relation on X. The main focus is on the open balls and the metrizable conditions of these spaces.

The core idea revolves around the definition of a ball $B(x, \alpha)$ in a T-equivalence space (X, E) centered at $x \in X$ with radius $\alpha \in [0, 1]$. This ball is defined as the set of points $y \in X$ such that $E(x, y) > \alpha$, which is an α-cut of the fuzzy equivalence relation E.

The foundation of such constructions is based on the fact that, in the case of Archimedean t-norms, fuzzy equivalences can be derived from metrics using specially designed decreasing functions mapping $[0, \infty)$ to $[0, 1]$. First, we utilize these fuzzy relations to establish a metrizable space and subsequently generalize this construction to arbitrary T-equivalence.

Further, we aim to prove that a ball $B(x, \alpha)$ is an open set. This will be done in two scenarios: one where the T-equivalence relation can be expressed through a metric and an additive generator, and another where the T-equivalence relation is considered independently of a metric.

The paper is structured as follows. In Sect. 2, we provide an overview of triangular norms. We then focus on fuzzy equivalence relations, where we define these relations in the context of t-norms. In Sect. 3, we explore the concept of T-equivalence generated metrizable spaces, focusing on the properties of open sets defined by T-equivalence relations. Finally, in Sect. 4, we conclude the paper.

2   Preliminaries

2.1   Triangular Norms

We start with the definition of a t-norm which plays the crucial role for the definition of transitivity for fuzzy relations:

Definition 1 ([17]). *A t-norm is a binary operation T on the unit interval $[0, 1]$, i.e. a function $T : [0, 1]^2 \to [0, 1]$ such that for all $x, y, z \in [0, 1]$ the following axioms are satisfied:*

- $T(x, y) = T(y, x)$ *(Commutativity);*
- $T(x, T(y, z)) = T(T(x, y), z)$ *(Associativity);*
- $T(x, y) \leq T(x, z)$ *whenever $y \leq z$ (Monotonicity);*
- $T(x, 1) = x$ *(A boundary condition).*

Often used t-norms are mentioned below:

- Minimum t-norm: $T_M(x, y) = \min(x, y)$;
- Product t-norm: $T_P(x, y) = x \cdot y$;
- Lukasiewicz t-norm: $T_L(x, y) = \max(x + y - 1, 0)$;
- Hamacher product t-norm: $T_{H_0}(x, y) = \begin{cases} \frac{x \cdot y}{x + y - x \cdot y} & \text{if } x^2 + y^2 \neq 0 \\ 0 & \text{otherwise} \end{cases}$.

A t-norm T is called Archimedean if and only if, for all pairs $(x, y) \in (0, 1)^2$, there is $n \in \mathbb{N}$ such that $T(\underbrace{x, x, \ldots, x}_{n \text{ times}}) < y$, where

$$T(\underbrace{x, x, \ldots, x}_{n \text{ times}}) = T(x, T(\underbrace{x, x, \ldots, x}_{n-1 \text{ times}})),$$

which means that the t-norm is applied n times to the input x. That is, when $n = 1$, the function becomes $T(x, x)$. When $n = 2$, it becomes $T(x, T(x, x))$, and so on.

Product and Lukasiewicz t-norms are Archimedean while minimum t-norm is not.

We will now proceed with the definitions of an additive generator and its pseudo-inverse.

Definition 2 ([17]). *An additive generator* $t : [0, 1] \rightarrow [0, \infty]$ *is a strictly decreasing function that is also right-continuous at 0 and satisfies* $t(1) = 0$, *such that for all* $(x, y) \in [0, 1]^2$ *we have*

$$t(x) + t(y) \in Ran(t) \cup [t(0), \infty],$$

where $Ran(t)$ *is the range of the function* t.

Definition 3 ([17]). *Let us assume that* $t : [0, 1] \rightarrow [0, \infty]$ *is an additive generator. Then the function*

$$t^{(-1)}(y) = \sup\{x \in [0, 1] | t(x) > y\}$$

is called the pseudo-inverse of t.

If the additive generator t is continuous, then the pseudo-inverse $t^{(-1)}$ is the inverse function of t.

Theorem 1 ([17]). *Let us assume that* t *is an additive generator, then the function* $T : [0, 1]^2 \rightarrow [0, 1]$ *defined as*

$$T(x, y) = t^{(-1)}(t(x) + t(y)),$$

where $t^{(-1)}(y)$ *is the pseudo-inverse function of* t *on* $Ran(t) \cup [t(0), \infty]$ *and* $t^{(-1)}(y) = 0$ *for all* $t \in [t(0), \infty]$, *is a t-norm.*

2.2   Fuzzy Equivalence Relations

We continue with an overview of basic definitions and results on fuzzy equivalence relations.

Definition 4 ([20]). *A fuzzy binary relation R on a set X is a function $R : X \times X \to [0,1]$.*

Definition 5 ([3]). *A fuzzy binary relation E on a set X is called a fuzzy equivalence relation with respect to a t-norm T (or a T-equivalence), if for all $x, y, z \in X$:*

1. $E(x,y) = 1 \iff x = y$ *(Reflexivity);*
2. $E(x,y) = E(y,x)$ *(Symmetry);*
3. $T(E(x,y), E(y,z)) \leq E(x,z)$ *(T-transitivity).*

Remark 1. Usually, in the definition of the fuzzy equivalence relation, the first condition is that for every $x \in X : E(x,x) = 1$. The condition that replaced it now requires that E "separates points". Due to its desirable properties, we will define the fuzzy equivalence as above and continue working with it.

Definition 6. *Metric space is an ordered pair (X, d) where X is a set and d is a metric on X, i.e., a function $d : X \times X \to [0, \infty)$ satisfying the following axioms for all points $x, y, z \in X$:*

1. $d(x,y) = 0 \iff x = y$ *(Identity of indiscernibles);*
2. $d(x,y) = d(y,x)$ *(Symmetry);*
3. $d(x,y) + d(y,z) \geq d(x,z)$ *(Triangle inequality).*

Now we will look at two theorems that show how continuous additive generators relate to fuzzy equivalence relations and metrics.

Theorem 2 ([3]). *Let t be continuous additive generator. Then for any T-equivalence E the mapping*

$$d(x,y) = t(E(x,y))$$

is a metric.

Theorem 3 ([3]). *Let t be a continuous additive generator for the t-norm T and $t^{(-1)}$ its pseudo-inverse. For any metric d, the mapping*

$$E(x,y) = t^{(-1)}(d(x,y))$$

is a T-equivalence.

The theorems demonstrate that it is possible to transition from metrics to T-equivalences with an additive generator and its pseudo-inverse, and vice versa. Now, let us examine a few examples of such constructed T-equivalences.

Example 1. Let $X = \mathbb{R}$, $d = |x - y|$ be a Euclidean metric, $t(x) = -\ln(x)$ be an additive generator for the product t-norm T_P, and $t^{(-1)}(y) = e^{-y}$ its pseudo-inverse. Then the function

$$E(x, y) = e^{-|x-y|}$$

is a T_P-equivalence.

Example 2. Let $X = \mathbb{R}$, $d(x, y) = \begin{cases} 0, & \text{if } x = y, \\ 1, & \text{if } x \neq y \end{cases}$ be the discrete metric,

$t(x) = \frac{1-x}{x}$ be an additive generator for Hamacher product t-norm T_{H_0}, and $t^{(-1)}(y) = \frac{1}{1+y}$ be its pseudo-inverse. Then the function

$$E(x, y) = \frac{1}{1 + d(x, y)}$$

is a T_{H_0}-equivalence.

It is evident, that the metric d in such T-equivalence constructions can be discontinuous. However, a discontinuous additive generator t and its pseudo-inverse $t^{(-1)}$ may fail to satisfy T-transitivity; therefore, it is essential to require that t be continuous. Let us look at an example where t is not continuous. Note that the following additive generator and t-norm are taken from [17].

Example 3. Let $X = \mathbb{R}$. Given an additive generator t:

$$t(x) = \begin{cases} 4 - 4x, & \text{if } x \in [0, 0.5), \\ 2 - x, & \text{if } x \in [0.5, 1), \\ 0, & \text{if } x = 1. \end{cases}$$

Its pseudo-inverse is:

$$t^{(-1)}(y) = \begin{cases} 1, & y \in [0, 1), \\ 2 - y, & y \in [1, \frac{3}{2}), \\ \frac{1}{2}, & y \in [\frac{3}{2}, 2), \\ 1 - \frac{y}{4}, & y \in [2, 4), \\ 0, & y \geq 4. \end{cases}$$

From functions t and $t^{(-1)}$, we get our discontinuous T-norm:

$$T(x, y) = t^{(-1)}(t(x) + t(y)) = \begin{cases} \min(x, y), & \text{if } \max(x, y) = 1, \\ \frac{1}{4}(x + y), & \text{if } (x, y) \in [0.5, 1)^2, \\ \frac{1}{4}(x + 4y - 2), & \text{if } x \in [0.5, 1) \text{ and } y \in [\frac{2-x}{4}, 0.5), \\ \frac{1}{4}(4x + y - 2), & \text{if } y \in [0.5, 1) \text{ and } x \in [\frac{2-y}{4}, 0.5), \\ 0, & \text{otherwise.} \end{cases}$$

If we choose $d(x, y) = |x - y|$, then $E(x, y) = t^{(-1)}(d(x, y))$ is constructed the following way:

$$E(x, y) = \begin{cases} 1, & d(x, y) \in [0, 1), \\ 2 - d(x, y), & d(x, y) \in [1, \frac{3}{2}), \\ \frac{1}{2}, & d(x, y) \in [\frac{3}{2}, 2), \\ 1 - \frac{d(x,y)}{4}, & d(x, y) \in [2, 4), \\ 0, & d(x, y) \geq 4. \end{cases}$$

However, the constructed function $E(x, y)$ does not satisfy T-transitivity, because for points $x = 0, y = 0.6$ and $z = 1.2$, we get:

$$T(E(x, y), E(y, z)) = T(1, 1) = 1 > 0.8 = E(x, z),$$

which contradicts T-transitivity of the fuzzy equivalence relation.

Taking into account above considerations, we will consider only cases where the t-norms and their additive generators are continuous.

3   T-Equivalence Generated Metrizable Space

Taking into account the conclusions from the previous section, let T be a continuous t-norm. We define T-equivalence space (X, E) as a pair, where X is a set and E is a T-equivalence relation on X. We now proceed with the defining the ball using T-equivalence relations.

Definition 7. *For a given T-equivalence space (X, E), we define the ball*

$$B(x, \alpha) = \{y \in X : E(x, y) > \alpha\}$$

with center $x \in X$ and radius $\alpha \in [0, 1]$ (Fig. 1).

The foundation of such constructions is based on the fact that, in the case of continuous Archimedean t-norms, a T-equivalence can be derived from metrics using the pseudo-inverse of an additive generator. By utilizing α-cuts of these fuzzy relations we obtain open balls in metric space:

Let (X, E) be a continuous T-equivalence space, where the T-equivalence E can be expressed as:

$$E(x, y) = t^{(-1)}(d(x, y)),$$

where $t^{(-1)}$ is the pseudo-inverse of the additive generator t and $d(x, y)$ is a metric on X. Then the ball $B(x, \alpha)$ is an open set.

If we can express the fuzzy equivalence E in the form

$$E(x, y) = t^{(-1)}(d(x, y)),$$

then the proof is trivial:

$$B(x, \alpha) = \{y \in X : E(x,y) > \alpha\} = \{y \in X : t^{(-1)}(d(x,y)) > \alpha\} =$$

$$= \{y \in X : t(t^{(-1)}(d(x,y))) < t(\alpha)\} = \{y \in X : d(x,y) < t(\alpha)\}.$$

Since $\{y \in X : d(x,y) < t(\alpha)\}$ is an open ball with centre x and radius $t(\alpha) \in [0, +\infty]$ in the metric space (X, d) and thus is an open set. We conclude that the set $B(x, \alpha)$ is an open set.

Now let us consider the general case, where we consider the T-equivalence relation independently.

Now we will prove that a ball $B(x, \alpha)$ is an open set in the following sense. Let us interpret a ball $B(x, \alpha)$ as a neighborhood of the point x and $\mathcal{B}_x = \{B(x, \alpha) : \alpha \in [0, 1)\}$ as a neighborhood system for x. In the next theorem we show that a ball $B(x, \alpha)$ is an open set in the sense that each element of it is included in it together with a neighborhood; that is, for every $z \in B(x, \alpha)$ there exists a level β such that $B(z, \beta) \subset B(x, \alpha)$. Therefore, we will call balls $B(x, \alpha)$ open balls.

Theorem 4. *Let T be a continuous t-norm and (X, E) be a T-equivalence space. Then the ball $B(x, \alpha)$ is an open set.*

Proof. If $\alpha = 1$, then $B(x, \alpha) = \emptyset$, and thus it is an open set. Now, we will consider the case when $0 \leq \alpha < 1$.

$$B(x, \alpha) = \{y \in X : E(x,y) > \alpha\},$$

and let $z \in B(x, \alpha)$. We need to prove that there exists a radius β such that:

$$B(z, \beta) \subset B(x, \alpha)$$

or, in other words, if $y \in B(z, \beta)$, then $y \in B(x, \alpha)$.

If $x = z$, then we can choose $\beta = \alpha$, and thus $B(z, \beta) \subset B(x, \alpha)$, implying that $B(x, \alpha)$ is an open set. Therefore, we only need to consider the case where $x \neq z$.

Let $z \in B(x, \alpha)$, then $E(x, z) > \alpha$. Now let $\delta = E(x, z) > \alpha$. Since $\delta > \alpha$, we can find a β, such that: $1 > \beta > \delta > \alpha$ and $T(\beta, \delta) > \alpha$. Thus, if $y \in B(z, \beta)$, then:

$$E(x, y) \geq T(E(x, z), E(z, y)) > T(\delta, \beta) > \alpha.$$

Therefore $B(z, \beta) \subset B(x, \alpha)$ and $B(x, \alpha)$ is an open set.

Remark 2. We can also notice that for continuous t-norms (or t-norms that are at least left-continuous at the point $(1, 1)$ [17]):

$$\lim_{\beta \to 1} T(\beta, \delta) = T(1, \delta) = \delta > \alpha.$$

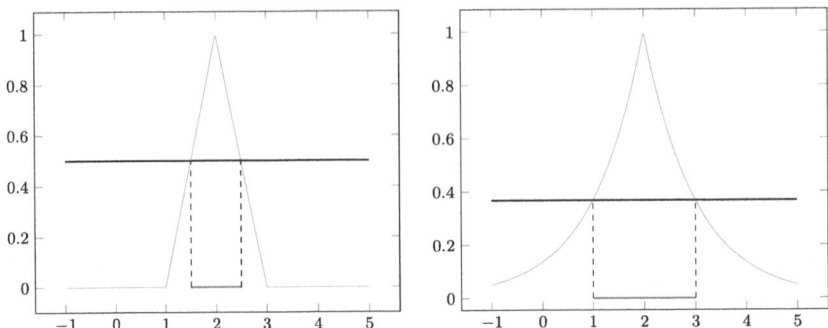

Fig. 1. A figure demonstrating the sets $B(x, \alpha)$, where $X = \mathbb{R}$, $x = 2$, and E is a fuzzy equivalence relation defined using a metric $d(x, y) = |x - y|$ and an additive generator. The left figure corresponds to the Łukasiewicz t-norm with $\alpha = 0.5$, while the right figure corresponds to the product t-norm with $\alpha \approx 0.4$.

Corollary 1. *Let E be a fuzzy equivalence on X. Then the set*

$$\tau_E = \{U \subset X : x \in U \text{ if } \exists \alpha \in [0, 1) : B(x, \alpha) \subset U\}$$

is a topology on X.

This topology τ_E is a topology generated by neighborhood system $\bigcup_{x \in X} \mathcal{B}_x$.

Now let us prove that the T-equivalence space (X, E), where T is a continuous t-norm, is Hausdorff.

Theorem 5. *Let T be a continuous t-norm. Every T-equivalence space (X, E) is Hausdorff.*

Proof. Let (X, E) be a T-equivelence space and $x, y \in X$. If $x \neq y$, then $0 \leq E(x, y) < 1$. Let $E(x, y) = \alpha$, $0 \leq \alpha < 1$. Then for all $\beta : \alpha < \beta < 1$, we can find a γ, such that $T(\gamma, \gamma) \geq \beta$.

Therefore, $B(x, \gamma) \cap B(y, \gamma) = \emptyset$. Suppose that there exists a $z \in X$, such that $z \in B(x, \gamma) \cap B(y, \gamma)$, then:

$$\alpha = E(x, y) \geq T(E(x, z), E(z, y)) \geq T(\gamma, \gamma) \geq \beta > \alpha,$$

which is a contradiction. Hence the space (X, E) is Hausdorff.

Theorem 6. *Let T be a continuous Archimedean t-norm and let E be a T-equivalence relation on X. Then the topological space (X, τ_E) is metrizable.*

Proof. We define a metric d by

$$d(x, y) = \inf\{ s : E(x, y) > t^{-1}(s) \},$$

where t is an additive generator of the t-norm T.

It is straightforward to verify that d is a metric. In particular, note that

$$\inf\{\, s : E(x,y) > t^{-1}(s)\,\} =$$

$$= \inf\{\, s : t(E(x,y)) < t(t^{-1}(s))\,\} = \inf\{\, s : d(x,y) < s\,\} = d(x,y),$$

where we have used Theorem 2, which establishes that $t(E(x,y))$ defines a metric.

Next, we show that d induces the same topology as τ_E by proving that the open balls coincide. That is, for every $B(x,\alpha) = \{y \in X : E(x,y) > \alpha\}$ there exists an $r \in (0, +\infty)$ such that the open ball in the metric space $O(x,r) = \{y \in X \mid d(x,y) < r\}$ satisfies $B(x,\alpha) = O(x,r)$. Indeed, by choosing $r = t(\alpha)$ we have

$$\{\, y \in X : E(x,y) > \alpha\,\} =$$

$$= \{\, y \in X : t(E(x,y)) < t(\alpha)\,\} = \{\, y \in X : d(x,y) < t(\alpha)\,\}.$$

Conversely, for every open ball $O(x,r) = \{y \in X : d(x,y) < r\}$, where $x \in X, r \in (0, +\infty)$, there exists $\alpha \in (0,1)$ such that $O(x,r) = B(x,\alpha)$. In fact, by setting $\alpha = t^{-1}(r)$, the wanted equality follows.

This shows that the open balls defined by E and those by d coincide, and hence the topology τ_E is induced by the metric d.

We now turn to a more general case.

Example 4. Let us prove that the function $d(x,y) = \inf\{1 - \alpha : E(x,y) > \alpha\}$, where E is a T-equivalence relation, defines a metric when T is the Łukasiewicz t-norm.

Proof. To show that d is a metric, we must verify the following properties of a metric. Since the T-equivalence relation is symmetric, the symmetry of d is trivial. Thus, we only need to check the identity of indiscernibles and the triangle inequality:

1. Identity of indiscernibles:
   (a) If $x = y$, then by reflexivity, $E(x,x) = 1$. Hence, $d(x,x) = \inf\{1 - \alpha : 1 - \alpha > 0\} = 0$.
   (b) Assume $d(x,y) = 0$. Then $\inf\{1 - \alpha : E(x,y) > \alpha\} = 0$. For every $\epsilon > 0$ there exists some α such that $E(x,y) > \alpha$ and $1 - \alpha < \epsilon$. This implies that $\alpha > 1 - \epsilon$. Since $\epsilon > 0$ is arbitrary, we conclude that $E(x,y)$ must be equal to 1. From the definition of a T-equivalence relation we get that $E(x,y) = 1$ if and only if $x = y$. Thus, $d(x,y) = 0$ implies $x = y$.
2. Triangle inequality: We need to prove that for all $x, y, z \in X$ the equality $d(x,y) + d(y,z) \geq d(x,z)$ holds.
   Let $x, y, z \in X$. If $E(x,y) = 1$, then $x = y$ and $d(x,y) = 0$, so the triangle inequality holds automatically in that case. The same applies if $E(y,z) = 1$. Otherwise, there exist numbers $\alpha, \beta \in [0,1)$ such that $d(x,y) = 1 - \alpha$ and $d(y,z) = 1 - \beta$, which implies that $E(x,y) > \alpha$ and $E(y,z) > \beta$.
   Using the T-transitivity property of E, we have $E(x,z) \geq T(E(x,y), E(y,z))$. Since $E(x,y) > \alpha$ and $E(y,z) > \beta$ and T is strictly monotone in each argument, it follows that $E(x,z) > T(\alpha, \beta)$. Thus, by the definition of d, we have

$d(x, z) \leq 1 - T(\alpha, \beta)$. Next, we analyze $1 - T(\alpha, \beta)$ using the Lukasiewicz t-norm, defined by $T(\alpha, \beta) = \max\{0, \alpha + \beta - 1\}$. We consider two cases:

Case 1: If $\alpha + \beta \leq 1$, then $T(\alpha, \beta) = 0$ and $1 - T(\alpha, \beta) = 1$. On the other hand,

$$(1 - \alpha) + (1 - \beta) = 2 - (\alpha + \beta) \geq 2 - 1 = 1 = 1 - T(\alpha, \beta).$$

Case 2: If $\alpha + \beta > 1$, then $T(\alpha, \beta) = \alpha + \beta - 1$, so that

$$1 - T(\alpha, \beta) = 1 - (\alpha + \beta - 1) = 2 - (\alpha + \beta).$$

Also, $(1 - \alpha) + (1 - \beta) = 2 - (\alpha + \beta)$.

In both cases, we obtain $1 - T(\alpha, \beta) \leq (1 - \alpha) + (1 - \beta)$. Therefore,

$$d(x, z) \leq 1 - T(\alpha, \beta) \leq (1 - \alpha) + (1 - \beta) = d(x, y) + d(y, z).$$

We note that in the previous example we verified the metric properties for a specific t-norm. Now, we turn to a more general situation. The following theorem provides sufficient conditions for the metrizability of the topological space (X, τ_E).

Theorem 7. *Topological space (X, τ_E) is metrizable if T-norm is strictly monotone and $T(1 - t, 1 - s) \geq 1 - (t + s)$ for all $t, s \in (0, 1)$.*

Proof. To establish that $d = \inf\{1 - \alpha : E(x, y) > \alpha\}$ is a metric, we must verify the properties of a metric. Since properties (1) and (2) of a metric can be proven similarly to Example 4, we can skip their proofs and focus on verifying the triangle inequality.

Now we prove that $d(x, y) + d(y, z) \geq d(x, z)$. Indeed, if $d(x, y) + d(y, z) < d(x, z)$, then there exist $t, s \in (0, 1)$, such that $d(x, y) + d(y, z) < t + s < d(x, z)$ and $d(x, y) < t$ & $d(y, z) < s$, where

$$d(x, y) = \inf\{1 - \alpha_1 : E(x, y) > \alpha_1\} < t \in (0, 1)$$

and

$$d(y, z) = \inf\{1 - \alpha_2 : E(y, z) > \alpha_2\} < s \in (0, 1).$$

Thus, $E(x, y) > 1 - t$ and $E(y, z) > 1 - s$, but

$$1 - (t + s) \leq T(1 - t, 1 - s) < T(E(x, y), E(y, z)) \leq E(x, z),$$

and thus $1 - (t + s) < E(x, z)$. However, this leads to contradiction with $t + s < d(x, z) = \inf\{1 - \alpha_3 : E(x, z) > \alpha_3\}$.

For example, the condition $T(1 - t, 1 - s) \geq 1 - (t + s)$ for all $t, s \in (0, 1)$ fulfills for product t-norm, for minimum t-norm.

The previous theorem could be generalized for

$$d(x, y) = \inf\{g(\alpha) : E(x, y) > \alpha\},$$

where $g : [0, 1] \rightarrow [0, \infty)$ is a strictly decreasing, continuous function such that $g(1) = 0$, and t-norm fulfills: $T(g^{-1}(t), g^{-1}(s)) \geq g^{-1}(t + s)$ for all $t, s \in (0, \infty)$.

4 Conclusion

In this work, we studied T-equivalence spaces, which are pairs (X, E) where X is a set and E is a fuzzy equivalence relation on X. Our main focus was on the open balls $B(x, \alpha)$ and the topology on X they induce.

We showed that if the fuzzy equivalence is defined using a metric and a continuous additive generator $E(x, y) = t^{(-1)}(d(x, y))$, then the fuzzy open balls coincide with the usual metric open balls and therefore are open sets. We also proved that, in general, these balls form a Hausdorff topology on X and under specific conditions, the topological space (X, τ_E) is metrizable.

This approach can be a useful tool in further studies, including fixed point theorems, applications in fuzzy clustering and decision-making. Moreover, it has the potential to contribute to a deeper understanding of the concepts of T-equivalence relations and t-norms.

References

1. Arboleda, L.C.: Contribution à l'étude des premières recherches topologiques (d'après la correspondance et les publications de Maurice Fréchet). Thesis, École des Hautes Études en Sciences Sociales, Paris (1980)
2. Cayley, A.: A sixth Memoir upon Quantics. Philos. Trans. R. Soc. Lond. **149**, 61–90 (1859)
3. De Baets, B., Mesiar, R.: Pseudo-metrics and T-equivalences. J. Fuzzy Math **5**, 471–481 (1997)
4. Deng, Z.: Fuzzy pseudo-metric spaces. J. Math. Anal. Appl. **86**, 85–95 (1982)
5. Engelking, R.: General Topology. Heldermann Verlag, Berlin (1989)
6. George, A., Veeramani, P.: On some results in fuzzy metric spaces. Fuzzy Sets Syst. **63**, 123–134 (1994)
7. Grabiec, M.: Fixed points in fuzzy metric spaces. Fuzzy Sets Syst. **27**, 385–389 (1988)
8. Gregori, V., Romaguera, S.: Some properties of fuzzy metric spaces. Fuzzy Sets Syst. **115**, 485–489 (2000)
9. Gregori, V., Romaguera, S.: On completion of fuzzy metric spaces. Fuzzy Sets Syst. **130**, 399–404 (2002)
10. Gregori, V., Romaguera, S.: Characterizing completable fuzzy metric spaces. Fuzzy Sets Syst. **144**, 411–420 (2004)
11. Gregori, V., Miñana, J.-J., Morillas, S., Sapena, A.: Cauchyness and convergence in fuzzy metric spaces. RACSAM **111**, 25–37 (2017)
12. Gregori, V., Miñana, J.-J., Morillas, S., Sapena, A.: On principal fuzzy metric spaces. Mathematics **10**, 2860 (2022)
13. Grigorenko, O., Šostak, A.: Fuzzy extension of crisp metric by means of fuzzy equivalence relation. Mathematics **10**(24), 78 (2022)
14. Gutiérrez-García, J., Rodríguez-López, J., Romaguera, S.: On fuzzy uniformities induced by a fuzzy metric space. Fuzzy Sets Syst. **330**, 52–78 (2018)
15. Hausdorff, F.: Grundzüge der Mengenlehre. Veit Comp, Leipzig (1914)
16. Kaleva, O., Seikkala, S.: On fuzzy metric spaces. Fuzzy Sets Syst. **13**, 51–56 (1984)

17. Klement, E.P., Mesiar, R., Pap, E.: Triangular Norms. Kluwer Academic Publishers, Dordrecht (2000)
18. Kramosil, I., Michálek, J.: Fuzzy metrics and statistical metric spaces. Kybernetika **11**, 26–41 (1975)
19. Zadeh, L.A.: Fuzzy sets. Inf. Control **8**, 338–353 (1965)
20. Zadeh, L.A.: Similarity relations and fuzzy orderings. Inform. Sci. **3**, 177–200 (1971)

On Fuzzy Metrics Constructed from Metrics and their Topology

Juan-José Miñana[1]([✉])[iD] and Simona Talia[2]

[1] Instituto de Investigación para la Gestión Integrada de Zonas Costeras,
Universitat Politècnica de València, C/ Paranimf,
1 Grao de Gandia, 46730 Gandia, Spain
juamiapr@mat.upv.es
[2] Universitat Politècnica de València, Camí de Vera, s/n, Algirós,
46022 València, Spain
stalia1@doctor.upv.es

Abstract. Fuzzy metrics have demonstrated to be useful in engineering problems. They show a better performance comparing with their classical counterparts. So, to obtain new examples of fuzzy metrics or methods to construct them is a topic of interest. Recently in [10] two new methods to construct fuzzy pseudo-metrics from pseudo-metrics have been established. The aim of this paper is to determine the relationship between the topology induced by the fuzzy pseudo-metric constructed using these two methods and the topology induced by the pseudo-metric from which is it constructed. In this direction, we show that for one of these two methods both topologies coincide whereas for the other one, two additional conditions on the one of the functions used in the method must be required to get such a conclusion. In addition, examples which justify and illustrate our study are provided in the paper.

Keywords: Fuzzy metric space · Continuous triangular norm · Induced Topology · Additive generator · Supperadditive function

1 Introduction

Fuzzy theory began in 1965 with the introduction of the notion of fuzzy set by Zadeh in [18]. Such a notion constituted a generalization of the classical concept of set, which is essential in the foundations of all Mathematics. Indeed, the most of mathematical concepts can be defined using set theory. Then, many authors have focussed on adapting different classical notions to the fuzzy framework. In this direction, some authors have tackled the problem of defining a notion of metric in keeping with the fuzzy theory. Among them we can find Kramosil and Michalek which defined in [12] a notion of fuzzy metric space based on the concept of probabilistic metric spaces (see Definition 1). Such a notion constituted an adaptation of the classical concept of metric to the fuzzy setting in the sense that the value $\mathcal{M}(x, y, t) \in [0, 1]$ can be understood as a degree of nearness between two points of a given set $\mathcal{X}$. As greater such a value is as larger is the

M. Baczyński et al. (Eds.): EUSFLAT 2025, LNCS 15883, pp. 219–228, 2025.
https://doi.org/10.1007/978-3-031-97225-6_18

proximity between both points, which is measured with respect to a parameter t. So, the "fuzzy distance" between two points does not provide a single value (as it does so a classical metric) but rather to a set of possible values, which fits with the essence of fuzzy theory. Later on, George and Veeramani slightly modified in [2] such a notion of fuzzy metric, which we will call GV-fuzzy metric, with the aim of obtaining a Hausdorff topology induced by it. So, George and Veeramani proved in [2] that each GV-fuzzy metric induces a Hausdorff topology $\mathcal{T}_\mathcal{M}$ on $\mathcal{X}$.

George and Veeramani also proved in [2] that for each metric space $(\mathcal{X}, d)$ we can define a GV-fuzzy metric $\mathcal{M}_d$ on $\mathcal{X}$, commonly known as the standard fuzzy metric, whose induced topology $\mathcal{T}_{\mathcal{M}_d}$ coincides with the topology $\mathcal{T}(d)$ induced by d on $\mathcal{X}$. Later on, Gregori and Romaguera proved in [7] that the topology induced by a $(GV\text{-})$fuzzy metric is metrizable. Even more, following the same arguments to those used in [2] and [7], the preceding affirmations are also concluded for fuzzy metrics (in the sense of Kramosil and Michalek). So, from the topological point of view, fuzzy metrics and classical ones are identical mathematical objects. Nonetheless, in some "purely metric" topics, as fixed point theory or completion, fuzzy metrics and classical ones show significant differences (see [8,9]). Moreover, fuzzy metrics have been used successfully in engineering problem comparing with their classical counterparts as image processing [1,14, 16], perceptual color difference [4,5], robust model estimation [15] or clustering [17]. So, the problem of obtaining new examples of fuzzy metric spaces have become of interest to supply a broader list of measurement tools with the aim of approaching the aforesaid problems or other which involve measuring with uncertainty. In this direction, in [6] the authors provided a wide list of examples of fuzzy metrics and their use in image filtering. Moreover, recently in [10] were established two new methods to construct fuzzy (pseudo-)metrics from classical ones, which allow to obtain as a particular case, among others, the standard fuzzy metric from them.

The aim of this paper is to explore further the aforementioned methods that were established in [10]. Concretely, we study the relationship between the topology induced by a pseudo-metric d and the topology induced by the fuzzy pseudo-metric $\mathcal{M}$ constructed from d following such methods. In this direction, we prove that for the first method, the aforesaid topologies coincide whereas for the second one, some additional conditions are required to get such a conclusion. Moreover, two examples show the need of demanding such two conditions for the second method.

The remaining of the paper is organized as follows. Section 2 is devoted to compile the main definitions and results required to carry out the subsequent study. Then, in Sect. 3 are presented the main results obtained concerning the relationship between the topologies induced by a pseudo-metric d and by the fuzzy pseudo-metric constructed from d by means of both methods provided in [10] aforementioned.

2 Preliminaries

Throughout the paper we will denote the set of all positive real numbers by $\mathbb{R}^+$. Besides, we will assume that the reader is familiar with triangular norms. To a deeper treatment on them one can look up [11].

We begin recalling the concept of fuzzy metric introduced by Kramosil and Michalek in [12]. However, such a concept is commonly used nowadays following as the reformulation provided by Grabiec in [3], which attending to what is detailed in [13] can be defined as follows.

Definition 1. *A fuzzy metric space is an ordered triple* $(\mathcal{X}, \mathcal{M}, *)$ *such that* $\mathcal{X}$ *is a (non-empty) set,* $*$ *is a continuous t-norm and* $\mathcal{M} : \mathcal{X} \times \mathcal{X} \times \mathbb{R}^+ \to [0,1]$ *is a mapping satisfying the following conditions, for all* $x, y, z \in \mathcal{X}$ *and* $t, s \in \mathbb{R}^+$.

(**KM1**) $\mathcal{M}(x, y, t) = 1$ *for all* $t \in \mathbb{R}^+$ *if and only if* $x = y$;
(**KM2**) $\mathcal{M}(x, y, t) = \mathcal{M}(y, x, t)$;
(**KM3**) $\mathcal{M}(x, y, t) * \mathcal{M}(y, z, s) \leq \mathcal{M}(x, z, t + s)$;
(**KM4**) *The function* $\mathcal{M}_{xy} : \mathbb{R}^+ \to [0,1]$ *is left-continuous, where* $\mathcal{M}_{xy}(t) = \mathcal{M}(x, y, t)$ *for each* $t \in \mathbb{R}^+$.

The modification of the preceding concept of fuzzy metric made by George and Veeramani in [2] is defined below.

Definition 2. *Let* $(\mathcal{X}, \mathcal{M}, *)$ *be fuzzy metric space.* $(\mathcal{X}, \mathcal{M}, *)$ *will be called a GV-fuzzy metric space if, in addition, the mapping* $\mathcal{M}$ *satisfies, for all* $x, y \in \mathcal{X}$ *and* $t \in \mathbb{R}^+$, *the following conditions.*

(**GV0**) $\mathcal{M}(x, y, t) > 0$;
(**GV1**) $\mathcal{M}(x, y, t_0) = 1$ *for some* $t_0 \in \mathbb{R}^+$ *implies* $x = y$;
(**GV2**) *The function* $\mathcal{M}_{xy} : \mathbb{R}^+ \to [0,1]$ *is continuous.*

As usual, we will say that $(\mathcal{M}, *)$, or simply $\mathcal{M}$ if confusion does not arise, is a $(GV\text{-})$fuzzy metric on $\mathcal{X}$. Similarly to the classical case, we will say that $(X, M, *)$ is a *fuzzy pseudo-metric space* if it satisfies all the axioms in Definition 1 except (**KM1**), which is replaced by the following weaker one:

(**KM1'**) $M(x, x, t) = 1$ for all $t \in \mathbb{R}^+$.

In the same way, if we replace axiom (**GV1**) in the Definition 2 by (**KM1'**) we also get the concept of GV-fuzzy pseudo-metric space.

George and Veeramani also proved in [2] that each GV-fuzzy metric induces a Hausdorff topology $\mathcal{T}_\mathcal{M}$ on $\mathcal{X}$ that has as a base the family of open balls $\{B_\mathcal{M}(x, r, t) \ : \ x \in \mathcal{X}, r \in]0,1[, t \in \mathbb{R}^+\}$, where $B_\mathcal{M}(x, r, t) = \{y \in \mathcal{X} : \mathcal{M}(x, y, t) > 1 - r\}$ for each $x \in \mathcal{X}$, $r \in]0,1[$ and $t \in \mathbb{R}^+$. Following the same arguments to those used in [2], the preceding assertions are also concluded for fuzzy metrics (in the sense of Kramosil and Michalek). Even more, as in the classical case, each $(GV\text{-})$fuzzy pseudo metric also induces a topology which has as a base the same family of open balls detailed above.

A well known example of fuzzy metric space is the so called standard GV-fuzzy metric, which was defined in [2].

Example 1. Let $(\mathcal{X}, d)$ be a metric space and define the mapping $\mathcal{M}_d : \mathcal{X} \times \mathcal{X} \times \mathbb{R}^+ \to [0,1]$ by

$$\mathcal{M}_d(x, y, t) = \frac{t}{t + d(x,y)}, \text{ for each } x, y \in \mathcal{X} \text{ and } t \in \mathbb{R}^+. \tag{1}$$

Then, $(\mathcal{X}, \mathcal{M}, *_P)$ is a fuzzy metric space, called standard fuzzy metric, where $*_P$ denotes the product t-norm, i.e. $a *_P b = a \cdot b$ for each $a, b \in [0,1]$. Besides, the topology $\mathcal{T}_{\mathcal{M}_d}$ coincides with the topology $\mathcal{T}(d)$ induced by d on $\mathcal{X}$.

To finish this section, we recall the concept of additive generator of a triangular norm and some observations on it.

Definition 3. *An additive generator of a t-norm $*$ is a strictly decreasing function $f_* : [0,1] \to [0,\infty]$ which is also right-continuous at 0 and satisfies that $f_*(1) = 0$ and, in addition, that*

$$f_*(a) + f_*(b) \in Ran(f) \cup [f_*(0), \infty] \tag{2}$$

and

$$a * b = f_*^{(-1)}(f_*(a) + f_*(b)) \tag{3}$$

for all $a, b \in [0,1]$, where $f_*^{(-1)} : [0,\infty] \to [0,1]$ denotes the pseudo-inverse of f_* which is defined by $f_*^{(-1)}(y) = \sup\{x \in [0,1] : f(x) > y\}$ for each $y \in [0,\infty]$.

Observe that in the preceding definition is assumed that $\sup \emptyset = 0$. Besides, note that if the function f is in addition continuous, then the pseudo-inverse $f^{(-1)}$ is given as follows:

$$f^{(-1)}(y) = \begin{cases} f^{-1}(y) & \text{if } 0 \leq y < f(0) \\ 0 & \text{if } f(0) \leq y \leq \infty \end{cases}. \tag{4}$$

Not all continuous t-norms admit an additive generator. The next result characterize those continuous t-norms that admit an additive generator. First, recall that an Archimedean t-norm $*$ is characterized by the property $a * a < a$ for each $a \in]0,1[$.

Theorem 1. *A binary operation $*$ on $[0,1]$ is a continuous Archimedean t-norm if and only if there exists a continuous additive generator f_* such that*

$$a * b = f_*^{(-1)}(f_*(a) + f_*(b)), \text{ for all } a, b \in [0,1].$$

3   The Results

As in the case of the standard fuzzy metric, when a fuzzy metric is constructed form a classical one, one would expect that the topology induced by the fuzzy (pseudo-)metric obtained coincides with the topology of the (pseudo-)metric from which is defined. This section is devoted to study the relationship between the topology induced by a pseudo-metric d and the topology induced by the fuzzy pseudo-metric constructed from d by means of the two methods established in [10]. With this aim, we recall the first one of these two methods.

Theorem 2. *Let $(\mathcal{X}, d)$ be a pseudo-metric space, let $\varphi : \mathbb{R}^+ \to \mathbb{R}^+$ be an increasing and left-continuous function, let $*$ be a continuous Archimedean t-norm and let f_* be an additive generator of $*$. Then $(X, \mathcal{M}_d^{f_*,\varphi}, *)$ is a strong fuzzy pseudo-metric space, where the fuzzy set $\mathcal{M}_d^{f_*,\varphi} : \mathcal{X} \times \mathcal{X} \times \mathbb{R}^+$ is given, for each $x, y \in \mathcal{X}$ and $t \in \mathbb{R}^+$, by*

$$\mathcal{M}_d^{f_*,\varphi}(x, y, t) = f_*^{(-1)}\left(\frac{d(x,y)}{\varphi(t)}\right). \tag{5}$$

Moreover, $\mathcal{M}_d^{f_*,\varphi}$ is a strong fuzzy metric if and only if d is a metric.

The next theorem establishes the relationship between the topologies induced by the fuzzy pseudo-metric and the classical one involved in the preceding theorem.

Theorem 3. *Let $(\mathcal{X}, d)$ be a pseudo-metric space, let $\varphi : \mathbb{R}^+ \to \mathbb{R}^+$ be an increasing and left-continuous function, let $*$ be a continuous Archimedean t-norm and let f_* be an additive generator of $*$. Then, the topology $\mathcal{T}(d)$ induced by d on $\mathcal{X}$ coincides with the topology $\mathcal{T}_{\mathcal{M}_d^{f_*,\varphi}}$ induced by $\mathcal{M}_d^{f_*,\varphi}$ on $\mathcal{X}$.*

Proof. We will show that $\mathcal{T}(d) = \mathcal{T}_{\mathcal{M}_d^{f_*,\varphi}}$. To this end, we will see first that $\mathcal{T}(d) \subseteq \mathcal{T}_{\mathcal{M}_d^{f_*,\varphi}}$ by proving that for each $x \in \mathcal{X}$ we have that, for all $\varepsilon > 0$ there exist $r_0 \in]0, 1[$ and $t_0 \in \mathbb{R}^+$ such $B_{\mathcal{M}_d^{f_*,\varphi}}(x, r_0, t_0) \subseteq B_d(x; \varepsilon)$.

Let $x \in \mathcal{X}$ and $\varepsilon > 0$. Fix an arbitrary $t_0 \in \mathbb{R}^+$ and consider $0 < \varepsilon' < \min\{f_*(0), \frac{\varepsilon}{\varphi(t_0)}\}$. Now, we take $r_0 = 1 - f_*^{(-1)}(\varepsilon') \in]0, 1[$ and consider $y \in B_{\mathcal{M}_d^{f_*,\varphi}}(x, r_0, t_0)$. Then,

$$1 - r_0 < \mathcal{M}_d^{f_*,\varphi}(x, y, t_0) = f_*^{(-1)}\left(\frac{d(x,y)}{\varphi(t_0)}\right).$$

Note that $\frac{d(x,y)}{\varphi(t_0)} < f_*(0)$, since by the contrary, by Eq. (4) we would conclude that $f_*^{(-1)}\left(\frac{d(x,y)}{\varphi(t_0)}\right) = 0 \le 1 - r$ for all $r \in]0, 1[$. Then, due to f_* is strictly decreasing and $f_*^{(-1)}$ is a bijection on $[0, f_*(0)]$ to $[0, 1]$ we have that

$$f_*^{(-1)}\left(\frac{d(x,y)}{\varphi(t_0)}\right) > 1 - r_0 \Leftrightarrow \frac{d(x,y)}{\varphi(t_0)} = f_*\left(f_*^{(-1)}\left(\frac{d(x,y)}{\varphi(t_0)}\right)\right) < f_*(1 - r_0).$$

Therefore, since $0 < \varepsilon' < f^{(-1)}(0)$ we get

$$\frac{d(x,y)}{\varphi(t_0)} < f_*(1 - r_0) = f_*\left(f_*^{(-1)}(\varepsilon')\right) = \varepsilon' < \frac{\varepsilon}{\varphi(t_0)}.$$

Then $d(x, y) < \varepsilon$ and so $y \in B_d(x; \varepsilon)$. Hence, $B_{\mathcal{M}_d^{f_*,\varphi}}(x, r_0, t_0) \subseteq B_d(x; \varepsilon)$.

Secondly, we will see that $\mathcal{T}_{\mathcal{M}_d^{f_*,\varphi}} \subseteq \mathcal{T}(d)$ by demonstrating that for each $x \in \mathcal{X}$ we have that, for all $r \in]0, 1[$ and $t \in \mathbb{R}^+$ we can find ε_0 satisfying $B_d(x; \varepsilon_0) \subseteq B_{\mathcal{M}_d^{f_*,\varphi}}(x, r, t)$.

Let $x \in \mathcal{X}$ and consider $r \in]0,1[$ and $t \in \mathbb{R}^+$. Take $\varepsilon_0 = f_*(1-r) \cdot \varphi(t)$ and let $y \in B_d(x; \varepsilon_0)$. Then, $d(x,y) < \varepsilon_0 = f_*(1-r) \cdot \varphi(t)$ and so $\frac{d(x,y)}{\varphi(t)} < f_*(1-r)$. Now, due to f_* is strictly decreasing and since $\left(f_*^{(-1)} \circ f_*\right)(a) = a$, for each $a \in [0,1]$, we get

$$\mathcal{M}_d^{f_*,\varphi}(x,y,t) = f_*^{(-1)}\left(\frac{d(x,y)}{\varphi(t)}\right) > f_*^{(-1)}\left(f_*(1-r)\right) = 1 - r.$$

Therefore, $y \in B_{\mathcal{M}_d^{f_*,\varphi}}(x,y,t)$ and so $B_d(x;\varepsilon_0) \subseteq B_{\mathcal{M}_d^{f_*,\varphi}}(x,r,t)$.

Remark 1. It should be noted that in [10, Theorem 3.2.] was provided a method to construct GV-fuzzy pseudo-metrics from classical ones following the ideas of Theorem 2. Concretely, to get a GV-fuzzy pseudo-metric it must be imposed continuity on φ and the continuous t-norm must be strict (i.e. $a*b > a*c$ for each $a,b,c \in (0,1]$ with $b > c$). Taking into account that GV-fuzzy pseudo-metrics are a subclass of fuzzy pseudo-metrics in the sense of Kramosil and Michalek (as they have been defined in this paper) and that none additional condition on the t-norm and φ is required to prove Theorem 3, the conclusion of Theorem 3 remains valid when GV-fuzzy pseudo-metrics are constructed by means of the aforesaid Theorem 3.2. in [10].

Now we focus on the second method to construct fuzzy metrics from metrics that was established in [10]. Such a method was given to obtain a fuzzy metric for the minimum t-norm $*_M$, where $a *_M b = \min\{a,b\}$ for all $a,b \in [0,1]$. It is well-known that $*_M$ is a continuous t-norm which is not Archimedean. Below, we formulate the aforesaid method but first recall that a function $\varphi : \mathbb{R}^+ \to \mathbb{R}^+$ is said to be superadditive if $\varphi(t+s) \geq \varphi(t) + \varphi(s)$, for each $t,s \in \mathbb{R}^+$.

Theorem 4. *Let (X,d) be a pseudo-metric space, let $\varphi : \mathbb{R}^+ \to \mathbb{R}^+$ be an increasing left-continuous superadditive function and let $g : [0,\infty] \to [0,1]$ be a decreasing left-continuous function such that $g(0) = 1$. Then $(X, \mathcal{M}_d^{g,\varphi}, *_M)$ is a fuzzy pseudo-metric space, where the fuzzy set $\mathcal{M}_d^{g,\varphi} : X \times X \times (0,\infty)$ is given, for each $x,y \in X$ and $t \in \mathbb{R}^+$, by*

$$\mathcal{M}_d^{g,\varphi}(x,y,t) = g\left(\frac{d(x,y)}{\varphi(t)}\right). \tag{6}$$

Moreover if, in addition, $g^{-1}(1) = \{0\}$ then $\mathcal{M}_d^{g,\varphi}$ is a fuzzy metric if and only if d is a metric.

As opposed to the conclusions detailed above on the first method, the topology induced $\mathcal{M}_d^{g,\varphi}$ does not coincide with the topology induced by d, in general, for this second method as shows the next example.

Example 2. Let $\varphi : \mathbb{R}^+ \to \mathbb{R}^+$ given by $\varphi(t) = t$ for all $t \in \mathbb{R}^+$ and $g : [0,\infty] \to [0,1]$ given by

$$g(t) = \begin{cases} 1, & \text{if } t = 0 \\ \frac{1}{2}, & \text{elsewhere} \end{cases}. \tag{7}$$

It is not hard to check that φ and g fulfils the conditions imposed in Theorem 4. Now, consider the metric space $(\mathcal{X}, d)$, where $\mathcal{X} = \mathbb{R}$ and d is the usual metric on $\mathbb{R}$, i.e. $d(x, y) = |x - y|$ for each $x, y \in \mathcal{X}$. Then, by Theorem 4 we have that $\mathcal{M}_d^{g,\varphi}$ is a fuzzy metric on $\mathcal{X}$ for the minimum t-norm $*_M$, since $g^{-1}(1) = \{0\}$. On account of the above considered φ and g, the expression of $\mathcal{M}_d^{g,\varphi}$ is given by

$$\mathcal{M}_d^{g,\varphi}(x, y, t) = \begin{cases} 1, & \text{if } x = y \\ \frac{1}{2}, & \text{if } x \neq y \end{cases}, \tag{8}$$

for each $x, y \in \mathcal{X}$ and $t \in \mathbb{R}^+$. Observe that the topology induced by $\mathcal{M}_d^{g,\varphi}$ is the discrete topology. Indeed, for each $x \in \mathcal{X}$ we have that $y \in B_{\mathcal{M}_d^{g,\varphi}}\left(x, \frac{1}{2}, 1\right)$ if and only if $y = x$, since $\mathcal{M}_d^{g,\varphi}(x, y, 1) = \frac{1}{2} \leq 1 - \frac{1}{2}$ for all $y \in \mathcal{X}$ with $y \neq x$. Taking into account that the topology induced by d on $\mathcal{X}$ is the usual topology of $\mathbb{R}$ we conclude that $\mathcal{T}(d)$ does not coincide with $\mathcal{T}_{\mathcal{M}_d^{g,\varphi}}$.

Note that in the preceding example, the function g considered is not continuous at 0. So, we wonder if by requiring continuity at 0 to be enough to show that both topologies are the same. The next example answers in a negative way to such a question.

Example 3. Let $\varphi : \mathbb{R}^+ \to \mathbb{R}^+$ given by $\varphi(t) = t$ for all $t \in \mathbb{R}^+$ and $g : [0, \infty] \to [0, 1]$ given by $g(t) = 1$ for all $t \in [0, \infty]$. Again, it is easy to verify that φ and g satisfies the conditions demanded in Theorem 4. Considering the (pseudo-)metric space $(\mathcal{X}, d)$ of the previous example we conclude that $\mathcal{M}_d^{g,\varphi}$ is a fuzzy pseudo-metric on $\mathcal{X}$ for the minimum t-norm $*_M$. Taking into account φ and g defined above, we have that $\mathcal{M}_d^{g,\varphi}(x, y, t) = 1$ for each $x, y \in \mathcal{X}$ and $t \in \mathbb{R}^+$. Then, the topology induced by $\mathcal{M}_d^{g,\varphi}$ on $\mathcal{X}$ is the so called trivial topology (the unique open sets are the empty set and $\mathcal{X}$) which does not coincide with the usual topology of $\mathbb{R}$, which is the topology induced by d on $\mathcal{X}$.

Below, we will establish a theorem in which two additional conditions on the function g are imposed to ensure that both topologies $\mathcal{T}(d)$ and $\mathcal{T}_{\mathcal{M}_d^{g,\varphi}}$ are the same. Before, we prove the following lemma.

Lemma 1. *Let* $\varphi : \mathbb{R}^+ \to \mathbb{R}^+$ *be an increasing superadditive function. Then,* $\lim_{t \to 0^+} \varphi(t) = 0$ *(where, as usual,* $\lim_{t \to 0^+}$ *denotes the one-sided limit as t approaches 0 from the right).*

Proof. We will make the demonstration by contradiction.

So, suppose that $\lim_{t \to 0^+} \varphi(t) \neq 0$. Taking into account that φ is an increasing function defined on $\mathbb{R}^+$ which takes values in $\mathbb{R}^+$ we have that there exists $L \in \mathbb{R}^+$ such that $\lim_{t \to 0^+} \varphi(t) = L$.

Now, fix $s_0 \in \mathbb{R}^+$. Due to φ is superadditive we have that $\varphi(t + s_0) \geq \varphi(t/2) + \varphi(t/2 + s_0)$ for all $t \in \mathbb{R}^+$. Taking the one-sided limit as t approaches 0 from the right on the preceding inequality we obtain

$$\lim_{t \to s_0^+} \varphi(s_0) = \lim_{t \to 0^+} \varphi(t + s_0) \geq \lim_{t \to 0^+} \varphi\left(\frac{t}{2}\right) + \lim_{t \to 0^+} \varphi\left(\frac{t}{2} + s_0\right) = L + \lim_{t \to s_0^+} \varphi(s_0).$$

Hence, we get a contradiction since $\lim\limits_{t \to s_0^+} \varphi(s_0) \geq \varphi(s_0) > 0$ and we conclude that $\lim\limits_{t \to 0^+} \varphi(t) = 0$.

Now, we are able to prove the next theorem.

Theorem 5. *Let (X, d) be a pseudo-metric space, let $\varphi : \mathbb{R}^+ \to \mathbb{R}^+$ be an increasing left-continuous superadditive function and let $g : [0, \infty] \to [0, 1]$ be a decreasing left-continuous function such that $g(0) = 1$. If g is continuous at 0 and there exists $a \in \mathbb{R}^+$ such that $g(a) < 1$, then the topology induced by d on $\mathcal{X}$ coincides with the topology induced by $\mathcal{M}_d^{g,\varphi}$ on $\mathcal{X}$.*

Proof. We will see that $\mathcal{T}(d) = \mathcal{T}_{\mathcal{M}_d^{g,\varphi}}$ following the same reasoning used in the proof of Theorem 3. First, we will prove that for each $x \in \mathcal{X}$ we have that given $\varepsilon > 0$ there exist $r_0 \in]0, 1[$ and $t_0 \in \mathbb{R}^+$ such $B_{\mathcal{M}_d^{g,\varphi}}(x, r_0, t_0) \subseteq B_d(x; \varepsilon)$.

Let $x \in \mathcal{X}$ and fix $\varepsilon > 0$. By our assumption, there exists $a \in \mathbb{R}^+$ such that $g(a) < 1$. On the one hand, there exists $r_0 \in]0, 1[$ such that $1 - r_0 < g(a)$. On the other hand, Lemma 1 ensures the existence of $t_0 \in \mathbb{R}^+$ such that $\frac{\varepsilon}{\varphi(t_0)} > a$. We will see that $B_{\mathcal{M}_d^{g,\varphi}}(x, r_0, t_0) \subseteq B_d(x; \varepsilon)$.

Suppose that $y \in B_{\mathcal{M}_d^{g,\varphi}}(x, r_0, t_0)$, then

$$g\left(\frac{d(x,y)}{\varphi(t_0)}\right) = \mathcal{M}_d^{g,\varphi}(x, y, t_0) > 1 - r_0 > g(a).$$

Now, taking into account that g is decreasing we get $\frac{d(x,y)}{\varphi(t_0)} < a < \frac{\varepsilon}{\varphi(t_0)}$ and so $d(x,y) < \varepsilon$. Thus, $B_{\mathcal{M}_d^{g,\varphi}}(x, r_0, t_0) \subseteq B_d(x; \varepsilon)$.

Secondly, we will see that for each $x \in \mathcal{X}$ is fulfilled that for all $r \in]0, 1[$ and $t \in \mathbb{R}^+$ we can find $\varepsilon_0 > 0$ satisfying $B_d(x; \varepsilon_0) \subseteq B_{\mathcal{M}_d^{f_*,\varphi}}(x, r, t)$.

Let $x \in \mathcal{X}$. Fix $r \in]0, 1[$ and $t \in \mathbb{R}^+$. Since g is continuous at 0 we have that for the previous fixed $r > 0$ there exists $\delta > 0$ such that for all $a \in [0, \delta[$ is satisfied $1 - g(a) = |g(0) - g(a)| < r$, or equivalently, $g(a) > 1 - r$. Then, for $\varepsilon_0 = \delta \cdot \varphi(t_0) > 0$ we get $B_d(x; \varepsilon_0) \subseteq B_{\mathcal{M}_d^{f_*,\varphi}}(x, r, t)$. Indeed, if $y \in B_d(x; \varepsilon_0)$ we have that $d(x,y) < \varepsilon_0 = \delta \cdot \varphi(t_0)$ and so, $\frac{d(x,y)}{\varphi(t_0)} < \delta$. Therefore, for the detailed above we conclude that

$$\mathcal{M}_d^{g,\varphi}(x, y, t) = g\left(\frac{d(x,y)}{\varphi(t_0}\right) > 1 - r$$

and we conclude that $y \in B_{\mathcal{M}_d^{f_*,\varphi}}(x, r, t)$. Hence, $B_d(x; \varepsilon_0) \subseteq B_{\mathcal{M}_d^{f_*,\varphi}}(x, r, t)$.

Remark 2. In [10] also was established a result which provides a way to construct a GV-fuzzy pseudo metric from a pseudo-metric following the ideas of Theorem 4 (see [10, Theorem 4.2.]). In such a case, the function g must be continuous and satisfying $g(a) > 0$ for each $a \in \mathbb{R}^+$. Again, the conclusion of Theorem 5 is obviously retrieved when a GV-fuzzy pseudo-metric is constructed following Theorem 4.2. in [10].

Acknowledgments. Financiado con Ayuda a Primeros Proyectos de Investigación (PAID-06-24), Vicerrectorado de Investigación de la Universitat Politècnica de València (UPV). This research is part of project CIAICO/2022/051 funded by Generalitat Valenciana and by projects PID2022-139248NB-I00 and PID2022-140189OB-C21 funded by MICIU/AEI/10.13039/501100011033 and ERDF/EU.

Disclosure of Interests. The authors have no competing interests to declare that are relevant to the content of this article.

References

1. Camarena, J.G., Gregori, V., Morillas, S., Sapena, A.: Fast detection and removal of impulsive noise using peer groups and fuzzy metrics. J. Vis. Commun. Image Represent. **19**, 20–29 (2008)
2. George, A., Veeramani, P.: On some results in fuzzy metric spaces. Fuzzy Sets Syst. **64**(3), 395–399 (1994)
3. Grabiec, M.: Fixed points in fuzzy metric spaces. Fuzzy Sets Syst. **27**(3), 385–389 (1988)
4. Grečova, S., Morillas, S.: Perceptual similarity between color images using fuzzy metrics. J. Vis. Commun. Image Represent. **34**, 230–235 (2016)
5. Gregori, V., Miñana, J.J., Morillas, S.: Some questions in fuzzy metric spaces. Fuzzy Sets Syst. **204**, 71–85 (2012)
6. Gregori, V., Morillas, S., Sapena, A.: Examples of fuzzy metrics and applications. Fuzzy Sets Syst. **170**, 95–111 (2011)
7. Gregori, V., Romaguera, S.: Some properties of fuzzy metric spaces. Fuzzy Sets Syst. **115**, 485–489 (2000)
8. Gregori, V., Romaguera, S.: On completion of fuzzy metric spaces. Fuzzy Sets Syst. **130**, 399–404 (2002)
9. Gregori, V., Sapena, A.: On fixed-point theorems in fuzzy metric spaces. Fuzzy Sets Syst. **125**, 245–252 (2002)
10. Grigorenko, O., Miñana, J.J., Valero, O.: Two new methods to construct fuzzy metrics from metrics. Fuzzy Sets Syst. **467**(108483), 1–18 (2023)
11. Klement, E.P., Mesiar, R., Pap, E.: Triangular Norms. Springer, Netherlands (2000)
12. Kramosil, I., Michalek, J.: Fuzzy metric and statistical metric spaces. Kybernetika **11**, 336–344 (1975)
13. Miñana, J.J., Valero, O.: A duality relationship between fuzzy metrics and metrics. Int. J. Gen. Syst. **47**(6), 593–612 (2018)
14. Morillas, S., Gregori, V., Peris-Fajarnés, G.: New adaptative vector filter using fuzzy metrics. J. Electron. Imaging **16**(3), 033007:1–15 (2007)

15. Ortiz, A., Ortiz, E., Miñana, J.J., Valero, Ó.: On the use of fuzzy metrics for robust model estimation: a RANSAC-based approach. In: Rojas, I., Joya, G., Català, A. (eds.) IWANN 2021. LNCS, vol. 12861, pp. 165–177. Springer, Cham (2021). https://doi.org/10.1007/978-3-030-85030-2_14
16. Ralević, N., Delić, M., Nedović, N.: Aggregation of fuzzy metrics and its application in image segmentation. Iran. J. Fuzzy Syst. **19**(3), 19–37 (2022)
17. Stamenković, A., Milosavljević, N., Ralević, N.: Application of fuzzy metrics in clustering problems of agricultural crop varieties. Ekonomika poljoprivrede **71**(1), 121–134 (2024)
18. Zadeh, L.A.: Fuzzy Sets. Inf. Control **8**(3), 338–353 (1965)

Some Metric-Like Structures and ⊕-Based Semi (Pseudo) Metric-Like

Şuara Onbaşıoğlu Altuhovs and Banu Pazar Varol$^{(\boxtimes)}$

Department of Mathematics, Kocaeli University, 41001 Kocaeli, Turkey
suaraonbasioglu@gmail.com, banupazar@kocaeli.edu.tr

Abstract. This study investigates metric-like spaces as generalization of partial metric spaces introduced by Harandi. We examine the properties of open balls and points in these spaces, along with the behaviour of convergent sequences. Additionally, we introduce the semi(pseudo) metric-like structure by using the concept of extended t-conorms.

Keywords: Equal-like points · Extended t-conorm · Metric-like · Semi(Pseudo)Metric-like

1 Introduction

Research on metric spaces and their various generalizations has been an ongoing topic in mathematics for many years. One notable extension is the concept of partial metric spaces, introduced by Matthews [12], which generalizes classical metric spaces by allowing the self-distance of a point to be nonzero. Building on this idea, Harandi [7] introduced metric-like spaces as a further generalization of partial metric spaces. Over time, these spaces have been studied under different names. For instance, Monika [13] referred to them as dislocated metric spaces, while Hitzler and Seda [8] used the term d-metric spaces. Despite these variations in terminology, most subsequent studies, including this one, adopt the definition given by Harandi (see [7]).

Building on these developments, some researchers have continued to analyze metric structures in fuzzy environments. Various studies in the literature combine partial metric and fuzzy metric structures from different perspectives into a single structure, as seen in [1,4,6]. For instance, Sedghi *et al.* [17] introduced the concept of partial fuzzy metric spaces to the literature in the sense of George and Veeramani (GV) [3] and generalized the structure of strong GV-fuzzy metric spaces. Shukla and Abbas [18] combined metric-like mappings in the sense of Harandi with fuzzy metric structures in the GV sense and proposed fuzzy metric-like spaces. Later, Onbaşıoğlu and Pazar Varol [14] extend this structure to intuitionistic fuzzy metric spaces in the sense of Park [16] and described the concept of intuitionistic fuzzy metric-like spaces.

This paper focuses on the structural properties of metric-like spaces, particularly the characteristics of open balls and the behaviour of points within these

M. Baczyński et al. (Eds.): EUSFLAT 2025, LNCS 15883, pp. 229–241, 2025.
https://doi.org/10.1007/978-3-031-97225-6_19

spaces. Inspired by recent developments in the field, we analyze how open balls in metric-like spaces behave under different conditions and investigate their role in understanding convergence and accumulation points. Furthermore, considering the approach of Šostak and Öner [15,19] and Grigorenko *et al.* [5], we examine the relationship between metric-like spaces and algebraic structures, particularly in the context of t-conorm extensions. Finally, we introduce a semi(pseudo) metric-like structure and provide various examples to illustrate its properties and potential applications.

2   Preliminaries

In this section, we recall the definition of partial metric spaces defined by Matthews [12] and the definition of metric-like spaces defined by Harandi [7] as a generalization of partial metric spaces. Due to the relationship between partial metric spaces and metric-like spaces, the definition of partial metric is given first. Throughout the paper, by $\mathbb{R}^+$ we mean $[0, +\infty)$; $\mathbb{R}$ and $\mathbb{N}$ will denote the set of all real numbers and the set of all positive integers, respectively and X is a non-empty initial universe.

Definition 1 [12]. *A mapping $\varrho : X \times X \to \mathbb{R}^+$ is called partial metric on X if the following conditions are hold:*

(PM1) $x = y \Leftrightarrow \varrho(x,x) = \varrho(y,y) = \varrho(x,y)$;
(PM2) $\varrho(x,x) \leq \varrho(x,y)$;
(PM3) $\varrho(x,y) = \varrho(y,x)$;
(PM4) $\varrho(x,z) \leq \varrho(x,y) + \varrho(y,z) - \varrho(y,y)$.

Then, the pair (X, ϱ) is called a partial metric space. A partial metric on X is a metric if $\varrho(x,x) = 0$ for all $x \in X$. However, the self-distance of any point in any partial metric space is not necessarily equal to zero. So, a partial metric is a generalization of a metric.

Example 1 [7]. *The pair $(\mathbb{R}^+, \varrho)$ is a partial metric space, where $\varrho(x,y) = max\{x,y\}$ for all $x,y \in \mathbb{R}^+$. In this setting, the self-distance of any point $x \in \mathbb{R}^+$ is equal to itself.*

Definition 2 [7]. *A mapping $\sigma : X \times X \to \mathbb{R}^+$ is called metric-like on X if the following conditions are hold:*

(ML1) $\sigma(x,y) = 0 \Rightarrow x = y$;
(ML2) $\sigma(x,y) = \sigma(y,x)$;
(ML3) $\sigma(x,z) \leq \sigma(x,y) + \sigma(y,z)$.

Then, the pair (X, σ) is called a metric-like space (also known as a dislocated metric or d-metric space). A metric-like mapping on X satisfies all the conditions of a metric except that $\sigma(x,x)$ may be positive for $x \in X$. Here, $\sigma(x,x)$ represents the size or weight of x, a feature used to describe the amount of information contained in x, unlike the usual meaning of a metric. If $\sigma(x,x) = 0$, it means that x is being defined and as $\sigma(x,x)$ increases, we gain more information about x.

Remark 1 [9]. Every partial metric space is a metric-like space, but the converse is not true in general. For example, let $X = \mathbb{R}$ and $\sigma(x, y) = max\{|x - 5|, |y - 5|\}$ for all $x, y \in \mathbb{R}$. Then, $(\mathbb{R}, \sigma)$ is a metric-like space but it is not a partial-metric space.

Example 2 [9]. Let $X = \mathbb{R}^+$ and $\sigma : X \times X \to \mathbb{R}^+$ defined as $\sigma(x, y) = x + y$ for all $x, y \in X$. Then, (X, σ) is a metric-like space.

Example 3 [10]. Let $X = \mathbb{R}$ and $\sigma : X \times X \to \mathbb{R}^+$ be defined as $\sigma(x, y) = |x| + |y|$ for all $x, y \in X$. Then, (X, σ) is a metric-like space.

Definition 3 [9]. *Each metric-like σ on X generates a topology τ_σ on X whose base is the family of $\sigma-$open balls. An open σ-ball, with center x, radius $r > 0$, is the set $\mathcal{B}_\sigma(x, r) = \{y \in X : |\sigma(x, y) - \sigma(x, x)| < r\}$ for all $x \in X$.*

Definition 4 [7]. *Let (X, σ) be a metric-like space. Then,*

(i) *A sequence $\{x_n\}$ in X converges to a point $x \in X$ if and only if $\lim_{n\to\infty} \sigma(x, x_n) = \sigma(x, x)$.*
(ii) *A sequence $\{x_n\}$ in X is said to be a $\sigma-$Cauchy sequence if the $\lim_{n,m\to\infty} \sigma(x_n, x_m)$ exists and is finite.*
(iii) *The space (X, σ) is said to be complete if every $\sigma-$Cauchy sequence $\{x_n\}$ in X converges to a point $x \in X$ such that $\lim_{n\to\infty} \sigma(x, x_n) = \sigma(x, x) = \lim_{n,m\to\infty} \sigma(x_n, x_m)$.*

Remark 2 [7]. The limit of a convergent sequence in a metric-like space need not be unique.

Definition 5 [9]. *Let (X, σ) be a metric-like space,*

(i) *x and y are called equal-like points if there exists a sequence $\{x_n\}$ of X converging to both x and y, i.e. $x_n \to x$ and $x_n \to y$.*
(ii) *x and y are called completely separate points if the following condition holds: $\sigma(x, y) > \sigma(x, x) + \sigma(y, y)$.*
(iii) *Let A be a subset of X, a point $x_0 \in X$ is said to be a cluster point of A whenever for every $\varepsilon > 0$ there exists $a \in A$ such that $|\sigma(a, x_0) - \sigma(x_0, x_0)| < \varepsilon$. The set of all cluster points of A is called the closure of A and is denoted by $\overline{A}$.*
(iv) *Let A be a non-empty subset of X, and let d be a metric on X. The distance between a point $x_0 \in X$ and the set A is defined as follows:*

$$d(x_0, A) := inf\{|\sigma(x_0, a) - \sigma(x_0, x_0)| : a \in A\}.$$

Theorem 1 [9]. *Let (X, σ) be a metric-like space and $\emptyset \neq A \subseteq X$, then $\overline{A} = \{x \in X : d(x, A) = 0\}$.*

Remark 3 If x and y are equal-like points, then they are not completely separated. If x and y are completely separated points, then they are not equal-like points.

The following Theorem states that the intersections of σ−open balls of equal-like points as centres have finitely many elements of the sequence. The proof of this theorem can be found in reference [9].

Theorem 2 [9]. *Let (X, σ) be a metric-like space. Two points x and y in X are said to be equal-like if and only if $\mathcal{B}_\sigma(x, \varepsilon) \cap \mathcal{B}_\sigma(y, \varepsilon) \neq \emptyset$ for all $\varepsilon > 0$.*

The extended t-conorm concept is defined below, and the following sections provide more detailed information about this structure.

Definition 6 [15]. *A binary operation $\oplus : \mathbb{R}^+ \times \mathbb{R}^+ \to \mathbb{R}^+$ is called extended t-conorm if, for all $\alpha, \beta, \gamma \in \mathbb{R}^+$ the following properties hold:*

($\oplus_1$) $\oplus$ *is commutative, that is $\alpha \oplus \beta = \beta \oplus \alpha$;*
($\oplus_2$) $\oplus$ *is associative, that is $\alpha \oplus (\beta \oplus \gamma) = (\alpha \oplus \beta) \oplus \gamma$;*
($\oplus_3$) $\oplus$ *is monotone, that is $\alpha \leq \beta \Rightarrow \alpha \oplus \gamma \leq \beta \oplus \gamma$;*
($\oplus_4$) *0 is the neutral element for $\oplus$, that is $\alpha \oplus 0 = \alpha$.*

Remark 4 [15]. In Definition 6, if $\oplus$ is defined on $[0, 1] \times [0, 1]$ and it takes its values in $[0, 1]$, then the definition of an extended t-conorm reduces to the concept of a t-conorm [11]. For this reason, we use the term 'extended t-conorm' to distinguish it from usual t-conorms.

Below, the special properties of the operation $\oplus$ are presented.

Definition 7 [15]. *A binary operation $\oplus : \mathbb{R}^+ \times \mathbb{R}^+ \to \mathbb{R}^+$ is called distributive, if for all $\alpha, \beta, \gamma \in \mathbb{R}^+$,*

($\oplus_5$) $k \cdot (\alpha \oplus \beta) = k \cdot \alpha \oplus k \cdot \beta$;
$\oplus$ *is called compressible, if,*
($\oplus_6$) $\alpha \leq \beta \oplus \gamma \Rightarrow \frac{\alpha}{\alpha+1} \leq \frac{\beta}{\beta+1} \oplus \frac{\gamma}{\gamma+1}$
$\oplus$ *is called continuous at the bottom level if this operation is continuous in all points of $\{0\} \times \mathbb{R}^+ \subseteq \mathbb{R}^+ \times \mathbb{R}^+$ (and, hence, by symmetry also on $\mathbb{R}^+ \times \{0\}$).*

3   Main Results

In this section, we primarily examine the structure of equal-like points and open balls centred at equal-like points. We compare equal-like points and completely separated points through the use of σ-open balls. Additionally, we define the Cartesian product space within the context of metric-like spaces. Furthermore, we define the semi(pseudo)-metric-like structure and present several examples.

3.1   Characteristics Structure of Metric-Like Spaces

In this section, we present results on equal-like points and completely separated points in a metric-like space and define Cartesian product space within the context of metric-like spaces.

Lemma 1. *Let (X, σ) be a metric-like space. For all $x, y, z \in X$, if x and y are equal-like points and y and z are equal-like points, then x and z are also equal-like points.*

Proof. Assume that the hypothesis is held. From Theorem 2,
$\mathcal{B}_\sigma(x, r) \cap \mathcal{B}_\sigma(y, r) \neq \emptyset$ and similarly $\mathcal{B}_\sigma(y, r) \cap \mathcal{B}_\sigma(z, r) \neq \emptyset$ satisfy for all $r > 0$.
Since $\mathcal{B}_\sigma(y, r) \cap \mathcal{B}_\sigma(z, r) \neq \emptyset$ and x and y are equal-like points, then we obtain
$\mathcal{B}_\sigma(x, r) \cap (\mathcal{B}_\sigma(y, r) \cap \mathcal{B}_\sigma(z, r)) \neq \emptyset$. It is clear from Theorem 2 that each of the sets centered at equal-like points must be non-empty. Therefore, we can conclude that the intersection of these three sets is non-empty.
$\Rightarrow \mathcal{B}_\sigma(x, r) \cap (\mathcal{B}_\sigma(y, r) \cap \mathcal{B}_\sigma(z, r)) \neq \mathcal{B}_\sigma(x, r) \cap \emptyset = \emptyset$
Since $\mathcal{B}_\sigma(y, r) \neq \emptyset$ and $\mathcal{B}_\sigma(x, r) \cap \mathcal{B}_\sigma(z, r) \neq \emptyset$,
$\Rightarrow \mathcal{B}_\sigma(y, r) \cap (\mathcal{B}_\sigma(x, r) \cap \mathcal{B}_\sigma(z, r)) \neq \emptyset$
$\Rightarrow \mathcal{B}_\sigma(x, r) \cap \mathcal{B}_\sigma(z, r) \neq \emptyset$ for all $r > 0$.
$\Rightarrow$ x and z are equal-like points.

Remark 5. A metric-like space of completely separate points is a Hausdorff space. Indeed, if x and y are completely separated points, there is at least one radius $r > 0$ that centres x and y such that $\mathcal{B}_\sigma(x, r) \cap \mathcal{B}_\sigma(y, r) = \emptyset$.

Remark 6. We can categorize the points of a metric-like space in three different ways: a group of equal-like points, a group of completely separate points, or a group of neither equal-like nor completely separate points. The set of equal-like points and completely separated points varies depending on the set and the metric-like mapping defined on it. For example, let E (determined using a convergent sequence $\{x_n\}$ in X) be the set of equal-like points in the metric-like space and let S be the set of completely separated points. From the Definition 5, E and S are disjoint sets. Since E and S are constructed with the help of $\{x_n\}$, thus $X \setminus (E \cup S)$ contains the rest of the other points which are neither equal-like nor completely separated points of a metric-like space.

In the next proposition, it was shown that the intersection of open balls taking as centers the equal-like points in a metric-like space is also an open set.

Proposition 1. *Let (X, d) be a metric space and $c \in X$ be a fixed element. Let (X, σ) be a metric-like space where $\sigma(c, c) = 0$ and $\sigma(x, y) = d(x, c) + d(c, y)$. Then, the intersection of two open sets centred by equal-like points is an open set in that space.*

Proof. Let begin by proving that (X, σ), with the metric-like mapping defined as above, is indeed a metric-like space.

If $\sigma(x, y) = d(x, c) + d(c, y) = 0$, then $d(x, c) = d(c, y) = 0 \Rightarrow x = y = c$ satisfy. From the Definition 2, it is clear that (ML2) is also satisfying. Now, we will show the triangle inequality. Since d is a metric on X, we have;

$\sigma(x, z) = d(x, c) + d(c, z) \leq (d(x, y) + d(y, c)) + d(c, z) \leq (d(x, c) + d(c, y)) + d(y, c) + d(c, z) = \sigma(x, y) + \sigma(y, z)$, and it implies that $\sigma(x, z) \leq \sigma(x, y) + \sigma(y, z)$.

Thus, (X, σ) is a metric-like space.

Let $x_1, x_2 \in X$ be equal-like points in this space. Then, from Theorem 2, for every $r \in \mathbb{R}^+$, we have $B_\sigma(x_1, r) \cap B_\sigma(x_2, r) \neq \emptyset$. We need to show that $B_\sigma(x_1, r) \cap B_\sigma(x_2, r)$ is an open set. Since $B_\sigma(x_1, r) \cap B_\sigma(x_2, r) \neq \emptyset$, there exists at least one $y \in B_\sigma(x_1, r) \cap B_\sigma(x_2, r)$ such that

$$|d(c, y) - d(c, x_1)| < r \quad \text{and} \quad |d(c, y) - d(c, x_2)| < r.$$

This implies that $d(c, y) \in \big(d(c, x_1) - r, d(c, x_1) + r\big) \cap \big(d(c, x_2) - r, d(c, x_2) + r\big)$. Taking the intersection, we obtain $\max\{d(c, x_1) - r, d(c, x_2) - r\} < d(c, y) < \min\{d(c, x_1) + r, d(c, x_2) + r\}$. Thus, $y \in B_\sigma(x_1, r) \cap B_\sigma(x_2, r)$.

Now, suppose that for all $\varepsilon > 0$, the following holds,

$$B_\sigma(y, \varepsilon) \not\subset B_\sigma(x_1, r) \cap B_\sigma(x_2, r).$$

By the definition of open balls, for any $z \in B_\sigma(y, \varepsilon)$, we have

$$|\sigma(y, z) - \sigma(y, y)| < \varepsilon$$

Expanding this, we get

$$|d(y, c) + d(c, z) - d(y, c) - d(c, y)| < \varepsilon,$$

which simplifies to $|d(c, z) - d(c, y)| < \varepsilon$. Thus,

$$d(c, y) - \varepsilon < d(c, z) < d(c, y) + \varepsilon.$$

Since $d(c, x_1), d(c, x_2) \in \mathbb{R}^+$, assume without loss of generality that $d(c, x_1) > d(c, x_2)$. Then,

$$d(c, x_1) - r < d(c, y) < d(c, x_2) + r.$$

From this, we obtain

$$d(c, z) < d(c, y) + \varepsilon < d(c, x_2) + r + \varepsilon.$$

Similarly,

$$d(c, x_1) - r - \varepsilon < d(c, y) - \varepsilon < d(c, z)$$

Thus, our assumption is false, and consequently, there exists an $\varepsilon > 0$, leading us to conclude that

$$B_\sigma(y, \varepsilon) \subset B_\sigma(x_1, r) \cap B_\sigma(x_2, r),$$

which proves that $B_\sigma(x_1, r) \cap B_\sigma(x_2, r)$ is open.

Below, we present an example that better illustrates open balls and equal-like points in metric-like spaces.

Example 4. Let $X = \mathbb{R}^+$ and $\sigma : X \times X \rightarrow \mathbb{R}^+$ be a metric-like mapping defined as $\sigma(x, y) = \max\{x, y\}$. Then,

   i) If $x, y \in \mathbb{R}^+$ with $x < y$, then $B_\sigma(x, \varepsilon) \subset B_\sigma(y, \varepsilon)$ for all $\varepsilon > 0$, and there exists $\varepsilon_0 > 0$ such that $y \notin B_\sigma(x, \varepsilon_0)$.
  ii) If $x = y$, then $B_\sigma(x, \varepsilon) = B_\sigma(y, \varepsilon)$ for all $\varepsilon > 0$.

(i) Let $x, y \in \mathbb{R}^+$ and assume that $x < y$. Since $\sigma(x, y) = \max\{x, y\}$ is a metric-like mapping on $\mathbb{R}^+$, we obtain $\sigma(y, y) > \sigma(x, x)$. Let $z \in B_\sigma(x, \varepsilon)$. From the definition of open balls in a metric-like mapping, we have

$$\sigma(x, x) - \varepsilon < \sigma(x, z) < \sigma(x, x) + \varepsilon < \sigma(y, y) + \varepsilon$$

From this assumption, we obtain three cases: $x < z < y$, $z < x < y$ and $x < y < z$.
If $x < z < y$, then $\sigma(x, z) = z$ and $\sigma(y, z) = y$, which leads to:

$$x < z < y < y + \varepsilon \Rightarrow \sigma(x, x) < \sigma(x, z) < \sigma(y, z) < \sigma(y, y) + \varepsilon$$

If $z < x < y$, then $\sigma(x, z) = x$ and $\sigma(y, z) = y$, which leads to:

$$z < x < y < y + \varepsilon \Rightarrow \sigma(z, z) < \sigma(x, z) < \sigma(y, z) < \sigma(y, y) + \varepsilon$$

If $x < y < z$, then $\sigma(x, y) = y$ and $\sigma(y, z) = z$, which leads to:

$$y - \varepsilon < x < y < z \Rightarrow \sigma(y, y) - \varepsilon < \sigma(x, x) < \sigma(x, y) < \sigma(y, z)$$

from all these cases, we conclude that $z \in B_\sigma(y, \varepsilon)$ for every $\varepsilon > 0$.
Now, we need to show that there exists $\varepsilon_0 > 0$ such that $y \notin B_\sigma(x, \varepsilon_0)$ if $x < y$.
Suppose, for contradiction, that $y \in B_\sigma(x, \varepsilon)$ for all $\varepsilon > 0$. Then,

$$y \in B_\sigma(x, \varepsilon) \Rightarrow \sigma(x, x) - \varepsilon < \sigma(x, y) < \sigma(x, x) + \varepsilon \Rightarrow x - \varepsilon < y < x + \varepsilon$$

Since $0 \leq x < y$, we have $0 < y - x$. If we choose $\varepsilon_0 = y - x$, then:

$$x - (y - x) < y < x + (y - x) \Rightarrow 2x - y < y < y$$

Thus, our assumption leads to a contradiction, and it follows that there exists $\varepsilon_0 > 0$ such that $y \notin B_\sigma(x, \varepsilon_0)$ satisfies.
(ii) Assuming $x \leq y$, it follows that $B_\sigma(x, \varepsilon) \subseteq B_\sigma(y, \varepsilon)$ for every $\varepsilon > 0$. On the other hand, if $y \leq x$, then again from (i), we have $B_\sigma(y, \varepsilon) \subseteq B_\sigma(x, \varepsilon)$, and if $x = y$, then we obtain $B_\sigma(x, \varepsilon) = B_\sigma(y, \varepsilon)$ for all $\varepsilon > 0$.

Theorem 3. *Let (X, σ) be a metric-like space and $A, B \subseteq X$, then following statements are hold;*

(i) $A \subseteq \overline{A}$;
(ii) $\overline{(\overline{A})} = \overline{A}$;
(iii) $\overline{(A \cup B)} = \overline{A} \cup \overline{B}$;
(iv) $\overline{\emptyset} = \emptyset$

Proof. The proofs of (i) and (iv) are clear. So, we give only (ii) and (iii).

(ii) First, from (i), it is clear that $\overline{A} \subseteq \overline{(\overline{A})}$. Now, we prove the reverse inclusion. Let $x_0 \in \overline{(\overline{A})}$. Then, for every $\varepsilon > 0$, we have $\mathcal{B}_\sigma(x_0, \varepsilon) \cap \overline{A} \neq \emptyset$. This implies that there exists at least one $a \in \overline{A}$ such that $|\sigma(x_0, a) - \sigma(x_0, x_0)| < \varepsilon$ for all $\varepsilon > 0$. By Theorem 1, it follows that $d(x_0, \overline{A}) = 0$. Thus, $x_0 \in \overline{A}$, which gives $\overline{(\overline{A})} \subseteq \overline{A}$. Consequently, we conclude that $\overline{(\overline{A})} = \overline{A}$.

(iii) Let $x_0 \in \overline{A \cup B}$. Then, we have $\mathcal{B}_\sigma(x_0, \varepsilon) \cap (A \cup B) \neq \emptyset$ for all $\varepsilon > 0$. This implies that

$$(\mathcal{B}_\sigma(x_0, \varepsilon) \cap A) \cup (\mathcal{B}_\sigma(x_0, \varepsilon) \cap B) \neq \emptyset$$

for all $\varepsilon > 0$, which further leads to $\mathcal{B}_\sigma(x_0, \varepsilon) \cap A \neq \emptyset$ or $\mathcal{B}_\sigma(x_0, \varepsilon) \cap B \neq \emptyset$. Assume, for contradiction, that there exist $\varepsilon_1, \varepsilon_2 > 0$ such that

$$\mathcal{B}_\sigma(x_0, \varepsilon_1) \cap A = \emptyset \quad \text{and} \quad \mathcal{B}_\sigma(x_0, \varepsilon_2) \cap B = \emptyset.$$

Taking $\varepsilon_0 = \min\{\varepsilon_1, \varepsilon_2\}$, we obtain

$$\mathcal{B}_\sigma(x_0, \varepsilon_0) \cap A = \emptyset \quad \text{and} \quad \mathcal{B}_\sigma(x_0, \varepsilon_0) \cap B = \emptyset.$$

This contradicts the assumption that $x_0 \in \overline{A \cup B}$, as it would imply

$$\mathcal{B}_\sigma(x_0, \varepsilon_0) \cap (A \cup B) = \emptyset.$$

Thus, we must have $\mathcal{B}_\sigma(x_0, \varepsilon) \cap A \neq \emptyset$ or $\mathcal{B}_\sigma(x_0, \varepsilon) \cap B \neq \emptyset$ for all $\varepsilon > 0$, which implies

$$x_0 \in \overline{A} \quad \text{or} \quad x_0 \in \overline{B}.$$

Hence, $x_0 \in \overline{A} \cup \overline{B}$.

On the other hand, if $A \subseteq B$, then by the monotonicity property of closure, we obtain $\overline{A} \subseteq \overline{B}$. The closure set

$$\overline{A} = \{x_0 \in X \mid \forall \varepsilon > 0, \exists \alpha \in A : |\sigma(x_0, \alpha) - \sigma(x_0, x_0)| < \varepsilon\}$$

is contained in

$$\overline{B} = \{x_0 \in X \mid \forall \varepsilon > 0 \, \exists \alpha \in A \subseteq B : |\sigma(x_0, \alpha) - \sigma(x_0, x_0)| < \varepsilon\}.$$

Since $A \subseteq A \cup B \Rightarrow \overline{A} \subseteq \overline{A \cup B}$ and $B \subseteq A \cup B \Rightarrow \overline{B} \subseteq \overline{A \cup B}$, we obtain $\overline{A} \cup \overline{B} \subseteq \overline{(A \cup B)}$. Thus, we conclude that $\overline{(A \cup B)} = \overline{A} \cup \overline{B}$.

Following, we give the concept of the Cartesian product space of two metric-like spaces and an example.

Proposition 2. *Let (X, σ_1) and (Y, σ_2) be two metric-like spaces. Let $\sigma : (X \times Y) \times (X \times Y) \to \mathbb{R}^+$ be defined by $\sigma(a, b) = \sqrt{\sigma_1(x_1, x_2)^2 + \sigma_2(y_1, y_2)^2}$, where $a = (x_1, y_1), b = (x_2, y_2) \in X \times Y$. Then σ is a metric-like mapping on $X \times Y$, and the space $(X \times Y, \sigma)$ is called the Cartesian product space of two metric-like spaces.*

Proof. To show that the mapping $\sigma : (X \times Y) \times (X \times Y) \to \mathbb{R}^+$ is a metric-like on $X \times Y$, it must satisfy the axioms of Definition 2. For all $a = (x_1, y_1)$, $b = (x_2, y_2), c = (x_3, y_3) \in X \times Y$,

(i) Since σ_1 and σ_2 are metric-like mappings on X and Y, respectively, we have:

$$\sigma_1(x_1, x_2) = 0 \Rightarrow x_1 = x_2 \quad \text{and} \quad \sigma_2(y_1, y_2) = 0 \Rightarrow y_1 = y_2,$$

Therefore,

$$\sigma(a, b) = \sqrt{\sigma_1(x_1, x_2)^2 + \sigma_2(y_1, y_2)^2} = 0 \Rightarrow \sigma_1(x_1, x_2)^2 + \sigma_2(y_1, y_2)^2 = 0$$

$$\Rightarrow \sigma_1(x_1, x_2) = 0 \quad \text{and} \quad \sigma_2(y_1, y_2) = 0 \Rightarrow (x_1, y_1) = (x_2, y_2) \Rightarrow a = b$$

(ii) Since σ_1 and σ_2 are symmetric functions:

$$\sigma_1(x_1, x_2) = \sigma_1(x_2, x_1), \quad \sigma_2(y_1, y_2) = \sigma_2(y_2, y_1),$$

it follows that:

$$\sigma(a, b) = \sqrt{\sigma_1(x_1, x_2)^2 + \sigma_2(y_1, y_2)^2} = \sqrt{\sigma_1(x_2, x_1)^2 + \sigma_2(y_2, y_1)^2} = \sigma(b, a).$$

(iii) Since σ_1 and σ_2 satisfy the triangle inequality:

$$\sigma_1(x_1, x_2) \leq \sigma_1(x_1, x_3) + \sigma_1(x_3, x_2), \quad \text{and} \quad \sigma_2(y_1, y_2) \leq \sigma_2(y_1, y_3) + \sigma_2(y_3, y_2).$$

By the triangle inequality of the Euclidean norm:

$$\begin{aligned}
\sigma(a, b) &= \sqrt{\sigma_1(x_1, x_2)^2 + \sigma_2(y_1, y_2)^2} \\
&\leq \sqrt{(\sigma_1(x_1, x_3) + \sigma_1(x_3, x_2))^2 + (\sigma_2(y_1, y_3) + \sigma_2(y_3, y_2))^2} \\
&\leq \sqrt{\sigma_1(x_1, x_3)^2 + \sigma_2(y_1, y_3)^2} + \sqrt{\sigma_1(x_3, x_2)^2 + \sigma_2(y_3, y_2)^2} \\
&= \sigma(a, c) + \sigma(c, b).
\end{aligned}$$

Hence, we obtain $(X \times Y, \sigma)$ is a Cartesian product space of two metric-like spaces.

The following example serves to illustrate Proposition 2.

Example 5. $(X \times Y, \sigma_m)$ and $(X \times Y, \sigma^*)$ are two metric-like spaces obtained as the Cartesian product of two metric-like spaces, where σ_m and σ^* defined as $\sigma_m(a, b) = \max\{\sigma_1(x_1, x_2), \sigma_2(y_1, y_2)\}$ and $\sigma^*(a, b) = \sigma_1(x_1, x_2) + \sigma_2(y_1, y_2)$.

Let consider the Cartesian product space $(X \times Y, \sigma_m)$, where the metric-like function σ_m is defined as

$$\sigma_m((x_1, y_1), (x_2, y_2)) = \max\{\sigma_1(x_1, x_2), \sigma_2(y_1, y_2)\},$$

for $a = (x_1, y_1)$, $b = (x_2, y_2)$, $c = (x_3, y_3) \in X \times Y$, and where σ_1 and σ_2 are metric-like mappings on X and Y, respectively.

We aim to prove that σ_m is a metric-like mapping on $X \times Y$. In order to do so, we shall verify the axioms given in Definition 2.

(i) $\sigma_m(a, b) = \max\{\sigma_1(x_1, x_2), \sigma_2(y_1, y_2)\} = 0 \Rightarrow \sigma_1(x_1, x_2) = 0, \sigma_2(y_1, y_2) = 0 \Rightarrow x_1 = x_2, y_1 = y_2 \Rightarrow a = b$.

(ii) $\sigma_m(a, b) = \max\{\sigma_1(x_1, x_2), \sigma_2(y_1, y_2)\} = \max\{\sigma_1(x_2, x_1), \sigma_2(y_2, y_1)\} = \sigma_m(b, a)$.

(iii) $\sigma_m(a, c) = \max\{\sigma_1(x_1, x_3), \sigma_2(y_1, y_3)\} \leq \max\{\sigma_1(x_1, x_2) + \sigma_1(x_2, x_3), \sigma_2(y_1, y_2) + \sigma_2(y_2, y_3)\} \leq \max\{\sigma_1(x_1, x_2), \sigma_2(y_1, y_2)\} + \max\{\sigma_1(x_2, x_3), \sigma_2(y_2, y_3)\} = \sigma_m(a, b) + \sigma_m(b, c)$.

Hence, $(X \times Y, \sigma_m)$ is a Cartesian product space of two metric-like spaces. $(X \times Y, \sigma^*)$ can be shown in similar way.

Definition 8. *An open ball with centre (u_1, v_1) and radius $r > 0$ in the Cartesian product space of two metric-like spaces is defined as below:*
$\mathcal{B}_\sigma((u_1, v_1), r) = \{(x_1, y_1) \in X \times Y : |\sigma((u_1, v_1), (x_1, y_1)) - \sigma((u_1, v_1), (u_1, v_1))| < r\}$.

Below we give an example for Definition 8 by considering Proposition 2.

Example 6. Let take $\sigma((u_1, v_1), (x_1, y_1)) = \sqrt{(\sigma_1(u_1, x_1))^2 + \sigma_2(v_1, y_1))^2}$. Then we obtain open ball with center (u_1, v_1) and radius $r > 0$ as :

$$\mathcal{B}_\sigma((u_1, v_1), r) = \left\{(x_1, y_1) \in X \times Y : \left|\sqrt{K_1} - \sqrt{K_2}\right| < r\right\}.$$

$(K_1 := (\sigma_1(u_1, x_1))^2 + (\sigma_2(v_1, y_1))^2$ and $K_2 := (\sigma_1(u_1, u_1))^2 + \sigma_2(v_1, v_1))^2$, respectively. Here, we use K_1, K_2 just as a notation).
On the other hand, if we take $X = Y = \mathbb{R}$ and σ_1, σ_2 as Euclid metric, then the open ball with center (u_1, v_1) and radius $r > 0$, $\mathcal{B}_\sigma((u_1, v_1), r) = \{(x_1, y_1) \in X \times Y : |\sqrt{|u_1 - x_1|^2 + |v_1 - y_1|^2}| < r\}$ is obtained. Here, $\sqrt{|u_1 - x_1|^2 + |v_1 - y_1|^2}$ is always greater than or equal to zero, so we obtain the graph of the open ball in the plane.

3.2   ⊕-Based Semi(pseudo) Metric-Like

In this section, we introduce the semi(pseudo)metric-like structure and give some examples in ⊕-based semi(pseudo) metric-like spaces to extend the metric-like structure.

Definition 9. *A mapping* $\rho : X \times X \to \mathbb{R}^+$ *is called semi(pseudo) metric-like if it satisfies the following two properties:*

(i) $\rho(x, x) \geq 0, \forall x, y \in \mathbb{R}^+$;
(ii) $\rho(x, y) = \rho(y, x), \forall x, y \in \mathbb{R}^+$.
A semi(pseudo) metric is a semi(pseudo) metric-like satisfying the following strengthened version of the first axiom:
(i' $\rho(x, y) = 0 \Rightarrow x = y$.

Definition 10. *Given an extended t-conorm* $\oplus$: $\mathbb{R}^+ \times \mathbb{R}^+ \to \mathbb{R}^+$, *a semi(pseudo) metric-like* $\rho : X \times X \to \mathbb{R}^+$ *is called*

(iii) $\oplus-$*based (pseudo) metric-like, or just* $\oplus-$*(pseudo) metric-like if*
$\rho(x, z) \leq \rho(x, y) \oplus \rho(y, z), \forall x, y, z \in X$.

Now, we show some examples for $\oplus-$based (pseudo) metric-like.

Example 7. Let $U = \{0, 3, 5\}$, and define
$$\rho(x, y) = \begin{cases} 7, & x = y = 0; \\ 6, & otherwise. \end{cases}$$
Then, (U, ρ) is a pseudo metric-like space and ρ is a $\oplus-$ based (pseudo) metric-like on U.

$(P_\ell 1)$ $x = y = 0 \Rightarrow \rho(x, y) = 7 > 0$;
otherwise $\Rightarrow \rho(x, y) = 6 > 0$.
$(P_\ell 2)$ $\rho(x, y) = \rho(y, x)$ is obvious.
$(P_\ell 3)$ If $x = y = z = 0 \Rightarrow 7 \leq 7 \oplus 7 = 7 + 7 = 14$
If $x = y \neq z \Rightarrow 7 \leq 6 \oplus 6 = 6 + 6 = 12$
If $x \neq y = z \Rightarrow 6 \leq 6 \oplus 7 = 6 + 7 = 13$
If $x \neq y \neq z \Rightarrow 6 \leq 6 \oplus 6 = 6 + 6 = 12$

Thus, ρ is a $\oplus-$based (pseudo) metric-like on U and (U, ρ) is a $\oplus-$based (pseudo) metric-like space.

Example 8. Let $U = \mathbb{R}^+$, define $\rho : U \times U \to \mathbb{R}^+$ such that $\rho(x, y) = x + y$. Then, ρ is a $\oplus-$based (pseudo) metric-like on U and (U, ρ) is a $\oplus-$based (pseudo) metric-like space.

$(P_\ell 1)$ $\rho(x, y) = x + y = 0 \Rightarrow x = y = 0 \; \forall x, y \in U$.
$(P_\ell 2)$ $\rho(x, y) = x + y = y + x = \rho(y, x)$
$(P_\ell 3)$ $x + z \leq (x + y) \oplus (y + z)$
$= (x + y) + (y + z)$
$= x + 2y + z$ since $2y \geq 0$,
$\Rightarrow x + z \leq (x + y) \oplus (y + z)$

Therefore, ρ is a $\oplus-$based (pseudo) metric-like on U and (U, ρ) is a $\oplus-$based (pseudo) metric-like space.

Example 9. Let (U, d) be a classical pseudo metric space where d is a $\oplus-$based (pseudo) metric and $\rho(x, y) = 1 + d(x, y), \forall x, y \in U$. Then, ρ is a $\oplus-$based (pseudo) metric-like on U.

4 Conclusion

This study presents the structure of open balls and results obtained on closed sets in metric-like spaces. It then examines the structures of points in metric-like spaces. It can be seen as an important source for establishing new topological structures in future. Next, a semi(pseudo) metric-like structure is introduced, and the extended t-conorm is generalized within this new framework. The obtained results, along with various examples, are presented. For further studies related to the use of extended t-conorms, we suggest referring to [2] *et al.*, as it presents a constructive framework for generalizing t-conorms to n-dimensional (a, b)-t-conorms for arbitrary $a, b \in \mathbb{R}$, with $a < b$. This framework provides a more general approach that allows the definition of (a, b)-t-conorms and other fuzzy operators over any arbitrary domain $[a, b]$. Additionally, the concept of an $\oplus$-based semi(pseudo) metric-like structure can be further extended to fuzzy sets and intuitionistic fuzzy sets in future research.

Acknowledgment. This study was conducted under the supervision of Prof. Alexander Šostak as part of the Erasmus+ internship program for graduate students between the University of Latvia and Kocaeli University, in which Şuara Onbaşıoğlu Altuhovs participated from September 2023 to January 2024. It is with great sadness that we bid farewell to Prof. Alexander Šostak, a highly esteemed scientist and a valued colleague. In recognition of his significant contributions to mathematics and the invaluable guidance he provided throughout this research, we hereby dedicate this study to his memory.

References

1. Aldemir, B., Güner, E., Aydoğdu, E., Aygün, H.: Some fixed point theorems in partial fuzzy metric spaces. J. Inst. Sci. Technol. **10**(4), 2889–2900 (2020)
2. Asmus, T.C., et al.: A constructive framework to define fusion functions with floating domains in arbitrary closed real intervals. Inf. Sci. **610**, 800–829 (2022)
3. George, A., Veeramani, P.: On some results in fuzzy metric spaces. Fuzzy Sets Syst. **64**(3), 395–399 (1994)
4. Gregori, V., Miñana, J.J., Miravet, D.: Fuzzy partial metric spaces. Int. J. Gen Syst **48**(3), 260–279 (2018)
5. Grigorenko, O., Miñana, J.J., Šostak, A., Valero, O.: On t-conorm based fuzzy (pseudo)metrics. Axioms **9**(3), 78 (2020)
6. Güner, E., Aygün, H.: A new approach to fuzzy partial metric spaces. Hacettepe J. Math. Stat. **51**(6), 1563–1576 (2022)
7. Harandi, A.A.: Metric-like spaces, partial metric spaces and fixed points. Fixed Point Theory Appl. **2012**(204), 1–10 (2012)
8. Hitzler, P., Seda, A.K.: Dislocated topologies. J. Electr. Eng. **21**(12), 3–7 (2000)
9. Hosseini, A., Fosner, A.: On the structure of metric-like spaces. Sahand Commun. Math. Anal. **1**(10), 159–171 (2019)
10. Hussain, N., Roshan, J. R., Parvaneh, V., Kadelburg, Z.: Fixed points of contractive mappings in b-metric-like spaces. Sci. World J. **2014**(2014), 471827, 1-15 (2014)

11. Klement, E.P., Mesiar, R., Pap, E.: Triangular Norms. Kluwer Academic Publishers, Dordrecht (2000)
12. Matthews, S.G.: Partial metric topology. General Topol. Appl. **728**(1), 183–197 (1994)
13. Monika: On metric-like spaces: a survey. Int. J. Appl. Eng. Res. **14**(6), 1390–1395 (2019)
14. Onbaşıoğlu, Ş, Pazar Varol, B.: Intuitionistic fuzzy metric-like spaces and fixed-point results. Mathematics **11**(8), 1902 (2023)
15. Öner, T., Šostak, A.: On metric-type spaces based on extended t-conorms. Mathematics **8**(7), 1097 (2020)
16. Park, J.H.: Intuitionistic fuzzy metric spaces. Chaos Solitons Fractals **22**, 1039–1046 (2004)
17. Sedghi, S., Shobkolaei, N., Altun, I.: Partial fuzzy metric space and some fixed point results. Commun. Math. **23**(2), 131–142 (2015)
18. Shukla, S., Abbas, M.: Fixed point results in fuzzy metric-like spaces. Iran. J. Fuzzy Syst. **11**(5), 81–92 (2014)
19. Šostak, A., Öner, T., Duman, İC.: On topological and metric properties of ⊕-sb-metric spaces. Mathematics **11**(19), 4090 (2023)

Information Fusion Techniques

Idempotence and Internality of Aggregations of Random Variables

Juan Baz[1]([✉])[iD], Irene Díaz[2][iD], and Susana Montes[1][iD]

[1] Department of Statistics, O.R. and D.M., University of Oviedo,
Fededrico García Lorca 18, 33007 Oviedo, Spain
{bazjuan,montes}@uniovi.es
[2] Department of Computer Science, University of Oviedo,
Campus de Gijón, 33204 Gijón, Spain
sirene@uniovi.es

Abstract. A classical result states that internality and idempotence are equivalent for aggregation functions. In the context of data analysis, it is natural to consider random variables as the inputs of the aggregation. In this direction, aggregations of random variables are functions that, given a random vector, return a random variable fulfilling monotonicity and some boundary conditions with respect to a stochastic order. This paper is focused on the definition of different notions of idempotence and internality for aggregations of random variables. The implications between the introduced concepts are studied in detail. In addition, families of aggregations of random variables that fulfill the defined properties are provided.

Keywords: Aggregation · Probability theory · Idempotence · Internality

1 Introduction

One of the most relevant families of aggregation functions are the means. This type of functions fulfill two equivalent properties, idempotence, $A(x, \ldots, x) = x$, and internality, $\min \boldsymbol{x} \leq A(\boldsymbol{x}) \leq \max(\boldsymbol{x})$. Means are usually used in Data Analysis in topic such as, for instance, time series [10,13], image analysis [1,15], risk analysis [19] or recommender systems [6].

In Statistics, means also appear as estimators for location parameters of distributions. For instance, the sample mean is one of the most widely used estimators for the expected value and the average between the minimum and the maximum is the most efficient estimator for the expectation value among uniform distributions [17]. In the aggregation of probabilities, see [2], idempotence (known as unanimity) is an important property.

Continuing in the context on Data Analysis, a quite reasonable assumption is to consider the data to be realizations of random variables. Starting from this idea, the concept of aggregation of random variables was defined in [5]. These

M. Baczyński et al. (Eds.): EUSFLAT 2025, LNCS 15883, pp. 245–257, 2025.
https://doi.org/10.1007/978-3-031-97225-6_20

functions take n random variables defined over a real interval and return another random variable over the same interval fulfilling monotonicity and boundary conditions with respect to a stochastic order.

However, although idempotence and internality seem to be very important in aggregation theory, there does not exist a concept of idempotent or internal aggregations of random variables. We devote this paper to the definition of such notions and the study of its properties. In general, it is hard to define these concepts uniquely, since the classical definitions can be extended in different ways. We propose five properties related to the idempotence and another five related to internality. The relation among these notions are studied in detail. Families of aggregations of random variables that satisfy these properties are provided.

The remainder of the paper is organized as follows. In Sect. 2 we recall and fix the notation for the basic concepts we need for the development of the paper. Idempotence of aggregations of random variables is studied in Sect. 3. In Sect. 4, a similar study is provided for the internality. We devoted Sect. 5 to prove some implications between both concepts when working with aggregations of random variables. The conclusions are discussed in Sect. 6.

2 Preliminaries

2.1 Aggregation Functions

An aggregation function is typically referred to as a function that fuses the information of different values by a unique number. Formally, if I is a possibly unbounded real interval, an aggregation function is defined as an increasing function $A : I^n \to I$ such that the infimum and the supremum of the image are, respectively, the infimum and the supremum of I.

Definition 1 [9]. *Let I be an interval of the real line $\mathbb{R}$. An aggregation function is a function $A : I^n \to I$ satisfying:*

(1) It is increasing (in each variable).
(2) The following boundary conditions are fulfilled:

$$\inf_{x \in I^n} A(x) = \inf I, \ \sup_{x \in I^n} A(x) = \sup I.$$

There exists a huge number of properties defined for aggregation functions. In this paper, we will focus on idempotence and internality. An aggregation function is idempotent if, when all the inputs are the same, the output equals the same value.

Definition 2 [9]. *Let $A : I^n \to I$ be an aggregation function. If for any $x \in I$ it holds $A(x, \ldots, x) = x$, then A is called an idempotent aggregation function.*

Henceforward, we will denote as $\mathbf{1} = (1,\ldots,1)$ the vector of ones of the adequate dimension.

Internal aggregation functions have the outputs bounded between the minimum and maximum of the inputs.

Definition 3 [9]. *Let $A : I^n \to I$ be an aggregation function. If for any $\boldsymbol{x} \in I^n$ it holds $\min \boldsymbol{x} \leq A(\boldsymbol{x}) \leq \max \boldsymbol{x}$, then A is called an internal aggregation function.*

The class of internal aggregation functions is also known as averages or means. The latter properties are, in fact, equivalent.

Proposition 1 [9]. *Let $A : I^n \to I$ be an aggregation function. Then, A is idempotent if and only if A is internal.*

2.2   Probability Concepts

A probability space is the trio (Ω, Σ, P), where Ω is a set, Σ is a σ-algebra consisting of subsets of Ω and $P : \Sigma \to [0,1]$ is a probability measure that assigns a probability to each element of Σ (see [3]).

A random variable is a measurable function from the set Ω of the probability space to the real numbers with the Borel σ-algebra [17]. A vector consisting of n different random variables is called a random vector. The distribution function of a random vector $\boldsymbol{X}$ is the function defined as

$$F_{\boldsymbol{X}}(x_1,\ldots,x_n) = P(X_1 \leq x_1,\ldots,X_n \leq x_n)$$

Similarly, the survival function is defined as $\overline{F}_{\boldsymbol{X}}(x_1,\ldots,x_n) = P(X_1 > x_1,\ldots,X_n > x_n)$. Both the distribution function and the survival function admit the following decompositions [20]:

$$F_{\boldsymbol{X}}(x_1,\ldots,x_n) = C(F_1(x_1),\ldots,F_n(x_n)),$$
$$\overline{F}_{\boldsymbol{X}}(x_1,\ldots,x_n) = \overline{C}(\overline{F}_1(x_1),\ldots,\overline{F}_n(x_n)),$$

where C and $\overline{C}$ are copulas (see [14]) and $F_1,\ldots,F_n$ and $\overline{F}_1,\ldots,\overline{F}_n$ denote the distribution and survival functions of the marginals of $\boldsymbol{X}$. Every copula is smaller than the minimum function [14].

In addition, the support of a random vector $\boldsymbol{X}$ is defined as the smallest closed subset $S(\boldsymbol{X})$ such that $P(\boldsymbol{X} \in S(\boldsymbol{X})) = 1$. The expectation of a random variable is defined as $E[X] = \int x dF(x)$, considering the Riemann-Stieltjes integral (see [8]). Another useful concept that will be needed are conditional distributions, that describe the behavior of random variables when a value or a range of values of other random variables is known.

Given two random variables X and Y, the conditional distribution of X given that $Y = y$ will be denoted, if well-defined, by $F_{X|Y=y}$. We will use $[X \mid Y = y]$ to denote a random variable with the associated conditional distribution. The conditional distribution given a range of values of one random variable or involving more than one condition can be defined similarly. We refer to [17] for more information in this regard.

Finally, the last concept we need are stochastic orders, which are partial orders between random vectors. In particular, we will use the following three.

Definition 4 [18]. *Let $\boldsymbol{X}$ and $\boldsymbol{Y}$ be two random vectors. Then,*

(1) If $P(\boldsymbol{X} \leq \boldsymbol{Y}) = 1$, then is said that $\boldsymbol{X}$ is almost surely smaller than or equal to $\boldsymbol{Y}$ and it is denoted by $\boldsymbol{X} \leq_{a.s.} \boldsymbol{Y}$.
(2) If for any increasing function $\phi : \mathbb{R}^n \to \mathbb{R}$ such that $E[\phi(\boldsymbol{X})]$ and $E[\phi(\boldsymbol{Y})]$ exist it holds $E[\phi(\boldsymbol{X})] \leq E[\phi(\boldsymbol{Y})]$, then $\boldsymbol{X}$ is said to be smaller than or equal to $\boldsymbol{Y}$ with respect to the usual stochastic order and is denoted by $\boldsymbol{X} \leq_{st} \boldsymbol{Y}$.
(3) If for any convex function $\phi : \mathbb{R}^n \to \mathbb{R}$ such that $E[\phi(\boldsymbol{X})]$ and $E[\phi(\boldsymbol{Y})]$ exist it holds $E[\phi(\boldsymbol{X})] \leq E[\phi(\boldsymbol{Y})]$, then $\boldsymbol{X}$ is said to be smaller than or equal to $\boldsymbol{Y}$ with respect to the convex stochastic order and is denoted by $\boldsymbol{X} \leq_{cx} \boldsymbol{Y}$.

Trivially, $\boldsymbol{X} \leq_{a.s.} \boldsymbol{Y} \implies \boldsymbol{X} \leq_{st} \boldsymbol{Y}$. For random variables, $X \leq_{st} Y$ is equivalent to having $F(x) \geq G(x)$ for any $x \in \mathbb{R}$, where F and G denote, respectively, the distribution functions of X and Y. We end this section with a characterization of the usual stochastic order and the convex order by a construction in a common probability space.

Theorem 1 [18]. *Let $\boldsymbol{X}$ and $\boldsymbol{Y}$ be two random vectors of dimension n. Then $\boldsymbol{X} \leq_{st} (\leq_{cx}) \boldsymbol{Y}$ if and only if there exist two random vectors $\hat{\boldsymbol{X}}$ and $\hat{\boldsymbol{Y}}$ defined in the same probability space such that $\hat{\boldsymbol{X}} =_{st} \boldsymbol{X}$, $\hat{\boldsymbol{Y}} =_{st} \boldsymbol{Y}$ and $\hat{\boldsymbol{X}} \leq_{a.s.} \hat{\boldsymbol{Y}}$ $\left(E\left[\hat{\boldsymbol{Y}} \mid \hat{\boldsymbol{X}} \right] =_{a.s.} \hat{\boldsymbol{X}} \right)$.*

2.3 Aggregation of Random Variables

Aggregation functions are widely used in data analysis, see [7,12,16]. In this context, it is quite natural to suppose that the inputs of the aggregation are observations of random variables. Following this direction, the concept of aggregation of random variables was introduced in [5] and refined in [4].

An aggregation of random variables takes a random vector with components having a support contained in a common interval and returns a random variable whose image is contained in the same interval. The properties of monotonicity and boundary conditions are extended by using stochastic orders. Considering a probability space (Ω, S, P), let us first introduce the following notation:

$$L_I^n(\Omega) = \{\boldsymbol{X} : \Omega \to I^n \mid \boldsymbol{X} \text{ is measurable}\}.$$

If $n = 1$, we will denote $L_I^1(\Omega)$ just as $L_I(\Omega)$. Then, the concept of aggregation of random variables is defined as follows.

Definition 5 [4,5]. *Let (Ω, Σ, P) be a probability space and I a real non empty interval. An aggregation of random variables is a function $A : L_I^n(\Omega) \to L_I(\Omega)$ which satisfies:*

(1) For any $\boldsymbol{X}, \boldsymbol{Y} \in L_I^n(\Omega)$ such that $\boldsymbol{X} \leq_{st} \boldsymbol{Y}$, $A(\boldsymbol{X}) \leq_{st} A(\boldsymbol{Y})$,

(2) For any $X \in L_I(\Omega)$, there exists $\boldsymbol{X} \in L_I^n(\Omega)$ such that $A(\boldsymbol{X}) \leq_{st} X$,
(3) For any $X \in L_I(\Omega)$, there exists $\boldsymbol{X} \in L_I^n(\Omega)$ such that $A(\boldsymbol{X}) \geq_{st} X$.

Along the paper, we will consider a standard probability space (see [11]) and we will simplify the notation by replacing $L_I^n(\Omega)$ with L_I^n.

Let us end this section by introducing two different types of aggregation of random variables. The first family is obtained by composing a usual aggregation function with random vectors. The proof of the fact that the resulting function is an aggregation of random variables with respect to the usual stochastic order can be found in [5].

Definition 6 [5]. *Let I be a real interval and let $\hat{A} : I^n \to I$ be a measurable aggregation function. Then, the aggregation of random variables $A : L_i^n \to L_I$ defined as $A(\boldsymbol{X}) = \hat{A} \circ \boldsymbol{X}$ for each $\boldsymbol{X} \in L_I^n$ is said to be induced by $\hat{A}$.*

The second family is related to the aggregation of distribution functions. Given an aggregation over the unit interval and a standard uniform random variable U, the aggregation is applied to the distribution functions to obtain a new distribution.

Proposition 2. *Let I be a real interval, U a standard uniform random variable and $\hat{A} : [0,1]^n \to [0,1]$ an internal continuous aggregation function. Then, if for each random vector $\boldsymbol{X} = (X_1, \ldots, X_n)$ with marginal distribution functions $F_1, \ldots, F_n$ the function $A : L_I^n \to L_I$ is defined as*

$$A(\boldsymbol{X}) = \left(\hat{A}(F_1, \ldots, F_n) \right)^{-1} (U),$$

then A is an aggregation of random variables.

Proof. Since $\hat{A}$ is an aggregation function, $\hat{A}(F_1, \ldots, F_n)$ is increasing. Moreover, since $\hat{A}$ is continuous, $\hat{A}(F_1, \ldots, F_n)$ is right-continuous, the limit in $-\infty$ is 0 and the limit in ∞ is 1. Therefore, $\hat{A}(F_1, \ldots, F_n)$ is a distribution function. In particular, it is the distribution function of $A(\boldsymbol{X})$.

For monotonicity, let $\boldsymbol{X}$ and $\boldsymbol{Y}$ be two random vectors with marginal distribution functions $F_1, \ldots, F_n$ and $G_1, \ldots, G_n$ such that $\boldsymbol{X} \leq_{st} \boldsymbol{Y}$. Then, the marginals are also ordered with respect to the usual stochastic order, so $F_i(x) \geq G_i(x)$ for each $x \in \mathbb{R}$ and $i \in [n]$. Then, since $\hat{A}$ is increasing, $\hat{A}(F_1, \ldots, F_n)(x) \geq \hat{A}(G_1, \ldots, G_n)(x)$ for all $x \in \mathbb{R}$. Therefore, it is concluded that $A(\boldsymbol{X}) \leq_{st} A(\boldsymbol{Y})$.

For the boundary conditions, if the interval I has a lower bound a, then it is clear that $A(a, \ldots, a) = a$ and the boundary conditions are fulfilled. If not, let $\boldsymbol{X} \in L_I$ with distribution function F. Then, consider the random vector $\boldsymbol{X} = (X, \ldots, X)$. Then, it is clear that $A(\boldsymbol{X})$ has distribution function $\hat{A}(F, \ldots, F) = F$ (since $\hat{A}$ is idempotent, see Proposition 1). Therefore, $A(\boldsymbol{X}) =_{st} X$ and both boundary conditions are met. $\qquad\square$

The aggregation of random variables A introduced in the latter result will be called distribution-based (on $\hat{A}$).

3 Idempotence

The idea behind idempotence is "if the inputs are the same, then the output is also the same". For random variables, this could be interpreted in different ways. In the next definition, 5 different alternatives are considered.

Definition 7. *Let I be a real interval and consider a function $A : L_I^n \to L_I$. Then,*

(1) If $A(\boldsymbol{X}) =_{a.s.} X_1$ for any $\boldsymbol{X} \in L_I^n$ such that $X_1 =_{a.s.} \cdots =_{a.s.} X_n$, it is said that A is almost surely idempotent.

(2) If $A(\boldsymbol{X}) =_{st} X_1$ for any $\boldsymbol{X} \in L_I^n$ such that $X_1 =_{st} \cdots =_{st} X_n$, it is said that A is idempotent in distribution.

(3) If $P(A(\boldsymbol{X}) = \lambda \mid X_1 = \cdots = X_n = \lambda) = 1$ for any $\boldsymbol{X} \in L_I^n$ and $\lambda \in I$ such that $[A(\boldsymbol{X}) \mid X_1 = \cdots = X_n = \lambda)]$ is well-defined, it is said that A is conditionally idempotent.

(4) If $E[A(\boldsymbol{X}) \mid X_1 = \cdots = X_n = \lambda] = \lambda$ for any $\boldsymbol{X} \in L_I^n$ and $\lambda \in I$ such that $[A(\boldsymbol{X}) \mid X_1 = \cdots = X_n = \lambda]$ is well-defined, it is said that A is martingale idempotent.

(5) If $P(A(\boldsymbol{X}) = \lambda) = 1$ for any $\boldsymbol{X} \in L_I^n$ such that $P(X_i = \lambda) = 1$ for any $i \in \{1, \ldots, n\}$, it is said that A is degenerate idempotent.

Almost surely idempotence and idempotence in distribution work with equalities between random variables. Conditionally idempotent and martingale idempotent, on the other hand, focus on the values that the random variables take. Finally, degenerate idempotence is just the classical definition of idempotence restricted to degenerate random vectors.

Some of the notions of idempotence are stronger than others. In the next result, we disclose the implications between the definitions. We want to remark that, at this point, we are not assuming the function $A : L_I^n \to L_I$ to be an aggregation of random variables, thus we are not using monotonicity for the proof.

Theorem 2. *Let I be a real interval and consider a function $A : L_I^n \to L_I$. Then,*

(1) A is conditionally idempotent $\implies$ A is almost surely idempotent

(2) A is conditionally idempotent $\implies$ A is martingale idempotent

(3) A is almost surely idempotent $\implies$ A is degenerate idempotent

(4) A is idempotent in distribution $\implies$ A is degenerate idempotent

Proof. (1) If $X_1 =_{a.s.} \cdots =_{a.s.} X_n$, then $P(X_1 = \cdots = X_n) = 1$. Since for any $\lambda \in I$ it holds $P(A(\boldsymbol{X}) = \lambda \mid X_1 = \cdots = X_n = \lambda) = 1$, then $P(A(\boldsymbol{X}) = X_1) = 1$ and $A(\boldsymbol{X}) =_{a.s.} X_1$.

(2) If $P(A(\boldsymbol{X}) = \lambda \mid X_1 = \cdots = X_n = \lambda) = 1$, then trivially $E[A(\boldsymbol{X}) \mid X_1 = \cdots = X_n = \lambda] = \lambda$.

(3) If $P(X_i = \lambda) = 1$ for any $i \in \{1, \ldots, n\}$, then $X_1 =_{a.s.} \cdots =_{a.s.} X_n$ so $A(\boldsymbol{X}) =_{a.s.} X_1$ and $P(A(\boldsymbol{X}) = \lambda) = 1$.

(4) If $P(X_i = \lambda) = 1$ for any $i \in \{1, \ldots, n\}$, then $X_1 =_{st} \cdots =_{st} X_n$ so $A(\boldsymbol{X}) =_{st} X_1$ and $P(A(\boldsymbol{X}) = \lambda) = 1$.   □

It is concluded that the strongest properties are conditionally idempotence and idempotence in distribution. The weakest is the degenerate idempotence. Martingale idempotence, although it seems to be the least intuitive notion of idempotence, has an interesting implication related to the convex stochastic order.

Proposition 3. *Let* $A : L_I^n \to L_I$ *be a martingale idempotent function. Then,*

$$[X_i \mid X_1 = \cdots = X_n] \leq_{cx} [A(\boldsymbol{X}) \mid X_1 = \cdots = X_n]$$

for any $i \in \{1, \ldots, n\}$

Proof. Notice that $E[[A(\boldsymbol{X}) \mid X_1 = \cdots = X_n] \mid [X_i \mid X_1 = \cdots = X_n] = \lambda] = E[A(\boldsymbol{X}) \mid X_1 = \cdots = X_n = \lambda] = \lambda$. The result holds by applying Theorem 1. □

We end this section by proving that aggregations of random variables induced by idempotent aggregations are conditionally idempotent.

Proposition 4. *Let* A *be an aggregation of random variables induced by an idempotent aggregation function. Then,* A *is conditionally idempotent.*

Proof. Let $\hat{A}$ be the idempotent aggregation function that induces A. If $X_1 = \cdots = X_n = \lambda$, then $\hat{A}(\lambda, \ldots, \lambda) = \lambda$ and $P(A(\boldsymbol{X}) = \lambda \mid X_1 = \cdots = X_n = \lambda) = 1$.   □

4   Internality

In this section, a similar study to the latter is carried out for the internality. The idea behind being internal is "to be between the maximum and the minimum". Again, 5 different notions can be defined following this idea.

Definition 8. *Let* $A : L_I^n \to L_I$ *be a function. Then:*

(1) *If* $\min \boldsymbol{X} \leq_{a.s.} A(\boldsymbol{X}) \leq_{a.s.} \max \boldsymbol{X}$ *for any* $\boldsymbol{X} \in L_I^n$, *it is said that* A *is almost surely internal.*

(2) *If* $\min \boldsymbol{X} \leq_{st} A(\boldsymbol{X}) \leq_{st} \max \boldsymbol{X}$ *for any* $\boldsymbol{X} \in L_I^n$, *it is said that* A *is internal in distribution.*

(3) *If* $\min_{i \in \{1, \ldots, n\}} P(X_i \leq \lambda) \leq P(A(\boldsymbol{X}) \leq \lambda) \leq \max_{i \in \{1, \ldots, n\}} P(X_i \leq \lambda)$ *for any* $\boldsymbol{X} \in L_I^n$ *and* $\lambda \in I$, *it is said that* A *is internal in probability.*

(4) *If* $S(A(\boldsymbol{X})) \subseteq [\inf \cup_{i=1}^n S(X_i), \sup \cup_{i=1}^n S(X_i)]$, *it is said that* A *is internal in support.*

(5) *If for any* $\boldsymbol{X} \in L_I^n$ *such that* $P(\boldsymbol{X} \in \boldsymbol{\lambda}) = 1$ *with* $\boldsymbol{\lambda} \in I^n$ *it holds* $P(A(\boldsymbol{X}) \in [\min \boldsymbol{\lambda}, \max \boldsymbol{\lambda}]) = 1$, *it is said that* A *is degenerate internal.*

For the first two properties, the maximum and minimum operators are applied to the random vectors and the aggregation is compared, using the almost surely order or the usual stochastic order, with them. The third and fourth alternatives take the maximum and minimum over distribution functions or the support of the random variables. Again, we have a notion for just the usual internality when working with degenerate distributions.

As in the other case, some implications, without using monotonicity, can be proved between the introduced properties.

Theorem 3. *Let* $A : L_I^n \to L_I$ *be a function. Then:*

(1) A is almost surely internal $\implies$ *A is internal in distribution*
(2) A is internal in probability $\implies$ *A is internal in distribution*
(3) A is internal in distribution $\implies$ *A is internal in support*
(4) A is internal in support $\implies$ *A is degenerate internal*

Proof. (1) Trivially from the fact that $X \leq_{a.s.} Y \implies X \leq_{st} Y$.
(2) Let $F(t)$, $F_{\min}(t)$ and $F_{\max}(t)$ be the distribution functions of $\boldsymbol{X}$, $\min \boldsymbol{X}$ and $\max \boldsymbol{X}$. In addition, denote as $F_1, \ldots, F_n$ the distribution functions of $X_1, \ldots, X_n$. Similarly, denote by $\overline{F}(t), \overline{F}_{\min}(t), \overline{F}_{\max}(t), \overline{F}_1, \ldots, \overline{F}_n$ the associated survival functions.
One has $F_{\max}(t) = F(t\boldsymbol{1}) = C\left(F_1(t), \ldots, F_n(t)\right)$, with C being a copula fulfilling that $C \leq \min$.
In addition, one has $\overline{F}_{\min}(t) = \overline{F}(t\boldsymbol{x}) = \overline{C}\left(\overline{F}_1(t), \ldots, \overline{F}_n(t)\right)$, with $\overline{C}$ copula fulfilling that $\overline{C} \leq \min$.
Therefore,

$$F_{\max}(\lambda) \leq \min_{i \in \{1, \ldots, n\}} F_i(\lambda) = \min_{i \in \{1, \ldots, n\}} P(X_i \leq \lambda),$$

and, since for any random variable X, $\overline{F}_X = 1 - F_X$,

$$F_{\min}(\lambda) \geq \max_{i \in \{1, \ldots, n\}} F_i(\lambda) = \max_{i \in \{1, \ldots, n\}} P(X_i \leq \lambda).$$

It is concluded that if

$$\min_{i \in \{1, \ldots, n\}} P(X_i \leq \lambda) \leq P(A(\boldsymbol{X}) \leq \lambda) \leq \max_{i \in \{1, \ldots, n\}} P(X_i \leq \lambda),$$

then $F_{\max}(\lambda) \leq P(A(\boldsymbol{X}) \leq \lambda) \leq F_{\min}(\lambda)$, thus $\min \boldsymbol{X} \leq_{st} A(\boldsymbol{X}) \leq_{st} \max \boldsymbol{X}$.
(3) Suppose that there exists $t \in \mathbb{R}$ such that $t < \inf U_{i=1}^n S(X_i)$ but $t \in S(A(\boldsymbol{X}))$. Then, there exists $\epsilon > 0$ such that $P(A(\boldsymbol{X}) \in (t - \epsilon, t + \epsilon)) > 0$ but $P(X_i \in (t - \epsilon, t + \epsilon)) = 0$ for every $i \in \{1, \ldots, n\}$. Moreover, one has $F_{X_i}(t+\epsilon) = 0$. Comparing the cumulative distribution functions of $A(\boldsymbol{X})$ and $\min \boldsymbol{X}$:

$$F_{A(\boldsymbol{X})}(t + \epsilon) \geq P(A(\boldsymbol{X}) \in (t - \epsilon, t + \epsilon)) > 0$$

$$F_{\min \boldsymbol{X}}(t + \epsilon) \leq \sum F_{X_i}(t + \epsilon) = 0$$

It is concluded that $\min \boldsymbol{X} \not\leq_{st} A(\boldsymbol{X})$, which is a contradiction to the fact of A being internal in distribution. If there exists $t \in \mathbb{R}$ such that $t > \sup U_{i=1}^{n} S(X_i)$ but $t \in S(A(\boldsymbol{X}))$, the contradiction can be reached similarly.

(4) Notice that if $P(X = \lambda) = 1$, $S(X) = \{\lambda\}$. $\qquad\qquad\qquad\square$

It is concluded that the strongest notions of internality are almost surely internality and internality in probability. It is easy to construct almost surely internal and internal in probability aggregations of random variables just by considering, respectively, induced aggregations of random variables by internal aggregation functions and distribution-based aggregations of random variables.

Proposition 5. *Let A be an aggregation of random variables induced by an internal aggregation function. Then, A is almost surely internal.*

Proof. Let $\hat{A} : I^n \to I$ the internal aggregation function that induces A. Since $\min \boldsymbol{x} \leq \hat{A}(\boldsymbol{x}) \leq \max \boldsymbol{x}$ for any $\boldsymbol{x} \in I^n$, then $\min \boldsymbol{X} \leq_{a.s.} A(\boldsymbol{X}) \leq_{a.s.} \max \boldsymbol{X}$ for any $\boldsymbol{X} \in L_I^n$.

Proposition 6. *Let A be an aggregation of random variables distribution-based on an internal aggregation function. Then, A is internal in probability.*

Proof. Let A be distribution-based on $\hat{A}$. For any $\boldsymbol{X} \in L_I^n$ with marginal distribution functions $F_1, \ldots, G_n$, the distribution function of $A(\boldsymbol{X})$ is $\hat{A}(F_1, \ldots, F_n)$. Since $\hat{A}$ is internal, $\min_{i \in \{1,\ldots,n\}} F_i(t) \leq \hat{A}(F_1, \ldots, F_n)(t) \leq \max_{i \in \{1,\ldots,n\}} F_i(t)$. From the definition of distribution function, it is concluded that A is internal in probability. $\qquad\qquad\qquad\square$

5   Relationship Between Idempotence and Internality

For increasing functions, idempotence and internality are equivalent, see Proposition 1. In this section, we explore the implications between the proposed notions of idempotence and internality when the function is assumed to be an aggregation of random variables.

Theorem 4. *Let $A : L_I^n \to L_I$ be an aggregation of random variables. Then,*

(1) A is degenerate idempotent $\iff$ A is degenerate internal,
(2) A is idempotent in distribution $\implies$ A is internal in distribution,
(3) A is almost surely idempotent $\implies$ A is internal in distribution,
(4) A is almost surely internal $\implies$ A almost surely idempotent,
(5) A is internal in probability $\implies$ A is idempotent in distribution.

Proof. (1) Let $\boldsymbol{X} \in L_I^n$ be a random vector such that $P(\boldsymbol{X} = \boldsymbol{\lambda}) = 1$ with $\boldsymbol{\lambda} \in I^n$. For the first implication, using monotonicity, since $(\min \boldsymbol{\lambda})\mathbf{1} \leq_{st} \boldsymbol{X} \leq_{st} (\max \boldsymbol{\lambda})\mathbf{1}$, then $\min \boldsymbol{\lambda} \leq_{st} A(\boldsymbol{X}) \leq_{st} \max \boldsymbol{\lambda}$, so $P(A(\boldsymbol{X}) \in [\min \boldsymbol{\lambda}, \max \boldsymbol{\lambda}]) = 1$. For the second implication, if $\boldsymbol{\lambda}$ is a constant vector with components equal to λ, $\lambda \leq_{st} A(\boldsymbol{X}) \leq_{st} \lambda$ and then $P(A(\boldsymbol{X}) = \lambda) = 1$.

(2) Starting from $(\min \boldsymbol{X})\mathbf{1} \leq_{st} \boldsymbol{X} \leq_{st} (\max \boldsymbol{X})\mathbf{1}$, from the monotonicity and the idempotence in distribution we have:

$$\min \boldsymbol{X} =_{st} A((\min \boldsymbol{X})\mathbf{1}) \leq_{st} A(\boldsymbol{X}) \leq_{st} A((\max \boldsymbol{X})\mathbf{1}) =_{st} \max \boldsymbol{X}$$

(3) Similarly as the previous case,

$$\min \boldsymbol{X} =_{a.s.} A((\min \boldsymbol{X})\mathbf{1}) \leq_{st} A(\boldsymbol{X}) \leq_{st} A((\max \boldsymbol{X})\mathbf{1}) =_{a.s.} \max \boldsymbol{X}$$

and the result follows since $X =_{a.s.} Y \implies X =_{st} Y$.

(4) If $X_1 =_{a.s.} \cdots =_{a.s.} X_n$, then $\min \boldsymbol{X} =_{a.s.} \max \boldsymbol{X} =_{a.s.} X_1$. Using that $\min \boldsymbol{X} \leq_{a.s} A(\boldsymbol{X}) \leq_{a.s.} \max \boldsymbol{X}$, one has that $A(\boldsymbol{X}) =_{a.s.} X_1$.

(5) If $X_1 =_{st} \cdots =_{st} X_n$, $F_1(t) = \cdots = F_n(t)$ and $F_1(t) = \min_{i \in \{1,\ldots,n\}} F_i(t) = \max_{i \in \{1,\ldots,n\}} F_i(t)$ for any $t \in \mathbb{R}$. Then,

$$F_1(t) = \min_{i \in \{1,\ldots,n\}} F_i(t) \leq F_{A(\boldsymbol{X})}(t) \leq \max_{i \in \{1,\ldots,n\}} F_i(t) = F_1(t)$$

for any $t \in \mathbb{R}$, thus $A(\boldsymbol{X}) =_{st} X_1$.   □

As a consequence of this result, there is an equivalence between the internality in support and degenerate internality for aggregations of random variables.

Corollary 1. *Let $A : L_I^n \to L_I$ be an aggregation of random variables. Then, A is internal in support if and only if A is degenerate internal.*

Proof. The first implication has been proved in Proposition 3. For the second one, using Theorem 4, any degenerate internal aggregation function is degenerate idempotent. Consider $\boldsymbol{X} \in L_I^n$. If $\inf \cup_{i=1}^n S(X_i) = -\infty$ the condition over the infimum is fulfilled. In other case, suppose $\inf \cup_{i=1}^n S(X_i) = a > -\infty$. Using monotonicity, since $a\mathbf{1} \leq_{st} \boldsymbol{X}$, then $a =_{a.s.} A(a\mathbf{1}) \leq_{st} \boldsymbol{X}$ and therefore $P(A(\boldsymbol{X} \geq a) = 1$. Similarly, we can obtain that $P(A(\boldsymbol{X} \leq b) = 1$ with $b = \sup \cup_{i=1}^n S(X_i)$. It is concluded that $S(A(\boldsymbol{X})) \subseteq [a, b] = [\inf \cup_{i=1}^n S(X_i), \sup \cup_{i=1}^n S(X_i)]$.   □

All the proved implications are summarized in the diagram of Fig. 1. As can be seen, the stronger properties are conditionally idempotence, almost surely internality and internality in probability. We want to remark that aggregations of random variables induced by idempotent/internal aggregation functions are both conditionally idempotent and almost surely internal, and those distribution-based on idempotent/internal aggregation functions are internal in probability. In addition, all the implications that cannot be deduced from transitivity are false. In the following, we briefly provide counterexamples for some of the implications.

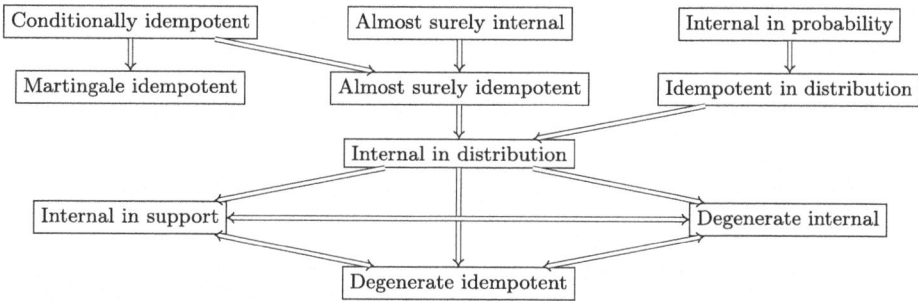

Fig. 1. Implications between the idempotence and internality notions for aggregations of random variables with respect to the usual stochastic order.

Example 1. (1) The aggregation of random variables given by $A(X_1, X_2) = \frac{1}{2}E\left[X_1 + X_2\right]$ is degenerate internal but not internal in distribution.

(2) The aggregation of random variables given by $A(X_1, X_2) = \frac{1}{2}(X_1 + X_2 + Y_{X_1,X_2})$, where Y_{X_1,X_2} is a non degenerate random variable with mean 0 and independent of X_1 and X_2, is martingale idempotent but not conditionally idempotent.

(3) The aggregation of random variables given by

$$A(\boldsymbol{X}) = \begin{cases} \max \boldsymbol{X} & \text{if } X_1 = \cdots = X_n, \\ \text{m\^ax } \boldsymbol{X} & \text{if } X_1 \neq X_2, \end{cases}$$

where $\text{m\^ax}(\boldsymbol{X})$ is a random variable with the same distribution as $\max \boldsymbol{X}$ but independent of $\boldsymbol{X}$. This aggregation of random variables is conditionally idempotent but is not almost surely internal.

(4) The aggregation of random variables induced by the maximum is conditionally idempotent and almost surely internal (by Propositions 4 and 5), but it is not idempotent in distribution.

(5) An aggregation of random variables distribution-based on the maximum is internal in probability (by Proposition 6), but it is not almost surely idempotent.

The ones that are not provided can be deduced from the counterexamples and Theorems 2, 3 and 4. For instance, suppose that internality in distribution implies almost surely idempotence. Then, since internality in probability implies internality in distribution, it should hold that internality in probability implies almost surely idempotence. This is not true, as (5) in Example 1 shows.

6   Conclusions

Different concepts of idempotence and internality for aggregations of random variables have been defined. The relations between the different properties have been studied in detail in both the cases of assuming monotonicity or not. In general, we can expect induced aggregation of random variables to fulfill idempotence and internality properties related to comparison of realizations and distribution-based aggregations of random variables to hold those based on comparing distributions and probabilities.

Funding Information. J. Baz is partially supported by Programa Severo Ochoa of Principality of Asturias (BP21042). J. Baz, S. Montes and I. Díaz are been supported by the Ministry of Science and Innovation (PID2022-139886NB-I00). S. Montes and I. Díaz are also been supported by the project UE Proyect SCIMIN-CRM-2024-00087-001.

References

1. Amorim, M., et al.: Systematic review of aggregation functions applied to image edge detection. Axioms **12**(4), 330 (2023)
2. Barrett, C.R., Pattanaik, P.K.: Aggregation of probability judgments. Econometrica: J. Econometric Soc., 1237–1241 (1987)
3. Bauer, H.: Measure and Integration Theory. de Gruyter, Berlin (2011)
4. Baz, J., Beliakov, G., Díaz, I., Montes, S.: Taxonomy of aggregations of random variables. In: Information Processing and Management of Uncertainty in Knowledge-Based Systems. Springer, Heidelberg (2025). https://doi.org/10.1007/978-3-031-74000-8_14
5. Baz, J., Díaz, I., Montes, S.: The choice of an appropriate stochastic order to aggregate random variables. In: Building Bridges between Soft and Statistical Methodologies for Data Science, pp. 40–47. Springer, Heidelberg (2022). https://doi.org/10.1007/978-3-031-15509-3_6
6. Beliakov, G., Calvo, T., James, S.: Aggregation functions for recommender systems. In: Recommender Systems Handbook, pp. 777–808 (2015)
7. Beliakov, G., Pradera, A., Calvo, T., et al.: Aggregation Functions: A Guide for Practitioners, vol. 221. Springer, Heidelberg (2007)
8. Bullock, G.L.: A geometric interpretation of the riemann-stieltjes integral. Am. Math. Mon. **95**(5), 448–455 (1988)
9. Grabisch, M., Marichal, J.L., Mesiar, R., Pap, E.: Aggregation Functions, vol. 127. Cambridge University Press, Cambridge (2009)
10. He, K., Yang, Q., Ji, L., Pan, J., Zou, Y.: Financial time series forecasting with the deep learning ensemble model. Mathematics **11**(4), 1054 (2023)
11. Itô, K., et al.: An Introduction to Probability Theory. Cambridge University Press, Cambridge (1984)
12. James, S.: An Introduction to Data Analysis Using Aggregation Functions in R. Springer, Heidelberg (2016)
13. Leite, D., Škrjanc, I.: Ensemble of evolving optimal granular experts, owa aggregation, and time series prediction. Inf. Sci. **504**, 95–112 (2019)
14. Nelsen, R.B.: An Introduction to Copulas. Springer, Heidelberg (2007)
15. Paternain, D., Fernández, J., Bustince, H., Mesiar, R., Beliakov, G.: Construction of image reduction operators using averaging aggregation functions. Fuzzy Sets Syst. **261**, 87–111 (2015)
16. Pollesch, N., Dale, V.H.: Applications of aggregation theory to sustainability assessment. Ecol. Econ. **114**, 117–127 (2015)

17. Rohatgi, V.K., Saleh, A.: An Introduction to Probability and Statistics. John Wiley & Sons, Hoboken (2015)
18. Shaked, M., Shanthikumar, J.G.: Stochastic Orders. Springer, Heidelberg (2007)
19. Shibzukhov, Z.M.: On the principle of empirical risk minimization based on averaging aggregation functions. Dokl. Math. **96**(2), 494–497 (2017). https://doi.org/10.1134/S106456241705026X
20. Sklar, M.: Fonctions de repartition an dimensions et leurs marges. Publ. Inst. Statist. Univ. Paris **8**, 229–231 (1959)

Input Importance in Aggregation Theory by Means of Dependence Stochastic Orders

Juan Baz[1]([✉])[iD] and Franco Pellerey[2][iD]

[1] Department of Statistics, O.R. and D.M., University of Oviedo,
Federico García Lorca 18, 33007 Oviedo, Spain
bazjuan@uniovi.es
[2] Dipartimento di Scienze Matematiche, Politecnico di Torino,
Corso Duca degli Abruzzi 24, 10129 Turin, Italy
franco.pellerey@polito.it

Abstract. Aggregation functions are usually used to summarize the information from different inputs into a unique value. Depending on the structure of the aggregation function and the behavior of the initial data, there are inputs that have a larger impact in the result of the aggregation. From a probabilistic approach, such an importance can be identified as the positive dependence between the input and the output. In this paper, sufficient conditions for the stochastic ordering with respect to positive dependence stochastic orders between bivariate random vectors consisting of an input and the output of aggregation functions are provided. In particular, quasi-arithmetic means and some OWA operators are considered, using as ordering the supermodular and concordance stochastic orders.

Keywords: Aggregation · Stochastic orders · Copulas · Dependence

1 Introduction

Aggregation functions [1,4] are widely used for fusing the information from different sources in different applications such as decision making [5,14] and prediction [7,10]. In some contexts, it is interesting to identify the inputs that have a larger importance in the aggregation process, since they have more impact in the output value.

The most simple example is the case of weighted means, in which the value of the weight is usually associated with the importance of the input. This can be shown by considering the associated partial derivatives, which equal

$$\frac{\partial \sum_{i=1}^{n} w_i x_i}{\partial x_k} = w_k, \ \forall k \in \{1, \dots, n\},$$

so that the variations of an input change more drastically the value of the aggregation if the weight is greater.

M. Baczyński et al. (Eds.): EUSFLAT 2025, LNCS 15883, pp. 258–269, 2025.
https://doi.org/10.1007/978-3-031-97225-6_21

From a probabilistic approach, the importance of an input can be measured by its dependence with the output of the aggregation. For instance, if one considers independent random variables $X_1, \ldots, X_n$ with the same distribution as the inputs of a weighted mean, the correlation coefficients between each of them and the aggregation can be easily computed. Denoting the variance of X_1 as σ^2,

$$\rho_{X_k, \sum_{i=1}^n w_i X_i} = \frac{Cov(X_k, \sum_{i=1}^n w_i X_i)}{\sqrt{Var(X_k)Var(\sum_{i=1}^n w_i X_i)}} = \frac{Cov(X_k, w_k X_k)}{\sqrt{\sigma^2 \sum_{i=1}^n w_i^2 \sigma^2}} =$$

$$= \frac{w_k \sigma^2}{\sigma^2 \sqrt{\sum_{i=1}^n w_i^2}} = \frac{w_k}{||\boldsymbol{w}||_2}.$$

Therefore, the linear dependence increases with the value of the weight, since

$$w_j \leq w_k \Rightarrow \rho_{X_j, \sum_{i=1}^n w_i X_i} \leq \rho_{X_k, \sum_{i=1}^n w_i X_i}. \tag{1}$$

However, the case of independent and identically distributed random variables is quite limited and there are some kinds of dependence that are not linear [8]. In this direction, this paper is devoted to extend the comparison in Eq. (1) by considering:

1. Dependence stochastic orders that not only take into account linear dependence,
2. Random variables that are dependent or have different distributions,
3. Other aggregation functions rather than the weighted mean.

More specifically, sufficient conditions for having the ordering

$$(X_i, A(\boldsymbol{X})) \leq_{dp} (X_j, A(\boldsymbol{X})),$$

where $\leq_{dp}$ is a positive dependence stochastic order and A an aggregation function are provided.

The rest of the paper is organized as follows. In Sect. 2, the basic notions about stochastic orders and copulas are provided. Then, Sect. 3 and 4 are devoted, respectively, to the cases of quasi-arithmetic means and OWA operators. Finally, the conclusions are discussed in Sect. 5.

2   Stochastic Orders and Copulas

Stochastic orders are relations that compare probability distributions and random vectors by means of their location, variability and dependence. The most known stochastic order is the usual stochastic order, which, for random variables, is defined as the pointwise comparison of the distribution functions.

Definition 1. *[9] Let X and Y be two random variables with distribution functions F_X and F_Y. If $F_X(t) \geq F_Y(t)$ for any $t \in \mathbb{R}$, it is said that X is smaller than or equal to Y in the usual stochastic order and it is denoted by $X \leq_{st} Y$.*

The usual stochastic order can also be characterized by the comparison of the expectation of increasing functions. If $X \leq_{st} Y$, the quantiles and the expectations (if they exist) are ordered.

Moving to variability stochastic orders, the dispersive order, which considers differences between quantiles, is usually considered.

Definition 2. *[9] Let X and Y be two random variables with quantile functions F^{-1} and G^{-1}. Then, X is said to be smaller than or equal to Y in the dispersive order, denoted as $X \leq_{disp} Y$, if*

$$F^{-1}(p) - F^{-1}(q) \leq G^{-1}(p) - G^{-1}(q) \text{ for any } 0 < q \leq p < 1.$$

In addition, variability can be also studied by using convex functions.

Definition 3. *[9] Let X and Y be two random variables. If $E[\varphi(X)] \leq E[\varphi(Y)]$ for any measurable convex function $\varphi : \mathbb{R}^n \to \mathbb{R}$ such that $E[\varphi(X)]$ and $E[\varphi(Y)]$ exist, then X is said to be smaller than or equal to Y in the convex stochastic order and it is denoted as $X \leq_{cx} Y$.*

Both the dispersive and the convex order imply the ordering of variances $Var(X) \leq Var(Y)$ and the convex order imposes the same expectation for X and Y. Moreover, if $E[X] = E[Y]$, then $X \leq_{disp} Y$ implies $X \leq_{cx} Y$. Regarding (positive) dependence stochastic orders, one of the most considered alternatives is the supermodular stochastic order. Recall that a function $f : \mathbb{R}^n \to \mathbb{R}$ is said to be supermodular if $f(x) + f(y) = f(x \wedge y) + f(x \vee y)$ for any $x, y \in \mathbb{R}^n$, where $\wedge$ and $\vee$ denote, respectively, the componentwise minimum and maximum.

Definition 4. *[9] Let X and Y be two random vectors. If $E[\varphi(X)] \leq E[\varphi(Y)]$ for any supermodular function $\varphi : \mathbb{R}^n \to \mathbb{R}$ such that $E[\varphi(X)]$ and $E[\varphi(Y)]$ exist, then X is said to be smaller than or equal to Y in the supermodular order, and it is denoted as $X \leq_{sm} Y$.*

If $X \leq_{sm} Y$, then both vectors have the same marginal distributions. This stochastic order implies the weaker PQD order.

Definition 5. *[9] Let X and Y be two random vectors that have the same marginal distributions. Then, X is said to be smaller than or equal to Y in the positive quadrant dependent order, and it is denoted as $X \leq_{PQD} Y$ if $P(X \leq x) \leq P(Y \leq x)$ and $P(X \geq x) \leq P(Y \geq x)$ for any $x \in \mathbb{R}^n$.*

Moreover, the PQD order implies inequalities for the main correlation measures such as the Pearson's correlation coefficient, Kendall's τ, Spearman's ρ and the Blomquist's q [13].

When the marginal distributions are different, one can use copulas to compare the dependence. These functions capture the dependence structure of the random vector and coincide with the distribution functions of random vectors with standard uniform marginals. The multivariate distribution function, defined as $F(x_1, \ldots, x_n) = P(X_1 \leq x_1, \ldots, X_n \leq x_n)$ of any random vector can be expressed as the composition of a copula and the marginal distribution functions by the so-called Sklar Theorem.

Theorem 1. *[3, 11] Let $\boldsymbol{X}$ be a random vector with marginal distribution functions $F_1, \ldots, F_n$ and joint distribution function F. Then, there exists a copula $C : [0,1]^n \to [0,1]$ such that*

$$F(x_1, \ldots, x_n) = C\left(F_1(x_1), \ldots, F_n(x_n)\right), \ \forall \boldsymbol{x} \in \mathbb{R}^n.$$

In addition, if $F_1, \ldots, F_n$ are continuous, the copula is unique.

Similarly, the survival function of $\boldsymbol{X}$, defined as $\hat{F}(x_1, \ldots, x_n) = P(X_1 > x_1, \ldots, X_n > x_n)$, can be decomposed as

$$\hat{F}(x_1, \ldots, x_n) = \hat{C}\left(\hat{F}_1(x_1), \ldots, \hat{F}_n(x_n)\right), \ \forall \boldsymbol{x} \in \mathbb{R}^n,$$

where $\hat{F}_1, \ldots, \hat{F}_n$ are the survival functions of the marginals and $\hat{C}$ is a copula, called the survival copula of $\boldsymbol{X}$.

Larger values of the copula and the survival copula are associated with a stronger positive dependence between the components of the random vector. In this direction, the concordance order is defined as follows.

Definition 6. *[6] Let $\boldsymbol{X}$ and $\boldsymbol{Y}$ be two random vectors with continuous marginal distributions with copulas C_X and C_Y and survival copulas $\hat{C}_X$ and $\hat{C}_Y$. If $C_X(\boldsymbol{x}) \le C_Y(\boldsymbol{x})$ and $\hat{C}_X(\boldsymbol{x}) \le \hat{C}_Y(\boldsymbol{x})$ for any $\boldsymbol{x} \in [0,1]^n$, it is said that $\boldsymbol{X}$ is smaller than or equal to $\boldsymbol{Y}$ in the concordance order and it is denoted as $\boldsymbol{X} \le_c \boldsymbol{Y}$.*

If the marginal distributions are the same, then the concordance order is equivalent to the PQD order, thus implied by the supermodular order. Moreover, for bivariate random vectors, the concordance order and the supermodular are equivalent when the vectors have the same marginal distributions. The following useful result is Theorem 2.4.3. in [3].

Theorem 2. *[3] Let $\boldsymbol{X} = (X_1, \ldots, X_n)$ be a random vector with continuous components and copula C and consider n continuous and strictly monotone mappings $\varphi_j : RanX_j \to \mathbb{R}$ with $j \in \{1, \ldots, n\}$. Then, the copula of the random vector $\boldsymbol{Y} = (\varphi_1 X_1, \ldots, \varphi_n X_n)$ is given by $C \circ \sigma_{i_1} \circ \cdots \circ \sigma_{i_k}$, where $\sigma_{i_j} : [0,1]^n \to [0,1]^n$ is defined as $\sigma_j(x_1, \ldots, x_j, \ldots, x_n) = (x_1, \ldots, 1-x_j, \ldots, x_n)$ and the indices $i_1, \ldots, i_k$ correspond to those mappings $\varphi_{i_1}, \ldots, \varphi_{i_k}$ that are strictly decreasing.*

That is, applying strictly increasing functions to the variables remains the copula of the random vector invariant, while applying a strictly decreasing function to a variable transforms the copula by reflecting the associated component. In particular, one has that $C_{-X,-Y}(x,y) = \hat{C}(x,y)$.

3   Input Importance for Quasi-Arithmetic Means

Quasi-arithmetic means transform the inputs of the aggregation using a strictly increasing monotone transformation, perform a convex linear combination of the values and then inverse the transformation. They include, as particular cases, weighted arithmetic means, weighted geometric means and weighted harmonic means. The general definition is the following.

Definition 7. *[2] A function $f : I^n \to I$ is said to be a quasi-arithmetic weighted mean if can expressed as*

$$f(\boldsymbol{x}) = g^{-1} \left(\sum_{k=1}^n w_i g(x_i) \right), \ \forall \boldsymbol{x} \in I^n,$$

where $g : I \to \mathbb{R}$ is any real-valued strictly monotone function and $\boldsymbol{w} \in [0,1]^n$ is a weighting vector such that $\sum_{k=1}^n w_i = 1$.

As already stated in the introduction, the value of the weight is usually interpreted as the importance of the associated input. However, the distribution of the input is also relevant. In the following, we will consider exchangeable random vectors, which are random vectors whose distribution is invariant when the order of their components is changed. In particular, all the marginal distributions of the input random vector have the same distribution. Therefore, it is reasonable to think that the following implication is true

$$w_i \le w_j \Rightarrow \left(X_i, g^{-1} \left(\sum_{k=1}^n w_i g(x_i) \right) \right) \le_{sm} \left(X_j, g^{-1} \left(\sum_{k=1}^n w_i g(x_i) \right) \right).$$

Let us start with a lemma that considers the bivariate case and a larger family of functions.

Lemma 1. *Let $f : \mathbb{R}^2 \to \mathbb{R}$ be a measurable function such that $f(x,y) \ge f(y,x)$ if $x \le y$. Then, for any exchangeable bivariate random vector $\boldsymbol{X} = (X_1, X_2)$, it holds that*
$$(X_1, f(X_1, X_2)) \le_{sm} (X_2, f(X_1, X_2)).$$

Proof. Let ϕ be a supermodular function. If $x_1 \le x_2$, then $f(x_1, x_2) \ge f(x_2, x_1)$ and, therefore,

$$\phi(x_2, f(x_2, x_1)) + \phi(x_1, f(x_1, x_2)) \le \phi(x_1, f(x_2, x_1)) + \phi(x_2, f(x_1, x_2)).$$

Similarly, if $x_1 \ge x_2$ then $f(x_1, x_2) \le f(x_2, x_1)$ and latter equation also holds. Then, since $\boldsymbol{X}$ is exchangeable one has that $(X_1, f(X_2, X_1)) =_{st} (X_2, f(X_1, X_2))$ and $(X_1, f(X_1, X_2)) =_{st} (X_2, f(X_2, X_1))$. Therefore,

$$E\left[\phi(X_1, f(X_1, X_2))\right] = \frac{1}{2} E\left[\phi(X_1, f(X_1, X_2))\right] + \frac{1}{2} E\left[\phi(X_2, f(X_2, X_1))\right] \le$$

$$\le \frac{1}{2} E\left[\phi(X_1, f(X_2, X_1))\right] + \frac{1}{2} E\left[\phi(X_2, f(X_1, X_2))\right] = E\left[\phi(X_2, f(X_1, X_2))\right]$$

$\square$

The inequality can be extended to random vectors of arbitrary dimensions by noting that exchangeability is preserved when considering some particular conditional distributions.

Theorem 3. *Let $f : \mathbb{R}^n \to \mathbb{R}$ be a measurable function such that $f(\boldsymbol{x}) \geq f(\pi_{i,j}\boldsymbol{x})$ if $x_i \leq x_j$ where $\pi_{i,j}$ denotes the permutation that changes the values of the i-th and j-th component. Then, for any exchangeable bivariate random vector $\boldsymbol{X}$, it holds that*

$$(X_i, f(\boldsymbol{X})) \leq_{sm} (X_j, f(\boldsymbol{X})).$$

Proof. Without lose of generality, consider $i = 1$ and $j = 2$. Define the random vector $\boldsymbol{Z} = (X_3, \ldots, X_n)$. For any possible value of $\boldsymbol{Z}$, $\boldsymbol{z}$, the exchangeability of $\boldsymbol{X}$ implies that the random vector

$$([X_1 \mid \boldsymbol{Z} = \boldsymbol{z}], [X_2 \mid \boldsymbol{Z} = \boldsymbol{z}]),$$

is exchangeable. Then, the result is a consequence of Lemma 1.   □

The result for quasi-arithmetic means can be obtained by adapting the latter result.

Corollary 1. *Let $\boldsymbol{X}$ be an exchangeable random vector. Then, for any quasi-arithmetic mean*

$$f(\boldsymbol{x}) = g^{-1}\left(\sum_{k=1}^{n} w_k g(x_k)\right), \qquad \forall \boldsymbol{x} \in I^n,$$

it holds that

$$w_i \leq w_j \Rightarrow (X_i, f(\boldsymbol{X})) \leq_{sm} (X_j, f(\boldsymbol{X})).$$

Proof. If $x_i \leq x_j$, since g is increasing then $g(x_i) \leq g(x_j)$. Therefore, using that $w_i \leq w_j$,

$$\sum_{k=1}^{n} w_k g(x_k) \geq \left(\sum_{k=1, k\neq i,j}^{n} w_k g(x_k)\right) + w_i g(x_j) + w_j g(x_i).$$

Applying that g^{-1} is increasing, then $f(\boldsymbol{x}) \geq f(\pi_{i,j}\boldsymbol{x})$ where $\pi_{i,j}$ denotes the permutation that changes the values of the i-th and j-th component. Then, the conditions of Theorem 3 are fulfilled and the result holds.   □

In words, Corollary 1 confirms the intuition that if $w_i < w_j$ then $f(\boldsymbol{X})$ is more dependent to the value assumed by X_j than the value assumed by X_i.

4   Input Importance for OWA Operators

Ordered Weighted Averagings (OWA) operators performs a convex linear combination of inputs of the aggregation after ordering them from the smallest to the greatest.

Definition 8. *[12] A function $f : I^n \to I$ is said to be an Ordered Weighted Averaging (OWA) operator if it can be expressed as*

$$f(\boldsymbol{x}) = \sum_{i=1}^{n} w_i x_{\sigma(i)},$$

where $\sigma : \{1, \ldots, n\} \to \{1, \ldots, n\}$ denotes the (bijective) permutation such that $x_{\sigma(1)} \leq \cdots \leq x_{\sigma(1)}$ and $\boldsymbol{w} \in [0,1]^n$ is a weighting vector satisfying $\sum_{i=1}^{n} w_i = 1$.

OWA operators include the maximum and the minimum. In general, it is reasonable to think that larger inputs have more impact in the output of the maximum and smaller inputs have more impact in the output of the minimum. Therefore, it is intuitive to conjecture

$$X_i \leq_{st} X_j \Rightarrow (X_i, \max(\boldsymbol{X})) \leq_c (X_j, \max(\boldsymbol{X})), \; (X_i, \min(\boldsymbol{X})) \geq_c (X_j, \min(\boldsymbol{X})).$$

Notice that the supermodular order cannot be achieved, since the marginal distributions are not necessarily the same. In the following result, the concordance order is proved for the maximum by directly computing the associated copulas.

Theorem 4. *Let $\boldsymbol{X}$ be a random vector with continuous independent components. Then*

$$X_i \leq_{st} X_j \Rightarrow (X_1, \max(\boldsymbol{X})) \leq_c (X_2, \max(\boldsymbol{X})), \quad \forall i, j \in \{1, \ldots, n\}.$$

Proof. Let us compute the copula of X_1 and $\max(\boldsymbol{X})$. The bivariate distribution function can be computed by considering conditional probabilities.

$$F_{X_1, \max(\boldsymbol{X})}(a, b) = P(X_1 \leq a) P(\max(\boldsymbol{X}) \leq b \mid X_1 \leq a).$$

If $a \leq b$, then $P(\max(\boldsymbol{X}) \leq b \mid X_1 \leq a) = P(\max(X_2, \ldots, X_n) \leq b) = \prod_{i=1}^{n} F_i(b)$. If $a \geq b$, then $P(\max(\boldsymbol{X}) \leq b \mid X_1 \leq a) = P(\max(X_2, \ldots, X_n) \leq b) P(X_1 \leq b \mid X_1 \leq a) = (\prod_{i=1}^{n} F_i(b)) \frac{F_1(b)}{F_1(a)}$. Moreover, notice that $F_{\max(\boldsymbol{X})}(x) = \prod_{i=1}^{n} F_i(x)$, thus $\prod_{i=2}^{n} F_i(x) = \frac{F_{\max(\boldsymbol{X})}(x)}{F_1(x)}$. Therefore, the expression of the joint distribution function is

$$F_{X_1, \max(\boldsymbol{X})}(a, b) = \begin{cases} \frac{F_1(a)}{F_1(b)} F_{\max(\boldsymbol{X})}(b) & \text{if } a \leq b, \\ F_{\max(\boldsymbol{X})}(b) & \text{if } a \geq b, \end{cases}$$

which can be summarized as $F_{X_1,\max(\boldsymbol{X})}(a,b) = \min\left(1, \frac{F_1(a)}{F_1(b)}\right) F_{\max(\boldsymbol{X})}(b)$. Since the components of $\boldsymbol{X}$ are continuous and independent, $\max(\boldsymbol{X})$ is also continuous. Therefore, the copula has the following expression.

$$C_{X_1,\max(\boldsymbol{X})}(x,y) = \min\left(1, \frac{x}{F_1\left(F_{\max(\boldsymbol{X})}^{-1}(y)\right)}\right) y,$$

since

$$F_{X_1,\max(\boldsymbol{X})}(a,b) = C_{X_1,\max(\boldsymbol{X})}(F_1(a), F_{\max(\boldsymbol{X})}(b)),$$

$$= \min\left(1, \frac{F_1(a)}{F_1\left(F_{\max(\boldsymbol{X})}^{-1}\left(F_{\max(\boldsymbol{X})}(b)\right)\right)}\right) F_{\max(\boldsymbol{X})}(b),$$

$$= \min\left(1, \frac{F_1(a)}{F_1(b)}\right) F_{\max(\boldsymbol{X})}(b).$$

Similarly, the copulas of $(X_i, \max(\boldsymbol{X}))$ and $(X_j, \max(\boldsymbol{X}))$ for any $i,j \in \{1,\ldots,n\}$ are of the form

$$C_{X_i,\max(\boldsymbol{X})}(x,y) = \min\left(1, \frac{x}{F_i\left(F_{\max(\boldsymbol{X})}^{-1}(y)\right)}\right) y,$$

$$C_{X_j,\max(\boldsymbol{X})}(x,y) = \min\left(1, \frac{x}{F_j\left(F_{\max(\boldsymbol{X})}^{-1}(y)\right)}\right) y.$$

If $X_i \leq_{st} X_j$, then $F_i(x) \geq F_j(x)$ for any $x \in \mathbb{R}$ and, therefore, it holds that $C_{X_i,\max(\boldsymbol{X})}(x,y) \leq C_{X_j,\max(\boldsymbol{X})}(x,y)$ for any $x,y \in [0,1]$. □

The case of the minimum can be achieved by changing the sign of the variables.

Corollary 2. *Let $\boldsymbol{X}$ be a random vector with continuous independent components. Then*

$$X_i \leq_{st} X_j \Rightarrow (X_i, \min(\boldsymbol{X})) \geq_c (X_j, \min(\boldsymbol{X})), \quad \forall i,j \in \{1,\ldots,n\}.$$

Proof. Consider the random vector $-\boldsymbol{X}$ and apply Theorem 4. If $X_i \leq_{st} X_j$, then $-X_i \geq_{st} -X_j$ and

$$(-X_i, \max(-\boldsymbol{X})) \geq_c (-X_j, \max(-\boldsymbol{X})),$$
$$(-X_i, -\min(\boldsymbol{X})) \geq_c (-X_j, -\min(\boldsymbol{X})).$$

Notice that, as a consequence of Theorem 2,

$$C_{-X_i,-\min(\boldsymbol{X})}(x,y) = \hat{C}_{X_i,\min(\boldsymbol{X})}(x,y),$$
$$C_{-X_i,-\min(\boldsymbol{X})}(x,y) = \hat{C}_{X_i,\min(\boldsymbol{X})}(x,y).$$

The result holds by applying that $(-X_i, -\min(\boldsymbol{X})) \geq_c (-X_j, -\min(\boldsymbol{X}))$ implies that $\hat{C}_{X_i,\min(\boldsymbol{X})}(x,y) \leq \hat{C}_{X_i,\min(\boldsymbol{X})}(x,y)$ for any $x,y \in [0,1]^2$. □

A more general result without assuming independence cannot be proved, since it is easy to construct random vectors $\boldsymbol{X} = (X_1, X_2)$ such that $X_1 =_{st} X_2$ but with $(X_1, \max(X_1, X_2))$ and $(X_2, \max(X_1, X_2))$ having different copula. In addition, other inequalities for OWA operators are hard to prove. For instance, if one has a random vector $\boldsymbol{X} = (X_1, X_2, X_3)$ with independent components such that $X_1 \leq_{cx} X_2 \leq_{cx} X_3$, one could expect X_1 having more impact when computing the median, since it has the same location but smaller variability than X_2 and X_3, thus is in the middle position with larger probability. In symbols

$$X_1 \leq_{cx} X_2 \leq_{cx} X_3 \Rightarrow (X_1, X_{(2)}) \geq_c (X_2, X_{(2)}) \geq_c (X_1, X_{(3)}).$$

However, next example shows that the intuition is false in this case.

Example 1. Consider three independent random variables X_1, X_2 and X_3 such that X_1 has uniform distribution over $[-1, 1]$ and X_2 and X_3 have uniform distribution over $[-2, 2]$. It is clear that $E[X_1] = E[X_2] = E[X_3] = E[X_{(2)}] = 0$ and $Var[X_1] = \frac{1}{3}$, $Var[X_2] = Var[X_3] = \frac{4}{3}$. Moreover, $X_1 \leq_{cx} X_2, X_3$ and $X_1 \leq_{disp} X_2, X_3$.

Let us compute $\rho_{X_1, X_{(2)}}$ and $\rho_{X_2, X_{(2)}}$. Compute the covariance between X_1 and $X_{(2)}$ as follows,

$$Cov(X_1, X_{(2)}) = \int_{-1}^{1} \int_{-2}^{2} \int_{-2}^{2} \frac{1}{32} x_1 x_{(2)} dx_3 dx_2 dx_1,$$

where $x_{(2)}$ denotes the median value of x_1, x_2 and x_3.

Define $C = [-1, 1] \times [-2, 2]^2$ and consider the following subsets:

$$C_1 = \{\boldsymbol{x} \in C \mid x_2 \leq x_1 \leq x_3\}, \quad C_2 = \{\boldsymbol{x} \in C \mid x_3 \leq x_1 \leq x_2\},$$
$$C_3 = \{\boldsymbol{x} \in C \mid x_1 \leq x_2 \leq x_3\}, \quad C_4 = \{\boldsymbol{x} \in C \mid x_1 \leq x_3 \leq x_2\},$$
$$C_5 = \{\boldsymbol{x} \in C \mid x_2 \leq x_3 \leq x_1\}, \quad C_6 = \{\boldsymbol{x} \in C \mid x_3 \leq x_2 \leq x_1\}.$$

Notice that the intersection of any pair of the latter subsets has Lebesgue measure 0, thus the integral over it is negligible. In addition, since the permutation of X_2 and X_3 and all the random variables are symmetric with respect to 0, the integrals over C_1 and C_2 are the same, as well as the integrals over C_3, C_4, C_5 and C_6. Thus,

$$Cov(X_1, X_{(2)}) = \int_{-1}^{1} \int_{-2}^{2} \int_{-2}^{2} \frac{1}{32} x_1 x_{(2)} dx_3 dx_2 dx_1 =$$

$$= \frac{2}{32} \int_{-1}^{1} \int_{-2}^{x_1} \int_{x_1}^{2} x_1^2 dx_3 dx_2 dx_1 + \frac{4}{32} \int_{-1}^{1} \int_{-2}^{x_1} \int_{-2}^{x_2} x_1 x_2 dx_3 dx_2 dx_1.$$

Let us compute each of the integrals in the latter expression.

$$\int_{-1}^{1} \int_{-2}^{x_1} \int_{x_1}^{2} x_1^2 dx_3 dx_2 dx_1 = \int_{-1}^{1} \int_{-2}^{x_1} \left(2x_1^2 - x_1^3\right) dx_2 dx_1 =$$

$$= \int_{-1}^{1} \left(2x_1^3 - x_1^4 + 4x_1^2 - 2x_1^3\right) dx_1 = -\frac{2}{5} + \frac{8}{3} = \frac{34}{15}.$$

$$\int_{-1}^{1}\int_{-2}^{x_1}\int_{-2}^{x_2} x_1 x_2 dx_3 dx_2 dx_1 = \int_{-1}^{1}\int_{-2}^{x_1} \left(x_1 x_2^2 + 2x_1 x_2 \right) dx_1 dx_2 =$$

$$= \int_{-1}^{1} \left(\frac{x_1^4}{3} + x_1^3 + \frac{8}{3}x_1 - 4x_1 \right) dx_1 = \frac{2}{15}.$$

Then, the covariance is

$$Cov(X_1, X_{(2)}) = \frac{2}{32}\frac{34}{15} + \frac{4}{32}\frac{2}{15} = \frac{19}{120}.$$

For the covariance of X_2 and $X_{(2)}$, similarly as in the latter case, the integral can be decomposed in three different cases, the first associated to C_1 and C_2, the second to C_3 and C_6 and the last one to C_4 and C_5. Then, it is obtained

$$Cov(X_2, X_{(2)}) = \frac{2}{32}\int_{-1}^{1}\int_{-2}^{x_1}\int_{x_1}^{2} x_2 x_1 dx_3 dx_2 dx_1 +$$

$$+\frac{2}{32}\int_{-1}^{1}\int_{-2}^{x_1}\int_{-2}^{x_2} x_2^2 dx_3 dx_2 dx_1 + \frac{2}{32}\int_{-1}^{1}\int_{-2}^{x_1}\int_{-2}^{x_3} x_2 x_3 dx_2 dx_3 dx_1.$$

$$\int_{-1}^{1}\int_{-2}^{x_1}\int_{x_1}^{2} x_2 x_1 dx_3 dx_2 dx_1 = \int_{-1}^{1}\int_{-2}^{x_1} \left(2x_1 x_2 - x_1^2 x_2 \right) dx_2 dx_1 =$$

$$= \int_{-1}^{1} \left(x_1^3 - 4x_1 - \frac{x_1^4}{2} + 2x_1^2 \right) dx_1 = -\frac{2}{10} + \frac{4}{3} = \frac{17}{15}.$$

$$\int_{-1}^{1}\int_{-2}^{x_1}\int_{-2}^{x_2} x_2^2 dx_3 dx_2 dx_1 = \int_{-1}^{1}\int_{-2}^{x_1} \left(x_2^3 + 2x_2^2 \right) dx_2 dx_1 =$$

$$= \int_{-1}^{1} \left(\frac{x_1^4}{4} - 4 + \frac{2}{3}x_1^3 + \frac{16}{3} \right) dx_1 = \frac{2}{20} - 8 + \frac{32}{3} = \frac{83}{30}.$$

$$\int_{-1}^{1}\int_{-2}^{x_1}\int_{-2}^{x_3} x_2 x_3 dx_2 dx_3 dx_1 = \int_{-1}^{1}\int_{-2}^{x_1} \left(\frac{x_3^3}{2} - 2x_3 \right) dx_3 dx_1 =$$

$$= \int_{-1}^{1} \left(\frac{x_1^4}{8} - 2 - x_1^2 + 4 \right) dx_1 = \frac{2}{40} - 4 - \frac{2}{3} + 8 = \frac{203}{60}.$$

Thus,

$$Cov(X_2, X_{(2)}) = \frac{2}{32}\frac{17}{15} + \frac{2}{32}\frac{83}{30} + \frac{2}{32}\frac{203}{60} = \frac{437}{960}.$$

Finally, it is necessary to compute the variance of the median, which involves previously computed integrals.

$$Var(X_{(2)}) = \frac{2}{32}\int_{-1}^{1}\int_{-2}^{x_1}\int_{x_1}^{2} x_1^2 dx_3 dx_2 dx_1 + \frac{4}{32}\int_{-1}^{1}\int_{-2}^{x_1}\int_{-2}^{x_2} x_2^2 dx_3 dx_2 dx_1 =$$

$$= \frac{2}{32}\frac{34}{15} + \frac{4}{32}\frac{83}{30} = \frac{39}{80}.$$

Then, the correlation coefficients can be computed as follows.

$$\rho_{X_1, X_{(2)}} = \frac{\frac{19}{120}}{\sqrt{\frac{1}{3}\frac{39}{80}}} = \frac{304\sqrt{65}}{6240} \approx 0.3928,$$

$$\rho_{X_2, X_{(2)}} = \frac{\frac{437}{960}}{\sqrt{\frac{4}{3}\frac{39}{80}}} = \frac{437\sqrt{65}}{6240} \approx 0.5646.$$

Suppose that $(X_1, X_{(2)}) \geq_c (X_2, X_{(2)})$. Then, applying Theorem 2, $(X_1, X_{(2)})$ has the same copula as $(2X_1, X_{(2)})$ and, therefore, $(2X_1, X_{(2)}) \geq_c (X_2, X_{(2)})$. Since $2X_1 =_{st} X_2$, $(2X_1, X_{(2)})$ and $(X_2, X_{(2)})$ have the same marginal distributions and then $(2X_1, X_{(2)}) \geq_{sm} (X_2, X_{(2)})$. This cannot be possible, since $(2X_1, X_{(2)}) \geq_{sm} (X_2, X_{(2)})$ would imply $\rho_{X_1, X_{(2)}} \geq \rho_{X_1, X_{(2)}}$, which is not true. Therefore, it is concluded that $(X_1, X_{(2)}) \not\geq_c (X_2, X_{(2)})$.

5   Conclusions

In this paper, the importance of the inputs in aggregation functions has been studied by using positive dependence stochastic orders. In particular, it has been proved that a larger weight in quasi-arithmetic means implies a larger positive dependence between the associated variable and the aggregation, with respect to the supermodular order, when dealing with exchangeable random vectors. For random vectors with independent components, the usual stochastic order implies the concordance order between the vectors consisting on the variable and the maximum, and the opposite for the minimum. However, for general OWA operators no general results seem to be achievable, so further analyses on specific cases could be the subject of further studies.

There are many other aggregation functions that can be analyzed using this approach. For instance, larger variability could imply more dependence when dealing with some permutation symmetric aggregations, as shown in Example 1. In addition, the results for the maximum and minimum might be extended by imposing conditions to probabilities of the form $P(X_1 > X_2)$.

Funding Details

J. Baz is supported by Programa Severo Ochoa of Principality of Asturias (BP21042) and by the Ministry of Science and Innovation (PID2022-139886NB-I00). F. Pellerey carried out this study within the FAIR - Future Artificial Intelligence Research and received funding from the European Union Next-GenerationEU (Piano Nazionale di Ripresa e Resilienza (PNRR) Missione 4 Componente 2, Investimento 1.3 D.D. 1555 11/10/2022, PE00000013).

References

1. Beliakov, G., Pradera, A., Calvo, T., et al.: Aggregation Functions: A Guide for Practitioners, vol. 221. Springer (2007)
2. Bullen, P.S.: Handbook of Means and Their Inequalities. Springer, Berlin (2013)
3. Durante, F., Sempi, C., et al.: Principles of Copula Theory, vol. 474. CRC Press, Boca Raton (2016)
4. Grabisch, M., Marichal, J.L., Mesiar, R., Pap, E.: Aggregation Functions, vol. 127. Cambridge University Press (2009)
5. Mohd, W.R.W., Abdullah, L.: Aggregation methods in group decision making: a decade survey. Informatica **41**(1) (2017)
6. Nelsen, R.B.: An Introduction to Copulas. Springer, New York (2006)
7. Nungesser, M.K., Joyce, L.A., McGuire, A.D.: Effects of spatial aggregation on predictions of forest climate change response. Climate Res. **11**(2), 109–124 (1999)
8. Rohatgi, V.K., Saleh, A.: An Introduction to Probability and Statistics. Wiley, New Jersey (2015)
9. Shaked, M., Shanthikumar, J.G.: Stochastic Orders. Springer, New York (2007)
10. Shanmugam, D., Blalock, D., Balakrishnan, G., Guttag, J.: Better aggregation in test-time augmentation. In: Proceedings of the IEEE/CVF International Conference on Computer Vision, pp. 1214–1223 (2021)
11. Sklar, A.: Fonctions de repartition an dimensions et leurs marges. Publ. Inst. Statist. Univ. Paris **8**, 229–231 (1959)
12. Yager, R.R.: Families of OWA operators. Fuzzy Sets Syst. **59**(2), 125–148 (1993)
13. Yanagimoto, T., Okamoto, M.: Partial orderings of permutations and monotonicity of a rank correlation statistic. Ann. Inst. Stat. Math. **21**, 489–506 (1969)
14. Zahedi Khameneh, A., Kilicman, A.: Some construction methods of aggregation operators in decision-making problems: an overview. Symmetry **12**(5), 694 (2020)

Insights into the q Exponent in Power Measure with Choquet-Based Generalizations for Classification Problems

Giancarlo Lucca[1]([⊠])(iD), Tiago C. Asmus[2](iD), Cedric Marco-Detchart[3](iD),
Helida S. Santos[2](iD), Heloisa A. Camargo[4](iD), Adenauer C. Yamin[5](iD),
Renata H. S. Reiser[5](iD), Humberto Bustince[3](iD), Alice Pintanel[2](iD),
and Graçaliz P. Dimuro[2](iD)

[1] Universidade Católica de Pelotas (UCPEL), Pelotas, RS, Brazil
giancarlo.lucca@ucpel.edu.br
[2] Universidade Federal do Rio Grande (FURG), Rio Grande, RS, Brazil
{tiagoasmus,helida,alicetissot,gracalizdimuro}@furg.br
[3] Universidade Pública de Navarra (UPNA), Pamplona, NA, Spain
{cedric.marco,bustince}@unavarra.es
[4] Universidade Federal de São Carlos (UFSCar), São Carlos, SP, Brazil
heloisa.camargo@ufscar.br
[5] Universidade Federal do Pelotas (UFPEL), Pelotas, RS, Brazil
{adenuaer,reiser}@inf.ufpel.edu.br

Abstract. Choquet-integrals are averaging aggregation functions based on a fuzzy measure that accounts for both the significance of each attribute being aggregated and the interactions between the variables. The effectiveness of a fuzzy measure can be characterized by its accuracy in modeling the relationship or association degree among the elements to be aggregated. In the literature, it is known that amid conventional fuzzy measures, the Power Measure (PM) presents statistically superior performance. This study explores the q exponent impact in the PM on the performance of different Choquet-based integrals when used in fuzzy rule-based classification systems. We aim to analyze how fixed q values influence classification accuracy across thirty-three benchmark datasets. The updated results reveal that smaller q values (e.g., $q = 0.1$ and $q = 0.5$) continue to yield superior accuracy, while larger values ($q \geq 100$) tend to a performance stabilization. Among the tested methods, the generalization named C_{F1F2}-integral achieves the highest classification accuracy, effectively adapting to different parameter settings.

Keywords: Power Measure · Choquet-based integrals · C_{F1F2}-integral · Fuzzy rule-based classification

1 Introduction

Fuzzy Rule-Based Classification Systems (FRBCS) [22] are an efficient way to deal with classification problems [17], by producing interpretable models

M. Baczyński et al. (Eds.): EUSFLAT 2025, LNCS 15883, pp. 270–281, 2025.
https://doi.org/10.1007/978-3-031-97225-6_22

using fuzzy logic [39]. A primal piece in FRBCS is the Fuzzy Reasoning Method (FRM) [13], an inference mechanism responsible for predicting a new input class. Barrenecha et al. [4] introduced an FRM that uses the well-known Choquet integral [11] based on a specific fuzzy measure [31] where the standard Cardinality measure is raised to a q exponent, called the Power Measure (PM). One advantage of the PM is that the q exponent can be adapted according to the application at hand.

Since the successful applications of the Choquet-integrals in several areas [15], further Choquet-based operators have appeared in the literature, like: Choquet-like integrals [30], C_T-integrals [24], CC-integrals [27], C_F-integrals [28], C_{F1F2}-integrals [23], gC_{F1F2}-integrals [16], d-Choquet integrals [9], dC_F-integrals [38], dXC-integrals [37], dCC-integrals [33] and VCI-integrals [18]. Generalizations of the Sugeno integral (and integrated frameworks) were also developed, e.g.: IV-Sugeno [19], FG-functionals [3], generalizations by a fusion function [20], Choquet-Sugeno-like [7] and IV-Choquet-Sugeno-like operators [6].

In the study by [25], power measure was the approach with the better performance considering several Choquet-based generalizations. Therefore, this study aims to analyze the relations of the Choquet-based generalizations performance according to different fixed values of the q exponent when defining the PM.

This article is organized as follows. Section 2 provides the basic concepts related to the paper. Section 2.2 demonstrates the importance of the q exponent in the classification process. In Sect. 3, we provide the methodology used in the study. The results are stated in Sect. 4, and finally, conclusions are drawn.

2   Preliminaries

This section recalls the main theoretical concepts related to this study. In what follows, consider $N = \{1, \ldots, n\}$, for an arbitrary integer $n > 0$. A function $F \colon [0,1]^n \to [0,1]$ is said to be averaging if for all $\boldsymbol{x} = (x_1, \ldots, x_n) \in [0,1]^n$: $\min(\boldsymbol{x}) \leq F(\boldsymbol{x}) \leq \max(\boldsymbol{x})$.

A restricted dissimilarity function (RDF) [8] is a mapping $\delta \colon [0,1]^2 \to [0,1]$ that satisfies, for all $x, y, z \in [0,1]$, the following conditions: ($\delta 1$) $\delta(x,y) = \delta(y,x)$; ($\delta 2$) $\delta(x,y) = 1$ if and only if $\{x,y\} = \{0,1\}$; ($\delta 3$) $\delta(x,y) = 0$ if and only if $x = y$; ($\delta 4$) if $x \leq y \leq z$, then $\delta(x,y) \leq \delta(x,z)$ and $\delta(y,z) \leq \delta(x,z)$.

A set function $\mathfrak{m} \colon 2^N \to [0,1]$ is called a fuzzy measure (FM) [34] if, for all $X, Y \subseteq N$, it satisfies the following properties: ($\mathfrak{m}1$) It is increasing: If $X \subseteq Y$, then $\mathfrak{m}(X) \leq \mathfrak{m}(Y)$; ($\mathfrak{m}2$) Boundary conditions: $\mathfrak{m}(\emptyset) = 0$ and $\mathfrak{m}(N) = 1$.

Example 1. In the following examples of fuzzy measures, let $A \subseteq N$.

  a) Uniform Measure (UM): $\mathfrak{m}_{\mathfrak{U}}(A) = \frac{|A|}{n}$;
  b) Power Measure (PM):

$$\mathfrak{m}_{\mathfrak{P}}(A) = \left(\frac{|A|}{n}\right)^q, \text{ with } q > 0. \tag{1}$$

Uniform Measure is one of the classic fuzzy measures and can be understood as the normalized cardinality of a set, the reason why sometimes called by the Cardinality Measure [27]. In this study, we focus on the Power Measure, since its flexibility and effectiveness have been demonstrated in previous works [23,28]. In particular, a comparison of different fuzzy measures in classification problems was done in [25].

An automorphism is a continuous, strictly increasing function $\varphi \colon [0,1] \to [0,1]$ with boundary conditions $\varphi(0) = 0$, $\varphi(1) = 1$. As an example, the function $\varphi^\alpha \colon [0,1] \to [0,1]$, given, for all $x \in [0,1]$, by $\varphi^\alpha(x) = x^\alpha$, $\alpha \in (0,+\infty)$, is an automorphism, which has been applied to seek optimal solutions in machine learning problems, by varying the value of α [32].

Now, observe that the Power Measure can be perceived as an adaptation of the Uniform Measure, by the action of the automorphism φ^α with $\alpha = q$, since $\mathfrak{m}_{\mathfrak{P}}(A) = (\mathfrak{m}_{\mathfrak{U}}(A))^q$, for any $A \subseteq N$ and $q > 0$. So, it is possible to search for the ideal value of q according to the application at hand, which contributes to the adaptability of the PM mentioned in the Introduction.

The discrete Choquet integral $\mathfrak{C}_{\mathfrak{m}} \colon [0,1]^n \to [0,1]$ related to a fuzzy measure $\mathfrak{m} \colon 2^N \to [0,1]$ is defined for all $\boldsymbol{x} = (x_1, \ldots, x_n) \in [0,1]^n$, as:

$$\mathfrak{C}_{\mathfrak{m}}(\boldsymbol{x}) = \sum_{i=1}^{n} \left(x_{(i)} - x_{(i-1)} \right) \cdot \mathfrak{m}\left(A_{(i)} \right), \tag{2}$$

where $\left(x_{(1)}, \ldots, x_{(n)} \right)$ is an increasing permutation of the components of $\boldsymbol{x}$ such that $0 \leq x_{(1)} \leq \ldots \leq x_{(n)}$, with $x_{(0)} = 0$, and $A_{(i)} = \{(i), \ldots, (n)\}$ is the subset of indices corresponding to the $n - i + 1$ largest components of $\boldsymbol{x}$.

Following this same constraints, there are several generalizations of the Choquet integral (CI), e.g.:

CT-Integral. Let $T \colon [0,1]^2 \to [0,1]$ be a t-norm [5]. The C_T-integral [24] with respect to an FM $\mathfrak{m}$ is the function $\mathfrak{C}_{\mathfrak{m}}^T \colon [0,1]^n \to [0,n]$, defined, for all $\boldsymbol{x} = (x_1, \ldots, x_n) \in [0,1]^n$, by

$$\mathfrak{C}_{\mathfrak{m}}^T(\boldsymbol{x}) = \sum_{i=1}^{n} T\left(x_{(i)} - x_{(i-1)}, \mathfrak{m}\left(A_{(i)} \right) \right). \tag{3}$$

CC-Integral. Take $C \colon [0,1]^2 \to [0,1]$ as a copula. The CC-integral [27] with respect to an FM $\mathfrak{m}$ is the mapping $\mathfrak{C}_{\mathfrak{m}}^C \colon [0,1]^n \to [0,1]$, given, for all $\boldsymbol{x} = (x_1, \ldots, x_n) \in [0,1]^n$, by

$$\mathfrak{C}_{\mathfrak{m}}^C(\boldsymbol{x}) = \sum_{i=1}^{n} C\left(x_{(i)}, \mathfrak{m}\left(A_{(i)} \right) \right) - C\left(x_{(i-1)}, \mathfrak{m}\left(A_{(i)} \right) \right). \tag{4}$$

C_F**-Integral.** The C_F-integral [28] for $F\colon [0,1]^2 \to [0,1]$, with respect to an FM $\mathfrak{m}$ is the function $\mathfrak{C}_\mathfrak{m}^F\colon [0,1]^n \to [0,1]$, given, for all $\boldsymbol{x} = (x_1, \ldots, x_n) \in [0,1]^n$, by

$$\mathfrak{C}_\mathfrak{m}^F(\boldsymbol{x}) = \min \left\{ 1, \sum_{i=1}^n F\left(x_{(i)} - x_{(i-1)}, \mathfrak{m}\left(A_{(i)}\right)\right) \right\}. \tag{5}$$

$C_{F_1 F_2}$**-Integral.** Let $\mathfrak{m}$ be a symmetric FM and take $F_1, F_2\colon [0,1]^2 \to [0,1]$ satisfying (i) F_1-dominance: $F_1(x,y) \geq F_2(x,y)$ for all $x,y \in [0,1]$; (ii) F_1 is $(1,0)$-increasing: $F_1(x+c,y) \geq F_1(x,y)$ for all $x,y \in [0,1], c > 0$. A $C_{F_1 F_2}$-integral [23] with respect to $\mathfrak{m}$ is a mapping $\mathfrak{C}_\mathfrak{m}^{(F_1, F_2)}\colon [0,1]^n \to [0,1]$, given, for all $\boldsymbol{x} = (x_1, \ldots, x_n) \in [0,1]^n$, as

$$\mathfrak{C}_\mathfrak{m}^{(F_1, F_2)}(\boldsymbol{x}) = \min \left\{ 1, x_{(1)} + \sum_{i=2}^n F_1\left(x_{(i)}, \mathfrak{m}\left(A_{(i)}\right)\right) - F_2\left(x_{(i-1)}, \mathfrak{m}\left(A_{(i)}\right)\right) \right\}. \tag{6}$$

dC_F**-Integral.** Consider $F\colon [0,1]^2 \to [0,1]$ having a left annihilator element $(\forall y \in [0,1]\colon F(0,y) = 0)$, and let $\delta\colon [0,1]^2 \to [0,1]$ be an RDF. The generalization of the CI by the function F, with respect to δ and an FM $\mathfrak{m}$, called dC_F-integral [38], is the function $\mathfrak{C}_{F,\mathfrak{m},\delta}\colon [0,1]^n \to [0,n]$, defined, for all $\boldsymbol{x} = (x_1, \ldots, x_n) \in [0,1]^n$, by:

$$\mathfrak{C}_{F,\mathfrak{m},\delta}(\boldsymbol{x}) = x_{(1)} + \sum_{i=2}^n F\left(\delta(x_{(i)}, x_{(i-1)}), \mathfrak{m}(A_{(i)})\right) \tag{7}$$

dXC_F**-Integral.** The generalization of the expanded form of the CI by RDFs $\delta\colon [0,1]^2 \to [0,1]$ with respect to an FM $\mathfrak{m}\colon 2^N \to [0,1]$, named d-XChoquet integral (d-XC) [37], is a mapping $X\mathfrak{C}_{\delta,\mathfrak{m}}\colon [0,1]^2 \to [0,n]$, defined, for all $\boldsymbol{x} = (x_1, \ldots, x_n) \in [0,1]^n$, by:

$$X\mathfrak{C}_{\delta,\mathfrak{m}}(\boldsymbol{x}) = x_{(1)} + \sum_{i=2}^n \delta\left(x_{(i)} \cdot \mathfrak{m}_{(i)}, \ x_{(i-1)} \cdot \mathfrak{m}_{(i)}\right). \tag{8}$$

In Table 1, we provide the definition of the basis function for each generalization, chosen due to the good results they achieved in previous works. The main property that is required for those generalizations when applied in FRBCs is some kind of increasingness, while the averaging property may impact negatively in the classification task, as discussed in [15]. Observe that an initial work analyzing Data Complexity Measure (DCM) and some of the generalized CIs were discussed in [26].

2.1   Fuzzy Rule-Based Classification Systems

Fuzzy Rule-Based Classification Systems (FRBCSs) [22] represent an extension of traditional rule-based systems [36], integrating fuzzy sets into the

Table 1. Functions used as the basis for Generalizations of the CI.

Generalization	Basis Function	Definition
C_T-integrals	Hamacher Product	$T_{HP}(x,y) = \begin{cases} 0, & \text{if } x=y=0, \\ \frac{xy}{x+y-xy}, & \text{otherwise.} \end{cases}$
CC-integral	Copula of the minimum	$C(x,y) = \min(x,y)$
C_F-integrals$_{\text{AVG}}$	pre-overlap function [10]	$F_{NA}(x,y) = \begin{cases} x, & \text{if } x \leq y, \\ \min\{\frac{x}{2}, y\}, & \text{otherwise.} \end{cases}$
C_F-integrals$_{\text{N-AVG}}$	pre-aggregation function [14]	$F_{NA2}(x,y) = \begin{cases} 0, & \text{if } x=0, \\ \frac{x+y}{2}, & \text{if } 0 < x \leq y, \\ \min\{\frac{x}{2}, y\}, & \text{otherwise.} \end{cases}$
$C_{F_1 F_2}$-integral	overlap functions	$GM(x,y) = \sqrt{x,y},\ F_{BPC}(x,y) = xy^2$
dC_F-integral	δ_5, Product t-norm	$P(x,y) = xy,\ \delta_5(x,y) = (\sqrt{x} - \sqrt{y})^{\frac{1}{2}}$
d-XC-integral	δ_5	$\delta_5(x,y) = (\sqrt{x} - \sqrt{y})^{\frac{1}{2}}$
AVG: averaging	N-AVG: non-averaging	

antecedents of rules. This integration enhances interpretability and provides a flexible framework for addressing complex classification tasks.

Two prominent types of FRBCSs, introduced by [35] and [29], form the basis of the models analyzed in this work. These systems comprise a collection of fuzzy rules expressed in a standard linguistic form:

$$\text{Rule } R_j : \text{ If } x_{p1} \text{ is } A_{j1} \text{ and } \ldots \text{ and } x_{pn} \text{ is } A_{jn}, \text{ then Class is } C_j \text{ with } RW_j, \tag{9}$$

where R_j denotes the j-th rule, A_{ji} represents fuzzy sets modeled by triangular membership functions, C_j indicates the class label, and $RW_j \in [0,1]$ is the rule weight [21]. The rule weight is calculated using the Certainty Factor (CF) [12]:

$$RW_j = CF_j = \frac{\sum_{x_p \in \text{Class } C_j} \mu_{A_j}(x_p)}{\sum_{p=1}^{N} \mu_{A_j}(x_p)}, \tag{10}$$

where N is the total number of training patterns, $\boldsymbol{x_p} = (x_{p1}, \ldots, x_{pm})$, and $p = 1, \ldots, N$.

Once the fuzzy rules composing the system have been created, the Fuzzy Reasoning Method (FRM) is responsible for classifying new examples. Let $\boldsymbol{x_p} = (x_{p1}, \ldots, x_{pn})$ represent a new example to be classified. Still, L denotes the number of rules in the rule base, and M denotes the number of classes in the problem. The FRM, which may incorporate Choquet-based integrals, consists of four steps:

1. **Matching Degree:** This step calculates the activation strength of the antecedents of the rules for the example x_p, using a t-norm $T' : [0,1]^n \to [0,1]$. The matching degree for each rule is given by:

$$\mu_{A_j}(x_p) = T'(\mu_{A_{j1}}(x_{p1}), \ldots, \mu_{A_{jn}}(x_{pn})), \text{ with } j = 1, \ldots, L.$$

2. **Association Degree:** For the class associated with each rule, the matching degree is weighted by the corresponding rule weight. This is expressed as:

$$b_j^k(x_p) = \mu_{A_j}(x_p) \cdot RW_j^k, \text{ with } k = \text{Class}(R_j), \ j = 1, \ldots, L.$$

3. **Classification Soundness Degree Computation:** The association degrees obtained in the previous step are aggregated with an aggregation function. In this case, using Choquet-based generalizations. The soundness degree for each class is computed as:

$$Y_k(x_p) = \mathfrak{C}_\mathfrak{m}\left(b_1^k(x_p), \ldots, b_L^k(x_p)\right), \text{ with } k = 1, \ldots, M, \tag{11}$$

where $\mathfrak{C}_\mathfrak{m}$ is the Choquet-based integral related to a fuzzy measure $\mathfrak{m}$. For practical reasons, only terms $b_j^k(x_p) > 0$ are considered in Eq. (11).

4. **Classification Decision:** A function $F \colon [0,1]^M \to \{1, \ldots, M\}$ is applied to decide the class corresponding to the maximum soundness degree:

$$F(Y_1, \ldots, Y_M) = \arg \max_{k=1, \ldots, M} (Y_k).$$

2.2   Illustrating the q Exponent Impact in the PM Performance

This section illustrates the importance of the q exponent in the considered fuzzy measure and, consequently, in the approach performance.

Example 2. Consider a generic example related to a classification problem with two classes (C_1 and C_2). Different generic fuzzy rules are activated for each class when classifying a new example. Precisely, class $C_1 = [0.9, 0.2]$, and $C_2 = [0.3, 0.7, 0.9]$. We provide the analysis of the FRM regarding the standard Choquet integral and the power measure as a fixed q exponent with $q = 1$ (standard cardinality) and $q = 5$. Thus, the following results are obtained:

- C_1 Class
    * $\mathfrak{C}_{PM_{q=1}}$: $(0.2 - 0) \cdot \left(\frac{2}{2}\right)^1 + (0.9 - 0.2) \cdot \left(\frac{1}{2}\right)^1 = 0.55$
    * $\mathfrak{C}_{PM_{q=5}}$: $(0.2 - 0) \cdot \left(\frac{2}{2}\right)^5 + (0.9 - 0.2) \cdot \left(\frac{1}{2}\right)^5 = 0.41$
- C_2 Class
    * $\mathfrak{C}_{PM_{q=1}}$: $(0.3 - 0) \cdot \left(\frac{3}{3}\right)^1 + (0.7 - 0.3) \cdot \left(\frac{2}{3}\right)^1 + (0.9 - 0.7) \cdot \left(\frac{1}{3}\right)^1 = 0.57$
    * $\mathfrak{C}_{PM_{q=5}}$: $(0.3 - 0) \cdot \left(\frac{3}{3}\right)^5 + (0.7 - 0.3) \cdot \left(\frac{2}{3}\right)^5 + (0.9 - 0.7) \cdot \left(\frac{1}{3}\right)^5 = 0.34$

After aggregating the values for each class, the predicted class corresponding to the most significant value is given as follows:

- $\mathfrak{C}_{PM_{q=1}}$: arg max$[0.55, \mathbf{0.57}] = C_2$
- $\mathfrak{C}_{PM_{q=5}}$: arg max$[\mathbf{0.41}, 0.34] = C_1$

Observing the results, the predicted class is C_2 when $q = 1$, while for $q = 5$ the prediction is C_1. So, one concludes the q exponent value in the PM directly influences the classifier's prediction.

3   Methodology

In this study, we evaluated the performance of the proposed method using the same datasets employed in the original generalizations of the Choquet Integral. Specifically, we elected thirty-three datasets from the KEEL repository [2] for the analysis, as presented in Table 2. This table provides a summary of these datasets, including their identification (ID), name, number of examples (#Ex.), number of attributes (#Atts.), and number of classes (#Class).

Table 2. Datasets summary used in the study.

ID	Dataset	#Ex.	#Atts.	#Class	ID	Dataset	#Ex.	#Atts.	#Class
App	Appendicitis	106	7	2	Pen	Penbased	10,992	16	10
Bal	Balance	625	4	3	Pho	Phoneme	5,404	5	2
Ban	Banana	5,300	2	2	Pim	Pima	768	8	2
Bnd	Bands	365	19	2	Rin	Ring	740	20	2
Bup	Bupa	345	6	2	Sah	Saheart	462	9	2
Cle	Cleveland	297	13	5	Sat	Satimage	6,435	36	7
Con	Contraceptive	1,473	9	3	Seg	Segment	2,310	19	7
Eco	Ecoli	336	7	8	Shu	Shuttle	58,000	9	7
Gla	Glass	214	9	6	Son	Sonar	208	60	2
Hab	Haberman	306	3	2	Spe	Spectfheart	267	44	2
Hay	Hayes-Roth	160	4	3	Tit	Titanic	2,201	3	2
Ion	Ionosphere	351	33	2	Two	Twonorm	740	20	2
Iri	Iris	150	4	3	Veh	Vehicle	846	18	4
Led	Led7digit	500	7	10	Win	Wine	178	13	3
Mag	Magic	1,902	10	2	Wis	Wisconsin	683	11	2
New	Newthyroid	215	5	3	Yea	Yeast	1,484	8	10
Pag	Pageblocks	5,472	10	5					

To streamline the training process, six datasets: *Magic, Page-blocks, Penbased, Ring, Satimage,* and *Twonorm* were stratified, and 10% of the examples were randomly sampled. Additionally, datasets with missing data, such as *wisconsin,* had incomplete examples removed to ensure consistency in the analysis. Each dataset was evaluated using 5-fold cross-validation, with classifier performance measured by the accuracy rate [17]. The final result, presented in Sect. 4, averages the accuracy rates across all test partitions. The algorithm configuration follows the specifications recommended for FARC-HD [1], which were also adopted in prior studies on the CI generalizations, as discussed in Sect. 2.

Finally, as previously stressed, we have fixed different values for the q exponent when aggregating the values in the FRM. We adopted an extensive range

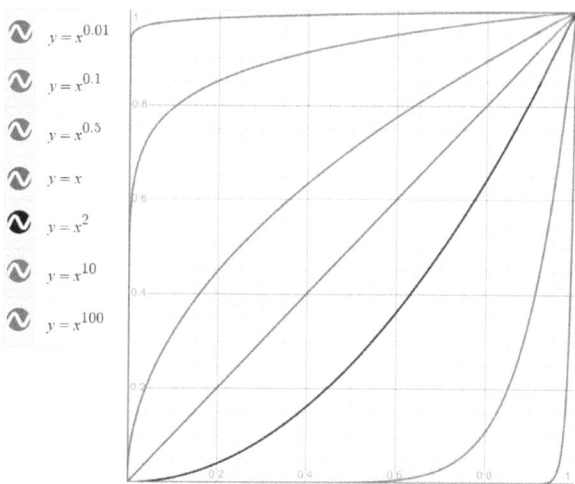

Fig. 1. Plot of the function $y = x^q$ for different q values.

Table 3. Accuracy mean obtained by the different approaches combined with the fixed q exponent in the power measure.

ID	Method	$q = 0.01$	$q = 0.1$	$q = 0.2$	$q = 0.5$	$q = 1$	$q = 2$	$q = 5$	$q = 10$	$q = 100$
A	$\mathfrak{C}_m$	79.40	79.33	79.54	79.16	78.72	77.98	77.07	76.63	76.68
B	$\mathfrak{C}_m^C$	79.20	79.17	79.05	78.93	78.92	78.61	77.89	76.90	76.62
C	$\mathfrak{C}_m^T$	79.09	79.40	79.51	79.61	79.44	78.95	78.00	76.94	76.61
D	$\mathfrak{C}_{m\,\text{AVG}}^F$	79.15	79.10	79.61	79.45	79.11	78.62	77.74	77.06	76.62
E	$\mathfrak{C}_{m\,\text{N-AVG}}^F$	79.87	80.16	80.14	80.31	80.10	80.26	79.58	78.18	76.56
F	$\mathfrak{C}_m^{(F_1, F_2)}$	80.44	80.67	80.92	80.78	80.57	80.27	79.63	78.31	76.86
G	$\mathfrak{C}_{F,m,\delta}$	80.32	80.16	80.07	80.14	80.22	79.64	78.37	77.74	76.72
H	$X\mathfrak{C}_{\delta,m}$	80.30	80.16	80.09	80.51	80.02	80.14	79.86	79.57	76.83

of values with $q = [0.01, 0.1, 0.2, 0.5, 1.0, 2, 5, 10, 100]$. These values were selected so that each constructed PM provides different results while avoiding redundancies. And, considering $\frac{|A|}{n} = x$, in Eq. (1), the result of the PM for a particular q is given by x^q. In Fig. 1, it is observed the graphs of the function $y = x^q$, for each chosen value of q, showing that we arrived at a somewhat even delimitation of the unit square. Values of q that are lesser than 0.01 or greater than 100 would not contribute to the intended analysis since they provided results similar to the cases where $q = 0.01$ and $q = 100$, respectively. We also considered other intermediate values to avoid similar situations.

=dum

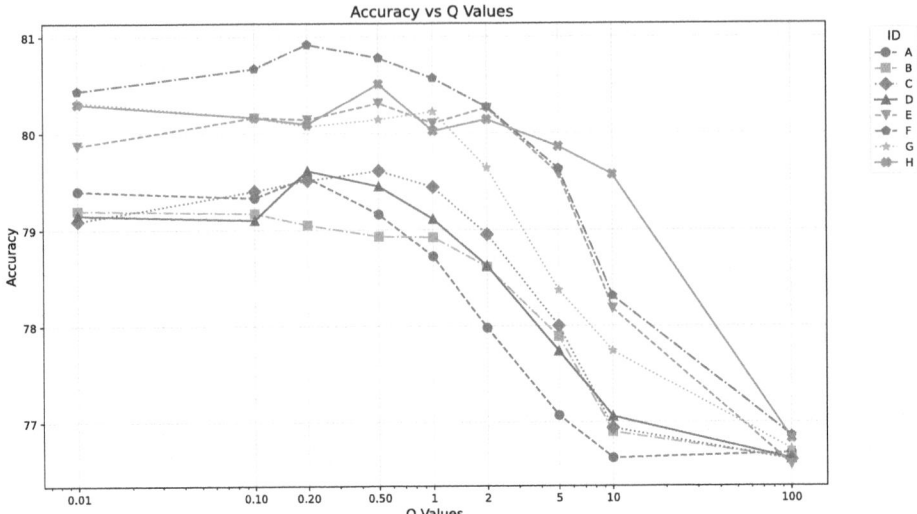

Fig. 2. Line Graph of the obtained results combining different Choquet-based generalizations and q values.

4 Obtained Results

This section discusses the main results based on the benchmark composed of thirty-three different datasets, considering the accuracy mean of these cases.

Table 3 summarizes the accuracy obtained by combining different values of q (columns) with different Choquet-based generalizations (rows). We also depict an identification (ID) for each approach, facilitating the visualization of the results.

In a first general analysis, we can notice that among the evaluated methods, $\mathfrak{C}_m^{(F_1,F_2)}$ (Method F) demonstrates the highest overall accuracy, reaching a maximum of 80.92% at $q = 0.2$. This analysis suggests a robust approach to variations in q, maintaining strong performance across a wide range of values.

The averaging generalizations, including $\mathfrak{C}_m$ (Method A) and its variants (Methods B, C and D), exhibit a more pronounced decline in accuracy as q increases. They demonstrate greater sensitivity to changes in this parameter, rapidly decreasing accuracy for larger q values. A similar behavior is observed for $\mathfrak{C}_{F,m,\delta}$ (Method G) and $X\mathfrak{C}_{\delta,m}$ (Method H). However, Method H slightly appears more resilient at intermediate q values (e.g., $q = 5, 10$).

We provide a graphical representation of the accuracy trends in Fig. 2 to complement the tabular results. This line graph illustrates how the accuracy of each method varies as the parameter q in the PM changes. The visualization helps to better understand the patterns and differences among the methods. Mainly, we notice the accuracy stabilization for larger q values. Additionally, the figure highlights the superior performance of specific methods, such as $\mathfrak{C}_m^{(F_1,F_2)}$ (F ID, in brown) which is the known state-of-the-art CI generalization so far.

5   Conclusions

This study addressed the problem of evaluating the influence of the q exponent in the PM on the performance of Choquet-based integrals for FRBCS. The main objective was to analyze how fixed q values affect classification accuracy across various generalizations and benchmark datasets.

The results confirm the relevance of the q parameter having a significant impact on the performance. Specifically, smaller q values ($q = 0.1$ and $q = 0.5$) yielded higher accuracy across most methods, whereas larger q values ($q \geq 1000$) resulted in stable but reduced accuracy. Moreover, among the tested methods, the $\mathfrak{C}_{\mathrm{m}}^{(F_1, F_2)}$-integral and $\mathfrak{C}_{\mathrm{m\,N\text{-}AVG}}^{F}$-integral achieved the highest accuracy, demonstrating their suitability for classification tasks under varying conditions. These findings emphasize the importance of effectively tuning the q parameter for optimizing classification performance.

Despite contributing to a better understanding of the interplay between the q exponent and Choquet-based integrals, offering practical insights for improving FRBCS, several avenues for future research remain open in this work. First, one may explore adaptive mechanisms to adjust the q parameter based on dataset characteristics to dynamically enhance the model robustness. In addition, investigating the application of these methods in other types of datasets and problem domains, such as regression or clustering, could expand their utility. Finally, integrating the PM with hybrid models combining other generalizations or machine learning techniques may be a promising direction for further improvements.

Acknowledgments. This study was partially funded by: CAPES, FAPERGS (24/2551 -0001396-2, 24/2551-0000723-7, 23/2551-0001865-9), CNPq (304118/2023-0, 407206/ 2023-0), FAPERGS/CNPq (23/ 2551-0000126-8), FAPESP (2022/09136-1), MCIN/ AEI/ 10.13039/5010 0011033/FEDER, UE (PID2022-13 6627NB-I00).

Disclosure of Interests. The authors have no competing interests to declare that are relevant to the content of this article.

References

1. Alcalá-Fdez, J., Alcala, R., Herrera, F.: A fuzzy association rule-based classification model for high-dimensional problems with genetic rule selection and lateral tuning. IEEE Trans. Fuzzy Syst. **19**(5), 857–872 (2011)
2. Alcalá-Fdez, J., et al.: Keel: a software tool to assess evolutionary algorithms for data mining problems. Soft. Comput. **13**(3), 307–318 (2009)
3. Bardozzo, F., et al.: Sugeno integral generalization applied to improve adaptive image binarization. Inf. Fusion **68**, 37–45 (2021). https://doi.org/10.1016/j.inffus. 2020.10.020
4. Barrenechea, E., Bustince, H., Fernandez, J., Paternain, D., Sanz, J.A.: Using the Choquet integral in the fuzzy reasoning method of fuzzy rule-based classification systems. Axioms **2**(2), 208–223 (2013)
5. Beliakov, G., Pradera, A., Calvo, T.: Aggregation Functions: A Guide for Practitioners. Springer, Berlin (2007)

6. Boczek, M., Jin, L., Kaluszka, M.: The interval-valued Choquet-Sugeno-like operator as a tool for aggregation of interval-valued functions. Fuzzy Sets Syst. **448**, 35–48 (2022). https://doi.org/10.1016/j.fss.2022.04.002
7. Boczek, M., Hutník, O., Kaluszka, M.: Choquet-Sugeno-like operator based on relation and conditional aggregation operators. Inf. Sci. **582**, 1–21 (2022). https://doi.org/10.1016/j.ins.2021.07.063
8. Bustince, H., Barrenechea, E., Pagola, M.: Relationship between restricted dissimilarity functions, restricted equivalence functions and normal en-functions: image thresholding invariant. Pattern Recogn. Lett. **29**(4), 525–536 (2008). https://doi.org/10.1016/j.patrec.2007.11.007
9. Bustince, H., et al.: d-Choquet integrals: Choquet integrals based on dissimilarities. Fuzzy Sets Syst. (2020). https://doi.org/10.1016/j.fss.2020.03.019
10. Bustince, H., et al.: On some classes of directionally monotone functions. Fuzzy Sets Syst. **386**, 161–178 (2020). https://doi.org/10.1016/j.fss.2019.01.024
11. Choquet, G.: Theory of capacities. Annales l'Inst. Fourier **5**, 131–295 (1953–1954)
12. Cordón, O., del Jesus, M.J., Herrera, F.: A proposal on reasoning methods in fuzzy rule-based classification systems. Int. J. Appl. e Reas. **20**(1), 21–45 (1999)
13. Cordón, O., del Jesus, M.J., Herrera, F.: Analyzing the reasoning mechanisms in fuzzy rule based classification systems. Math. Soft Comp. **5**(2–3), 321–332 (1998)
14. Dimuro, G.P., Bedregal, B., Bustince, H., Fernandez, J., Lucca, G., Mesiar, R.: New results on pre-aggregation functions. In: Uncertainty Modelling in Knowledge Engineering and Decision Making, Proceedings of 12th International FLINS Conference (FLINS 2016), Series on Computer Engineering and Information Science, vol. 10, pp. 213–219. World Scientific, Singapura (2016)
15. Dimuro, G.P., et al.: The state-of-art of the generalizations of the choquet integral: from aggregation and pre-aggregation to ordered directionally monotone functions. Inf. Fusion **57**, 27–43 (2020). https://doi.org/10.1016/j.inffus.2019.10.005
16. Dimuro, G.P., Lucca, G., Bedregal, B., Mesiar, R., Sanz, J.A., Lin, C.T., Bustince, H.: Generalized CF1F2-integrals: from choquet-like aggregation to ordered directionally monotone functions. Fuzzy Sets Syst. **378**, 44–67 (2020). https://doi.org/10.1016/j.fss.2019.01.009
17. Duda, R.O., Hart, P.E., Stork, D.G.: Pattern Classification. Wiley (2000)
18. Ferrero-Jaurrieta, M., et al.: VCI-LSTM: vector choquet integral-based long short-term memory. IEEE Trans. Fuzzy Syst. **31**(7), 2238–2250 (2023). https://doi.org/10.1109/TFUZZ.2022.3222035
19. Fumanal-Idocin, J., et al.: A generalization of the sugeno integral to aggregate interval-valued data: an application to brain computer interface and social network analysis. Fuzzy Sets Syst. **451**, 320–341 (2022). https://doi.org/10.1016/j.fss.2022.10.003
20. Horanská, Ľ, Šipošová, A.: A generalization of the discrete choquet and sugeno integrals based on a fusion function. Inf. Sci. **451–452**, 83–99 (2018). https://doi.org/10.1016/j.ins.2018.03.059
21. Ishibuchi, H., Nakashima, T.: Effect of rule weights in fuzzy rule-based classification systems. IEEE Trans. Fuzzy Syst. **9**(4), 506–515 (2001)
22. Ishibuchi, H., Nakashima, T., Nii, M.: Classification and Modeling with Linguistic Information Granules. Advanced Approaches to Linguistic Data Mining. Advanced Information Processing. Springer, Berlin (2005)
23. Lucca, G., Dimuro, G.P., Fernandez, J., Bustince, H., Bedregal, B., Sanz, J.A.: Improving the performance of fuzzy rule-based classification systems based on a nonaveraging generalization of CC-integrals named $C_{F_1 F_2}$-integrals. IEEE Trans. Fuzzy Syst. **27**(1), 124–134 (2019). https://doi.org/10.1109/TFUZZ.2018.2871000

24. Lucca, G., et al.: Pre-aggregation functions: construction and an application. IEEE Trans. Fuzzy Syst. **24**(2), 260–272 (2016)
25. Lucca, G., Sanz, J.A., Dimuro, G.P., Borges, E.N., Santos, H., Bustince, H.: Analyzing the performance of different fuzzy measures with generalizations of the choquet integral in classification problems. In: 2019 IEEE International Conference on Fuzzy Systems (FUZZ-IEEE), pp. 1–6 (2019). https://doi.org/10.1109/FUZZ-IEEE.2019.8858815
26. Lucca, G., Sanz, J., Dimuro, G.P., Bedregal, B., Bustince, H.: Analyzing the behavior of aggregation and pre-aggregation functions in fuzzy rule-based classification systems with data complexity measures. In: Kacprzyk, J., Szmidt, E., Zadrożny, S., Atanassov, K.T., Krawczak, M. (eds.) IWIFSGN/EUSFLAT -2017. AISC, vol. 642, pp. 443–455. Springer, Cham (2018). https://doi.org/10.1007/978-3-319-66824-6_39
27. Lucca, G., et al.: CC-integrals: choquet-like copula-based aggregation functions and its application in fuzzy rule-based classification systems. Knowl.-Based Syst. **119**, 32–43 (2017)
28. Lucca, G., Sanz, J.A., Dimuro, G.P., Bedregal, B., Bustince, H., Mesiar, R.: CF-integrals: a new family of pre-aggregation functions with application to fuzzy rule-based classification systems. Inf. Sci. **435**, 94–110 (2018). https://doi.org/10.1016/j.ins.2017.12.029
29. Mamdani, E.H.: Application of fuzzy algorithms for control of simple dynamic plant. Proc. Inst. Electr. Eng. **121**(12), 1585–1588 (1974)
30. Mesiar, R., Kolesárová, A., Bustince, H., Dimuro, G., Bedregal, B.: Fusion functions based discrete Choquet-like integrals. Eur. J. Oper. Res. **252**(2), 601–609 (2016). https://doi.org/10.1016/j.ejor.2016.01.027
31. Murofushi, T., Sugeno, M., Machida, M.: Non-monotonic fuzzy measures and the Choquet integral. Fuzzy Sets Syst. **64**(1), 73–86 (1994)
32. Sanz, J., Fernández, A., Bustince, H., Herrera, F.: IVTURS: a linguistic fuzzy rule-based classification system based on a new interval-valued fuzzy reasoning method with tuning and rule selection. IEEE Trans. Fuzzy Syst. **21**(3), 399–411 (2013)
33. Sartori, J., et al.: d-CC integrals: generalizing CC-integrals by restricted dissimilarity functions with applications to fuzzy-rule based systems. In: Naldi, M.C., Bianchi, R. (eds.) Intell. Syst., pp. 243–258. Springer, Cham (2023)
34. Sugeno, M.: Theory of fuzzy integrals and its applications. Ph.D. thesis, Tokyo Institute of Technology, Tokyo (1974)
35. Takagi, T., Sugeno, M.: Fuzzy identification of systems and its applications to modeling and control. IEEE Trans. Syst. Man Cyb. **SMC-15**(1), 116–132 (1985)
36. Tung, A.K.H.: Rule-based classification. In: Encyclopedia of Database Systems, pp. 2459–2462. Springer, Boston (2009)
37. Wieczynski, J., et al.: d-XC integrals: on the generalization of the expanded form of the choquet integral by restricted dissimilarity functions and their applications. IEEE Trans. Fuzzy Syst. **30**(12), 5376–5389 (2022). https://doi.org/10.1109/TFUZZ.2022.3176916
38. Wieczynski, J., et al.: dc_F-integrals: generalizing C_F-integrals by means of restricted dissimilarity functions. IEEE Trans. Fuzzy Syst. **31**(1), 160–173 (2023). https://doi.org/10.1109/TFUZZ.2022.3184054
39. Zadeh, L.A.: Fuzzy sets. Inf. Control **8**(3), 338–353 (1965)

Measuring Representativeness Through Coverage Degrees and Indexes

Inmaculada Gutiérrez[1]([✉]) [iD], J. Tinguaro Rodríguez[2] [iD], Xabier González[3] [iD], Daniel Gómez[1] [iD], Javier Montero[2] [iD], and Humberto Bustince[3] [iD]

[1] Faculty of Statistical Studies, Complutense University of Madrid, Madrid, Spain
{inmaguti,dagomez}@ucm.es
[2] Faculty of Mathematics, Complutense University of Madrid, Madrid, Spain
{jtrodrig,monty}@ucm.es
[3] Department of Statistics, Computer Science and Mathematics,
Universidad Pública de Navarra, Pamplona, Spain
{xabier.gonzalez,bustince}@unavarra.es

Abstract. This paper first introduces the notion of representativeness system (RS) in order to capture the essential aspects of different systems in which a set of sources or representatives are intended to represent or provide a service to a given set of objects. The paper focuses on formally elaborating the notion of coverage indexes as mathematical tools to study and assess the quality of representativeness systems, defining different subfamilies of this type of indexes as well as providing a construction method for them. The practicality of these indexes is briefly illustrated in the context of cluster quality assessment, highlighting some promising features.

Keywords: Coverage · Representativeness Systems · Aggregation Functions

1 Introduction

Representativeness constitutes a key notion when dealing with systems in which a certain set of entities are intended to act as representatives of a given population of objects or individuals. We will refer to these systems as *representativeness systems* (RS). For instance, representativeness can be understood in terms of the feasibility of the objects to be identified (or even identify themselves) with the available representatives, either due to the ability of the representative to be seen as a model of the objects, because of their similarity regarding a set of relevant aspects, or due to their common interests or aims. Alternatively, representatives can also be seen as entities that either address the needs of the objects or potentially provide a service that the objects may eventually require or benefit from.

Here, following the seminal ideas in [1], we deal with this concept of representativeness from the perspective that the extent to which an object is represented

M. Baczyński et al. (Eds.): EUSFLAT 2025, LNCS 15883, pp. 282–293, 2025.
https://doi.org/10.1007/978-3-031-97225-6_23

by a representative can be identified with the *coverage* level of the former by the latter. In this way, a natural modeling of such representativeness could consider it as a gradable property, which can be assessed in terms of coverage levels or degrees, in the sense that, depending on how they are related, a given representative might only partially represent an object or cover its needs, e.g. because the former is not fully able to effectively provide the latter with the required service, or because a maximum quality service can not always be provided.

This abstract concept of representativeness systems can be applied to a wide range of specific contexts. For instance, in an election, voters usually feel or perceive themselves as being represented to varying degrees by different candidates, based on the candidates' expressed political ideologies, the adequacy of their election manifestos to the voters' needs, the trust they inspire, and so forth. The extent to which voters feel adequately represented by any candidate is, of course, a key element in assessing the quality of the political system in the district under consideration. Similarly, when purchasing a house, buyers often perceive different properties as fulfilling their needs to varying degrees, based on factors such as the property's location, its condition, its size and features, and the asking price. A buyer may prioritize a well-maintained home in a desirable neighborhood, while another might prioritize affordability or a larger living space, even if it means compromising on certain amenities or location. The degree to which each property represents the different characteristics and their alignment with the buyer's preferences ultimately influences their decision. Likewise, when considering an individual residing in a specific city location or experiencing a particular medical condition, the available hospitals or medical centers in the city may offer diverse levels of coverage for the individual's medical needs, depending on factors such as the location of the centers or their medical specialization. Similar considerations can be applied to media outlets and news across different topics, telecommunications antennas and their coverage of devices, students and educational facilities, consumers and suppliers of a certain commodity, citizens and administrative centers, and so forth.

Despite the wide conceptual applicability of RSs, establishing a single formal definition that determines coverage degrees across all possible contexts may prove challenging—or even undesirable. Rather, it seems natural for the definition of such degrees to vary depending on the specific context and the relevant aspects of the relationship between the representatives and the objects to be covered. For example, in certain contexts, degrees may be derived as a function of the similarity or distance between them, while in other situations, they may depend on the matching between the offered and required services, the presence of connections between the entities, and so on.

But once an operational definition is established for a particular context, the information provided by coverage degrees can be highly valuable for assessing different quality aspects of the analyzed RSs, such as whether a satisfactory level of coverage by the considered representatives is attained for most objects, the potential redundancy of certain representatives as well as their relevance (see [1, 5]), the existence of uncovered or inadequately covered objects, the assignment of objects to representatives when partitioning is necessary, evaluating the relative quality of existing partitions assigning objects to representatives, and other.

Clearly, information aggregation (or fusion), understood as the application of mathematical or computational procedures to combine and reduce the available information into meaningful indexes reflecting diverse dimensions of the considered system (see [1,3,4,7,9]), must be an important tool in exploiting the coverage information for previous purposes. Roughly speaking, in the context of RSs, any such aggregation can be seen as a procedure that takes the coverage information as input and returns a single value summarizing it. This summary may exhibit different meanings (i.e., capture diverse quality dimensions) depending on the specific features of such an aggregation procedure.

In this paper, we first provide a formal definition of RSs. Next, we focus on evaluating the representation of the analyzed objects within it. To do so, we also propose a formal definition of a *coverage index* as a function with several desirable properties that form the basis for further development of quality indexes for RSs. These properties must encompass some intuitive ideas, focusing particularly on the fairness or symmetry of the aggregation, in order to guarantee that the evaluated RS remains invariant under permutations of objects. Following the intuitive idea that, in general, a good coverage situation is one where, globally, the majority of objects are reasonably covered by at least one source, we work on characterizing a quality index that captures this global perspective. This leads to the so-called global coverage index (GCI). We place special emphasis on its characterization in terms of function composition. In this context, grouping functions [2] allow us to model a disjunctive behavior, approaching the ideal situation where every object is fully covered by one representative.

The remainder of the paper is organized as follows. In Sect. 2, some formal concepts related to RS and coverage indexes are introduced, and we also analyze their desirable properties. Then, Sect. 3 formally describes the construction of global coverage indexes. Some useful features of the proposed indexes are illustrated in the context of cluster analysis in Sect. 4. Some conclusions are finally exposed in Sect. 5 together with directions for further research.

2   From Representativeness Systems to Global Coverage Indexes

This section is devoted to present a first formal approach to the notions of representativeness systems and coverage indexes.

2.1   Representativeness Systems

Let $X = \{x_1, \ldots, x_N\}$ denote a set of objects and $S = \{s_1, \ldots, s_K\}$ denote a set of representatives or coverage sources. Given $i \in \{1, \ldots, N\}$ and $j \in \{1, \ldots, K\}$, let $\mathbf{U} = (u_{ij})$ be an $N \times K$ matrix where $u_{ij} \in I = [0,1]$ represents the level or degree of coverage of object $x_i \in X$ by representative $s_j \in S$. The upper bound of I, 1, represents the maximum level of representativeness, i.e., total coverage of an object by a representative. Conversely, the lower bound, 0, represents the minimum level, corresponding to a total lack of coverage. Other values within $[0,1]$ indicate intermediate levels of representativeness. However, the choice of the interval $[0,1]$ is not essential, as it is possible to use a general interval $I = [a,b]$ instead. The matrix $\mathbf{U} = (u_{ij})_{N \times K}$ is referred to as the '*coverage matrix*'. If $\mathcal{U}_{N,K}(I)$ denotes the set of all $N \times K$ matrices with entries $u_{ij} \in I$, then it clearly holds that $\mathbf{U} \in \mathcal{U}_{N,K}(I)$. A representativeness system (RS) is thus defined as the combination of the three elements, $X, S, \mathbf{U}$, i.e., as the triplet $\mathcal{RS} = (X, S, \mathbf{U})$.

2.2   Coverage Indexes

To evaluate how well the objects in X are represented by the sources in S from the information in the coverage matrix $\mathbf{U}$, the development of a general notion of a quality index for an RS is explored. Any quality index F should depart from the system's coverage matrix $\mathbf{U}$ and provide a single quality degree $F(\mathbf{U}) \in I$ as the system's quality assessment. As a starting point, perhaps the most obvious and general approach is to regard these coverage indexes as aggregation functions. (see e.g. [9]).

Definition 1 (Coverage index).   *Let* $\mathbf{0}_{N \times K}, \mathbf{1}_{N \times K} \in \mathcal{U}_{N,K}(I)$ *respectively denote matrices with all entries equal to 0 or 1. A coverage index is an aggregation function on* $\mathcal{U}_{N,K}(I)$, *i.e. a function* $F : \mathcal{U}_{N,K}(I) \to I$ *fulfilling:*

(A1) *F is non-decreasing in each matrix entry.*
(A2) *F satisfies the boundary condition $F(\mathbf{0}_{N \times K}) = 0$.*
(A3) *F satisfies the boundary condition $F(\mathbf{1}_{N \times K}) = 1$.*

Although a specific characterization has been provided, one might consider any aggregation defined in $[0,1]^{N \times K}$.

Conditions $(A1) - (A3)$ provide the minimum basis for developing sound quality indexes for an RS: the quality of an RS should be maximum (resp. minimum) when all objects are represented in maximum (minimum) degree by all representatives; and the system quality should be a nondecreasing function of coverage levels. However, the generality of Definition 1 allows reflecting quite different notions of quality, and particularly admits inequitable or *unfair* quality measures, meaning indexes that do not consider objects and/or sources as indistinguishable. For example, $F(\mathbf{U}) = u_{11}$ verifies Definition 1 and associates quality with the coverage of x_1 by s_1, neglecting the representation status of all other objects and the influence of other sources. Equitable or *fair* indexes thus need to verify an additional symmetry condition.

Definition 2 (Fair coverage index).   *A fair coverage index is a coverage index F that satisfies the condition*

(A4) *$F(\mathbf{U}) = F(\sigma_1(\mathbf{u}_{\sigma(1)}), \ldots, \sigma_N(\mathbf{u}_{\sigma(N)}))$ for any $\mathbf{U} \in \mathcal{U}_{N,K}(I)$, where $\mathbf{u}_i$ denotes the i-th row of $\mathbf{U}$, and σ_i respectively denotes permutations of K and N elements, $i = 1, \ldots, N$.*

Notice that condition $(A4)$ guarantees that any fair index is invariant under permutations of the objects, as well as under permutations of any object's coverage degrees. Note also that $(A4)$ is a more strict symmetry condition than general symmetry of aggregation operators.

Quite different conceptions of an RS's quality can still be modeled under Definition 2, as the next example illustrates.

Example 1. The operator $F_1(U) = \max_{i,j}(u_{ij})$ is symmetric in a general sense, and thus it particularly verifies $(A4)$. It models quality in terms of how well represented is the object that is best covered by any representative in S. A high value of F_1 implies that at least one object is highly covered by at least one representative, whereas a low value indicates that, in general, the coverage of all objects by all representatives is low. On the other extreme, $F_2(U) = \min_{i,j}(u_{ij})$ also models quality in a totally symmetrical way, but now focusing on the lowest representation level reached by any object from any representative: a low value of F_2 implies that at least one object is poorly represented by at least one representative, whereas a high value indicates that all objects are, in some sense, well represented by all representatives. However, the operator $F_3(U) = \min_i(\max_j(u_{ij}))$ also verifies $(A4)$, but is not a symmetric aggregation in the general sense. It associates quality to a situation in which every object has at least one representative that covers it adequately. Thus, it allows detecting objects that are poorly represented by all representatives. Finally, $F_4(U) = \frac{1}{N}\sum_i \max_j(u_{ij})$ measures how well are the objects covered, in average, when considering the best representative for each of them. For this reason, this index can be understood as a *global* quality metric for an RS.

2.3   Global Coverage Indexes

Now we focus on studying coverage indexes expressing the *global* conception of quality shown by operator F_4 in Example 1. The essence of this global quality notion, to be captured by *global coverage index*, (GCI) is that most objects have to be reasonably well covered by at least one source. For instance, when determining the location of service points, a global quality index should assess an RS as *good* if it ensures feasible access to the service for most objects. On the contrary, if most objects fail to be adequately covered by at least one representative, the quality of the system should be assessed as *low*.

Definition 3 (Global coverage index (GCI)).   *A mapping* GCI : $\mathcal{U}_{N,K}(I) \rightarrow I$ *is a global coverage index (GCI) if it is a continuous fair coverage index, and for any* $\mathbf{U} \in \mathcal{U}_{N,K}(I)$ *it also verifies:*

    $(GCI1)$ $GCI(\mathbf{U}) = 0$ *if and only if* $\max_j u_{ij} = 0$ $\forall i = 1, \ldots, N$.
    $(GCI2)$ $GCI(\mathbf{U}) = 1$ *if and only if* $\max_j u_{ij} = 1$ $\forall i = 1, \ldots, N$.

Therefore, any GCI is particularly a fair coverage index satisfying conditions $(A1) - (A4)$, plus continuity (to prevent abrupt changes in the index values) and properties $(GCI1)$ and $(GCI2)$, which extend the boundary conditions

$(A2)$ and $(A3)$ to ensure GCIs exhibit the global behavior previously discussed. Specifically, $(GCI1)$ entails that **i)** $GCI(\mathbf{0}_{N\times K}) = 0$, i.e., it holds $(A2)$; and **ii)** $GCI(\mathbf{U}) = 0$ only when $\mathbf{U} = \mathbf{0}_{N\times K}$. Thus, the minimum quality valuation a is *reserved* exclusively for the worst-case input scenario where no representative manages to cover any of the objects. This aligns with the goal of assigning low quality index values only when most objects are inadequately covered by *all* representatives. Similarly, $(CGI2)$ entails that **i)** $GCI(\mathbf{U})$ must be equal to 1 when $\mathbf{U}$ contains a value 1 in each row (thus $(A3)$ has to hold), meaning that all objects have at least one representative fully covering them; and **ii)** $GCI(\mathbf{U}) = 1$ only in that case, i.e. the maximum quality valuation 1 is *reserved* for situations where each object is fully covered by at least one representative. This aligns with the objective of attaining high quality index values only when most objects are sufficiently covered by at least one representative.

Note that operator F_4 introduced above is indeed a GCI, while operators F_1-F_3 are not GCIs, as they do not express quality in the exposed global sense.

3   Construction of GCIs

Once the intuitive concept behind a GCI has been outlined, we analyze the construction of GCIs through compositions. Noting that operators F_1–F_4 can be expressed as a composition $M \circ \mathbf{G}$ of two functions. The first one is a vector function $\mathbf{G} : \mathcal{U}_{N,K}(I) \rightarrow I^N$ with all its components being equal, i.e. such that for any $\mathbf{U} \in \mathcal{U}_{N,K}(I)$ it is $\mathbf{G}(\mathbf{U}) = (G(\mathbf{u}_1), \dots, G(\mathbf{u}_N)) \in I^N$, where $G : I^K \rightarrow I$. The second function, $M : I^N \rightarrow I$, produces the final aggregated value $M(G(\mathbf{u}_1), \dots, G(\mathbf{u}_N)) = (M \circ \mathbf{G})(\mathbf{U}) \in I$. For example, $F_1(U) = \max_{i,j}(u_{ij}) = \max_i(\max_j(u_{ij}))$, i.e. in this case $G = \max$ and $M = \max$, while for F_4 it is $G = \max$ and $M = \text{mean}$. We then focus on obtaining sufficient conditions on the functions G and M to ensure that the composition $M \circ \mathbf{G}$ captures the intended meaning of a GCI as a quality metric that measures the extent to which *most* objects in X are *adequately* covered by the set of representatives S.

Since a situation in which each object is totally covered by one representative is regarded in terms of quality as an ideal one, independently of the coverage offered by the rest of representatives, it seems quite evident that a kind of disjunctive behavior has to be imposed on the function G [1]. That is, if a row $\mathbf{u}_i$ contains an element equal to the maximum coverage degree 1, then $G(\mathbf{u}_i)$ should be equal to 1 independently of the degrees observed in the remaining positions. Moreover, the maximum valuation $G(\mathbf{u}_i) = 1$ should be reserved for just such situations. On the other hand, the minimum valuation $G(\mathbf{u}_i) = 0$ should only happen when all elements of $\mathbf{u}_i$ are equal to 0. As said, all these considerations points to the function G needing to exhibit a disjunctive character.

This kind of disjunctive behavior can be conveniently captured by grouping functions [2]. Let us recall that a K-dimensional grouping function [7] is any mapping $G : I^K \rightarrow I$ that is $(G1)$ non-decreasing, $(G2)$ continuous, $(G3)$ symmetric, and verifies the boundary conditions $(G4)$ $G(\mathbf{u}) = 0$ if and only if $\mathbf{u} = \mathbf{0}_K$, and $(G5)$ $G(\mathbf{u}) = 1$ if and only if $\mathbf{u} = \mathbf{1}_k$, for any $\mathbf{u} \in I^K$ and where $\mathbf{0}_K$ (resp.

$\mathbf{1}_K$) denotes a K-dimensional vector with all its elements equal to 0 (resp. 1). Therefore, through this notion, the meaning of an object $x_i \in X$ being *adequately* covered by the representatives in S can be identified with a maximum or relatively high value of $G(\mathbf{u}_i)$, where G is a K-dimensional grouping function. Let us refer to the vector $\mathbf{G}(\mathbf{U}) = (G(\mathbf{u}_1), \ldots, G(\mathbf{u}_N))$ as the adequacy vector.

Then, once this adequacy vector is available, the function $M : I^N \to I$ has to reflect whether *most* objects are being adequately covered by the representatives in S. The intuition derived from the operators F_2 and F_3 described above suggests that the function M should lie between the minimum and the maximum. This is typically associated to the notion of *averaging* functions (see e.g. [7,9]). Indeed, it seems natural to consider a kind of average to capture the intended quality meaning of *most* objects being well represented, as it would tend to reflect the adequacy degree of the average object, i.e., that with a central or intermediate value in the adequacy vector provided by $\mathbf{G}$.

Moreover, it seems also convenient to consider mappings M that are compensative, in the sense of balancing all the available information in the vector $\mathbf{G}(\mathbf{U})$. This would leave out non-compensative measures of central tendency such as the median, which would for instance assess the quality of the system to be maximum if just half of the objects are totally covered, even when the remaining half is not covered at all. The necessary aspects of this compensativeness for the purpose of obtaining GCI functions through the combination $M \circ \mathbf{G}$ can be captured by the following conditions:

($M1$) $M(\mathbf{v}) = 0$ if and only if $\mathbf{v} = \mathbf{0}_N$.
($M2$) $M(\mathbf{v}) = 1$ if and only if $\mathbf{v} = \mathbf{1}_N$.

Additionally, a continuous function M verifying conditions ($M1$) and ($M2$) can exhibit neither a purely disjunctive nor a purely conjunctive behavior, and thus it has to be averaging at least to some extent. Of course, for the reasons before discussed, M has also to exhibit a sound behavior in terms of continuity, symmetry and monotonicity. The following result is then straightforward.

Proposition 1. *Let $G : I^K \to I$ be a K-dimensional grouping function, and let $M : I^N \to I$ be a function. The mapping $GCI : \mathcal{U}_{N,K}(I) \to I$ defined as $GCI(\mathbf{U}) = M(G(\mathbf{u}_1), \ldots, G(\mathbf{u}_N))$ is a global coverage index if and only if M is continuous, non-decreasing, symmetric, and verifies conditions ($M1$) and ($M2$).*

Example 2. Let us briefly consider some examples resulting from different choices of G and M. Firstly, as already mentioned, the operator F_4 is a GCI arising from the composition of $G = \max$ and $M = mean$. Regardless of the choice of G, if $M = median$ then $M \circ \mathbf{G}$ is not generally a GCI, as for the median of N values in I to be 0 it is only needed that at least $\lfloor N/2 + 1 \rfloor$ of such values are equal to 0, thus failing to verify condition ($GC1$). It is not difficult to see that in general this is also the case for any function $M = P_p$, where P_p denotes the p-th sample percentile operator. Similarly, if M is a weighted mean, the composition $M \circ \mathbf{G}$ generally fails to verify the symmetry condition ($A4$) for general weighting vectors $\mathbf{w} = (w_1, \ldots, w_N)$. Moreover, it is possible to obtain

GCIs such that *all* the elements of the row vectors $\mathbf{u}_i$ have actual influence on the index, rather than only the element u_{ih} such that $h = \arg \max \mathbf{u}_i$, which reflects the object's coverage degree by its best representative, as it is implicitly imposed when $G = \max$ is chosen. For instance, it can be seen that the combination $M \circ \mathbf{G}$ given by $M = mean$ and the Einstein sum operator $G(\mathbf{u}_i) = 1 - \frac{\Pi_j (1-u_{ij})}{\Pi_j u_{ij}}$ is a GCI providing that kind of behavior. Notice that for this G it holds that $G(\mathbf{u}) \geq max(\mathbf{u})$ for any $\mathbf{u} \in I^K$, and thus $G(\mathbf{u}_i)$ may assess the coverage level of $x_i \in X$ by the whole set of representatives S to be greater than its coverage degree by its best representative. This can be understood as modeling a kind of collaborative coverage by the different representatives, in the sense of the coverage effect of the different representatives adding up in order to provide the object with a level of representativeness better than those individually permitted by each representative.

4   Coverage Indexes in the Context of Cluster Analysis

In this section we briefly illustrate the potential usefulness of coverage indexes for cluster validation analysis. To this aim, we restrict to the context of prototype-based clustering, in which a centroid s_j can be associated with each cluster C_j in a given partition $\mathcal{P} = \{C_1, \ldots, C_K\}$ of a set of objects (i.e. data) X. In this preliminary approach, representativeness or coverage of an object $x_i \in X$ by cluster $C_j \in \mathcal{P}$ is identified with its closeness to the corresponding centroid s_j. Then, a possible operative definition of coverage degrees is given as follows:

$$u_{ij} = e^{-\frac{r}{s} d(x_i, s_j)} \tag{1}$$

where $d(x_i, s_j)$ denotes the distance from object x_i to s_j, the centroid of the j-th cluster, $r > 0$ is an amplitude parameter and $s > 0$ is an scale parameter. The coverage matrix is then formed as $\mathbf{U} = (u_{ij})_{N \times K}$. Note that the right-hand side of Eq. 1 is related to the mountain function introduced in [10] for density estimation purposes when selecting centroids from a grid of candidate points.

As a consequence of the exponentially decaying behavior modeled in Eq. 1, u_{ij} fades out quite quickly as x_i moves further from s_j. This is convenient to reflect that objects in relatively well-separated clusters should be scarcely covered by the other clusters' representatives. Parameters r and s provide flexibility in modulating that exponential behavior. Specifically, the role of the scale parameter s is to set the unit of measure in terms of the distance d; the amplitude parameter r then allows to set the desired coverage degree $u_{ij} = e^{-r}$ to be attained for such a unit dissimilarity $d'(x_i, s_j) = s$. Ideally, the ratio r/s should be low enough to guarantee that all objects in a cluster are adequately covered by its representative, but also great enough to avoid redundant coverage of any cluster's objects by other clusters' representatives. Notice also that with these assumptions coverage indexes, and particularly GCIs, can be understood as a particular, new kind of cluster cohesion (or compacity) measure.

We next provide some examples illustrating how coverage indexes can be useful in capturing different aspects of a partition quality.

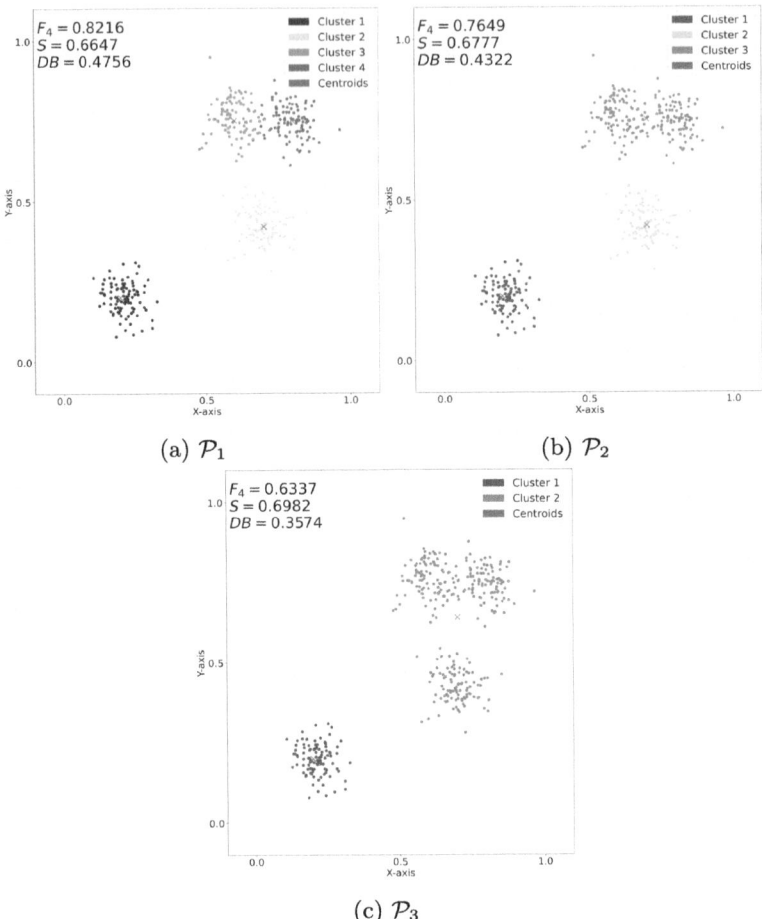

Fig. 1. Synthetic data and indexes values for Example 3.

Example 3. Figure 1 shows a 2-D synthetic dataset featuring 4 relatively non-overlapped clusters. In Fig. 1a, a partition $\mathcal{P}_1$ is shown that correctly captures these 4 groups, while in Fig. 1b former clusters 3 and 4 are merged into a single cluster (partition $\mathcal{P}_2$), which in Fig. 1c also merges with the former cluster 2 (partition $\mathcal{P}_3$). Clearly, $\mathcal{P}_1$ is the partition with the highest quality, while $\mathcal{P}_3$ is that with the lowest. We then apply Eq. 1 using the Euclidean distance, $r = 2\ln 10$ and $s = \sqrt{2}$. This leads to the coverage matrices $\mathbf{U}_1, \mathbf{U}_2$ and $\mathbf{U}_3$, over which we apply the GCI F_4 providing the coverage quality indexes $F_4(\mathbf{U}_1) = 0.8216$, $F_4(\mathbf{U}_2) = 0.7649$ and $F_4(\mathbf{U}_3) = 0.6337$. These values correctly ranks the correlative quality of the three partitions. However, this correct ranking is not attained by using two widely-extended internal clustering validity indexes, namely the Silhouette (S) coefficient [11] and the Davies-Bouldin (DB) index [6]: both indexes reverse the ranking, declaring $\mathcal{P}_3$ as the highest quality partition

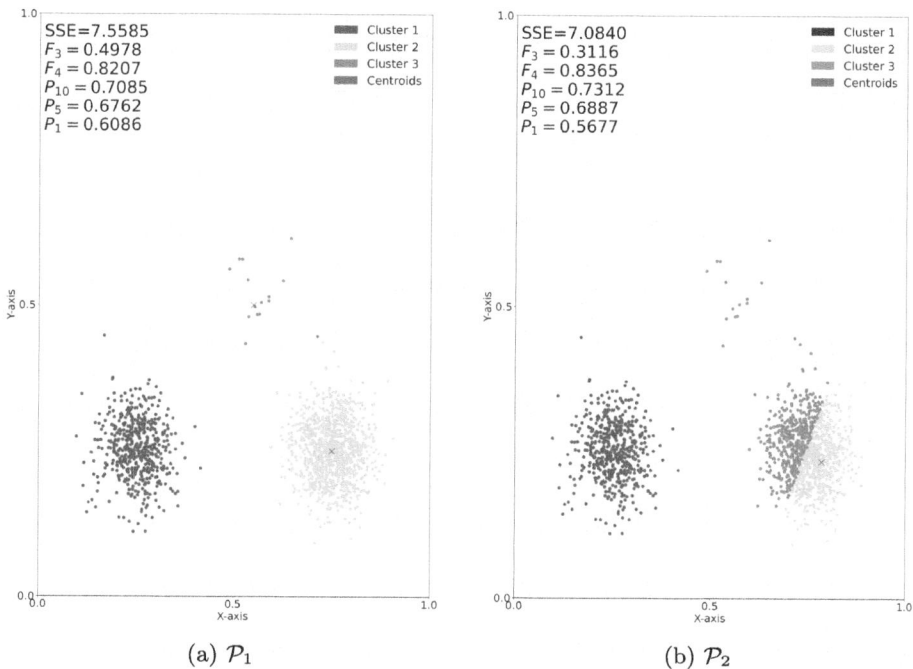

Fig. 2. Synthetic data and indexes values for Example 4.

and $\mathcal{P}_1$ as the lowest quality one (recall that greater, resp. lower, values of Silhouette, resp. Davies-Bouldin, are supposed to identify better partitions). This shows that coverage indexes, even when only expressing cluster cohesion, can provide a more accurate estimation of a partition's quality than some well-known cluster validation indexes that also incorporate notions of cluster separation.

Example 4. Figure 2 now depicts 3 well-separated synthetic clusters, which are however quite unbalanced regarding their number of elements: it is $|C_1| = 500, |C_2| = 1010, |C_3| = 15$ (see Fig. 2a). Due to this unbalanced size, prototype-based clustering algorithms such as K-Means, using a sum of squared errors (SSE) or inertia as objective function, typically present a strong bias towards ignoring the smallest cluster C_3 and merging it with the biggest one, C_2, which is also usually separated into two clusters. Figure 2a presents the partition $\mathcal{P}_1$ obtained from the correct cluster centers, while Fig. 2b shows the partition $\mathcal{P}_2$ provided by K-Means when applied with $K = 3$ and using 10 K-Means++ initializations. The corresponding values of inertia as well as of several fair coverage indexes (FCIs) using $G = \max$ are presented in each subfigure. Notice that F_4 (using $M = mean$) and FCIs using percentiles $M = P_p$ with $p \geq 5$ all declare $\mathcal{P}_2$ to represent a higher quality partition than $\mathcal{P}_1$. On the other hand, F_3 (using $M = \min$) and P_1 instead assess $\mathcal{P}_1$ as the highest-quality partition. This shows that providing a greater attention to the least covered objects can be important in analyzing the quality of a partition, and that some FCIs provide a significant tool to this aim due to their capability to modulate this attention.

5   Conclusions and Further Research

Representativeness systems (RSs) are a basic tool to capture the essential aspects of diverse real-world systems in which a set of objects receive a service from a set of sources or representatives delivering it. Coverage Indexes (CIs), and particularly Global Coverage Indexes (GCIs), then offer a flexible framework for measuring the quality of RSs through different criteria or perspectives, providing room for a wide range of alternative metrics. Moreover, such indexes can be easily constructed by combining two meaningful operations, i.e. adequacy computation and aggregation. These features have been illustrated in the context of cluster analysis, suggesting the practicality of these indexes to address some problems associated to cluster quality assessment. Future work will be devoted to a more-in-depth study of the mathematical properties of the different families of CIs, as well as to develop their application in different fields, such as social network analysis [8,14]. Another line of research will touch on the usage of OWA [12] operators, particularly MEOWA [13], for fulfilling the averaging role of function M in Proposition 1.

Acknowledgements. This research has been partially funded by the Government of Spain, Grant Plan Nacional de I+D+i, PID2021-122905NB-C21 and the PID2022-136627NB-I00, supported by MCIN/AEI/10.13039/501100011033/FEDER.

References

1. Amo, A., Montero, J., Biging, G., Cutello, V.: Fuzzy classification systems. Eur. J. Oper. Res. **156**(2), 495–507 (2004)
2. Bustince, H., Pagola, M., Mesiar, R., Hüllermeier, E., Herrera, F.: Grouping, overlap, and generalized bientropic functions for fuzzy modeling of pairwise comparisons. IEEE Trans. Fuzzy Syst. (2012)
3. Calvo, T., Kolesárová, A., Komorníková, M., Mesiar, R.: Aggregation operators: properties, classes and construction methods. In: Studies in Fuzziness and Soft Computing, pp. 3–104. Springer (2002). https://doi.org/10.1007/978-3-7908-1787-4_1
4. Castiblanco, F., Franco, C., Montero, J., Rodriguez, J.T.: Degree of global covering and global overlapping in solvency fuzzy classification. In: León-Castro, E., Blanco-Mesa, F., Gil-Lafuente, A.M., Merigó, J.M., Kacprzyk, J. (eds.) Intelligent and Complex Systems in Economics and Business. AISC, vol. 1249, pp. 21–32. Springer, Cham (2021). https://doi.org/10.1007/978-3-030-59191-5_2
5. Castiblanco, F., Franco, C., Rodríguez, J.T., Montero, J.: Evaluation of the quality and relevance of a fuzzy partition. J. Intell. Fuzzy Syst. **39**(3), 4211–4226 (2020)
6. Davies, D.L., Bouldin, D.W.: A cluster separation measure. IEEE Trans. Pattern Anal. Mach. Intell. **1**(2), 224–227 (1979)

7. Gómez, D., Rodríguez, J.T., Montero, J., Bustince, H., Barrenechea, E.: N-Dimensional overlap functions. Fuzzy Sets Syst. **287**, 57–75 (2016)
8. Gutiérrez, I., Barroso, M., Gómez, D., Castro, C.: Improving community detection algorithms in directed graphs with fuzzy measures. an application to mobility networks. Expert Syst. Appl. **269**, 126305 (2025)
9. Messiar, R., Kolesárová, A., Calvo, T., Komorníková, M.: A review of aggregation functions, vol. 20, pp. 121–144. Springer (2008)
10. Rickard, J., Yager, R., Miller, W.: Mountain clustering on nonuniform grids. In: AIPR 2004: 33rd Applied Imagery Pattern Recognition Workshop, Proceedings: Emerging Technologies and Applications for Imagery Patterns Recognition, pp. 106–111 (2005)
11. Rousseeuw, P.J.: Silhouettes: a graphical aid to the interpretation and validation of cluster analysis. J. Comput. Appl. Math. **20**, 53–65 (1987)
12. Yager, R.R.: On ordered weighted averaging aggregation operators in multicriteria decision-making. IEEE Trans. Syst. Cybern. **18**(1), 183–190 (1988)
13. Yager, R.R.: Weighted maximum entropy OWA aggregation with applications to decision making under risk. IEEE Trans. Syst. Man Cybern. Part A Syst. Hum. **39**(3), 555–564 (2009)
14. Zhang, S., Yu, J., Hu, M.: An edge server placement based on graph clustering in mobile edge computing. Sci. Rep. **14**(1) (2024)

Understanding Data Properties in the Mallows Model: Impact of Voter Count Variability

Mario Villar$^{(\boxtimes)}$ (ID), Noelia Rico (ID), and Irene Díaz (ID)

Department of Computer Science, University of Oviedo, Oviedo, Spain
villarmario@uniovi.es

Abstract. The Mallows model is a sampling technique frequently used to create synthetic election datasets and evaluate ranking aggregation algorithms. It provides flexibility, as authors can recreate different election scenarios by modifying the model's parameters. When applying this model, results from data with different numbers of voters are often compared without adequate consideration, mistakenly assuming a consistent underlying structure in the preference distribution. However, experimental results have shown that this practice may be problematic because some intrinsic properties of the data fluctuate when modifying this parameter. In this paper, we address this issue by studying the behaviour of Mallows model for producing elections when increasing the number of voters. We generate a synthetic dataset that contains simulations of elections for different numbers of voters and alternatives and measure some structural characteristics of the generated data. Afterwards, we analyse the behaviour of these properties as the number of voters increases. Results show that some aspects, such as the modal ranking, are affected by this variation. This leads to the conclusion that the performance of ranking aggregation algorithms, particularly those based on the Condorcet method, cannot be directly compared to data with different numbers of voters due to varying aggregation difficulty.

Keywords: ranking aggregation · Mallows model · algorithm evaluation · Condorcet method

1 Introduction

In many scenarios, items can be ranked using different criteria, yet a unified ordering is required. For example, shopping platforms must present customers with the most advantageous arrangement of products based on multiple factors, such as user ratings or return rates. Similarly, in participatory budgeting, community members rank proposed projects according to their priorities, necessitating a consensus ranking to guide decision-making. All these scenarios are considered elections, as a set of alternatives (e.g. products, projects) is ordered by some voters (e.g. metrics, community members) based on their preferences.

M. Baczyński et al. (Eds.): EUSFLAT 2025, LNCS 15883, pp. 294–305, 2025.
https://doi.org/10.1007/978-3-031-97225-6_24

Typically, those preferences are expressed through rankings of the alternatives, where one is above another if it is preferable. Thus, the desired overall order is a ranking that aggregates the individual ones while maximizing the satisfaction of the voter's preferences.

The field that studies ranking aggregation is Social Choice Theory and its first studies date back to the 18th century [16]. One of its earliest contributors was the Marquis of Condorcet [29], who introduced a technique based on majorities (the Condorcet method) that is still popular today. In the last two decades, a subfield called Computational Social Choice (COMSOC) gained popularity [10]. Studies in this area focus on the computational complexity of Social Choice techniques, for example, by analysing the computational difficulty of applying ranking aggregation methods to some elections. One prominent research line in COMSOC is the development of efficient implementations of ranking aggregation algorithms, as it has been demonstrated that some theoretical techniques represent NP-Hard problems [3, 26].

Evaluating algorithms on election data represents a critical stage in comparing execution times and performance of different implementations of ranking aggregation methods. Usually, two data sources can be used: real-life data from election datasets and synthetic data generated through some statistical model. However, real-world data usually offers limited flexibility due to a restricted number of alternatives and voters [9], and over 60% of the literature relies just on artificial data, according to Boehmer et al. [6]. One of the most popular approaches to generating election data is the Mallows model [22], where a fixed central ranking works as the ground truth. Its dispersion parameter controls the divergence of the sampled rankings from the central one, providing more flexibility than other methods like Impartial Culture [18]. This model enables the generation of data with diverse characteristics by adjusting the number of alternatives, voters, and the level of dispersion.

There is no established standard for selecting the appropriate parameter configuration, and authors take different approaches [6]. For instance, some fix values for all three parameters and evaluate the algorithms on a single election dataset, while others resort to a range of values for each parameter and generate multiple datasets of variable natures. However, results obtained in different datasets are frequently compared arbitrarily without studying if varying parameter values preserve the same structural properties of the sampled data. This lack of analysis represents a problem, as Boehmer et al. [7] have shown that different numbers of alternatives produce data of distinct nature. Moreover, one of our prior studies [28] discovered that changing the numbers of voters also seems to alter the performance of some algorithms, but no comprehensive analysis has been done yet regarding the impact of this parameter.

Therefore, there is still a need to understand the influence of the number of voters when generating Mallows' data to compare results from different election scenarios. Bridging this gap would enable a proper assessment of the robustness and consistency of ranking aggregation techniques, ensuring their applicability in diverse real-world contexts. Thus, this work aims to examine possible changes in structural properties of Mallows' data when varying the number of voters to determine the effect they could have in ranking aggregation algorithms. We revise existing studies in Sect. 2. Then, we introduce some theoretical concepts needed for the development of the paper in Sect. 3. Finally, we detail the experiments carried out and analyse some structural properties of the sampled data in Sect. 4, and summarize the work done and propose some next steps in Sect. 5.

2   Related Work

The Mallows model is a probabilistic model introduced by Colin L. Mallows in 1957 [22] to model elections by learning approximate distributions. It can also be used to generate election data of different natures to evaluate algorithms in COMSOC studies. In fact, according to Boehmer et al. [6], it is currently the second most popular sampling technique in the literature.

However, there are no standard values for the model's parameters. Authors take multiple approaches: fixing specific values and generating a single election dataset [12,24], randomly selecting a range of dispersion values while fixing the number of alternatives and voters to sample multiple datasets [20,25], using various numbers of alternatives [13,21] or voters [2,4], or testing with a range of values for all three parameters [8,11]. The aim of utilising multiple values is usually comparing the performance in diverse election scenarios.

Szufa et al. [27] designed a 2D map that visualises election data generated with different parameters. This type of map demonstrates that the Mallows model can produce data similar to most real-world datasets [5]. Although this study justified the widespread use of this model, it also showed that the coverage of the election space fluctuated when modifying the number of alternatives. The normalised version proposed in [7] adapts the dispersion of the model to maintain the same space coverage independently of the number of alternatives.

The above-mentioned studies have set some good foundations for fully comprehending the behaviour of the Mallows model. Nevertheless, they only analysed the influence of the number of alternatives and not the number of voters, and we have detected, in a prior study, that some Condorcet properties fluctuate in profiles generated with different voter counts [28]. This result suggested that the number of voters may also influence the Mallows model sampling process. We have not found any studies analysing the structural properties of Mallows' data when varying the number of voters and doing so would be crucial to establish a fair evaluation process.

3   Preliminaries

Let $\mathcal{A} = \{a_1, a_2, ..., a_m\}$ be a set of m alternatives. The set of all the possible permutations of alternatives is denoted $\mathcal{L}(\mathcal{A})$. A strict ranking v is a linear order over the set $\mathcal{A}$, i.e., a permutation $v \in \mathcal{L}(\mathcal{A})$ such that either $a_i \succ_v a_j$ or $a_j \succ_v a_i$ for any $a_i, a_j \in \mathcal{A} \mid a_i \neq a_j$. Thus, the number of possible rankings is the factorial of the number of alternatives, $m!$. Note that strict rankings establish complete, transitive and antisymmetric relations on $\mathcal{A}$, which means that no ties (having two different alternatives where neither is above the other) are allowed.

When n independent voters express their preferences over the entire set $\mathcal{A}$, a profile π of rankings is obtained. Guaranteeing the anonymity of the voters, profiles only consider the number of votes of each unique ranking, so that which voter selected which ranking is not significant. A ranking aggregation algorithm is a method that extracts a consensus ranking from a profile of rankings.

3.1   The Mallows Model

The Mallows model [22] is a statistical model initially designed for modelling ranking elections, but that can also be used to sample data from a probabilistic distribution [15]. The model is defined over a central ranking $\sigma \in \mathcal{L}(\mathcal{A})$, for some specific number of alternatives, and a dispersion value ϕ. When sampling artificial data, this central ranking is considered the ground truth and can be selected arbitrarily. To facilitate notation, from now on we are going to follow the lexicographical order of the alternatives, fixing $\sigma = a_1 \succ a_2 \succ \ldots \succ a_m$. The other parameter of the model, the dispersion, regulates the divergence of the sampled rankings to the central one.

The probabilistic distribution modelled by the Mallows model is based on the Kendall-tau distance [19]. The Kendall-tau distance $\kappa(u, v)$ between two rankings $u, v \in \mathcal{L}(\mathcal{A})$ is the number of pairs of alternatives $a_i, a_j \in \mathcal{A} \mid a_i \neq a_j$ whose relative order in u is different than in v (either $a_i \succ_u a_j$ and $a_j \succ_v a_i$ or $a_j \succ_u a_i$ and $a_i \succ_v a_j$). The probability of sampling a new ranking $r \in \mathcal{L}(\mathcal{A})$ is defined as

$$P(r) = \frac{1}{Z(\phi, m)} \phi^{\kappa(r,\sigma)} \tag{1}$$

where the normalising constant $Z(\phi, m)$ is defined as

$$Z(\phi, m) = \prod_{i=1}^{m-1} \left(1 + \sum_{j=1}^{i} \phi^j \right)$$

Using minimum dispersion ($\phi = 0$) would always yield the central ranking, while maximum dispersion ($\phi = 1$) allows to sample all possible rankings uniformly (Impartial Culture). For n voters, a profile is generated by sampling n rankings independently using the prior probability distribution. Note that these events (sampling each ranking) are independent of one another, i.e. the probability of generating a ranking does not depend on the past ones.

The Normalised Mallows Model. A normalised variant of the model has been recently proposed to tackle an issue when increasing the number of alternatives [7]. This adaptation uses a new dispersion parameter, norm-ϕ, which is internally converted to the dispersion value ϕ of the classical version so that norm-$\phi = \frac{exp\text{-}\kappa(m,\phi)}{m\cdot(m-1)/2}$, where $exp\text{-}\kappa(m, \phi)$ is the expected Kendall-tau distance between the central ranking and any ranking of m alternatives. Under this criterion, fixing norm-ϕ and varying the number of alternatives preserves the expected Kendall-tau distance between the sampled rankings and the central one. Therefore, this normalised version enables fair comparisons of ranking aggregation algorithms across elections with varying numbers of alternatives.

3.2 The Condorcet Method

As mentioned in Sect. 1, the Condorcet method is one of the earliest ranking aggregation techniques, laying the foundation for many others that followed. This method favours alternatives which are preferred to others by more than half of the voters: an alternative is ranked above another in the consensus ranking (Condorcet ranking, CR) only if more than half of the rankings of the profile rank the first above the second.

Therefore, the CR is obtained by pairwise comparisons of all the alternatives. To facilitate this process, the outranking matrix $\mathbf{O}$ can be used, as it holds the number of voters that prefer one alternative above another for every pair of them [1]. Formally, it is a square matrix of size m, where row i corresponds to alternative $a_i \in \mathcal{A}$ and column j to $a_j \in \mathcal{A}$. The element $o_{ij} \in \mathbf{O}$ is the number of rankings in which $a_i \succ a_j$. The diagonal is set to zero and the sum $o_{ij}+o_{ji} = n$ (representing the total number of voters) holds for any pair $a_i, a_j \mid i \neq j$.

The CR is constructed by placing an alternative a_i above another a_j if and only if $o_{ij} > o_{ji}$ or, equivalently since rankings are strict, when $o_{ij} > \frac{n}{2}$. However, this method encounters a fundamental issue known as the Condorcet paradox [17]. Consider three alternatives $a_i, a_j, a_h \in \mathcal{A}$ where each one is preferred by a majority of voters over another in the group, yet none is preferred over both others, i.e. $o_{ij} > \frac{n}{2}$, $o_{jh} > \frac{n}{2}$, $o_{hi} > \frac{n}{2}$. In such case, a cycle emerges in the consensus ranking because no single alternative is superior to the other two, and a CR does not exist for that profile.

The Condorcet winner (CW) is an alternative that beats any other in pairwise comparisons, that is, an alternative a_c that verifies $o_{cj} > \frac{m}{2} \forall a_j \in \mathcal{A} \setminus \{a_c\}$. A profile does not have a CW if no alternative is preferred to the others by the majority of voters. In that case, a CR will not exist either. However, profiles can have a CW without a CR if cycles do not appear for that top alternative but do appear for any other alternative. Therefore, there are three possible scenarios given a profile: 1) there is a CR, 2) the CR does not exists but a CW can still be found, and 3) neither of them exist.

4 Analysing Different Structural Properties

In a prior study [28], we observed that the Condorcet method had fluctuating behaviour depending on the number of voters of synthetic datasets of profiles of rankings. In particular, fixing the number of alternatives, profiles exhibited CRs and CWs more frequently when the number of voters was incremented. This trend occurred for all numbers of alternatives. Therefore, we believe that assessing the performance of algorithms that leverage the presence of a CW or CR, such as Kemeny's, may lead to overly optimistic results when using profiles generated by the Mallows model with a large number of voters. In this study, we aim to analyse key properties of elections generated under the Mallows model to better understand the underlying reasons for these observations.

Firstly, let us introduce the experimental set up used for this research. We have sampled profiles using the Mallows model through the repeated insertion model [15], as it is the sampling technique considered in the library *PrefLib* [23]. We normalised the dispersion of the model following the procedure described in Sect. 3.1. We generated profiles covering a wide range of election scenarios, from low numbers of alternatives and voters to larger ones, and considering multiples values of dispersion. The dispersion values are not evenly distributed because the effect of increasing the dispersion is more pronounced at higher values. The Table 1 gathers the values we have considered for the three parameters. For every combination of the listed values, we sampled 1000 profiles, while always keeping $\sigma = a_1 \succ a_2 \succ \ldots \succ a_m$ as the central ranking. The reason for generating such a high number of profiles is to ensure a proper statistical data analysis.

Table 1. Parameter space considered for sampling profiles of rankings. All combinations of the three parameters were used: we sampled 1000 profiles for each of the 3157 combinations.

Number of alternatives	$\{3, 5, 10, 15, 20, 25, 30\}$
Number of voters	$\{10\} \cup \{x \in \mathbb{N} \mid 25 \leq x \leq 1000 \text{ and } x \equiv 0 \pmod{25}\}$
Mallows model normalised dispersion	$\{0.1, 0.4, 0.5, 0.6, 0.7, 0.75, 0.8, 0.85, 0.9, 0.95, 1.0\}$

In the rest of this section, we analyse various structural properties of the described dataset of profiles and examine the results obtained using the Condorcet method. To ensure clarity and due to space constraints, we focus our discussion on profiles with a small number of alternatives. However, our experiments confirm that the findings presented in this work generalize to any number of alternatives and dispersion levels.

The first aspect we are going to analyse is the positions of the alternatives in the sampled rankings and in the CRs. To do so, we considered profiles for a specific number of alternatives and dispersion, and averaged the position of each alternative in all the generated rankings of all the profiles. Then, we separately considered profiles where the CR existed, and averaged for each alternative its position in all the CRs. We calculated the standard deviation (from now on STD) of the positions taken by the alternatives in both cases. Figure 1 compares the positions in the sampled rankings and the CRs for 3 and 5 alternatives and 0.9 normalised dispersion. The left plot shows the evolution of their mean position and the right one visualizes the evolution of the STD of their position. Although alternatives can only take integer positions (from 1 to m), this chart considers decimals resulting from the average value. This figure suggests that the number of voters impacts the overall profile characteristics rather than the individual positions of the alternatives in the sampled rankings, as these are stable.

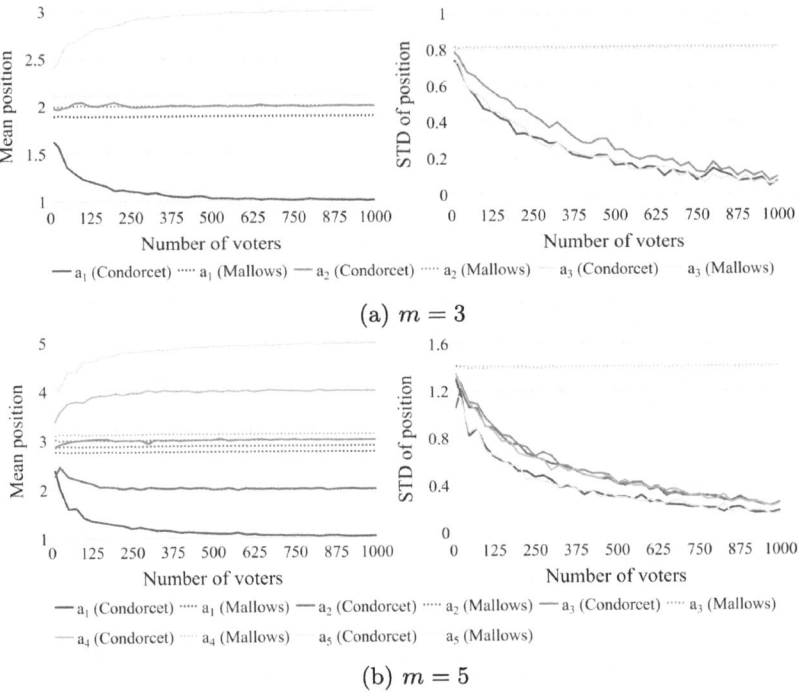

Fig. 1. Comparison of the evolution of the position of the alternatives in the Mallows rankings (dotted lines) and in the CRs (solid lines) for profiles with 3 and 5 alternatives and 0.9 normalised dispersion. All the sampled rankings were considered for the Mallows position, while only profiles with CR were contemplated for the CR position. The mean (left) and the STD of the position (right) are shown.

We can observe a notable variation in CR positions as the number of voters increases, despite the fixed dispersion. The alternative in the top position of the central ranking σ (a_1) tends to be placed also in the top position of the CR for larger numbers of voters, while the alternative in the last position in σ (a_3 or a_5 for $m = 3$ or $m = 5$ respectively) leans towards the bottom of the CR. In addition, the STD of the CR position of every alternative narrows significantly, approaching zero even for the middle alternative (whose average position seems relatively stable). These new observations align with the previous findings we have [28]: CRs tend to the central ranking for larger numbers of voters and become more prevalent. Despite these shifts in CR positions, the average position of alternatives in the sampled rankings, as well as their STD, are approximately constant.

Let us consider the scenario with three alternatives, where there are six possible rankings (see Table 2). Fixing a value for the normalized dispersion, the internal dispersion value to which it gets converted is also fixed for any number of voters. Thus, the probability of sampling each ranking, given by the Eq. 1, is the same for any number of voters. We expect the Mallows model to generate each ranking at the same ratio independently of the number of voters chosen.

Table 2. Possible rankings for three alternatives. The right column shows the Kendall-tau distance when the central ranking $\sigma = a_1 \succ a_2 \succ a_3$ is considered.

Ranking	Kendall-tau distance to σ
$a_1 \succ a_2 \succ a_3$	0
$a_1 \succ a_3 \succ a_2$	1
$a_2 \succ a_1 \succ a_3$	1
$a_2 \succ a_3 \succ a_1$	2
$a_3 \succ a_1 \succ a_2$	2
$a_3 \succ a_2 \succ a_1$	3

To verify it, Fig. 2 visualizes the frequencies with which each ranking was generated as the number of voters increases. We use the percentage of appearances rather than its absolute value because the total number of rankings of the profiles depends on the number of voters. The solid lines represent the mean percentage of appearances in profiles with the same voter count, while the shaded areas depict the STD of those percentages. A wider shaded area implies higher variability in the appearance frequency between profiles with the same number of voters.

The results confirm that each ranking is sampled at a constant ratio, as the percentage of appearances remains stable when increasing the voter count. Rankings with more pairwise swaps relative to the central ranking appear less frequently, as the Mallows model bases the probability of sampling a ranking on its Kendall-tau distance to the central ranking. This relationship is reflected in the equal sampling ratios of rankings with identical Kendall-tau distances from the central one, e.g. $a_1 \succ a_3 \succ a_2$ and $a_2 \succ a_1 \succ a_3$, with distance 1 to σ, and $a_2 \succ a_3 \succ a_1$ and $a_3 \succ a_1 \succ a_2$, with distance 2. However, the STD of the percentage decreases significantly as the number of voters grows. The distribution of rankings varies greatly between sampled profiles for lower voter counts, whereas it becomes more uniform for larger ones. This fact highlights an interesting dynamic: while the sampling rates of individual rankings remain unaffected, the differences in CR positions suggest variable underlying characteristics of the profiles when modifying the number of voters.

To inspect the changes in the nature of the profiles, let us analyse the evolution of the modal rankings. The modal ranking of a profile is the ranking sampled the most times [14]. A tie occurs when two or more rankings in a profile share the same number of votes. Figure 3 shows an important increment in the percentage of profiles where the central ranking is the modal one when the number of voters increases. In compensation, every other ranking tends to be modal

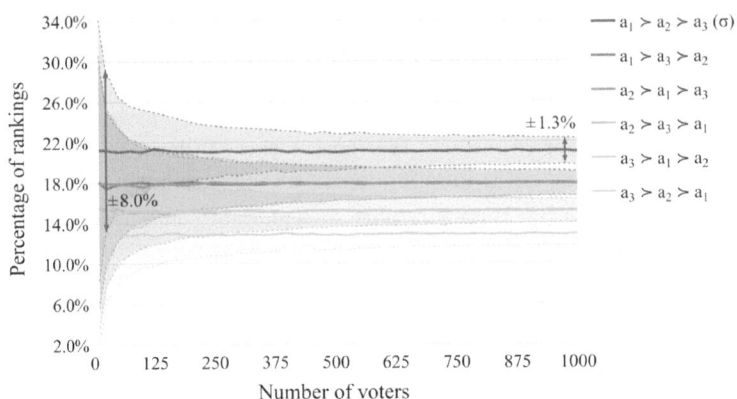

Fig. 2. Evolution of the mean percentage of appearances of every unique ranking for 3 alternatives when incrementing the number of voters with 0.9 normalised dispersion. The average percentage is then calculated for the 1000 profiles and the shaded area corresponds to the STD of the percentage of appearances across the profiles. The ranking σ is the central ranking used for sampling.

fewer times, and the number of ties also diminishes. As seen for the percentage of appearances, rankings with the same Kendall-tau distance to the central one follow the same decreasing trend. This discovery is linked to the diminishing STD of the percentage of appearances, as the sampling ratio of the central ranking is the largest for any voter count. When the STD of all other rankings is low, the likelihood of sampling any other ranking more times than the central one is also low.

Both the decreasing STD of the percentage of appearances and the growing ratio at which the central ranking is the modal one support the fact that CWs and CRs exist more frequently for bigger voter counts. Taking a look again at Fig. 2, the rankings in which alternative a_1 is above a_2 are sampled approximately 54% of the times, while those where a_1 is above a_3 are sampled 57% of times. Therefore, the average number of voters that prefer a_1 over a_2 is $0.54 \cdot n > \frac{n}{2}$, and for those that prefer a_1 over a_3 it is $0.57 \cdot n > \frac{n}{2}$, implying that in the average case a_1 would be the CW. A lower STD of the percentage of appearances of those rankings means that fewer profiles differ from that average case, resulting in an increasing rate of profiles exhibiting CW when escalating the number of voters. The same reasoning applies to the CR when the remaining pairwise comparison is taken into account: rankings where a_2 is over a_3 are sampled 54% of times, so a_2 is preferred over a_3 by $0.54 \cdot n > \frac{n}{2}$ of the voters on average. In the average case, the CR is the central ranking, and lower STDs of the percentage of appearances imply that this case occurs more often, which matches with the central ranking being the modal one at an increasing rate. These observations justify the behaviour of the average CR positions seen in Fig. 1.

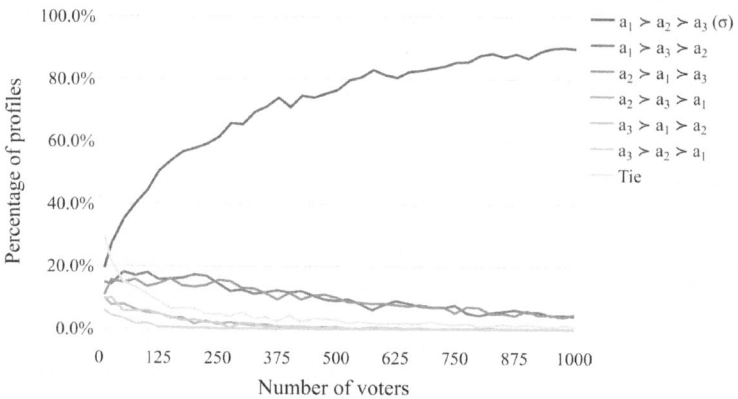

Fig. 3. Evolution of the percentage of profiles in which each ranking for 3 alternatives was the modal one with the number of voters, for 0.9 normalised dispersion, using the 1000 profiles. The ranking σ is the central ranking used for sampling.

5   Final Remarks and Future Work

In this paper, we have shown that varying the number of voters of synthetic profiles generated with the Mallows model changes the difficulty of obtaining a CR for a fixed number of alternatives and dispersion. Thus, the performance of ranking aggregation algorithms based on the Condorcet method is affected by this parameter, as evidenced by variations detected in Condorcet rankings (CRs), and consequently its evaluation on this type of datasets. To investigate the underlying causes of this fluctuating behaviour, we analysed a dataset of profiles sampled using multiple configurations of the Mallows model, focusing on various structural properties of the generated data.

As expected, incrementing the number of voters does not modify the mean or STD of the position of the alternatives in the sampled rankings, as their sampling probabilities do not depend on this parameter. For the same reason, the rankings' average percentage of appearances on the profiles is almost constant. However, the STD of this percentage decreases significantly when escalating the number of voters, which leads to sampled profiles being more similar for higher counts. The modal ranking of the profiles also changes significantly, tending to be the central one more frequently.

Both novel discoveries align with the findings we presented in a prior study [28], and explain why CRs lean towards the central ranking for larger voter counts. Since the central ranking is considered the ground truth in the Mallows model, an algorithm based on the Condorcet method is going to see its performance boosted when evaluated on data sampled with bigger numbers of voters. However, the theoretical reasons behind the variations observed in the properties of the sampled profiles still remain open and need to be addressed in future works.

Acknowledgments. This research has been funded by the Government of Spain through project MCINN-23-PID2022-139886NB-I00 and by grant Project PAPI-24-TESIS-14 of the University of Oviedo.

References

1. Arrow, K., Raynaud, H.: Social Choice and Multicriterion Decision-Making, 1st edn. The MIT Press (1986)
2. Ayadi, M., Amor, N.B., Lang, J., Peters, D.: Single transferable vote: incomplete knowledge and communication issues. In: Proceedings of the 18th International Conference on Autonomous Agents and MultiAgent Systems, pp. 1288–1296 (2019)
3. Bartholdi, J., Tovey, C.A., Trick, M.A.: Voting schemes for which it can be difficult to tell who won the election. Soc. Choice Welfare **6**, 157–165 (1989). https://doi.org/10.1007/BF00303169
4. Bentert, M., Skowron, P.: Comparing election methods where each voter ranks only few candidates. In: Proceedings of the AAAI Conference on Artificial Intelligence, vol. 34, pp. 2218–2225 (2020). https://doi.org/10.1609/aaai.v34i02.5598
5. Boehmer, N., Bredereck, R., Faliszewski, P., Niedermeier, R., Szufa, S.: Putting a compass on the map of elections. In: Zhou, Z.H. (ed.) Proceedings of the Thirtieth International Joint Conference on Artificial Intelligence, pp. 59–65 (2021). https://doi.org/10.24963/ijcai.2021/9
6. Boehmer, N., et al.: Guide to numerical experiments on elections in computational social choice. In: Proceedings of the Thirty-Third International Joint Conference on Artificial Intelligence, pp. 7962–7970 (2024). https://doi.org/10.24963/ijcai.2024/881
7. Boehmer, N., Faliszewski, P., Kraiczy, S.: Properties of the mallows model depending on the number of alternatives: a warning for an experimentalist. In: Proceedings of Machine Learning Research, vol. 202, pp. 2689–2711 (2023)
8. Boehmer, N., Faliszewski, P., Niedermeier, R., Szufa, S., Was, T.: Understanding distance measures among elections. In: Proceedings of the Thirty-First International Joint Conference on Artificial Intelligence, pp. 102–108 (2022). https://doi.org/10.24963/ijcai.2022/15
9. Boehmer, N., Schaar, N.: Collecting, classifying, analyzing, and using real-world ranking data. In: Proceedings of the 2023 International Conference on Autonomous Agents and Multiagent Systems, pp. 1706–1715 (2023). https://doi.org/10.48550/arXiv.2204.03589
10. Brandt, F., Conitzer, V., Endriss, U., Lang, J., Procaccia, A.: Handbook of Computational Social Choice. Cambridge University Press (2016). https://doi.org/10.1017/CBO9781107446984
11. Brandt, F., Hofbauer, J., Strobel, M.: Exploring the no-show paradox for condorcet extensions using ehrhart theory and computer simulations. In: Proceedings of the 18th International Conference on Autonomous Agents and MultiAgent Systems, pp. 520–528 (2019)
12. Brill, M., Israel, J., Micha, E., Peters, J.: Individual representation in approval-based committee voting. Soc. Choice Welfare **64**, 69–96 (2025). https://doi.org/10.1007/s00355-024-01563-w
13. Brill, M., Schmidt-Kraepelin, U., Suksompong, W.: Margin of victory for tournament solutions. Artif. Intell. **302**, 103600 (2022). https://doi.org/10.1016/j.artint.2021.103600

14. Caragiannis, I., Procaccia, A., Shah, N.: Modal ranking: a uniquely robust voting rule. In: Proceedings of the AAAI Conference on Artificial Intelligence, vol. 28 (2014). https://doi.org/10.1609/aaai.v28i1.8811
15. Doignon, J.P., Pekeč, A., Regenwetter, M.: The repeated insertion model for rankings: missing link between two subset choice models. Psychometrika **69**, 33–54 (2004). https://doi.org/10.1007/BF02295838
16. Fishburn, P.C.: The Theory of Social Choice. Princeton University Press (1973)
17. Fishburn, P.C.: Paradoxes of voting. Am. Polit. Sci. Rev. **68**, 537–546 (1974). https://doi.org/10.2307/1959503
18. Guilbaud, G.T.: Les théories de l'intérêt général et le problème logique de l'agrégation. Revue économique **63**, 659–720 (1952). https://doi.org/10.3917/reco.634.0659
19. Kendall, M.G.: A new measure of rank correlation. Biometrika **30**, 81–93 (1938). https://doi.org/10.2307/2332226
20. Kliachkin, A., Psaroudaki, E., Mareček, J., Fotakis, D.: Fairness in ranking: robustness through randomization without the protected attribute. In: 40th International Conference on Data Engineering Workshops, pp. 201–208 (2024). https://doi.org/10.1109/ICDEW61823.2024.00032
21. Lu, T., Boutilier, C.: Multi-winner social choice with incomplete preferences. In: Proceedings of the Twenty-Third International Joint Conference on Artificial Intelligence, pp. 263–270 (2013)
22. Mallows, C.L.: Non-null ranking models. I. Biometrika **44**, 114–130 (1957). https://doi.org/10.2307/2333244
23. Mattei, N., Walsh, T.: PREFLIB: a library for preferences http://www.preflib.org. In: Perny, P., Pirlot, M., Tsoukiàs, A. (eds.) ADT 2013. LNCS (LNAI), vol. 8176, pp. 259–270. Springer, Heidelberg (2013). https://doi.org/10.1007/978-3-642-41575-3_20
24. Micha, E., Shah, N.: Can we predict the election outcome from sampled votes? In: Proceedings of the AAAI Conference on Artificial Intelligence, vol. 34, pp. 2176–2183 (2020). https://doi.org/10.1609/aaai.v34i02.5593
25. Relia, K.: Dire committee: diversity and representation constraints in multiwinner elections. In: Proceedings of the Thirty-First International Joint Conference on Artificial Intelligence, pp. 5143–5149 (2022). https://doi.org/10.24963/ijcai.2022/714
26. Rico, N., Vela, C.R., Díaz, I.: Reducing the time required to find the Kemeny ranking by exploiting a necessary condition for being a winner. Eur. J. Oper. Res. **305**, 1323–1336 (2023)
27. Szufa, S., Faliszewski, P., Skowron, P., Slinko, A., Talmon, N.: Drawing a map of elections in the space of statistical cultures. In: Proceedings of the 19th International Conference on Autonomous Agents and MultiAgent Systems, pp. 1341–1349 (2020)
28. Villar, M., Rico, N., Díaz, I.: Exploring condorcet properties in mallows model-generated preferences. In: 20th Conference of the Spanish Association for Artificial Intelligence, pp. 65–70 (2024)
29. Young, H.P.: Condorcet's theory of voting. Am. Polit. Sci. Rev. **82**, 1231–1244 (1988). https://doi.org/10.2307/1961757

Mathematical Fuzzy Logic

Foulis Quantales and Complete Orthomodular Lattices

Michal Botur[1] (ID), Jan Paseka[2]([✉]) (ID), and Richard Smolka[2] (ID)

[1] Department of Algebra and Geometry, Faculty of Science, Palacký University
Olomouc, 17. listopadu 12, 771 46 Olomouc, Czech Republic
michal.botur@upol.cz
[2] Department of Mathematics and Statistics, Faculty of Science, Masaryk University,
Kotlářská 2, 611 37 Brno, Czech Republic
paseka@math.muni.cz

Abstract. Our approach establishes a natural correspondence between complete orthomodular lattices and certain types of quantales.

Firstly, given a complete orthomodular lattice X, we associate with it a Foulis quantale $\mathbf{Lin}(X)$ consisting of its endomorphisms. This allows us to view X as a left module over $\mathbf{Lin}(X)$, thereby introducing a novel fuzzy-theoretic perspective to the study of complete orthomodular lattices.

Conversely, for any Foulis quantale Q, we associate a complete orthomodular lattice $[\,Q\,]$ that naturally forms a left Q-module. Furthermore, there exists a canonical homomorphism of Foulis quantales from Q to $\mathbf{Lin}([\,Q\,])$.

Keywords: quantale · quantale module · orthomodular lattice · linear map · Foulis semigroup · Sasaki projection · dagger category

1 Introduction

Fuzzy logic, a framework for reasoning with uncertainty, is fundamentally connected to residuation, a concept central to various branches of mathematics and computer science. Notable examples include Hájek's Basic Logic (BL) [9] and Esteva and Godo's Monoidal T-norm Based Logic (MTL) [6], which arise from continuous and left-continuous t-norms respectively. The essential role of residuated structures in characterizing these and other fuzzy logics has driven extensive research in this area.

Quantales [14] are essential structures in theoretical computer science and mathematical physics. They underpin significant frameworks like process algebras and quantum logics, developed by Abramsky and Vickers [2], as well as the quantum mechanical formalisms of Birkhoff and von Neumann [3]. Quantales naturally model concurrent processes and algebraically represent quantum mechanics. Their semantics can be formally described using quantale modules, leading to extensive study of quantales and their modules for their relevance in quantum logic, concurrency theory, and related fields.

M. Baczyński et al. (Eds.): EUSFLAT 2025, LNCS 15883, pp. 309–321, 2025.
https://doi.org/10.1007/978-3-031-97225-6_25

We study Foulis quantales and their modules as quantale-like structures for complete orthomodular lattices. This approach introduces a fuzzy-theoretic perspective, as every quantale module naturally carries a fuzzy order [19].

This paper is structured as follows. Section 2 provides an overview of fundamental algebraic concepts, including orthomodular lattices, dagger categories, quantales, and quantaloids. Drawing inspiration from research on orthomodular lattices [4,11] and complete orthomodular lattices [5], we investigate the essential properties of the involutive quantale of endomorphisms of a complete orthomodular lattice. This investigation lays the groundwork for a fuzzy-logic-inspired approach to quantum logic.

Section 3 delves into the core theme of the paper: Foulis quantales and their modules. We explore their key characteristics and examine their applications within the context of complete orthomodular lattices.

This work assumes familiarity with the foundational concepts and results pertaining to quantales, dagger categories and orthomodular lattices. Readers seeking further information on these topics are encouraged to consult [10,11,16, 17], and [12].

2   Complete Orthomodular Lattices, Dagger Categories and Quantales

2.1   Complete Orthomodular Lattices

The concept of ortholattices provides a broader mathematical framework that extends beyond traditional Boolean algebras. These structures are distinguished by their orthocomplement operation - a sophisticated counterpart to Boolean negation. When we add the property of orthomodularity, we arrive at orthomodular ortholattices, which form a special class with unique characteristics. This refinement proves especially valuable in quantum logic and related fields, where the additional structure captures important mathematical and logical relationships that Boolean algebras cannot express.

Definition 1. [11] A meet semi-lattice $(X, \wedge, 1)$ is called an ortholattice if it comes equipped with a function $(-)^\perp \colon X \to X$ satisfying:

- $x^{\perp\perp} = x$;
- $x \leq y$ implies $y^\perp \leq x^\perp$;
- $x \wedge x^\perp = 1^\perp$.

One can then define a bottom element as $0 = 1 \wedge 1^\perp = 1^\perp$ and join by $x \vee y = (x^\perp \wedge y^\perp)^\perp$, satisfying $x \vee x^\perp = 1$.

We write $x \perp y$ if and only if $x \leq y^\perp$.

Such an ortholattice is called orthomodular lattice if it satisfies (one of) the three equivalent conditions:

- $x \leq y$ implies $y = x \vee (x^\perp \wedge y)$;
- $x \leq y$ implies $x = y \wedge (y^\perp \vee x)$;

– $x \leq y$ and $x^{\perp} \wedge y = 0$ implies $x = y$.

An orthomodular lattice X is called a complete orthomodular lattice if it is also a complete lattice.

We introduce a categorical framework for complete orthomodular lattices by constructing a category **SupOMLatLin**. The objects are complete orthomodular lattices, and morphisms are linear maps between them (following the treatment in [4,5]).

Definition 2. [5] The category **SupOMLatLin** has complete orthomodular lattices as objects. A morphism $f\colon X \to Y$ in **SupOMLatLin** is a function $f\colon X \to Y$ between the underlying sets such that there is a function $h\colon Y \to X$ and, for any $x \in X$ and $y \in Y$,

$$f(x) \perp y \text{ if and only if } x \perp h(y).$$

We say that h is an *adjoint* of a *linear map* f. It is clear that adjointness is a symmetric property: if a map f possesses an adjoint h, then f is also an adjoint of h. We denote $\mathbf{Lin}(X, Y)$ the set of all linear maps from X to Y. If $X = Y$ we put $\mathbf{Lin}(X) = \mathbf{Lin}(X, X)$.

Moreover, a map $f\colon X \to X$ is called *self-adjoint* if f is an adjoint of itself.

The identity morphism on X is the self-adjoint identity map $\mathrm{id}_X\colon X \to X$. Composition of $X \xrightarrow{f} Y \xrightarrow{g} Z$ is given by usual composition of maps.

Our guiding example is the following construction. Let $\mathcal{H}$ be a Hilbert space and consider $\mathcal{C}(\mathcal{H})$, the set of all closed subspaces of $\mathcal{H}$. When equipped with the operations $\wedge$ (intersection) and $\perp$ (orthogonal complementation), $\mathcal{C}(\mathcal{H})$ forms a complete orthomodular lattice. Moreover, for Hilbert spaces $\mathcal{H}_1$ and $\mathcal{H}_2$, any bounded linear operator $T : \mathcal{H}_1 \to \mathcal{H}_2$ induces a linear map $\Phi_T : \mathcal{C}(\mathcal{H}_1) \to \mathcal{C}(\mathcal{H}_2)$ between the corresponding lattices of closed subspaces. The adjoint map Φ_T^* is naturally determined by T^*, the adjoint of the original operator.

Lemma 1. [5, Lemma 2.6] *Let $f : X \to Y$ be a map between complete orthomodular lattices. The following three key properties of f are equivalent:*

1. *f possesses a right order-adjoint;*
2. *f admits an adjoint in the sense of Definition 1;*
3. *f preserves arbitrary joins (i.e., is join-complete).*

This equivalence provides multiple perspectives for understanding linear maps in the context of complete orthomodular lattices.

The Sasaki projection, named after Shôichirô Sasaki, is a crucial concept in orthomodular lattice theory. It defines a unique projection operation that reflects the non-classical, quantum-like behavior of these structures, offering insights into relationships between elements beyond the scope of classical Boolean logic.

Definition 3. *Let X be an orthomodular lattice. Then the map $\pi_a : X \to X$, $y \mapsto a \wedge (a^{\perp} \vee y)$ is called the* Sasaki projection *to $a \in X$.*

The following properties of Sasaki projections are established in [13] and are crucial for our discussion:

Lemma 2. *Let X be an orthomodular lattice, and let $a \in X$. Then for each $y, z \in L$ we have*

(a) $y \leq a$ *if and only if* $\pi_a(y) = y$;
(b) $\pi_a(\pi_a(y^\perp)^\perp)) \leq y$;
(c) $\pi_a(y) = 0$ *if and only if* $y \leq a^\perp$;
(d) $\pi_a(y) \perp z$ *if and only if* $y \perp \pi_a(z)$.

The definition that follows brings to mind the kernel and range, two key ideas in the study of morphisms between complete orthomodular lattices. One important difference between them is that the range only produces a complete lattice, but a kernel always forms a complete orthomodular lattice.

Definition 4. *Let $f \colon X \to Y$ be a morphism of complete orthomodular lattices. We define the kernel and the range of f, respectively, by*

$$\ker f = \{x \in X \colon f(x) = 0\},$$
$$\operatorname{im} f = \{f(x) \colon x \in X\}.$$

2.2 Dagger Categories

Dagger categories, crucial in categorical quantum mechanics, are categories with an involutive functor (the dagger) defining adjoints for morphisms. This structure enables the representation and analysis of quantum processes and reversible computations.

We observe that this idea has been present in the literature since the 1960s and was usually taken into consideration in a particular context. With the publication of Abramsky and Coecke's work [1], it became part of the mainstream discourse regarding the fundamentals of quantum mechanics. P. Selinger is credited with coining the term "dagger category" [18].

Definition 5. *A dagger on a category $\mathcal{C}$ is a functor $^\star \colon \mathcal{C}^{\mathrm{op}} \to \mathcal{C}$ that is involutive and the identity on objects. A category equipped with a dagger is called a dagger category.*

Let $\mathcal{C}$ be a dagger category. A morphism $f \colon A \to B$ is called a dagger monomorphism if $f^\star \circ f = \mathrm{id}_A$, and f is called a dagger isomorphism if $f^\star \circ f = \mathrm{id}_A$ and $f \circ f^\star = \mathrm{id}_B$. A dagger automorphism is a dagger isomorphism $f \colon A \to A$.

Limits and colimits are dual in dagger categories. Applying the dagger * to a limit cone yields a colimit cone, and conversely.

The category of complete orthomodular lattices with linear maps is shown to constitute a dagger category by the following theorem.

Theorem 1. [5, Theorem 2.7] **SupOMLatLin** *is a dagger category.*

Two significant findings that are worth mentioning are as follows.

Corollary 1. [5, Corollary 3.5, Corollary 4.6] *Let X be a complete orthomodular lattice, and let $a \in X$. Then π_a is self-adjoint, idempotent and $\operatorname{im} \pi_a = {\downarrow}a = {\downarrow}\pi_a(1)$. Moreover, we have a factorization*

$$
\begin{array}{ccc}
{\downarrow}a & \xrightarrow{\ \pi_a|_{\downarrow a}\ } & X \\
{\scriptstyle \pi_a|^{\downarrow a}} \uparrow & \nearrow{\scriptstyle \pi_a} & \\
X & &
\end{array}
\tag{1}
$$

such that $\pi_a|^{\downarrow a}$ is dagger epi, $\pi_a|_{\downarrow a}$ is dagger mono, $\pi_a|_{\downarrow a} \circ \pi_a|^{\downarrow a} = \pi_a$, $\pi_a|^{\downarrow a} = (\pi_a|_{\downarrow a})^*$, and $\pi_a|^{\downarrow a} \circ \pi_a|_{\downarrow a} = \operatorname{id}_{\downarrow a}$.

Lemma 3. [5, Corollary 3.9] *Let $f\colon X \to Y$ be a morphism of complete orthomodular lattices. Then $\ker f = {\downarrow}f^*(1)^\perp$ is a complete orthomodular lattice.*

The category **SupOMLatLin** possesses a zero object $\underline{0}$ (see [5]), characterized by the existence of unique morphisms to and from any object. This zero object is the one-element orthomodular lattice $\{0\}$. For any complete orthomodular lattice X, the unique morphism $\underline{0} \to X$ maps 0 to 0.

Identifying $\underline{0}$ with the principal downset ${\downarrow}0$, this morphism is a dagger monomorphism with adjoint $f^* \colon X \to \underline{0}$ given by $f^*(x) = \pi_0(x) = 0$. We denote by $0_{X,Y} \colon X \to \underline{0} \to Y$ the unique morphism factoring through the zero object for any objects X and Y.

The following definition introduces kernels and their dagger counterparts, laying the foundation for studying algebraic structures within the framework of category theory.

Definition 6. [10]

1. For a morphism $f\colon A \to B$ in arbitrary category with zero morphisms, we say that a morphism $k\colon K \to A$ is a kernel of f if $fk = 0_{K,B}$, and if $m\colon M \to A$ satisfies $fm = 0_{M,B}$ then there is a unique morphism $u\colon M \to K$ such that $ku = m$.

We sometimes write $\ker f$ for k or K.

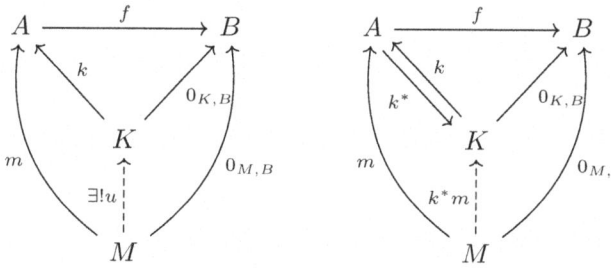

2. For a morphism $f\colon A \to B$ in arbitrary dagger category with zero morphisms, we say that a morphism $k\colon K \to A$ is a weak dagger kernel of f if $fk = 0_{K,B}$, and if $m\colon M \to A$ satisfies $fm = 0_{M,B}$ then $kk^*m = m$.
   A weak dagger kernel category is a dagger category with zero morphisms where every morphism has a weak dagger kernel.
3. A dagger kernel category is a dagger category with a zero object, hence zero morphisms, where each morphism f has a weak dagger kernel k (called dagger kernel) that additionally satisfies $k^*k = 1_K$.

Every dagger kernel is a kernel, and in **SupOMLatLin**, the converse holds: all kernels are dagger kernels. Theorem 2 thus shows that **SupOMLatLin** forms a dagger kernel category.

Theorem 2. [5, Theorem 3.12] *The category* **SupOMLatLin** *is a dagger kernel category. The dagger kernel of a morphism* $f\colon X \to Y$ *is* $\ker(f) = \pi_k|_{\downarrow k}\colon \downarrow k \to X$, *where* $k = f^*(1)^\perp \in X$, *like in Lemma 3. Moreover,* $f \circ \ker(f) = 0_{\downarrow k, Y}$, $\pi_k = \ker(f) \circ \ker(f)^*$ *and* $\mathrm{id}_{\downarrow k} = \ker(f)^* \circ \ker(f)$.

2.3   Quantales and Quantaloids

While complete orthomodular lattices give us a snapshot of a quantum system's possible states, focusing on testable properties, quantales take a different viewpoint. They provide a dynamic perspective, allowing us to reason about the evolution of the system and the structure of quantum actions that cause these changes.

Mulvey [14] coined the term "quantales" as a "quantization" of the term "location" during the Oberwolfach Category Meeting in the early 1980s. Quantales, which were first inspired by studies in topology and functional analysis, provide a strong foundation for simulating complex systems with non-classical logics, especially in domains such as computer science, abstract algebra, and quantum mechanics. The realization that quantales, like Boolean algebras for classical propositional logic, give semantics for propositional linear logic was a crucial advancement in quantales theory. Naturally, quantales appear as subgroups, lattices of ideals, or other appropriate algebraic substructures.

Definition 7. [16]

1. A quantale is a complete lattice Q with an associative binary multiplication satisfying

$$x \cdot \bigsqcup_{i \in I} x_i = \bigsqcup_{i \in I}(x \cdot x_i) \quad \text{and} \quad \left(\bigsqcup_{i \in I} x_i\right) \cdot x = \bigsqcup_{i \in I}(x_i \cdot x)$$

for all x, $x_i \in Q$, $i \in I$ (I is a set). Here $\bigsqcup_{i \in I} x_i$ denotes the join of the set $\{x_i\colon i \in I\}$. A quantale Q is said to be unital if there is an element $e \in Q$ called unit such that

$$e \cdot a = a = a \cdot e$$

for all $a \in Q$. The element $0 = \bigsqcup \emptyset$ is a zero element of Q: $0 \cdot s = 0 = s \cdot 0$. We denote by $\sqsubseteq$ the order relation on Q.

2. By an involutive quantale will be meant a quantale Q together with a semi-group involution $*$ satisfying

$$\left(\bigsqcup a_i\right)^* = \bigsqcup a_i^*$$

for all $a_i \in Q$. In the event that Q is also unital, then necessarily e is selfad-joint, i.e.,

$$e = e^*.$$

We also define $s \leq t$ if and only if $s = t \cdot s$, and $s \perp t$ if and only if $0 = s^* \cdot t$ for all $s, t \in Q$.

Quantaloids [17] are a versatile and powerful generalization of quantales, enriched in sup-lattices, and are used extensively in category theory and logic. They provide a robust framework for studying enriched categories, automata theory, and other mathematical structures, highlighting their importance in both theoretical and applied mathematics.

Definition 8. 1. A quantaloid **Q** is a category enriched over the category **Sup** of complete lattices with supremum preserving maps.
This means that for any objects A and B in the quantaloid, the hom-object $Hom(A, B)$ is not merely a set but a complete lattice, such that the composition of morphisms preserves all joins:

$$\left(\bigvee_{i \in I} f_i\right) \circ \left(\bigvee_{j \in J} g_j\right) = \left(\bigvee_{i \in I, j \in J} f_i \circ g_j\right)$$

2. A quantaloid **Q** with involution, i.e., a dagger category for which

$$\left(\bigvee_i p_i\right)^* = \bigvee_i p_i^*$$

for all morphisms $p_i \in \mathbf{Q}$, will be called *involutive*.

Example 1. (see [15, page 355] and [8, Example 2.4]) Let **SupOLatLin** be the category of complete orthocomplemented lattices with join-preserving maps as morphisms. The composition in **SupOLatLin** is given by the standard composition of mappings, and the identity morphisms serve as units. One can naturally view **SupOLatLin** as an involutive quantaloid, where the join is defined by the pointwise ordering of mappings, and the involution † on **SupOLatLin** is given by

$$f^\dagger(t) = \left(\bigvee\{s \in X \mid f(s) \leq t^\perp\}\right)^\perp$$

for each morphism $f \colon X \to Y$ in **SupOLatLin** and every element $t \in Y$.

Lemma 4. *Let* $f : X \to Y$ *be a linear map between complete orthomodular lattices. Then* $f^\dagger = f^\star$.

Proof. Let $x \in X$ and $y \in Y$. We compute:

$$x \perp f^\dagger(y) \text{ if and only if } x \leq \bigvee \{s \in X \mid f(s) \leq y^\perp\} \text{ if and only if}$$

$$x \leq \bigvee \{s \in X \mid f(s) \perp y\} \text{ if and only if } x \leq \bigvee \{s \in X \mid s \perp f^\star(y)\}$$

$$\text{if and only if } x \perp f^\star(y).$$

We conclude that $f^\dagger = f^\star$.

Given that the category **SupOLatLin** of complete orthocomplemented lattices satisfies the definition of an involutive quantaloid, we can directly derive the following theorem based on Theorem 1 and Lemma 4.

Theorem 3. SupOMLatLin *is an involutive quantaloid that is a full dagger subcategory of* **SupOLatLin**.

The intrinsic structure of sets of linear maps between complete orthomodular lattices is the focus of our current discussion. We derive the following as a corollary of Theorem 3.

Corollary 2. *Let* X *and* Y *be complete orthomodular lattices. Then*

(i) $\mathbf{Lin}(X, Y)$ *is a complete lattice,*
(ii) $\mathbf{Lin}(X)$ *is a unital involutive quantale.*

3   Foulis Quantales and Their Modules

In the 1960s, David Foulis introduced a novel mathematical structure known as a "Baer *-semigroup", later termed a "Foulis semigroup". Properties of the multiplicative semigroup of bounded operators on a Hilbert space served as the basis for Foulis' initial set of characteristics.

This structure provides a framework for modeling various aspects of quantum mechanics. While it has been referenced under different names throughout the literature, its fundamental properties have remained unchanged. For a concise overview, we refer to Chap. 5, Sect. 18 of Kalmbach's book [12]. The Foulis quantales we introduce here can be characterized precisely as unital involutive quantales that additionally exhibit the structural properties of Foulis semigroups.

Definition 9. A Foulis quantale is a unital involutive quantale Q together with an endomap $[-] : Q \to Q$ satisfying:

(a) $[s]$ is a self-adjoint idempotent, i.e., satisfies $[s] \cdot [s] = [s] = [s]^*$;
(b) $0 = [e]$;
(c) $s \cdot x = 0$ iff $\exists_y . x = [s] \cdot y$.

For an arbitrary $t \in Q$ put $t^\perp \stackrel{def}{=} [t^*] \in [Q]$. Hence from (a) we get equations $t^\perp \cdot t^\perp = t^\perp = (t^\perp)^*$. We will call elements of $[Q]$ Sasaki projections.

A homomorphism of Foulis quantales is a map $h \colon Q_1 \to Q_2$ between Foulis quantales that preserves arbitrary joins, finite multiplication, unit, involution, and $^\perp$. In particular, h maps Sasaki projections to Sasaki projections.

Remark 1. A quantale is a Foulis quantale if and only if it is a unital involutive quantale Q equipped with an endomap $-^\perp \colon Q \to Q$ satisfying the following conditions:

(1) $s^\perp$ is a self-adjoint idempotent, i.e., $s^\perp \cdot s^\perp = s^\perp = (s^\perp)^*$;
(2) $0 = e^\perp$;
(3) $s \perp x = 0$ if and only if there exists y such that $x = s^\perp \cdot y$.

When considering a complete orthomodular lattice, its associated endomorphism quantale exhibits the specific algebraic properties that characterize a Foulis quantale. The fact that $\mathbf{Lin}(X)$ forms a Foulis semigroup for any orthomodular lattice X is a classical result from [7], later elaborated via Galois connections in [12, Chapter 5, §§18], dating back six decades.

Proposition 1. *Let X be a complete orthomodular lattice. Then $\mathbf{Lin}(X)$ is a Foulis quantale.*

Proof. We know from Corollary 2 that $\mathbf{Lin}(X)$ is a unital involutive quantale. Let us define the endomap $[-] \colon \mathbf{Lin}(X) \to \mathbf{Lin}(X)$ by $[s] = \pi_{s^*(1)^\perp}$ for all $s \in \mathbf{Lin}(X)$. Evidently, $[s]$ is a self-adjoint idempotent. We compute:

$$[\mathrm{id}_X] = \pi_{\mathrm{id}_X^*(1)^\perp} = \pi_{1^\perp} = \pi_0 = 0_{X,X}.$$

Suppose that $s, t \in \mathbf{Lin}(X)$. Let $t = [s] \circ r$. From Theorem 2 we conclude

$$s \circ t = s \circ \pi_{s^*(1)^\perp} \circ r = s \circ \ker(s) \circ \ker(s)^* \circ r$$
$$= 0_{\downarrow s^*(1)^\perp, X} \circ \ker(s)^* \circ r = 0_{X,X} = 0_{\mathbf{Lin}(X)}.$$

Conversely, if $s \circ t = 0_{\mathbf{Lin}(X)} = 0_{X,X}$, then there is a linear map $f \colon X \to {\downarrow}s^*(1)^\perp$ such that $\ker(s) \circ f = t$ and $0_{\downarrow s^*(1)^\perp, X} \circ f = 0_{X,X}$. Hence t satisfies:

$$[s] \circ t = \pi_{s^*(1)^\perp} \circ t = \ker(s) \circ \ker(s)^* \circ \ker(s) \circ f = \ker(s) \circ f = t.$$

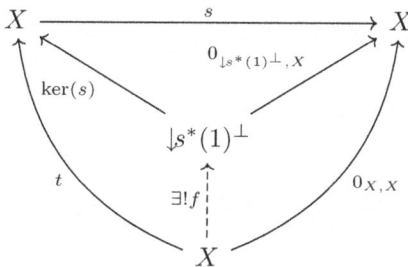

Theorem 4. *Let Q be a Foulis quantale. Then, for all $t, r \in Q$ and $k \in [Q]$,*

$$r^* \cdot t = 0 \iff t = [r^*] \cdot t, \tag{*}$$

$$t \leq r \implies r^\perp \leq t^\perp \text{ and } k^{\perp\perp} = k, \tag{**}$$

$$t \leq r^\perp \iff r \leq t^\perp. \tag{***}$$

and the subset

$$[Q] = \{[t] \mid t \in Q\} \subseteq Q,$$

is a complete orthomodular lattice with the following structure.

Order	$k_1 \leq k_2 \Leftrightarrow k_1 = k_2 \cdot k_1$
Top	$1 = [0]$
Orthocomplementquad	$k^\perp = [k]$
Meet	$k_1 \wedge k_2 = \left(k_1 \cdot [[k_2] \cdot k_1]\right)^{\perp\perp}$
Join	$\bigvee S = [[\bigsqcup S]].$

Proof. A significant portion of this statement, including its proof for Foulis semigroups, aligns with the established findings presented in [11, Lemma 4.6.]. To complete the demonstration, it is necessary only to establish that

$$[[\bigsqcup S]] = \bigvee S$$

where S is a subset of $[Q]$. As this portion of the proof is identical to the argument presented in [4, Theorem 21] for a finite subset, we refer the reader there for the complete details.

Quantale modules formalize the interaction between quantum operations and quantum states. Specifically, elements of a quantale Q represent quantum operations, while points in a module A correspond to the possible states of a quantum system. The action of the quantale on its module captures how quantum operations transform the system state: each operation $q \in Q$ induces a state transition $q \cdot m \mapsto m'$, where $m, m' \in A$.

Definition 10. Given a quantale Q, a left Q-module is a complete lattice A and a map $\bullet \colon Q \times A \longrightarrow A$ *satisfying:*

(A1) $s \bullet (\bigvee B) = \bigvee_{x \in B}(s \bullet x)$ for every $B \subseteq A$ and $s \in Q$.
(A2) $(\bigsqcup T) \bullet a = \bigvee_{t \in T}(t \bullet a)$ for every $T \subseteq Q$ and $a \in A$.
(A3) $u \bullet (v \bullet a) = (u \cdot v) \bullet a$ for every $u, v \in Q$ and every $a \in A$.
(A4) $e \bullet a = a$ for all $a \in A$ (unitality).

The definition of right Q-modules follows analogously. It is readily apparent that every complete lattice A forms a right **2**-module. Here, **2** represents a two-element chain equipped with a meet operation as its multiplication and the identity map as its involution.

The following statement says that a complete orthomodular lattice X can be acted upon from the left by its linear transformations and from the right by a specific two-element structure, giving it two different but compatible ways of being transformed or modified.

Proposition 2. *Let X be a complete orthomodular lattice. Then X is a left* **Lin**(X)-*module and also a right* **2**-*module.*

Proof. We define the action $\bullet\colon \mathbf{Lin}(X) \times X \longrightarrow X$ by $f \bullet x = f(x)$ for all $f \in \mathbf{Lin}(X)$ and all $x \in X$. The verification of conditions (A1)-(A4) is transparent.

The following theorem demonstrates that the complete orthomodular lattice of Sasaki projections in a Foulis quantale carries both a left module structure over the quantale itself and a right module structure over the two-element Boolean algebra. This bimodule structure illuminates the algebraic nature of Sasaki projections.

Theorem 5. *Let Q be a Foulis quantale. Then $[Q]$ is a left Q-module with action $\bullet$ defined as $u \bullet k = (u \cdot k)^{\perp\perp}$ for all $u \in Q$ and $k \in [Q]$ and also a right* **2**-*module.*

Proof. The proof proceeds analogously to [4, Theorem 24], with the sole modification that arbitrary subsets are used in place of finite subsets throughout the argument.

Definition 11. *Let Q be a Foulis quantale and $u \in Q$. Then the map $\sigma_u \colon [Q] \to [Q]$, $y \mapsto u \bullet y$ is called the* Sasaki action *to $u \in Q$.*

Evidently, $\sigma_u \in \mathbf{Lin}([Q])$. Moreover, if $u \in [Q]$ then σ_u is self-adjoint linear, idempotent and $\operatorname{im} \sigma_u = {\downarrow}u$ in $[Q]$ (see [4, Proposition 26]).

The following theorem establishes a canonical correspondence between elements of a Foulis quantale and linear transformations acting on its Sasaki projections, illuminating the structural relationship between these components.

Theorem 6. *Let Q be a Foulis quantale. Then there is a natural homomorphism $h\colon Q \to \mathbf{Lin}([Q])$ of Foulis quantales such that $h(u) = \sigma_u$ for all $u \in Q$.*

Proof. Since $[S]$ is a left Q-module, we obtain that h preserves multiplication, arbitrary joins, and the unit. It remains to show that h preserves involution and $\perp$.

Assume that $u \in Q$ and $k, l \in [Q]$. We compute:

$h(u)^\star(k) \le l^\perp$ if and only if $h(u)^\star(k) \perp l$ if and only if $k \perp h(u)(l)$

if and only if $h(u)(l) \le k^\perp$ if and only if $u \bullet l \le k^\perp$ if and only if

$k^\perp \cdot u \cdot l = u \cdot l$ if and only if $k \cdot u \cdot l = 0$ if and only if $l^\star \cdot u^\star \cdot k^\star = 0$

if and only if $l \cdot u^\star \cdot k = 0$ if and only if $l^\perp \cdot u^\star \cdot k = u^\star \cdot k$

if and only if $u^\star \bullet k \le l^\perp$ if and only if $h(u^\star)(k) \le l^\perp$.

Since $u^\perp \in [Q]$ we have that $h(u^\perp) = \sigma_{u^\perp}$ is the classical Sasaki projection $\pi_{u^\perp}$ by [5, Proposition 3.6]. From Proposition 1 we obtain

$$h(u)^\perp = \pi_{h(u)(e)^\perp} = \pi_{(u^{\perp\perp})^\perp} = \pi_{u^\perp}.$$

We conclude that $h(u)^\star = h(u^\star)$ and $h(u)^\perp = h(u^\perp)$ for all $u \in Q$.

Acknowledgments. The first author acknowledges support from the Czech Science Foundation (GAČR) project 23-14386L "Representations of algebraic semantics for substructural logics". The second author was supported by the Austrian Science Fund (FWF) [10.55776/PIN5424624] and the Czech Science Foundation (GAČR) project 24-14386L "Orthogonality and Symmetry". The third author acknowledges support from the Masaryk University project MUNI/A/1457/2023.

We thank the anonymous referees for the very thorough reading and contributions to improve our presentation of the paper.

References

1. Abramsky, S., Coecke, B.: A categorical semantics of quantum protocols. In: Proceedings of the 19th Annual IEEE Symposium on Logic in Computer Science, pp. 415–225 (2004)
2. Abramsky, S., Vickers, S.J.: Quantales, observational logic and process semantics. Math. Struct. Comput. Sci. **3**(2), 161–227 (1993)
3. Birkhoff, G., von Neumann, J.: The logic of quantum mechanics. Ann. Math. **37**(4), 823–843 (1936)
4. Botur, M., Paseka, J., Lekár, M.: Foulis m-semilattices and their modules. In: Proc. 2025 IEEE 55rd Internat. Symp. Multiple-Valued Logic, pp. 196–201. Springer (2025). https://doi.org/10.1109/ISMVL64713.2025.00044
5. Botur, M., Paseka, J., Smolka, R.: A dagger kernel category of complete orthomodular lattices. Int. J. Theor. Phys. **64**, 111 (2025). https://doi.org/10.1007/s10773-025-05965-z
6. Esteva, F., Godo, L.: Monoidal t-norm based logic: towards a logic for left-continuous t-norms. Fuzzy Sets Syst. **124**(3), 271–288 (2001)
7. Foulis, D.J.: Baer *-Semigroups. Proc. Am. Math. Soc. **11**(4), 648–654 (1960)
8. Gylys, R.: Involutive and relational quantaloids. Lith. Math. J. **39**, 376–388 (1999)
9. Hájek, P.: Metamathematics of Fuzzy Logic. Trends in Logic, vol. 4. Kluwer Academic Publishers, Dordrecht (1998)
10. Heunen, C., Jacobs, B.: Quantum logic in dagger kernel categories. Electr. Notes Theor. Comput. Sci. **270**(2), 79–103 (2011)
11. Jacobs, B.: Orthomodular lattices, Foulis semigroups and dagger kernel categories. Logical Methods Comput. Sci. **6**(2:1), 1–26 (2010)
12. Kalmbach, G.: Orthomodular Lattices. Academic Press, London (1983)
13. Lindenhovius, B., Vetterlein, T.: A characterisation of orthomodular spaces by Sasaki maps. Int. J. Theor. Phys. **62**, Article no. 59 (2023)
14. Mulvey, C.J.: §. Suppl. Rend. Circ. Mat. Palermo ser. II, **12**, 99–104 (1986)
15. Mulvey, C.J., Pelletier, J.W.: A quantisation of the calculus of relations. In: Canadian Mathematical Society Conference Proceedings, vol. 13, pp. 345–360. American Mathematical Society, Providence (1992)

16. Rosenthal, K.I.: Quantales and Their Applications. Pitman Research Notes in Mathematics, vol. 234, Longman Scientific & Technical (1990)
17. Rosenthal, K.I.: The Theory of Quantaloids, Pitman Research Notes in Mathematics Series, vol. 348, Longman Scientific & Technical (1996)
18. Selinger, P.: Dagger compact closed categories and completely positive maps. In: Selinger, P. (ed.) Proceedings of the 3rd International Workshop on Quantum Programming Languages (QPL 2005), pp. 139–163. Elsevier, Amsterdam (2007)
19. Solovjovs, S.: Quantale algebras as a generalization of lattice-valued frames. Hacettepe J. Math. Stat. **45**(3), 781–809 (2016)

On Some Properties of Tabular Varieties of MTL-Algebras and Their Decidability

Stefano Aguzzoli and Matteo Bianchi[(✉)]

Department of Computer Science "Giovanni degli Antoni", Università degli Studi di Milano, Via Celoria 18, 20133 Milan, Italy
{stefano.aguzzoli,matteo.bianchi}@unimi.it

Abstract. A variety is called tabular (T) whenever it is generated by one finite algebra. A pretabular (PT) variety is a non tabular variety whose proper subvarieties are all tabular. Those notions were firstly studied for Heyting algebras, in the sixties and seventies. An important role of PT varieties is to check if the tabularity problem (*i.e.* deciding if a certain variety is tabular or not) is decidable. In a recent work we started studying T and PT varieties of MTL-algebras, finding some preliminary results. In this paper we take a step further, by studying the decidability issues for some properties for tabular varieties of MTL-algebras, like tabularity, consistent tabularity, non-boolean tabularity, single chain generation and amalgamation property. We study the decidability and the computational complexity of those problems.

Keywords: MTL-algebras · Tabular Varieties · Pretabular Varieties · Decidability · Tabularity problem · Amalgamation Property · Single-chain completeness

1   Introduction

Tabular logics have been studied since the sixties [26], while the notion of a pretabular variety was firstly introduced and studied some years later for the case of Heyting algebras [22,23]. During the years the analysis has been extended to modal algebras and to other classes of algebras [9,13,21,24]. Monoidal t-norm based logic MTL was introduced in [14], together with MTL-algebras, the corresponding algebraic semantics. MTL-algebras are special types of residuated lattices [16], and every axiomatic extension of MTL is algebraizable in the sense of [10]. This means that for every axiomatic extension L of MTL there exists a unique subvariety of MTL-algebras, the variety of L-algebras, that provides the corresponding algebraic semantics for L. In [5] we started a preliminary analysis of tabular (T) and pretabular (PT) varieties of MTL-algebras, by providing the full classification for PT varieties of BL and WNM-algebras, as well as some general results about tabular and pretabular varieties. However, the PT varieties were originally also studied as a tool connected to the tabularity problem, namely deciding if a certain variety is tabular or not. Indeed, the tabularity problem was

© The Author(s), under exclusive license to Springer Nature Switzerland AG 2025
M. Baczyński et al. (Eds.): EUSFLAT 2025, LNCS 15883, pp. 322–334, 2025.
https://doi.org/10.1007/978-3-031-97225-6_26

already mentioned in [24]. In this paper we tackle some decidability issues for some properties related to tabular varieties. PT varieties play a pivotal role in the decidability for the tabularity problem: a variety of MTL-algebras is non tabular if and only if it does contain a PT subvariety. Let $\mathbb{L}$ be a variety of MTL-algebras. Let $\mathbb{M}$ be a subvariety of $\mathbb{L}$, such that $\mathbb{M}$ is finitely axiomatizable from MTL. We say that the tabularity property for $\mathbb{L}$ is decidable whenever there is an algorithm that decides if $\mathbb{M}$ is tabular or not. We also study two variations of the tabularity problem, namely consistent and non-boolean tabularity, and we provide computational complexity results. Let $\mathbb{L}$ be a tabular variety of MTL-algebras. The single chain generated problem consists in deciding if there exists a chain $\mathcal{A} \in \mathbb{L}$ which generates $\mathbb{L}$ as a variety or not. Finally, the amalgamation property (see Sect. 5) problem consists in deciding if $\mathbb{L}$ has the amalgamation property or not.

We prove the following results.

- The tabularity problem for the varieties of BL and WNM-algebras is NP-complete.
- The consistent tabularity problem for the varieties of BL and WNM-algebras is in BH_2 as well as the non-Boolean tabularity problem for WNM.
- The single chain generated problem and the amalgamation property problem for tabular varieties of MTL-algebras are decidable.

2   Preliminaries

Let $\mathbb{L}$ be a variety of MTL-algebras. With $\mathcal{L}(\mathbb{L})$ we denote its lattice of subvarieties, ordered by inclusion. Given a class of algebras we denote with $\mathbf{V}(K)$ the variety generated by K. Analogously, given a set of equations Ax, we denote with $\mathbf{V}(Ax)$ the equational class of all algebras satisfying identically all equations in Ax. We shall use $\mathbf{V}_{\mathbb{L}}(Ax)$ to denote the variety axiomatized as $\mathbb{L}$ plus Ax.

Theorem 1 ([20]).   *Let $\mathbb{L}$ be a variety of algebras. Then $\mathcal{L}(\mathbb{L})$ is a dually-algebraic lattice, and the varieties finitely axiomatizable from $\mathbb{L}$ are the dually-compact elements of $\mathcal{L}(\mathbb{L})$.*

Definition 1.   *An MTL algebra is an algebra $(A, *, \rightarrow, \wedge, \vee, 0, 1)$ such that:*

1. *$(A, \wedge, \vee, 0, 1)$ is a bounded lattice with minimum 0 and maximum 1.*
2. *$(A, *, 1)$ is a commutative monoid.*
3. *$(*, \rightarrow)$ forms a residuated pair: $z * x \leq y$ iff $z \leq x \rightarrow y$ for all $x, y, z \in A$.*
4. *The following identity holds, for all $x, y \in A$:*

$$(x \rightarrow y) \vee (y \rightarrow x) = 1. \qquad \text{(Prelinearity)}$$

A totally ordered MTL-algebra is called MTL-chain.

In the rest of the paper the notation $\neg x$ denotes $x \to 0$. The class of all MTL-algebras forms a variety of algebras: see [14, §2.2],[12, Page 30] for details. Given a class K of MTL-algebras, with $Ch(K)$ we denote the class of chains in $\mathbf{V}(K)$. If $K = \{\mathcal{A}\}$ we write $Ch(\mathcal{A})$ for $Ch(\{\mathcal{A}\})$. We now list some varieties of MTL-algebras that will be used in the rest of the paper.

- The variety of BL-algebras, $\mathbb{BL}$, axiomatized as $\mathbb{MTL}$ plus (DIV): $x \wedge y = x * (x \to y)$.
- The variety of WNM-algebras, $\mathbb{WNM}$, axiomatized as $\mathbb{MTL}$ plus (WNM): $\neg(x * y) \vee ((x \wedge y) \to (x * y)) = 1$.

We will also mention a number of subvarieties of BL and WNM-algebras. Specifically, the varieties of: MV-algebras $\mathbb{MV}$, perfect MV-algebras $\mathbb{C}$, product algebras $\mathbb{P}$, strict basic algebras $\mathbb{SBL}$, drastic product algebras $\mathbb{DP}$, F-algebras $\mathbb{F}$, Gödel algebras $\mathbb{G}$, NM$^-$-algebras $\mathbb{NM}^-$. We refer to [3,6,11,17,18] for all the details. We recall that, for $n \in \mathbb{N}$ and $V \in \{DP, NM, G, F\}$, all the V-chains with n elements are isomorphic (see [1,3,6]). So, with the notation $\mathcal{V}_n$ we denote an arbitrarily fixed V-chain with n elements, and by $\mathbb{V}_n$ the variety it generates. Moreover, $\mathcal{L}_k$ denotes the k element MV-chain, and $\mathbb{MV}_k = \mathbf{V}(\mathcal{L}_k)$.

3 Tabular and Pretabular Varieties of MTL-Algebras

In this section we recall some general properties of tabular and pretabular varieties of MTL-algebras. For further details we refer to [5].

Definition 2. *Let $\mathbb{L}$ be a variety of MTL-algebras.*

- *$\mathbb{L}$ is said to be* tabular *(T), whenever $\mathbb{L}$ is generated by one finite algebra.*
- *$\mathbb{L}$ is said to be* pretabular *(PT) if every proper subvariety of $\mathbb{L}$ is tabular, whilst $\mathbb{L}$ is not tabular.*

Definition 3. *A a variety $\mathbb{L}$ of MTL-algebras is said to be almost minimal (AM), whenever $\mathbb{B} \subsetneq \mathbb{L}$ is the only proper non-trivial subvariety of $\mathbb{L}$.*

We have the following characterization for tabular varieties of MTL-algebras.

Theorem 2 ([5]). *Let $\mathbb{L}$ be a variety of MTL-algebras. The following are equivalent.*

a) $\mathbb{L}$ *is tabular.*
b) $\mathbb{L}$ *does not contain any infinite chain.*
c) $\mathbb{L}$ *is generated by one finite set of finite chains.*

By Baker's theorem, every T variety of MTL-algebras is finitely axiomatizable. For PT varieties of MTL-algebras we have the following result.

Theorem 3. *Let $\mathbb{L}$ be a variety of MTL-algebras. Then $\mathbb{L}$ is PT if and only if the following hold.*

1) $\mathbb{L}$ *is not tabular.*
2) *For every infinite chain $\mathcal{C} \in \mathbb{L}$, $\mathbf{V}(\mathcal{C}) = \mathbb{L}$.*

4 The Complexity of Deciding Tabularity

Let $\mathbb{L}$ be a variety of MTL-algebras, and let $\mathbb{M} \in \mathcal{L}(\mathbb{L})$ be finitely axiomatizable, via a finite set of equations S, from $\mathbb{L}$. We say that the tabularity property for $\mathbb{L}$ is decidable whenever there is an algorithm that decides if $\mathbb{M}$ is tabular or not. To tackle this problem the notion of PT variety is essential. We will show that a variety is non-tabular if and only if it has a PT subvariety. Therefore, we have that $\mathbb{M}$ is non-tabular if and only if S holds true in some PT variety in $\mathbb{M} \in \mathcal{L}(\mathbb{L})$. In particular, if the set of PT varieties in $\mathbb{M} \in \mathcal{L}(\mathbb{L})$ is finite, then the tabularity problem for $\mathbb{L}$ is decidable.

Notice that every PT variety $\mathbb{L} \in \mathcal{L}(\mathrm{MTL})$ is a minimal non-tabular variety, since $\mathcal{L}(\mathbb{M}) \setminus \{\mathbb{M}\}$ contains only tabular varieties.

Proposition 1. *Let $\mathbb{L}$ be a non-tabular variety of MTL-algebras, and let $NT(\mathbb{L})$ be the poset of all non-tabular varieties in $\mathcal{L}(\mathbb{L})$. Then*

- $NT(\mathbb{L})$ *is a join semilattice.*
- *every chain in $NT(\mathbb{L})$ has a greatest lower bound in $NT(\mathbb{L})$.*

Proof. Let $\mathbb{L}$ be a non-tabular variety of MTL-algebras, and let $NT(\mathbb{L})$ be the poset of all non-tabular varieties in $\mathcal{L}(\mathbb{L})$. Since $\mathcal{L}(\mathbb{L})$ is a complete lattice, and $NT(\mathbb{L})$ is obtained from it by removing tabular varieties, an easy check shows that $NT(\mathbb{L})$ is a join semilattice. We now show that every chain in $NT(\mathbb{L})$ has a greatest lower bound. Suppose not. Then there is a chain in $NT(\mathbb{L})$, say $\mathcal{A}$ such that $\mathcal{A}$ has no greatest lower bound in $NT(\mathbb{L})$. By Theorem 1 $\mathcal{L}(\mathbb{L})$ is a complete lattice, and then every chain in $\mathcal{L}(\mathbb{L})$ has a greatest lower bound. Therefore the greatest lower bound of $\mathcal{A}$ is a tabular variety, say $\mathbb{M}$. Then $\mathbb{M}$ is finitely axiomatizable, and therefore it is a dually-compact element in $\mathcal{L}(\mathbb{L})$. Since $\mathbb{M} = \inf(\mathcal{A})$, then $\mathbb{M} \geq \inf(T)$, for some finite subset T of $\mathcal{A}$. Since T is a finite totally ordered set of non-tabular varieties, then $\inf(T) \in T$, but this would imply that $\mathbb{M}$ contains a non-tabular subvariety, which is impossible. The proof is settled. □

Remark 1. Notice that the poset of non-tabular varieties is not a lattice, in general. Consider the variety $\mathbb{P} \vee \mathbb{C}$, where $\mathbb{P}$ and $\mathbb{C}$ are the variety of product algebras and the variety generated by Chang's MV-algebra, respectively. Then the poset P of non-tabular varieties of $\mathbb{P} \vee \mathbb{C}$ is the following one:

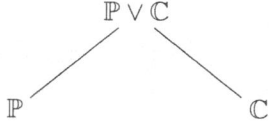

Clearly this is not a lattice, since $\mathbb{P} \wedge \mathbb{C} = \mathbb{B}$ is not contained in P.

A moment's reflection shows that each join semilattice of non-tabular varieties containing at least two distinct pretabular varieties is not a lattice, since they are incomparable and their meet is tabular (the meet does not need to be $\mathbb{B}$, for instance $\mathbb{F} \wedge \mathrm{NM}^- = \mathrm{NM}_4$).

Theorem 4. *A variety* $\mathbb{L}$ *of MTL-algebras is non-tabular if and only if* $\mathcal{L}(\mathbb{L})$ *does contain some PT variety.*

Proof. The right to left direction is trivial. For the left to right direction, let $\mathbb{L}$ be a non-tabular variety, and let C be the poset of all the non-tabular subvarieties in $\mathcal{L}(\mathbb{L})$. By Proposition 1, every chain in C has a greatest lower bound. By an easy application of Zorn lemma, C must have a minimal element, which is necessarily a PT variety. The proof is settled.   □

In the next sections we shall deal with the computational complexity of deciding tabularity for some subvarieties of MTL. Since we shall deal with axiomatisations we recall here the reader that each subvariety of MTL is axiomatisable with a set of identities of the form $\mathcal{E} = 1$, for $\mathcal{E}$ a term in the language of MTL. As a matter of fact, an MTL-algebra $\mathcal{A}$ satisfies an identity of the form $\mathcal{E}_1 = \mathcal{E}_2$ if and only if it satisfies $\mathcal{E}_1 \leftrightarrow \mathcal{E}_2 = 1$.

We shall need also some of the following definitions and results about the complexity of decision problems for satisfiability and validity for some subvarieties of BL and MTL.

Definition 4. *Let* $\mathbb{V}$ *be a variety of MTL-algebras. Then the Problem* $TAUT(\mathbb{V})$ *is defined as:*

- *INSTANCE: An identity* $\mathcal{E} = 1$.
- *QUESTION: Does* $\mathcal{E} = 1$ *hold in all algebras in* $\mathcal{V}$?

The name $TAUT(\mathbb{V})$ we have given to the problem defined in Definition 4 comes from logic as it correspond to the problem of tautologousness of formulas in the propositional logic whose associated algebraic semantics is the variety $\mathbb{V}$. Therefore, a formula is a tautology if and only the corresponding identity holds in all algebras in the variety. We recall that $SAT(\mathbb{B})$ and $TAUT(\mathbb{B})$ corresponds to satisfiability and tautologousness of formulas in classical propositional logic, so $SAT(\mathbb{B})$ is NP-complete and $TAUT(\mathbb{B})$ is coNP-complete.

We recall some complexity results about deciding tautologousness for varieties of MTL-algebras. See [7,19] for a thorough investigation of these topics.

Lemma 1. *Let* $\mathbb{V}$ *be a variety of WNM-algebras generated by a single chain. Then* $TAUT(\mathbb{V})$ *is in coNP.*

Proof. It is well known that the universe of each WNM chain $\mathcal{C}$ generated by a finite set $\{x_1, \ldots, x_n\}$ of elements is $\{0, 1\} \cup \{x_i, \neg x_i, \neg\neg x_i \mid i \in \{1, \ldots, n\}\}$, that is, it counts at most $3n + 2$ elements. It is then trivial that checking that a valuation $\sigma: Var \to \mathcal{C}$ is such that $\sigma(\mathcal{E}) \neq 1$ requires polynomial time in the number of variables occurring in $\mathcal{E}$. This observation proves that $TAUT(\mathbb{V})$ is in coNP.   □

Notice that we can apply Lemma 1 to the varieties $\mathbb{G}, \mathbb{NM}^-, \mathbb{DP}$ and $\mathbb{F}$, as well as their finitely valued variants, since all of them are subvarieties of WNM that are generated by a single chain.

Lemma 2. *Let* $\mathbb{V}$ *be any subvariety of* $\mathbb{SBL}$. *Then* $TAUT(\mathbb{V})$ *is coNP-hard.*

Proof. For each identity $\mathcal{E} = 1$, the map $\mathcal{E} \mapsto \neg\neg\mathcal{E}$ is a polynomial time reduction of TAUT($\mathbb{B}$) to TAUT($\mathbb{V}$). □

We can apply Lemma 2 to both $\mathbb{G}$ and $\mathbb{P}$ as they both are subvarieties of $\mathbb{SBL}$. The following lemma was shown in [18], but it follows also by Lemma 1 and Lemma 2.

Lemma 3. $TAUT(\mathbb{G})$ *is coNP-complete*

The proof of the following lemma can be found in [19, Thm. 4.2.5, Cor. 5.1.5].

Lemma 4. *Let* $\mathbb{V} \in \{\mathbb{P}, \mathbb{C}\}$. *Then* $TAUT(\mathbb{V})$ *is coNP-complete.*

4.1 Tabularity for Subvarieties of $\mathbb{BL}$

We recall the following result from [5].

Theorem 5. *The pretabular subvarieties of* $\mathbb{BL}$ *are exactly* $\mathbb{G}, \mathbb{P}, \mathbb{C}$.

We are ready to establish the computational complexity of the problem of tabularity for subvarieties of $\mathbb{BL}$.

Definition 5. *We define the Problem TABULARITY_FOR_BL:*

> *INSTANCE:* A finite set Ax of identities of the form $\mathcal{E} = 1$.
> *QUESTION:* Is the subvariety of $\mathbb{BL}$ axiomatised by Ax tabular?

Lemma 5. *TABULARITY_FOR_BL is in NP.*

Proof. We have to check whether the subvariety $\mathbf{V}_{\mathbb{BL}}(Ax)$ of $\mathbb{BL}$ is tabular. To prove that $\mathbf{V}_{\mathbb{BL}}(Ax)$ is tabular, for each variety $\mathbb{W} \in \{\mathbb{G}, \mathbb{P}, \mathbb{C}\}$ one guesses an identity $\mathcal{E}_\mathbb{W} = 1 \in Ax$ that fails in $\mathbb{W}$. Then the set of identities $\{\mathcal{E}_\mathbb{W} = 1 \mid \mathbb{W} \in \{\mathbb{G}, \mathbb{P}, \mathbb{C}\}\}$ does not hold in any supervariety of any one of $\mathbb{G}, \mathbb{P}, \mathbb{C}$. Whence, by Theorem 4, the set of identities Ax cannot axiomatise any non-tabular subvariety of $\mathbb{BL}$, therefore it axiomatises a tabular (maybe trivial) subvariety of $\mathbb{BL}$.

Since $\mathcal{E}_\mathbb{W} = 1$ is not in TAUT($\mathbb{W}$), by Lemma 1 and Lemma 4, TABULARITY_FOR_BL is in NP. □

Lemma 6. *TABULARITY_FOR_BL is NP-hard.*

Proof. By Lemma 3, it suffices to reduce the complement of TAUT($\mathbb{G}$) to TABULARITY_FOR_BL in polynomial time.

Let $\mathcal{E} = 1$ be an identity. Consider the finite set of identities $E(\mathcal{E}) = Ax(\mathbb{G}) \cup \{\mathcal{E} = 1\}$, where $Ax(\mathbb{G})$ axiomatises Gödel algebras, that is $Ax(\mathbb{G}) = \{x \to (x * x) = 1\}$. Then, if $\mathcal{E} = 1$ fails in $\mathbb{G}$, the set of identities $E(\mathcal{E})$ fails in $\mathbb{G}$, too, and clearly fails both in $\mathbb{P}$ and $\mathbb{C}$. By Theorem 4, then $E(\mathcal{E})$ must fail in every supervariety of any one of $\mathbb{G}, \mathbb{P}, \mathbb{C}$. That is, $E(\mathcal{E})$ axiomatises a tabular (maybe trivial) subvariety of $\mathbb{BL}$. Trivially, the reduction $\mathcal{E} \mapsto E(\mathcal{E})$ can be computed in polynomial time. By Lemma 3, we conclude that TABULARITY_FOR_BL is NP-hard. □

Theorem 6. *TABULARITY_FOR_BL is NP-complete.*

Proof. By Lemma 5 and Lemma 6. □

4.2   Tabularity for Subvarieties of WNM

We recall another result from [5].

Theorem 7 ([5]). *The pretabular subvarieties of* $\mathbb{BL}$ *are exactly* $\mathbb{G}, \mathrm{NM}^-, \mathbb{DP}, \mathbb{F}$.

In analogy with the previous subsection we are going to establish the computational complexity of the problem of tabularity for subvarieties of WNM.

Definition 6. *We define the Problem TABULARITY_FOR_WNM:*

> INSTANCE: *A finite set Ax of identities of the form* $\mathcal{E} = 1$.
> QUESTION: *Is the subvariety of* WNM *axiomatised by Ax tabular?*

Lemma 7. *TABULARITY_FOR_WNM is in NP.*

Proof. We proceed in analogous fashion as in the proof of Lemma 5. One just need to guess for each $\mathbb{W} \in \{\mathbb{G}, \mathrm{NM}^-, \mathbb{DP}, \mathbb{F}\}$, an identity $\mathcal{E}_{\mathbb{W}} = 1 \in Ax$ failing in $\mathbb{W}$. By Lemma 1, we conclude TABULARITY_FOR_WNM is in NP.   □

Lemma 8. *TABULARITY_FOR_WNM is NP-hard.*

Proof. In complete analogy with the proof of Lemma 6, we reduce polynomially the complement of $\mathrm{TAUT}(\mathbb{G})$ to TABULARITY_FOR_WNM, by mapping each identity $\mathcal{E} = 1$ to $E(\mathcal{E}) = Ax(\mathbb{G}) \cup \{\mathcal{E} = 1\}$.   □

Theorem 8. *TABULARITY_FOR_WNM is NP-complete.*

Proof. By Lemma 7 and Lemma 8.   □

4.3   Tabularity for Subvarieties of MTL

Results of Theorem 6 and Theorem 8 can be extended to decide tabularity for subvarieties of $\mathbb{BL} \vee \mathrm{WNM}$.

Definition 7. *For any subvariety* $\mathbb{V}$ *of* $\mathbb{BL} \vee \mathrm{WNM}$ *we define the Problem TABULARITY_FOR_V:*

> INSTANCE: *A finite set Ax of identities of the form* $\mathcal{E} = 1$.
> QUESTION: *Is the subvariety of* $\mathbb{V}$ *axiomatised by Ax tabular?*

Theorem 9. *TABULARITY_FOR_V is NP-complete for any subvariety* $\mathbb{V}$ *of* $\mathbb{BL} \vee \mathrm{WNM}$.

Proof. By Theorem 3 every PT variety is single chain generated, and by [4] $Ch(\mathbb{BL} \vee \mathrm{WNM}) = Ch(\mathbb{BL}) \cup Ch(\mathrm{WNM})$. Therefore the PT varieties in $\mathbb{BL} \vee \mathrm{WNM}$ coincide with the PT varieties in $\mathbb{BL} \cup \mathrm{WNM}$. Since the pretabular subvarieties of $\mathbb{V}$ form a subset of the pretabular subvarieties of $\mathbb{BL} \vee \mathrm{WNM}$, the proof is the same as the proofs of Theorem 6 and Theorem 8, *mutatis mutandis.*
□

How about the more general case of $\mathbb{V} = \mathrm{MTL}$? Unfortunately, we cannot use the strategies described before, as in [5, Theorem 2] it has been shown that there are uncountably many PT varieties of MTL-algebras. Therefore,

Problem 1. Is TABULARITY_FOR_MTL decidable?

4.4 Consistent Tabularity for $\mathbb{BL}$ and $\mathbb{WNM}$

In Definition 5 and Definition 6, we allow the case of a finite axiomatisation that actually gives the trivial variety. Therefore we propose the following variant:

Definition 8. *We define the Problems CONSISTENT_TABULARITY_FOR_$\mathbb{BL}$, and CONSISTENT_TABULARITY_FOR_$\mathbb{WNM}$:*
Let $\mathbb{V} \in \{\mathbb{BL}, \mathbb{WNM}\}$.

  INSTANCE: A finite set Ax of identities of the form $\mathcal{E} = 1$.
  QUESTION: Is $\mathbf{V}_\mathbb{V}(Ax)$ tabular and non-trivial?

Recall that DP, is the class of decision problems which are set differences of two problems in NP [25]. Equivalently, DP coincides with BH_2 in the Boolean hierarchy.

Theorem 10. *The Problems CONSISTENT_TABULARITY_FOR_$\mathbb{BL}$, and CONSISTENT_TABULARITY_FOR_$\mathbb{WNM}$ are in BH_2.*

Proof. By Lemma 5 and Lemma 7, checking that a given finite set of identities Ax axiomatises a tabular subvariety of $\mathbb{BL}$ or $\mathbb{WNM}$ is in NP. Let $\mathbb{W} \in \{\mathbb{BL}, \mathbb{WNM}\}$. We have to exclude that $\mathbf{V}_\mathbb{W}(Ax)$ is the trivial variety. But if it is not the trivial variety then the identity $0 = 1$ fails in any of its non-trivial subvarieties, for instance in the variety of Boolean algebras. So we must only check that Boolean algebras are a subvariety of $\mathbf{V}_\mathbb{W}(Ax)$. To check that this is not the case it is sufficient to guess $\mathcal{E} \in Ax$ and a Boolean valuation σ such that $\sigma(\mathcal{E}) \neq 1$. This check is clearly performed in polynomial time. $\square$

Clearly, an analogous result to Theorem 10 holds for any subvariety of $\mathbb{MTL}$ such that the tabularity problem for the finite axiomatisations of its subvarieties happens to be in NP. In particular, we have the following result.

Definition 9. *Let $\mathbb{V}$ be a subvariety of $\mathbb{BL} \vee \mathbb{WNM}$. We define the Problem CONSISTENT_TABULARITY_FOR_$\mathbb{V}$:*

  INSTANCE: A finite set Ax of identities of the form $\mathcal{E} = 1$.
  QUESTION: Is $\mathbf{V}_\mathbb{V}(Ax)$ tabular and non-trivial?

Theorem 11. *Problem CONSISTENT_TABULARITY_FOR_$\mathbb{V}$ is in BH_2.*

4.5 Non-Boolean Tabularity for $\mathbb{BL}$ and $\mathbb{WNM}$

It may be interesting to the many-valued logician to decide whether a set of identities axiomatises a non-trivial tabular variety which is not the variety of Boolean algebras.

Definition 10. *We define the Problems NON-BOOLEAN_TABULARITY_FOR_BL, and NON-BOOLEAN_TABULARITY_FOR_WNM:*
   Let $\mathbb{V} \in \{\mathbb{BL}, \mathbb{WNM}\}$.

   INSTANCE: A finite set Ax of identities of the form $\mathcal{E} = 1$.
   QUESTION: Is $\mathbf{V}_{\mathbb{V}}(Ax)$ tabular, non-trivial and distinct from $\mathbb{B}$?

Theorem 12. *NON-BOOLEAN_TABULARITY_FOR_WNM is in BH_2.*

Proof. Let $\mathbf{V}_{\mathrm{WNM}}(Ax)$ be a tabular variety. By [2] the almost minimal subvarieties of $\mathbb{WNM}$ are exactly $\mathbb{G}_3$, $\mathbb{NM}_4$, $\mathbb{DP}_3$. If an identity does not hold in any of $\mathbb{G}_3$, $\mathbb{NM}_4$, $\mathbb{DP}_3$ then, clearly, $\mathbf{V}_{\mathrm{WNM}}(Ax) = \mathbb{B}$ or it is trivial. Therefore NON-BOOLEAN_TABULARITY_FOR_WNM is in BH_2, as by Lemma 1, TAUT($\mathbb{V}$) is in coNP for any variety among $\mathbb{G}_3$, $\mathbb{NM}_4$, $\mathbb{DP}_3$. while TABULARITY_FOR_WNM is in NP by Lemma 7.   □

   In sharp contrast with Theorem 12, we cannot apply the same method to NON-BOOLEAN_TABULARITY_FOR_BL, since there are infinitely many almost minimal subvarieties of $\mathbb{BL}$, namely $\mathbb{G}_3$, $\mathbb{P}$, $\mathbb{C}$ and $\mathbb{MV}_{p+1}$ for each prime number p (see [2,3]). Therefore, the problem of establishing that an identity fails in all almost minimal subvarieties of $\mathbb{BL}$ is not likely to be in NP. Since one has to guess an almost minimal subvariety where to check that all equations of Ax hold identically, we can prove containment in Σ_2^p of the polynomial hierarchy.

5   Decidable Problems Concerning Tabular Subvarieties of $\mathbb{MTL}$

As any tabular subvariety of $\mathbb{MTL}$ is generated by a finite set of finite chains, every problem that consists of checking (even by brute force) that some property holds for any relevant (to the problem) combination of generators must be decidable. Here we give two examples of such problems, which also have an interesting equivalent logical version.

5.1   Single Chain Generated Problem for Tabular Varieties

A variety $\mathbb{L}$ of MTL-algebras is *single-chain generated* (SCG) whenever there exists a chain $\mathcal{A}$ such that $\mathbf{V}(\mathcal{A}) = \mathbb{L}$.

Theorem 13. *Let $\mathbb{L}$ be a tabular variety of MTL-algebras. The following are equivalent.*

1 $\mathbb{L}$ is SCG.
2 There exists a finite chain $\mathcal{A}$ such that $\mathbb{L} = \mathbf{V}(\mathcal{A})$.
3 $Ch(\mathbb{L}) = \mathbf{HS}(\mathcal{A})$, for some finite chain $\mathcal{A}$.
4 There exists a finite chain $\mathcal{A} \in \mathbb{L}$ such that every chain in $\mathbb{L}$ embeds in some quotient of $\mathcal{A}$.

Proof. Let $\mathbb{L}$ be a tabular variety of MTL-algebras. By Theorem 2 1) is equivalent to 2). By Jónsson's lemma and Theorem 2, 2) is equivalent to 3). Since every variety of MTL-algebras has the congruence extension property, $\mathbf{HS}(K) = \mathbf{SH}(K)$, for every class of MTL-chains K. Therefore 3) and 4) are equivalent. $\qquad\square$

We say that the SCG problem is decidable, for a tabular variety $\mathbb{L}$ of MTL-algebras, if there exists an algorithm to decide if $\mathbb{L}$ is SCG.

A key point in defining the problem is how a tabular variety $\mathbb{L}$ is given in input. By Theorem 2, $\mathbb{L}$ is generated by one finite set of finite chains, and by Baker's theorem [8] $\mathbb{L}$ is finitely axiomatizable. We thus propose two options.

– $\mathbb{L}$ is specified via generators, *i.e.* via one finite set K of finite chains such that $\mathbb{L} = \mathbf{V}(K)$.
– $\mathbb{L}$ is specified axiomatically, via a finite set S of equations s.t. $\mathbb{L} = \mathbf{V}(S)$.

Theorem 14. *Let K be a finite set of finite chains. Then the SCG problem for $\mathbf{V}(K)$ is decidable.*

Proof. Let $\mathbb{L}$ be a tabular variety, generated by a finite set of finite chains K. By Jónsson's lemma, $Ch(\mathbb{L}) = \mathbf{HS}(K)$. By Theorem 13, to check the SCG it is sufficient to verify if there exists a chain $\mathcal{A} \in \mathbf{HS}(K)$ such that every member of $\mathbf{HS}(K)$ embeds into some quotient of $\mathcal{A}$. Since K is a finite set of finite chains, then every member of $\mathbf{HS}(K)$ is a finite chain, and only finitely many of them are non-isomorphic. Therefore in a finite time we can compute if the required $\mathcal{A}$ exists or not. Therefore the SCG problem for $\mathbb{L}$ is decidable. $\qquad\square$

Problem 2. Let S be a finite set of equations. Is the SCG problem for $\mathbf{V}(S)$ decidable?

Remark 2. As shown in [1,16], a variety $\mathbb{L}$ of MTL-algebras is single-chain generated if and only if the corresponding logic L has the Halldén completeness (HC), which is basically a weakened version of the disjunction property. Let $\mathbb{L} = \mathbf{V}(S)$ be a tabular variety specified via a finite set of equations S. Then deciding the SCG for $\mathbb{L}$ is equivalent to deciding the HC for L.

5.2 Amalgamation Property Problem for Tabular Varieties

We start with the definition of two versions of amalgamation property.

Definition 11. *Let $\mathbb{L}$ be a class of algebras. A V-formation is a tuple $(\mathcal{A}, \mathcal{B}, \mathcal{C}, i, j)$ such that $\mathcal{A}, \mathcal{B}, \mathcal{C} \in \mathbb{L}$, $\mathcal{A} \overset{i}{\hookrightarrow} \mathcal{B}$, and $\mathcal{A} \overset{j}{\hookrightarrow} \mathcal{C}$.*

– *We say that $\mathbb{L}$ has the* one-sided amalgamation property *(1AP), whenever for every V-formation $(\mathcal{A}, \mathcal{B}, \mathcal{C}, i, j)$ there is a tuple $(\mathcal{D}, h, k)$, called 1-amalgam, such that $\mathcal{D} \in \mathbb{L}$, $\mathcal{B} \overset{h}{\hookrightarrow} \mathcal{D}$, k is a homomorphism from $\mathcal{C}$ to $\mathcal{D}$, and $h \circ i = k \circ j$.*

- *We say that* $\mathbb{L}$ *has the* amalgamation property *(AP), whenever for every V-formation* $(\mathcal{A}, \mathcal{B}, \mathcal{C}, i, j)$ *there is a tuple* $(\mathcal{D}, h, k)$, *called an amalgam, such that* $\mathcal{D} \in \mathbb{L}$, $\mathcal{B} \overset{h}{\hookrightarrow} \mathcal{D}$, $\mathcal{C} \overset{k}{\hookrightarrow} \mathcal{D}$, *and* $h \circ i = k \circ j$.

Theorem 15 ([15]). *Let* $\mathbb{L}$ *be a variety of MTL-algebras. The following are equivalent:*

- $\mathbb{L}$ *has the amalgamation property.*
- $\mathbb{L}$ *has the one-sided amalgamation property.*
- $Ch(\mathbb{L})$ *has the one-sided amalgamation property.*

Let $\mathbb{L}$ be a tabular variety of MTL-algebras. We say that the AP problem is decidable whenever there exists an algorithm that allows to establish if $\mathbb{L}$ has the AP or not. As in the previous section, we can specify a tabular variety either via generators or axiomatically. For the first case we have the following result.

Theorem 16. *Let* K *be a finite set of finite chains. Then the AP problem for* $\mathbf{V}(K)$ *is decidable.*

Proof. Let $\mathbb{L}$ be a tabular variety, characterized via a finite set of finite chains K. By Jónsson's lemma, $Ch(\mathbb{L}) = \mathbf{HS}(K)$. By Theorem 15, to check the AP for $\mathbb{L}$ it is sufficient to check the 1AP for $\mathbf{HS}(K)$. Since K is a finite set of finite chains, all the members of $\mathbf{HS}(K)$ are also finite chains, and only finitely many of them are non isomorphic. This implies that the 1AP for $\mathbf{HS}(K)$ is decidable, since it is sufficient to check if there exists a V-formation in $\mathbf{HS}(K)$ that does not have a 1-amalgam in $\mathbf{HS}(K)$, and this can be done in a finite time. Therefore the AP for $\mathbb{L}$ is also decidable, and the proof is settled.   □

Problem 3. Let S be a finite set of equations. Is the AP problem for $\mathbf{V}(S)$ decidable?

Remark 3. As shown in [16], a variety $\mathbb{L}$ of MTL-algebras has the AP if and only if the corresponding logic L has the deductive interpolation property (DIP). Let $\mathbb{L} = \mathbf{V}(S)$ be a tabular variety specified via a finite set of equations S. Then deciding the AP for $\mathbb{L}$ is equivalent to deciding the DIP for L.

Acknowledgements. This work has been partially supported by Istituto Nazionale di Alta Matematica (Indam).

References

1. Aguzzoli, S., Bianchi, M.: Single chain completeness and some related properties. Fuzzy Sets Syst. **301**, 51–63 (2016). https://doi.org/10.1016/j.fss.2016.03.008
2. Aguzzoli, S., Bianchi, M.: Minimally many-valued extensions of the monoidal t-norm based logic MTL. In: Petrosino, A., Loia, V., Pedrycz, W. (eds.) WILF 2016. LNCS (LNAI), vol. 10147, pp. 106–115. Springer, Cham (2017). https://doi.org/10.1007/978-3-319-52962-2_9

3. Aguzzoli, S., Bianchi, M.: On linear varieties of MTL-algebras. Soft. Comput. **23**(7), 2129–2146 (2018). https://doi.org/10.1007/s00500-018-3423-3
4. Aguzzoli, S., Bianchi, M.: Strictly join irreducible varieties of BL-algebras: the missing pieces. Fuzzy Sets Syst. **418**, 84–100 (2021). https://doi.org/10.1016/j.fss.2020.12.008
5. Aguzzoli, S., Bianchi, M.: Tabular and pretabular varieties of MTL-algebras. In: Fahrenberg, U., Fussner, W., Glück, R. (eds.) Relational and Algebraic Methods in Computer Science. LNCS, vol. 14787, pp. 1–18. Springer, Cham (2024). https://doi.org/10.1007/978-3-031-68279-7_1
6. Aguzzoli, S., Bianchi, M., Valota, D.: The classification of all the subvarieties of DNMG. In: Kacprzyk, J., Szmidt, E., Zadrożny, S., Atanassov, K.T., Krawczak, M. (eds.) IWIFSGN/EUSFLAT -2017. AISC, vol. 641, pp. 12–24. Springer, Cham (2018). https://doi.org/10.1007/978-3-319-66830-7_2
7. Aguzzoli, S., Gerla, B., Haniková, Z.: Complexity issues in basic logic. Soft. Comput. **9**(12), 919–934 (2005)
8. Baker, K.: Finite equational bases for finite algebras in a congruence-distributive equational class. Adv. Math. **24**(3), 207–243 (1977). https://doi.org/10.1016/0001-8708(77)90056-1
9. Blok, W.J.: Pretabular varieties of modal algebras. Stud. Logica. **39**, 101–124 (1980). https://doi.org/10.1007/BF00370315
10. Blok, W., Pigozzi, D.: Algebraizable Logics. Memoirs of The American Mathematical Society, vol. 77. American Mathematical Society (1989). http://tinyurl.com/o89ug5o
11. Cignoli, R., D'Ottaviano, I., Mundici, D.: Algebraic Foundations of Many-Valued Reasoning, Trends in Logic, vol. 7. Kluwer Academic Publishers (1999)
12. Cintula, P., Hájek, P., Noguera, C.: Handbook of Mathematical Fuzzy Logic, vol. 1. College Publications (2011)
13. Esakia, L., Meskhi, V.: 5 critical modal systems. Theoria **43**, 52–60 (1977)
14. Esteva, F., Godo, L.: Monoidal t-norm based logic: towards a logic for left-continuous t-norms. Fuzzy Sets Syst. **124**(3), 271–288 (2001). https://doi.org/10.1016/S0165-0114(01)00098-7
15. Fussner, W., Metcalfe, G.: Transfer theorems for finitely subdirectly irreducible algebras. J. Algebra **640**, 1–20 (2024). https://doi.org/10.1016/j.jalgebra.2023.11.003
16. Galatos, N., Jipsen, P., Kowalski, T., Ono, H.: Residuated Lattices: An Algebraic Glimpse at Substructural Logics, Studies in Logic and The Foundations of Mathematics, vol. 151. Elsevier (2007)
17. Gispert, J.: Axiomatic extensions of the nilpotent minimum logic. Rep. Math. Log. **37**, 113–123 (2003). http://tinyurl.com/nqsle2f
18. Hájek, P.: Metamathematics of Fuzzy Logic, Trends in Logic, vol. 4. Kluwer Academic Publishers, paperback edn. (1998)
19. Haniková, Z.: Computational complexity of propositional fuzzy logics. In: Handbook of Mathematical Fuzzy Logic, vol. 2, pp. 793–851. College Publications (2011)
20. Jipsen, P., Rose, H.: Varieties of Lattices. Lecture Notes in Mathematics, vol. 1533. Springer, Cham (1992). https://tinyurl.com/yhtbnmc3
21. Kowalski, T.: Pretabular varieties of equivalential algebras. Reports Math. Log. **33**, 3–10 (1999)
22. Kuznetsov, A.: Some properties of the lattice of varieties of pseudo-boolean algebras. In: 11th All-Union Algebraic Colloquium, pp. 255–256 (1971). (in Russian)
23. Maksimova, L.: Pretabular superintuitionist logic. Algebra Logic **11**(5), 308–314 (1972). https://doi.org/10.1007/BF02330744

24. Maksimova, L.: Pretabular extensions of Lewis S4. Algebra Logic **14**(1), 16–33 (1975). https://doi.org/10.1007/BF01668576
25. Papadimitriou, C., Yannakakis, M.: The complexity of facets (and some facets of complexity). J. Comput. Syst. Sci. **28**(2), 244–259 (1984)
26. Troelstra, A.: On intermediate propositional logics. Indagationes Mathematicae (Proceedings) **68**, 141–152 (1965). https://doi.org/10.1016/S1385-7258(65)50019-6

On the Non-falsity and Threshold Preserving Variants of MTL Logics

Francesc Esteva[1] , Joan Gispert[2] , and Lluís Godo[1(✉)]

[1] Artificial Intelligence Research Institute (IIIA - CSIC),
Campus de la Univ. Autònoma de Barcelona, 08193 Bellaterra, Spain
{esteva,godo}@iiia.csic.es
[2] Department Maths and Computer Science, Univ. de Barcelona,
08007 Barcelona, Spain
jgispert@ub.edu

Abstract. In this paper we study the definition and axiomatisation of non-falsity preserving and threshold preserving companions of several extensions of the Monoidal t-norm based fuzzy logic MTL. More in detail, we first extend some recent preliminary results on non-falsity preserving logics, and then we present a new study on threshold-preserving companions of the main three fuzzy logics, Łukasiewicz, Product and Gödel logics.

Keywords: Mathematical fuzzy logic · monoidal t-norm based logic · non-falsity preserving logics · threshold preserving logics

1 Introduction

Fuzzy logics are logics of *graded truth* that have been proposed as a suitable tool for reasoning with imprecise information, in particular for reasoning with propositions containing vague predicates. Their main feature is that they allow to interpret formulas in a linearly ordered scale of truth-values, and this is specially suited for representing the gradual aspects of vagueness. In particular, systems of fuzzy logic have been in-depth developed within the frame of mathematical fuzzy logic (MFL) [8,15]. In deductive systems in MFL, mostly with semantics in the real unit interval $[0, 1]$, the usual notion of deduction is defined by requiring the preservation of the truth-value 1 (full *truth-preservation*), which is understood as representing the absolute truth. Namely, generalizing the classical notion of consequence, in these systems a formula follows from a set of premises if every algebraic evaluation that interprets the premises as 1-true also interprets the conclusion as 1-true. All the fuzzy logics under the truth-preserving paradigm are explosive in the sense of validating the ¬-explosion rule

$$\frac{\varphi \quad \neg\varphi}{\psi}$$

M. Baczyński et al. (Eds.): EUSFLAT 2025, LNCS 15883, pp. 335–346, 2025.
https://doi.org/10.1007/978-3-031-97225-6_27

where $\neg$ is the definable negation in systems of MFL. A logic not satisfying this rule is called $\neg$-paraconsistent [4, 9, 17].

In the last years, there have been several works studying paraconsistent variants of fuzzy logics (see e.g. [5, 7, 11]), mainly by moving from the (full) truth-preserving paradigm to the *degree-preserving paradigm*, in which a conclusion follows from a set of premises if, for all evaluations, the truth degree of the conclusion is greater or equal than those of the premises, see e.g. [3]. Still, another way of defining paraconsistent variants of a fuzzy logic is put forward in [1], although for the particular case of Łukasiewicz fuzzy logic. In this approach, the notion of consequence at work is the *non-falsity preservation*, according to which a conclusion follows from a set of premises whenever if the premises are non-false, so must be the conclusion. In other words, assuming a $[0, 1]$-valued semantics, this is the case when, for any evaluation, if truth degrees of the premises are above 0, then the truth-degree of the conclusion is so as well. While this notion of consequence is not weaker than the one in the truth-preserving logics, it is stronger than the one of degree-preserving logics, and has been preliminary studied in [12]. For instance, while all tautologies in a truth-preserving logic keep being obviously valid in the non-falsity preserving variant, usually Modus Ponens is not a valid inference rule any longer, e.g. in the case of Łukasiewicz logic. On the other hand, the excluded-middle axiom $\varphi \vee \neg\varphi$ is a valid formula in the non-falsity variant (it always take a positive truth-value), while this is neither a valid in the truth-preserving and degree-preserving variants.

In this paper, we first further explore non-falsity preserving companions of two classes of extensions of the MTL logic, and second we address the question of defining and syntactically characterising logics that preserve a given truth-value threshold, that can be any real value $a \in (0, 1]$, focusing the study on the three most prominent extensions of MTL, namely Łukasiewicz, Product and Gödel fuzzy logics. In more detail, after this introduction, in Sect. 2 we gather some preliminaries on various systems of t-norm based fuzzy logics and present basic definitions about variants of these systems corresponding to logical matrices on MTL-chains with lattice filters as sets of designated values. Then in Sect. 3 we focus on the paraconsistent non-falsity preserving companions of MTL logics, overviewing basic results for the case of Involutive MTL logics from [12] and providing new insights for MTL logics validating a suitable inference rule. Finally in Sect. 4 we deal with threshold-preserving logics for the above mentioned three particular cases. We conclude with some final remarks in Sect. 5.

2   Preliminaries

Most well known and studied system of mathematical fuzzy logic are the so-called *t-norm based fuzzy logics*, corresponding to formal many-valued calculi with truth-values in the real unit interval $[0, 1]$ and with a conjunction and an implication interpreted respectively by a (left-) continuous t-norm and its residuum, and thus, including e.g. the well-known Łukasiewicz, Gödel and Product infinitely-valued logics, corresponding to the calculi defined by Łukasiewicz, min and product t-norms respectively. The most general t-norm based fuzzy logic is the logic MTL (monoidal t-norm based logic) introduced in [14], whose theorems correspond to the common tautologies of all many-valued calculi defined by a left-continuous t-norm and its residuum [16].

The language of MTL consists of denumerably many propositional variables $p_1, p_2, \ldots$, binary connectives $\wedge, \&, \rightarrow$, and the truth constant $\overline{0}$. Formulas, which will be denoted by lower case greek letters $\varphi, \psi, \chi, \ldots$, are recursively defined from propositional variables, connectives and truth-constant as usual. Further connectives and constants are definable, in particular: $\neg\varphi$ stands for $\varphi \rightarrow \overline{0}$ and $\overline{1}$ stands for $\neg\overline{0}$. A Hilbert-style calculus for MTL was introduced in [14] with the following set of axioms:

(A1) $(\varphi \rightarrow \psi) \rightarrow ((\psi \rightarrow \chi) \rightarrow (\varphi \rightarrow \chi))$
(A2) $\varphi\&\psi \rightarrow \varphi$
(A3) $\varphi\&\psi \rightarrow \psi\&\varphi$
(A4) $\varphi \wedge \psi \rightarrow \varphi$
(A5) $\varphi \wedge \psi \rightarrow \psi \wedge \varphi$
(A6) $\varphi\&(\varphi \rightarrow \psi) \rightarrow \varphi \wedge \psi$
(A7a) $(\varphi \rightarrow (\psi \rightarrow \chi)) \rightarrow (\varphi\&\psi \rightarrow \chi)$
(A7b) $(\varphi\&\psi \rightarrow \chi) \rightarrow (\varphi \rightarrow (\psi \rightarrow \chi))$
(A8) $((\varphi \rightarrow \psi) \rightarrow \chi) \rightarrow (((\psi \rightarrow \varphi) \rightarrow \chi) \rightarrow \chi)$
(A9) $\overline{0} \rightarrow \varphi$

and whose unique inference rule is *modus ponens*: from φ and $\varphi \rightarrow \psi$ derive ψ.

In Table 1 we gather some of the main axiomatic extensions of MTL together with their additional axioms. Of particular interest in this paper is the Involutive MTL logic (IMTL for short), i.e. the axiomatic extension of MTL with the axiom (INV) which enforces the negation $\neg$ to be involutive [14]. The well-known Łukasiewicz logic is the extension of IMTL with the divisibility axiom (Div), Gödel logic is the extension of MTL with the contraction axiom (Con) while Product logic is the extension of MTL with the (Div) and the cancellation axiom (C) [15]. Both Gödel and Product logics are extensions of SMTL, the extension of MTL with the axiom (PC). In this paper we will also consider in Sect. 3.2 the extension of non-SMTL logics (i.e. MTL logics that are not SMTL logics) with an additional rule of inference.

MTL is an algebraizable logic in the sense of Blok and Pigozzi [2] and its equivalent algebraic semantics is given by the variety of MTL-algebras. MTL-algebras can be equivalently introduced as commutative, bounded, integral residuated lattices $\langle A, \wedge, \vee, *, \rightarrow, \overline{0}, \overline{1} \rangle$ further satisfying the following prelinearity condition: $(x \rightarrow y) \vee (y \rightarrow x) = \overline{1}$. Algebras of IMTL are MTL-algebras satisfying the equation $x = \neg\neg x$, algebras of L are usually called MV-algebras and are IMTL-algebras further satisfying the equation $x * (x \rightarrow y) = x \wedge y$, Gödel-algebras are MTL-algebras satisfying the equation $x * y = x \wedge y$, while Product algebras are MTL-algebras satifsying $x \wedge y = x * (x \rightarrow y)$ and $\neg x \vee ((x \rightarrow x * y) \rightarrow y) = 1$.

Besides enjoying strong completeness as a consequence of their algebraizability, all the logics in Table 1, enjoy completeness with respect to their corresponding classes of algebras on the real-unit interval $[0, 1]$, as proved e.g. in

Table 1. Some axiomatic extensions of MTL obtained by adding the corresponding additional axiom schemata.

Axiom schema	Name	Logic	Additional axioms
		Strict MTL (SMTL)	(PC)
$\neg\neg\varphi \to \varphi$	(Inv)	Involutive MTL (IMTL)	(Inv)
$\neg\varphi \vee ((\varphi \to \varphi\&\psi) \to \psi)$	(C)	Nilpotent Minimum (NM)	(Inv) and (WNM)
$\varphi \to \varphi\&\varphi$	(Con)	Basic Logic (BL)	(Div)
$\varphi \wedge \psi \to \varphi\&(\varphi \to \psi)$	(Div)	Strict Basic Logic (SBL)	(Div) and (PC)
$\neg(\varphi \wedge \neg\varphi)$	(PC)	Łukasiewicz Logic (L)	(Div) and (Inv)
$\neg(\varphi\&\psi) \vee (\varphi \wedge \psi \to \varphi\&\psi)$	(WNM)	Product Logic (Π)	(Div) and (C)
$\varphi \vee \neg\varphi$	(EM)	Gödel Logic (G)	(Con)
		Classical Logic (CL)	(EM)

[16] for MTL and in [13] for IMTL. Furthermore, Łukasiewicz logic, Gödel logic and Product logic are even complete w.r.t. a *single* algebra over $[0, 1]$, the standard MV-algebra, the standard Gödel algebra and the standard Product algebra respectively, see e.g. [15].

In the following, given a left-continuous t-norm $*$, we will denote by $[\mathbf{0}, \mathbf{1}]_*$ the standard MTL-algebra determined by $*$, i.e. $[\mathbf{0}, \mathbf{1}]_* = ([0, 1], \min, \max, *, \to, 0, 1)$, where $\to$ is the residuum of $*$ and the negation $\neg$ is defined as $\neg \mathrm{x} = x \to 0$. In the systems of mathematical fuzzy logic considered above, the usual notion of logical consequence has been defined as preservation of the *truth*, represented by the top element of the corresponding algebras. For instance let L be any extension of MTL, which we assume to be complete w.r.t. the family $\mathcal{C}_L = \{[\mathbf{0}, \mathbf{1}]_* \mid [\mathbf{0}, \mathbf{1}]_*$ is a L-algebra$\}$ of standard L-algebras. Then the typical notion of logical consequence is the following for every set of formulas $\Gamma \cup \{\varphi\}$:

$$\Gamma \models_L \varphi \quad \text{if,} \quad \text{for any } [\mathbf{0}, \mathbf{1}]_* \in \mathcal{C}_L \text{ and any } [\mathbf{0}, \mathbf{1}]_*\text{-evaluation } e,$$
$$\text{if } e(\psi) = 1 \text{ for any } \psi \in \Gamma, \text{ then } e(\varphi) = 1 \text{ as well.}$$

This can be generalised by considering logics defined by logical matrices $M = \langle \mathbf{A}, F \rangle$, where $\mathbf{A}$ is a standard L-chain and F is a non-trivial lattice filter of $\mathbf{A}$ i.e. F is either a closed interval $F_a = [a, 1]$ with $a \in (0, 1]$, or a semi-open interval $F_{(a} = (a, 1]$ with $a \in [0, 1)$. Considering the filters as sets of designated values, then the companions of the logic L given by the classes of matrices $\mathcal{C}_L^a = \{\langle [\mathbf{0}, \mathbf{1}]_*, F_a \rangle \mid [\mathbf{0}, \mathbf{1}]_*$ is a L-algebra$\}$ and $\mathcal{C}_L^{(a} = \{\langle [\mathbf{0}, \mathbf{1}]_*, F_{(a} \rangle \mid [\mathbf{0}, \mathbf{1}]_*$ is a L-algebra$\}$ are defined respectively as follows:

$$\Gamma \models_L^a \varphi \quad \text{if,} \quad \text{for any } [\mathbf{0}, \mathbf{1}]_* \in \mathcal{C}_L \text{ and any } [\mathbf{0}, \mathbf{1}]_*\text{-evaluation } e,$$
$$\text{if } e(\psi) \geq a \text{ for any } \psi \in \Gamma, \text{ then } e(\varphi) \geq a \text{ as well.}$$

$$\Gamma \models_L^{(a} \varphi \quad \text{if,} \quad \text{for any } [\mathbf{0}, \mathbf{1}]_* \in \mathcal{C}_L \text{ and any } [\mathbf{0}, \mathbf{1}]_*\text{-evaluation } e,$$
$$\text{if } e(\psi) > a \text{ for any } \psi \in \Gamma, \text{ then } e(\varphi) > a \text{ as well.}$$

The extreme cases are the 1-preserving logic $\models_L^1 = \models_L$, which is explosive, and the non-falsity preserving logic $\models_L^{(0}$, which is paraconsistent w.r.t. $\neg$. Observe that the finitary versions of both logics are strongly related because, for any L-evaluation e, the condition $e(\neg\varphi) = 1$ if and only if $e(\varphi) = 0$ holds due to the fact the implication in MTL is residuated and thus $e(\varphi \to \psi) = 1$ iff $e(\varphi) \le e(\psi)$.

Lemma 1. *For every pair of formulas φ, ψ the following relation holds:* $\varphi \models_L^{(0} \psi$ *iff* $\neg\psi \models_L^1 \neg\varphi$.

Moreover, if $[\mathbf{0}, \mathbf{1}]_*$ is a standard IMTL-algebra, with c being the fixpoint of the involutive negation $n(x) = x \to 0$, then it is easy to check that

(i) The logic of the matrix $M^a = \langle [\mathbf{0}, \mathbf{1}]_*, F_a \rangle$ is paraconsistent iff $a \le c$,
(ii) The logic of the matrix $M^{(a} = \langle [\mathbf{0}, \mathbf{1}]_*, F_{(a} \rangle$ is paraconsistent iff $a < c$.

3 Non-falsity Preserving Companions of Two Classes of MTL Extensions

3.1 The Case of Extensions of IMTL

In this section we recall from [12] the characterisation of logics defined by (sets of) matrices of the form $\langle [\mathbf{0}, \mathbf{1}]_*, F_{(0} \rangle$, with $[\mathbf{0}, \mathbf{1}]_*$ being a standard IMTL-algebra. We remind that this means that $*$ is a left-continuous t-norm such that the residual negation $\neg$, defined as $\neg x = x \to 0 = \sup\{y \in [0, 1] \mid x * y = 0\}$ satisfies the involutivity condition $\neg(\neg x) = x$. Notable examples of such t-norms are Łukasiewicz t-norm (which is continuous) and Nilpotent Minimum t-norm.

Assume L is an axiomatic extension of IMTL, complete with respect to a class of standard algebras $\mathcal{C}_L$, and whose corresponding notion of proof is denoted $\vdash_L$. It is immediate to observe that in the case of a IMTL logic L, Lemma 1 can be strengthened in the sense that the 1-preserving logic $\models_L^1$ and the non-falsity preserving logic $\models_L^{(0}$ become interdefinable. Namely, in this case we have both:

(i) $\varphi \models_L^1 \psi$ iff $\neg\psi \models_L^{(0} \neg\varphi$,   (ii) $\varphi \models_L^{(0} \psi$ iff $\neg\psi \models_L^1 \neg\varphi$.

In order to syntactically characterise $\models_L^{(0}$, defined by the class of matrices

$$\mathcal{C}_L^{(0} = \{\langle [0, 1]_*, F_{(0} \rangle \mid \langle [0, 1]_*, F_1 \rangle \in \mathcal{C}_L\},$$

the following system nf-L, called the *non-falsity preserving companion* of L, is defined in [12] as follows.

Definition 1. *The calculus* nf-L *is defined by the axioms of* L *and the following rules:*

- *Rule of Adjunction: (Adj)* $\dfrac{\varphi, \quad \psi}{\varphi \wedge \psi}$

- *Reverse Modus Ponens: (MP^r)* $\dfrac{\neg\psi \vee \chi}{\neg\varphi \vee \neg(\varphi \to \psi) \vee \chi}$

– *Restricted Modus Ponens: (r-MP)* $\dfrac{\varphi, \quad \varphi \to \psi}{\psi}$,   *if* $\vdash_L \varphi \to \psi$

The corresponding notion of proof will be denoted by $\vdash_{\mathsf{nf}-L}$.

The above (MP^r) rule captures the following form of reverse of modus ponens: if $\neg\psi$ is non-false then either $\neg\varphi$ is non-false or $\neg(\varphi \to \psi)$ is non-false. The addition of the disjunct χ both in the premise and in the conclusion of the rule is needed for technical reasons. On the other hand, note the usual Modus Ponens rule is not valid in $\models_L^{(0}$ (e.g. we may have $e(\varphi) = e(\neg\varphi) = e(\varphi \to \bar{0}) = a > 0$, with a being the negation fix point in $[0,1]_*$, while $e(\bar{0}) = 0$), thus we need to have the above restricted form.

The following is a syntactic counterpart of part of Lemma 1.

Proposition 1. *[12] If* $\psi \vdash_L \varphi$ *then* $\neg\varphi \vdash_{\mathsf{nf}-L} \neg\psi$.

Thanks to this relation, the logic nf-L has been shown to be complete in [12] with respect to the intended semantics.

Theorem 1. *Let* L *be an axiomatic extension of IMTL. The calculus* nf-L *is sound and complete w.r.t. to the class of matrices* $\mathcal{C}_L^{(0}$.

Note that, as a direct corollary, Definition 1 provides us with complete axiomatisations of non-falsity preserving companions of prominent IMTL logics like Lukasiewicz or Nilpotent Minimum logics.

3.2   The Non-falsity Preserving Variant of Non-SMTL Logics Validating the Rule (R$^{\neg\neg}$)

In this section we show that to prove the results in the previous section the requirement of the negation $\neg$ to be involutive, as it happens in IMTL logics, can be significantly weakened. Indeed, let MTL$^{\neg\neg}$ be the (non-axiomatic) extension of MTL with the rule

$$(\mathrm{R}^{\neg\neg}) \quad \dfrac{\neg\neg\varphi}{\varphi},$$

introduced in [5]. The algebraic semantics of MTL$^{\neg\neg}$ consists of the quasi-variety generated by the class of MTL-chains **A** whose negation $\neg$ is such that, for any $a \in A$, $\neg a = 0$ iff $a = 1$, or equivalently $\neg a > 0$ iff $a < 1$.

If L is an axiomatic extension of MTL, let us denote by L$^{\neg\neg}$ the extension of L with the rule (R$^{\neg\neg}$). If L is complete w.r.t. a class of standard matrices $\mathcal{C}_L$ over the real unit interval $[0,1]$, then L$^{\neg\neg}$ is complete w.r.t. the class of matrices $\mathcal{C}_{L^{\neg\neg}} = \{\langle [0,1]_*, \{1\}\rangle \mid \langle [0,1]_*, \{1\}\rangle \in \mathcal{C}_L$ s.t. for all $x, \neg x = 0$ iff $x = 1\}$, see [5].

In L$^{\neg\neg}$ we keep having at the semantical level the equivalence between the 1-preserving logic and the non-falsity preserving logic, in the following sense.

Lemma 2. *For any logic L extension of MTL, the following conditions hold:*

(i) $\varphi \models_{L^{\neg\neg}}^1 \psi$ *iff* $\neg\psi \models_{L^{\neg\neg}}^{(0} \neg\varphi$,   *(ii)* $\varphi \models_{L^{\neg\neg}}^{(0} \psi$ *iff* $\neg\psi \models_{L^{\neg\neg}}^1 \neg\varphi$.

Proof. Straighforward: (ii) is Lemma 1, and to prove (i), note that if $[0, 1]_*$ is a standard MTL$^{\neg\neg}$-algebra then "$x = 1$ implies $y = 1$" is equivalent to "$y < 1$ implies $x < 1$", and this is in turn equivalent to "$\neg y > 0$ implies $\neg x > 0$".   □

Then one can define the non-falsity preserving companion of a MTL$^{\neg\neg}$-logic and prove its completeness as follows. In fact, we can restrict ourselves to extensions of *non-SMTL* logics with the rule (R$^{\neg\neg}$). By a non-SMTL logic we mean a MTL logic that does not satisfy the axiom (PC) $\neg(\varphi \wedge \neg\varphi)$. Indeed, note that if L is a SMTL logic, then L$^{\neg\neg}$ collapses into classical logic. This is so because, using the rule (R$^{\neg\neg}$), from axiom (PC), which can be equivalently expressed in MTL as $\neg\varphi \vee \neg\neg\varphi$, L$^{\neg\neg}$ then derives the Excluded-Middle axiom $\neg\varphi \vee \varphi$.

Theorem 2. *Let L be a non-SMTL logic. Then the calculus* nf-L$^{\neg\neg}$*, defined by the axioms of L following rules:*

- *The rule (R$^{\neg\neg}$)*
- *The rule of Adjunction (Adj)*
- *The rule of Reverse Modus Ponens (MP^r)*
- *The rule of Restricted Modus Ponens (r-MP)*

is a sound and complete axiomatisation w.r.t. to the class of matrices $\mathcal{C}^0_{L^{\neg\neg}}$.

The proof is an easy adaptation of the proof of Theorem 1 for IMTL logics in [12].

4   Threshold-Preserving Logics

In this section we turn our attention to logics preserving lower bounds of truth-values, in other words, logics whose semantic consequence relations are of the form $\models^a_L$ and $\models^{(a}_L$ for some positive value $a \in (0, 1]$ (as introduced in Sect. 2) for some logics L extensions of MTL that are complete with respect to some class of standard L-algebras $\mathcal{C}_L$.

We state two general but sufficient conditions for a logic L to guarantee a finitary axiomatisation $\models^a_L$. Consider the following two conditions on L:

(C1) L satisfies a form of global Deduction Theorem in the sense that there exists a term t such that:

$$\Gamma \cup \{\varphi\} \vdash_L \psi \quad \text{iff} \quad \Gamma \vdash_L t(\varphi) \to \psi$$

(C2) The logic $\models^a_L$ is interpretable in L, that is, there exists a term r such that:

$$\varphi \models_a \psi \quad \text{iff} \quad r(\varphi) \models_L r(\psi)$$

Theorem 3. *Let L be an extension of MTL satisfying conditions (C1) and (C2). Then the calculus L_a defined syntactically by the axioms of L and the following rules:*

- *the rules of L restricted to theorems of L,*
- *the rule of Adjunction, and*
- *the restricted rule:* $(R_{t,r})$ $\dfrac{\varphi, \quad \vdash_L t(r(\varphi)) \to r(\psi)}{\psi}$

is a sound and complete axiomatisation of the finitary $\models^a_L$.

Proof. The following is a sketch of the proof:

(i) $\varphi_1, \ldots, \varphi_n \models^a_L \psi$ iff
(i) $\varphi_1 \wedge \ldots \wedge \varphi_n \models^a_L \psi$ iff
(ii) $r(\varphi) \models_L r(\psi)$ iff –by condition (C2), where $\varphi = \varphi_1 \wedge \ldots \wedge \varphi_n$
(iii) $\models_L t(r(\varphi)) \to r(\psi)$ iff –by condition (C1)
(iv) $\vdash_L t(r(\varphi)) \to r(\psi)$ iff –by completeness of L
(v) in L there is a proof $\langle \Pi_1, \ldots, \Pi_n \rangle$ where $\Pi_n = t(r(\varphi) \to r(\psi))$ iff
(vi) in L_a there is a proof $\langle \Pi_0, \Pi_1, \ldots, \Pi_n, \Pi_{n+1} \rangle$, where the steps $\Pi_1, \ldots, \Pi_n$ (with applications of the rules restricted to theorems) are as above and where Π_0 is an initial step to obtain φ by the adjunction rule from $\varphi_1, \ldots, \varphi_n$, and a final step $\Pi_{n+1} = \psi$, where ψ is obtained from Π_0 and Π_n by the application of the rule $(R_{t,r})$. $\square$

4.1   The Case of Łukasiewicz logics

A particular instantiation of the above setting is for finite-valued Łukasiewicz logics[1] L_n and for the infinite-valued Łukasiewicz logic L expanded with Baaz-Monteiro Δ operator L_Δ.

Finite-valued Łukasiewicz logics L_n are complete with respect to the matrices $\langle \mathbf{MV}_n, \{1\} \rangle$, where $\mathbf{MV}_n$ is the MV-chain over the n-element set $MV_n = \{0, 1/(n-1), \ldots, (n-2)/(n-1), 1\}$, and they satisfy the above conditions (C1) and (C2). Namely, as is well-known, Baaz-Monteiro operator Δ is definable in L_n as $\Delta\varphi := \varphi \& .\overset{n}{\ldots}. \& \varphi$ and L_n enjoys a global deduction theorem: $\varphi \vdash_{L_n} \psi$ iff $\vdash_{L_n} \Delta\varphi \to \psi$. On the other hand, it is also well-known that, for every $a \in MV_n$, there is a McNaughton term $r_a(x)$ such that $r_a(x) = 1$ iff $x \geq a$. Therefore, it holds that $\varphi \vdash^a_{L_n} \psi$ iff $r_a(\varphi) \models_{L_n} r_a(\psi)$. As a consequence, according to Theorem 3, the logic L^a_n defined there provides a complete axiomatisation of the semantic consequence relation $\models^a_{L_n}$. In this case the rule $(R_{t,r})$ takes this form:

$$\frac{\varphi, \quad \vdash_{L_n} \Delta(r_a(\varphi)) \to r_a(\psi)}{\psi}.$$

Note that for $n = 3$ and $a = 1/2$, the resulting logic $L_3^{1/2}$ provides an alternative axiomatisation (in the language of L_n) of the well-known D'Ottaviano and da Costa's paraconsistent logic J_3 [10].

When we move to the case of infinite-valued Łukasiewicz logic L, condition (C2) keeps holding at least for every rational a thanks to the McNaughton terms, but (C1) fails since L does not have a global deduction theorem. To overcome this

---

[1] This case was partially studied in [6], here we provide more elegant axiomatisations.

problem we can consider the logic L_Δ, the expansion of L with the Δ operator, already axiomatised by Hájek in [15]. Then in L_Δ condition (C2) keeps holding for rational values a, while now condition (C1) is satisfied as well taking $t = \Delta$. Therefore, Theorem 3 can be applied to L_Δ to get axiomatisations of L_Δ^a for every rational a.

In particular, if we are interested on the logic to reason with *half-true* propositions, it is enough to instantiate Theorem 3 with $a = 1/2$, $t(\varphi) = \Delta\varphi$ and $r(\varphi) = \varphi \otimes \varphi$.

4.2   The Cases of Gödel and Product Logics

In this final section we consider the cases of Gödel and Product logics. These logics fall outside the scope of Theorem 3, and hence they require a specific consideration.

The Case of Gödel Logic. The analysis of Gödel logic turns out to be very simple. Gödel logic can be seen as the axiomatic extension of MTL with the axiom (Con), see Table 1. In fact, Gödel logic is standard complete with respect to the single matrix $M_1 = \langle [\mathbf{0}, \mathbf{1}]_\mathbf{G}, \{1\}\rangle$, where $[\mathbf{0}, \mathbf{1}]_\mathbf{G}$ denotes the standard Gödel algebra $([0, 1], \min, \max, *_G, \to_G, 0, 1)$, with $*_G = \min$ and $\to_G$ is its residuum.

For $a \in (0, 1)$, let us denote by $\models_G^a$ and $\models_G^{(a}$ the logics defined by the logical matrices $M^a = \langle [\mathbf{0}, \mathbf{1}]_\mathbf{G}, [a, 1]\rangle$ and $M^{(a} = \langle [\mathbf{0}, \mathbf{1}]_\mathbf{G}, (a, 1]\rangle$ respectively. We will also denote the logic $\models_G^1$ simply as $\models_G$.

As is well-known, a distinctive characteristic of Gödel logic is that, for any $a \in [0, 1]$, the mapping $g^a : [0, 1] \to [0, 1]$, defined by $g^a(x) = x$ for $x \in [0, a)$ and $g^a(x) = 1$ for $x \in [a, 1]$, is a morphism of Gödel-algebras, analogously with the mapping $g^{(a} : [0, 1] \to [0, 1]$ defined by $g^a(x) = x$ for $x \in [0, a]$ and $g^a(x) = 1$ for $x \in (a, 1]$. Note that, in particular, $g^{(0}$ maps $[0, 1]$ into $\{0, 1\}$. These well-known facts allow us to prove the following result, see also the left-hand lattice of logics in Fig. 1.

Proposition 2. $\models_G^{(0}$ *coincides with classical logic, while for any* $a \in (0, 1]$, $\models_G^a = \models_G^{(a} = \models_G$.

The Case of Product Logic. Product logic is defined as the axiomatic extension of MTL with axioms (Div) and (C), see Table 1. Product logic is standard complete with respect to the single matrix $M_1 = \langle [\mathbf{0}, \mathbf{1}]_\mathbf{\Pi}, \{1\}\rangle$, where $[\mathbf{0}, \mathbf{1}]_\mathbf{\Pi}$ denotes the standard product algebra $([0, 1], \min, \max, *_\Pi, \to_\Pi, 0, 1)$, with $*_\Pi$ being the product t-norm and $\to_\Pi$ is its residuum.

For $a \in (0, 1)$, let us denote by $\models_\Pi^a$ and $\models_\Pi^{(a}$ the logics defined by the logical matrices $M^a = \langle [\mathbf{0}, \mathbf{1}]_\mathbf{\Pi}, [a, 1]\rangle$ and $M^{(a} = \langle [\mathbf{0}, \mathbf{1}]_\mathbf{\Pi}, (a, 1]\rangle$ respectively. We will also denote the logic $\models_\Pi^1$ simply as $\models_\Pi$.

In the following we will make use of a known result about automorphisms of the standard product algebra $[\mathbf{0}, \mathbf{1}]_\mathbf{\Pi}$. Namely, let $\alpha \in \mathbb{R}^+$ and define the mapping

$h^\alpha : [0,1] \to [0,1]$ by $h(x) = x^\alpha$. Then h^α is an automorphism of $[\mathbf{0,1}]_\mathbf{\Pi}$.[2] This means that, for $\otimes \in \{\min, \max, *_\Pi, \to_\Pi\}$ and every α, $h^\alpha(e(\varphi \otimes \psi)) = h^\alpha(e(\varphi)) \otimes h^\alpha(e(\psi))$, for any formulas φ, ψ, every $[0,1]_\Pi$-evaluation e.

Now we can prove a series of results that we will allow to completely characterise all the $\models_\Pi^a$ and $\models_\Pi^{(a}$ logics.

Proposition 3. *The following conditions hold:*

(1) For any $a \in (0,1)$, $\models_\Pi \varphi$ iff $\models_\Pi^a \varphi$.
(2) For any $a, b \in (0,1)$, $\models_\Pi^a = \models_\Pi^b$.
(3) $\models_\Pi^{(0}$ coincides with classical logic, and for $a \in (0,1]$, $\models_\Pi^a = \models_\Pi^{(a}$
(4) For any $a \in (0,1)$, $\varphi \models_\Pi^a \psi$ iff $\models_\Pi^a \varphi \to \psi$.

Proof. We prove the above conditions:

(1) It is clear that if $\models_\Pi \varphi$ then $\models_\Pi^a \varphi$. Conversely, assume $\not\models_\Pi \varphi$. Then there is e such that $e(\varphi) < 1$. Let $b = e(\varphi)$. Then $\not\models_\Pi^a \varphi$ for all a such that $b < a < 1$. Hence, by (i), $\not\models_\Pi^a \varphi$ for any $a \in (0,1)$ as well.

(2) Indeed, assume $\varphi \not\models_\Pi^a \psi$. Then there exists an evaluation e such that $e(\varphi) \geq a$ and $e(\psi) < a$. We know there exists $\alpha \in \mathbb{R}^+$ such that $a^\alpha = b$. Then, if we let $e' = h^\alpha \circ e$, we have that $e'(\varphi) \geq a^\alpha = b$ and $e'(\psi) < a^\alpha = b$, hence $\varphi \not\models_\Pi^b \psi$.

(3) That $\models_\Pi^{(0}$ coincides with classical logic is a direct consequence of the fact that the mapping $k : [0,1] \to \{0,1\}$ such that $h(0) = 0$ and $h(x) = 1$ for $x \in (0,1]$ is a morphism of product algebras.

To show that $\models_\Pi^a = \models_\Pi^{(a}$, first assume $\varphi \not\models_\Pi^a \psi$, and hence there is e such that $e(\varphi) \geq a > e(\psi)$. Let $\alpha < 1$ such that $(e(\psi))^\alpha = a$, then $(e(\varphi))^\alpha \geq a^\alpha > a = (e(\psi))^\alpha$. Therefore, for $e' = h^\alpha \circ e$, we have $e'(\varphi) > a \geq e'(\psi)$, and hence $\varphi \not\models_\Pi^{(a} \psi$. Conversely, assume $\varphi \not\models_\Pi^{(a} \psi$. Then there is e such that $e(\varphi) > a \geq e(\psi)$. Let $\alpha > 1$ be such that $(e(\varphi))^\alpha = a$ and hence we have $a = (e(\varphi))^\alpha > (e(\psi))^\alpha$. This means that $e'(\varphi) \geq a > e'(\psi)$, where $e' = h^\alpha \circ e$, that is, $\varphi \not\models_\Pi^a \psi$. □

(4) Assume $\varphi \not\models_\Pi^a \psi$. Then there is e such that $e(\varphi) \geq a > e(\psi)$. It follows that $1 > e(\varphi \to \psi) = e(\psi)/e(\varphi)$, and thus there is α such that $(e(\psi)/e(\varphi))^\alpha < a$, that is, $e'(\varphi \to \psi) < a$, where $e' = h^\alpha \circ e$. Thus, $\not\models_\Pi^a \varphi \to \psi$. Conversely, assume $\not\models_\Pi^a \varphi \to \psi$. Then there is e such that $e(\varphi \to \psi) < a$, hence $e(\psi)/e(\varphi) < a$, that is, $e(\psi) < a \cdot e(\varphi)$. Let α such that $(e(\varphi))^\alpha = a$. Then we have $(e(\psi))^\alpha < a^\alpha \cdot (e(\varphi))^\alpha = a^\alpha \cdot a < a$. Hence, we have $e'(\varphi) = a$ while $e'(\psi) < a$, where again $e' = h^\alpha \circ e$. Therefore, $\varphi \not\models_\Pi^a \psi$. □

The intersection of all the logics $\models_\Pi^b$ for all $b \in (0,1]$ is what is known as the degree-preserving companion of $\models_\Pi$, and is denoted as $\models_\Pi^{\leq}$, see [3]. Then as a consequence of (1) and (2) of Proposition 3 we have that $\models_\Pi^{\leq} = \models_\Pi \cap \models_\Pi^a$ for any $a \in (0,1)$. Next is the final summary result, which is also graphically shown in the right-hand lattice of logics in Fig. 1.

---

[2] In fact, all the automorphisms of $[\mathbf{0,1}]_\mathbf{\Pi}$ are of form h^α [18].

Theorem 4.   - *For every* $a \in (0,1)$, $\models_\Pi^a = \models_\Pi^{\leq}$.

- $\models_\Pi^{(0}$ *is classical logic, while for any* $a \in (0,1]$, $\models_\Pi^a = \models_\Pi^{(a} \subsetneq \models_\Pi$.

Proof. The inclusion $\models_\Pi^{\leq} \subseteq \models_\Pi^a$ is clear. Assume $\varphi \not\models_\Pi^{\leq} \psi$. Then there exists e such that $e(\varphi) > e(\psi)$. Let α such that $(e(\varphi))^\alpha = a$, hence $(e(\psi))^\alpha < a$. Therefore, if $e' = h^\alpha \circ e$, then $e'(\varphi) = a > e'(\psi)$, and thus $\varphi \not\models_\Pi^a \psi$. Therefore $\models_\Pi^a \subseteq \models_\Pi^{\leq}$. □

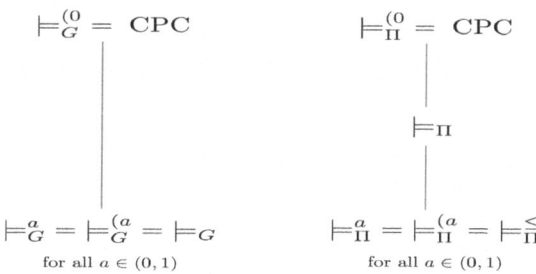

Fig. 1. Lattice of threshold-preserving Gödel and Product logics

5   Conclusions

In this paper we have been concerned with the definition and axiomatisation of both non-falsity preserving and threshold preserving companions of several extensions of the Monoidal t-norm based fuzzy logic MTL, extending some preliminary results in the recent paper [12]. All the axiomatisarions provided make use of restricted inference rules. The question whether we could find axiomatisations with "pure" inference rules is currently an open problem. On the other hand, while the study and characterisation of non-falsity preserving companions of MTL logics is already quite exhaustive, the general study of threshold-preserving companions is only partial, with the exception of the main three fuzzy logics, Lukasiewicz, Product and Gödel logics. In future work we aim at filling this gap, and consider possible applications of these logics to reasoning under uncertainty or with preferences.

Acknowledgements. The authors are indebted to the anonymous reviewers for their comments and suggestions. They also acknowledge support by the MOSAIC project (EU H2020-MSCA-RISE Project 101007627). Esteva and Godo acknowledge partial support by the Spanish project LINEXSYS (PID2022-139835NB-C21), and Gispert by the Spanish project SHORE (PID2022-141529NB-C21), both funded by MCIU/AEI/10.13039/501100011033. Gispert also acknowledges the project 2021 SGR 00348 funded by AGAUR.

References

1. Avron, A.: Paraconsistent fuzzy logic preserving non-falsity. Fuzzy Sets Syst. **292**, 75–84 (2016)
2. Blok, W.-J., Pigozzi, D.-J.: Algebraizable Logics. Memoirs of the American Mathematical Society, vol. 396 (1989)
3. Bou, F., et al.: Logics preserving degrees of truth from varieties of residuated lattices. J. Log. Comput. **19**(6), 1031–1069 (2009)
4. Carnielli, W., Coniglio, M.-E.: Paraconsistent Logic: Consistency, Contradiction and Negation. Logic, Epistemology, and the Unity of Science, vol. 40. Springer (2016)
5. Coniglio, M.-E., Esteva, F., Godo, L.: Logics of formal inconsistency arising from systems of fuzzy logic. Logic J. IGPL **22**(6), 880–904 (2014)
6. Coniglio, M.-E., Esteva, F., Godo, L.: On the set of intermediate logics between truth and degree preserving Lukasiewicz logic. Logical J. IGPL **24**(3), 288–320 (2016)
7. Coniglio, M.-E., Esteva, F., Gispert, J., Godo, L.: Degree-preserving Gödel logics with an involution: intermediate logics and (ideal) paraconsistency. In: Arielli, O., Zamansky, A. (eds.), Arnon Avron on Semantics and Proof Theory of Non-Classical Logics, Outstanding Contributions to Logic, vol. 21, pp. 107–139. Springer (2021)
8. Cintula, P., Noguera, C.: A general framework for mathematical fuzzy logic. In: Cintula, P., Hájek, P., Noguera, C. (eds.) Handbook of Mathematical Fuzzy Logic - Volume 1, Studies in logic, Mathematical Logic and Foundations, vol. 37, pp. 103–207. College Publications, London (2011)
9. da Costa, N.: On the theory of inconsistent formal systems. Notre Dame J. Form. Log. **15**, 497–510 (1974)
10. D'Ottaviano, I., da Costa, N.: Sur un problème de Jáskowski. Comp. Rend. Acad. Sci. Paris (A-B) **270**, 1349–1353 (1970)
11. Ertola, R.-C., Esteva, F., Flaminio, T., Godo, L., Noguera, C.: Paraconsistency properties in degree-preserving fuzzy logics. Soft. Comput. **19**(3), 531–546 (2015)
12. Esteva, F., Gispert, J., Godo, L.: On the paraconsistent companions of involutive fuzzy logics that preserve non-falsity. In: Lesot, M.-J., et al. (eds.) IPMU 2024. Lecture Notes in Networks and Systems 1175, pp. 375-389. Springer (2025)
13. Esteva, F., Gispert, J., Godo, L., Montagna, F.: On the standard and rational completeness of some axiomatic extensions of the monoidal T-norm logic. Stud. Logica. **71**(2), 199–226 (2002)
14. Esteva, F., Godo, L.: Monoidal t-norm based logic: towards a logic for left-continuous t-norms. Fuzzy Sets Syst. **124**, 271–288 (2001)
15. Hájek, P.: Metamathematics of Fuzzy Logic. Trends in Logic - Studia Logica Library, vol. 4. Kluwer (1998)
16. Jenei, S., Montagna, F.: A proof of standard completeness for Esteva and Godo's logic MTL. Stud. Logica. **70**(2), 183–192 (2002)
17. Priest, G.: Paraconsistent logic. In: Gabbay, D.-M., Guenthner, F. (eds.) Handbook of Philosophical Logic, vol. 6, 2nd edn, pp. 287–393. Kluwer Academic Publishers, Dordrecht (2002)
18. Savický, P., Cignoli, R., Esteva, F., Godo, L., Noguera, C.: On product logic with truth-constants. J. Log. Comput. **16**(2), 205–225 (2006)

Quantitative Lockean Thesis and its Logical Representation

Tommaso Flaminio[1]([⊠]) and Lluis Subirana[2]

[1] Artificial Intelligence Research Institute, IIIA - CSIC, Bellaterra, Barcelona, Spain
tommaso@iiia.csic.es
[2] Department of Mathematics, University of Barcelona, Barcelona, Spain

Abstract. The present paper considers a generalization of the Lockean thesis to a quantitative, many-valued, setting. The aim of such generalization is to handle the conjunctive closure principle, that usually fails in the classical setting, by a gradual approach. Being the Lockean thesis probabilistic in nature, we also show how its quantitative version can be formalized within the language of the probability logic FP(RŁ). Our analysis shows that the belief operator definable in FP(RŁ) recovers the satisfiability of belief sets that might be classically contradictory. In other words, there are belief set whose conjunctive closure is classically unsatisfiable, but whose generalized representation in FP(RŁ) are not contradictory.

1 Introduction

The *Lockean thesis* is a philosophical principle formulated by Foley in [7] that defines *beliefs* in terms of *degree of confidence*. Precisely, Foley claims that it is rational to believe in a certain statement φ (expressed in the classical logical language $\mathcal{L}$) if the (subjective) probability of it overcomes a certain numerical value. This can be informally introduced as follows.

Lockean Thesis: For any φ, it is rational to believe in φ provided that its probability $P(\varphi)$ overcomes a certain threshold λ.

Given a threshold λ and a probability function P, one can hence define a belief set, i.e. the epistemic state of an agent, as:

$$\mathscr{B}_{\lambda,P} = \{\varphi \mid P(\varphi) \geq \lambda\}.$$

Appealing to (subjective) probability functions to define belief yields some consequences that we now recall for a better understanding of, and to get acquainted with the present framework.

1. The arithmetic of probability theory, plus the intuitive principle stating that a rational agent believing φ should be more confident of φ rather than its negation $\neg\varphi$, fixes the threshold value λ to be higher than $1/2$.

© The Author(s), under exclusive license to Springer Nature Switzerland AG 2025
M. Baczyński et al. (Eds.): EUSFLAT 2025, LNCS 15883, pp. 347–358, 2025.
https://doi.org/10.1007/978-3-031-97225-6_28

2. Taking $\lambda > 1/2$, besides ensuring the previously recalled intuitive principle, also yields that every belief set $\mathscr{B}_{\lambda,P}$ is not contradictory, in the sense that there is no φ such that $\varphi, \neg\varphi \in \mathscr{B}_{\lambda,P}$.
3. The belief set $\mathscr{B}_{\lambda,P}$ is not usually closed under conjunctions: a rational agent can believe in two statement φ_1 and φ_2, but not in their (logical) conjunction $\varphi_1 \wedge \varphi_2$. Indeed, it might be the case that $P(\varphi_i) \geq \lambda$, while $P(\varphi_1 \wedge \varphi_2) < \lambda$.

The third argument above involves a principle known in the literature under the name of "conjunctive closure". We will meet again this principle in the rest of the present paper and it is hence convenient to highlight it as follows.

Conjunctive Closure: For any belief set $\mathscr{B}$, if $\varphi_1 \in \mathscr{B}, \ldots, \varphi_n \in \mathscr{B}$, then $\varphi_1 \wedge \ldots \wedge \varphi_n \in \mathscr{B}$.

This principle has been widely studied in the literature and it is involved in the discussions concerning some paradoxical situations, the best known being Kyburg's lottery paradox [17] and Makinson's preface paradox [19]. Several proposals to overcome those paradoxical cases have been considered and most of them focus on coherently keep together Lockean thesis and conjunctive closures. For instance, [2] proposes to employ non-standard probability functions to ensure conjunctive closure, and a similar analysis has been also proposed in [23]. The paper [3] computes the minimal real-valued thresholds to ensure the conjunctive closure of a fixed number of believes.

Besides that general formulation, that indeed generates paradoxical behaviors when framed in a classical logical setting, the conjunctive closure principle might reasonably fail in a probabilistic context like the one that we are taking here into account. For instance, let us consider the following case.

Example 1 (The die example). Consider a fair six-faces die that we throw on a table, and the events

- $\varphi =$ "the outcome is a number greater or equal than 2";
- $\psi =$ "the outcome is a number smaller or equal than 5".

Being the die fair, we assign probability $P(\varphi) = P(\psi) = 5/6$ and we could hence agree that both events are element of our belief set that can hence be defined by reasonable $\lambda = 0.7$. However $P(\varphi \wedge \psi) = 2/3$ which is strictly smaller than the Lockean threshold λ. Thus, $\varphi \wedge \psi \notin \mathscr{B} = \{\varphi, \psi\}$ which is not closed under conjunction. In logical terms, the failure of conjunctive closure can be represented as follows: let $\mathbf{b}_{5/6}(\cdot)$ be the function that assigns to each formula δ in our language, the classical values 1 if $P(\delta) \geq 5/6$ while it gives value 0 if $P(\delta) \leq 5/6$. Then there is no classical model that can extend the assignment $\varphi \mapsto \mathbf{b}_{5/6}(\varphi)$, $\psi \mapsto \mathbf{b}_{5/6}(\psi)$, $\varphi \wedge \psi \mapsto \mathbf{b}_{5/6}(\varphi \wedge \psi)$ because clearly $\mathbf{b}_{5/6}(\varphi) = \mathbf{b}_{5/6}(\psi) = 1$ while $\mathbf{b}_{5/6}(\varphi \wedge \psi) = 0$.

In this paper we propose an extension of the Lockean thesis to a many-valued setting that allows to handle conjunctive closure in a *graded, many-valued* way, so supporting the idea that "belief comes in degrees". By doing so, however, we do not aim at requiring the conjunctive closure principle to hold, but our goal is to understand up to which extent it can be treated in a multi-valued setting by studying real-valued degrees of belief that depend on probabilistic values. Given the probabilistic and quantitative nature of this approach, we will also show how the belief operator that arises from the Lockean thesis can be formalized and studied within the probability logic FP(RŁ). More in details, we will first define and comment on a quantitative version of Lockean thesis, and then we will formalize it within the language of FP(RŁ). Finally we will observe that, although conjunctive closure leads to a classical contradiction in several cases, its satisfiability can be recovered in our probabilistic-logical setting.

The present paper is structured as follows: the quantitative version of Lockean thesis, together with basic properties for the so arising function assigning degrees of belief, is the subject of the next Sect. 2. Section 3 recalls how the logic FP(RŁ) is defined and it hence paves the way for the logical representation of qualitative Lockean beliefs that will be studied in Sect. 4. Precisely, in Subsect. 4.1 we will show how to formalize Lockean beliefs within FP(RŁ), while Subsect. 4.2 will more directly consider the property of conjunctive closure in this setting. We will end this paper with Sect. 5 where we will go through some final considerations and present some future research directions.

2   The Quantitative Lockean Thesis

Although (quantitative) probabilities are adopted in the formulation of the Lockean thesis, the consequent analysis concerning believed statements and belief sets is purely qualitative: φ is either believed ($P(\varphi) \geq \lambda$) or it is not believed ($P(\varphi) < \lambda$) and hence the epistemic state $\mathscr{B}_{\lambda,P}$ is a (classical) subset of the set of formulas from $\mathcal{L}$. It is hence reasonable to extend the quantitative and numerical setting provided by probability functions to the layer of belief, by defining a *degree of belief* for a classical formula φ that is proportional its probability $P(\varphi)$.

The generalization of the belief set to a fuzzy set is done as follows: consider a threshold value $1/2 < \lambda \leq 1$ and a function $m_\lambda : [0,1] \to [0,1]$ such that $m_\lambda(x) = 1$ for all $x \geq \lambda$, $m_\lambda(x) = 0$ for all $x \leq 1 - \lambda$ and $m_\lambda(x)$ is monotone in the open interval $(1 - \lambda, \lambda)$ (see Fig. 1 for an example). In a sense, m_λ can be seen as a truth function for the predicate *high* and of parameter λ. The one represented in Fig. 1 below is an example of a function that might work for the purpose. In general, we can use the following.

Definition 1. *For every $1/2 < \lambda \leq 1$ a monotone function $m_\lambda : [0,1] \to [0,1]$ is a* Lockean modifier *if it satisfies:*

- $m_\lambda(x) = 1$ *for all $x \geq \lambda$ and $m_\lambda(x) = 0$ for all $x \leq 1 - \lambda$;*
- $m_\lambda(x) \leq x$ *for all $x \leq 1/2$ and $m_\lambda(x) \geq x$ for all $x \geq 1/2$.*

In what follows we will focus in particular on Lockean modifiers m_λ that are linear between $1 - \lambda$ and λ, and hence they are depicted as in Fig. 1. These functions are denoted by ℓ_λ for simplicity and they are defined as follows:

$$\ell_\lambda(x) = \min\left\{ \max\left\{ 0, \frac{x - (1 - \lambda)}{2\lambda - 1} \right\}, 1 \right\}.$$

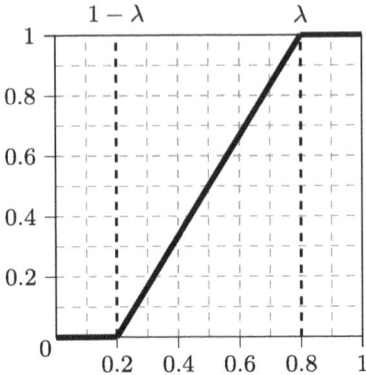

Fig. 1. A piecewise linear Lockean modifier function for $\lambda = 0.8$.

Now, let us consider again the previously discussed in Example 1, and let us take $\lambda = 0.7$ and $\ell_\lambda(x) = \min\left\{\max\left\{0, \frac{x-0.3}{0.4}\right\}, 1\right\}$. In this way we can hence compute the degree of belief of a formula γ as

$$\mathbf{b}_\lambda(\gamma) = \ell_\lambda(P(\gamma)) = \min\left\{\max\left\{0, \frac{P(\gamma) - 0.3}{0.4}\right\}, 1\right\}.$$

Thus, recalling that $P(\varphi) = P(\psi) = 5/6$ and $P(\varphi \wedge \psi) = 2/3$, we get the following:

$\mathbf{b}_\lambda(\varphi) = \ell_\lambda(P(\varphi)) = 1$;
$\mathbf{b}_\lambda(\psi) = \ell_\lambda(P(\psi)) = 1$;
$\mathbf{b}_\lambda(\varphi \wedge \psi) = \ell_\lambda(P(\varphi \wedge \psi)) \approx 0.916$;

Therefore, if $\varphi \wedge \psi$ was just rejected by the classical Lockean formulation of belief, with the proposed approach we can appreciate that the conjunction $\varphi \wedge \psi$ is actually "almost" (in the sense of being "very close to be") believed.

The next collect some basic properties about linear Lockean modifiers ℓ_λ.

Proposition 1. *For every* $\lambda > 1/2$ *the function* ℓ_λ *satisfies the following properties for all* $x, y \in [0, 1]$

1. $\ell_\lambda(1 - x) = 1 - \ell_\lambda(x)$;
2. *if* $x \odot y = \max\{0, x + y - 1\} = 0$, *then* $\ell_\lambda(x + y) \geq \ell_\lambda(x) + \ell_\lambda(y)$.

Proof. (1) If $x \leq 1 - \lambda$ or $x \geq \lambda$, $\ell_\lambda(x) \in \{0, 1\}$ and the claim is trivially true. If $1 - \lambda < x < \lambda$ then $\ell_\lambda(1 - x) = \frac{(1-x)-(1-\lambda)}{2\lambda-1} = \frac{-x+\lambda}{2\lambda-1} = \frac{2\lambda-1-x+1-\lambda}{2\lambda-1} = 1 - \frac{x-(1-\lambda)}{2\lambda-1} = 1 - \ell_\lambda(x)$.
(2) It is known that $x \odot y = 0$ iff $x \leq 1 - y$. If $x = 1 - y$, then $x + y = 1$ and $\ell_\lambda(x + y) = 1$ so the claim follows. Indeed, by (1) above one has that $\ell_\lambda(x + y) = 1 = \ell_\lambda(x) + \ell_\lambda(y)$.

Then, let us assume that $x < 1 - y$ and, without loss of generality, that $x \leq y$ as well. So, if $x \leq 1 - \lambda$, $\ell_\lambda(x) = 0$ and by monotonicity of ℓ_λ, $\ell_\lambda(x+y) \geq \ell_\lambda(y) = \ell_\lambda(x) + \ell_\lambda(y)$. Conversely, if $x > 1 - \lambda$, $\ell_\lambda(x) > 0$ and then:

- if $x + y < \lambda$ then $\ell_\lambda(x + y) = \ell_\lambda(x) + \ell_\lambda(y)$ because ℓ_λ is linear in that interval;
- if $x + y \geq \lambda$ then $\ell_\lambda(x + y) = 1$ and, since we are assuming that $x < 1 - y$, by monotonicity and (1) above, $\ell_\lambda(x) + \ell_\lambda(y) \leq \ell_\lambda(1 - y) + \ell_\lambda(y) = 1 - \ell_\lambda(y) + \ell_\lambda(y) = 1$.

This concludes the proof.   □

For every $\lambda > 1/2$ and for every probability function P, the function $\mathbf{b}_\lambda$ computing *degrees of belief* of every formula φ can be defined as

$$\mathbf{b}_\lambda(\varphi) = \ell_\lambda(P(\varphi)). \tag{1}$$

As a consequence of the above Proposition 1, $\mathbf{b}_\lambda$ is superadditive in the following sense.

Corollary 1. *For all φ, ψ such that $\varphi \wedge \psi = \bot$, $\mathbf{b}_\lambda(\varphi \vee \psi) \geq \mathbf{b}_\lambda(\varphi) + \mathbf{b}_\lambda(\psi)$.*

Proof. Immediate observing that $\varphi \wedge \psi = \bot$ implies that $P(\varphi) + P(\psi) \leq 1$ and hence $P(\varphi) \odot P(\psi) = 0$. Thus the claim follows from Proposition 1(2).   □

3   The Logic FP(RŁ) and its Models

Among the family of t-norm based fuzzy logics, the one that have received more attention from the community of mathematical logicians surely is Łukasiewicz logic. It is not the aim of this section to give a formal presentation of it, but it is necessary to highlight the following facts:

(1) The language of Łukasiewicz calculus (Ł in symbols), [14], is usually presented in the signature $\oplus, \neg, \bot$ of type (2,1,0). The binary connective $\oplus$ is called "strong disjunction" (or "Łukasiewicz sum" for a reason that will be evident in a short while); the unary connective $\neg$ is "negation"; the constant $\bot$ stands for "falsum". Other connectives are definable by the following stipulations: for all formulas φ and ψ,

$\top := \neg\bot$ (the constant "true"); $\varphi \odot \psi := \neg(\neg\varphi \oplus \neg\psi)$ (strong conjunction); $\varphi \to \psi := \neg\varphi \oplus \psi$ (implication); $\varphi \equiv \psi := (\varphi \to \psi) \odot (\psi \to \varphi)$ (double implication, or equivalence); $\varphi \ominus \psi := \neg(\varphi \to \psi)$ (difference); $\varphi \vee \psi := (\varphi \to \psi) \to \psi$ (weak disjunction); $\varphi \wedge \psi := \neg(\neg\varphi \vee \neg\psi)$ (weak conjunction).

In what follows we will use the following abbreviation: for every $m \in \mathbb{N}$, $m \geq 1$, and for every formula φ, $m.\varphi$ stands for $\varphi \oplus \ldots \oplus \varphi$ (m-times).

(2) The (equivalent) algebraic semantics of Ł is the variety $\mathbb{MV}$ of MV-algebras [5]. In the same way the two element boolean algebra generated the variety of boolean algebras, $\mathbb{MV}$ is generated by the structure $[0,1]_{MV} = ([0,1], \oplus, \neg, 0)$ where $[0,1]$ is the real unit interval and for all $x, y \in [0,1]$, $x \oplus y = \min\{1, x + y\}$ and $\neg x = 1 - x$. The additional connectives defined above have a semantics in $[0,1]_{MV}$ as follows: for all $x, y \in [0,1]$,

⊤ is interpreted in 1; $x \odot y = \max\{0, x+y-1\}$; $x \to y = \min\{1, 1-x+y\}$; $x \equiv y = 1 - |x-y|$; $x \ominus y = \max\{0, x-y\}$; $x \vee y = \max\{x, y\}$; $x \wedge y = \min\{x, y\}$.

(3) The logic RŁ (see [12]) is obtained by expanding the language of Ł by countably many unary connectives δ_n (for each $n \in \mathbb{N}$ and $n > 0$). Formulas are defined accordingly. The semantics on $[0, 1]$ is expanded by the condition: for all $x \in [0, 1]$ and for all $n > 0$,

$\delta_n(x) = \frac{x}{n}$, the division by n.

As a consequence, for every rational number $r = \frac{m}{n} \in [0, 1]$ one can define the constant $\bar{r}$ in the language of RŁ as $m.\delta_n(1)$ and its interpretation in $[0, 1]$ will be precisely r.

By a general construction firstly discussed in [15], we can now expand the language of RŁ by a unary modality P to read as "it is probable that" and introduce the logic FP(RŁ) that we are now going to recall. Its formulas are defined according to the following identifications.

(EF): the set of *event* formulas which contains all classical formulas of Łukasiewicz language; these formulas will be those defined by means of the connectives ¬ and ∧ and the constant ⊥ and they will be denoted by lowercase Greek letter $\varphi, \psi, \ldots$ with possible subscripts;

(MF): the set of *modal* formulas which contains expressions of the form $P(\varphi)$ for every event formula φ, the constants ⊤ and ⊥ and which is closed under the connectives of RŁ language. Modal formulas will be denoted by uppercase Greek letters $\Phi, \Psi, \ldots$ with possible subscripts.

A remark is in order: by its definition, modal formulas are just RŁ-terms $\Phi(x_1, \ldots, x_n)$ where the variables x_i are replaced by atomic modal formulas. In other words, every (compound) modal formula Φ is of the form $\Phi[P(\psi_1), \ldots, P(\psi_k)]$ for $P(\psi_1), \ldots, P(\psi_k)$ atomic modal formulas (regarded as variables) and Φ being an RŁ-term.

Definition 2. *The logic FP(RŁ) is defined by the following axioms and rules:*
(CL): all axioms and rules of classical calculus for event formulas;
(RŁ): all axioms and rules of RŁ for modal formulas;
(P): the following axioms and rules specific for the modality P:

(P1) ¬$P(\varphi) \leftrightarrow P(\neg\varphi)$;
(P2) $P(\varphi \to \psi) \to (P(\varphi) \to P(\psi))$;
(P3) $P(\varphi \vee \psi) \leftrightarrow [(P(\varphi) \to P(\varphi \wedge \psi)) \to P(\psi)]$;
(N) *The* necessitation rule: *from φ derive $P(\varphi)$.*

The notion of proof *is defined as usual and for every modal formula Φ, we will henceforth write $\vdash_{FP} \Phi$ to denote that Φ is a theorem of FP(RŁ).*

Semantics for FP(RŁ) is given in terms of probability spaces based on finitely additive probability functions.

Definition 3. *A probability Kripke model for FP(RŁ) and with respect to a finite language $\mathcal{L}$ is a pair $\mathcal{M} = (W, \mu)$ where*

- *W is the (finite) set of classical valuations to the boolean algebra $\{0, 1\}$;*
- *$\mu : W \to [0, 1]$ is a probability distribution, i.e., $\sum_{w \in W} \mu(w) = 1$.*

Given a formula ϕ of FP(RŁ), a probability Kripke model $\mathcal{M} = (W, \mu)$ and a $w \in W$, the truth value $\|\phi\|_{\mathcal{M},w}$ of ϕ in $\mathcal{M}$ and w is defined as follows:

(EF) if ϕ is an event formula, then $\|\phi\|_{\mathcal{M},w} = w(\phi)$. For every event formula ϕ, we will write W_ϕ to denote the set of models of ϕ, i.e., $W_\phi = \{w \in W \mid w(\phi) = 1\}$.

(MF) if $\phi = P(\varphi)$ is an atomic modal formula, $\|\phi\|_{\mathcal{M},w} = \sum_{w \in W_\phi} \mu(w)$; if ϕ is a compound modal formula, its truth value is computed by the truth functionality of the RŁ connectives involved in its definition.

Notice that if ϕ is modal its truth value is independent on the chosen world w and hence we will henceforth simply write $\|\phi\|_{\mathcal{M}}$ instead of $\|\phi\|_{\mathcal{M},w}$. Also, we will write $\mu(W_\phi)$ for $\sum_{w \in W_\phi} \mu(w)$.

The next result has been proved in [8], but the proof technique is standard and it can be directly adapted from the proof given in [14,15], see also [9].

Theorem 1. *The logic FP(RŁ) is sound and finite strong complete with respect to the class of probability Kripke models. In other words, for every finite set Γ of modal formulas and for every modal formula Φ, $\Gamma \vdash_{FP} \Phi$ if and only if $\|\Phi\|_{\mathcal{M}} = 1$ for every probability Kripke model $\mathcal{M}$ such that $\|\Psi\|_{\mathcal{M}} = 1$ for all $\Psi \in \Gamma$.*

4 Believing in Highly Probable Formulas

An interesting application prompt by the logical analysis of the concept of "belief" is the possibility of defining *knowledge* through it. Such a framework has been analyzed following by several paths most of which have been studied and formalized within the formal setting of modal logic. The main idea in that framework is that of adopting (or refusing) the standard Plato's argument according to which *knowledge* is a belief that is *justified* and *true*. Among them, it is worth to recall the work of Ayer [1] and Gettier [11], the former adopting Plato's view, the latter refusing it. More recently similar analysis have been formalized in a standard modal logic setting; we recall [21] and [22]; [13] (and references therein) where the authors study ways to define a knowledge operator (generally formalized as an S5 necessity modality) is treated in terms of a belief KD45-like modality.

Now, according to the (qualitative or quantitative) Lockean thesis, belief itself can be treated as a derived notion and, as we have seen, it can be described via probability functions and confidence degrees. In this section we aim at presenting a logical representation of notion of belief that arises by the quantitative Lockean thesis, and we will discuss the property of conjunctive closure in this setting. By doing so we prepare the ground to analyze the following questions:

- what belief operator can be formalized via probability and Lockean thesis?
- what is the corresponding notion of knowledge that so arises?

We will present some more details on these issues in the last section of this paper.

4.1   Logical Representation of Lockean Beliefs

Let φ be a classical formula (that is definable in the language of FP(RŁ) as an event formula) and let $\lambda > 1/2$ be a rational value that we take for a fixed Lockean threshold. We want to define a unary modality $B_\lambda(\cdot)$ within FP(RŁ) so that $B_\lambda(\varphi)$ takes value: 1 if $P(\varphi) \geq \lambda$; 0 if $P(\varphi) \leq 1 - \lambda$ and it is linear between on the interval $[1 - \lambda, \lambda]$. In other words we want to define an operator that behaves as the function $\mathbf{b}_\lambda(\cdot)$ defined as in (1) in every model $\mathcal{M} = (W, \mu)$ and where the Lockean modifier is piecewise linear as discussed in Sect. 2. Thus, writing $\lambda = n/m$, let us consider the FP(RŁ)-formula:

$$B_\lambda(\varphi) := m.\delta_{(2n-m)}(P(\varphi) \ominus \overline{1 - \lambda})$$

where, for every rational number r, $\overline{r}$ is the rational truth-constant for it and for a positive integer k, $k.y = y \oplus \ldots \oplus y$ (k-times) as previously recalled.

By Theorem 1, the logic FP(RŁ) is sound and complete with respect to probability Kripke models that, we recall, are models (W, μ) where W is the set of classical valuations for a finite set of variables and μ is a probability distribution on W. Thus, it is not difficult to see that, for every event formula φ and for all canonical model $\mathcal{M} = (W, \mu)$,

$$\|B_\lambda(\varphi)\|_{\mathcal{M}} = \min\left\{1, \max\left\{0, \frac{\mu(W_\varphi) - (1 - \lambda)}{2\lambda - 1}\right\}\right\} = \mathbf{b}_\lambda(\mu(W_\varphi)).$$

The next example is meant to clarify the above equations.

Example 2. Let us consider $\lambda = \frac{n}{m} = \frac{4}{5}$. The above formula $B_{4/5}(\varphi)$, evaluated in a model (W, μ), takes value:

$$
\begin{aligned}
\|B_{\frac{4}{5}}(\varphi)\|_{\mathcal{M}} &= \min\{1, \|5.\delta_{(2\cdot4)-5}(P(\varphi) \ominus (1 - (4/5)))\|_{\mathcal{M}}\} \\
&= \min\{1, \tfrac{5}{3} \cdot \|P(\varphi) \ominus (1/5)\|_{\mathcal{M}}\} \\
&= \min\{1, \tfrac{5}{3} \cdot (\max\{0, \mu(W_\varphi) - 1/5\})\} \\
&= \min\left\{1, \max\left\{0, \tfrac{\mu(W_\varphi) - 1/5}{3/5}\right\}\right\} \\
&= \mathbf{b}_{\frac{4}{5}}(\mu(W_\varphi)).
\end{aligned}
$$

Therefore, if $\mu(W_\varphi) \geq \frac{4}{5}$, the above takes value 1; if $\mu(W_\varphi) \leq \frac{1}{5}$, it takes value 0 and for all $1/5 < \mu(W_\varphi) < 4/5$, the function $\|B_{4/5}(\varphi)\|_{(W, \mu)}$ is linear.

Although other proposals for the definition of $B_\lambda(\cdot)$ are possible, for instance employing other Lockean modifiers, the present one can be taken to be the standard one within the FP(RŁ)-setting. Notice that, according to the previous formulation, when $P(\varphi) = 1/2$, i.e., when φ is fully uncertain, its degree of belief mirrors this fact as both φ and $\neg\varphi$ are partially believed in the same degree.

The next lemma, and indeed most of the results of this section, is proved by semantic means.

Lemma 1. *For every RŁ theorem $\phi(x_1, \ldots, x_k)$ (with possible truth constants), the compound probability formula $\phi(P(\varphi_1), \ldots, P(\varphi_k))$ is a theorem of FP(RŁ) for all events $\varphi_1, \ldots, \varphi_k$.*

Proof. By contrapositive, assume that $\phi(P(\varphi_1), \ldots, P(\varphi_k))$ is not a theorem of FP(RŁ); whence there exists a model (W, μ) that does not evaluate the above formula to 1. Then, the map $v : x_i \mapsto \|P(\varphi_i)\|_{(W,\mu)}$ is an RŁ assignment to $[0, 1]$ such that

$$v(\phi(x_1, \ldots, x_k)) = \|\phi(P(\varphi_1), \ldots, P(\varphi_k))\|_{(W,\mu)} < 1.$$

Therefore, $\phi(x_1, \ldots, x_k)$ is not valid in the RŁ algebra on $[0, 1]$, and so it is not a theorem of RŁ.   □

Let us close this section by observing that defining the operator B_λ within the same language of our logic allows to immediately solve the problem highlighted in Example 1. Indeed, in this setting, the assignment $B_\lambda(\varphi) \mapsto \mathbf{b}_\lambda(\varphi)$, where the later is computed as in (1), is clearly satisfiable because $B_\lambda(\varphi)$ is definable.

4.2 Dealing with Conjunctive Closure

We are now interested in understanding up to which extent the operator B_λ can handle the conjunctive closure. In other words, we want to understand if, or under which conditions, $(B_\lambda(\varphi) \wedge B_\lambda(\psi)) \leftrightarrow B_\lambda(\varphi \wedge \psi)$ holds true in FP(RŁ).

Let us start noticing that, by Axiom (P2) of Definition 2, the probability operator P of FP(RŁ) is monotone. Therefore, since $\varphi \wedge \psi \to \varphi$ and $\varphi \wedge \psi \to \psi$ holds in classical logic, one has that $P(\varphi \wedge \psi) \to P(\varphi)$ and $P(\varphi \wedge \psi) \to P(\psi)$ are theorems of FP(RŁ). Thus, since $((\phi_1 \to \phi_2) \wedge (\phi_1 \to \phi_3)) \to (\phi_1 \to (\phi_2 \wedge \phi_3))$ holds in MTL (see [6, Proposition 1]) and hence it holds in RŁ in particular, by Lemma 1 and the aforementioned facts, by modus ponens, we get that in FP(RŁ) it holds that $P(\varphi \wedge \psi) \to (P(\varphi) \wedge P(\psi))$. Semantically, $P(\varphi \wedge \psi) \to (P(\varphi) \wedge P(\psi))$ holds because by the Fréchet-Hoeffding theorem,

$$\mu(W_{\varphi \wedge \psi}) = \mu(W_\varphi \cap W_\psi) \leq \min\{\mu(W_\varphi), \mu(W_\psi)\}.$$

By the monotonicity of Lockean modifiers (recall Definition 1), it is hence easy to prove that $B_\lambda(\varphi \wedge \psi) \to (B_\lambda(\varphi) \wedge B_\lambda(\psi))$. This result is in fact not surprising because it just states that if the conjunction $\varphi \wedge \psi$ is believed (according to our Lockean setting), then φ and ψ are believed as well. Indeed, the interesting direction is the other one: if φ and ψ are believed, their conjunction $\varphi \wedge \psi$ is also believed. In the next two propositions we will analyze the validity of the formula

$(C\lambda)$ $(B_\lambda(\varphi) \wedge B_\lambda(\psi)) \to B_\lambda(\varphi \wedge \psi)$

within the logic FP(RŁ) where the operator B_λ is defined. What these results prove is that, while $(C\lambda)$ is not generally a logical theorem (Proposition 2), it becomes valid only under quite strong assumptions for the probability operator (Proposition 3).

Proposition 2. *There are φ and ψ classical formulas of FP(RŁ) and $\lambda > 1/2$ such that $(C\lambda)$ is not a theorem of FP(RŁ).*

Proof. By the completeness theorem of FP(RŁ) with respect to canonical probability models (Theorem 1), let us prove that there exists a model $\mathcal{M} = (W, \mu)$ in which $(\mathrm{B}_\lambda(\varphi) \wedge \mathrm{B}_\lambda(\psi)) \rightarrow \mathrm{B}_\lambda(\varphi \wedge \psi)$ fails. Indeed, take W having at least two possible worlds w_1, w_2 (i.e., atoms of a free Boolean algebra) and let μ be such that $\mu(w_1) = \mu(w_2) = 1/2$. Then, $\mathrm{B}_\lambda(w_1) = \mathrm{B}_\lambda(w_2) > 0$ because $\lambda > 1/2$. However, $w_1 \wedge w_2 = \bot$ and hence $\mu(w_1 \wedge w_2) = 0$ and $\mathrm{B}_\lambda(w_1 \wedge w_2) = 0$ as well. Therefore, if φ is the minterm for w_1 and ψ is the minterm for w_2, one has: $\|\mathrm{B}_\lambda(\varphi) \wedge \mathrm{B}_\lambda(\psi)\|_{(W,\mu)} > \|\mathrm{B}_\lambda(\varphi \wedge \psi)\|_{(W,\mu)}$ and hence $(C\lambda)$ is not a theorem. $\square$

Proposition 3. *$(C\lambda)$ is a theorem of FP(RŁ) for all $\lambda > 1/2$ iff P satisfies $P(\varphi \wedge \psi) \leftrightarrow P(\varphi) \wedge P(\psi)$.*

Proof. The left-to-right direction is trivially true because if $(C\lambda)$ is a theorem for all $\lambda > 1/2$, the so is for $\lambda = 1$, in particular. Now, notice that $\mathrm{B}_1(\varphi) = P(\varphi)$. Thus, for $(C1) = (P(\varphi) \wedge P(\psi)) \rightarrow P(\varphi \wedge \psi)$. Since $P(\varphi \wedge \psi) \rightarrow (P(\varphi) \wedge P(\psi))$ is indeed a theorem of FP(RŁ), it follows that P satisfies $P(\varphi \wedge \psi) \leftrightarrow P(\varphi) \wedge P(\psi)$.

Conversely, assume that $P(\varphi \wedge \psi) \leftrightarrow P(\varphi) \wedge P(\psi)$ is true for the probability operator P. By Lemma 1, and since $\bar{r}x \wedge \bar{r}y \leftrightarrow \bar{r}(x \wedge y)$ and $(x \ominus \bar{r}) \wedge (y \ominus \bar{r}) \leftrightarrow (x \wedge y) \ominus \bar{\alpha}$ are RŁ theorems for all $r \in [0,1]$, for all events φ, ψ we have that

1. $\bar{r}P(\varphi) \wedge \bar{r}P(\psi) \leftrightarrow \bar{r}(P(\varphi) \wedge P(\psi))$ and
2. $(P(\varphi) \ominus \bar{r}) \wedge (P(\psi) \ominus \bar{r}) \leftrightarrow (P(\varphi) \wedge P(\psi)) \ominus \bar{r}$

are theorems of FP(RŁ) and hence they translate into valid equations in every model (W, μ). As a consequence, writing $\bar{r}$ for $m.\delta_{2n-m}$, $\mathrm{B}_\lambda(\varphi) \wedge \mathrm{B}_\lambda(\psi) = \bar{r}(P(\varphi) \ominus \overline{1-\lambda}) \wedge \bar{r}(P(\psi) \ominus \overline{1-\lambda}) = \bar{r}(P(\varphi) \ominus \overline{1-\lambda} \wedge P(\psi) \ominus \overline{1-\lambda}) = \bar{r}((P(\varphi) \wedge P(\psi)) \ominus \overline{1-\lambda})$. The latter, by the assumption $P(\varphi \wedge \psi) \leftrightarrow P(\varphi) \wedge P(\psi)$ hence gives $\bar{r}((P(\varphi \wedge \psi)) \ominus \overline{1-\lambda}) = \mathrm{B}_\lambda(\varphi \wedge \psi)$. This proves the last claim. $\square$

A final comment about the last result. A probability function μ is a model of $P(\varphi \wedge \psi) \leftrightarrow P(\varphi) \wedge P(\psi)$, that in turn ensures conjunctive closure for all Lockean threshold λ iff μ is a Boolean homomorphism to $\{0, 1\}$, i.e. if it is a logical valuation. In terms of distribution such a μ assigns value 1 to a unique possible world w and 0 to all the other ones. In this sense, the above Proposition 3 tells us that conjunctive closure is satisfied only under the trivial assumption that probabilities are $\{0, 1\}$-valued.

5   Conclusion and Future Work

In this short paper we have discussed the possibility of generalizing Lockean thesis to a many-valued setting, we discussed the validity of the key property of conjunctive closure in this context, and we show how this analysis can be formalized within the probability logic FP(RŁ).

Although the present paper does not present deep technical results, we believe that the topic could be of particular interest. Indeed, much work in this direction has to be done; in what follows we highlight three possible directions that we retain to be of particular interest.

(1) Analyze the paradoxes that arise by the failure of conjunctive closure, within the logical context provided by the logic FP(RŁ). Particular interesting in this setting are the already recalled lottery and preface paradoxes (see [17] and [19] respectively), but also the sorites paradox could be apporached in this setting. Indeed, as remarked in [18] this latter and the lottery paradoxes seems to be the two faces of the same coin. Also, and interestingly, formal and many-valued approaches to resolve the sorites paradox have been studied [16].

(2) For every $\lambda > 1/2$ the unary operator B_λ, as defined in this setting, can be seen as a doxastic and gradual modal operator that, in contrast with the usual modal approach to belief, does not satisfy the $(C\lambda)$ equation and hence it is not a typical KD45 modality. This remark might open new directions of research to investigate, in the line of [13], what type of knowledge could be defined (or approximated) in this setting.

(3) Following [2,3], another way to overcome the limitation of belief representation via the Lockean thesis employs the use of hyperreal-valued probability functions by which one could define that a formula φ is "highly probable" whenever $P(\varphi) > 1-\varepsilon$ for a positive infinitesimal ε. To do that, we then need a probability logic in the style of FP(RŁ) but that can handle infinitesimal values. This can be defined in a similar way to what has been done in [10] where the probability operator P was added to the language of a logic called SLΠ whose domains of truth values are non-trivial ultrapowers $[0,1]^*$ of the segment $[0,1]$.

Finally we would like to highlight that the (qualitative) Lockean thesis received some attentions in several areas of logic, philosophy and knowledge representation. Of particular interest are for us the recent works that employ it to extend the classical AGM belief revision realm (see e.g. [4,20] and references therein). The qualitative version of the Lockean thesis that we propose here has, in our opinion, a great potentiality in providing generalizations of those approaches.

Acknowledgments. The authors are grateful to the anonymous referees for their careful reading and for pointing us out an imprecision in the formulation of $B_\lambda(\varphi)$. Flaminio acknowledges partial support by the Spanish project SHORE (PID2022-141529NB-C22) funded by MCIN/AEI/10.13039/501100011033, and the H2020-MSCA-RISE-2020 project MOSAIC (Grant Agreement number 101007627).

References

1. Ayer, A.J.: The Problem of Knowledge. Macmillan, London (1956)
2. Benci, V., Horsten, L., Wenmackers, S.: Infinitesimal Probabilities. Br. J. Philos. Sci. **69**(2), 509–552 (2016)
3. Bonzio, S., Cevolani, G., Flaminio, T.: How to believe long conjunctions of beliefs: probability, quasi-dogmatism and contextualism. Erkenntnis **88**(3), 965–990 (2023)

4. Cantwell, J., Rott, H.: Probability, coherent belief and coherent belief changes. Ann. Math. Artif. Intell. **87**(3), 259–291 (2019). https://doi.org/10.1007/s10472-019-09649-3

5. Cignoli, R., D'Ottaviano, I.M.L., Mundici, D.: Algebraic Foundations of Many-Valued Reasoning. Kluwer (2000)

6. Esteva, F., Godo, L.: Monoidal t-norm based logic: towards a logic for left-continuous t-norms. Fuzzy Sets Syst. **124**, 271–288 (2001)

7. Foley, R.: Working Without a Net. Oxford University Press, Oxford (1992)

8. Flaminio, T.: NP-containment for the coherence tests of assessment of conditional probability: a fuzzy-logical approach. Arch. Math. Logic **46**(3–4), 301–319 (2007)

9. Flaminio, T., Godo, L., Marchioni, E.: Reasoning about uncertainty of fuzzy events: an overview. In: Cintula, P., et al. (eds.) Understanding Vagueness - Logical, Philosophical, and Linguistic Perspectives, pp. 367–400. College Publications (2011)

10. Flaminio, T., Montagna, F.: A logical and algebraic treatment of conditional probability. Arch. Math. Logic **44**, 245–262 (2005)

11. Gettier, E.: Is justified true belief knowledge? Analysis **23**, 121–123 (1963)

12. Gerla, B.: Rational Łukasiewicz logic and DMV-algebras. Neural Netw. World **11**, 579–584 (2001)

13. Halpern, J.Y., Samet, D., Segev, E.: Defining knowledge in terms of belief: the modal logic perspective. Rev. Symb. Logic **2**(3), 469–487 (2009)

14. Hájek, P.: Metamathematics of Fuzzy Logic. Kluwer (1998)

15. Hájek, P., Godo, L., Esteva, F.: Probability and fuzzy logic. In: Besnard, P., Hanks, S. (eds.) Proceedings of Uncertainty in Artificial Intelligence UAI 1995, pp. 237–244. Morgan Kaufmann, San Francisco (1995)

16. Hájek, P., Novák, V.: The sorites paradox and fuzzy logic. Int. J. Gen. Syst. **32**(4), 373–383 (2003)

17. Kyburg, H.: Probability and the Logic of Rational Belief. Wesleyan University Press, Middletown (1967)

18. Lissia, L.M.: Cut-off points for the rational believer. Synthese **200**(2), 1–19 (2022). https://doi.org/10.1007/s11229-022-03510-7

19. Makinson, D.: The paradox of the preface. Analysis **25**(6), 205–207 (1965)

20. Shear, T., Fittelson, B.: Two approaches to belief revision. Erkenntnis **84**, 487–518 (2019)

21. Stalnaker, R.: On logics of knowledge and belief. Philos. Stud. **128**(1), 169–199 (2006)

22. van Benthem, J.: Epistemic logic and epistemology: the state of their affairs. Philos. Stud. **128**(1), 49–76 (2006)

23. Wenmackers, S.: Ultralarge lotteries: analyzing the Lottery Paradox using nonstandard analysis. J. Appl. Log. **11**, 452–467 (2013)

Author Index

M. Baczyński et al. (Eds.): EUSFLAT 2025, LNCS 15883, pp. 359–360, 2025.
https://doi.org/10.1007/978-3-031-97225-6

The manufacturer's authorised representative in the EU is Springer
Nature Customer Service Centre GmbH, Europaplatz 3, 69115 Heidelberg,
Germany. If you have any concerns regarding our products, please
contact ProductSafety@springernature.com

Printed and bound by CPI Group (UK) Ltd, Croydon, CR0 4YY
29/04/2026
02099461-0012